FUNDAMENTALS OF
MOTOR
CONTROL

IN PARTNERSHIP WITH THE NJATC

Learning Solutions

New York   Boston   San Francisco
London   Toronto   Sydney   Tokyo   Singapore   Madrid
Mexico City   Munich   Paris   Cape Town   Hong Kong   Montreal

Published by Pearson Learning Solutions, 501 Boylston Street, Suite 900, Boston, MA 02116
A Pearson Education Company
www.pearsoned.com

Printed in the United States of America

10   18

2009520021

RG/SB

ISBN 10: 0-558-21689-7
ISBN 13: 978-0-558-21689-4

Contents

SECTION 2

CHAPTER 9   Evolution of Motor Controls: Transitioning from Magnetics to Electronics   167

CHAPTER 10   Solid State Devices   189

About the Authors

James A. Rehg is a freelance writer and co-owner of *Text On Demand*, a company specializing in information presentation and documentation. His industrial experience includes instrumentation system design at McDonnell Douglas Corporation, administration of industrial automation training centers, and consulting on the design of automated manufacturing systems. During almost 35 years as an engineering educator, he taught community college, technical college, and university students before retiring from Penn State University where he was an Associate Professor of Engineering. During his teaching career, Jim received recognition for excellence in teaching at the college, state, and national levels. He has authored numerous technical reports, research papers, white papers, and industrial manuals. In addition, he has authored *Introduction to Robotics in CIM Systems,* 6th edition for Pearson/Prentice Hall publishers and co-authored the following college and industrial training textbooks: *Programmable Logic Controllers*, 1st edition for the NJATC, *Programmable Logic Controllers*, 2nd edition, *Industrial Electronics*, 1st edition, *Computer Integrated Manufacturing*, 3rd edition. The later three texts were published by Pearson/Prentice Hall publishing. Jim's current projects include co-authoring two textbooks for Pearson/Prentice Hall publishers with the following titles: *Motors and Control Systems* and *Semiconductors and Electronic Circuits*.

Glenn J. Sartori is a freelance writer and co-owner of *Text On Demand*, a company that specializes in presenting and documenting technical information. Glenn spent 40 years in the aerospace industry at several companies and recently retired from *The Boeing Company*. His education includes a BS and MS in Electrical Engineering plus numerous in-house courses from state-of-the-art digital design and imbedded controller programming to management and team building. At various positions in his career, Glenn was responsible for the design, development, and production support of electronic control and test equipment integrated into various aircraft and missile platforms and for managing design teams with those responsibilities. On-site training and support for the sophisticated hardware and operational software took Glenn to customer locations across the world. He developed and conducted classes for production personnel and customers on electronic system operation, testing, and troubleshooting. Glenn has co-authored the following textbooks for Pearson/Prentice Hall publishers: *Programmable Logic Controllers*, 1st edition for the NJATC, *Programmable Logic Controllers*, 2nd edition, *Industrial Electronics*, 1st edition. His current projects for Pearson/Prentice Hall publishers include two textbooks: *Motors and Control Systems* and *Semiconductors and Electronic Circuits*.

Michael A. Hassell is the academic coordinator for the Columbus Ohio Electrical JATC. As a 37 year member of the IBEW, Michael has worked as a journeyman wireman, foreman, general foreman and superintendant on various projects around the world from Alaska to the Middle East. He has been educating students in electrical systems and computer technologies for over 30 years. As an adjunct faculty member of Columbus State Community College, Michael currently teaches apprentice and journeyman electrical courses in theory, motor control, telecommunications and Microsoft Office applications. A 1999 graduate of the National Training Institute, Michael has returned to NTI for the past 8 years to teach Powerpoint for Instructional Use and How to Teach the AC and DC Theory Lessons. He is the primary author of the NJATC's *Motor Control* textbook, 1st edition, and a contributing editor for *Conduit Bending and Fabrication*.

Preface

Every motor requires some method of control regardless of its size or application. If the control is only to start and stop the motor, the control device is rather simple. However, in many applications, automatic operations such as starting the motor under a specific set of conditions or reversing the direction of the motor during a process cycle requires more complex control devices. In other cases, the status of process variables such as flow, pressure and temperature determines when motor power is applied, how much power is applied, and the length of time for the motor to operate. The various modes and methods of motor control operation require a variety of control devices. These control devices are necessary for control of the motor and its driven components for proper operation in commercial and industrial applications.

Because commercial and industrial applications have unique operating requirements, much of the control equipment is built for a specific function. The proper choice of appropriate control equipment, an understanding of the overall control scheme, and the knowledge to install all of the components into a motor control system are necessary skills of an electrical worker. Specific procedures have been developed over the years and have become industry standards when installing, troubleshooting, and repairing motor control systems. Today's advanced motor control systems use electronically controlled smart devices, which provide highly efficient performance, reduced power consumption, and built-in diagnostics. Many have integrated micro-computers that require programming for sequential motor and machine control.

This book addresses the complete range of motor control from manual/mechanical devices to intelligent systems. It is formatted into three sections, which have a systematic approach to the presentation of motor control. The basic concepts are built on a clear and concise description of the control devices, motor control theory, and the methods that are required to perform successful motor control installation, maintenance and troubleshooting. Each section contains motor control technical notes, safety tips, and commercial and industrial applications. Section 1 is structured to introduce motor controls for apprenticeship classes, Section 2 for intermediate or elective classes, and Section 3 for journeymen classes.

Section 1: Chapters 1 through 8 discuss manually-, mechanically-, and automatically-operated input control devices. Both NEMA and IEC contactors and manual and magnetic motor starters are addressed with emphasis on types, functions, and applications. The section concludes with the development and purpose of schematic, wiring, logic, and ladder diagrams, including details on standard drawing conventions and techniques for generating and interpreting of ladder diagrams.

Section 2: Chapters 9 through 16 discuss solid state input and output devices. Unique motor control devices including special purpose motor starters, programmable timers, and function specific control components are presented. The function and operation of AC and DC motor speed control devices are discussed, including troubleshooting techniques and a variety of applications.

Section 3: Chapters 17 through 24 discuss analog signal types and analog devices used in motor control. Advanced topics such as variable speed drives, programmable logic controllers and networks are presented. The section concludes with detailed methods for system-wide troubleshooting of motor control systems using real-world applications.

The authors greatly appreciate the support of the entire motor control team: LeeAnne Fischer and Dianne Fortier from Pearson Learning Solutions; Rich Gomes, Tim Waters, and the entire production crew from Pearson Learning Solutions; Jim Boyd from NJATC; and especially to Mike Hassell from The Electrical Trades Center in Columbus, Ohio, for his insightful comments to our text and illustrations.

Jim Rehg (jamesrehg@plcteacher.com)
Glenn Sartori (glennsartori@plcteacher.com)

We dedicate this book to the men and women of the IBEW and NECA organizations who are in the field, installing, operating, maintaining, and troubleshooting motor control systems; and to our wives, Marci Rehg and Rosanne Sartori, for their support and understanding over the many months that we worked to generate the contents of this book.

—Jim Rehg and Glenn Sartori

CHAPTER 1

Evolution of Motor Control— The Development of Motor Control in Industry

GOALS AND OBJECTIVES

The primary goal of this chapter is to describe the industrial scope of motor control and introduce the NEMA and IEC standards that govern how motor control is implemented in North America and across the globe.

After completing this chapter you will be able to:

1. Define motor control and the evolution of the industry.
2. Describe the nature of NEMA and IEC standard devices.
3. Explain the differences between the NEMA and IEC standards' philosophy.

1-1 INTRODUCTION TO MOTOR CONTROL

From the beginning of time, civilization searched for *prime movers* to reduce the daily work load. Early prime movers converted *natural energy* sources, such as wind and moving water, to *rotational energy* to pump water or mill grain. The invention of the *steam engine* by Thomas Savery in 1698 provided factories, not located near natural energy sources, a powerful prime mover to drive machines. Typically, a single steam engine was used to turn an overhead drive system, and long leather belts delivered the rotational power to individual machines. Prime mover advancements have generally been driven by the need for enhanced energy conversion efficiency and improved ease of use. The steam engine offers *portable* power source but not *individual* power sources at each machine.

The first conversion of *electrical* energy into *rotational mechanical* energy was demonstrated by Michael Faraday in 1821. Faraday's machine, Figure 1-1, demonstrated that a *current flow* in a *magnetic field* produces a *force* on the current carrying conductor. In this simple demonstration the copper wire hangs from the support wire with the end in the mercury pool. A magnet, which stands in the center of the pool, produces the magnetic flux or magnetic lines of force as shown. When a battery is connected between the pool of mercury and the support wire, a current flows in the wire. The *left-hand rule* indicates that a force is produced on the wire due to the wire current crossing the magnetic flux at a ninety degree angle. The force causes the wire to rotate around the magnet dragging the loose end in the mercury pool.

Based on the work of Faraday and other scientists, the *DC motor*, Figure 1-2, is invented by Zénobe Gramme in 1873. The Gramme machine is the first

FIGURE 1-3: Nikola Tesla's first practicable AC motor.

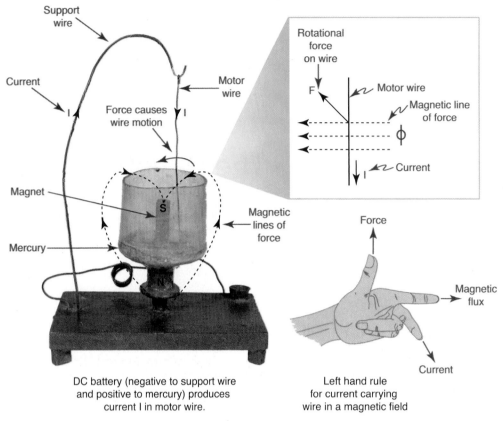

DC battery (negative to support wire and positive to mercury) produces current I in motor wire.

Left hand rule for current carrying wire in a magnetic field

Courtesy of John D. Jenkins, "Where Discovery Sparks Imagination," AMRE, 2009.

FIGURE 1-3: Nikola Tesla's first practicable AC motor.

Courtesy of John D. Jenkins, "Where Discovery Sparks Imagination," AMRE, 2009.

electric motor successfully used in industry to put a *prime mover* at each machine. In 1888 Nikola Tesla invents the first practicable *AC motor*, Figure 1-3, and the *polyphase transmission system* used to distribute AC electric power. George Westinghouse teamed with Tesla in 1890, and the company bearing his name established *AC power generation* and *distribution* as it is used today. By the turn of the century, factories have an AC motor, a *more efficient* prime mover, available for individual machines and a power distribution system to drive the motors.

The development of the electric motor provides a prime mover that revolutionizes *manufacturing*, *agriculture*, *transportation*, and *household appliances*. With the successful introduction of the motor into manufacturing, motor development shifts to improvement in *motor efficiency* and a means for *motor control*.

FIGURE 1-3: Nikola Tesla's first practicable AC motor.

Courtesy of John D. Jenkins, "Where Discovery Sparks Imagination,"
AMRE, 2009.

Motor Controllers

A motor controller is a device that *governs* the performance of an electric motor in a *predefined* manner. Motor controllers include *manual* or *automatic* devices *to start* and *stop* the motor, *select forward* or *reverse rotation*, *set* and *regulate* the *speed*, and *regulate* or *limit* the *torque*. The scope of motor control applications includes: *domestic applications*, *office equipment*, *medical equipment*, *commercial applications*, *industrial applications*, *transportation applications*, *power tools*, and *hobby equipment*. This text focuses on motor control as it relates to industrial and commercial motor control.

Today, efficient motors and equally efficient motor control systems are critical because electric motors consume *more than half* of all generated electrical energy. A Department of Energy (DOE) study in 1998 found that electric motor-driven systems used in industrial processes consume 679 billion kWh or 63 percent of all electricity used in U.S. Efficient use of power in motor driven applications is a goal of manufacturing and two standards organizations the *National Electrical Manufacturers Association* (NEMA) and the *International Electrotechnical Commission* (IEC).

1-2 NATIONAL ELECTRICAL MANUFACTURERS ASSOCIATION

By 1910 the *Associated Manufacturers of Electrical Supplies* and the *Electric Power Club*, which included manufacturers of motors and generators, actively promoted *standardization* for the growing electrical industry. On September 1, 1926, these two organizations united to form the *National Electrical Manufacturers Association* or NEMA, which is currently located in Washington, DC. NEMA's first national standards effort, called the "Safe Electrical Cord" Program, brought attention in 1929 to the use of safe power cords on new electrical appliances. NEMA's standards played a major role in efficient production of material for the army and navy during WW II. The same standards helped industries return to production of consumer products after the war. By the early 1990s, NEMA company membership numbered over 600 and represented a broad cross-section of domestic electrical manufacturing. Globalization in the decade fueled active cooperation with European standards-writing organizations as products from off-shore manufacturers merged with domestic products in North America's factories. In the last ten years, energy conservation took on renewed importance as power disruptions in various parts of the country raised questions about the nation's electrical infrastructure and its energy efficiency technologies. *Standards development* remains the primary mission of NEMA, but *globalization* requires a much broader agenda. Figure 1-4 illustrates a NEMA device used to start motors.

Understanding NEMA Standards

NEMA is one of two standards for motor control devices used in industries in the US, Canada, and Mexico. Two NEMA sections, *Industrial Automation Control Products and Systems* and *Motors and Generators*, govern devices used in motor control. NEMA publications for *installers*, *contractors*, *inspectors*, and *MRO* (maintenance/ repair operations) are

NEMA Standard—A Standard of the National Electrical Manufacturers Association defines a *product*, *process*, or *procedure* with reference to one or more of the following: *nomenclature*, *composition*, *construction*, *dimensions*, *tolerances*, *safety*, *operating characteristics*, *performance*, *rating*, *testing*, and the *service* for which it is designed. NEMA standards have *two classes*: standards for current products in production, suggested standards for future design on products in development.

TECH NOTES

FIGURE 1-4: NEMA starting device for 10 horsepower motor.

Courtesy of Rockwell Automation, Inc.

of greatest interest in this text. These four topics are found in NEMA *standards* and *application guides*. The latter publication is for *installers*, *inspectors*, and *employees working with the product*. A NEMA standards publication contains a combination of the items in Figure 1-5.

1-3 INTERNATIONAL ELECTROTECHNICAL COMMISSION

The *International Electrotechnical Commission* (IEC), which is located in Geneva, Switzerland, was formed in 1906 to secure the co-operation of the technical societies of the world through standardization of electrical apparatus and machinery. The IEC is a non-profit, non-governmental international standards organization that produces international standards for *electrical*, *electronic* and *related technologies*. Examples of IEC standards' areas include: *power generation*, *power transmission and distribution*, *semiconductors*, *fiber optics*, *batteries*, *solar energy*, *nanotechnology*, and *marine energy*. Standards work started soon after formation. In 1938 the IEC produced the *International Electrotechnical Vocabulary* (IEV), now known as *Electropedia*. The first edition included 2,000 terms in French, English, German, Italian, Spanish, and Esperanto, with definitions in French and English. Tracking changes in technology in the 1950s and 60s, the IEC initiated standards for electroacoustics, radio, television, semiconductors, medical and maritime equipment, and lasers. The IEC's four-class system for lasers is now the global reference. In 2005, the Commission published the current edition of the IEC *Multilingual Dictionary* (IEV), which now contains 19,400 electrotechnical definitions in French and English and equivalent terms in 13 languages.

FIGURE 1-5: Data included in a NEMA standard.

Standard Item	Description
Scope	Scope includes a clear, concise, and comprehensive statement of the coverage.
Definitions	Definition includes new terms used in the standard.
Rating	Rating includes rated values or methods of rating the equipment.
Manufacturing	Manufacturing includes construction, materials, dimensions, provisions for mounting, spacings between live parts, precautionary labels, and nameplate markings.
Dimensions	Dimensions are given for interchangeability purposes.
Performance	Performance covers temperature rise, interrupting capacity, voltage regulation, speed regulation, number of operations without deterioration, and the ability to withstand specified conditions.
Testing	Testing includes procedures for tests to determine compliance with manufacturing ratings and performance standards included in testing standards.
Marking	Marking includes manufacturer's symbol and identification.
Application	Application includes product information.

IEC Standards—The IEC impacted global standards immediately by setting an international standard for the *resistance for copper* and *international letter symbols* related to units of measurement. In addition the following electrical units were defined: *Hertz* for frequency, *Oersted* for magnetic field strength, *Gauss* for magnetic flux density, *Maxwell* of magnetic flux, *Gilbert* for magnetomotive force, *Var* for reactive power, and *Weber* for the practical unit of magnetic flux. In the 1930s, the IEC established a comprehensive system of physical units, called the "*Giorgi*" system." Later this system is expanded into the "*Système international*" or in English, the *International System of Units* (SI). SI is the current standard for *scientific units* and *symbols*.

Consolidated indexes are also available in English, French, German, and Spanish. The IEC currently has 67 country members, while another 69 participate in the Affiliate Country Program. The *Affiliate Program* helps third-world countries work with the IEC. The IEC is the *largest* international standards organization and IEC standard equipment and devices are present in factories around the world. Figure 1-6 illustrates an IEC device used to start motors.

Understanding IEC Standards

The IEC cooperates closely with the *International Organization for Standardization* (ISO) and currently has over 16,000 ISO/IEC standards. IEC standards are numbered 60000 through 79999 and standards are listed by number and title; for example, IEC 60417: Graphical symbols for use on equipment.

FIGURE 1-6: IEC starting device for 10 horsepower motor.

Courtesy of Rockwell Automation, Inc.

The IEC produces standard publications under a number of document formats: *International Standards*—IS (published standards), *Technical Specifications*—TS (standards under consideration and development), *Technical Reports*—TR (additional standard specifications), *Industry Technical Agreement* (documents that specify the parameters of a new product or service), *Publicly Available Specifications* (documents that represent a consensus among industry experts) and *Guides* (general information on standards).

1-4 APPLICATION OF THE STANDARDS

Manufacturing systems include *motors* and *motor controls*. All components in these systems meet standards set by one or more standards organizations. Figure 1-7 lists the standards and testing organizations most often associated with manufacturing equipment. The figure lists the traditional national boundaries for the groups along with the symbol placed on equipment they test and certify. The traditional boundaries no longer limit product movement, since manufacturers in North America, Europe, and Asia produce automation components to both NEMA and IEC standards for markets around the globe. If you are an electrical worker in the U.S., you must know both standards, because the machines in the factory come from many countries. For example, a conveyor and operator station from the U.S. uses NEMA standard motors, sensors, switches, and indicators. While the Japanese machine tool feeding the conveyor uses motors and motor controls with an IEC standard. Learning to recognize the symbols for the standards organizations is also important since that is how the hardware is labeled.

Comparison of the NEMA and IEC Standards

Both standards started early in the 20th century in parallel with the development of electricity. Both standards organizations focus on the creation and

FIGURE 1-7: Primary manufacturing equipment certification organizations.

Standards Organization	Primary Area of Coverage	Symbol
National Electrical Manufacturers Association	United States, Canada, Mexico	**NEMA**
Canadian Standards Association	Canada	CSA®
Underwriters Laboratories, Inc.	United States	UL®
International Electrotechnical Commission	Worldwide with 136 countries participating	IEC
Conformité Européenne	Western and Eastern Europe	CE
VDE Testing and Certification Institute	Western and Eastern Europe	VDE

distribution of criteria to influence the design, development, and production of components for the electrical industries they support. Both standards offer guidelines and a process for the implementation of electrical systems from these components. As motor control devices are presented in the text, the influence of both standards on the device is compared. An introduction to the *differences in the standards* is presented in Figure 1-8 to emphasize the importance of learning how the standards define motor control.

Figure 1-8 *compares* the NEMA and IEC standards. While the comparisons are general, they show that knowledge of the standards helps electrical workers to install and replace NEMA and IEC hardware. The comparison table in the figure shows:

- A need to convert between *English* and *metric* electrical units.
- Two different methods to specify *enclosure protection* from environmental conditions.

- Motor and motor control parameters are *defined differently* in the two standards but equivalent devices are available.
- IEC is more *application* specific than NEMA.
- NEMA devices are typically *larger* and *more costly* but have *longer* mean-time-between-failures.
- Some devices, like switches and pilot lamps, have *similar* standard specifications, so that some manufacturers produce *one device* under both standards.

In general, IEC definitions are more *narrow*, *comprehensive*, and *specific*. Therefore, IEC devices are used by original equipment manufacturers (OEMs) where machine specifications are well defined. NEMA ratings are more *conservative*. As a result, NEMA devices with fewer sizes and wider ranges of parameter values are used in applications where *requirements are less predictable* or may vary.

FIGURE 1-8: Comparison of NEMA and IEC standards.

Item	NEMA Standard	IEC Standard
Parameter units	English	Metric
Degrees of ingress protection	NEMA type sets standard	IP code sets standard
Size	Larger footprint for equivalent device	Smaller footprint for equivalent device
Performance	Life as much as 4 times higher than equivalent IEC device	Life of 1,000,000 operations is typical
Application areas	Fewer application specific parameters	Device selection driven by application so more application sensitivity
Cost	Higher equivalent device cost	Lower equivalent device cost
Motors	Frame and flange size in English units, horsepower, speed, 60 hertz power, voltage rating, terminal box location, duty cycle, and temperature classes	Frame and flange size in metric units, Kilowatts, speed, 50 hertz power, voltage rating, terminal box location, duty cycle, and temperature classes
Motor controls	Supplied in standardized sizes, rated in horsepower, mounting not standard, limited terminal markings	No size standards, rated in Utilization Category, mounting standard in some categories, complete terminal identification
Pilot lamps and switches	NEMA type enclosure rating, similar electrical performance, panel opening three sizes, and no styling standard	IP code enclosure rating, similar electrical performance, panel opening not in standard, and no styling standard
Other areas	Typical hand reset only mechanism	Typical hand or auto-reset or stop mechanism
	Designed for time delay fuses and circuit breakers	Designed for fast-acting, current-limiting European fuses

CHAPTER 2

Manually-Operated Devices

GOALS AND OBJECTIVES

The primary goals for this chapter are to identify manually-operated input devices, and to describe the operation of and applications for these discrete control devices in manufacturing systems. In addition, the operation of and applications for visual and audible signaling devices are described. Finally, troubleshooting tips and procedures for typical failure modes are presented.

After completing this chapter, you will be able to:

1. Identify and describe the components of a manually-operated device.
2. Identify and discuss the operation of toggle, pushbutton, selector, key, drum foot switches, and joystick.
3. Identify and discuss the functions of signaling devices.
4. Identify the symbols for manually-operated devices and signaling devices.
5. Describe troubleshooting techniques for manually-operated devices.

2-1   INPUT SWITCHING DEVICES

Manually-operated input devices are switches with an internal switching mechanism that is actuated by a human operator. *Pushbutton switches* are the most common manually operated interface devices followed by *selector switches*. Other switch operators electrical workers encounter are the *key, drum, foot,* and *joystick.* All of these switch types are addressed in this chapter.

Switches have: a *mechanical device* to change the switch contact position, some number of *contact poles,* and some number of *contact positions*. In switches these three criteria are called: the *operator,* the *pole,* and the *throw.*

Toggle switches are used infrequently in industrial control. However, the easy to understand toggle switch cross section in Figure 2-1 is a good illustration for learning switch fundamentals and components.

Switch Operator

The operator is the device or mechanism used to change the contact positions in the contact block. The operator changes with each switch type; for example, in a *pushbutton switch* the operator is a *button* and in the *key switch* it is a *key and tumbler mechanism.* Switch operators with two states or positions, Figure 2-1, are the most common in industrial control. Switch contacts are designated as *normally open* (NO) or *normally closed* (NC). With the switch operator in the *non-actuated* position, the NO contacts are *open* and the NC contacts are *closed* or *shorted.* When the switch operator is placed in the *actuated* state the

FIGURE 2-1: Toggle switch.

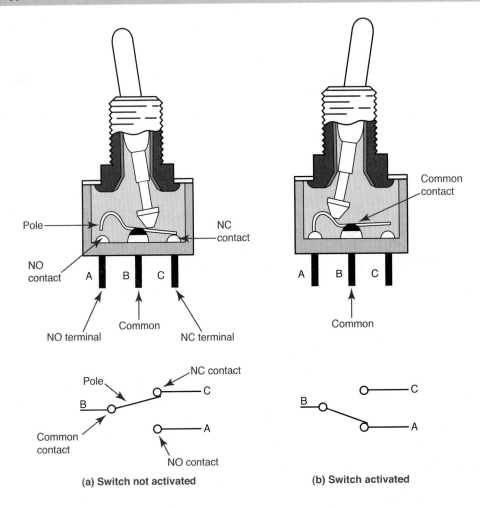

(a) Switch not activated

(b) Switch activated

NO contacts are *closed* or *shorted* and the NC contacts are *open*.

In many industry references the term "Normally" is used to indicate the *original position* of the operator or the *non-actuated position* of the operator. In some circumstances this leads to confusion or an incorrect assumption on the position of the operator or contact state. In this text only the terms *activated* (held) and *non-activated* (not held and original) are used. Terms in parenthesis are used, but less frequently. When the term "Normally" is used, it refers to the condition of the device off the shelf, out of the box, or not yet installed.

Switch Pole

The term *pole* indicates the number of isolated (not electrically connected) sets of contacts within a switch assembly. The switch in Figure 2-1 has one pole. Switches commonly have one, two or three poles, but

more are possible. Figure 2-2(a) illustrates the NEMA and IEC control symbols for the switches. Figure 2-2(b) illustrates other NEMA pole combinations. With two or more poles present, every pole is an *independent circuit* and all move *at the same time* when the operator is moved. For example, a switch for three phase power would require a three pole switch with three NO contacts. Each phase is switched by one of the three poles.

Switch Throw

The term *throw* indicates the number of current conducting positions or contact positions associated with each pole. Switches are commonly manufactured in *single throw* or *double throw* configurations. In a *single throw* (ST) configuration, the pole has contacts that are either normally open (NO) or normally closed (NC). Activating the switch operator in this configuration, closes the NO contact or opens the NC con-

FIGURE 2-2: NEMA and IEC switch symbols.

Letter Code	NEMA		IEC	
	NO	NC	NO	NC
NEMA – SW IEC – SW	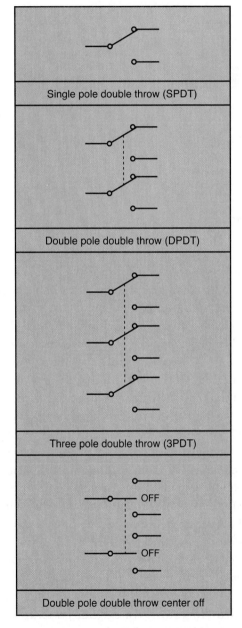			

(a) NEMA and IEC single pole single throw (SPST) symbols and letter codes

Single pole double throw (SPDT)

Double pole double throw (DPDT)

Three pole double throw (3PDT)

OFF

OFF

Double pole double throw center off

(b) Other commonly used NEMA contact configurations

tact. Moving the switch operator back to the original state, returns the NO contact to open or the NC contact to closed. A residential light switch is an example of a single throw device. Standard symbols and letter codes are in Figure 2-2(a).

In the *double throw* (DT) configuration, the pole has two contact positions, NO and NC, with a common wire between them. Study the double throw configurations in Figure 2-2(b). Some switches have a *center off* position as illustrated in Figure 2-2(b). When the operator is switched to the center off position, the operator holds the pole so no contact with either the NO or NC contacts occurs.

Single and Double Break Contacts

When contacts are opened, *single break* (SB) switches interrupt circuit current flow at *one point*. However, *double break* (DB) switches use two sets of contacts to interrupt the circuit current at *two points*. Single break (SB) type contacts are illustrated in Figure 2-2, and a double break (DB) type contacts are illustrated in Figure 2-3. The notation for the four switch symbols (left to right) in Figure 2-3(d) is SPST DB normally open contacts, SPST DB normally closed contacts, SPDT DB, DPDT DB. Single break contacts have *lower* current ratings because they break the current at only one point. Double break contacts, sized like a single break contact, are rated for *higher* currents because the current is broken at two points.

Momentary and Maintained Operator

Switch operators use two methods, *momentary* and *maintained,* to set the condition of switch contacts. In a *momentary* operator, the contacts change state when the operator is actuated. They remain in the actuated condition only while the switch operator is *physically* held in the actuated position. Momentary operators are also called *spring back* and *spring return* by some manufacturers. When the *machine* operator releases the switch, the *switch* operator returns to its *original position* and the contacts return to their *original state*.

In a *maintained* operator, the contacts change state when the switch operator is actuated, and *remain* in that state after the operator is *released*. The next actuation of the switch operator returns the contacts to the non-actuated or original state. *Momentary* and

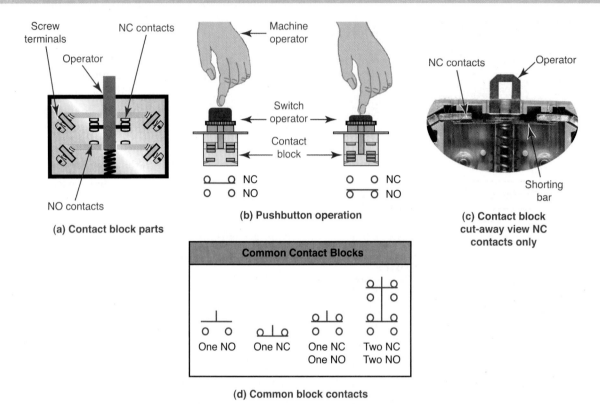

(a) Contact block parts

(b) Pushbutton operation

(c) Contact block cut-away view NC contacts only

(d) Common block contacts

maintained positions are controlled by the *switch operator* with the contact block inheriting the condition set by the operator. However, frequently the terms *momentary contacts* or *maintained contacts* are used, but the contacts do not determine momentary and maintained switch operation.

Pushbutton Switches

Pushbuttons are the most frequently used manual switch in commercial and industrial motor control applications. Pushbutton switches, found in most motor control circuits, are used to *manually start* and *stop* machines, and to *control* and *override* industrial processes. The standard pushbutton consists of two main components, the *operator* and the *contact block(s)*. Figure 2-3 illustrates a SPDT contact block in (a), the operation of the pushbutton in (b), a view of a NC double break contact and contact bar in (c), and the standard symbols and letter codes in (d). The cut-away in Figure 2-3(c) is not from a pushbutton contact block but is presented to show how a NC contact set with contact bar and operator are constructed.

The pushbutton operator is the red button in Figure 2-3(b) that is pressed by the machine operator to actuate the switch. Note how the operator moves the contact bar from the NC position to the NO position when activated. The SPDT pushbutton switch is pictured in Figure 2-4(a), and a separate pushbutton operator and SPDT contact block are shown in Figure 2-4(d). When actuated, the operator mechanically forces the contacts in the block to change state. For example, if the contact block contains NO contacts, actuation causes the contacts to close. If the contact block contains NC contacts, the contacts open.

Pushbutton switch styles include operators that are *pushed*, *pulled*, and *turned* to actuate the switch or return an actuated switch to the non-actuated state. In addition, pushbutton operators have four styles: *extended operator, flush operator, guarded operator,* and *mushroom.*

Extended Operator—An extended operator pushbutton, Figure 2-4(a), has the actuator *protruding* 1/4″ or more beyond the top edge of the mounting ring. The extension permits the machine operator

FIGURE 2-4: Pushbutton operators with three degrees of operator guarding.

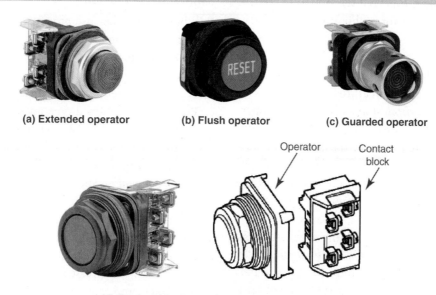

(a) Extended operator   (b) Flush operator   (c) Guarded operator

(d) Contact blocks stack under pushbutton operators

Letter Code	NEMA			IEC	
	NO	NC	NO & NC (double circuit)	NO	NC
NEMA - PB IEC - SB					

(e) NEMA and IEC control symbols and letter codes

Courtesy of Rockwell Automation, Inc.

to *easily actuate* the pushbutton with pressure from a flat hand or fingers placed anywhere on the operator. This style is often used for STOP buttons because the operator color is seen easily. Unintended operation of the motor control system and personal injury are possibly due to incidental operator contact when the operators are extending beyond the mounting ring.

Flush Operator—Flush pushbuttons have the operator surface *even* with the mounting ring as pictured in Figure 2-4(b). Flush operators *curb* unintended operator actuation from incidental operator contact because actuation requires finger pressure on the center of the operator. Motor control systems frequently use flush operators to protect against accidental initiation. The *reset* pushbutton in Figure 2-4(b) is a flush operator because preventing unscheduled system reset is often critical in a production system.

Guarded Operator—Two types of guarded pushbuttons, *half shroud* and *extended guard*, provide the greatest level of protection from unintended operator actuation. Half-shroud pushbuttons surround the top half of the pushbutton operator with a raised guard. The half-shroud provides more protection from incidental contact than a standard flush operator. In addition, operator access with gloved hands using the thumb is better compared to gloved hand access to flush pushbuttons.

Extended guards, shown in Figure 2-4(c), offer the highest level of protection from accidental actuation by surrounding the pushbutton with a cylinder extending above the surface of operator. Access to the pushbutton is restricted to an opening the size of the operator. However, actuation with gloved hands is difficult and removal of the gloves to press the operator is often required. Numerous combinations of contacts in contact blocks, see Figure 2-3(d) and 2-4(d), are attached to operators. NEMA and IEC control symbols and letter codes for pushbuttons are shown in Figure 2-4(e).

Mushroom Operator—The *mushroom-type* pushbutton as shown in Figure 2-5 features an operator with a large circular mushroom shaped surface. The operators of both pushbuttons in Figure 2-5 are *maintained* types. In Figure 2-5(a) the mushroom operator extends over the edges of the mounting ring and typically has a diameter larger than the operator of the standard pushbutton. Motor control systems that require quick operator reaction, such as *emergency stop* circuits, use mushroom head pushbuttons. In these applications, the *size, shape, quick identification,* and *easy actuation* of mushroom operators makes them an ideal choice. NEMA and IEC control symbols and letter codes for a NC mushroom pushbutton are illustrated in Figure 2-5. The mushroom symbols are the same as pushbuttons in Figure 2-4 except that the pushbutton symbols have a mushroom cap added. Contact blocks between pushbuttons and mushroom pushbuttons from the same manufacturer are generally *interchangeable,* so contact configurations and specifications are the same.

FIGURE 2-5: Mushroom pushbutton switch.

| (a) Mushroom 2 position push-pull | (b) Mushroom 2 position push-pull/twist |

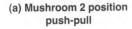

Letter Code	NEMA	IEC
	NC	NC
NEMA - PB IEC - SB		

Courtesy of Rockwell Automation, Inc.

Pushbutton Momentary and Maintained Operation

Pushbutton switches use *momentary* and *maintained* operators. Pressing a momentary type operator causes all NO contacts to *close* and all NC contacts to *open*. Releasing the operator causes all contacts to immediately return to their *original* position.

Pressing a maintained type operator causes all NO contacts to *close* and all NC contacts to *open*. However, when the operator is *released*, all contacts remain in their *actuated* position. Manually returning the operator to its *original* position returns the contacts to their *original* state.

Momentary contact pushbuttons are shown in Figure 2-4(a) through (c). A maintained contact pushbutton with a *push-pull operator* is shown in Figure 2-5(a). A depressed operator changes NC and NO contacts and remains depressed until the operator is *pulled out* to return the contacts to their original position. A maintained contact pushbutton with a *push-pull/twist operator* is shown in Figure 2-5(b). The operator is rotated and pulled to return contacts to their original position.

Maintained contact pushbuttons are usually mushroom type and commonly used as emergency stop pushbuttons in motor control applications. The NC contacts, of an emergency stop pushbutton, opens the control circuit and halts the process when the pushbutton is pressed. The operator remains depressed until physically reset to the original position. The production process does not restart if the start pushbuttons are pressed. The restart is inhibited until a machine operator physically resets NC stop pushbutton contacts back to the original position. Strategically placing several emergency stop pushbuttons in a production area adds an increased level of safety to the production system.

Interlocking Pushbuttons

An *interlocking pushbutton* switch is shown in Figure 2-6(a) with one mushroom operator and one extended operator. Any combination of available operator styles is used in either operator location. The two pushbutton operators are linked to a single or multiple contact block(s). One operator changes the contacts in the contact block(s) to their *actuated posi-*

FIGURE 2-6: Interlocking and three position pushbutton switches.

(a) NEMA—interlocking pushbutton

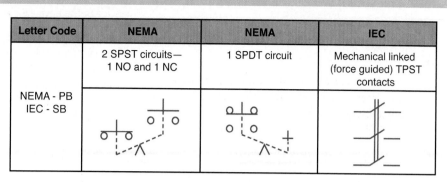

Letter Code	NEMA	NEMA	IEC
NEMA - PB IEC - SB	2 SPST circuits— 1 NO and 1 NC	1 SPDT circuit	Mechanical linked (force guided) TPST contacts

(c) Control symbols and letter code

(b) IEC—three position push-pull pushbutton operator

	Three Position Pushbutton Operator Position		
	Out	Center	In
Operator options	Momentary	Maintained	Momentary
	Momentary	Maintained	Maintained

(d) Three position push-pull pushbutton operator

Courtesy of Rockwell Automation, Inc.

tion(s), and the other operator returns the contacts to their *original condition(s)*. Interlocks have *maintained contacts* so the operator that is actuated is in and the not actuated operator is out. Many manual motor starters use interlocked pushbuttons as *start* and *stop* buttons. The maintained operator symbols are shown in Figure 2-6(c) with a dotted line (NEMA) or solid line (IEC) to indicate the mechanically linked feature of the pushbutton.

Three Position Push-Pull Pushbuttons

Figure 2-6(d) shows the operator for a *three position push-pull pushbutton* and the contact momentary and maintained position options. The *momentary out, maintained center,* and *momentary in* operator incorporates two momentary pushbuttons into a single switch and prevents both momentary operations to occur simultaneously. The second option, *momentary out, maintained center,* and *maintained in* incorporates two different switch control options into a single switch.

Other Contact Configurations

Normally open and normally closed contact blocks are just two options for use with switch operators, especially for emergency stop applications. Variations include:

- NCLB—*Normally closed late break contacts*— When the operator is actuated, the NCLB contacts open after the change in regular NO or NC contacts. When the operator is returned to the original position, the open NCLB contacts close before the change in regular NO or NC contacts.
- NOEM—*Normally open early make contacts*— When the operator is actuated, the NOEM contacts close before the change in regular NO or NC contacts. When the operator is reset to the original position the closed NOEM contacts open before the change in regular NO or NC contacts.
- SMCB—*Self-Monitoring contact blocks*—The self monitoring contact block is composed of a NCLB contact wired in series with a NO *monitoring*

contact. The NO monitoring contact automatically closes when the SMCB contact block is properly installed onto the emergency-stop operator. If the SMCB contact block is separated from the operator, the NO monitoring contact automatically opens the control circuit.

Manufacturers use a variety of terms to describe NCLB and NOEM operation. For example, Square D identifies *late-break* with the term *late-opening* and early make with *early-make closing*. However, the operation described earlier is the same.

Selector Switches

Selector switches are control devices in which the operator is rotated to actuate contacts in the attached contact block(s). Switch configuration options that determine the operation and application of a selector switch include:

- **The physical style of the operator**—Figure 2-7(a) through (c) illustrates three selector switch styles based on the technique used to rotate the operator. The *standard knob* operator in Figure 2-7(a) is used for *general purpose* applications. In Figure 2-7(b), a *knob lever operator,* an extend lever handle makes changing switch position *easier* for machine operators wearing gloves. Finally, the *cylinder lock* operator in Figure 2-7(c) requires a key to rotate the operator. This provides a level of security by only allowing authorized personnel with a key to operate the switch. The standard operator is *not illuminated,* but *illuminated operators* are available to identify operator position in low ambient light conditions. Illuminated operators offer a wide range of AC/DC voltage choices from 6 to 600 volts and 50/60 hertz transformer options.

- **The number of positions**—In most industrial applications, selector switches have *two, three,* or *four positions* with two and three position switches used more often than four. Figure 2-7(e) and (f) illustrates the control symbol for two and three position selectors respectively.

- **Selection of maintained or spring return operator for each position**—The operator at each position is *maintained* (M) or *spring return* (S). Spring return indicates a *momentary position,* where actuation requires the machine operator to physically hold the operator in the actuated position. For example, a three position selector designated S→M←S, illustrated in Figure 2-7(f), indicates that the center position is *maintained* and the left and right positions are *momentary* or *spring return.* The graphic below the S→M←S in the figure indicates the same operator action. Other options are MMM, *maintained* at each position, S→MM and MM←S, *two maintained positions* and *one spring return.* If a spring return position is present it is *always* located at the far left and/or far right positions.

- **The number and type of contacts**—The standard switchable contact configurations include 1 NO, 1 NC, 1 NO and 1 NC, or 2 NO and 2 NC. The number of contact blocks is a function of the contact configurations and the number of positions. For example, Figure 2-7(d) shows a four position selector with four contact blocks. While the two position cylinder lock operator, as in Figure 2-7(c), has a single contact block with 1 NO and 1 NC contact set. Two and four position selectors are available with *make-before-break* and break-before-make switch characteristics, when NCLB and NOEM contact blocks are used.

- **The type of contact blocks**—Contact blocks are available with contacts designed to switch differ-

FIGURE 2-7: Selector switches.

(a) Standard knob operator

(b) Knob lever operator

(c) Cylinder lock operator

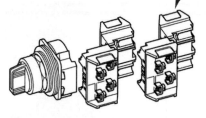

(d) Switch operator with four contact blocks

Letter Code	NEMA	IEC
NEMA - SS IEC - SA	o ⏌ o ⋮ o o	

(e) Standard symbols and letter

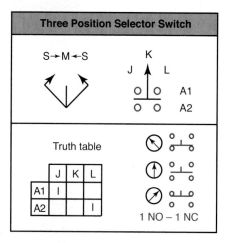

(f) Truth table and operator

Courtesy of Rockwell Automation, Inc.

ent size loads. A typical selection includes: *standard (general purpose)*, *maximum duty* with horsepower ratings, *low voltage (dry contact rating)*, *logic reed*, *sealed*, and *stackable sealed* switches.

• **The type of legend plate**—Most of the frequently used *switch name plates* or *legend plates*, such as Hand Off Auto, are available pre-printed by the switch manufacturers. Custom legends with special words are also available.

Two position selector switches are the most common with the majority of the operators configured for *maintained contacts*. Figure 2-7(e) shows the NEMA and IEC control symbols and letter codes for a two position selector.

Multi-position selector switches are either three or four position. Truth tables, Figure 2-7(f), are used to indicate closed and open contacts for *each* switch position. For example in the figure, the *A1* contacts are closed in the *J* switch position, and *A2* is closed in the *L* position. In the center, both A1 and A2 are open. Figure 2-7(f) illustrates a NEMA three position switch with center off. Three position selector switches usually have a center or neutral OFF position as illustrated in the figure. Multi-position switches, while not used as frequently, are important because of their flexibility and multiple contact positions. Three position selector switches, such as shown in Figure 2-7(f), can be *maintained*, *momentary* or a *combination* of both. Four position selector switch operators are generally *maintained*; however, one momentary position is permitted, but the location is restricted to the first or last contact position.

NEMA Versus IEC Pushbutton and Selector Switches

Physical installation and features differ between the NEMA style and the IEC style pushbuttons. Figure 2-8 compares differences in *operator style*, *connection terminations*, *panel opening*, and *panel sealing*.

FIGURE 2-8: Pushbutton options.

Pushbutton and Selector Comparison	NEMA versus IEC
Operator Style	There is no specific NEMA or IEC standard that governs operator styles. As a result, operator features reflect a manufacturer's or customer's preference. The figure below illustrates typical NEMA and IEC operator styles. In the United States, NEMA operators are constructed with a high proportion of metallic components; whereas, European IEC designs use a higher proportion of plastic components, which permits lower cost and modern appearance. (Pushbuttons top—selectors below) NEMA style IEC style
Connection Terminations	Both NEMA and IEC style pushbuttons offer a wide range of wire termination options. The figure below illustrates connection styles that are available in both NEMA and IEC. Note pressure plate terminals in (a), and barrel terminals in (b). Also, available are stab-on-connectors to make the electrical termination and spring-clamp technology is gaining acceptance as an alternate to the standard screw-type styles. (a) (b)
Panel Opening	Industrial pushbuttons have three standard panel opening sizes: 16mm, 22.5mm and 30.5mm. The 16mm and the 22.5mm sizes originated in Europe, and the 30.5mm size is generally used in United States. Today, all sizes enjoy global acceptance. Hole sizes are specified in the IEC standards, but not in NEMA standards.
Panel Sealing	IEC pushbuttons are inserted from the front of the panel and secured from the rear with sealing gaskets located on the front of the panel. By contrast, NEMA pushbuttons have panel seals located inside the panel, and switches are inserted from the rear.

Courtesy of Rockwell Automation, Inc.

Figure 2-9 shows an annotated three-position selector switch with maintained contacts in a heating control circuit. When the selector switch is in the HAND position, the motor starting system has power applied as long as the system temperature is below the set-point value for the high temperature cutout switch. When the selector switch is in the AUTO posi- tion, the motor starting system is controlled by the temperature thermostat. Power is applied to the blower motor when the system temperatures falls below the set-point value and the NO system temperature thermostat switch closes. Finally, when the selector switch is in the OFF position, the circuit is open.

FIGURE 2-9: Thermostat controlled motor.

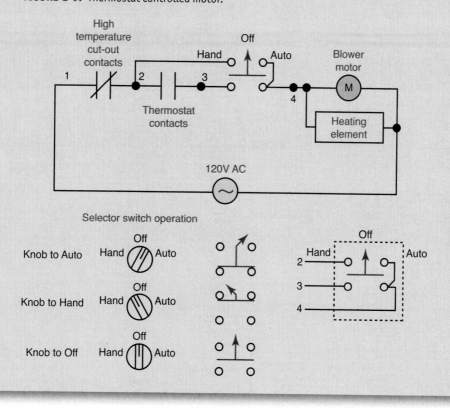

Drum Switches

The drum switch, a variation of the selector switch, is another type of manually operated switch used in motor control and is a variation of the selector switch. Drum switches are generally three-position switches that are used for the directional control of smaller single phase and polyphase motors. Figure 2-10(a) shows the drum switch, and Figure 2-10(b) shows its contact configuration. Note that the center off position has all contacts

FIGURE 2-10: Drum switch.

	Handle Position		
	Reverse	**Off**	**Forward**
	1○——○2	1○ ○2	1○ ○2
	3○——○4	3○ ○4	3○ ○4
	5○——○6	5○ ○6	5○——○6

(a) Drum switch

(b) NEMA contact terminal symbols with shared contacts for non-activated operator

Figure 2-11 shows a drum switch used as a reversing switch for a three phase motor. The switch inputs are L1, L2, and L3, and the switch outputs are T1, T2, and T3. Note that in Figure 2-11(a) there is no connection between the inputs and the outputs, which is the off position. Figure 2-11(b) has L1 connected to T1, L2 connected to T2, and L3 con-

nected to T3, which forces the motor to run in the forward direction. Whereas, in Figure 2-11(c), the connections to T1 and T3 are reversed, that is, L1 is connected to T3 and L3 is connected to T1, which forces the motor to run in the reverse direction.

FIGURE 2-11: Three phase AC motor reversing with a drum switch.

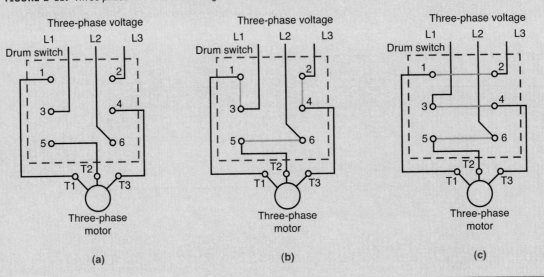

(a)   (b)   (c)

open. The other two positions that are labeled forward and reverse have internally connected contacts.

Foot Switches

The *foot switch* gives a machine operator full use of their hands while starting a machine with their foot. Most foot switches are configured with *NO contacts* and a *momentary* operator. When the machine operator presses the switch with their foot, the NO contacts close. The contacts return to their original position only when the foot is removed from the switch. Foot switches are manufactured in a variety of styles, but most have a foot shroud that protects the switch from being accidentally actuated. Figure 2-12 illustrates a shrouded and unshrouded style. Also, the NEMA and IEC foot switch symbols for NO and NC contacts are shown along with the letter codes.

A common field task for electrical workers, conduit threading, requires a foot switch. Large free standing conduit threading machines are often equipped with a foot switch for hands-free operation. In addition, machine control with a foot switch provides a level of safety for the operators—simply lifting their foot shuts down the machine in an emergency.

Joysticks

Industrial joysticks, like video game controllers, offer users many control functions from a single device. A *durable* industrial joystick with a *high* duty cycle is pictured in Figure 2-13(a). Environmentally *sealed* contacts are available in a variety of contact configurations with *NO contacts* used most often. Most joysticks have *spring-back* or *spring-return* operators configured with 2, 3, 4, or 8 positions. Each joystick position or direction has an assigned contact to sense the stick movement. Study the positions and movement in Figure 2-13(b).

Movement of the handle to one of the stick positions actuates the contact for that position. The con-

FIGURE 2-12: Foot switch, control symbols, and letter code.

Letter Code	NEMA		IEC	
	NO	NC	NO	NC
NEMA – FT IEC – FT				

Courtesy of AutomationDirect.

FIGURE 2-13: Joystick positions and contact symbols.

Dot indicates position of joystick in which contact will close

Description	Function
2 positions 2 contacts	
2/4 positions 4 contacts	
4 positions 4 contacts	
8 positions 8 contacts	

Right   A

Left   B

Up   C

Down   D

(a) Joystick   **(b) Positions and contacts**   **(c) Joystick contact symbols**

Courtesy of J. R. Merritt.

tact remains actuated until the handle is moved to another position or returned to the center position. Study the stick contact symbols for a four-position device in Figure 2-13(c). The *dot* in the figure indicates the handle motion to actuate the position contact. The spring mechanism in the handle returns the joystick to the *center* or *neutral* position whenever the joystick is released. Also, accidental actuation is prevented on some joysticks by a *locking mechanism*.

The joystick's major advantage is *single-hand multi-input* process or machine control with continuous *visual contact* of the operation. Typical applications include: *cranes, steel mill process control, logging, mining machinery,* and *offshore drilling equipment.*

Figure 2-14 shows an overhead crane and a four-position joystick control. The joystick controls the movement of the crane with the four position contacts. Forward joystick movement toward the 12 o'clock position in Figure 2-14(b) causes the crane's hoist to lift the load. Backward handle movement (toward the 6 o'clock position) causes the crane to lower the load. Left or right movement causes the crane trolley to traverse left and right. Joysticks offer the flexibility to control multiple directions of hoist and crane trolley at the same time. For example, pushing the joystick handle to the upper right raises and traverses the load to the right. The circuit used to produce the crane control is illustrated in Figure 2-14(c).

FIGURE 2-14: Joystick crane control application.

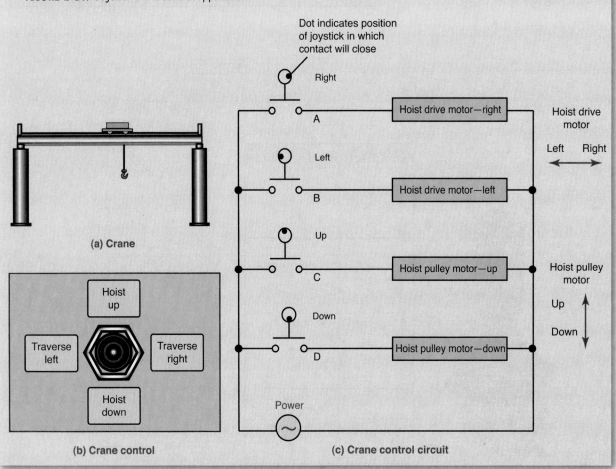

(a) Crane

(b) Crane control

(c) Crane control circuit

2-2 OUTPUT SIGNALING DEVICES

Signaling devices have eight classifications: *illuminated pushbutton switches, pilot lights, beacons, hazardous location devices, horns, panel alarms,* and *tower lights.* These devices provide a visual and/or sound indication about the status of an industrial process. The indication alerts the machine operator to *monitor* the process, *determine* process status, or *react* to a process malfunction. Signaling devices prevent: process problems from going *unnoticed, serious damage* to machine components, and *injury* to shop-floor personnel. Signaling devices are an integral part of most motor control systems. The illuminated pushbutton functions as both an *input* (manual contact closures) device and an *output* (illuminated operator) device. Figure 2-15 shows an overview of the types of output signaling devices used in manufacturing.

FIGURE 2-15: Overview of output signaling devices.

Output Signaling Devices	Description
	Round Beacons—six colors, many diameters, and light sources include: steady, flashing, strobe, and rotating halogen, and variable rotational speeds.
	Square Beacons—six colors with a high intensity strobe.
	Panel Alarms—special purpose panel alarms offer sounders, LED beacons, xenon strobes, and sounder with LED combination.
	Tower Lights 30 mm—offer one to five modules in combinations of sound and light units with six lens colors matched to LED color for improved optics.
	Tower Lights 70 mm—offer steady and flashing LED light modules with six color lens and sound modules with pulsing and steady sound.

Courtesy of Rockwell Automation, Inc.

2-3   VISUAL SIGNALING DEVICES

Visual signaling devices have a *visual* indicator or a combination of *visual and sound* indicators. *Pilot lights* and other *panel mounted alarm lights* are the most frequently used, but the visual range is limited to operators close to the panel. *Beacon* and *stack* or *tower lights* offer a large visual range depending on the device size used. Typical visual ranges for devices are illustrated in Figure 2-16(a). Three luminous sources are used in visual signaling devices:

- **Incandescent lamp**—Incandescent lamps are good for continuous and blinking applications with adequate performance at a relatively low cost. However, the filament light bulb's life time is the shortest of the three choices and decreases with exposure to any level of vibration.
- **Xenon (strobe) tube**—The high voltage xenon tube creates a brilliant flash of light at ignition that is further enhanced by a *Fresnel lens*. Tube life varies from 10–20 million flashes.
- **LED (Light Emitting Diode)**—LEDs emit a *single color* and have *lower brilliance* than incandescent lamps and xenon tubes. However, LEDs operate at low current levels and have long operational life. They are the best choice for high shock and vibration applications.

Figure 2-16(b) indicates the meaning and expected operator reaction for a variety of lens colors associated with visual signaling devices.

Illuminated Pushbuttons and Pilot Lights

Illuminated pushbuttons, back-lighted with an LED or incandescent lamp, provide a visual indication of system status with the illuminated pushbutton operator. *Pilot lights* are industrial-grade lamps installed in control panels and machine front panels to provide a *visual indication* of events and conditions of the system. For example, pilot lights indicate *operational motor status*, *level of material in a storage bin*, or a *system malfunction*. The variety of signaling devices is as varied as the applications that use them.

FIGURE 2-16: Visual distance and color guidelines.

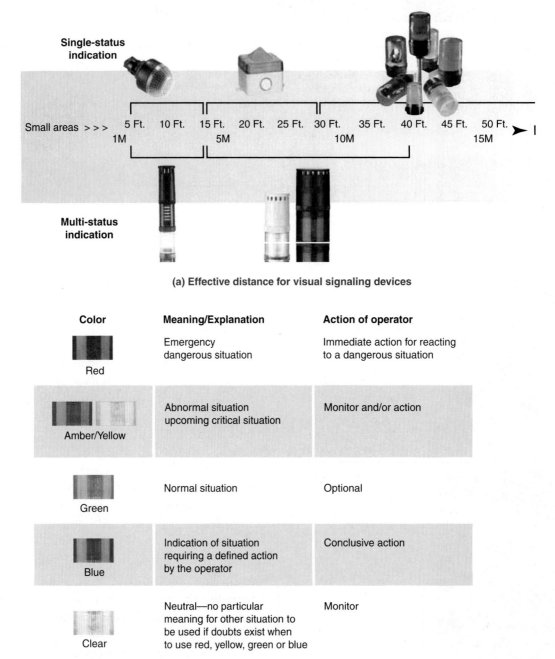

Single-status indication

Small areas > > >

| 5 Ft. | 10 Ft. | 15 Ft. | 20 Ft. | 25 Ft. | 30 Ft. | 35 Ft. | 40 Ft. | 45 Ft. | 50 Ft. |
| 1M | | 5M | | | 10M | | | | 15M |

Multi-status indication

(a) Effective distance for visual signaling devices

Color	Meaning/Explanation	Action of operator
Red	Emergency dangerous situation	Immediate action for reacting to a dangerous situation
Amber/Yellow	Abnormal situation upcoming critical situation	Monitor and/or action
Green	Normal situation	Optional
Blue	Indication of situation requiring a defined action by the operator	Conclusive action
Clear	Neutral—no particular meaning for other situation to be used if doubts exist when to use red, yellow, green or blue	Monitor

(b) General use and meanings of colors for visual signaling equipment

Courtesy of Rockwell Automation, Inc.

Single Pilot Lights

The basic single pilot light consists of a *lens cap*, the *lamp*, and a *power module* as illustrated in Figure 2-17(a). The basic pilot light has two terminals that are connected to a DC or AC power source. Pilot lights are not polarity sensitive, thus, either terminal can be connected to either side of a DC power source.

Lens caps are available in a variety of colors: *red, green, amber, white*, and *clear*. For the most part, lens caps are *interchangeable* within a manufacturer's

FIGURE 2-17: Pilot lights, symbols, and letter codes.

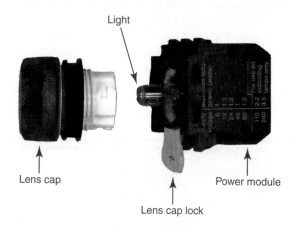

(a) Basic NEMA single pilot light

Light

Lens cap

Lens cap lock

Power module

(b) NEMA pilot lamp for hazardous areas

Letter Code	NEMA	IEC
NEMA – L IEC – HL	(R)	⊗

(c) Pilot lamp symbols and letter code

product line, but not between different product lines or different manufacturers. NEMA lens caps are generally made from a break-resistant plastic and are usually threaded for screwing on and off the pilot light. Figure 2-17(b) shows a well guarded pilot light for hazardous locations, and Figure 2-17(c) illustrates the NEMA and IEC symbols for pilot lights and their letter codes. However, in NEMA devices the letter *L*, in the letter code, is usually replaced by a letter that designates the lens cap color. For example, an *R*, inside the circle, indicates a red lens cap. For IEC devices, the lens color letter is placed adjacent to the symbol.

The voltage range for lamps is 6 to 240 volts, AC or DC, but most applications use 24 or 120 volts AC or DC for power. As a result, verification of supply voltage before changing lamps is important.

Transformer Input Pilot Lights

A *transformer*, Figure 2-18, is placed in the *power module* of some pilot lights to permit use of lower voltage lamps. The primary (input) transformer voltage is the L1 and L2 control voltage. The transformer secondary voltage matches the lamp voltage. Common input voltages are 48 to 600 volts AC, the lamp voltage from the secondary is typically 6 volts. Pilot lights with transformers are safer when lamps are replaced while the control circuit is energized. An electrical worker can simply remove the lens cap and replace a suspected faulty lamp without the need to shut down the motor control system. However, transformers add cost and an additional point of failure to the device.

FIGURE 2-18: Dual input transformer relay type pilot light.

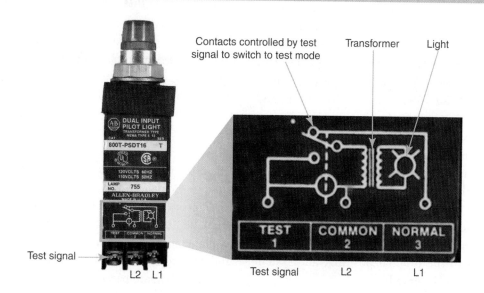

Contacts controlled by test signal to switch to test mode

Transformer

Light

Test signal

L2   L1

TEST 1   COMMON 2   NORMAL 3

Test signal   L2   L1

Incandescent lamps have long been the standard in pilot lights. However, the light-emitting diode (LED) replaced the incandescent lamp where possible in industrial applications. Incandescent lamps are less efficient, generate more heat, and have shorter life spans than LED pilot lights. Incandescent lamps operate on either AC or DC, but the LED requires DC,

usually 3 to 12 volts. Standard oil-tight LED indicating devices are available with 120V AC input. The electronics that are required to drive the LED are contained within device's terminal block. Figure 2-19(a) shows the indicator as viewed from the front of the panel, and Figure 2-19(b) illustrates the indicating device as viewed from the back of the panel.

FIGURE 2-19: Standard oil-tight LED indicating device.

(a) Panel view

(b) Back panel view

Pilot Light Test Options

Descriptions of three pilot light test circuits are included in Figure 2-20 with example test circuits. One standard *push-to-test* and two with *dual inputs* are illustrated in the figure along with their circuit descriptions. All three permit a test on the lamp in the indicator, but the circuit in (a) requires that the lens cap is pushed. The dual input circuits in Figure 2-20(b) and (c) have a second input to apply the lamp test voltage or signal. The test circuit on the side of the pilot light in Figure 2-18 is like the circuit in Figure 2-20(c).

The *push-to-test* feature, Figure 2-20(a), provides a quick method to verify that the lamp is good or bad by pressing on the lens cap. Some pilot lights have three terminals labeled *Test*, *Com(mon)*, and *Normal*. L_1 and L_2 are wired to Test and Com respectively. The monitored system parameter is connected to the *Normal* input, so when push-to-test is inactive the system parameter status is displayed by the light. Pressing the lens cap opens the NC contacts and closes the NO contacts. With the cap pressed, the test power is applied to the lamp and illumination indicates a good lamp. When the machine operator releases the lens cap, the switch returns to the original position, and system parameter status is displayed.

System panels often have numerous pilot lights, and individual lamp checks with push-to-test type devices takes too long. In those cases, *dual input* type pilot lights shown in Figure 2-20(b) and (c) are used. The dual inputs permit a *single* test button connected to the *Test* input on every pilot light to *simultaneously* test all lamps. Read the description of each test circuit in Figure 2-20.

Cluster Pilot Lights

The *cluster* style pilot light allows up to four lamps in one pilot light. Figure 2-21 shows a model with three lamps, labeled fan 1, fan 2, and fan 3. Each cluster lamp operates as the single pilot light. While used less frequently, the cluster pilot light is ideal where panel space is limited.

Beacon Indicator Lights

The usual range for pilot lights is limited to personnel close to the panel where it is installed. *Beacon* indicator lights permit a visual indication of system status as much as 100 feet away. Beacon indicator lights are available in the *round* and *square* styles with *rotating* and *flashing* or *strobe* indicators. Figure 2-22 illustrates round and square beacon lights.

FIGURE 2-20: Pilot light test circuit options.

Test Circuit	Description
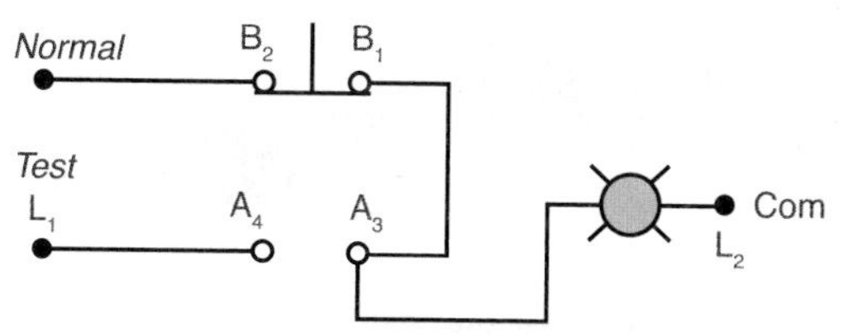 (a)	**Push-to-Test Pilot Light Device**—Push-to-test (PTT) pilot lights reduce the time required to troubleshoot a faulty indicator circuit. L_1 and L_2 are wired as shown to the lamp and the NO contacts of momentary SPDT push-to-test switch. The system signal is connected to the *Normal* terminal and to the lamp through the NC contacts on the PTT switch. In operation the lamp is on when power is applied to the *Normal* input. The lens cap is attached to the SPDT switch actuator, so pressing the lens cap opens B_1 to B_2 and shorts A_3 to A_4. As a result of the PTT action, the lamp turns on. Full voltage and transformer model push to test pilot lights are available.
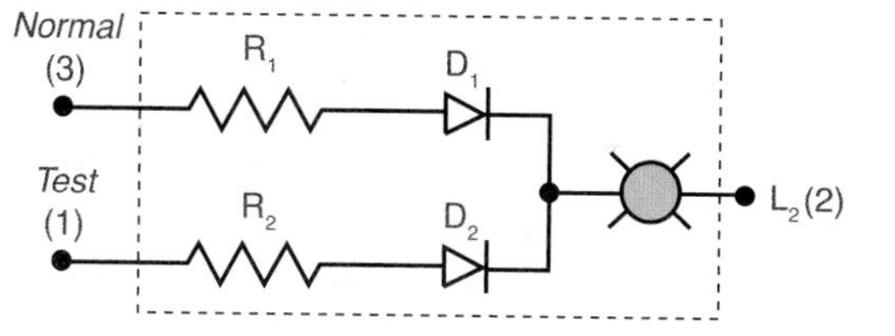 (b)	**Dual Input Diode Pilot Light Device**—Pilot light has two inputs *Normal* and *Test*. The diodes isolate the two inputs so current from one cannot flow into the other. The resistor limits lamp and diode current.
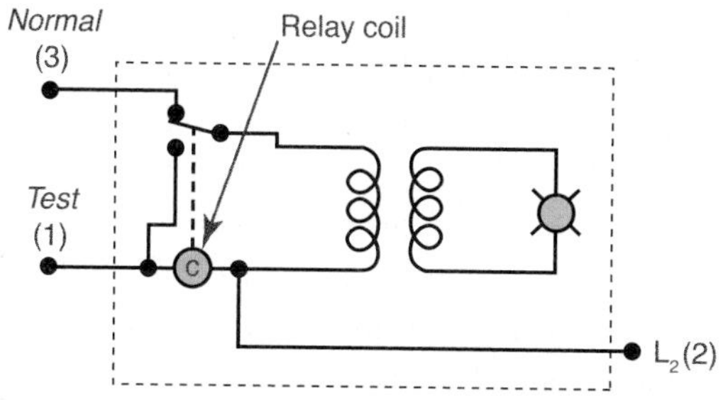 (c)	**Dual Input Transformer Relay Pilot Light Device**—Pilot light has two inputs *Normal* and *Test*, a transformer to reduce lamp voltage, and a relay to switch *Test* voltage to the transformer primary. Application of the test voltage energizes the coil, C, and changes the state of the SPDT relay contacts. In the energized state, the test signal is applied to the transformer to test the light.

FIGURE 2-21: Cluster pilot light with four segments.

Rotating or flashing beacon warning lights are generally associated with a *hazard problem* or a *proceed-with-caution* indication. The beacon lights in Figure 2-22 have input control to *rotate, flash,* or *rotate and flash* the beacon light simultaneously. Beacon warning lights are available in voltage ranges from 24 to 277 volts with 120 volts as the most common voltage used in industry.

Tower Indicator Lights

Tower indicators or *stack lights* permit multiple indicators and signaling devices to be assembled into a column with both *lights* and *sound* devices present. Towers with multicolored lights are visible from

FIGURE 2-22: Round and square beacon lights.

(a) Round beacons

(b) Square beacons

Courtesy of Rockwell Automation, Inc.

FIGURE 2-23: Tower or stack lights.

(a) Three and four light stacks

(b) Tower with horn at top

distances of 50 or more feet. Figure 2-16 illustrates light codes used to build the stack or tower signaling devices, and Figure 2-23(a) towers with a variety of lens color options. In addition, tower indicators are available in versions that include *audible alarms* within the same stack, as in Figure 2-23(b).

2-4 AUDIBLE SIGNALING DEVICES

Rotating and *flashing* beacon lights usually provide adequate visual indication of system status. However, in some situations a visual warning is not sufficient due to brightly illuminated environments or obstructions between operators and the signaling device.

Audible signaling devices generate a *sound* output signal or a combination of *sound and visual* outputs. Sound signaling devices include *tone sounders, buzzers, bells, standard horns,* and *hazardous location horns*. Devices are *panel* mounted, *tower* mounted, and combined in *horn/beacon combinations* as in Figure 2-23(b). In new applications, electronic tone sounders and horns replace the *older buzzer* and *bell* technology. Machine operators must identify the system status condition based on the sound from the audible devices in the production system.

Figure 2-24 shows an overview of newer audible signaling devices and their symbols. The sound level for audible devices, listed in Figure 2-24, is measured in *decibels* or *db*. A decibel is a statement of sound level based on a *logarithmic* scale. The logarithmic scale is not a straight line; as a result an 80 db sound level is not twice as loud as a 40 db level, but many times louder than 40 db.

Audible Alarms

Audible alarms combined with visual indicators ensure that operators know the system's status. However, ambient noise and bright ambient light interferes with an operator's ability to distinguish the alarm light and sound in the presence of other ambient conditions. For example, the sound of a buzzer in the grinding machines area easily blends in with grinder noise; so a horn is a better audible alarm selection. A good rule-of-thumb sets the signaling device sound level *15 db higher* than the loudest ambient noise present. Sound devices with different tones and tone sequences or combinations of both horns and tone are often used. That sets apart the *process status* message delivered by the audible signals from the background noise.

FIGURE 2-24: Overview of audible signaling devices.

Audible Signaling Device	Description	Symbol
30 mm—72 db 65 mm—105 db	**Panel Mounted Sounders**—Single circuit sounders for panel mount are shown. Sound output is a selectable continuous, pulsing tone, or wobble. The sound output varies from 72 to 105 db. All have sound plus light combination options.	**NEMA**
General purpose High performance Horn/beacon combination	**General Purpose Horns**—General purpose electronic horns, suitable for most midrange industrial applications, have 108 dB maximum sound output with multi-tone and volume control capability. With no moving parts, electronic horns are more reliable than electromechanical models. An electronic horn has 2 million hour life time, while electromechanical horns last approximately 500 hours. **High-Performance Electronic Horns**—High-performance horns have three differentiated tones from 100 to 126 dB for specific signal requirements, such as a machine start up, material shortage, or fault condition. Also, forty-five selectable tone sets with optimal frequency sweep or whoop are available for noisy environments. Attached xenon strobe beacons in six lens colors are also available.	**IEC**
Hazardous location devices	**Hazardous Location Devices**—These devices include alarm horn sounders and loudspeakers. The features include multiple tones, selectable tone stages, 110 dB or 117 dB and 15 watt output at either 8 or 16 ohms, volume control, and multiple voltage levels.	

Courtesy of Rockwell Automation, Inc.

2-5 TROUBLESHOOTING MANUALLY-OPERATED DEVICES

In general, processes stop because of a component failure or the actuation of devices/switches/operators. If a bad component is the cause, identify the faulty component and determine the reason for the component failure. If possible, correct the system so future failures of that component do not occur, and then restart the process.

Processes are also stopped with an emergency stop switch when a process or unsafe operation problem is present. When an emergency stop operator is pressed, the switch is not reset to the original position until the process situation is *fixed* or the safety concern for the emergency stop is *corrected*.

All of the switches covered in this chapter have a common troubleshooting approach. Switch failures are grouped into two categories: *operator problems* and *contact problems*.

Operator Problems

Operators are the mechanical elements that force the contacts from their normal position to the opposite state. Often the operator changes positions, but the contacts do not move. When operators fail, the contacts remain in either the not activated state or

LEGACY SIGNALING DEVICES—Examples of signaling of production system status are found in earliest manufacturing systems. Figure 2-25 shows three signaling devices that are still in place in production systems, but often not installed in new systems. The mechanical bell and electromechanical buzzer are replaced with their audible counterparts, the electronic tone sounder and horn. The electronic versions have no moving parts so they are more reliable, longer lasting, and provide greater output flexibility. The annunciator is a visual indicator that displays system status by lighting a rectangular block when the system status changes. The technology was developed initially for the process control industry but has application across all of manufacturing. LED and plasma screen displays with system status screens configured with software have replaced the electrical annunciator in many applications.

FIGURE 2-25: Legacy signaling devices.

Legacy Device	NEMA Symbol
	Bell 
	Buzzer 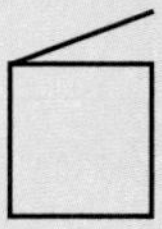
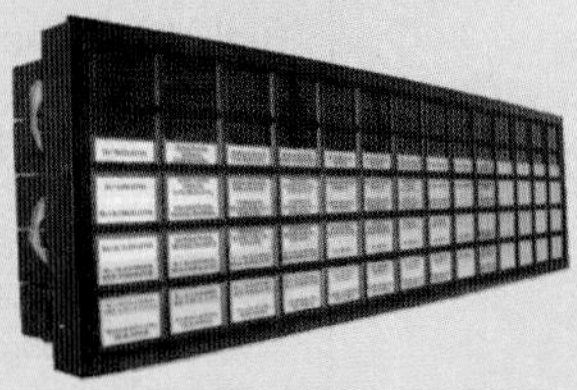	Annunciator 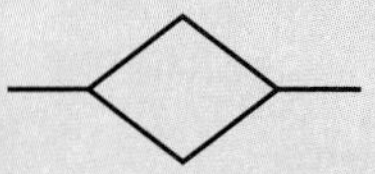

Courtesy of Apex Automation Solutions.

Figure 2-26 illustrates a simple fault detection circuit. When a fault is detected, the fault sensing device switches 120V AC to the buzzer and to the pilot light. The red pilot light provides a visual alarm, and the buzzer provides an audible alarm.

FIGURE 2-26: Fault detection circuit.

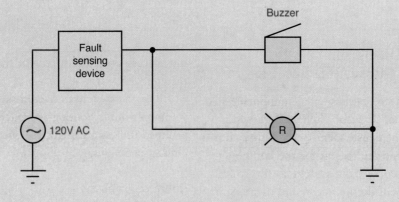

Safety control devices are designed for control of systems where *failure free operation* of the control system is a primary concern. Failure free operation is achieved through *redundant contacts*, *self monitoring contact blocks*, and a *safety control device*.

Pushbutton emergency stops are *self-latching*, which means after an emergency stop actuator is depressed and the contacts open, the emergency stop device remains in the actuated position until deliberately reset. Resetting the operator means that a person manually *rotates the actuator, pulls the actuator, or inserts and turns a key*. Figure 2-27(a) shows three cable pull emergency stop switches and two E stop pushbuttons.

Figure 2-27(b) shows the *self monitoring normally open* (SMNO) contact in series with the NC pushbutton contact. When the contact block is properly installed, the SMNO contact is held closed, and the NC contact is controlled by the pushbutton operator. If the contact block is improperly installed or damaged the SMNO is open and the system cannot be activated.

Safety switching devices use two sets of contact to record an actuation. The contacts are used by a safety control device to determine that the actuation occurred. An IEC switch with dual contacts connected to a safety control device is shown in Figure 2-27(b).

FIGURE 2-27: Safety switches.

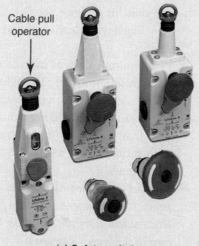

Cable pull operator

(a) Safety switches

Courtesy of Rockwell Automation, Inc.

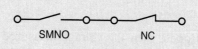

SMNO   NC

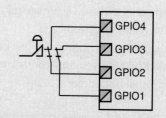

GPIO4
GPIO3
GPIO2
GPIO1

(b) SMNO and redundant contacts

Motor control circuits often require an emergency stop pushbutton with NC contacts in the contact block. In an emergency situation, depressing the emergency stop pushbutton opens the NC contacts and stops the motor. If the contact block is removed during maintenance and not properly reinstalled, the NC contacts may not open when the operator

is actuated to stop the motor. When performing maintenance on motor control circuits, verify: (a) that the emergency stop pushbutton operator works properly, (b) that contact block is properly engaged and seated on the pushbutton operator, and (c) that the pushbutton is prepared to open the motor control circuit when depressed.

the opposite state. Operator problems usually affect all the contacts in the multi-pole multi-throw configuration.

Contact Problems

Contact failures on switches include: *always open, always closed,* or *excessive resistance* for closed contacts. *Fused* or *welded* contacts occur when contacts carry excessive *current* or have excessive *arcing*. These

same switching conditions burn the contacts and the closed resistance is much higher than normal.

When a switch is the suspected cause of a system problem, the following procedure is used.

* Apply all related National Fire Protection Association (NFPA) 70e standards for electrical safety in the workplace in troubleshooting the suspected switched control circuit.

FIGURE 2-28: Manual switch troubleshooting guide.

Observed Symptom	Possible Reason for Failure
Excessive contact resistance	Grounds, shorts, incorrect fuse or circuit breaker size, inductive loads produced excessive arcing or excessive contact current; severe vibration
Switch is not closing a contact (always open)	Broken external connection; foreign material in switch; operator speed or pressure exceeds specifications; physical damage to operator or contacts
Switch is not opening a contact (always closed)	Shorted external terminals; foreign material buildup in switch; operator speed or pressure exceeds specifications; switch physical damage

- If a contact is open, then the voltage measured across the contacts is the voltage being switched.
- If a contact is closed, then the voltage measured across the contacts is near zero. A higher reading indicates excessive contact resistance.
- If excessive contact resistance is suspected, one of the switch wires should be removed and contact resistance measured with an ohmmeter.

Continuity tests for NO and NC contacts with operators in the actuated and non-actuated positions should *not* be made with field wiring attached. Remove the field wire from one side of the contact before performing the continuity check. Figure 2-28 provides a list of observed symptoms for failed or faulty switches and the possible reasons for the symptom that should be investigated.

CRITICAL CONCEPTS

The need to know content from Chapter 2 is summarized in the following statements.

- Manually operated input devices are switches whose operation is performed by an internal mechanism, which is activated by a human operator.
- *Pole* refers to an internal conductor in the switch that is moved by the switching mechanism. *Contacts* refer to the switch outputs, NC and NO. *Throw* refers to the number of switch positions. *Operator* refers to the external switch component that is physically moved to cause the switching action.

- Toggle switches are mechanical devices that are manually set in one of two positions—not activated and activated.
- Pushbuttons are either configured as momentary or maintained.
- Selector switches are control devices in which the operator is rotated or turned to actuate the switching action.
- Drum switches are generally three-position switches that are used in motor control.
- Foot switches allow shop-floor personnel to have full use of their hands while operating a machine with the foot.
- Joysticks integrate up to eight control contacts into one switching device.
- Signaling devices include visual and audible output devices.
- Visual output devices include pilot lights, illuminated pushbuttons, beacon lights, and tower lights.
- Visual devices use incandescent lamps, xenon (strobe) tubes, and LEDs as sources of illumination.
- Pilot lights are tested individually with a push-to-test feature or with a single test switch if they have dual inputs.
- Current aural alarms include: *buzzers, bells, electronic tone sounders, standard electronic horns*, and *electronic hazardous location horns* with the first two in the legacy category.

QUESTIONS

1. Describe the switch terms—pole, contacts, throw, and operator.
2. How are selector switches different from standard toggle switches?
3. The drum switch is used for what application?
4. What is the advantage of using a foot switch in an industrial application?
5. What is the advantage of using a joystick in an industrial application?
6. What shop floor environment makes visual signaling devices difficult to detect?
7. What is the difference between beacon lights and tower lights?
8. What is the functional difference between push-to-test and dual-input testing features of pilot lights?
9. Why are similar alarm sounds for different situations to be avoided?
10. What are the two basic categories for switch failures?

3

Mechanically and Automatically Operated Devices

GOALS AND OBJECTIVES

The primary goals for this chapter are to identify mechanically- and automatically-operated input devices, and to describe the operation of and applications for these discrete control devices in manufacturing systems. In addition, troubleshooting tips and procedures for typical failure modes are presented.

After completing this chapter, you should be able to:

1. Identify and describe mechanically-operated limit switches in typical control applications.
2. Identify and describe automatically-operated *flow, level, pressure,* and *temperature* switches in typical control applications.
3. Identify the *symbols* for mechanically- and automatically-operated devices.
4. Troubleshoot *limit, flow, level, pressure,* and *temperature* switches in typical control applications.

3-1 MECHANICALLY OPERATED INPUT DEVICES

Mechanically operated input devices are opened or closed by the *physical contact* between a moving part in an industrial process, sometimes called a trip dog, and the actuator of the device. The *limit switch* is the most frequently used mechanically operated input device. *Miniature or micro switches* are smaller than limit switches and have a snap-action switching mechanism. Micro switches are sometimes used inside limit switches for the switching mechanism.

Limit Switches

Limit switches are mechanical devices that are activated by physical contact with a moving object. The physical contact opens or closes a set of electrical contacts within the limit switch enclosure. The contacts start or stop the flow of current in an external electrical circuit. Limit switches' industrial applications include *setting travel limits* for machine parts, *starting and stopping* production sequences, *detecting* moving objects, *monitoring* an object's position, and numerous *safety conditions,* such as *detecting* that machine guards are in place. As shown in Figure 3-1(a), the limit switch is composed of three basic components—a *body,* an *operator head* and an *actuator.* Each of these components is discussed in detail in the following sections. Figure 3-1(b) illustrates the NEMA and the IEC symbols and letter codes for the limit switch.

Limit Switch Components

The *limit switch body* is shown in Figure 3-2(a). The limit switch body houses the mechanical switch and the wiring between the switch and the input connections. The input wiring configurations include: *screw*

FIGURE 3-1: Limit switch and symbols.

Actuator

Operator head

Body

(a) Limit switch components

Letter Code	NEMA		IEC	
	NO	NC	NO	NC
NEMA – LS IEC – SQ				
	NO held closed	NC held open		

Other NEMA Contact Symbols		
Center Neutral Operator		Maintain Operator
Non-actuated	Actuated	
NP	NP	

(b) NEMA and IEC limit switch contact symbols and letter codes

FIGURE 3-2: Limit switch body and sample contact ratings.

(a) Limit switch body

(b) Name plate

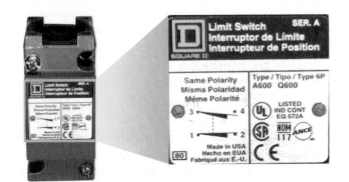

Circuit	Rated Voltage	Amperes		Continuous Carrying Current	Voltamperes	
		Make	Break		Make	Break
SPDT	120V AC	60	6	10	7200	720
	240V AC	30	3	10	7200	720
	480V AC	15	1.5	10	7200	720
	600V AC	12	1.2	10	7200	720

(c) SPDT NEMA contact ratings

terminals, *threaded hub* that accepts an electrical conduit for most environmental installations, or a *connector*. Each limit switch has a nameplate on the side of the body. The nameplate, Figure 3-2(b), indicates the switch's *contact configuration* and *standards* and *testing organizations* for switch compliance. The most common contact configurations are single pole double throw (SPDT) and double pole double throw (DPDT). The NO contact is across one set of terminals and the NC across another set of terminals with double-break contacts used most often. The contacts are designed for control circuits and are not intended to carry larger motor currents. NEMA contact ratings for the A600 NEMA limit switch are listed in Figure 3-2(c).

The *operator head*, Figure 3-3(a), is a *plunger* type and attaches to the switch body. Plunger operators are blunt tipped or have a roller tip. The *roller lever* type operator head in Figure 3-3(b) has a *knurled shaft* to attach numerous lever configurations available for every application.

FIGURE 3-3: Operator heads.

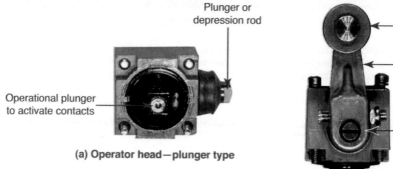

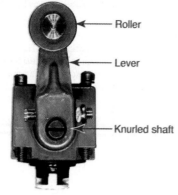

(a) Operator head—plunger type

(b) Operator head—roller-lever type

Limit switches rely on external pressure or movement against the *actuator* to open or close the contacts inside the body. Some actuator styles trip the switch contacts with an external force of a few ounces. Other operator options detect movements of a few millimeters to several inches. To support a range of industrial applications, limit switches utilize a variety of actuators. Figure 3-4 illustrates four switches and actuator options with actuator descriptions and typical applications.

Limit Switch Installation

In order for proper limit switch operation, two important installation factors must be considered. First, the limit switch range of operation must match the systems mechanical requirements for degree of rotation and direction of linear travel. Secondly, the correct mounting placement for the switch body is crucial for proper performance and damage free operation. Figure 3-5 illustrates correct and incorrect implementations of limit switches from an actuator standpoint. The following good practice guidelines aid in limit switch installations:

- Mount limit switches rigidly and in easily accessible locations.
- Provide adequate clearance for easy service and replacement.
- Mount switch bodies so cover plates face maintenance access points.

- Never mount where heat exceeds specified limits.
- Never mount where false trigger from the machine operator is possible.
- Mount away from coolant liquid spray, machine oil drips, and where machined chips accumulate.

Figure 3-6 illustrates the operating positions of a limit switch. The figure also provides the definitions of operator characteristics for the travel positions of lever and plunger type limit switches.

A correctly installed limit switch permits allowed-travel and prevents over-travel. Incorrect installations, Figure 3-5, cause the majority of premature limit switch failures. Review all the installation precautions that are covered in Figure 3-5.

Trip Dogs

The physical contact between a moving machine part and a limit switch operator is used to monitor and control the production system. The cams designed to move limit switch operators are called *trip dogs*. Figure 3-5 illustrates cam designs and their interaction with operators. The trip dog's *unique shape* produces proper limit switch lever rotation and plunger or pushrod depression. The examples in Figure 3-5 demonstrate that the speed of the moving part dictates the *shape*, *style*, and *location* of the trip dog used to activate the limit switch.

FIGURE 3-4: Limit switch actuators.

Actuator	Description and Application
	**Lever** **Description**—The lever actuator is a single arm usually with a roller attached at the end. The lever is calibrated by sliding it up or down on the shaft of the limit switch arm. Most lever type actuators are designed to work in either direction of travel but generally are used where the actuating object is moving in one direction. **Application**—Detection of moving objects on an assembly line conveyor system
	**Fork Lever** **Description**—The fork lever actuator is available with either *maintained* contact or *momentary* contact limit switches. Proper location of the limit switch body is important because fork levers are not adjustable. They are used where the actuating object travels in two directions. **Application**—Detection of end-of-travel on grinder table that automatically travels back and forth
	**Wobble Stick** **Description**—The wobble stick actuator consists of a single actuating lever protruding from the top of the limit switch. Although most actuators are metallic, wobble sticks are available in plastic, Teflon or nylon. Wobble stick actuators allow the limit switch to be actuated from any lateral direction. This makes the actuator less likely to be damaged by over-travel or misalignment. **Application**—Detection of an object moved by a robot arm with several different lateral movements in an automated cell
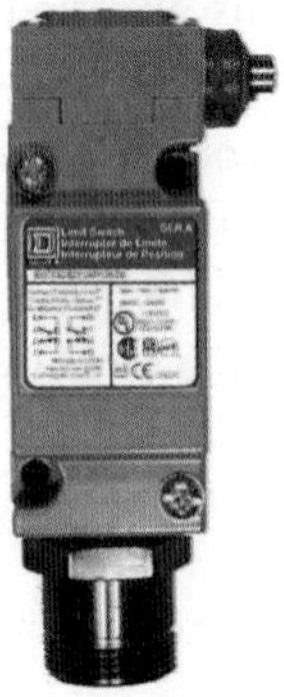	**Push Rod** **Description**—The push rod actuator has the least amount of travel compared to other actuators. It has a short rod on the *side* or *top* of a limit switch head that operates the switch contacts when depressed. The required force to actuate the switch is applied parallel with the rod position. Excessive wear occurs in installations where the trip device moves 90 degrees to the push rod. In those applications, a *push roller* limit switch solves the problem by adding a roller assembly so friction is reduced/eliminated between the trip device and the push rod. **Application**—Detection of end of travel for a linear actuator on a production machine

FIGURE 3-5: Limit switch actuator considerations.

Incorrect	Correct	Description
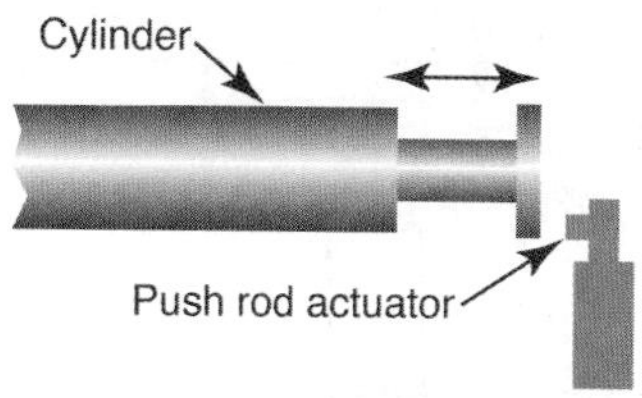	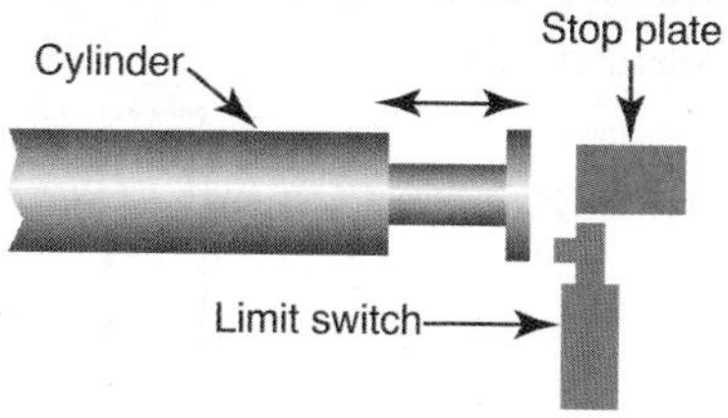	The operating mechanism for limit switches should never be operated beyond the switch's over-travel limit under any operational condition. A limit switch should not be used as a mechanical stop.
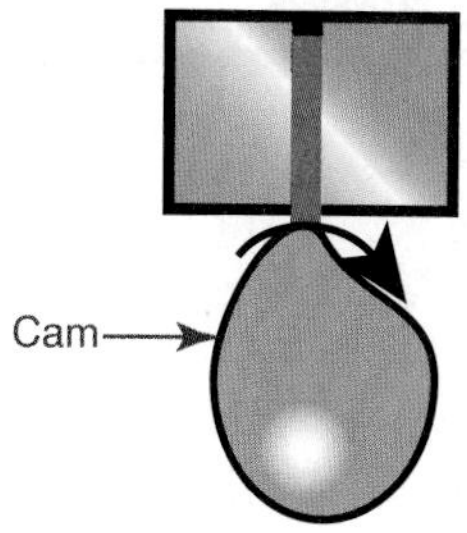	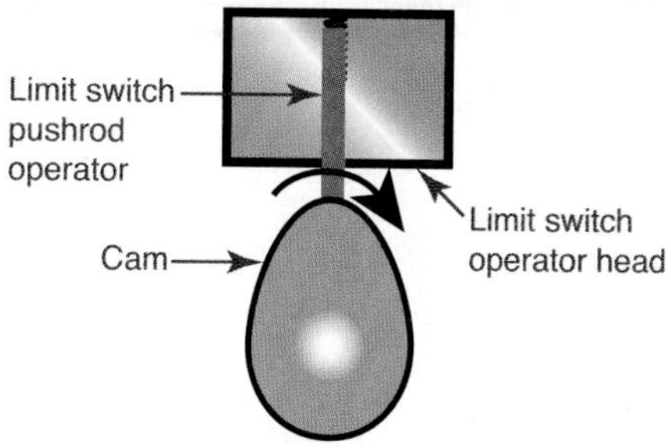	When fast motions are present the cam should never apply a severe impact to the actuator. Cams should hold operators long enough to operate relays, pneumatic valves, and other slower acting devices.
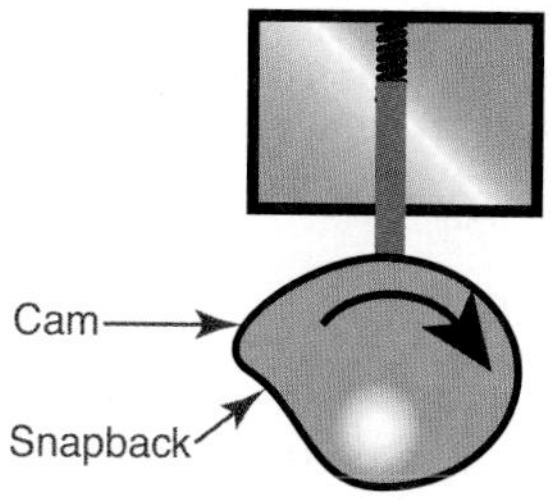	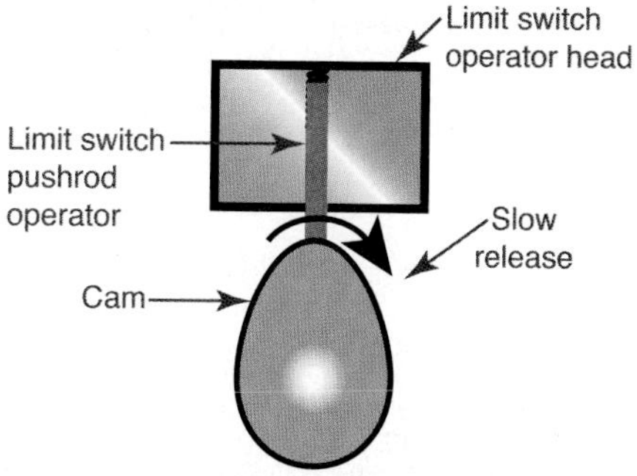	A cam or trip dog installation should never allow the actuator to suddenly snapback or release freely to the neutral position.
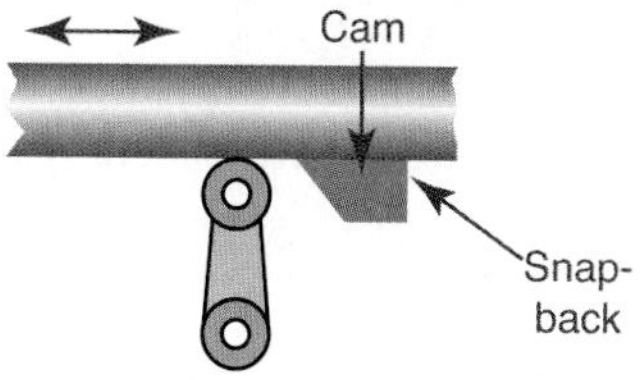	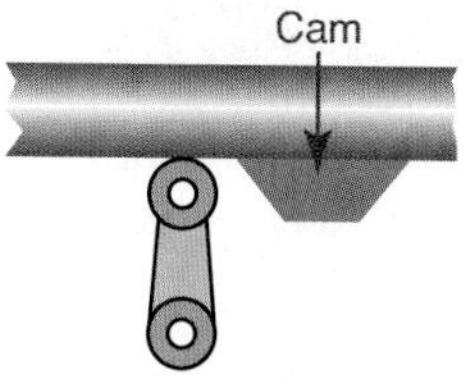	
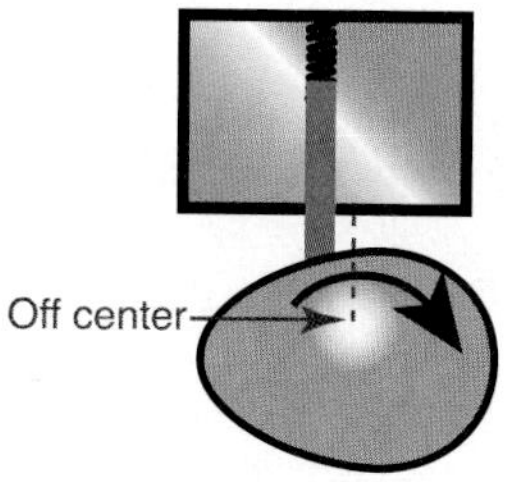	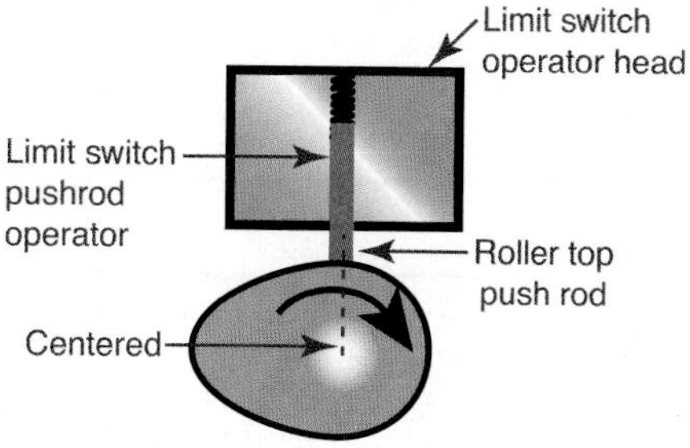	For limit switches with pushrod actuators the actuating force should be applied as nearly as possible in line with the pushrod axis.

- - - - - - - - - - - - - - - - Definitions of Operating Characteristics - - - - - - - - - - - - - - - -

Operating force (OF):
The force applied to the actuator required to operate the switch contacts.

Releasing force (RF):
The value to which the force on the actuator must be reduced to allow the contacts to return to the normal position.

Free position (FP):
The initial position of the acutator when there is no external force applied.

Operating position (OP):
The position of the actuator at which the contacts snap to the operated contact position.

Releasing position (RP):
The position of the actuator at which the contacts snap from the operated contact position to their normal position.

Total travel position (TTP):
The position of the actuator when it reaches the stopper.

Pretravel (PT):
The distance or angle through which the actuator moves from the free position to the operating position.

Overtravel (OT):
The distance or angle of the actuator movement beyond the operating position.

Movement differential (MD):
The distance or angle from the operating position to the releasing position.

Total travel (TT):
The sum of the pretravel and total overtravel expressed by distance or angle.

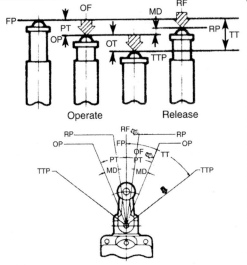

OF: Operating force   **TTP:** Total travel position
RF: Releasing force   **PT:** Pretravel
FP: Free position   **OT:** Overtravel
OP: Operating position   **MD:** Movement differential
RP: Releasing position   **TT:** Total Travel

APPLICATION

Figure 3-7 illustrates a hydraulic platform system. The platform is used to raise material from a lower level to an upper level. A hydraulic cylinder is used to raise the platform. Limit switch LS1 is located on the lower level and detects when the platform is in that position. Limit switch LS2 is located on the upper level and detects when the platform is in that position. Review the platform diagram, Figure 3-7(a), and the control circuit in Figure 3-7(b). The up and down hydraulic control is activated by the up and down pushbuttons respectively. While the momentary pushbutton is held in the platform is driven to a new position. When the platform activates the limit switch at the end of travel, the LS1 or LS2 NC contact opens and the platform remains at that level.

FIGURE 3-7: Hydraulic platform system.

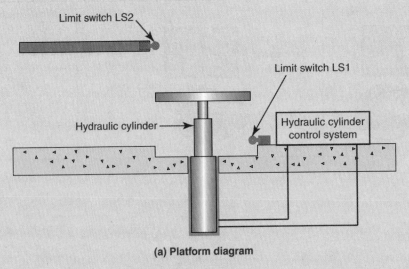

(a) Platform diagram

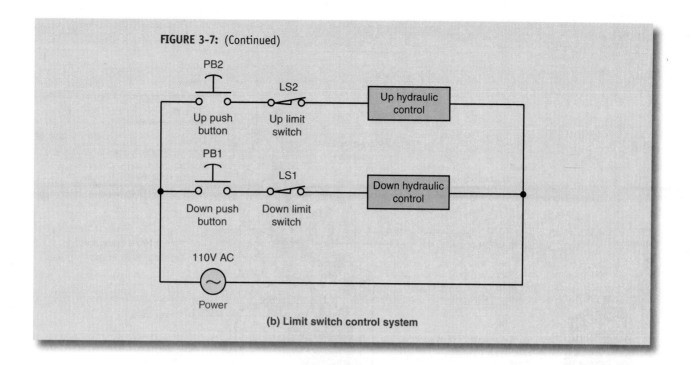

FIGURE 3-7: (Continued)

(b) Limit switch control system

Miniature Switches

Miniature switches or *micro switches,* a sub class of limit switches, have similar physical and electrical characteristics. Figure 3-8 illustrates a miniature switch, often called a *micro-switch*. Numerous operators are available, and these switches are also mounted inside larger switches to provide the switching action. This switching action is visible in the cut-away. The pole has a spring that maintains contact with the NC con-

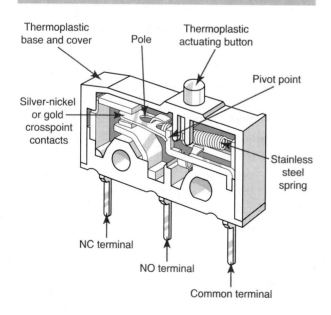

FIGURE 3-8: Miniature switch and snap-action operation.

tact on the top. When the operator is depressed, the pole moves to the NO contact. Upon release of the operator the pole is pulled back to the NC position. With the actuator in the up position (as shown in Figure 3-8), the spring is above the pivot point. As a result, the pole is held on the NC contact above the pivot point. When the actuating button is depressed, the spring is forced below the pivot point. This causes the pole to snap to the NO contact below the pivot point. In mechanical systems, this is called an over center switching configuration. Miniature switches have fast switching action and are often called *snap-action* switches.

Some limit switches have a miniature switch inside the body to produce the switching action. Figure 3-9 shows a cut-away of a limit switch with miniature switch inside and all parts of the limit switch identified. The contact configuration for a miniature switch is SPDT with one terminal used as a common between the NO and NC contacts of the switch. The miniature switch body is usually composed of molded plastic offering minimal electrical isolation and little physical protection for the contacts. Due to this minimal physical protection, miniature switches are normally mounted inside machinery where there is little risk of physical damage. Miniature switches have fewer operator options and their actuators have a short travel distance compared to limit switches. Miniature switches are often used in equipment enclosures to detect open panel doors and missing equipment guards.

FIGURE 3-9: Limit switch with built-in miniature snap-action switch.

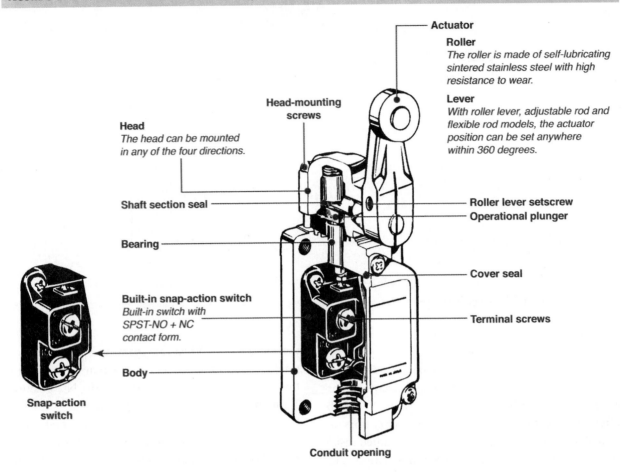

Actuator

Roller
The roller is made of self-lubricating sintered stainless steel with high resistance to wear.

Lever
With roller lever, adjustable rod and flexible rod models, the actuator position can be set anywhere within 360 degrees.

Head-mounting screws

Head
The head can be mounted in any of the four directions.

Shaft section seal

Bearing

Built-in snap-action switch
Built-in switch with SPST-NO + NC contact form.

Body

Snap-action switch

Roller lever setscrew
Operational plunger

Cover seal

Terminal screws

Conduit opening

3-2 AUTOMATICALLY OPERATED INPUT DEVICES

Automatically operated input devices are switches triggered by a change in a *process parameter*. Examples of process parameters include: *liquid level and pressure, fluid flow,* and *material temperature.* In general, these devices measure process parameters as either a *discrete* or *analog* variable value. The set points for discrete devices are specific process parameter values. For example, a liquid level in a tank closes discrete float switch contacts when the liquid level reaches the set point depth. In contrast, the analog device produces a *continuously changing* electrical output that is proportional to the change in the process parameter. For example, an analog level sensor produces a voltage output that is *proportional* to the level of liquid in a tank

as the liquid depth changes. The analog type process sensors are covered in Section 3, while the discrete devices are addressed in this chapter. The most commonly used switches in this discrete group are *flow, level, pressure, vacuum,* and *temperature.*

The electrical properties of all automatically operated discrete process switches are similar. All offer contact configurations that include: *single* and *double pole* options, *single* throw or *double* throw contacts, and *single* or *double* break contact bars. Most devices switch voltages from 120 to 600 volts AC with typical make and break currents of 6 amps to 2 amps, respectively (maximum make = 60 amps @ 125V AC, maximum break = 6 amps @ 125V AC). These devices can switch small AC and DC motors and resistive and inductive loads.

FIGURE 3-10: Flow switch.

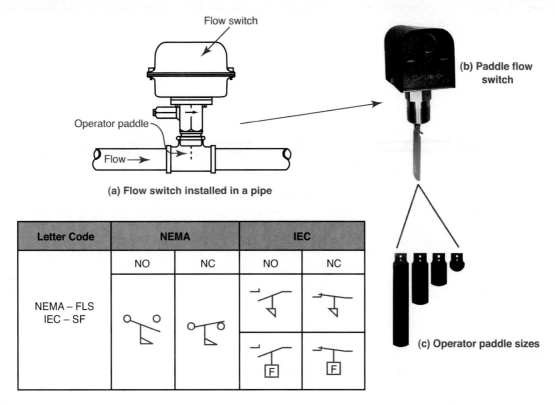

(a) Flow switch installed in a pipe

(b) Paddle flow switch

(c) Operator paddle sizes

Letter Code	NEMA		IEC	
	NO	NC	NO	NC
NEMA – FLS IEC – SF				

(d) NEMA and IEC flow switch symbols and letter code

Flow Switches

Automatically or *process actuated* flow switches detect a change in a pipe's *liquid flow* or a duct's *gas flow*. Most industrial processes depend on fluids flowing from one location to another. A *flow switch* for a liquid flow pipe is illustrated in Figure 3-10(a) with a close up of the *switch* and *operator* or *paddle* in Figure 3-10(b). Various paddle sizes, Figure 3-10(c), are available depending on the pipe diameter in the system. Switch contacts are *activated* by the operator or paddle suspended in the flow. The paddle movement indicates when the flow is above or below the set point. Switches are available for liquids flowing in pipes with varying viscosities and detection of air and gas movement in ducts. The NEMA and IEC flow switch letter codes and symbols for NO and NC contacts are shown in Figure 3-10(d).

Flow switches are used to detect the presence or absent of flow in a variety of systems such as boilers, *cooling lines, air compressors,* and *fluid pumps.* For example, a liquid flow switch is used to monitor a fire protection system's automatic sprinklers. In this application, water flow in the sprinkler pipe closes the flow switch's NO contact to trigger an alarm. Similarly, if a liquid normally flows through a pipe, the NC flow switch contact is held open. When the flow stops, the NC contact closes, thus activating an alarm.

Level Switches

Level switches, also called *float* switches, are discrete switches used for the control of liquid or granular material levels in tanks and bins. Level switches use the elevation of a float on a liquid's surface to trigger

Figure 3-11(a) illustrates an air duct with air moved through the duct by a continuously operating fan. The return air is heated when the system thermostat turns on the heating elements. The flow switch is used to detect airflow through the heating elements of a heater. The control circuit in Figure 3-11(b) uses the flow switch and thermostat to control power to the heaters.

FIGURE 3-11: Flow control switch and duct flow control circuit.

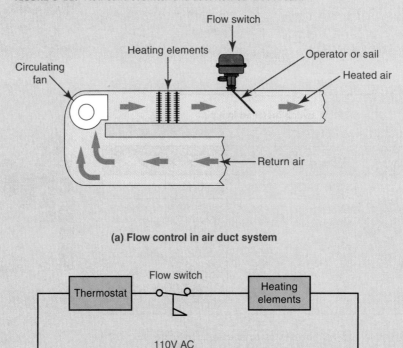

(a) Flow control in air duct system

(b) Control circuit for air duct system

When replacing or installing a new level switch, the operating environment is an important aspect that the electrical worker must consider. Factors to consider when an older switch is replaced with a newer or different model include:

- **Corrosiveness**—Monitoring the level in a vessel that contains corrosive chemicals requires a level device made of a non-corrosive material such as plastic, stainless steel or some type of polymer.

- **Temperature**—If the temperature of the product that is monitored is excessive, a hi-temp level device is required.
- **Adhesiveness**—A product that is adhesive in nature such as paint could build up on the level device, which prevents an actuation or causes a false actuation.
- **Turbulence**—The mixing operation motion may cause the level device to chatter on and off, thus requiring a less sensitive device.

a change in the switch contacts. Figure 3-12(a) shows a level switch with a vertically attached float, and Figure 3-12(b) pictures a level switch with a horizontally attached float. The switch includes a snap action mechanism that provides quick-make and quick-break contact operation; similar to the miniature switch mechanism. When the float rises to the trigger level the switching action occurs with rapid snap-through force. The NEMA and IEC symbols and letter codes for the float switch are illustrated in Figure 3-12(c).

Level sensing devices used in a variety of commercial and industrial applications require different and unique configurations for each installation. For example, level device models are available for *open* or closed tank processes. Open-tank models are used in *unsealed* tanks that are open to atmospheric pressure.

FIGURE 3-12: Level switches.

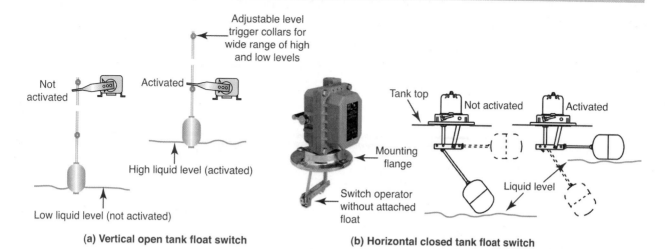

Adjustable level trigger collars for wide range of high and low levels

Not activated

Activated

Low liquid level (not activated)

High liquid level (activated)

(a) Vertical open tank float switch

Tank top

Not activated

Activated

Mounting flange

Switch operator without attached float

Liquid level

(b) Horizontal closed tank float switch

Letter Code	NEMA		IEC	
	NO	NC	NO	NC
NEMA – FL IEC – SL				

(c) NEMA and IEC level switch symbols and letter code

Figure 3-13(b) illustrates a tank where level switches are use to monitor the liquid level in a sealed tank. A closed-tank type level device [Figure 3-13(a)] is used that mounts through openings in the side of the tank. The low liquid level switch, near the bottom of the tank, controls the minimum liquid level. The high liquid level switch, near the top of the tank, controls the maximum liquid level. The control circuit in Figure 3-13(c) uses a momentary pushbutton

FIGURE 3-13: Process tank fill and drain application.

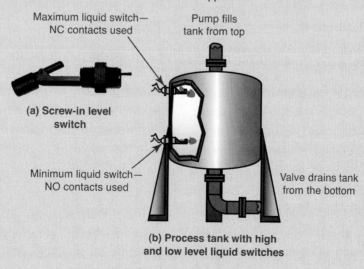

Maximum liquid switch— NC contacts used

Pump fills tank from top

(a) Screw-in level switch

Minimum liquid switch— NO contacts used

Valve drains tank from the bottom

(b) Process tank with high and low level liquid switches

(continued)

APPLICATION

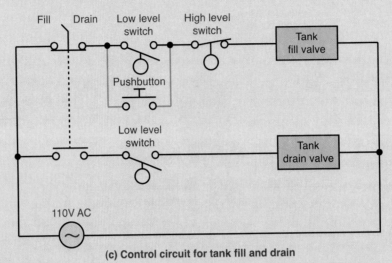

FIGURE 3-13: (Continued)

(c) Control circuit for tank fill and drain

switch and the level switches to control a fill pump for the tank. A two position selector switch is used to control a valve to fill and empty the tank. The tank fills when the fill valve is energized and drains when the drain valve has power applied. The fill momentary pushbutton is depressed until the liquid is above the low liquid level switch.

Closed tank models are used in applications where the tank is *sealed* and typically is pressurized.

It is often necessary to trigger a process action for liquid levels between maximum and minimum levels. To satisfy that need, multi-level liquid level sensing is required. Figure 3-14 illustrates two automatically actuated discrete input switch options for multi-level sensing. Read the descriptions in the figure.

Pressure Switches

Pressure switches change the state of a contact (open or close) based on the pressure applied to the device by *water, air, or another fluid* such as oil. These switches sense pressure changes of less than 1 psi (pounds per square inch) to over 15,000 psi. There are three categories of pressure devices illustrated in Figure 3-15(a): *positive pressure, vacuum (negative pressure),* and *differential pressure.* Most of these devices work on two principles:

- Principle one states that a gas is compressible so a gas at *higher* pressure occupies less volume than the same gas at a *lower* pressure.
- Principle two states that liquids are not compressible and transfer pressure applied to them.

Positive pressure switches are actuated when additional gas or liquid is added to the system, while *vacuum* switches function when gas or liquid is removed from a system. *Differential pressure* switches measure the difference in pressure from two different sources. Both positive and negative pressure devices monitor the rise and fall of the pressure and actuate their contacts when the desired pressure, called the *set point*, is reached.

Figure 3-15(a) illustrates and describes the operation of pressure switches. In the top row in the figure, the application of positive pressure moves the shaft up, causing the NC contacts to open and the NO contacts close. In the middle row, the NO contacts are held closed by the internal pressure and the NC contacts are held open. When negative pressure is applied (gas or air is withdrawn), the shaft move down, and both contacts return to their original position. In the bottom row, different pressures are applied to each side of the cylinder, the shaft moves toward the side with the lowest pressure. The movement of the shaft is driven by the difference between the two pressures. This closes the NO contacts and opens the NC contacts. Finally, in Figure 3-15(b), the NEMA and the IEC symbols and letter codes are shown for the three types of pressure switches.

FIGURE 3-14: Multi-level options for liquid level sensing.

Multi-level Option	Operation Description
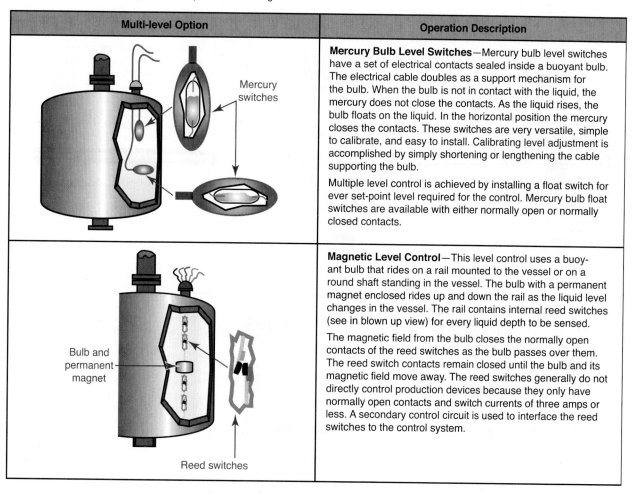	**Mercury Bulb Level Switches**—Mercury bulb level switches have a set of electrical contacts sealed inside a buoyant bulb. The electrical cable doubles as a support mechanism for the bulb. When the bulb is not in contact with the liquid, the mercury does not close the contacts. As the liquid rises, the bulb floats on the liquid. In the horizontal position the mercury closes the contacts. These switches are very versatile, simple to calibrate, and easy to install. Calibrating level adjustment is accomplished by simply shortening or lengthening the cable supporting the bulb.

Multiple level control is achieved by installing a float switch for ever set-point level required for the control. Mercury bulb float switches are available with either normally open or normally closed contacts. |
| | **Magnetic Level Control**—This level control uses a buoyant bulb that rides on a rail mounted to the vessel or on a round shaft standing in the vessel. The bulb with a permanent magnet enclosed rides up and down the rail as the liquid level changes in the vessel. The rail contains internal reed switches (see in blown up view) for every liquid depth to be sensed.

The magnetic field from the bulb closes the normally open contacts of the reed switches as the bulb passes over them. The reed switch contacts remain closed until the bulb and its magnetic field move away. The reed switches generally do not directly control production devices because they only have normally open contacts and switch currents of three amps or less. A secondary control circuit is used to interface the reed switches to the control system. |

FIGURE 3-15: Pressure switch operation, symbols, and letter codes.

Not Activated Position	Activated Position	Switch Type
NC and NO contacts · Pressure switch · Atmospheric pressure · Actuating pressure		**Positive Pressure Switch**—The larger purple arrow in the activated position column indicates that an increase in pressure compared to atmospheric pressure activates the NO and NC contacts of the SPDT switch. The green arrow indicates the direction of plate movement when pressure increases.

(a) Pressure switch operation

(continued)

FIGURE 3-15: (Continued)

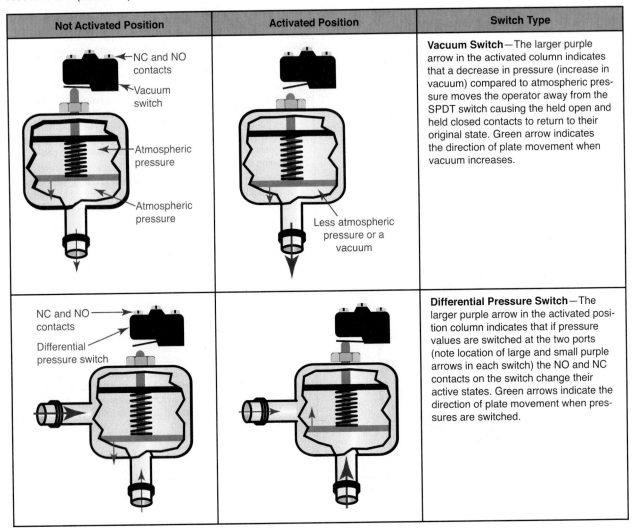

(a) Pressure switch operation (*continued*)

(b) Pressure switch symbols and letter codes

Pressure switches use different sensing devices to detect pressure. Most common sensing devices are the *diaphragm, bellows,* and *piston.* The diaphragm sensing device is used for *low-pressure* applications, bellows for *medium-pressure,* and the piston for *high-pressure.* Figure 3-16 illustrates these three pressure sensing devices. Read the accompanying description.

Deadband

Deadband, a characteristic used in process sensing and switching devices, is defined as follows:

> *A deadband, also called a neutral zone, is an area within a signal range where no action occurs (the system is dead). Deadband is embedded into the*

FIGURE 3-16: Pressure sensing devices.

Pressure Sensing Device	Description
	Diaphragm—The diaphragm is a flexible membrane, which is rubber for low-pressure measurements and metal for higher-pressure measurements of about 300 psi. The diaphragm is mounted in a cylinder, creating space on both sides. One space is open to the atmosphere, and the other is connected to the pressure source to be sensed. When pressure is applied, the diaphragm expands into the open space. The amount of movement is proportional to the pressure being applied. The spring tension is adjustable to allow for different pressure set point values.
	Bellows—The bellows is a thin sealed metal cylinder with corrugated sides like pleats. When pressure is applied to the bellows, the bellows expands and opens the pleats, producing a displacement that is proportional to the applied pressure. This type of switch is used to measure medium-level pressures up to 2,000 psi. While the bellows can sense higher pressure than the diaphragm, a bellows is less sensitive. It takes a greater change in pressure to cause the bellows to expand enough to activate a switch. The spring tension is adjusted for different pressure set point values.
	Piston—The stainless-steel cylindrical piston moves within a cylinder. The tight-fitting piston is held at one end of the chamber by tension from a compressed spring. Pressure enters the chamber and moves the piston and switch actuator rod as the spring compresses. Electrical contacts are actuated at the adjustable set point or pressure setting. The piston pressure switch device is used for high-pressure applications of 15,000 psi or greater. The spring tension is adjusted for different pressure set point values.

input sensor or switch, or it is built into the system controllers. The neutral zone prevents oscillation or repeated activation-deactivation cycles, called hunting. Hunting occurs when an output devices is turned on and off by small input parameter changes above and below a single set-point value.

Pressure and temperature devices utilize deadband control more often than other types of automatic control, but all automatically operated process switches have some deadband present. Deadband control works the same for all types of automatically operated switches. However, deadband changes with each set point on mechanical and automatically operated process switches. The deadband is small at the low end of the set-point range and larger at the high end. Deadband is illustrated for a pressure switch in Figure 3-17(a) and (b).

Figure 3-17(b) illustrates deadband control for a pressure switch on an air compressor system. Any pressure above the upper pressure limit turns off the compressor motor. Any pressure below the lower pressure limit turns on the compressor. No action occurs between the upper and lower pressure values. The upper and lower limits are referred to as *set points*.

Deadband is both useful and harmful. Without deadband or with a small deadband, the switch contacts cycle open and closed when the pressure hovers near the set point. However, a large deadband is also a problem in applications that require the pressure to be held within a small range. A deadband is used in *pressure, temperature, flow* and *level* switch control systems.

Temperature Switches

Temperature switches use a temperature sensing device to *mechanically* change electrical contacts at a user specified *temperature*. Temperature switches are used in a variety of applications such as *HVAC* and *fire alarm* systems, and numerous *process control* systems. The three frequently used mechanical temperature sensing devices include: the *bimetallic strip,* the *capillary tube,* and the *direct immersion probe.*

Temperature switches also use a deadband to reduce the on and off cycling of the temperature switch and the device it controls. Processes that change quickly, like heating air flow in a heat exchanger, need a wider deadband. Slower processes, like heating of liquids, use a narrower deadband. Temperature sensing devices, often called *temperature sensors,* replace the mechanical contact activation with electronic switches. Temperature sensors that interface resistance temperature detectors, thermistors, and thermocouples with electronic controls are discussed in Section 3.

FIGURE 3-17: Deadband versus hysteresis.

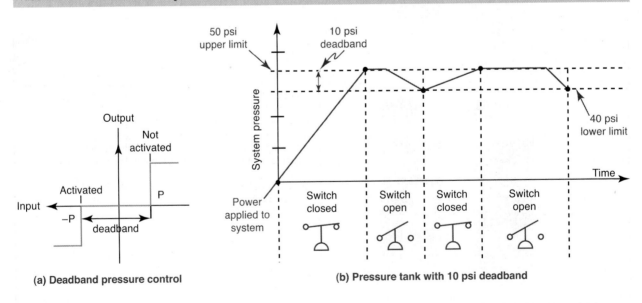

(a) Deadband pressure control

(b) Pressure tank with 10 psi deadband

Figure 3-18(a) illustrates a pressure switch that controls the gas pressure in the gas over liquid sealed tank system. The pump forces liquid into the closed system and compresses the gas above the liquid in the tank. The maximum gas pressure is 50 psi with a deadband of 10 psi to prevent cycling of the pump motor. The pressure switch turns the pump on at 40 psi and off at 50 psi. Figure 3-18(b) illustrates the control system used to maintain tank pressure.

FIGURE 3-18: Pressure controlled liquid pump system.

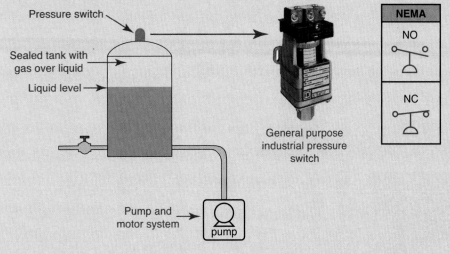

(a) Pump and tank system with pressure switch to monitor gas pressure over liquid

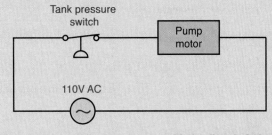

(b) Control circuit for tank system with deadband of 10 psi

Bimetallic Strip

The *bimetallic strip* is a temperature sensing device that bends when the temperature changes. The strip is made with *two different metals* with different expansion and contraction rates when heated and cooled as shown in Figure 3-19. Both the steel and brass expand when heated and contract when cooled. However, the brass expands and contracts at a greater rate, forcing the sandwiched metal strip to bend. The movement of the strip is used to open and close electrical contacts. A longer strip produces greater movement with a change in temperature. When the strip is formed into a coil shape, the coil tightens when heated and opens when cooled. A long bimetallic strip produces a greater deflection with change in temperature. So a long strip is formed into a coil to reduce the space required for a more sensitive temperature sensor. The coil in Figure 3-20 is inside a commercial thermostat used to open and close a mercury switch as room temperature changes. Note that the coil is anchored to the thermostat at the inside end. The mercury switch is attached to the end that is free to move with changes in temperature. As the figure indicates, the coiling of the bimetallic strip permits a longer strip to be used in a small space.

Capillary Tubes

Capillary tube temperature devices, one of the oldest types of temperature switches, consist of two

FIGURE 3-19: Bimetallic strip temperature sensing device.

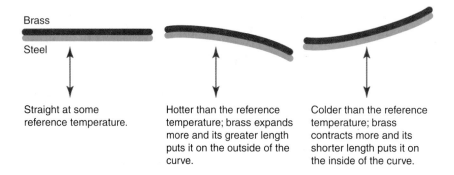

Brass

Steel

Straight at some reference temperature.

Hotter than the reference temperature; brass expands more and its greater length puts it on the outside of the curve.

Colder than the reference temperature; brass contracts more and its shorter length puts it on the inside of the curve.

FIGURE 3-20: Bimetallic strip temperature switch.

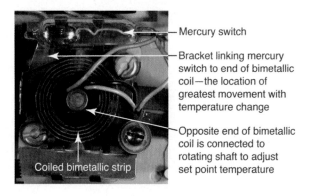

— Mercury switch

— Bracket linking mercury switch to end of bimetallic coil—the location of greatest movement with temperature change

— Opposite end of bimetallic coil is connected to rotating shaft to adjust set point temperature

Coiled bimetallic strip

components: the *bulb* and *capillary tube* plus *bellows* and *main sensor body*. The tube, which can be several feet long, connects the bulb to the bellows in the main sensor body. The bellows is mechanically linked to the electrical contacts. Figure 3-21 is a simplified drawing of a capillary tube temperature switch and an image of an operational device. The *bellows, capillary,* and *bulb* are filled with fluid. The fluid has a high *positive coefficient of expansion*—the fluid volume increases as the temperature increases and decreases for a drop in temperature. As the stainless steel bulb warms the fluid expands, increasing the pressure against every surface in the *bulb, tube,* and *bellows.* Since only the bellows moves under pressure,

FIGURE 3-21: Capillary temperature switch components.

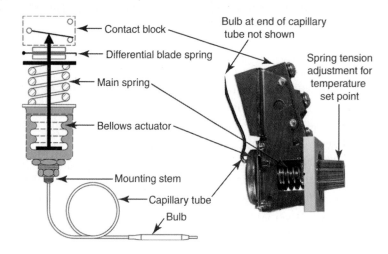

← Contact block

Bulb at end of capillary tube not shown

← Differential blade spring

Spring tension adjustment for temperature set point

← Main spring

← Bellows actuator

— Mounting stem

— Capillary tube

Bulb

FIGURE 3-22: Capillary temperature switch.

Letter Code	NEMA		IEC	
	NO	NC	NO	NC
NEMA - TS IEC - ST				

(b) NEMA and IEC control symbols and letter codes

(a) Capillary temperature switch

Courtesy of Rockwell Automation, Inc.

it exerts a *force* on the main spring and differential blade spring in Figure 3-21. As the force of these springs is overcome, the bellow's motion is transferred to the contact block and actuates the contacts—this is referred to as the *trip setting*. As temperature decreases, the main spring retracts, but the differential blade spring keeps the contact block actuated. When the threshold force on the *differential blade spring* is overcome, the contacts returns to their normal state—this is referred to as *reset setting*. Adjusting the force of the main spring (by turning the *operating range* adjustment screw) determines the temperature necessary to *trip* the contacts. Adjusting the force on the differential blade spring (by turning the *differential* adjustment screw) determines when the contacts *reset*. The trip and reset settings determine the deadband for the temperature switch. Figure 3-22 shows a capillary temperature switch and the standard control symbols and letter codes for temperature switches.

Direct Immersion Probe

Figure 3-23 illustrates a *direct immersion* temperature switch. It operates as the capillary tube temper-

FIGURE 3-23: Direct immersion temperature switch.

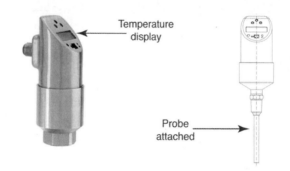

Temperature display

Probe attached

Courtesy of Rockwell Automation, Inc.

ature switch with the vertically attached probe replacing the bulb and capillary tube. The direct immersion type switch is also available with a horizontally attached probe. The direct immersion switch is used in applications where the switch is installed through the tank wall or the side of the pipe into the liquid to be measured.

The direct immersion temperature switch is installed in the hot air section of the duct and controls the duct heating elements. The deadband temperature control requirements are pictured in Figure 3-24(a). The control circuit in Figure 3-24(b) turns the heating element on when the temperature drops below 80°. The heating elements are cycled off at 90°. The temperature switch's set point is 90° and the deadband is set at 10°. Note that air flow must be present for the heating system to function.

FIGURE 3-24: Air duct temperature control with 10 °F of deadband.

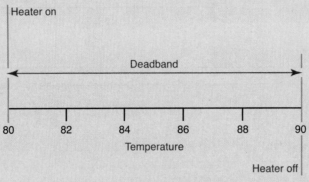

(a) Air duct temperature control deadband

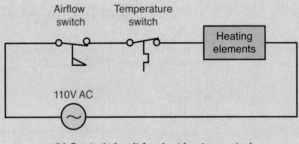

(b) Control circuit for duct heater control

Safety limit switches are used in production areas to guard operators and machines from unsafe production practices. Figure 3-25(a) illustrates safety limit switch models with top and side push rollers plus a standard lever. Example of best practices for location and motion of trip dogs with these types of operators are shown in Figure 3-25(c). The top push spring return model is used in Figure 3-25(b) to verify that a machine guard is in place before a machine cycle is permitted to start. Safety limit switches have *direct opening action*, which forces the normally closed contacts to open when the limit switch is actuated. This opening will occur even in the event of a *welded contact condition* that requires up to 10 Newtons of force to break the welded contact.

Switches are available in NEMA and IEC models with a variety of actuators and contact configurations.

Operation of the limit switches in the figure is achieved by the sliding action of the machine guard door, which depresses the plunger. For safety applications, it is important that upon actuation, the guard or moving object should not pass completely beyond the switch to allow the plunger to return to its original position—the plunger must remain engaged by the guard or object. In the figure this precaution is achieved by the location of the two limit switches and control circuit wiring of the switch contacts.

(continued)

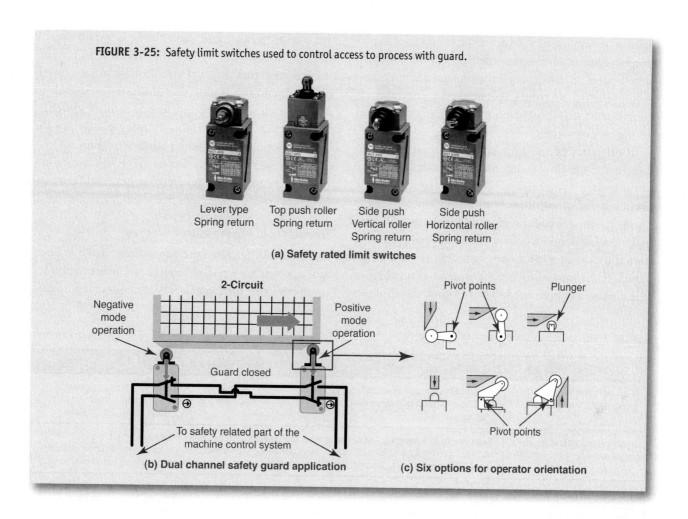

FIGURE 3-25: Safety limit switches used to control access to process with guard.

Lever type
Spring return

Top push roller
Spring return

Side push
Vertical roller
Spring return

Side push
Horizontal roller
Spring return

(a) Safety rated limit switches

2-Circuit

Negative
mode
operation

Positive
mode
operation

Guard closed

Pivot points

Plunger

To safety related part of the
machine control system

Pivot points

(b) Dual channel safety guard application

(c) Six options for operator orientation

3-3 TROUBLESHOOTING MECHANICALLY AND AUTOMATICALLY OPERATED DEVICES

Every minute a production system is not producing due to a problem, the company is losing money. That is why competent system troubleshooters are worth their weight in gold. The best way to make your mark in a career is to demonstrate that you can solve problems. This section presents lists of observable symptoms for failed or faulty devices and the possible reason for the symptom that should be investigated.

Troubleshooting Limit Switches

Limit switch problems can be grouped into two categories: *operator problems* and *contact problems*. Operators include the levers, plungers, wobble sticks, and adjustable rod levers plus the mechanical linkage in the head of the switch. These operators are the mechanical elements that force the contacts from their original position to the opposite state. Often the operator will change positions from activated to not acti-

vated but the contacts may not move. When the operator fails, the contacts are left in either the activated position or the not activated one. Operator problems usually affect all the contacts in the limit switch body.

Contact problems on switches include: always open, always closed, or excessive resistance for closed contacts. Often when a contact is forced to carry excessive current or has arcing, the contacts fuse or are welded together and never open. The excessive current conditions can cause the contacts to be burned and the resistance when closed is much higher than normal. When a limit switch is suspected for this system problem, use the procedure for troubleshooting manual switch contacts in Chapter 2.

Figure 3-26 provides a list of observable symptoms for failed or faulty limit switches and the possible reason for the symptom that should be investigated.

Troubleshooting Flow and Level Switches

Automatically operated switches have an operator and set of switchable contacts. The procedure for troubleshooting the contacts is the same as that presented in troubleshooting limit switches. Flow and level switch contacts are usually accessible through a removable access panel on the switch. If the contacts are not accessible at the switch, troubleshoot the contacts at the terminal or control box where the switch is connected to the control circuit.

If all parts of the flow control circuit are good except for the flow switch then troubleshooting the flow switch is necessary. The operators for flow switches are often difficult to access since they are inside the measured flow. However, if the flow is manually cycled between off and on, then the operator is tested by looking for a corresponding change in the contacts. In some switch designs manual toggling of the contacts is permitted to verify that the contacts

are operating. In some cases the only way to verify the operational state of a flow switch is to remove it. The operators on level switches are more accessible on open tank installations but are as difficult to access on closed tank applications as flow switches. Use the flow switch troubleshooting procedure for troubleshooting level switch control circuits.

Figure 3-27 provides a list of observable symptoms for failed or faulty flow and level switches and the possible reason for the symptom that should be investigated.

Troubleshooting Pressure Switches

Automatically operated pressure switches have an operator and set of switchable contacts. The procedure for troubleshooting the contacts is the same as that presented

FIGURE 3-26: Limit switch troubleshooting guide.

Observed Symptom	Possible Reason for Failure
Failure in the insulation of control and internal wires	Moisture inside switch enclosure; incorrect NEMA enclosure type; corrosive fumes; excessive heat from other maintenance work in area or from voltage surges or short circuits; foreign material buildup
High closed contact resistance	Evidence of filing or dressing of contacts, a prohibited practice; contact damage from grounds, shorts, incorrect fuse or circuit breaker size, or excessive contact current from burned contacts; incorrect NEMA enclosure type; oxidation, oil or other foreign material on contacts; loose terminal screws
Burned contacts or contacts welded close	Contact damage from grounds, shorts, incorrect fuse or circuit breaker size; inductive loads produced excessive arcing or excessive contact current from burned or welded contacts; severe vibration
Mechanical failure	Abrasive dust or foreign material on mechanical linkage; incorrect application of lever, plunger, wobble lever, or adjustable rod lever; incorrect mounting location for switch body; improper design or location of trip dog, operator speed or pressure exceeds switch specifications; physical damage
Sticking or sluggish operator	Dirt or foreign material buildup on mechanical linkages; improper adjustment of linkage arms and cams; corrosion of bearings in rotational linkages and mechanisms; mechanical binding; incorrect NEMA enclosure type

FIGURE 3-27: Flow and level switch troubleshooting guide.

Observed Symptom	Possible Reason for Failure
Failure in the insulation of control and internal wires	Moisture inside switch enclosure; incorrect NEMA enclosure type; corrosive fumes; excessive heat from other maintenance work in area, from voltage surges or from short circuits; foreign material buildup insulation material; process temperature and pressures exceed switch specifications
High closed contact resistance	Evidence of filing or dressing of contacts, a prohibited practice; contact damage from grounds, shorts, incorrect fuse or circuit breaker size, or excessive contact current from burned contacts; incorrect NEMA enclosure type; oxidation, oil or other foreign material on contacts; loose terminal screws
Burned contacts or contacts welded close	Contact damage from grounds, shorts, incorrect fuse or circuit breaker size; inductive loads produced excessive arcing or excessive contact current from burned or welded contacts; severe vibration
Mechanical failure	Abrasive dust or foreign material on mechanical linkage; incorrect application of float or flow operator; incorrect mounting location for switch body; improper location of switch operator, operator speed or pressure exceeds switch specifications; physical damage
Sticking or sluggish operator	Dirt or foreign material buildup on mechanical linkages; improper adjustment of linkage arms, counter balance weights, and cams; corrosion of bearings in rotational linkages and mechanisms; mechanical binding; incorrect NEMA enclosure type

in troubleshooting limit switches. Pressure switch contacts are usually accessible through a removable access panel on the switch. If the contacts are not accessible at the switch, troubleshoot the contacts at the terminal or control box where the switch is connected to the control circuit. Always check the amount of deadband when using pressure switches in different applications.

If all parts of the pressure control circuit are good except for the pressure switch then troubleshooting the pressure switch is necessary. The operators for pressure switches are often difficult to access since they are part of the pressure system. Use the flow and level switch troubleshooting procedure for troubleshooting pressure switch control circuits.

Figure 3-28 provides a list of observable symptoms for failed or faulty pressure switches and the possible reason for the symptom that should be investigated.

Troubleshooting Temperature Switches

Automatically operated temperature switches have a set of switchable contacts. The procedure for troubleshooting the contacts is the same as that presented in troubleshooting limit switches.

If all parts of the temperature control circuit are good except for the temperature switch then troubleshooting the temperature switch is necessary. The operators for temperature switches are easy to access since only the capillary tube bulb is in the process system. Use the flow and level switch troubleshooting procedure for troubleshooting temperature switch control circuits.

Figure 3-29 provides a list of observable symptoms for failed or faulty temperature switches and the possible reason for the symptom that should be investigated.

FIGURE 3-28: Pressure switch troubleshooting guide.

Observed Symptom	Possible Reason for Failure
Failure in the insulation of control and internal wires	Moisture inside switch enclosure; incorrect NEMA enclosure type; corrosive fumes; excessive heat from other maintenance work in area, from voltage surges or from short circuits; foreign material buildup on insulation material; process pressures exceed switch specifications
High closed contact resistance	Evidence of filing or dressing of contacts, a prohibited practice; contact damage from grounds, shorts, incorrect fuse or circuit breaker size, or excessive contact current from burned contacts; incorrect NEMA enclosure type; oxidation, oil or other foreign material on contacts; loose terminal screws
Burned contacts or contacts welded close	Contact damage from grounds, shorts, incorrect fuse or circuit breaker size; inductive loads that produced excessive arcing or excessive contact current from burned or welded contacts; severe vibration
Mechanical failure	Abrasive dust or foreign material on mechanical linkage; incorrect mounting location for switch body; pressure exceeds switch specifications; physical damage
Sticking or sluggish operator	Dirt or foreign material buildup on mechanical linkages; improper adjustment of linkage arms; corrosion of bearings in linkages and mechanisms; mechanical binding; incorrect NEMA enclosure type
Leaks	Corrosion of bearings in linkages and mechanical damage and binding; incorrect pressure applied

FIGURE 3-29: Temperature switch troubleshooting guide.

Observed Symptom	Possible Reason for Failure
Failure in the insulation of control and internal wires	Moisture inside switch enclosure; incorrect NEMA enclosure type; corrosive fumes; excessive heat from other maintenance work in area, from voltage surges or from short circuits; foreign material buildup on insulation material; process temperature exceeds switch specifications
Arcing and burning contacts	Misapplied—contact ratings insufficient for application; switching currents above maximum level; switching inductive loads
Burned contacts or contacts welded close	Contact damage from grounds, shorts, incorrect fuse or circuit breaker size; inductive loads produced excessive arcing or excessive contact current from burned or welded contacts; severe vibration
Bimetallic strip distorted	Mechanical binding; measured temperature allowed to overshoot above device specification
Capillary bulb/tube or probe distorted	Ambient or storage temperature is allowed to decrease below device specification and liquid froze in capillary tube or probe

CRITICAL CONCEPTS

The need-to-know content from Chapter 3 is summarized in the following statements.

- Mechanically operated devices operate by physical contact with a system object, and automatically operated devices operate by physical contact with a measured process variable.
- Limit switch actuators include: roller lever, plunger, wobble sticks, and fork lever.
- Process actuated flow switches are used to detect a change in the flow of a liquid or a gas in a pipe or duct. Automatically operated types use mechanical linkages to couple process flow to changes in an electrical contact position.
- Flow switches are automatically or process actuated switches used to detect a change in the flow of a liquid or a gas in a pipe or duct.
- Level switches, also called float switches, are discrete switches used for the control of liquid or granular material levels in tanks and bins.
- Pressure switches change the state of a contact (open or closed) based on the pressure applied to the device by water, air, or another fluid such as oil.
- The diaphragm is a flexible membrane, which is rubber for low-pressure measurements and metal for higher-pressure measurements.
- The bellows is a thin sealed metal cylinder with corrugated sides like the pleats of an accordion. When pressure is applied to the bellows, the bellows expands and opens the pleats, producing a displacement that is proportional to the applied pressure.
- The piston is a cylinder that moves within a tight-fitting chamber. This sensing device uses a stainless-steel piston that moves against a tension spring to operate electrical contacts.
- The differential pressure sensing device is a modified diaphragm where pressure is applied to both ends of the cylinder. When different pressures are applied to the ends of the cylinder, the diaphragm moves toward the end with the lowest pressure.
- Deadband is the difference between the start point and the stop point of an automatically operated switch. It is inherent in all pressure, temperature, flow and level switches.
- Temperature switches, which are activated by a temperature sensing device, cause electrical contacts to change state at a specific temperature.
- The bimetallic strip is a temperature sensing device that bends when the temperature changes. It is made of two different metals that expand at different rates when heated.
- The capillary tube is a temperature sensing device, which is a sealed chamber filled with an expandable fluid.

QUESTIONS

1. What is the difference between mechanically- and automatically-operated input devices?
2. What are the three basic components of a limit switch?
3. What actuator allows the limit switch to be actuated from almost any direction?
4. What actuator has the least amount of travel compared to other limit switch actuators?
5. Name one method to prevent the limit switch from snapping back to the at rest position.
6. Name the four operating positions of a limit switch.
7. How does a flow switch function differ from a level switch function?
8. Describe how the diaphragm, bellows and piston function as pressure sensing devices?
9. How is the deadband phenomenon both beneficial and detrimental?
10. Describe how the bimetallic strip and capillary tube are used as temperature sensing devices.

CHAPTER 4

Control Relays (Mechanical)

GOALS AND OBJECTIVES

The primary goals for this chapter are to identify mechanical control relay devices, and to describe the operation of and applications for these discrete control devices in manufacturing systems. Also, troubleshooting tips and procedures for typical failure modes are presented.

After completing this chapter, you will be able to:

1. Identify and describe the components of a NEMA and IEC standard mechanical relays.
2. Identify and discuss the operation of panel mount, plug-in, and DIN-rail mounted relays.
3. Identify and discuss the operation and function of configurable relays.
4. Describe troubleshooting techniques for mechanical relay devices.

4-1 THEORY

The *control relay* is an *electromechanical device* that is activated by a magnetic field produced by a current flow in a conductor.

Figure 4-1(a) illustrates this current induced magnetic field discovered by Hans Oersted in the early 1800s. The *magnetic field* is present all along the *full length* of the conductor. The *direction* of the *electron* current flow through the conductor determines the *direction* of the magnetic field around it. The magnetic field generates *lines of force*, also called *flux, magnetic field lines,* and *lines of induction*. The variable used for the value of the lines of force is the Greek symbol ϕ (pronounced phi).

If a conductor is bent to form a single loop, as in Figure 4-1(b), all the lines of force circling the conductor *enter one side* of the loop and *exit from the other side* of the loop. Note that a *north pole* is created on the side of the loop where flux exits, and a *south pole* is present on the side where the flux enters.

If a conductor is wound into a *multiple-loop coil,* the magnetic lines of force combine as shown in Figure 4-1(c). The magnetic force of the multiple-loop coil is *stronger* than the magnetic force of the single coil. The *strength* of magnetic field is further increased by adding additional loops in the coil, as in Figure 4-2(a), and by insertion of an iron core, as in Figure 4-2(b).

FIGURE 4-1: Current and magnetic fields.

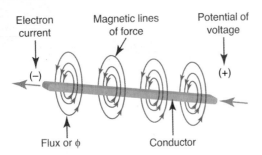

Electron current

Magnetic lines of force

Potential of voltage

(−)

(+)

Flux or φ

Conductor

(a) Induced magnetic field from current in conductor

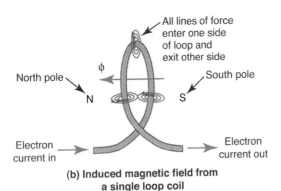

All lines of force enter one side of loop and exit other side

φ

North pole

South pole

N

S

Electron current in

Electron current out

(b) Induced magnetic field from a single loop coil

Magnetic lines of force, flux, or φ

North pole

N

South pole

S

Electron current out

Electron current in

(c) Induced magnetic field from multi-turn loop coil

The wire coiled around an air or iron core forms an electromagnet.

An electromagnet is defined as a magnet whose magnetic energy is produced by the flow of electric current.

Electromagnets are available is a variety of shapes and sizes—very large, which are strong enough to lift tons of metal, and very small, which are used in relays.

Solenoids

A *solenoid* is a specific type of *electromagnet*. The solenoid is defined as:

> *A coil of insulated or enamel covered wire with a movable metal core in the shape of a rod made of solid iron, solid steel, or powdered iron.*

Solenoids convert electrical energy directly into linear mechanical motion.

FIGURE 4-2: Increase magnetic field with increased turns and current.

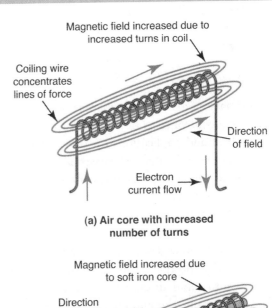

Magnetic field increased due to increased turns in coil

Coiling wire concentrates lines of force

Direction of field

Electron current flow

(a) Air core with increased number of turns

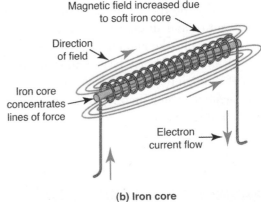

Magnetic field increased due to soft iron core

Direction of field

Iron core concentrates lines of force

Electron current flow

(b) Iron core

Left-Hand Rule—In an electromagnet, the core concentrates the lines of force that are produced by the current flow through the coil. With the core in place and the coil energized, the polarity of the magnet, *north* and *south,* is determined by the *left hand rule* as shown in Figure 4-3. The rule states:

The thumb of the left hand points in the direction of the flux, φ, and toward the magnetic north pole of the coil, when the fingers of the left hand wrap the coil in the direction of the electron current flow.

FIGURE 4-3: Left-hand rule to identify flux direction and north pole.

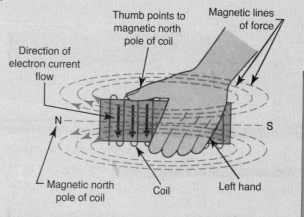

Solenoid Construction and Operation—The basic *DC solenoid,* illustrated in Figure 4-4, has *two* components: a *coil of wire* and an *iron core plunger* or *armature.* In the de-energized case as shown in Figure 4-4(a), the only force acting on the iron core is the spring pushing it out of the coil. When the switch is closed, current through the coil creates an electromagnet with a magnetic flux that flows out of the top of

FIGURE 4-4: Solenoid operation and symbols.

F_S —Spring force

F_M —Magnetic force

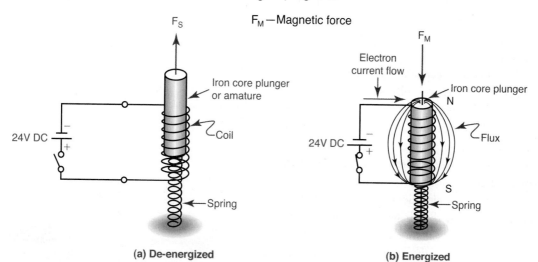

(a) De-energized

(b) Energized

Letter Code	NEMA	IEC
NEMA – SOL IEC – YV		

(c) Solenoid symbols

the coil (north pole) and flows into the bottom of the coil (south pole). As shown in Figure 4-4(b), the magnetic field pulls the iron core into the coil because the magnetic force, F_M, is greater than the spring force, F_S. The length of core movement between the de-energized and energized positions of the core is called the *stroke*. The control symbols and letter codes for solenoids are shown in Figure 4-4(c).

Figure 4-5 illustrates the operation and construction of an AC powered solenoid. Solenoids powered from AC sources are more common in industry and have a third component, called a *frame*. The top cut-away image in Figure 4-5(a) identifies solenoid components. The *frame* and the *armature* are made of high-grade silicon steel, which is constructed of multiple layers called *laminations*. The lamination construction in Figure 4-5(b) is necessary for AC solenoids to reduce the heat caused by eddy currents flowing in the frame and plunger. *Eddy currents* or *circular currents* are generated because of the alternating magnetic field produced by the continuous changing AC source. Eddy current size and generated heat are reduced by the lamination because the eddy currents are confined to each lamination. DC solenoids operate with solid core or laminated cores because the coil current flows in one direction.

Figure 4-5(a) illustrates solenoid operation at three time intervals: (1) lower view—just after the coil is energized where inrush current is highest; (2) middle view—as the armature is closing with reduced inrush current; and (3) upper view—fully energized when the armature is *pulled in* with minimum *sealing current*. The reason for the variation in the coil current is the energy required to generate the magnetic circuit flux [Figure 4-5(a), top image] in the frame and armature as the solenoid closes. *Magnetic circuit flux* is analogous to current in an electrical circuit, and the *air gap* is like a resistor. If the air gap is wider then the energy required to push the flux around the magnetic circuit is higher. As a result, a larger coil current is required in the just energized solenoids compared to the fully energized sealed solenoid. Finally, note the small *air gap* in Figure 4-5(a), top image, when the solenoid is fully closed. The small gap allows the armature to release when the solenoid is de-energized.

The AC solenoid coil source current periodically passes through zero, so the armature starts to open. When the AC source increases with the opposite polarity the armature reseals. As a result, AC solenoids tend to chatter unless a *shading coil* is added.

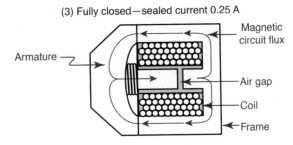

(3) Fully closed—sealed current 0.25 A

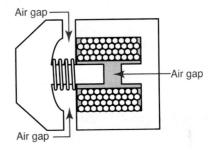

(2) Partially closed—current 1.25 A

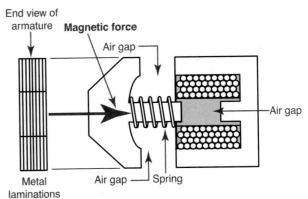

(1) Just energized—inrush current 2.5 A

(a) Solenoid cut away operation

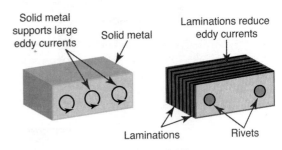

(b) Eddy current reduction

A *shading coil*, illustrated in Figure 4-6, is a single turn of conducting material, typically copper or aluminum that is mounted on the face of the laminated armature assembly. The shading coil's induced current sets up an auxiliary magnetic field to hold the armature closed when the AC source passes through zero. The shading coil keeps the armature sealed, which eliminates chatter. Without the shad-

ing coil, excessive noise, wear, and heat occurs, which reduces solenoid life.

Solenoid Configurations—Figure 4-7 shows four configurations that control contact movement with solenoids and electromagnets. Study the figure and note the movement of the relay armature. The *clapper* type pivots to close contacts. The *bell-crank* type converts vertical motion into horizontal motion with a central pivot point to close contacts. The *vertical-* and *horizontal-action* types move the armature in vertical and horizontal directions to close the contacts. Horizontal-action solenoids are one of the most common configurations.

Solenoid Applications—The relays in Figure 4-7 represent the primary application for solenoids. This solenoid action opens and closes sets of contacts used to control a wide variety of electrical devices.

FIGURE 4-6: Shading coils.

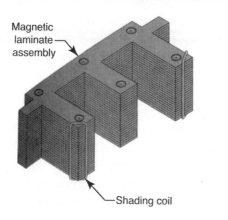

FIGURE 4-7: Types of solenoids used to close contacts.

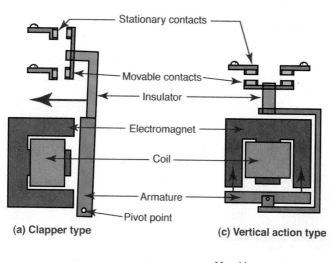

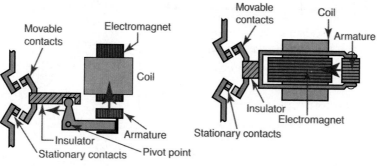

Solenoids are also used in mechanical applications; such as, door locks and safety applications that require lock in and/or lockout operations. For example, a solenoid is used to lock doors on control panels and machine guards so access is permitted only when personnel and machine safety is assured. In addition, industrial applications rely on the precise control of liquids and gases, and solenoid operated values provide a cost effective solution. When solenoid actuation is used, remote pilot devices control the process through electrical signals to the solenoids.

4-2 NEMA VERSUS IEC RELAYS

The relay, invented by Joseph Henry in 1835, is an electromagnetic controlled switch that opens and closes one or more sets of contacts under the control of an external circuit. Control relays are used extensively in industrial processes and in commercial equipment to control power to: *motor starters, heating elements, pilot lights, audible alarms,* and *small motors.* A *small volt-* age applied to a relay coil permits control of a *larger voltage* connected to a load. Figure 4-8 illustrates the *elements* of a relay with its associated *external* circuitry. This illustration is redrawn as two control circuits—one with *IEC* symbols and one with *NEMA* symbols. Refer to Figure 4-9 for the NEMA and IEC symbols for each relay element. Note in Figure 4-8 that each control circuit has an *input circuit,* a *relay,* and an *output circuit.* When a control switch is closed, 24V DC is applied to the relay coil in the input circuit. The relay contact then closes in the output circuit, applying the higher AC voltage in the load.

Control Relay Contact Configurations

Relay contacts, similar to mechanically-operated switches, *open* and *close* electrical paths with a variety of contact configurations. These configurations are identified by their number of *poles,* type of *throws,* and number of *breaks.* Figure 4-10(a) through (c) illustrates the *single pole single throw* (SPST), the *single pole double throw* (SPDT), and the *double pole double throw* (DPDT) contact arrangement.

FIGURE 4-8: NEMA and IEC sample relay control circuits.

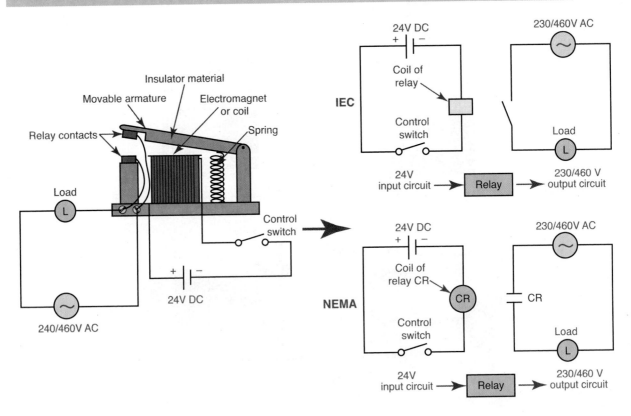

Figure 4-10(d) lists the *single-break, double-break,* and *make-before-break* contact configurations. The term *break* is defined as:

The term break in contact applications refers to the number of separate places on a contact that open or close an electrical circuit.

For example, a *single-break* (SB) contact breaks an electrical circuit in *one place*, and a *double-break* (DB) contact breaks an electrical circuit in *two places*. In Figure 4-10(c) the dotted line indicates that all contacts *change* together. In the far right table of Figure 4-10(d), *make-before-break* configurations are shown. Upon actuation in Case 1, contact (1) is *closed* before contact (2) is *opened*. Upon actuation in Case 2, contact (1) is *opened*, before contact (2) is *closed*; and contact (2) is *closed* before contact (3) is *opened*.

NEMA and IEC relay *terminal identifications* are shown in Figure 4-11. In Figure 4-11(a), the NEMA relay coil is identified as CR1, and all contacts for the relay are identified by the coil number. Multiple *poles* on the same relay are numbered as 1 CR1, 2 CR1 and so forth. Multiple relays are numbered so that the second relay is identified as CR2, the third as CR3 and so forth. In addition, the manufacturer numbers each terminal of the relay in sequence starting at one. Relay terminal numbers, Figure 4-11(a), are generally stamped on the relay case.

In Figures 4-11(b) and (c), the IEC relay coil *terminals* are identified as A1 and A2, and the *poles/contacts* are identified by a two number sequence. The *first*

FIGURE 4-9: NEMA and IEC control relay symbols.

Letter Code	NEMA		IEC	
Coil NEMA – CR IEC – KA	CR		▭	
Contacts NEMA – CR IEC – KA	NO	NC	NO	NC
	⊣⊢	⊣/⊢	⟋	⌐

FIGURE 4-10: Contact configurations and terms.

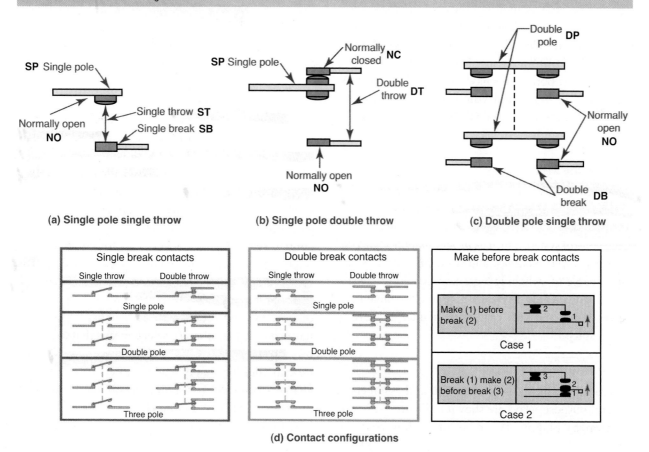

(a) Single pole single throw

(b) Single pole double throw

(c) Double pole single throw

(d) Contact configurations

FIGURE 4-11: NEMA and IEC relay symbols and terminal identifications.

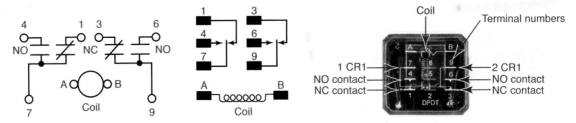

(a) NEMA DPDT SB control relay with two relay contact drawing styles

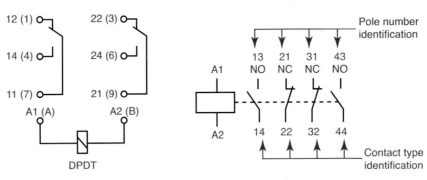

(b) IEC DPDT SB control relay with two NO and two NC contacts

(c) IEC 4PST SB control relay with two NO and two NC contacts

number is the *pole* number—1, 2, 3, 4 and so forth. The *second number* indicates the *contact type*—if it is a NO contact, it is identified as a 3 and 4, and if it is NC contact, it's identified as a 1 and 2. Figure 4-11(b) illustrates a DPDT relay, and Figure 4-11(c) illustrates a 4PST relay. Both relays have NO and NC contacts. Study Figure 4-11 until you are familiar with the NEMA and the IEC terminal identifications for the relays.

Interposing Relay

Interposing relay is term used to describe a relay that enables the energy in a high-power circuit to be switched by a low-power control signal. Discrete output circuits from control systems, such as *programmable logic controllers, output modules,* and some *pilot devices,* are not capable of switching high currents. So to control higher power field devices, such as electromagnetic valves or motor starters or heaters, an interposing relay is necessary.

General Purpose Relays

Several different styles of industrial and commercial general purpose relays are shown in Figure 4-12. The throwaway plug-in style relay offers low cost and quick replacement. Most general purpose relay contacts have a current rating of 5A to 15A. Contacts generally have a lower contact rating for DC currents than for AC currents. For example, a 15A AC-rated contact is only rated for 8A to 10A DC.

Machine or Industrial Control Relays

The *machine control relay* is an electromagnetic relay that consists of several contacts, typically two to eight, but are available with up to twelve contacts. The machine control relay is also called a *heavy-duty* or *machine tool* relay because they are used extensively in machine tools for direct switching of *solenoids, contactors* and *motor starters.* Machine control relays provide *easy access* for contact maintenance and generally have a *long life.* The IEC machine tool relays typically have a life of *one million operations* with the NEMA relays expected to operate at least *twice as long.* Usually, these relays have *convertible contacts,* which means that each contact can be configured as a *NO contact* or a *NC contact.* In addition, many manufacturers offer DIN rail adapters as an alternate mounting option. Figure 4-13 illustrates a *NEMA* and an *IEC machine relay.* Note that the terminal numbers on the face of IEC con-

FIGURE 4-12: General purpose control relays.

General Purpose Relay	Description
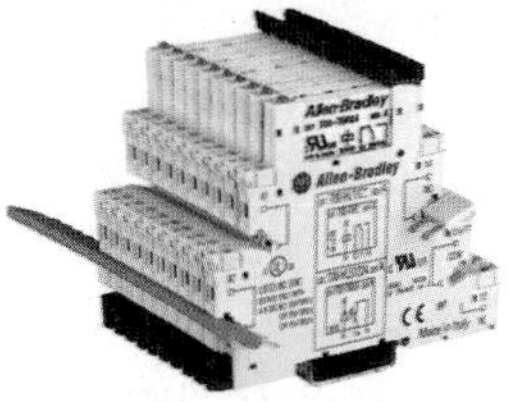	Terminal block relays with one and two pole contacts, DIN rail mount, and selectable jumpers for common coil, pole, or NO connections
	Square base cube relay with flange mount and tab terminals
	Power relay with flange mount and screw terminal
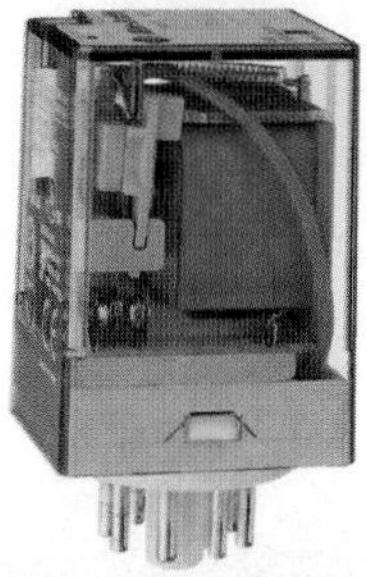	Tube base relay with eight pin configuration
	Mounting plate for eight pin tube base relay—eleven pin bases are also available
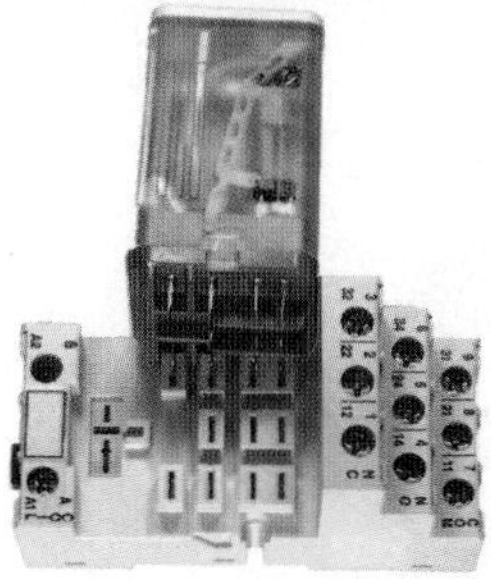	Square base eight tab relay with eight socket mounting plate

trol relay illustrate the numbering convention discussed in Figure 4-11.

Figure 4-14 lists the voltage and current contact ratings for a variety of relay styles. Note that the NEMA style relay has a broader range of voltage and current ratings.

FIGURE 4-13: Machine or industrial control relays.

(a) NEMA relay

(b) IEC relay

FIGURE 4-14: Comparison of relay ratings.

Contact Voltage and Current Ratings for Control Relays		
Relay Type	Voltage	Current
NEMA—Machine Control	300 to 600 V	Most 10 A some to 20 A
IEC—Machine Control	600 V	Most 10 A some to 15 A
General Purpose	600 V	Most 10 A some to 60 A
General Purpose—Plug-in	120 to 240 V some rated in motor hp	10 to 30 A load dependent

4-3 CONFIGURABLE RELAYS

NEMA and IEC configurable machine control relays are defined as follows:

A configurable relay is designed to accept additional sets of contacts called add-on contacts or adder decks.

Figure 4-15 illustrates a DIN rail mounted machine control relay and an example of an adder deck. Most conferrable relays accept one or two adder decks, which increases the contact count to as many as *twelve* contacts. The adder contact decks are single throw, double break contacts. Many NEMA machine relays have the capability of adding at least one adder deck, which adds two or four additional contacts. Contacts are added to the IEC machine relays through the use of *auxiliary* side mounting *contact blocks*. In addition, *reversible* contact cartridges, Figure 4-16, permit the NC *contacts* to be changed to NO *contacts*.

FIGURE 4-15: Configurable machine control relay with adder blocks or decks.

Machine Control Relay	Adder Decks

FIGURE 4-16: Reversible contact set with NC contact configuration.

SAFETY

Safety Control Relays—Safety control relays provide the mechanically linked contacts required in feedback circuits for *e-stops, safety gates, light curtains,* and *master control relay safety* applications. Mechanically linked contacts allow detection of a welded contact condition. Mechanically linked contacts do not work independently, so an open NC contact cannot close when the closed NO contact has welded. Double-break contacts provide *better protection* against contact *welding, greater DC load breaking capability, better isolation,* and *separation of NO and NC* circuits. Double-break contacts open the circuits in two places, creating two air gaps and reducing the probability of welded contacts by more that 50 percent.

The *red faceplate* identifies the control relay as a safety device with the IEC mechanically linked symbol displayed. An anti-tamper feature ensures that all contact blocks are permanently fixed to ensure that the safety function is not altered. Also, manual operation is prevented and field modifications are not permitted. Figure 4-17 displays *safety control relays* for both *IEC and NEMA* standards.

FIGURE 4-17: NEMA and IEC safety control relays.

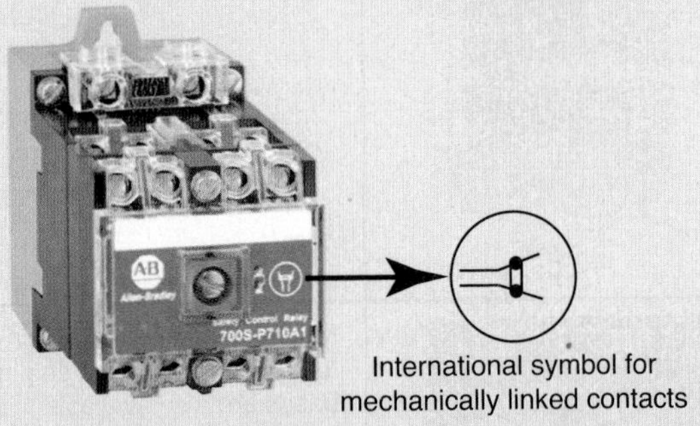

International symbol for mechanically linked contacts

(a) NEMA

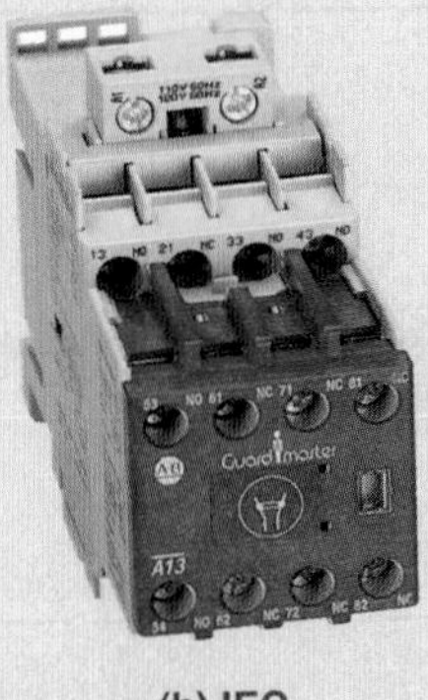

(b) IEC

Manufacturers provide a variety of adder decks and reversible contact cartridges for machine control relays. Relay families provide various types of contact cartridges that are combined into one relay to yield a custom-tailored application solution. Relays are available with standard 10A contact cartridges and a *double-break, bifurcated* design. Bifurcation provides excellent *contact reliability* and *low-contact bounce*, while the double-break contact design reduces the possibility of contacts welding and enhances the relay's ability to break DC circuits. Adder decks are generally available with a maximum of 12 NO or 12 NC contacts. Other relay options include 20A contact cartridges with large single-contact pads on each side of the contact bar for twice the current rating to control heavy loads and for system master control.

4-4 TROUBLESHOOTING SOLENOIDS AND CONTROL RELAYS

Solenoid and control relay problems fall into two main categories—operator failure and contact failure. The operator for solenoids and relays are the electromagnetic coil plus the mechanical linkage to the contact poles. All of the problems and troubleshooting procedures discussed for switch operators and contacts in Chapter 2 apply to relays.

Troubleshooting Solenoids

First, perform the troubleshooting procedures for switches in Chapter 2. Secondly, verify that the applied voltage and frequency are correct, verify power line transients are suppressed, and verify the environmental conditions are within specifications. If the solenoid is suspect, perform the following steps:

1. Turn the solenoid voltage off and measure the voltage to insure the power is off
2. Remove the solenoid cover and visually inspect the solenoid. Replaced damaged parts. If there is no damage, disconnect the solenoid from the circuit
3. Check for solenoid continuity. The resistance reading on the DVM should be close to the coil's nominal value.

A plating process creates fumes that are exhausted from the production area with a fume hood and blower. A flow switch is used in the exhaust duct to detect no air flow or air flow too low for safe plating tank operation. The system is illustrated in Figure 4-18. A control relay with a DPDT contact set is used for system control. A NO contact (1 CR1) on one pole of CR1 is used to seal in the momentary start switch in the 24VAC control circuit. A second NO contact (2 CR1) on the other pole of CR1 is used to energize the blower motor starter. When the system is started, the operator observes that the duct airflow off light is on until the blower air flow opens the NC flow switch. The light returns to the on state whenever air flow drops below the flow switch set-point value.

FIGURE 4-18: Plating process fume blower control.

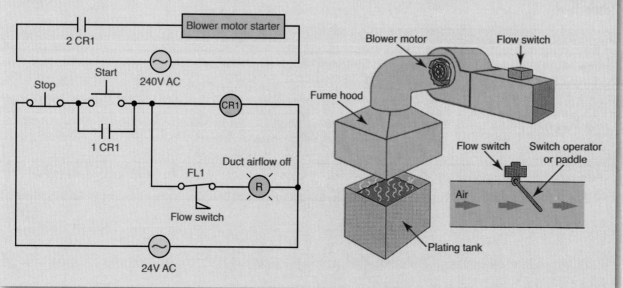

Figures 4-19 and 4-20 provide a list of observed symptoms for failed or faulty AC and DC solenoids and the possible reasons for the fault or failure.

Troubleshooting Control Relays

Perform the troubleshooting procedures for switches in Chapter 2. If the relay is still suspect after it has passed the troubleshooting procedure for switches, an examination of the contacts is in order. In some low current applications, the contacts look clean but may have a thin film of *sulfide, oxidation,* or *contaminants* on the contact surface. Contacts may also be *pitted* due to arcing. Arcing is the discharge of an electric current across the gap of an electric contact when it is opened or closed. Arcing in relay contacts is shown in Figure 4-21. Inductive loads produce the largest arcs when switched. Contact *surface film* and lack of *surface to surface contact* when closed increases the closed contact resistance and contact heat. Burnishing the contacts eliminates the pitting and cleans the contact surface, which permits proper current flow. Figure 4-21 also illustrates contacts before and after burnishing.

Figure 4-22 provides a list of observed symptoms for failed or faulty relays and the possible reasons for the symptom that should be investigated.

FIGURE 4-19: AC solenoid troubleshooting guide.

Observed Symptom	Possible Reason for Failure
Noisy or humming magnet	Open shading coil; too much lateral movement of core in frame due to wear; contamination on core or frame face; voltage below minimum
Broken shading coil	Voltage above maximum; improperly sized device; line frequency below rated value
Coil failure	Excessive moisture or improper NEMA enclosure; high ambient temperature; failure of seal in on pick-up causes high current; armature chatter; corrosive environment; voltage above maximum; mechanical load too high or too low; too high of a duty cycle; improperly sized device
Frame or armature wear	Improperly sized device; open shading coil; voltage above maximum; mechanical load too high or too low
Failure of contacts to pick up	Voltage too low or not present; coil has open or shorted winding; mechanical binding between armature and frame; improperly sized device; frame to armature air gap too large; mechanical load too high
Failure of contacts to drop out	Voltage present; welded contacts; mechanical binding between armature and frame; frame to armature air gap too small; sticky substance on frame and armature faces

FIGURE 4-20: DC solenoid troubleshooting guide.

Observed Symptom	Possible Reason for Failure
Coil failure	Excessive moisture or improper NEMA enclosure; high ambient temperature; failure of seal in on pick-up causes high current; armature chatter; corrosive environment; voltage above maximum; mechanical load too high or too low; too high of a duty cycle; continuous use of intermittent coil; improperly sized device
Failure of contacts to pick up	Voltage too low or not present; coil has open or shorted winding; mechanical binding between armature and frame; improperly sized device; frame to core air gap too large; mechanical load too high
Failure of contacts to drop out	Voltage present; welded contacts; mechanical binding between armature and frame; frame to armature air gap too small; sticky substance on frame and armature faces

FIGURE 4-21: Contact arcing and cleaning technique.

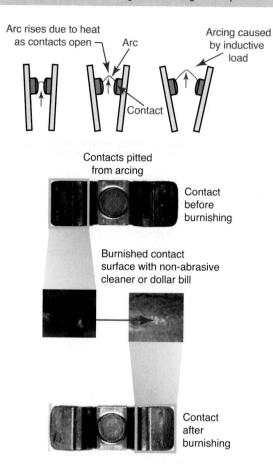

Arc rises due to heat as contacts open — Arc

Arcing caused by inductive load

Contact

Contacts pitted from arcing

Contact before burnishing

Burnished contact surface with non-abrasive cleaner or dollar bill

Contact after burnishing

CRITICAL CONCEPTS

The need to know content from Chapter 4 is summarized in the following statements.

- Electromagnetism is the magnetism that is produced when an electric current is passed through a conductor.
- The strength of magnetic field is further increased by increasing the number of turns of the coil and by inserting an iron core through the coil.
- The solenoid is a coil of insulated or enameled wire wound on a rod-shaped form, which is made of solid iron, solid steel, powdered iron or air.
- The DC solenoid has two components: a coil of wire and an armature.
- The IEC relay coils are identified as A1 and A2, and the contacts are identified by a two number—the contact number and the contact type.
- The term break is defined as the number of separate places on a contact that open or close an electrical circuit.
- A shading coil is a single turn of conducting material, typically copper or aluminum, which is mounted face of the laminated armature assembly.
- Four configurations that control contact movement with solenoids and electromagnets are the clapper

FIGURE 4-22: Relay troubleshooting guide.

Observed Symptom	Possible Reason for Failure
Wear on electromagnet	Improperly sized device; voltage above maximum; armature chatter; cycling of armature at too high a rate
Insulation failure	Excessive moisture or improper NEMA enclosure; temperature above maximum; voltage or current spikes; toxic environment; contaminants on surface
Coil failure	Excessive moisture or improper NEMA enclosure; high ambient temperature; failure of seal in on pick-up causes high current; armature chatter; corrosive environment; voltage above maximum; mechanical load too high or too low
Failure to drop out	Binding in mechanical linkage; contaminant on linkage
Mechanical wear	Excessive or too rapid cycling; toxic or abrasive environment; improper NEMA enclosure
Low trip point	Improperly sized device; damaged armature spring
High trip point	Improperly selected device; improper replacement coil; binding in mechanical linkage; shorted coil

type, the bell-crank type, and the vertical and horizontal action types.

- Interposing relay is term used to describe a relay that enables the energy in a high-power circuit to be switched by a low-power control signal

- General purpose relays are designed for industrial and commercial applications that use a throwaway plug-in style relay for quick replacement and where economy is a high priority.

- The machine control relay is called a heavy-duty or machine tool relay and is used extensively in machine tools for direct switching of solenoids, contactors and motor starters.

- Configurable relays are NEMA and IEC machine control relays that accept additional sets of contacts called add-on contacts or adder decks.

QUESTIONS

1. Define electromagnetism.
2. Describe the magnetic lines of force in a conductor that is bent to form a loop.
3. Define an electromagnet.
4. Describe the operation of a DC solenoid.
5. How is a laminated armature constructed?
6. In a relay, the terms magnetic circuit flux and air gap relate to what terms in an electrical circuit?
7. What is the function of a shading coil?
8. What function do control relays perform in industrial processes and commercial equipment?
9. What are interposing relays?
10. What applications use general purpose relays?
11. What is a configurable relay?

5

Control Transformers

GOALS AND OBJECTIVES

The primary goals for this chapter are to identify and to describe control transformer configurations and to describe how control transformers are selected. In addition, control transformer overcurrent protection with fuses is described. Finally, troubleshooting tips and procedures for typical failure modes are presented.

After completing this chapter, you will be able to:

1. Identify and describe control transformer configurations and wiring.
2. Describe how branch control circuits are protected at the control transformer from overcurrent conditions.
3. Describe how control transformers are rated and selected.
4. Describe troubleshooting techniques for control transformers.

5-1 RATINGS

The *control transformer* is a transformer that is used to step down the voltage to control circuits in an industrial motor control system. Control transformers are rated by the amount of volt-amperes (VA) they supply at a steady-state rate, plus the amount of VA they

supply on system turn on—the inrush VA. The VA demand for control transformers assumes a forty percent power factor to account for non-resistive loads in the control system. Figure 5-1 shows typical control transformers. Figures 5-2 and 5-3 illustrate control symbols and the configuration options for numerous voltage conditions. Many manufacturers provide transformers that match the 50 and 60 cycle operation frequencies required by NEMA and IEC standards.

FIGURE 5-1: Three sizes of control transformers.

Courtesy of AutomationDirect.

FIGURE 5-2: Control transformer configurations.

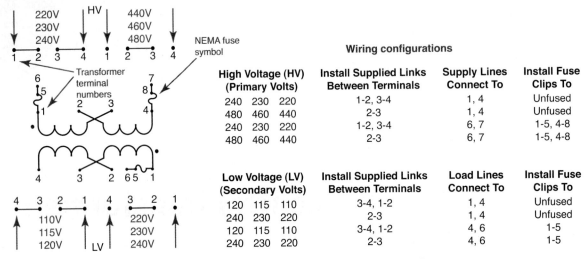

High Voltage (HV) (Primary Volts)			Install Supplied Links Between Terminals	Supply Lines Connect To	Install Fuse Clips To
240	230	220	1-2, 3-4	1, 4	Unfused
480	460	440	2-3	1, 4	Unfused
240	230	220	1-2, 3-4	6, 7	1-5, 4-8
480	460	440	2-3	6, 7	1-5, 4-8

Low Voltage (LV) (Secondary Volts)			Install Supplied Links Between Terminals	Load Lines Connect To	Install Fuse Clips To
120	115	110	3-4, 1-2	1, 4	Unfused
240	230	220	2-3	1, 4	Unfused
120	115	110	3-4, 1-2	4, 6	1-5
240	230	220	2-3	4, 6	1-5

(a) Jumper connections at primary and secondary windings

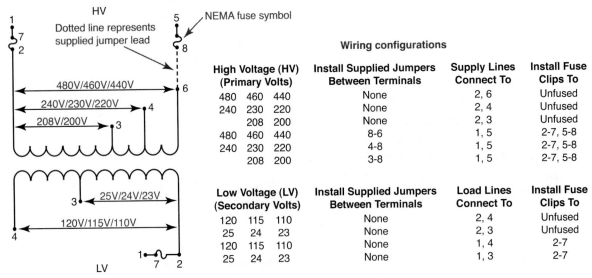

High Voltage (HV) (Primary Volts)			Install Supplied Jumpers Between Terminals	Supply Lines Connect To	Install Fuse Clips To
480	460	440	None	2, 6	Unfused
240	230	220	None	2, 4	Unfused
	208	200	None	2, 3	Unfused
480	460	440	8-6	1, 5	2-7, 5-8
240	230	220	4-8	1, 5	2-7, 5-8
	208	200	3-8	1, 5	2-7, 5-8

Low Voltage (LV) (Secondary Volts)			Install Supplied Jumpers Between Terminals	Load Lines Connect To	Install Fuse Clips To
120	115	110	None	2, 4	Unfused
25	24	23	None	2, 3	Unfused
120	115	110	None	1, 4	2-7
25	24	23	None	1, 3	2-7

(b) Multi-tapped primary and secondary

5-2 CONFIGURATIONS

Control transformers are generally configured to step down the main line voltage to a control voltage of 120 or 24V AC. Figure 5-2(a) illustrates transformer to step 240 or 480V AC down to 240 or 120V AC. To transform 240V AC down to 120V AC jumpers configure the primary and secondary transformer windings. The primary winding (HV side) jumpers connect the two primary windings in parallel. The jumpers on the secondary or LV side connect the secondary coils in parallel as well. To step down 480V AC to 120V AC, the two primary windings are connected in series, and the secondary windings remain in parallel. Note that both control transformers in the figures support fuses in the HV and LV winding sides.

The winding terminals are generally tied together with a metal link to minimize the voltage drop across the connection and to provide a quick and easy way to reconfigure the winding (e.g. parallel to serial). When terminal are linked with wire, follow the manufacturers recommended wire types and sizes. Figure 5-3 illustrates the links used to connect transformer terminals. In Figure 5-2(a), the link location for all the voltage combinations is illustrated above the HV winding and below the LV winding. Also, link requirements for all input and output voltage combinations for the transformer are indicated in the wiring configuration tables in Figures 5-2 along with fuse clip terminal locations.

NEMA versus IEC Standards

Control transformer manufacturers often indicated that their products comply with both *NEMA* and *IEC* standards and carry both a *CE* and *UL* compliance symbols. Since the CE standards changed in 2004, it is not clear if a CE marked device meets the current or previous standards. Also, when *self-certification* is performed by the manufacturer for CE certification, access to all test documentation is required. As a result, it is difficult to verify that control transformers with

the CE symbol meet the current standards of the European Union. The surest indication that current standards are satisfied is the presence of a *third-party certification* symbol, the TÜV Rheinland mark as

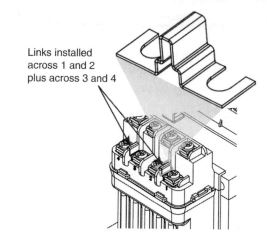

FIGURE 5-3: Links to connect terminals on control transformers.

Links installed across 1 and 2 plus across 3 and 4

Courtesy of AutomationDirect.

APPLICATION

In Figure 5-4, terminals H1 and H3 are connected together, and terminals H2 and H4 are connected together, which parallels the primary windings. The two primary windings in parallel yield an effective number of turns of 200, the same as if there was only one primary winding. With a secondary winding of 100 turns, the turns ratio is 2:1. Therefore, the primary voltage of 240V AC is reduced by a factor of 2, yielding a secondary voltage of 120V AC.

In Figure 5-5, terminals H2 and H3 are connected together, which forms a series connection of the primary windings. The two primary windings in series yield an effective number of turns of 400. With a secondary winding of 100 turns, the turns ratio is 4:1. Therefore, the primary voltage of 480V AC is reduced by a factor of 4, yielding a secondary voltage of 120V AC.

FIGURE 5-4: Primary windings connected in parallel.

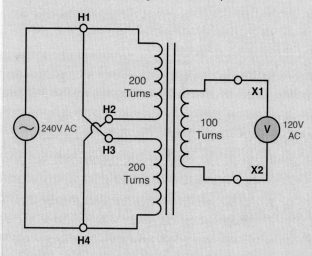

FIGURE 5-5: Primary windings connected in series.

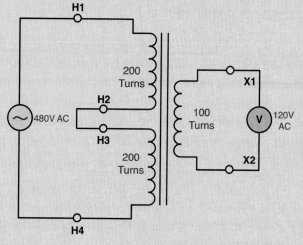

FIGURE 5-6: TÜV Rheinland mark certification symbol.

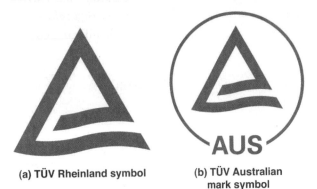

(a) TÜV Rheinland symbol   **(b) TÜV Australian mark symbol**

shown in Figure 5-6. The TÜV Rheinland mark certifies that the control transformer meets the standards required by the European Common Market based on tests performed by TÜV Rheinland group.

5-3   CONTROL TRANSFORMER SIZING

Control transformers are selected based on two motor control circuit criteria: a *high current* for a short time period and *steady-state current* indefinitely. The high current, called *in-rush current,* occurs when power is applied to magnetic devices, like relays and solenoids. A review of the pull-in sequence for a solenoid in Figure 4-5 illustrates the difference between the inrush or starting current and steady-state current. The steady-state current is also called the *sealed current.* The term sealed implies that *relays* and *solenoids* are *pulled-in,* and the *magnetic path air-gaps* are *closed* or sealed. The volt-ampere (VA) rating for a control transformer is also impacted by the load power factor. Therefore, the three characteristics of the load circuit used to determine the proper transformer size include: *total steady-state* (sealed) *VA, total inrush VA,* and *inrush load power factor.*

- *Total steady-state* (sealed) *VA* is the total amount of VA that the transformer must supply to the load circuit for an extended length of time or the amount of current at the secondary voltage required to hold in the *sealed* devices in the circuit. This is determined by adding the total steady-state VA of all devices in a control circuit. This includes the resistive loads like lamps.
- *Total inrush VA* is the amount of VA that the transformer delivers when the control circuit is initially

energized. Electromagnetic devices draw many times normal current, 3 to 10 times normal is typical, for 30 to 50 milliseconds after voltage is applied. The VA supplied by the transformer during this time is called the *total in-rush VA.* In-rush VA values for control circuit devices are available from the device manufacturer.

- *In-rush load power factor* is difficult to determine without detailed vector analysis of all the load components. Such an analysis is generally not feasible. Therefore, a safe assumption is a *forty percent* power factor.

Impact of In-Rush Current

The NEMA Standard specifies that alternating current magnetic motor starting devices must function at 85% of the rated coil voltage. For example, a 120V AC rated coil must pull-in at 102 volts, which is 85 percent of the rated voltage. As a result, the control transformer's secondary voltage drop due to input voltage variation and inrush current drop cannot exceed 15 percent. For example, a 480 to 120V AC transformer operating at 90 percent of the line voltage has 432 (480 – 48) volts on the primary and 108 (120 –12) volts on the secondary. This is based on the turns-ratio and assuming no voltage drop through the transformer. Therefore, the voltage drop in the control transformer under inrush current conditions must not exceed 5 percent or 6 volts. In other words, during inrush conditions 90 percent of the rated secondary voltage is present. Combining these two conditions result in a secondary voltage of approximately 102 (120 – 12 – 6) volts, which meets the motor starting devices *pick-up* or *pull-in* requirement.

Control transformers are selected using the following process:

1. Determine the total inrush VA of the control circuit devices by adding the inrush VA and steady-state VA of all devices including resistive loads, like pilot lights, that do not have inrush values.
2. Identify the supply voltage variation and round it up to either 5 or 10 percent.
3. Use the data from step 2 to identify the inrush VA column to use in the table in Figure 5-7 as follows: a) 10 percent supply voltage variation permits only a 5 percent drop due to inrush current—so use 95 percent column; b) 5 percent supply voltage variation permits a 10 per-

FIGURE 5-7: Inrush current for control transformer selection.

Inrush VA at 40% Power Factor			
Nominal VA Rating	85%	90%	95%
63	347	289	216
80	338	290	229
130	907	745	541
200	1267	1039	754
250	1394	1116	781
350	2870	2298	1584
500	3786	3013	2065
750	7360	5763	3786
800	7360	5763	3786
1000	8837	6785	4329
1600	14921	11328	7070
2000	20500	14850	9100

cent drop due to inrush current—so use 90 percent column.

4. Go down the column selected in step 3 and locate the inrush VA closest to, but not less than, the total inrush VA value from step 1.
5. Locate the corresponding continuous nominal VA rating on the left side of the table.
6. Verify that the total sealed VA of the control circuit does not exceed the nominal VA rating of the selected transformer. If it does, select the next largest sealed VA value.
7. Identify a transformer model with voltage and VA values specified by the process.

Control transformer suppliers provide a transformer VA table, like that in Figure 5-7, to identify the correct VA rating for a control circuit application. The VA rating determine by the sizing process is used to select a transformer model. Verify that the selected device matches the primary and secondary voltages, has a VA rating equal to or slightly higher than the required value, and supports primary and secondary protection devices required in the application. Some suppliers provide power factor correction multipliers for power factors larger or smaller than forty percent.

5-4 SYSTEM PROTECTION AND GROUNDING

Control transformers generally have overcurrent protection provided by *fuses* or *circuit breakers*. Overcurrent protection has two purposes:

- To protect components, equipment and people from risk of hazards caused by overcurrents.
- To isolate sub-systems from the main system once a fault has occurred.

Overcurrents exist when the normal load for a circuit is exceeded. An overload condition is any current flow in the normal current path that is higher than the circuit's normal full load current.

A short circuit is an overcurrent condition that leaves the normal current path and greatly exceeds the normal full load current of the circuit. Components and equipment can be damaged by both types of overcurrents.

Fuses

A fuse is defined as an overcurrent protective device with a fusible link that permanently opens the circuit when an overcurrent condition occurs. A fuse, installed in line with the transformer's primary and/or secondary windings, is the most common protection used for control transformers. Some industrial applications require fuse protection on one secondary line and in both *primary lines*. Fuse locations on control transformers are illustrated in Figure 5-2.

Common installation options for control transformer fuses include: *fuse clips* on the transformer terminals, panel and transformer mounted *fuse holders*, and *DIN rail* mounted fuse holders. Figure 5-8 illustrates an installation of fuse clips on the HV terminals of the primary line. The fuse is located between terminal one and five in the transformer coil symbol as noted in Figure 5-2 for the smaller of the three transformers in Figure 5-1.

Finger protection to protect personnel from accidental shocks is provided with a fuse cover as illustrated in Figure 5-9. The figure also illustrate a cartridge style fuse for fuse clips and the NEMA and IEC standard fuse symbols and letter code.

Other fuse holders, illustrated in Figure 5-10, include panel and transformer mounted fuse blocks and DIN rail mounted holders. One style fuse holder in Figure 5-10(b) indicates if the fuse is open.

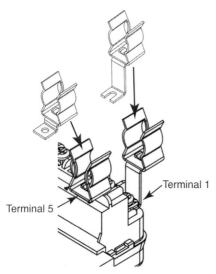

Terminal 1

Terminal 5

Courtesy of AutomationDirect.

(a) Panel mount fuse block

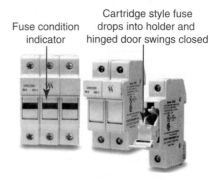

Fuse condition indicator

Cartridge style fuse drops into holder and hinged door swings closed

(b) DIN mount fuse block

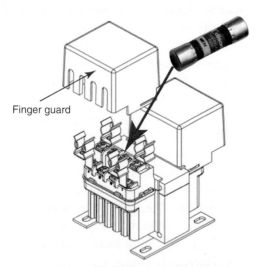

Finger guard

Letter Code	NEMA	IEC
FU		

Courtesy of AutomationDirect.

During normal load conditions, the fuse carries the steady-state operating current of the circuit. However, when an overcurrent occurs, the link inside the fuse goes through a *melt* and *arc* sequence that opens the link and interrupts the overcurrent. Fuse sizing for control systems is based on the following items:

- Current and voltage rating and characteristics of protected equipment
- Normal operating and overload current conditions
- Ambient temperature
- Fuse melting characteristics
- Pulse and inrush characteristics
- Physical size and available space
- NEMA and IEC standards requirements

The number of different types and styles of fuses do not permit descriptions of each. In the field, open fuses should be replaced with the same model and style specified by the equipment manufacturer or by an equivalent fuse from another fuse producer. Fuses are available in five speed categories identified by an international standard letter symbol:

F—Quick-acting, FF—Super-quick-acting, M—Medium-time-lag, T—Time-lag or Anti-surge, and TT—Super-time-lag.

NEMA and IEC Fuse Standards

The NEMA's UL/CSA standard devices have significantly different *time versus current* characteristics for overcurrent when compared to IEC equivalents. While the dimensional units for the NEMA and IEC fuses are different, the materials used in construction are similar. However, substitution of one standard device with one from the other standard is difficult because of differences in melting and opening times for the same magnitude of current. For example, UL listed time delay fuses typically open in 2 seconds maximum when subjected to 200% to 250% of rated current. In contrast, IEC has two categories of time delay fuses:

* T—time lag, opens with 10 times rated current within 0.01 seconds to 0.1 seconds
* TT—long time lag, opens with 10 times rated current within 0.1 seconds to 1 second

Control Circuit Protection

The use of fuses on the primary and secondary side of the control transformer, as noted in Figure 5-2, is specified by the National Electric Code (NEC). Primary protection [NEC Sections 430, 450, and 725] specifies protection device requirements based on primary current values. Secondary protection [NEC Section 240] specifies protection device requirements based on secondary conductor size.

Control transformers suppliers recommend fuse sizes based on the NEC for their transformer models. The tables indicate primary and secondary fuse size for each VA rating in two table formats. One table is for fuses only on the primary side, and a second table lists fuse sizes when both the primary and secondary sides are fused. Figure 5-11 illustrates the tables for Allen Bradley control transformers fused in both the primary and secondary lines. Note that the primary side uses a Class CC type time-delay fuse and the secondary uses a Midget style fuse. The time-delay class fuses provide uninterrupted power during the in-rush current and steady-state operation. A typical current versus time curve for a time-delay fuse is shown in Figure 5-12. Note the allowed current at 0.01 seconds after current flow starts and at 100 seconds. The high initial current and lower steady-state current meets motor control circuit requirements.

Grounded and Floating Control Circuits

Grounding guidelines for control transformers are addressed in the NEC Section 250 plus the NFPA and UL. Alternating current circuits of 50 volts or more must be grounded according to NEC Section 250, which requires a neutral to ground bond at the transformer with a grounding electrode. Figure 5-13 illustrates a grounded system with the X2 lead of the secondary connected to the grounded panel or enclosure. The *grounded system* is the most common in industrial control applications and offers two benefits:

* Voltage measurements at any point in the control system are made easily with one meter lead connected to the panel or enclosure ground.
* A short of the control system to the control panel or enclosure (see accidental ground fault in Figure 5-13) opens the fuse and removes power to the control circuit.

The fused secondary protects the control circuit from damage from any overcurrent condition. The digital multimeter (DMM) in Figure 5-13 demonstrates that measurements anywhere along the control circuit are made easily when one side of the secondary is grounded (be aware of possible ground faults).

NEC Section 250 specifies that alternating-current circuits operating at less than 50 volts do not have a grounding requirement, except for the following conditions:

1. Where the transformer supply system exceeds 150 volts to ground.
2. Where the transformer supply system is ungrounded.
3. Where installed overhead outside the buildings.

As a result, a *floating* control system is used in some electrical machinery. In a *floating system,* Figure 5-14, neither side of the secondary of the control transformer is grounded. The fuse in the secondary line provides some protection for the branch circuit but not protection for ground fault conditions. Measurements on a floating system with a digital multimeter (DMM) between the panel ground and any point in the control system produces false voltage readings because X2 is not grounded. Troubleshooting a floating system requires that the one side of the meter be connected to the X2 secondary lead, as in Figure 5-14, while the other meter probe checks voltages in the circuit. Probe access to the X2 lead on the secondary is often a problem when the control circuit switches are located some distance from the placement of the control transformer and control relay.

Maximum Amp Rating for Current Limiting Class CC Fuses Based on Transformer Primary Voltage													
VA	208V	220V	240V	277V	347V	380V	400V	415V	440V	480V	500V	550V	600V	690V
63	0.75	0.75	0.5	0.5	0.4	0.4	0.4	0.4	0.3	0.3	0.3	0.25	0.25	0.25
80	1.5	1.5	1.5	1	1	1	1	0.75	0.75	0.75	0.75	0.5	0.5	0.5
130	3	2.5	2.5	2	1.5	1.5	1.5	1.5	1.25	1.25	1.25	1	1	0.75
200	4	4	4	3	2.5	2.5	2.5	2	2	2	2	1.5	1.5	1
250	6	5	5	4	3	3	3	3	2.5	2.5	2.5	2	2	1.5
350	8	7	7	6	5	4	4	4	3	3	3	3	2.5	2.5
500	6	5	5	9	7	6	6	6	5	5	5	4	4	3
750	9	8	7	6	5	9	9	9	8	7	7	6	6	5
800	9	9	8	7	5	5	5	8	8	8	8	7	6	5
1000	12	10	10	9	7	6	6	6	5	5	5	8	8	7
1600	15	15	15	12	11	10	10	9	9	8	8	7	6	5
2000	20	20	20	18	14	12	12	12	10	10	10	9	8	7

(a) Primary fuse sizing chart

Maximum Amp Rating for Current Limiting Midget Fuses					
VA	24V	110V	115V	120V	230V
63	4	0.75	0.75	0.75	0.4
80	5	1	1	1	0.5
130	9	1.8	1.8	1.8	0.9
200	13	2.5	2.5	2.5	1.25
250	15	3.2	3.2	3.2	1.5
350	20	4.5	4.5	4.5	2.5
500	30	6.25	6.25	6.25	3
750	45	9	9	9	4.5
800	45	9	9	9	4.5
1000	60	12	12	12	6
1600	100	20	20	20	10
2000	—	25	25	25	12

(b) Secondary fuse sizing chart

FIGURE 5-12: Average fuse melt current as a function of time.

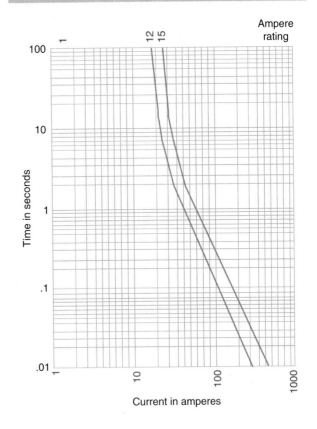

FIGURE 5-13: Grounded system.

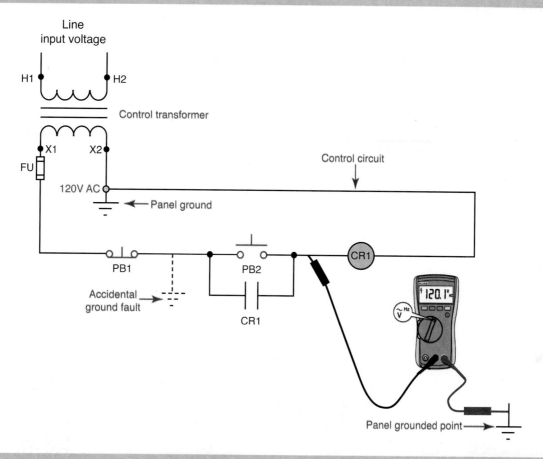

FIGURE 5-14: Floating system.

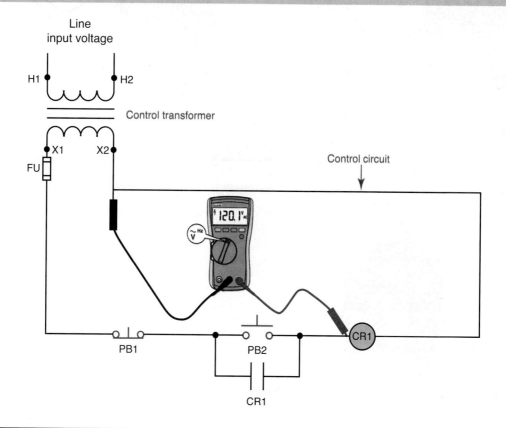

5-5 TROUBLESHOOTING CONTROL TRANSFORMERS

Transformer failures are often an open circuit or a shorted circuit in the windings. Two methods are typically used to troubleshoot transformer failure—measure the input and output voltages and measure the winding resistance.

Input and Output Voltage Measurements

Measure the *primary* and *secondary* voltage at the transformer in the energized control circuit. Perform the measurements under *no load* and *full load* conditions. If the voltages match the rated values within the normal line voltage variation, then the transformer is good.

Coil Resistance Measurements

Check for open coils, coils shorted together or coils shorted to the core with a digital multimeter (DMM). Disconnect the transformer from the control circuit and primary power source for these measurements. Figure 5-15 illustrates the following checks:

1. *Open windings,* Figure 5-15(a)—Check the resistance of each primary and secondary coil with the DMM. A *low resistance* reading (resistance of the coil) verifies that the transformer is good. An *infinite reading* indicates that the primary or secondary coil is open and a faulty transformer.

FIGURE 5-15: Transformer testing procedures.

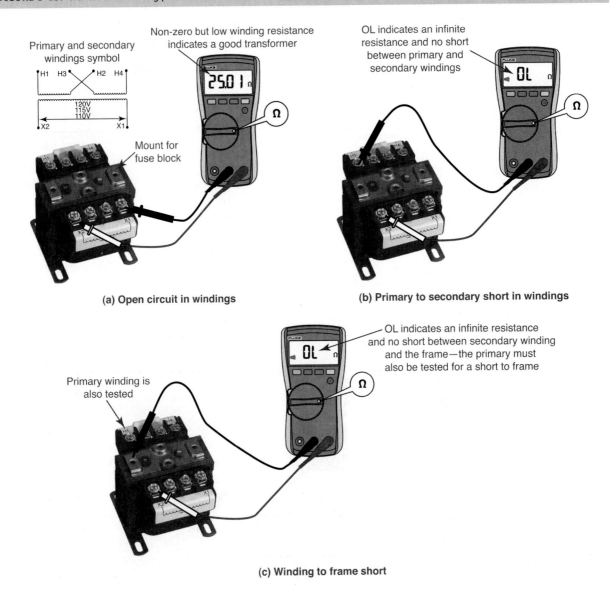

(a) Open circuit in windings

(b) Primary to secondary short in windings

(c) Winding to frame short

FIGURE 5-16: Control transformer troubleshooting guide.

Observed Symptom	Possible Reason for Failure
Overheating	Improperly sized transformer; excessive secondary current surges; excessive primary voltage; shorted windings in primary or secondary
Insulation failure	Improperly sized transformer; excessive secondary current surges; excessive primary voltage or voltage surges; physical damage; excessive moisture or contaminant due to improper NEMA enclosure type
Repeatedly blown primary fuse	Shorted primary or secondary windings; primary or secondary windings shorted to frame; ground fault on secondary side
No primary current	No primary voltage; open primary fuse; open primary winding
No secondary voltage	No primary voltage; open primary fuse; open primary winding; open secondary winding

2. *Short between primary and secondary windings,* Figure 5-15(b)—Check the resistance between the primary winding terminals and the secondary winding terminals with a DMM. An *infinite reading* verifies that the primary and secondary windings are not shorted. A zero or low reading indicates a short between the primary and secondary windings and a faulty transformer.

3. *Windings shorted to the frame,* Figure 5-15(c)—Check the resistance between the transformer frame and the primary windings and between the frame and the secondary windings with a DMM. An *infinite reading* verifies that the frame is not shorted to the winding. A zero or low reading indicates a short between the frame and the winding and a faulty transformer.

Figure 5-16 provides a list of observed symptoms for failed or faulty transformers and possible reasons for the symptom to be investigated.

CRITICAL CONCEPTS

The need to know content from Chapter 5 is summarized in the following statements.

- Control transformers are used to step down the voltage to control circuits in an industrial system.

- The three characteristics of the load circuit used to determine the proper transformer VA size include: *total steady-state* (sealed) *VA, total inrush VA,* and *inrush load power factor.*

- *Total steady-state* (sealed) *VA* is the total amount of VA that the transformer must supply to the load circuit for an extended length of time or the amount of current at the secondary voltage required to hold the *sealed* contacts in the circuit.

- *Total inrush VA* is the amount of VA that the transformer delivers when the control circuit is initial energized.

- Control transformers have a range of primary and secondary voltages for the many different control application requirements.

- A fuse is defined as an overcurrent protective device with a fusible link that permanently opens the circuit when an overcurrent condition occurs.

- Fuses are installed in line with control transformers on the primary and secondary side of the transformer based on several sections in the NEC and on control requirements.

- Fuses are installed on transformer terminal clips, in panel or transformer mounted fuse blocks, and in DIN rail mounted fuse holders.

- The requirement to ground the secondary side of the control transformer is based on the secondary voltage value and requirements specified in several sections in the NEC.

- In a grounded control system, one side of the secondary winding of the control transformer is grounded.

- In a floating control system, neither side of the secondary of the control transformer is grounded.

QUESTIONS

1. What two parameters are used to rate control transformers?

2. Indicate the location of links and line connections to configure the control transformer in Figure 5-2 to step 480V AC down to 120V AC with both primary inputs fused and the secondary line fused.

3. Indicate the location of links and line connections to configure the control transformer in Figure 5-3 to step 208V AC down to 24V AC with both primary inputs fused and the secondary line fused.

4. Describe in-rush current.
5. Describe how primary voltage variation and in-rush VA are related to control transformer size determination.

6. What is the difference between a grounded system and a floating system?
7. What are the benefits of a grounded system?
8. What is the purpose of overcurrent protection?
9. What advantage does a fused secondary provide?

CHAPTER 6

Contactors and Motor Starters

GOALS AND OBJECTIVES

The primary goals for this chapter are to identify contactor and motor starting devices, and to describe the operation of and applications for these motor control devices in manufacturing systems. Also, troubleshooting tips and procedures for typical failure modes are presented.

After completing this chapter, you will be able to:

1. Identify and describe the components of a NEMA and IEC manual and magnetic contactors.
2. Identify and discuss the operation of manual and magnetic motor starters.
3. Identify and discuss the operation of motor overload protections
4. Identify the symbols for contactors and motor starters
5. Describe troubleshooting techniques for contactors and motor starters

6-1 THEORY

Power for factory machines started with machine drive pulleys connected by leather belts to a pulley on a common overhead drive shaft. Figure 6-1 illustrates this early motor drive system. The power source for the drive shaft evolved from *waterwheel* to *steam engine,* and finally to *electric motors* in the 1800s. Changing machine speeds required multiple size pulleys.

Once started, the motor and machinery operated *continuously.* Machines only stopped at the end of a shift or for maintenance requirements or production problems. Starting and stopping the drive shaft motor a few times each day was a simple process. Eventually, less expensive AC motors and practical power distribution permitted each machine and/or process to have a dedicated electric motor. As a result, machine control required efficient techniques for motor and speed that focused on individual motors and/or processes.

FIGURE 6-1: Early industrial motor control.

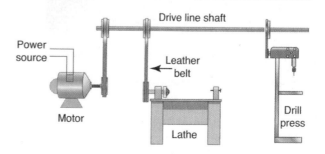

The knife switch (Figure 6-2) is one of the earliest techniques for starting and stopping motors. A knife switch would commonly be used to switch each lead of the motor in Figure 6-1. Knife switches are low cost and easy to operate, but introduced numerous problems to early motor control applications. Safety concerns for switch operators emerged due to the exposure to dangerous shocks from the exposed live electrical circuits. In addition, each opening and closing of the soft copper switch reduced the switch life span due to electrical arcing that caused *pitting* and *contact* damage. Switch damage accelerates when switches are opened and closed slowly, which leads to further heat stress and eventual mechanical failure.

Knife switch improvements included: *insulated handles* for safety and *spring loaded* blades to speed the *make-and-break* process for the motor current. This switch evolution produce the current knife switch, shown in Figure 6-2, which is mounted inside steel enclosures and called a *disconnect* switch. Disconnects are used primarily to switch line power to the motor branch circuit. The design and assembly of these motor control devices are governed by the NEMA and IEC standards. Comparison of NEMA and IEC standards in previous chapters helped us understand how the standards shaped the products. That process is equally important for contactors and motor starters.

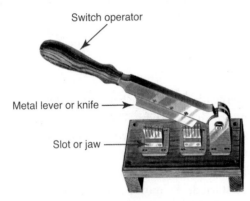

Switch operator

Metal lever or knife

Slot or jaw

(a) Original knife switch—SPST

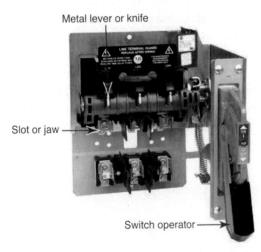

Metal lever or knife

Slot or jaw

Switch operator

(b) Present day knife switch called a disconnect—TPST

Courtesy of Rockwell Automation, Inc.

6-2 NEMA VERSUS IEC CONTACTORS AND MOTOR STARTERS

The differences between NEMA and IEC standards for contactors and motor starters expand upon the differences described in previous chapters for switches and relays. Common differences identified earlier include *dimensional units, cost, operational life time, control drawing figure styles, terminal numbering techniques, device styling,* and *size.* However, the major difference between the standard for contactors and motor starters is the sizing of the control device for a given motor or resistive load.

The capacity of magnetic and manual motor starters is determined by the *current ratings* of their power contacts for *continuous* and *inrush* current conditions. In general, IEC devices are more *application specific.* As a result, IEC devices are often found on OEM machines where the motor and load parameters are known and where the machine will operate under reasonably controlled conditions.

The table in Figure 6-3 compares the two standards for motor starter devices. Study the information in the tables so you understand how the two standards differ for motor starter selection and sizing. Examples of IEC and NEMA contactors are pictured in Figures 6-4

FIGURE 6-3: Comparison of NEMA and IEC contactors and motor starters.

Item	NEMA Standard	IEC Standard
Physical size or footprint	Larger footprint (30 to 70 percent) for equivalent device or a given current draw	Smaller footprint for equivalent device or current draw. Most dramatic size difference at 50 HP and below, where 80 percent of the world's motors are rated.
Cost	Higher equivalent device cost	Lower equivalent device cost
Contacts	Contacts are replaceable and relatively easy to change	Contacts are replaceable but harder to change so labor cost dictates device replacement not repair.
Overload protection	Melting alloy (Eutectic) heater based overload relays are not calibrated, adjustable (except by changing heaters), and ambient temperature compensated with no automatic or remote reset. Solid state electronic overload relays replace melting alloy and have the same features as the IEC models.	Bimetallic overload relays are calibrated, adjustable, and ambient temperature compensated with automatic reset but no remote reset. Solid state electronic overload relays replace bimetallic and are calibrated, adjustable, and not sensitive to ambient temperature with electrical remote reset. Field selectable trip classes are available.
Performance	Life as much as 2 to 3 times higher than equivalent IEC device	Contact life is typically 1 to 2 million under full load. Mechanical life cycle of 10 million is typical.
Motor starter size	Selected from eleven *standard sizes* from 00 to 9 based on a defined current and motor HP rating	Selected not from standard sizes but based on the application and the capability of the IEC device from four AC and five DC Utilization Categories
Interchangeability	Meets AC-3 and limited AC-4 use	Many do not meet NEMA standards
Fault current	Meets NEC requirements	Generally a smaller fault current
Mounting	No standardization	Below 20 HP equivalent size a standard DIN rail mounting is used
Terminal markings	Power in—out—L1, L2, L3—T1, T2, T3 Coil power—No standardization Contacts—No standardization	Power in—out—1, 3, 5—2, 4, 6 Coil power—A1, A2 Contacts—Two digits—first digit for pole number, second digit for contact type: 1–2 for normally closed and 3–4 for normally open

FIGURE 6-4: IEC 3 pole contactor.

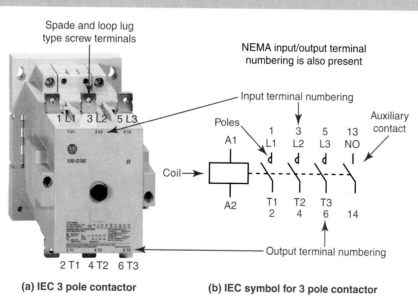

(a) IEC 3 pole contactor   (b) IEC symbol for 3 pole contactor

Courtesy of Rockwell Automation, Inc.

FIGURE 6-5: NEMA 3 pole contactor.

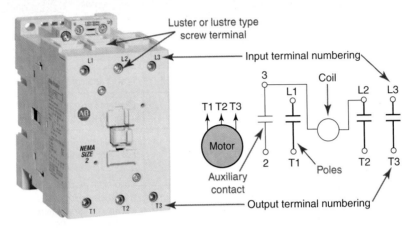

(a) NEMA 3 pole contactor

(b) NEMA symbol for 3 pole

Courtesy of Rockwell Automation, Inc.

and 6-5 respectively. The control symbol for each standard is illustrated along side each contactor. Note the numbering system for the terminals on each device, and note that the Rockwell IEC device also lists the NEMA numbering.

6-3 CONTACT CONSTRUCTION

The electrical contacts for power control devices are similar in shape and in the material used to produce them. Figure 6-6 shows a three pole starter contact bar set and a magnified view of a contact. The contacts used in motor starters must withstand the electrical and physical conditions created while starting and stopping motors. Generally, contacts are a silver and cadmium alloy with about 90 percent silver. This composite provides good *conductivity*, resists *arc damage*, and promotes *long contact life*. In addition, *silver oxide*, that eventually coats the surface, is an excellent electrical conductor.

Contacts used in motor starters are not flat, but shaped with a slight curve to their surface. The curved surface is visible in Figures 6-6 and 6-7. The curved shape promotes a better connection between the con-

FIGURE 6-6: Contactor and magnetic starter contact construction.

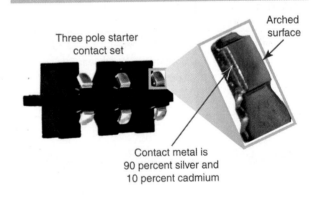

tact surfaces and allows for a "self-cleaning" process. Foreign material or raised burrs on the surface of flat contacts may prevent a good connection. Figure 6-7 shows the angular orientation for the movable contact bar or pole and the stationary circuit contacts. This angled design and the curved contact surface allow the contact surfaces to close with movement between the surfaces. This produces a lower contact resistance and better connection.

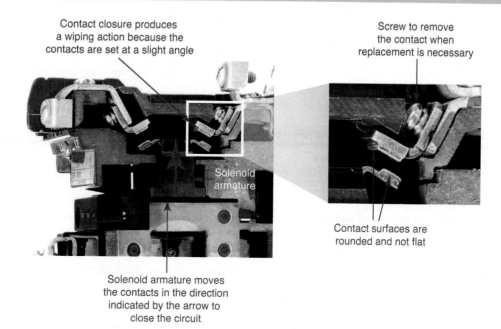

Contact closure produces a wiping action because the contacts are set at a slight angle

Screw to remove the contact when replacement is necessary

Solenoid armature

Contact surfaces are rounded and not flat

Solenoid armature moves the contacts in the direction indicated by the arrow to close the circuit

6-4 CONTACTORS

Electrical workers in the field often hear the terms *contactor* and *motor starters* used incorrectly. In this text those terms are used in the following context:

Manual contactor—activated switching device, without an overload protection device attached, to switch single-phase or three-phase AC power or DC power to the load.

Magnetic contactor—magnetically activated switching device, without an overload protection device attached, to switch single-phase or three-phase AC power or DC power to the load.

Definite Purpose magnetic contactor—magnetically activated switching device, without an overload protection device attached, to switch power to a load other than an AC or DC motor. Devices have multiple power poles and offer several options to keep the contacts pulled-in when coil power is removed. Some manufacturers call these *Definite Purpose* contactors.

Magnetic motor starter—magnetically activated switching device that includes a magnetic contactor and an attached overload protection device,

to switch single-phase and three-phase power for AC motor control and power for DC motor control.

The term *motor starter* implies that the manual starting switch, magnetic motor starter, or electronic motor control includes overload protection for the motor. *Contactors*, as the name suggests, have the contacts to switch or control power to loads. *Overloads* offer protection from excessive current flow to the switched load. When the contactor and overload are combined into a single device or separate devices are wired together, the combination is a *motor starter*. Some smaller motors and other higher loads, like heaters, have *integrated overloads*. When overload protection is included in the load, it is not duplicated elsewhere in the branch circuit. *Magnetic contactors* are covered in this section, *magnetic motor starters* are covered later in this chapter, and *electronic motor control* is discussed later in the book.

Power Poles

Contactors are much like the general purpose control relays discussed in Chapter 4 because they:

• Use *horizontal* and *vertical* electromagnetic solenoids to open and close electrical contacts.

- Use pilot devices to remotely actuate the magnetic coil.
- Switch higher voltage AC and DC circuits with lower voltage control circuits.
- Use similar contact configurations.

However, some important exceptions include:

- Contactor contacts are divided into categories: *normally open power poles* and *normally open or normally closed auxiliary contacts*.
- They are not general purpose devices but designed for *specific application categories* to control AC or DC power for *motors, heaters,* and *lighting*.
- Most often they switch *single-phase, two-phase,* or *three-phase* AC power for AC motors or DC power for DC motor applications.
- *Double break* contacts are the predominant configuration.
- Contactors most often have *two* or *three* NO power poles and *one* to *eight* auxiliary contacts with a combination of NO and NC configurations.

NEMA contactors normally show only NEMA terminal markings. IEC contactors usually show both IEC and NEMA terminal markings. Therefore, both the NEMA and IEC contactors in Figures 6-4 and 6-5 have the power poles marked L1, L2, and L3 on the input side and T1, T2, and T3 on the output side. Input terminals for NEMA power poles are marked L1, L2, and L3 and outputs are T1, T2, and T3. The IEC input power circuit terminals are marked 1, 3, and 5 and the outputs are 2, 4, and 6.

Motor starting systems have a power circuit to switch the main power to the motor and a control circuit that switches power to the coil of the contactor in the motor starter. The NO power circuit contacts are closed by the double-break contact bar attached to the armature as shown in Figure 6-7. When a control transformer is used, the power circuit and control circuit are electrically isolated; therefore *higher voltage power* circuits can be actuated by *lower voltage* control circuits. With contactors you can control a greater number of circuits with a single pilot device. This permits *large horsepower motors, high voltage heaters,* or *large banks of lights* to be controlled with *lower voltage pilot devices* at a remote location. When the control voltage comes from the motor supply voltage both are de-energized when the motor controller disconnect is opened, this concept is covered in greater detail later in this chapter. The coils for both NEMA and IEC contactors are available in a variety of voltages. Typical ranges include 24V AC to 600V AC or 12 to 250V DC.

AC contactors used for motor control applications are available in single-phase and three-phase configurations with *one, two, three,* and *four* power pole models offered by many manufacturers.

Contactors for DC power switching have power pole contacts designed to *reduce arcing* during switching with arc suppression construction and greater contact separation in their open state. Contactors are available with either AC or DC coils in a wide range of control voltages.

NEMA and IEC Contactor Size Guide

NEMA magnetic contactors have *eleven sizes* from 00 to 9 as shown in Figure 6-8(a). The continuous current contact rating for each size is across from the size number. NEMA sizes are related to motor voltage and horsepower rating in Figure 6-8(b) for single-phase motors. A similar table in Figure 6-8(c) relates NEMA sizes to voltage and horsepower when three-phase motors are used. A study of Figure 6-8 indicates that NEMA magnetic contactor and motor starter size is linked to motor current, which is translated to horsepower.

IEC magnetic contactor and motor starters sizes are designed to be much more application specific with more sizes over the same range of application current requirements. IEC starter ratings are based on three parameters: *operational current, thermal current,* and *utilization categories. Operational* current refers to the ability of the starter to make and break current values in specific applications called *utilization categories*. Thermal current refers to the amount of I^2R heat the starter can withstand without damage. The AC and DC utilization categories are listed in Figures 6-9(a) and 6-9(b) respectively.

Translating a utilization category and the application voltage and current conditions into a specific

FIGURE 6-8: NEMA contactor sizes for single- and three-phase motor starters.

NEMA Size	Continuous Amps
00	9
0	18
1	27
2	45
3	90
4	135
5	270
6	540
7	810
8	1215
9	2250

(a) NEMA continuous ampere ratings

Motor Voltage	Max HP	NEMA Size
120	.33	00
	1	0
	2	1
	3	2
	7.5	3
240	1	00
	2	0
	3	1
	7.5	2
	15	3

(b) Single phase motor starters

Motor Voltage	Max HP	NEMA Size
208	3	0
	7.5	1
	10	2
	25	3
	40	4
	75	5
	150	6
240	3	0
	7.5	1
	15	2
	30	3
	50	4
	100	5
	200	6
	300	7
	450	8
	800	9
480 and 600	5	0
	10	1
	25	2
	50	3
	100	4
	200	5
	400	6
	600	7
	900	8
	1600	9

(c) Three phase motor starters

IEC magnetic contactor or motor starter is more difficult than finding a NEMA device size. A review of manufactures data indicates that twenty-four IEC contactors are available to cover the ten NEMA sizes (00 to 8) listed in Figure 6-8(a). The table in Figure 6-10 illustrates this difference. Study the highlighted rows for a size 2 NEMA device. Note that it covers 10 to 25 horsepower motors with up to 45 amps of current. In contrast, there are three IEC devices (first column) one for 10, 15, and 25 horsepower. NEMA horsepower brackets are wider than the IEC standard devices. In summary, there are only 10 basic NEMA

FIGURE 6-9: IEC contactor utilization categories.

Utilization Category	Definition	
AC-1	Resistance furnaces	Non-inductive or slightly inductive loads, resistive furnaces
AC-2	Slip-ring motors	Starting and stopping of running motors
AC-3	Squirrel-cage motors	Starting and stopping of running motors
AC-4	Squirrel-cage motors	Starting, plugging, and inching (Note 1)
AC-15	Electro-magnets	Electromagnets for contactors, valves, solenoid actuators

Note 1: Plugging is defined as stopping or reversing the motor rapidly by reversing the motor primary connections while the motor is running. Inching or jogging is defined as energizing a motor once or repeatedly for short periods to obtain small rotations.

(a) IEC AC utilization categories

Category	Typical Applications
DC-1	Non-inductive or slightly inductive loads, resistance furnaces
DC-2	Shunt-motors: Starting, switching off motors during running
DC-3	Shunt-motors: Starting, plugging, inching
DC-4	Series-motors: Starting, switching off motors during running
DC-5	Series-motors: Starting, plugging, inching
DC-15	Electromagnets for contactors, valves, solenoid actuators

(b) IEC DC utilization categories

contactor sizes for motors ranging from 2 to 900 horsepower. However, some IEC contactor manufacturers offer as many as 20 contactor sizes to cover this same horsepower range.

Arc Suppression

Switching AC and DC current in power poles introduces the possibility of arcs when the switching contacts are opened and in some cases as the contacts closed. The degree of arcing and contact damage is based on the following factors:

The level of the voltage and current that is switched—contacts switching higher voltage and current have a higher likelihood of arc damage.

The type of voltage that is switched—contacts switching AC loads have less arc damage than those used for DC powered devices.

The type of load, resistive versus inductive—inductive loads produce larger and more damaging arcs than resistive load of comparable size.

The speed of the switched contacts—generally the slower the contacts are opened and closed the greater that the possibility of arc damage.

The state or condition of the contact surface—contact surfaces with pitting and whiskers produced by previous arcing are more likely to experience arc damage when power is switched.

The type of contact protection and arc suppression present—minimizing arc damage to contacts starts with the selection of properly sized contactors for a motor control application. Also, the use of arc suppression circuits and devices reduces arc damage.

FIGURE 6-10: Comparison of IEC and NEMA contactor models/sizes for a similar HP motor.

Maximum HP @ 460 VAC 3 Phase 60 hertz	IEC Contactor Model AC-3 Current (max)	NEMA Contactor HP—Size—Current (max)
5	9 A	5—0—18 A
10	16 A	5 to 10—1—27 A
15	23 A	10 to 25—2—45 A
25	30 A	10 to 25—2—45 A
30	37 A	25 to 50—3—90 A

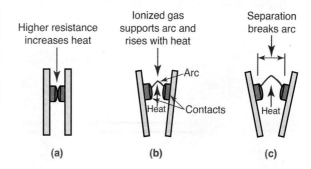

FIGURE 6-11: Arc development.

Contacts opened under a motor's *full load current* (FLC) have an increased risk of arcing. As the contact surfaces begin to separate, the cross-sectional area conducting the FLC is reduced, so higher resistance is present. As the resistance increases, the *resistive power losses* increase and *contact temperature* increases. Immediately before the contacts separate, the heat produced by the small conducting surface melts and vaporizes some of the contact metal. This condition is illustrated in Figure 6-11(a). As the contact surfaces physically separate, an arc forms in the conductive ionized metal gas between the separated contacts. This condition is illustrated in Figure 6-11(b). At some point, contact separation and the rising heat from the arc make the arc length too long and the arcing stops. This condition is illustrated in Figure 6-11(c). Continued arcing conditions with persistent arcs causes contact damaged due to the heat. Arcing also causes oxidation of the silver alloy on the contact surface. This is actually a benefit, as the oxide is an excellent conductor.

AC arcs are *self-extinguishing* when the AC current passes through the zero point on the sinusoidal alternating current waveform. Therefore, AC arcs have a maximum life span of *one half cycle*. However, even short duration arcs reduce the life span of contacts and must be eliminated or reduced when possible.

Arc suppressing devices, such as *arc chutes*, quickly extinguish arcs. Arc chutes are designed to quench the arc by *dividing, confining* and *extinguishing* the arc produced by each set of contacts. Isolating each contact in a separate arc chute reduces the possibility of arcing between phases.

Arcs across power poles switching DC current are not *self-extinguishing* and the hardest to extinguish. The constant DC current remains at a fixed high level

so arcing across wider contact gaps is possible. Suppressing arcs in DC contactors requires contacts that open and close rapidly and open wider in their open state. However, rapidly closing contacts must be inhibited from contact bounce through mechanical design techniques.

Auxiliary Contacts

The power poles in the contactor carry the motor current, while other contacts, called *auxiliary contacts* or *electrical interlocks,* are used for the control circuit. Auxiliary contacts are available in *normally open* (NO), *normally closed* (NC) or *combinations* of each.

All contactor manufacturers offer a variety of auxiliary contact configurations for their electromagnetic products. The control application dictates the *type* and *number* of auxiliary contacts with *one* to *eight* generally available. As a rule, they are *interchangeable* between models from one manufacturer, but *not interchangeable* between different contactor manufacturers. Most magnetic motor starters are supplied with at least one NO auxiliary contact. This contact is used for *electrical hold* or start pushbutton *sealing* requirements in the control circuit. The application of auxiliary contacts into the control circuit is fully described in Chapter 8.

Generally, the single auxiliary contact is supplemented with additional auxiliary contacts mounted on the *front, top, left,* and *right* sides of the contactor or magnetic motor starter. Figure 6-12(a) illustrates an IEC contactor with one auxiliary contact installed on the right side and a second contact ready to be attached. An *operator* on the auxiliary contact picks

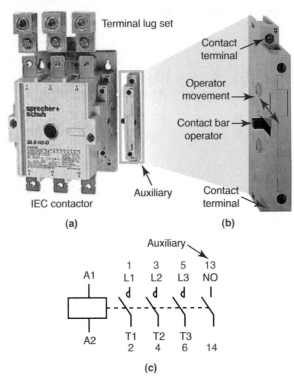

FIGURE 6-13: NEMA contactors and auxiliary contacts.

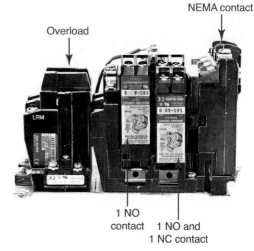

(a) Allen Bradley magnetic motor starter auxiliary contacts

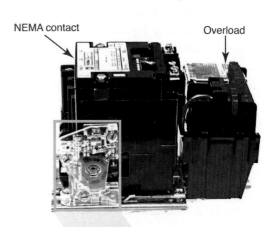

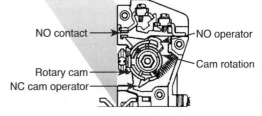

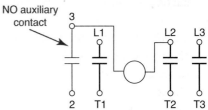

(b) Square D magnetic motor starter auxiliary contacts and control symbol

Courtesy of Sprecher + Schuh, Inc.

up the contactor's armature through a hole in the side of the contactor. Additional auxiliary contacts *stack* on existing auxiliary contacts. Operator operation is passed through from the attached auxiliary contact to next attached contact. The larger view of the auxiliary contact in Figure 6-12(b) shows the *contact bar operator* and the *operator motion*. Figure 6-12(a) pictures the *hole* in the side of the attached auxiliary contact. Two visible terminals indicate that the enlarged auxiliary is a *single throw* contact with either *NO* or *NC* contacts. The IEC control symbol for an auxiliary contact is shown in Figure 6-12(c).

NEMA magnetic motor starters with auxiliary contacts attached are shown in Figure 6-13(a) and (b). The motor starter in Figure 6-13(a) from Allen Bradley has two auxiliary contact blocks attached for a total of three auxiliary contacts. In Figure 6-13(b), the Square D NO auxiliary contact is enlarged to demonstrate how a counter-clockwise cam rotation closes the NO contacts. To change this field configurable auxiliary from a NO to a NC contact device, remove the cam, flip 180 degrees, and place it back into the auxiliary contact. The NC cam operator, identified in Figure 6-13(b), is now at the top, and the pointed operator holds the contacts closed in the non-actuated state. The NEMA control symbol for a three-phase magnetic motor starter with an auxiliary contact is also in the figure.

Normally open and normally closed auxiliary contacts function like other magnetic control relay devices. When the contactor is actuated normally open contacts close and normally closed contacts open. Auxiliary contacts are available in logic voltage rated and in standard control voltage rated contacts. Logic level contacts have *dry circuit* rated *bifurcated contacts* for signals down to 5V DC with currents as low as 2 mA. Dry circuit contacts are used to switch low voltage and current in electronic control applications such as programmable logic controller discrete input module signals.

Bifurcated auxiliary contacts provide a higher degree of reliability than the standard auxiliary contacts because it divides each movable contact into two sections at the tip of the contact. They are used in low-voltage low-current dry circuit applications. Standard contacts are typically reliable for a minimum of 5mA at 17 volts, while bifurcated contacts are good for dry circuit operation.

Definite Purpose Contactors

Contactors designed for power control applications other than motors are called *Definite Purpose* or *Special Use contactors* by the manufacturer. *Definite Purpose (DP)* contactors switch power for loads other than AC and DC motors. There are numerous types of DP contactors for loads that include: *lighting, heaters, capacitors, hydraulic elevators,* and *HVAC* devices. The loads for DP contactors are generally resistive but experience high inrush or closing currents in some applications. For example, the tungsten filaments of incandescent lamps have a very low resistance value when cold. As a result, the pole closing or inrush current is very high and brief. The turn on characteristics of discharge lamps (lighting with ballast) is highly inductive due to series-connected transformers or chokes. As a result, the inrush current is very high with the duration dependent on the lamp type. Also, switching capacitor banks onto a power line for power factor correction creates extremely high inrush currents to charge the capacitors.

Overload protection is present in the branch circuit but not normally a part of the DP contactors. Figure 6-14 includes an image of a *heater* and *capacitor* DP contactor, a description of their operation, and the standard control symbol used for each.

Lighting Contactors

Lighting contactors are the most common definite use (DU) contactor applications. Lamp categories include:

- Filament lamps (incandescent, infrared, and halogen)
- Ballast type discharge lamps (fluorescent, mercury vapor, and sodium)
- LED
- Mixed lamp groups

In general, North American applications group lighting contactor current ratings without distinction between incandescent or ballast type of load. As a result, contactor selection table are often for mixed lamp loads; therefore higher incandescent inrush current is included in the ratings. Europeans applications usually separate the values for incandescent from discharge (ballast) lighting in contactor sizing.

Contactors used for *lighting control systems* are constructed in the same manner as contactors used for motor starting. However, lighting circuits are single-phase and generally rated at 120 volts or 277 volts. Contactors used in motor starter circuits often carry very large currents required for motors; whereas lighting circuits are commonly rated at 15 amps to 20 amps. When lighting contactors are used to control outside lighting such as parking lot lights, they may

FIGURE 6-14: Special use contactors for heaters and capacitors.

Special Use Heater Contactor and NEMA Symbol

Heater switching—the contactor is used to switch *resistive heater loads*. Four power poles, L1/T1 to L4/T4, are available for two single phase heater banks. Current capacity of the poles is matched to the lamp inrush and continuous current requirements and to the lamp type. This contactor is also used in *HVAC applications*. The symbol shows one non-power pole called an auxiliary contact. Auxiliary contact blocks are added to the side of the contactor. One auxiliary contact is included in the circuit symbol, but the contactor model in the picture does not have auxiliary contacts.

Special Use Capacitor Contactor and IEC Symbol

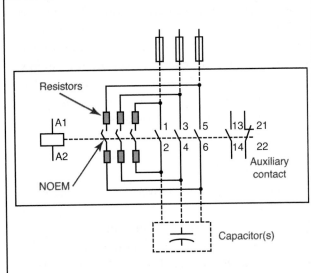

Capacitor and capacitor bank switching—the contactor is used to switch capacitors onto the power line for power factor correction. Inrush currents 30 times (single capacitor) or 200 times (capacitor bank) are possible in this application. Inrush current is reduced by resistors that pre-charge the capacitors to minimize the large inrush current. Contactor has three power poles and one non-power pole called an auxiliary contact. NO early make contacts (NOEM) close to pre-charge the capacitors before main contactor contacts close. Two auxiliary contacts are included in the circuit symbol, but the device in the picture does not have auxiliary contacts attached.

Courtesy of Sprecher + Schuh, Inc.

have as many as 12 poles on one contactor assembly. Figure 6-15 illustrates the variety of lighting contactor configurations with 8 and 4 pole devices. The NEMA control symbol for a 12 power pole devices is also present.

Lighting Contactor Operation

Lighting contactors operate on the same principle as motor control contactors. The coil of the contactor is controlled by automatic or manual pilot devices. A pilot device acts as a switching mechanism to energize and de-energizes the coil that controls the lighting contactor. The most common pilot devices are *time clocks*, *photocells* or *manual switches*. Lighting contactors that are controlled by automatic means such as time clocks or photocells commonly have a manually operated switch to act as an override.

Light contactors from different manufacturers vary to some degree, but general operational characteristics include:

- Coil power options include 24 to 480V AC at 50 or 60 hertz.
- Ballast and incandescent ampere contact ratings offer 15 to 400 amperes.
- Power poles include 2 to 12 poles in NO and NC configurations.
- Auxiliary contact options are one to four in choice of NO or NC contacts.
- Control transformer options from 45 to 250 VA.
- Lighting contactors are held in the actuated position *electrically*, *mechanically*, and *magnetically*. In each case a pilot device actuates the contactor then one of the four holding mechanisms or techniques is employed.

Electrically Latched Contactors—Electrically held contactors are used where the control signal is activated by a *maintained operator switch*, *timer*, or other *maintained electrical signal*. The contactor is closed as long as the coil is energized. This design is well suited for applications where lights are operated frequently or where the control panel is in a remote location. The operation of mechanical and magnetic latching contactors and relays is covered in Chapter 14.

FIGURE 6-15: Lighting contactors.

(a) 8 power poles and 4 auxiliary contacts

(b) 4 power poles

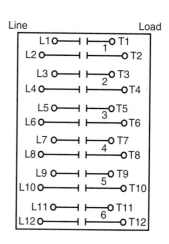

(c) NEMA symbol for 12 power pole and 4 auxiliary contacts

Courtesy of Rockwell Automation, Inc.

A lighting control application requires control of two single-phase incandescent light circuits from two locations with ON and OFF momentary operator pushbuttons. In addition, the system has ON and OFF light indicators and uses an *electrically latched* magnetic lighting contactor. The lights are located on a loading dock, and the lighting control hardware and enclosure are located in the manufacturing area. Indicator lights provide dock light status in the manufacturing area. A second set of ON and OFF

remote momentary pushbutton devices are located on the dock. Two single-phase incandescent light circuits are required and the four power pole lighting contactor in Figure 6-15(b) is used. Two auxiliary contacts are added for the control requirements. The control circuit for the light control is drawn in Figure 6-16. The contactor's NC auxiliary contact controls the OFF indicator and the contactors NO auxiliary contact seals in the contactor coil. Power poles for the two incandescent lamp circuits are not shown.

FIGURE 6-16: Electrically held lighting contactor with remote on, remote off, and on and off pilot lights.

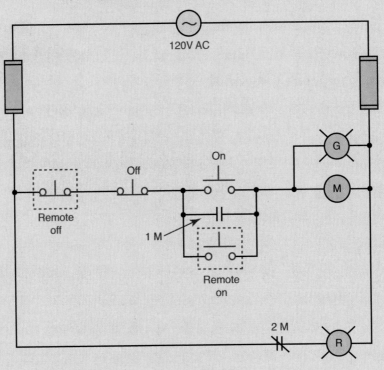

6-5 MANUAL MOTOR STARTERS

Manual motor starters are hand-operated devices consisting of an on-off switch and motor overload protection. Manual motor starters are operated by physically moving levers or pressing buttons that close physical contacts. Manual motor starters are used to control small motors, such as *fractional horsepower* and *inte-*

gral horsepower motors, found in commercial and industrial applications.

Fractional Horsepower Motor Starters

Fractional horsepower motors are often used in stand-alone applications where remote control is not required. Typical examples of fractional horsepower

A lighting control application requires control of four single-phase incandescent light circuits for a parking lot with an ON OFF AUTO selector switch and a clock timer with a NO SPST contact. The clock timer controls the lights in the AUTO position, the lights are off in the OFF position, and the ON position bypasses the clock timer. In addition, the system has ON and OFF light indicators. The lighting contactor in Figure 6-12(a) is used with a NC auxiliary contact for control of the OFF indicator. The control circuit for the light control is drawn in Figure 6-17. The contactors power poles for the two incandescent lamp circuits are not shown.

FIGURE 6-17: Electrically held lighting contactor with ON OFF AUTO three-position selector, remote on pilot device, and on and off pilot lights.

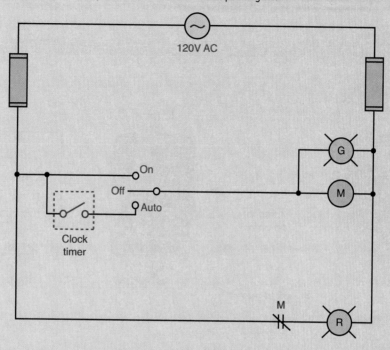

motors controlled by manual motor starters are *exhaust fans, small drill presses* and *commercial garbage disposals.* Figure 6-18 illustrates a toggle-style fractional motor starter and the NEMA symbol. It is shown with and without its enclosure. Note in the control drawing that the starter controls a single-phase motor and has a manually-operated overload reset pushbutton. The toggle lever is a snap action switch designed to open and close the starter contacts as *quickly* as possible to reduce *arcing* and *pitting.* Switch positions on the enclosure are labeled "I" for start and "O" for stop. When the toggle lever is moved to the *on* or *start* position, the motor is connected directly across the line and in series with the starter contact

and overload protection. The current used by the motor flows through the starter contact and the overload protection. The motor overload protection device is intended to open the circuit if the motor draws too much current. Fractional horsepower manual motor starters generally use thermal motor overload protection devices to prevent motor damage due to overload conditions. If an overload occurs, the overload pushbutton pops out, indicating the starter contact is open, and the circuit to the motor is disconnected. The overload contact is reset by depressing the pushbutton. Operation of thermal overloads is covered later in this chapter.

Figure 6-19 illustrates a selector-style fractional motor starter and the IEC symbol. Note that the

During a power interruption, the contacts of a manual motor starter remain closed. When power is restored, the motor immediately restarts. For applications where the motor normally operates continuously, this is an advantage. However, the automatic restart characteristic presents problems to personnel and equipment. If the motor restarts during a manufacturing process, the product may be damaged or improperly made. Of greater concern is the safety for the electrical worker and maintenance personnel due to an unpredictable and unexpected restart of the motor. Electrical workers who operate motor starters are to verify the power switch is in the *off* position prior to troubleshooting. Proper lockout/tagout procedures are to be followed. Failure to observe simple safety precautions could result in injury or loss of life.

FIGURE 6-18: Toggle style manual motor starter for fractional horsepower motors with NEMA control symbol.

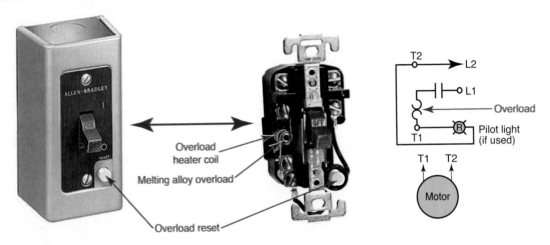

Courtesy of Rockwell Automation, Inc.

FIGURE 6-19: Motor circuit protectors and IEC control symbol.

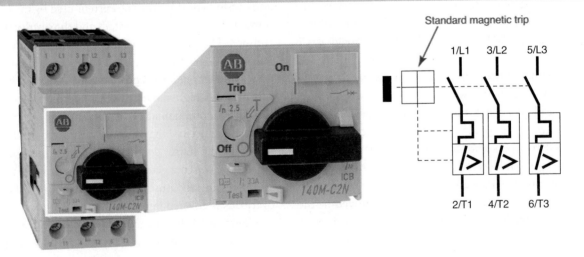

Courtesy of Rockwell Automation, Inc.

starter controls a three-phase motor by a selector switch with three positions—OFF, TRIP, and ON. Position notation on the switch is "I" for start, "O" for stop, and "T" for trip. The L1, L2 and L3 are the line input terminals, and the T1, T2, and T3 are load (motor) terminals. Note that the motor starter has a magnetic trip overload protection. If an overload occurs, the switch is driven to the TRIP position.

Integral Horsepower Motor Starters

Integral horsepower manual motor starters typically use *built-in pushbuttons* for operation as opposed to *toggle switches* found on fractional horsepower manual motor starters. Integral horsepower motors, which are one horsepower or greater, are available in sizes up to *fifteen* horsepower. Applications for these manual motor starters include *large industrial power tools, milling machines, lathes* and *exhaust fans.* Figure 6-20 illustrates a manual integral motor starter and the NEMA symbol.

Integral horsepower motor starters are available in *one-* or *two-pole* for single-phase and *three-pole* for three-phase motor applications. One- and two-pole starters are constructed with one or two sets of double break contacts that *simultaneously connect* or *disconnect* the line or lines to the circuit. Three-pole starters are constructed with three sets of double break contacts that *simultaneously connect* or *disconnect* each

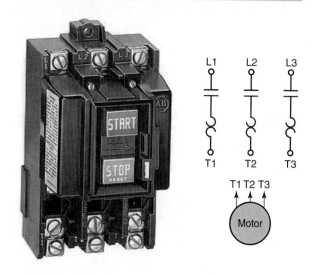

FIGURE 6-20: Manual push button integral motor starter with thermal overloads and NEMA control symbol.

phase to the circuit. Figure 6-21 illustrates the components of an integral horsepower manual motor starter with an exploded view.

Selection of Manual Motor Starters

The electrical worker specifies certain characteristics of the starter to match operational requirements.

FIGURE 6-21: Exploded view of NEMA manual motor starter shown in Figure 6-20.

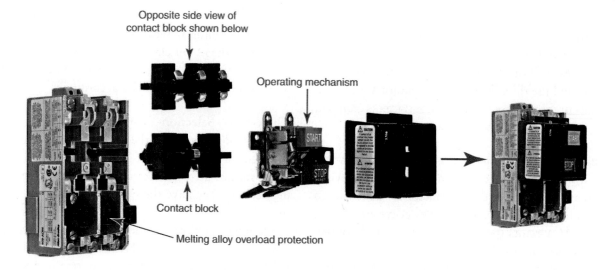

Opposite side view of contact block shown below

Operating mechanism

Contact block

Melting alloy overload protection

Figure 6-22 illustrates the manual motor starter used in a conveyor system. Note the two manual starters, one for the feed conveyor and one for the wrapper. The feed conveyor gets pallets from the pallet stacker, and then moves the pal- let onto the pallet wrapper. The operator controls both man- ual starters, which are close to each other, allowing for quick shut down in case of a conveyor or wrapping problem. An auto- matic guided vehicle picks up the pallets from the wrapper.

FIGURE 6-22: Feed conveyor and pallet wrapper manual motor control.

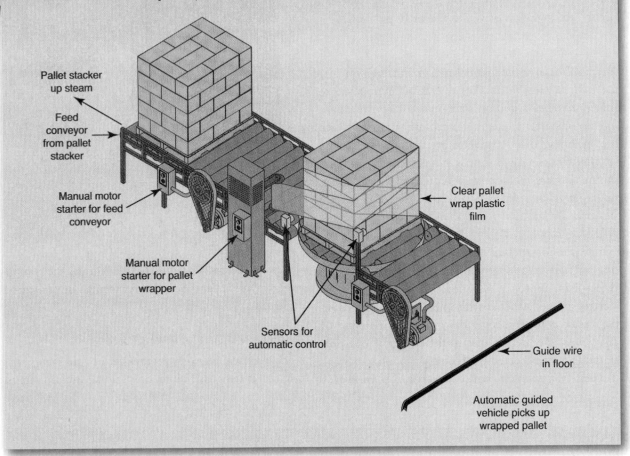

Manual motor starters are selected on: *the number of phases, number of poles, voltage level* and *motor size.* Figure 6-23 illustrates a selection tree for the single-phase and the three-phase manual motor starter. If a single- or three-phase manual motor starter is required, the figure shows the various selection choices.

Single-Phase Selection—Single-phase manual starters are available as *single-pole* and *double-pole* devices so that each ungrounded conductor is opened when disconnecting a device. Single-pole devices are used on 120V AC circuits (power and neutral), and double-pole devices are used on 240V AC circuits.

Single-phase manual starters are typically available in only one size, have limited horsepower ratings, and are used in motor applications of one horsepower or less. The NEMA 00 classification is used for single phase starters. IEC manual starters/contactors are horsepower rated and selected accordingly.

Three-Phase Selection—Three-phase manual starters are *physically larger* than the single-phase starters and are used for motors up to fifteen horsepower. Three-phase starters are constructed with three-pole switch-ing because they have three ungrounded conductors to connect and disconnect. Three-phase devices, like single-phase devices, use double-break contacts and have quick-make and quick-break mechanisms. Three-phase contactors and starters are normally designed to be used on circuits from 208V AC up to and includ-

6-6 MAGNETIC MOTOR STARTERS

A *magnetic motor starter* is an electrically operated contactor with overload protection as shown in Figures 6-24 and 6-25. Figure 6-24 is a NEMA style three-phase starter with contactor and overload integrated into a single unit. Figure 6-24 is a IEC style starter with similar configuration.

The magnetic motor starter's coil, overload contacts, and auxiliary contacts are in the *motor control* circuit. The contacts to switch the three phase power to the motor are in the *higher current power control* circuit.

The contactor uses an electromagnetic solenoid (coil) to open and close the *three phase motor* contacts and the *auxiliary* contacts. The magnetic motor starter is an electrical version of the manual motor starter shown in Figure 6-21.

The overload protection device in the motor starter detects excessive over-current conditions in the motor by measuring motor current through the contactor's power control circuit. When an overload condition exists, overload contacts in the motor control circuit de-energize the contactor. The de-energized contactor opens the power control circuit, which removes power from the motor. Magnetic motor starters are available in sizes that can switch loads of a few amperes to hundreds of amperes.

ing 600V AC. Three-phase manual starters are also used for motors where no low-voltage protection is required, motors used in some intermittent duty applications, and motors that do not need remote operation by pilot devices.

FIGURE 6-23: Single- and three-phase manual starter selection tree.

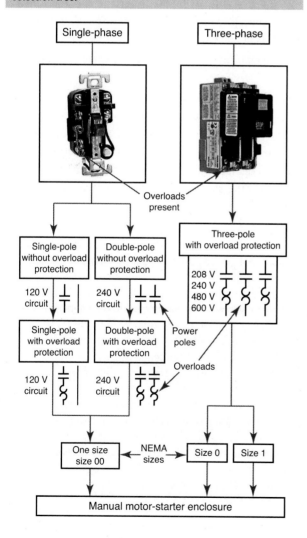

FIGURE 6-24: NEMA standard magnetic motor starter.

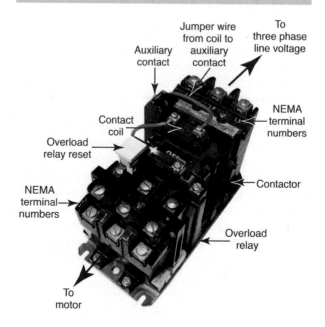

FIGURE 6-25: IEC standard magnetic motor starter.

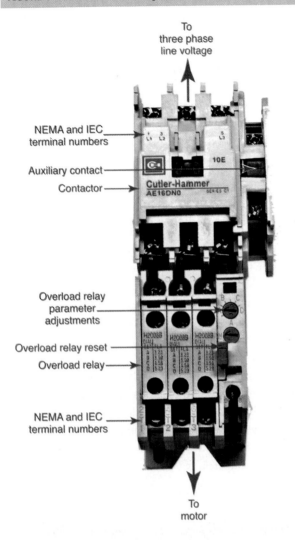

To
three phase
line voltage

NEMA and IEC terminal numbers

Auxiliary contact

Contactor

Overload relay parameter adjustments

Overload relay reset

Overload relay

NEMA and IEC terminal numbers

To
motor

The electromagnetic coil permits control of large horsepower, high-voltage motors with remote pilot devices and a lower coil voltage. The coils for both NEMA and IEC magnetic starters are available in a variety of voltages ranging from 24V AC to 600V AC. The magnetic force required to close the starter contacts is directly proportional to the size of the contacts and the frame on which the contacts are mounted. Electromagnetic coils are basically inductive devices, and the magnetic force produced by any coil is a product of the current flowing through the coil and the number of turns in the coil.

Construction

The magnetic motor starter consists of a *magnetic contactor* and a set of *overload protection devices*. Magnetic contactors use an electromagnetic solenoid (coil) to open and close the contacts. As motor current increases, the size of the starter contacts increases. So

The use of remote pilot devices allows multiple machines and processes to be controlled by operators or computers from a single location. Virtually every aspect of machine operation is controlled by: (a) electrical workers using manual pilot devices such as pushbuttons and selector switches, (b) mechanical actuated limit switches, automatically actuated process switches, such as float switches, mechanical and electronic timers, and (c) automation controllers, such as programmable logic controllers. Centrally located pilot and control devices in the same area with monitoring equipment allows electrical workers to constantly and more closely oversee the entire production system. Personnel can react to situations or make timely process changes that can reduce the overall operational cost. In locations where several machines are grouped together to perform a single operation, a problem with one machine may cause damage to some or all of the other machines.

An example is a conveyor feeding large stones into a crusher that pounds the stones into gravel. If the motor driving the crusher were to stop and the conveyor continued to feed large stones, the crusher overflows with stones and possibly jams when restarted. With magnetic starters, a system is designed to immediately stop the conveyor if the crusher stops. In addition, with magnetic starters many safety devices such as emergency stop buttons and equipment guard switches are used to stop any and all associated motors.

Because of their flexibility and control integration capabilities, magnetic motor starters have practically replaced manual starters in most commercial and industrial applications. Magnetic motor starters control virtually every motor-driven industrial process such as conveyor systems, pumping operations, packaging systems, chemical mixing processes, and painting booths.

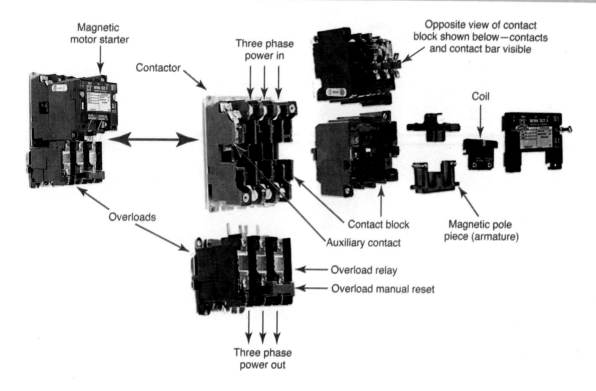

Magnetic motor starter

Contactor

Three phase power in

Opposite view of contact block shown below—contacts and contact bar visible

Coil

Overloads

Contact block

Auxiliary contact

Magnetic pole piece (armature)

Overload relay

Overload manual reset

Three phase power out

manufacturers use coils that develop greater electromagnetic force. Motors in excess of 1500 HP can be controlled with magnetic starters. The motor control circuit with the remote pilot device and the contactor coil are often at a lower voltage than the voltage used in the motor power circuit. This feature allows high voltage motors to be controlled by lower voltage and less expensive pilot devices, reducing the overall cost and reducing safety concerns. Starter construction is illustrated in Figure 6-26 with an exploded assembly of a NEMA magnetic motor starter. Note the exploded view of the *contactor* shows the *contact block*, *the armature*, and the *coil*. Plus the exploded view of the *overload assembly* shows the *overload relay* and the *overload manual reset*.

Combination Starters

Combination starters consist of a *safety disconnect, short circuit* and *overload protection*, and *magnetic motor starter* placed in a *common enclosure*. Figure 6-27 illustrates a combination starter with all the components just listed plus the control transformer, and the thru-panel disconnect operator. With few exceptions, the NEC requires all motors to have a disconnecting device to disengage the power from the motor and the motor

FIGURE 6-27: Combination starter.

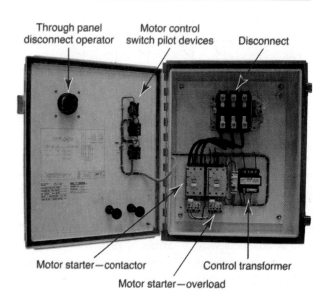

Through panel disconnect operator

Motor control switch pilot devices

Disconnect

Motor starter—contactor

Control transformer

Motor starter—overload

starter. Motor control pushbutton switches and indicator light are mounted through the enclosure cover. Combination starters offer space and cost savings over separate components.

Figure 6-28 illustrates a typical disconnect switch that is used in a combination starter. This type of disconnect

(a) Three phase manual disconnect

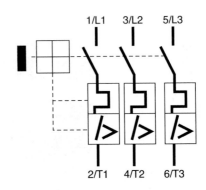

**(b) IEC manual three phase
disconnect with thermal OL**

FIGURE 6-29: Three phase manual branch circuit disconnect NEMA symbols for a variety of devices.

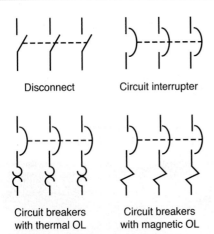

Disconnect   Circuit interrupter

Circuit breakers   Circuit breakers
with thermal OL   with magnetic OL

is used to remove power from the entire motor starter. In general, AC disconnect switches are used to isolate a component of an electrical system from the power source. Figure 6-29 illustrates three phase branch circuit *disconnects* with a variety of protection devices. Electrical workers use disconnects for many reasons, including *fault isolation* and opening of branch circuits for maintenance.

6-7 OVERLOAD RELAYS

The basic difference between a *magnetic contactor* and a *magnetic motor starter* is the addition of an *overload relay*, as illustrated in Figure 6-30. The relationship

between the overload relay's current *sensing devices*, the *overload contacts*, and the *contacts* used to switch the three phase motor power is important to understand. The distinction between these devices is restated here for emphasis.

> *The overload protection device in the motor starter detects excessive over-current conditions in the motor by measuring motor current through the contactor's power control circuit. When an overload condition exists, the overload contacts in the lower power motor control circuit de-energize the contactor. The de-energized contactor opens the power control circuit, which removes power from the motor.*

Overloads protect the motor from damage and satisfy a National Electrical Code requirement. Overload motor currents most often result from: *loss of a phase on a three-phase motor, operation with too much load* or *low line voltage*.

Branch Circuit Versus Overload Protection

Branch circuit *fuses* and *circuit breakers* protect conductors and control circuit components from excessive current caused by: *high current draws over time, short circuits* and *ground faults*. Overload relays are present only for motor protection. The union of a magnetic contactor with an overload device creates a magnetic motor starter. Figure 6-30 illustrates the combination of a contactor with an overload relay. The NEMA symbols for an overload relay are included in the figure.

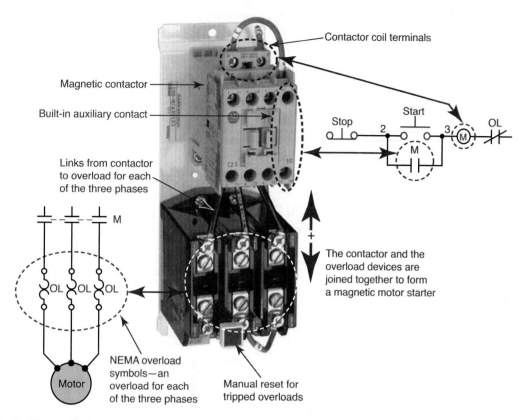

Courtesy of Rockwell Automation, Inc.

When a manual or magnetic motor starter *initially* connects power to a motor, the motor *momentarily* draws *six* to *eight times* the normal operating current. This initial high current, called *inrush* current, is normal for a short duration and not harmful to the motor. Branch circuit protection, including fuses and circuit breakers located ahead of the motor starter, is designed to *ignore* this initially high inrush current required in motor startup and acceleration. Unnecessary disruption of motor current, when the current is within normal operating values, is called a *nuisance interrupt*. Nuisance interrupts occur most often when branch circuit fuses or circuit breakers and overload relays are not sized properly.

Motors are designed to operate efficiently from no load current values no load attached to full load current (FLC) values (at maximum load or horsepower). Motor operation above the FLC, an *overload condition*, increases the winding temperature, which damages the wire insulation and shortens motor life. This

damage is proportional to the *magnitude* and the *duration* of the overload current. Extremely high short duration currents and currents just above the FLC for long time periods cause damaging heat and eventually motor failure. It is estimated that *thirty percent* of motor failures are due to frequent operation at overload current levels.

Types of Overload Relays

Three types of overload relays, *thermal (heat)*, *magnetic*, and *electronic*, with *different* operational principles, protect the motor from overload current. Thermal types are subdivided into *melting alloy* or *eutectic alloy* and *bimetallic strip*. Protection against the two other causes of overload current, *loss of a phase voltage* and *low line voltage*, are discussed in a later chapter

Motor current is *proportional* to motor load and an *indication* of the heat in the windings. Overload relays, located on the motor starter, *monitor* the current in the motor power circuit and *open* the power circuit when excessive motor current occurs. Overload relays are an indirect monitor of motor heat because they are not located on the motor but some distance away on the motor starter device. After overload conditions are *corrected*, overload relays are *manually* or *automatically reset*. However, the three-phase power circuit contacts in the contactor remain open until the start contacts in the motor control circuit are manually closed for a restart.

Thermal overload relays are usually *less expensive* than magnetic and electronic overload control devices. The thermal units are sized electrically to the motor's full load current and sized physically to the NEMA motor starter where they mount. Within these limitation, thermal units are often interchangeable across different size NEMA starters.

Overload Relay Trip Classes

NEMA and IEC overload relays respond to overload conditions based on *trip curves*. These trip curves are defined by the *class* of protection required. The class designations based on *tripping time* are:

- Class 10—10 Seconds or less
- Class 20—20 Seconds or less
- Class 30—30 Seconds or less

IEC motor starters are typically application rated. This means the controller is sized very close to its operational limit for a given application. IEC motors are also generally more application rated. As a result, Class 10 trip is most common on IEC overload applications. NEMA devices have a broader capacity because there are fewer motor starter sizes to bridge the full range of motor horsepowers used. As a result, Class 20 trip is most common on NEMA overload applications.

The class designation is typically dictated by the application and motor selected for process. Class 10 operation is often used with *hermetically-sealed motors, submersible pumps,* or motors with *short locked rotor time* capability. Class 20 operation is recommended for *general applications*. Class 30 is used with motors driving *high inertia loads*, where additional accelerating time is needed and the safe permissible locked rotor time of the motor is within Class 30 performance requirements.

Melting or Eutectic Alloy Overload Relays

Thermal overload relays, often just called *heaters*, are available in two types—*melting* or *eutectic alloy* and *bimetallic strip*. The melting alloy style is generally used by NEMA rated motor starters and the bimetallic strip type are used in IEC rated starters. While both are tripped by heat generated from motor current in the motor power circuit, their methods of operation are quite different.

At the heart of the melting alloy overload is the *eutectic alloy*, a metal that has a *low* but *fixed* melting point and is not affected by repeated *melting* and *solidifying*. The melting properties of the eutectic alloy are similar to electrical solder; as a result, these devices are often called *solder pot* relays. Figure 6-31 illustrates how the

FIGURE 6-31: Operation of eutectic alloy thermal overload.

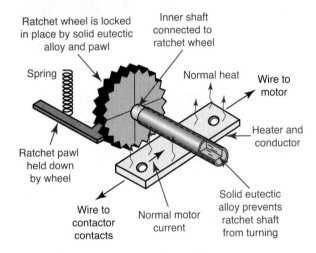

(a) Non-overload current

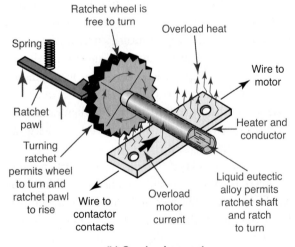

(b) Overload current

eutectic alloy is used to trigger a change in contacts when the alloy is heated to a temperature that causes the alloy to melt. Study the figure before continuing with the description of the operation.

An understanding of the mechanism in Figure 6-31 is a critical starting point in the understanding of eutectic alloy overload operation. The heart of the process is the *ratchet wheel* with its *shaft* inside the *tube* filled with eutectic alloy metal. At currents below the trigger current/overload condition, the alloy is a solid so the ratchet shaft is fixed to the inside of the tube. As a result, no rotation of ratchet and the ratchet shaft inside the tube is possible. The tube temperature is set by the overload heater based on the current in one phase of the three-phase motor. A ratchet pawl applies rotational pressure on the ratchet wheel with upward tension created by a spring. However, ratchet rotation is inhibited because the ratchet wheel shaft is locked in the solid eutectic alloy.

Figure 6-31(a) illustrates this *non-overload* condition where the motor current through the heater produces *too little heat* to melt the eutectic alloy in the tube. The illustration in Figure 6-31(b) is an *overload* condition. The motor current produced sufficient heat in the heater link to *melt* the eutectic alloy. Depending on the overload heater class, the alloy goes from a *solid* to a *liquid* in 10, 20, or 30 seconds at a specific temperature in a narrow range. With the metal alloy *liquefied,* the ratchet wheel shaft is free to *turn* inside the tube fixed to the heater. Wheel rotation permits the spring loaded pawl to rise.

The information learned in Figure 6-31 is now applied to the operation of eutectic alloy thermal overload relay in Figure 6-32. This figure integrates the ratchet and eutectic/heater unit with a set of contacts controlled by the ratchet pawl. A rotating cam is used to link the motion of the ratchet wheel with movement in the contact operator.

Figure 6-32(e) shows the heater wire wrapped around the eutectic tube. A review of the eutectic overload operation starts with Figure 6-32(a)—operation *without* an overload condition present. The ratchet is *locked* in place by the *solid* eutectic alloy and the pawl *engages* the ratchet, which *holds* the contacts in their NC state. The NC contacts in the control circuit permit the motor to be *started* and *run* with current in the nominal operational range.

If the motor load *exceeds* the horsepower rating, motor current *climbs* to the *overload* level and the condition in Figure 6-32(b) occurs. Heat from the increased current *melts* the eutectic alloy, which *frees* the ratchet shaft and the ratchet wheel *rotates.* Rotation of the ratchet permits the pawl cam to *pivot* and the compressed spring *opens* the NC control contacts. Since the overload control contacts are in series with the contactor coil, the circuit to the coil is opened. With the coil de-energized, the contactor armature opens the motor power circuit stopping the motor. The motor restart is not possible until the overload relay is manually reset.

With motor power circuit current at zero, the temperature of the eutectic alloy overload drops. After the alloy solidifies, the ratchet shaft is lock to prevent rotation. With the condition that generated the overload removed, the overload is *reset* with reset pushbutton. The *reset action* drags the pawl across the ratchet wheel to a point where the control contacts are again *locked* in their NC position. The start sequence pilot devices are now prepared for a restart of the motor.

Figure 6-30 pictures a eutectic alloy overload wired to a NEMA contactor. The mechanism illustrated in Figure 6-32 is embedded in each of the three-phase power overloads in Figure 6-30. A single reset on the overload resets all three phases. Figure 6-33 shows a eutectic alloy overload with the trip indicator, reset pushbutton and NC control circuit contact indicated. A portion of a control circuit is present with the location of the overload NC contact marked. Some overload relays permit additional control contacts to trigger alarms when a motor overload current trips the overload. The alarm alerts operators that a motor is shut down, an overload condition is present, and a reset and restart is necessary.

Bimetallic Overload Relays

Bimetallic overload relays are constructed by joining *two strips* of *dissimilar* metals back to back. Review Chapter 3 Figures 3-19 and 3-20 and the associated text that describes the construction and operation of bimetallic temperature sensors. As the Chapter 3 material indicates, the two joined metals expand and contract at different rates; as a result, the

FIGURE 6-32: Eutectic alloy overload relay operation.

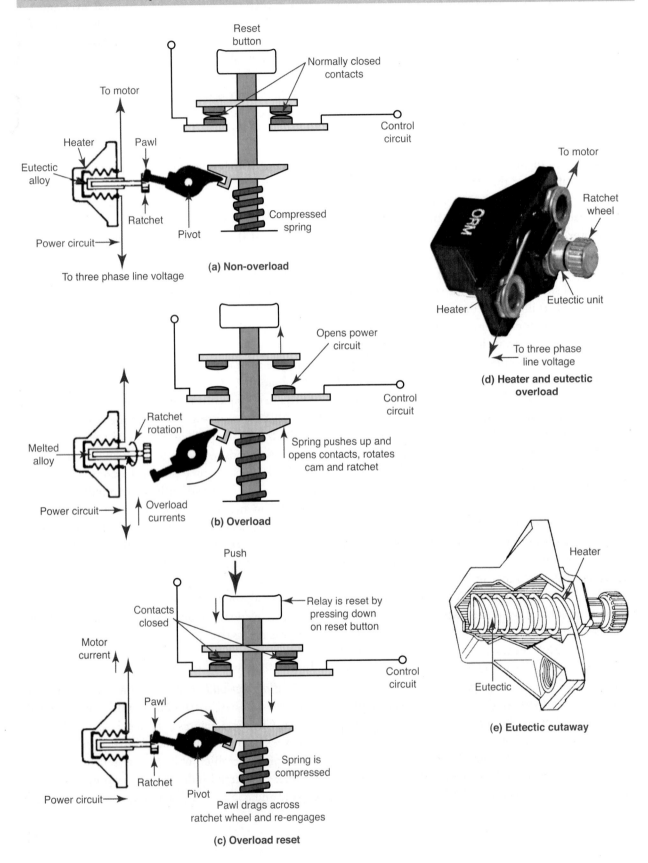

(a) **Non-overload**

(b) **Overload**

(c) **Overload reset**

(d) **Heater and eutectic overload**

(e) **Eutectic cutaway**

FIGURE 6-33: NEMA eutectic overload relay.

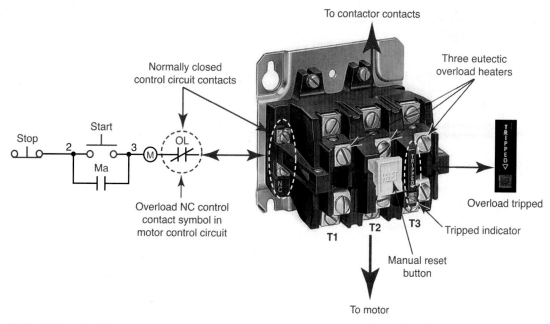

To contactor contacts

Normally closed
control circuit contacts

Three eutectic
overload heaters

Stop   Start

OL

Ma

Overload NC control
contact symbol in
motor control circuit

T1   T2   T3

Manual reset
button

Overload tripped

Tripped indicator

To motor

Courtesy of Rockwell Automation, Inc.

strip bends when heated. Figure 6-34(a) is a cut away showing one phase of a bimetallic overload. The motor phase current flows thought a *heater* located *close* to the *bimetallic* sensors. As the sensor's *temperature increases*, the top ends of the bimetallic strip *move apart*. The right end pushes against the trip adjustment screw, and the left end pushes against the NC control contact's operator. The NC contact operator is a *maintain* type, so it remain in the actuated position (NC contacts open) after the operator is actuated by the bimetallic strip. A return to the *original* position requires a *manually* reset.

In some designs the motor current flows *through* a portion of the bimetallic strip and heats it *directly* with the motor current. Such a system is illustrated in Figure 6-34(b) and (c) with a bimetallic strip for each phase, L1, L2, and L3, as shown. This bimetallic strip overload has *two slide bars* connected in a four-bar linkage. The control contacts' operator is actuated by the vertical bar on the left end in Figure 6-34(b).

Overload Tripping Due to Excess Motor Load—

Figure 6-34(b) illustrates normal motor operation without an overload present. The gray slide bars move left and right independently. The lower bar (slide bar 1) is pushed to the left when the bimetallic strip bends

to the left. Spring 1 keeps slide bar 1 in contact with the bimetallic strip. The upper bar (slide bar 2) is pushed to the right when the bimetallic strip bends to the right. Spring 2 keeps slide bar 2 in contact with the bimetallic strip. This bar mechanism tracks all three phase currents for the motor for two conditions: *motor overload* on three phases and *loss* of a single phase.

Figure 6-34(b) illustrates the position of slide bars 1 and 2 with equal phase currents below the overload trip point. Note that each slide bar moved to the left an equal amount. The bar linking the two slide bars remains vertical and approaches the overload contacts operator. If all three phase currents continued to increase equally, the vertical bar at point "A" would trip the overload operator. The NC overload contacts 95 and 96 are opened and de-energize the motor contactor. This is a motor overload condition with all three current exceeding the current trip point value. When the motor current is off, the bimetallic strips cool. All three strips bend back to the right and the overload NC contacts return to their original positions (95 and 96 are closed). After the cause of the overload is removed, the motor is restarted with the start switch. Some bimetallic overload relays are available with a switch selectable option for automatic reset or manual only reset.

FIGURE 6-34: Operation of bimetallic strip overload relays.

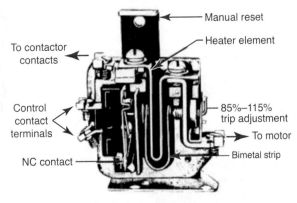

Manual reset

Heater element

To contactor contacts

Control contact terminals

85%–115% trip adjustment

To motor

Bimetal strip

NC contact

(a) Cut away view of bimetallic strip overload

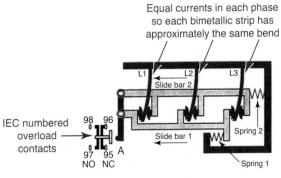

Equal currents in each phase so each bimetallic strip has approximately the same bend

L1   L2   L3

Slide bar 2

IEC numbered overload contacts

98   96

Slide bar 1

Spring 2

97   95   A
NO   NC

Spring 1

(b) Motor current below

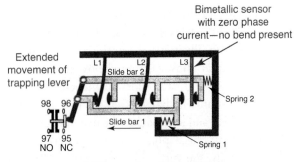

Bimetallic sensor with zero phase current—no bend present

Extended movement of trapping lever

L1   L2   L3

Slide bar 2

Spring 2

98   96

Slide bar 1

97   95
NO   NC

Spring 1

(c) Two motor phase currents below FLC and one phase open

Overload Tripping Due to Single-Phase Failure—

Figure 6-34(c) illustrates a single phase failure (L3) and the corresponding increased currents in the two other phases (L1 and L2). With no motor current in L3, the bimetallic strip is in the zero current vertical position. This holds slide bar 2 in the far right position with spring 2 compressed. The excess current in L1 and L2 moves slide bar 1 to the left. The deferential movement of the two bars (top bar fixed in place and bottom bar moving to the left) causes the bottom

of the vertical link on the left side of the bars to move to the left and trips the overload contact.

A *unique function* of a bimetallic overload is the ability to *automatically* reset. In some motor control circuits, the motor is restarted as soon as the overload control contacts are automatically reset. For example, automatic restart has some *advantages* in applications like *industrial refrigerators*, *freezers*, and *pumping operations*. With automatic restart, products are not damaged by loss of refrigeration and tanks do not overflow.

However, obvious disadvantages exist when a motor in some applications restart automatically. Without removal of the *problem* that caused the overload, *motor damage* is highly likely due to exposure to *overload* current conditions after every restart. Motors exposed to this repeated cycling are often destroyed. In addition, motor restarts in a manufacturing process are capable of damaging products partially finished or still engaged with the production machines. Also, the automatic restart feature presents significant hazards to operation and maintenance personnel. A motor restart, while electrical workers are investigating the cause of the fault or operators are clearing products from a machine, has the potential for serious injury or loss of life.

Figure 6-35(a) and (b) illustrates a bimetallic overload relay with accompanying IEC motor power circuit and motor control circuit. Both NO and NC motor control contacts are present, but only the NC contact is used in the motor control circuit. The enlarge view of the relay front shows the manual or automatic reset selection, trip indicator, test button to manually actuate the control contacts, motor current adjustment, manual reset, and stop.

The bimetal overload relay is ambient temperature compensated for constant tripping characteristic over a –20° to +60°C ambient temperature range. It has a class 10 thermal rating with a differential mechanism (Figure 6-34) for high sensitivity to phase loss conditions and reliable motor protection in normal duty applications. A remote reset attachment permits manual overload reset with a switch pilot device.

Comparison of Eutectic Alloy and Bimetallic Strip Overloads

Eutectic alloy and bimetallic overload relays are both legacy devices because they have been in use for many years. Electrical workers must know how to work with

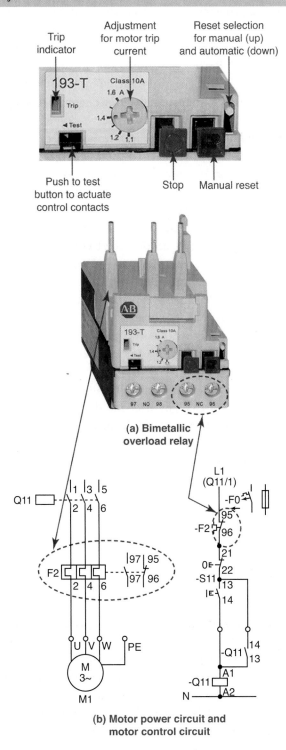

(a) Bimetallic overload relay

(b) Motor power circuit and motor control circuit

devices, and IEC standard motor starters with thermal overloads use the bimetallic devices. General observations for the two types of thermal overloads includes:

- Eutectic alloy typically perform better in high vibration environments because the solid alloy resists vibration.
- Eutectic alloy cannot provide automatic reset, ambient temperature compensation, and phase fault protection.
- Eutectic alloy generally use a class 20 trip curve and bimetallic use a class 10 curve.
- Eutectic alloy uses interchangeable heater elements that allow the selection and installation of heaters designed to match the motor and applications in terms of trip times and trip current. Bimetallic overloads with integral heater elements are available for a range of motor currents, and a provision to externally adjust the overload trip point is provided.

Magnetic Overload Relay

Magnetic overload relays offer greater *flexibility* and *quicker* reset times than thermal overloads because no heat is require for operation. Magnetic overloads include *adjustment* to compensate for motors with a *prolonged inrush* current due to unusual duty cycles or *longer acceleration* times. Some magnetic overload relays permit independent adjustments for both *trip current* and *trip time*.

The magnetic overload relay solenoid coil, wound with wire to handle full load current, is connected in *series* with the motor power circuit. Figure 6-36 illustrates the operation of a magnetic overload. Note the power lugs for connection to the *motor* and *contactor* contacts. The operator for the overload control contacts is actuated by the *armature* or *piston* of the overload solenoid. With the piston assembly mounted in an oil-filled *dashpot*, the relay provides the *inverse-time* characteristics or *time lag* required in some motor starting applications. The oil-filled dashpot acts like a *shock absorber* to slow the upward movement of the piston assembly, which is pulled by the high inrush motor current. The dashpot slows the armature movement so inrush current does not trip the overload. A spring (not shown) returns the armature to the position dictated by the normal motor running current. A sustained motor overload condition moves the armature up and trips the NC control contacts. If the dashpot is not used the magnetic overload relay trips instantaneously at the preset current.

these legacy devices and also the newer electronic overload relays. The following list of characteristics for eutectic alloy and bimetallic overloads provides a comparison of the two devices. In general, older NEMA rated motor starters with thermal overloads have eutectic alloy

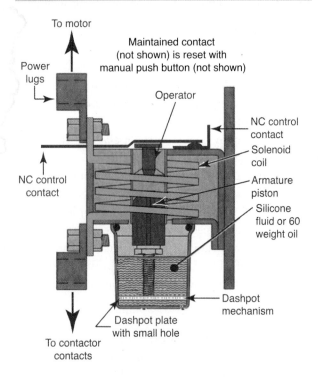

FIGURE 6-36: Magnetic overload relay symbolic operational illustration.

To motor

Maintained contact
(not shown) is reset with
manual push button (not shown)

Power
lugs

Operator

NC control
contact

Solenoid
coil

Armature
piston

Silicone
fluid or 60
weight oil

NC control
contact

Dashpot
mechanism

Dashpot plate
with small hole

To contactor
contacts

Magnetic overload relays operate on *current intensity* and *not heat*. As the motor current increases, the solenoid's magnetic field increases, lifting the solenoid piston assembly upwards. At the preset trip current, the piston assembly opens a normally closed contact, which opens the control circuit for the motor starter. The motor remains off until the maintained control contact in the overload is manually reset, and the control pilot devices for starting are actuated. Immediate reset of magnetic overload relays, after the overload condition is removed, is possible since the cool down period required by thermal overload is not necessary.

Mechanical overload relays are used in heavy duty applications such as *rolling mills, large metal processing machines,* and *large pumping stations* where motors are operated in a *stressful* environment. They are also ideal for motor applications with *long acceleration times* and *extremely high inrush* current that do not fit into the normal time and current curves of thermal overload protection devices. The benefits mechanical overloads provide include: *instantaneous* and *inverse time tripping* (time lag) characteristics, independent *trip time* adjustment, and independent *trip current* adjustment.

Electronic Overload Relays

The newest overload technology, *electronic* overload devices, provides *motor protection* and *control flexibility* not available in *thermal* and *magnetic* overload relays. An electronic overload relay is pictured in Figure 6-37. Review the information in the figure now and as you read the features offered by electronic overloads in this paragraph. Their superiority includes: *instantaneous resets, low energy consumption, faster reaction time to overloads, adjustable range settings, dip switch selectable standard class designation of 10, 15, 20, or 30,* and *instant phase loss protection.* Motor power current is measured with small built-in *current transformers,* which are covered in the next section. As a result, electronic overloads draw much less power from the motor circuit compared to the thermal and magnetic devices and permit immediate reset after tripping. In addition, the overload trips the motor contactor if one or more of the power phases supplying the motor is lost; a feature called *phase loss protection.* Another useful feature is *front panel adjustment* of motor overload trip point current.

For example, if the ambient temperature for the motor location changes after the system is installed, then adjustment of the level of the overload trip current setting is required. *Absolute motor temperature* above rated values damages winding wire insulation. The absolute motor temperature is the *temperature rise* due to motor operation plus the current *ambient temperature.* If the ambient temperature changes significantly, a change in the motor overload current trip point is required.

A motor controller with eutectic overload devices requires a change in the heaters for each phase to match the new condition. The motor controller with an electronic overload requires a quick "tweak" with a screwdriver to change in the current setting on the front panel. However, maintenance procedures never permit an increase in the overload set point on the front panel as a quick fix for an overload condition. A poor maintenance procedures like this, leads to dramatically shortened motor life due to operation in a constant overload condition.

Current Transformers

To measure and respond to the motor overloads, thermal and magnetic overload relays have the motor phase currents flowing through their respective heaters or coils.

FIGURE 6-37: Electronic overload relay.

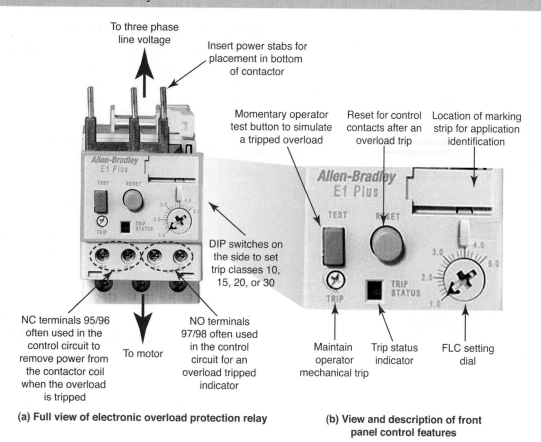

(a) Full view of electronic overload protection relay

(b) View and description of front panel control features

Courtesy of Rockwell Automation, Inc.

As motor horsepower increases the size of the heater elements and coil wires increases to handle the higher motor currents. At some point it is not practical to pass all the motor current through the sensing elements in the overload relay. The problem is solved with a *current transformer* (CT).

Figure 6-38(a) shows a current transformer used in motor control circuits, and Figure 6-38(b) shows Rockwell Automation's CT turns ratios for their overload relays. These *donut-shaped* devices function in a similar manner as traditional power transformers. AC electrical energy is coupled between the primary and secondary windings by an electro-magnetic field that switches direction at a rate set by the frequency of the AC source current. Traditional power transformers connect an AC power source to the primary winding and draw transformed AC power from the secondary winding. Figure 6-38(c) illustrates the construction and operation of a current transformer. The motor current wire passing through the center of the CT is the primary winding with a single turn. The secondary winding wraps around an iron core with the number of turns dictated by the turns ratios listed in Figure 6-38(b). A magnetic field circles the single turn primary motor power wire. The AC current causes the field to grow with clockwise orientation around the wire, to collapse, and then grow in a counterclockwise orientation. This changing magnetic field cuts across the wires in the donut shaped CT. This induces a proportional current to the motor's phase current with a value determined by the CT turns ratio. Figure 6-38(b) indicates that the second ratio value is always 5. The maximum secondary current is a standard 5 amps, and the motor control wire's FLC maximum value is close to the upper value of the turns ratio. For example, the first CT has 50 turns and the maximum FLC is 45 amps. Therefore, a 45 amp motor current produces 4.5 amps of CT current for the overload. Current transformers are used with electronic overload relays to monitor the current drawn by large horsepower

FIGURE 6-38: Current transformer or CT for use with overload relays.

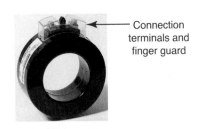

(a) Current transformer or CT

CT Ratio	FLC Setting Range [A]	CT Ratio	FLC Setting Range [A]	CT Ratio	FLC Setting Range [A]
50:5	9...45	300:5	60...302	1200:5	240...1215
100:5	18...90	500:5	84...420	2500:5	450...2250
150:5	28...140	600:5	125...630	5000:5	1000...5000
200:5	42...210	800:5	172...860	—	—

(b) CT ratios and FLC ranges

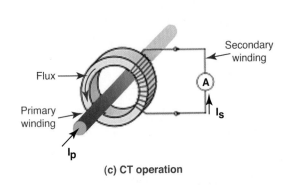

(c) CT operation

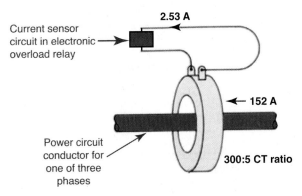

(d) CT connected to bimetallic heater strip

An electronic overload relay uses a current transformer in each leg of the three-phase motor power circuit to sense motor current. The estimated motor FLC for the applications is 152 amps. A 300:5 turns ratio current transformer is selected from the table in Figure 6-38(b). The electrical worker must determine what the secondary output from the CT is for the motor FLC. A turns ratio of 300 to 5 means that 5 amps flows in the secondary when 300 amps flows in the primary or motor current wire. 300 divided by 5 equals 60. So, 1 amp flows to the electronic overload for every 60 amps flowing in the motor power circuit. Divide the FLC, 152 amps, by 60 and the result is 2.53 amps—the current flow to the overload. The solution is illustrated in Figure 6-38(d).

motors as the CT in Figure 6-38(d) illustrates. CTs are also used with large electrical services to drive current and power meters from service entrance feed lines.

Service Factor

Exceeding the FLC has the potential for damage to the motor winding insulation. However, most motor applications have operational situations where the FLC is exceeded for short periods of time. To accommodate these situations motor manufactures provide a *Service Factor* (SF) rating for the motor. The SF indicates the *additional motor horsepower* available for a limited time

period that does not damage the motor. Service Factor values range from 1.0 to 1.25. An SF of 1.00 or 100 percent indicates that only the rated nameplate FLC loading is permitted. An SF of 1.25 or 125 percent indicates

The motor nameplate full load current (FLC) is 11.0 amps and the motor has a SF of 1.2. A 1.2 service factor permits operation at 20 percent over FLC for short periods of time. As a result, a motor current of 13.2 [11 A + (0.2 x 11 A) = 13.2 A] amps is permitted for short periods of time.

that 25 percent of the rated horsepower is in reserve for use in short burst without any danger of motor damage.

Heater sizing for thermal overloads considers: motor FLC current, contactor size, the motor's SF, motor and motor starter ambient temperature, and the overload class number requirement. To select the proper size heater, manufacturers provide procedures and tables, which guide electrical workers to the correct choice.

Sizing Overloads

Full load current (FLC) is the maximum current in amps a motor is expected to draw while running under normal operating *voltage, speed* and *torque* conditions. Manufacturers list the FLC on the motor's permanently attached nameplate. However, the FLC is affected by *changes* that take the motor outside of the normal operating conditions. Overloads are sized based on: *motor FLC current, contactor size, the motor's SF, motor and motor starter ambient temperature,* and *the overload class number requirement.*

Thermal overload relays, bimetallic and melting alloy, protect motor windings based on motor current flow through the overload relay. As motor current rises, the heat generated by the current in the overload relay rises as well. The overload's trip temperatures assumes an ambient temperature of (40°C or 104°F) plus a temperature increase above ambient by a specific level of motor current. Overloads do not differentiate heat sources. They *trip* when a specific temperature is *reached,* regardless of the *source* (ambient or motor current) for the heat.

Motor starter locations range from inside *freezers* to near *blast furnaces,* so ambient temperatures fluctuate widely. Manufacturers of thermal overload relays provide a *procedure* to select the overload heater. These selection procedures consider *ambient temperature* and *current levels* in the overload relay. While the procedures vary among the manufacturers, they all provide tables to identify a thermal heater device sized to stop the motor before damage to the windings occurs when a overload is present.

The following procedure is used by *Rockwell Automation* for their eutectic type thermal overload relays.

Heater Element Selection—Selection processes are for motors rated for *continuous duty.* If *intermittent duty* is required, contact with the manufacturer is recommended for sizing information.

A. For motors with service factor of not less than 1.15, or motors with a temperature rise not over +40°C (+104°F), apply the following rules 1 through 3. Apply rules 2 and 3 when the temperature between the starter and motor is different, but not by more than 10°C (18°F).

  1. The same temperature at the motor starter and the motor—Select the heater element with a listed FLC nearest the full load current value shown on the motor nameplate.

  2. Ambient temperature at the motor starter is higher than the ambient temperature at the motor—If the full load current value shown on the motor nameplate falls between two listed FLC values on the selection table, use the higher value FLC in the table to select the *heater element number.*

  3. Ambient temperature at the motor starter is lower than at the ambient temperature at the motor—If the full load current value shown on the motor nameplate falls between two listed FLC values on the selection table, use the lower value FLC in the table to select the *heater element number.*

B. For motors with a service factor of less than 1.15, apply rules 1, 2 and 3 above for selection of a *heater element number,* but use the next smaller *heater element* than the one determined by the rules.

Review the following application sidebar that illustrates how a heater element is selected using these rules.

Ambient Temperature Correction—The ambient temperature at the motor and controller is the same in most applications. Under this condition, the overload relay is designed to sense changes in ambient temperature and also protect the motor over a range of temperatures.

The output that a motor can safely deliver varies with temperature. The motor delivers its full rated horsepower at an ambient temperature specified by the motor manufacturers, normally +40 °C (+104 °F). At high temperatures (higher than +40 °C) less than 100% of the FLC can be drawn by the motor without shortening the insulation life. At lower temperatures (less than +40 °C) more than 100% of the FLC can be drawn by the motor without shortening the insulation life. Thus, there is an inverse relationship between motor ambient temperature and motor output. In any motor, allowable output decreases as the ambient temperature is raised.

Sizing overload relay heaters for large variations in ambient temperature requires an application of a correction factor to the motor FLC. The correction factors' graphs are provided by the motor manufacturers.

APPLICATION

Select overload heaters for a motor starter with eutectic overload protection used in the following control: motor nameplate FLC is 46.7 amps with a 1.15 service factor, class 20 overload protection with an open enclosure, protection on all three phases, a NEMA size 3 Bulletin 509 starter, the starter ambient temperature is 113°F while the motor ambient temperature is 105°F. Starter specifications and sizing charts are in Figures 6-39(a) through 6-39(c).

FIGURE 6-39: (a) Index to heater selection tables. (b) Rockwell notation for overload classes.

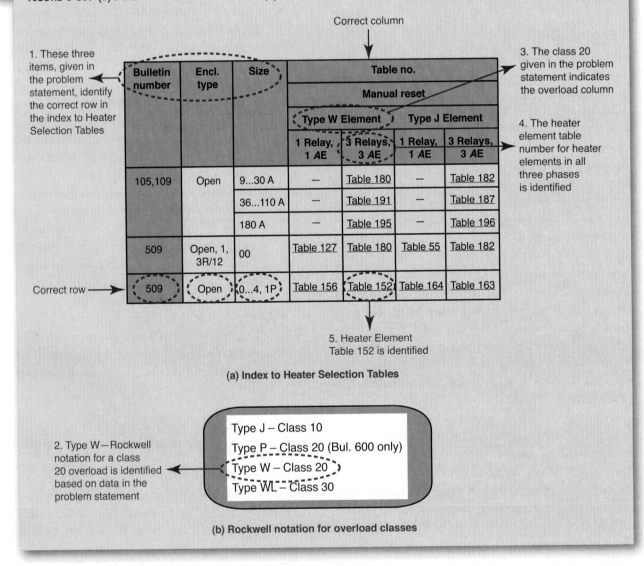

1. These three items, given in the problem statement, identify the correct row in the index to Heater Selection Tables

3. The class 20 given in the problem statement indicates the overload column

4. The heater element table number for heater elements in all three phases is identified

Correct column

Bulletin number	Encl. type	Size	Table no.				
			Manual reset				
			Type W Element		Type J Element		
			1 Relay, 1 AE	3 Relays, 3 AE	1 Relay, 1 AE	3 Relays, 3 AE	
105,109	Open	9...30 A	—	Table 180	—	Table 182	
		36...110 A	—	Table 191	—	Table 187	
		180 A	—	Table 195	—	Table 196	
509	Open, 1, 3R/12	00	Table 127	Table 180	Table 55	Table 182	
509	Open	0...4, 1P	Table 156	Table 152	Table 164	Table 163	

Correct row

5. Heater Element Table 152 is identified

(a) Index to Heater Selection Tables

2. Type W—Rockwell notation for a class 20 overload is identified based on data in the problem statement

Type J – Class 10
Type P – Class 20 (Bul. 600 only)
Type W – Class 20
Type WL – Class 30

(b) Rockwell notation for overload classes

Selecting the heater element size starts with identifying the correct Heater Element Table Number. Review the five steps, listed in Figures 6-39(a) and 6-39(b), to identify and understand why Heater Element Table 152 is used for element number identification.

The starter and motor have different ambient temperatures. Conversion from 105 and 113°F to degrees Celsius yields 40.5 and 45°C respectively. The starter ambient is 45°C and the motor ambient is 40.5°C, so the difference is less than 10°C. Therefore, rule two identified earlier is used. Rule two is listed below.

Higher Temperature at the Controller than at the Motor—If the full load current value shown on the motor nameplate falls between two listed "Full Load Amperes" values, select the "Heater Type Number" with the higher value.

Review steps 6, 7, and 8 listed in Figure 6-39(c), to identify and understand why the Heater Element number W68 is required for this application.

FIGURE 6-39: (c) Segments of Table 152 listing heater element numbers.

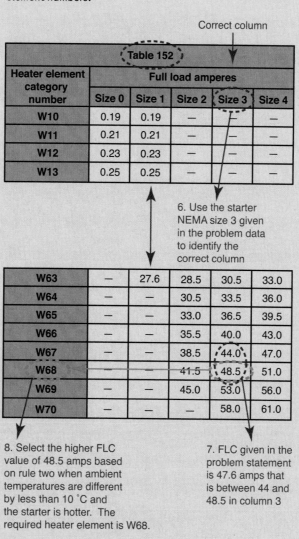

Correct column

Heater element category number	Full load amperes				
	Size 0	Size 1	Size 2	Size 3	Size 4
W10	0.19	0.19	—	—	—
W11	0.21	0.21	—	—	—
W12	0.23	0.23	—	—	—
W13	0.25	0.25	—	—	—

6. Use the starter NEMA size 3 given in the problem data to identify the correct column

W63	—	27.6	28.5	30.5	33.0
W64	—	—	30.5	33.5	36.0
W65	—	—	33.0	36.5	39.5
W66	—	—	35.5	40.0	43.0
W67	—	—	38.5	44.0	47.0
W68	—	—	41.5	48.5	51.0
W69	—	—	45.0	53.0	56.0
W70	—	—	—	58.0	61.0

8. Select the higher FLC value of 48.5 amps based on rule two when ambient temperatures are different by less than 10 °C and the starter is hotter. The required heater element is W68.

7. FLC given in the problem statement is 47.6 amps that is between 44 and 48.5 in column 3

(c) Segments of Table 152 listing heater element numbers

The correction factor lowers the motor nameplate FLC for higher ambient temperature and raises it for lower ambient temperatures.

Integral Motor Protection Devices

The motor overload relay protection devices discussed thus far are mounted on the motor starter inside an enclosure. The distance from this enclosure to the protected motor is dictated by the application with the distance ranging from a few feet to many feet. As a result, the protection for motor overheating is performed indirectly using the motor current. Physical measurement of the motor winding temperature is not performed by the overload relays.

Inherent motor protection accurately measures motor temperature because these devices are mounted on the motor housing or located inside the motor. Signals from these devices are integrated into the motor control circuit for additional overload protection in some applications. In smaller single-phase motors applications integral protection devices are connected in series with

A visual picture of motor protection is presented in a Trip Time versus Multiples of FLC log-log graph. Figure 6-39(d) illustrates the class 10, 20, and 30 overload trip time graphs with two different inrush currents shown. The curves for the inrush currents are straight line approximations. The actual curves are not as vertical or horizontal as the approximations. The plots clearly illustrate that nuisance tripping would occur if a class 10 overload is used with the motor that has a 7 times FLC inrush current. However, operation of the 6 times FLC motor with a class 10 overload is possible.

The log-log Trip Time versus Multiple of FLC graph in Figure 6-39(e) demonstrates how coordinated protection functions. Protection against short circuits and ground faults is provided by the short circuit protection device (SCPD) in the form of fuses or circuit breakers at a branch disconnect. The motor overload protection is provided by a class 20 overload relay. Study the annotated graphs to learn safe and unsafe operation areas for the motor with different multiples of FLC for varying lengths of time.

FIGURE 6-39: (d) Class 10, 20, and 30 trip time curves.

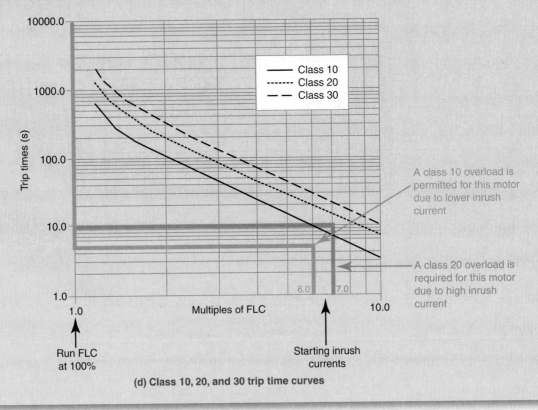

(d) Class 10, 20, and 30 trip time curves

FIGURE 6-39: (e) Overload and combination protection analysis.

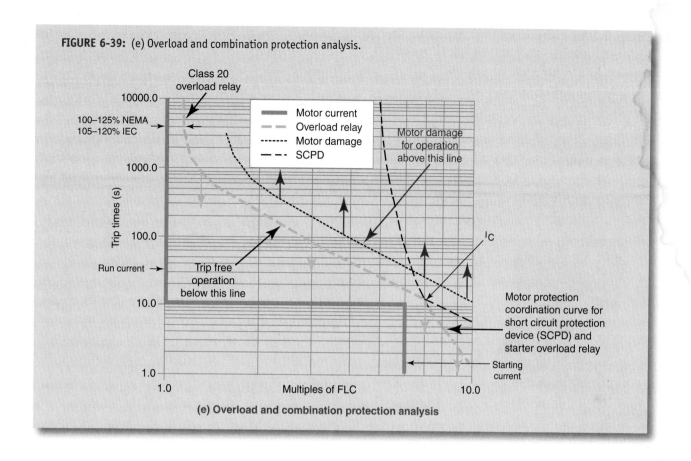

(e) Overload and combination protection analysis

the motor windings. In this case the protection device opens the motor power circuit when an overload occurs.

Thermistor Overload Protection

Thermistor overload protection devices are integrated into special purpose electronic controllers to open motor power circuits when overload currents situations are present. As the name implies, a thermistor is a temperature sensitive resistor. When used for motor overload protection, the thermistor mounted on the motor changes resistance as the motor temperature increases. A sufficient change in resistance is interpreted by the electronic controller as an overload condition and the motor is shut down. These devices are very expensive because each system is a unique design for specific motor control application.

Bimetallic Thermodiscs

Bimetallic thermodiscs are similar to bimetallic strips with two dissimilar metals joined together. However, bimetallic thermodiscs are formed into a round saucer shaped device. As these devices are heated, the depth of the saucer shape is increased. This increased bow-

ing in the shape is used to mechanically open NC contacts in the motor power circuit and stop the motor. This inexpensive overload device is used on many fractional horsepower single-phase motors to protect motor windings from over heating. The thermodisc is mounted on the frame of the motor so its temperature tracks the winding temperature. Automatic reset after the motor cools is the most common, but manual reset thermodisc devices are also available.

6-8 ENCLOSURES

Enclosures provide mechanical and electrical protection for the electrical worker and for the contactors and motor starters. Enclosures provide protection from a variety of elements such as water, dust, oil and hazardous environmental conditions. The option of locating a motor starter in a non-hazardous area allows for the use of a much less expensive enclosure. Motor starters used in hazardous locations, such as grain silos and chemical plants where an arc could result in explosions or fires, are mounted in special enclosures. These enclosures are designed to prevent the arc and the hazardous environment from coming into contact with each other. Because of their special construction, these enclosures are more expensive.

NEMA and IEC classify enclosures based on the usage and service conditions. A range of NEMA enclosures are available for both indoors and outdoors. Enclosures are also available that protects from explosive environments. Figure 6-40 shows an explosion proof enclosure. Note the disconnect switch inside the enclosure and the disconnect operator on the outside of the enclosure.

The NEMA classifications of enclosures are shown in Figure 6-41. Note that the type is specified by number or a number and a letter. Each type specifies a use (indoor or outdoor) and a service condition. For example, a 6P enclosure is used indoors or outdoors and can survive prolonged submersion in water at a limited depth.

The IEC classifications of enclosures are shown in Figure 6-42. Note that the enclosure type is specified by the letters IP, followed by two numbers. The first number specifies protection of persons against access to hazardous parts and protection against penetration of solid foreign objects. The second number specifies protection against a variety of water conditions under specified test conditions. For example, an IP21 enclosure provides protection against objects up to 12mm in diameter and against vertically falling drops of water under specified test conditions.

FIGURE 6-40: Explosion proof enclosure.

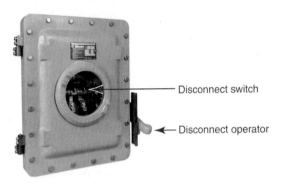

Disconnect switch

Disconnect operator

Courtesy of Rockwell Automation, Inc.

FIGURE 6-41: NEMA enclosure classifications.

Type	Usage	Service Conditions
1	Indoor	No unusual
3	Outdoor	Windblown dust, rain, sleet, and ice on enclosure
3R	Outdoor	Falling rain and ice on enclosure
4	Indoor/outdoor	Windblown dust and rain, splashing water, hose-directed water, and ice on enclosure
4X	Indoor/outdoor	Corrosion, windblown dust and rain, splashing water, hose-directed water, and ice on enclosure
6	Indoor/outdoor	Occasional temporary submersion at a limited depth
6P	Indoor/outdoor	Prolonged submersion at a limited depth
7	Indoor locations classified as Class I, Groups A, B, C, or D, as defined in the NEC®	Withstand and contain an internal explosion of specified gases, contain an explosion of specified gases, contain an explosion sufficiently so an explosive gas-air mixture in the atmosphere is not ignited
9	Indoor locations classified as Class II, Groups E or G, as defined in the NEC®	Dust
12	Indoor	Dust, falling dirt, and dripping noncorrosive liquids
13	Indoor	Dust, spraying water, oil, and noncorrosive coolant

FIGURE 6-42: IEC enclosure standard chart.

IP Ratings Definitions*	No protection	Protected against vertically falling drops of water (condensation)	Protected against dripping water with enclosure up to 15° from vertical	Protected against sprayed water up to 60° from vertical	Protected against sprayed water from all directions (limited ingress permitted)	Protected against low pressure water jets from all directions (limited ingress permitted)	Protected against strong jets of water from all directions	Protected against immersion up to one meter	Protected against long periods of immersion under pressure
	IP...0	IP...1	IP...2	IP...3	IP...4	IP...5	IP...6	IP...7	IP...8
IP0... No protection	IP00								
IP1... Protected against solid objects up to 50mm (accidental touch by hands)	IP10	IP11	IP12						
IP2... Protected against solid objects up to 12mm (fingers, knuckles)	IP20	IP21	IP22	IP23					
IP3... Protected against solid objects up to 2.5mm (tools, wires)	IP30	IP31	IP32	IP33	IP34				
IP4... Protected against solid objects up to 1mm (wires)	IP40	IP41	IP42	IP43	IP44				
IP5... Protected against dust (limited engress permitted)	IP50			IP53	IP54	IP55	IP56		
IP6... Totally protected against dust	IP60					IP65	IP66	IP67	

*The first IP number (left side of chart) is protection against solid objects. The second IP number (across top) is protection against liquids. The chart itself shows degrees of protection according to IEC 529.

6-9 TROUBLESHOOTING CONTACTORS AND MOTOR STARTERS

Contactors and motor starters are checked first in motor control systems because they are the point where the incoming power, load and control circuits are connected. Before addressing troubleshooting techniques and contactor and motor starter failures, let's look at some of the reasons why motors fail.

Motor Failures

Today's T-Frame motors introduced in 1964 are smaller and less expensive than older U-Frame models. However, T-Frame motors also have a lower tolerance for thermal overload since they're built with less copper and steel. Consequently, the overload relays used on T-Frame motors must have a faster response time than those used on U-Frames. Applying that added protection is a must if you want to get the most life from these new motors. Most manufacturers rate the life expectancy of a T-Frame motor at 25 years. However, they also tell you that each occurrence of a ten degree centigrade increase above the motor's insulation rating cuts that motor's life in half. NEMA controls were designed for use with U-frame motors and have simply been adapted to T-frame motors. IEC controls are engineered specifically for use with today's advanced motors, but can also be used with the older U-frames.

Recently the Electrical Research Association studied more than 9,000 damaged motors. From this sample, the group was able to identify the leading causes of motor failure. Figure 6-43 shows a pie chart, which highlights causes of motor failures. Note that only 10 percent of the motors studied failed as a result of old age. An astounding 44 percent of the failures are directly attributed to thermal overload or single phasing. Single phasing occurs when power is lost in one of the three phases supplying a three-phase motor. Instantly the current through the two remaining phases jumps significantly. Unless promptly disconnected, the two powered windings are soon destroyed from over current.

IEC technology directly addresses overload and temperature compensation. IEC overload relays shut down motors twice as fast as standard NEMA controls. Plus, IEC devices detect single-phase conditions and quickly shut down the motors in the event of this

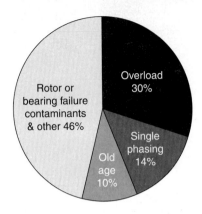

FIGURE 6-43: Leading causes of motor failure.

hazard. IEC overload relays detect single phasing and react before motors can be damaged. The bimetal strips in these devices monitor the current drawn through each of the three phases, bending a proportionate distance. If a phase is lost, the bimetal strip straightens and, using a double slide-bar ripping mechanism, instantly disconnects the motor from power. In addition, most IEC devices are equipped with automatic ambient temperature compensation, allowing them to continually monitor and adjust to surrounding temperatures. As a result, trip times remain constant regardless of conditions.

Troubleshooting Techniques

Contactors and motor starters are checked first in motor control systems because they are the point where the incoming power, plus load and control circuit are connected. Basic voltage and current readings are taken at a contactor or motor starter to determine where the problem lies. Some of the basic troubleshooting procedures for a motor starter apply to contactors because a motor starter is a contactor with an overload protection.

First, check the tightness of all terminals and bus-bar connections. Loose connections in the power circuit of contactors and motor starters can cause overheating, which leads to equipment malfunction or failure. Loose connections of power and control terminals cause system malfunctions. Loose grounding terminals lead to electrical shock and electromagnetic-generated interference. When troubleshooting a motor starter, use the following procedure:

1. Visually inspect the motor starter. Service or replace motor starters that show wear, heat damage, or exhibit burn marks due to arcing. Inspect the motor and the load for signs of an overload or other damage. Figure 6-44 shows burnt and pitted contacts due to arcing.

2. Reset the overload relay if there is no visual indication of damage, or replace the overload relay if there is visual indication of damage.

3. Observe the motor starter for several minutes if the motor runs after the overload relay is reset. The overload relay continues to open if an overload problem continues to exist.

4. Check the starter input voltages if resetting the overload relay does not start the motor. Check voltages on the path to the starter if the voltage reading is zero volts. The voltage is acceptable if the voltage reading is within the manufacturer's specified voltage range.

Figure 6-45 provides a list of observed symptoms for failed or faulty contactors and motor starters and possible reasons for the symptom to be investigated.

FIGURE 6-44: Contact damage from arcing and heat from switching high voltage and current.

Pitting and burning from arcing as contacts open

One pole on the lower half of a contact set

CRITICAL CONCEPTS

The need to know content from Chapter 6 is summarized in the following statements.

- The major difference between the NEMA and the IEC standards for contactors and motor starters is the sizing of the control device for a given motor or resistive load.
- The capacity of magnetic and manual motor starters is determined by the *current ratings* of their power contacts for *continuous* and *inrush* current conditions.
- Contacts used in motor starters are not flat, but rather shaped with a slight curve to their surface.
- The term *motor starter* implies that the manual starting switch, magnetic motor starter, or electronic motor control includes overload protection for the motor.
- NEMA magnetic contactors have *eleven sizes* from 00 to 9. Whereas IEC magnetic contactor and motor starters sizes are designed to be much more application specific with more sizes over the same range of application current requirements.
- Switching AC and DC current in power poles introduces the possibility of arcs when the switching contacts are opened and in some cases as the contacts closed.
- Arc suppressing devices, such as *arc chutes*, quickly extinguish arcs. Arc chutes are designed to quench the arc by dividing, confining and extinguishing the arc produced by each set of contacts.
- The power poles in the contactor carry the motor current, while other contacts, called *auxiliary contacts* or *electrical interlocks*, are used for the

FIGURE 6-45: Contactor and motor starter troubleshooting guide.

Observed Symptom	Possible Reason for Failure
Humming or loud buzzing noise	Magnetic pole faces misaligned; too low of voltage at the coil; pole face obstructed by foreign object, dirt or rust; shading coil broken
Contactor fails to drop out	Voltage to coil not being removed; worn or contaminated parts causing binding; contact poles sticking; mechanical interlock binding; too small a gap between armature and frame
Contactor fails to pull in	No coil voltage; too low of voltage; open coil; shorted coil; mechanical obstruction; excessive gap between armature and frame; loose coil connections
Contacts badly burned or welded	Too high of inrush current; over current protection set too high; load cycling too fast; shorted circuit; insufficient contact pressure; incorrect model of device
Nuisance tripping	Incorrect overload size; lack of temperature compensation; loose coil connections

control circuit. Normally open and normally closed auxiliary contacts function like other magnetic control relay devices.

- *Definite Purpose* contactors switch power for loads other than AC and DC motors. Such loads include: *lighting, heaters, capacitors, hydraulic elevators,* and *HVAC devices.*
- Contactors used for *lighting control systems* are constructed in the same manner as contactors used for motor starting. However, lighting circuits are single-phase and generally rated at 120 volts or 277 volts.
- *Manual motor starters* are hand-operated devices consisting of an on-off switch and motor overload protection.
- Manual motor starters are used to control small motors such as fractional horsepower and integral horsepower motors.
- Manual motor starters are selected on the number of phases, number of poles, voltage level and motor size.
- A magnetic motor starter is an electrically operated contactor with overload protection and uses an electromagnetic solenoid to open and close the starter contacts, which distinguishes a magnetic starter from a manual starter.
- Combination starters consist of a safety disconnect, short circuit and overload protection and magnetic motor starter placed in a common enclosure.
- Enclosures provide mechanical and electrical protection for the electrical worker and for the contactors and motor starters, protection from a variety of elements such as water, dust, oil and hazardous environmental conditions.
- NEMA and IEC classifies enclosures based on usage and service conditions—NEMA by a number or a number and a letter, IEC by the letters IP, followed by two numbers.

QUESTIONS

1. Describe the differences between NEMA and IEC contactor and motor starters for physical size, cost and contacts.
2. Describe the differences between NEMA and IEC motor starters sizes.
3. Describe the differences between magnet contactor, defined purpose magnetic contactor and magnetic starter.
4. What is the purpose of auxiliary contacts?
5. How does an arc chute suppress arcing?
6. What are the differences between a fractional horsepower motor and an integral horsepower motor?
7. What are the bases of selecting a manual motor starter?
8. What are difference between a manual motor starter and a magnetic motor starter?
9. How does overload protection in a motor starter protect the motor?
10. What is inrush current?
11. Compare eutectic alloy to bimetallic strip overloads.
12. Describe the operation of the magnetic overload relay.
13. What does the service factor indicate?
14. What are the advantages of an electronic overload relay?
15. What factors determine the size of an overload protection?
16. Describe thermistor and thermodisc overload protection.
17. Describe how NEMA and IEC specify enclosures for motor starters.
18. What are the causes of motor failures?

Timing Devices

GOALS AND OBJECTIVES

The primary goals for this chapter are to identify timing devices, and to describe the operation of and applications for these devices in manufacturing systems. In addition, troubleshooting tips and procedures for typical timer failure modes are presented.

After completing this chapter you should be able to:

1. Describe the *four* timer configurations and identify the associated symbols.
2. Identify and describe the components of mechanical timers such as the *synchronous clock timer* and the *dashpot timer.*
3. Identify and discuss the operation of *non-programmable* electronic timers such as the *on-delay* and *off-delay* timers.
4. Describe troubleshooting techniques for mechanical and electronic timers.

7-1 INTRODUCTION TO TIMERS

Timers serve a critical function in motor control by *managing events* in industrial processes. Timers enable process events that are *started* and *stopped* at different intervals. They eliminate the labor intense effort of manually controlling the time of each process operation. Timers reduce the need for multiple machine operators, and some processes are managed entirely with one or more timing devices. Timers are available in many different types and configurations to meet a wide variety of system requirements. The *number* and *type* of timing functions present and the *mechanical, electrical,* or *electronic* technique used to establish the time base divide industrial timers into three general categories. Timed events are managed with *dashpot controlled* timers (mechanical timers), *synchronous clock* timers (electrical timers), and *solid-state* timers (electronic timers). *Solid state* timers offer *programmable* and *non-programmable models* with *single-function* and *multifunction* operation.

The mechanical, electrical, and on- and off-delay non-programmable solid state timers are covered in this chapter. The multifunction type non-programmable timers and the programmable timers are discussed in Chapter 13.

Figure 7-1 illustrates the three types of timers covered in this chapter. While the older style mechanical and clock type timers are used in production systems, the solid-state or electronic timer is rapidly replacing the legacy models. *Mechanical* and *electronic timers* are often called *timing relays,* so both terms are used in this text.

FIGURE 7-1: Overview of industrial timing devices.

(a) Mechanical pneumatic timer   (b) Electrical synchronous clock timer   (c) Single function electronic timer

Courtesy of Siemens and Omron Corporation.

Mechanical versus Electronic Timers

A large number of mechanical and electronic timing relays are used in industrial control, and the electrical worker must understand how each functions. Both relays produce a time delay. However, the mechanical timing relay typically uses a pneumatic device, and the slow release of air produces the delay. An electrical solenoid is normally used to activate the pneumatic device. As a result, the mechanical timing relay has two input terminals to initiate and end the time delay process. In a timing relay, multiple configurations of contacts are controlled by the delay device. Changes to these NO and NC contacts are used to energize and de-energize electrical process devices.

In contrast, the electronic timing relay uses an electronic circuit to produce the time delay. The addition of the electronics gives the electronic timing relay greater flexibility. For example, both solid state switches and mechanical contacts are available to control process devices. In addition, electronic timing relays offer time delays over a greater range and with far better accuracy. They also have better reliability due to fewer or no mechanical parts, and have many more timing options available. Another difference in the electronic timing relay is the presence of two trigger mechanisms for the time delay. Some electronic timing relays have two inputs, often labeled A1 and A2, that power the electronic timer and start the timing process. Others have the same two terminals, A1 and A2, but their sole function is to provide power to the electronics. Then a third input is used to start the timing process.

Timer Functions

The reaction of the timer's *output* to a change in the *input* is set by the timer function. Timer manufacturers offer a range of output functions; however, the timer functions available from most suppliers include: *on-delay, off-delay, on- and off-delay, one-shot, fleeting off delay,* and *repeat cycle (flasher).* While all are used in process timing applications, the on-delay and off-delay timer functions are used most often and are the ones discussed in this chapter.

Understanding mechanical and electronic timing relay operation in a complex production system is often difficult because timers *delay the start* of some processes and *delay the termination* of others. As a result, mastering the application and troubleshooting of the numerous timers used in manufacturing is a challenge for electrical workers. Understanding *timing relays* and *timers* starts with the terms used to describe the timing functions and the control symbols used to represent them in control diagrams. The two most common timing functions are *on-delay* and *off-delay.*

On-Delay Timers

The *on-delay timer* is defined as follows:

An on-delay timer is a device with a preset time period between energizing the timer or applying the input signal and the action of the timer output contacts. During the timing period no change occurs in the timer output contacts.

FIGURE 7-2: On-delay timing relay contact operations.

Timer Diagram			Description
Timer status	ENERGIZED	DE-ENERGIZED	When the timer's energized, the timed-delay starts. When the On-Delay timed-delay is complete, the contacts change state from open to closed. When the timer's de-energized, the contacts go back to open.
	On-Delay		
Contact status	OPEN / CLOSED	OPEN	
(a) Normally Open, Timed Closed (NOTC)			
Timer status	ENERGIZED	DE-ENERGIZED	When the timer's energized, the timed-delay starts. When the On-Delay timed-delay is complete, the contacts change state from closed to open. When the timer's de-energized, the contacts go back to closed.
	On-Delay		
Contact status	CLOSED / OPEN	CLOSED	
(b) Normally Closed, Timed Open (NCTO)			
Instantaneous contact	OPEN / CLOSED	OPEN	The instantaneous contacts close, only when the timer is energized as indicated in (a) and (b).

The operation of the on-delay function is similar on mechanical and electronic timing relays without a remote trigger. When a remote trigger is present, power is applied to the electronic timer and timing is triggered through the external trigger input. The on-delay timer is used to apply or remove power to a load at a preset time after the on-delay timing relay is energized. For example, this timing function is used in pumping systems to delay the start of a large pump motor until the pumps are fully primed.

On-delay timer function is also called *delay on energize (DOE)*, *delay on make*, and *delay on operate*. These names identify the type of control provided by this timing relay. Namely, the delay starts when the timer is activated, and the output contacts change after the delay.

Many dashpot timers have DPST timed contacts; however, clock timers usually have SPST contacts. In addition, timing relays often have one or more *instantaneous* contacts with multiple configurations. Instantaneous contacts activate when the timing relay is energized and return to their original state when the timing relay is de-energized. The contact operates like a *control relay* contact or an *auxiliary* contact on a contactor; as a result, some manufacturers call them *auxiliary contacts*.

Figure 7-2 illustrates the operation of the on-delay timer. The Timer Status line indicates the energized condition of the timer input or the energized state of a timer with a remote trigger. Read the descriptions in the figure for the operation of on-delay NO contacts, Figure 7-2(a), on-delay NC contacts, Figure 7-2(b), and instantaneous contacts.

The notation NOTC (*normally open timed closed*) is given to the NO contact operation, and NCTO (*normally closed timed open*) is given to the NC contact operation. Figure 7-3(a) illustrates an on-delay *mechanical* timer with *NEMA* control symbols. Figure 7-3(b) shows an *electronic* on-delay timer with *IEC* control symbols. Note that the NOTC and NCTO contacts are identified in each timer relay coil and contact drawing. Figure 7-3(c) provides the NEMA and IEC standard coil and contact symbols for on-delay timing relays and their letter codes.

Off-Delay Timers

The *off-delay timer* is defined as follows:

An off-delay timer is a device with a preset time period that starts after the input signal is removed from an electronic timing relay or power is removed from a mechanical timing relay. The timer output contacts change when the input signal or external trigger is applied to an electronic timer or power is applied to the mechanical timer. The contacts remain in the changed state until after the timing period.

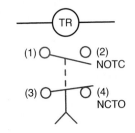

(a) NEMA on-delay timing relay
wiring diagram for the pneumatic
timer in Figure 7-1(a)

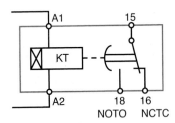

(b) IEC on-delay timing relay
wiring diagram for the electronic
timer in Figure 7-1(c)

Letter Code	NEMA		IEC
Coil NEMA – TR IEC – KT	TR		KT / KT
Contacts NEMA – TR IEC – KT	NO	NC	NO and NC
	NOTC	NCTO	NCTO / NOTC

(c) NEMA and IEC on-delay timing relay coil and
contact symbols plus the letter codes

As the definition indicates, electronic off-delay timing relays have power applied continuously and trigger the off-delay timer with a separate input trigger signal. Also, the mechanical off-delay timer uses the coil contacts to trigger the delay as in the on-delay operation. The timed contacts of the off-delay timer *immediately change* state when the timer is energized or initialized and return to their original state after the set time delay has elapsed. The *total time* for the *activated* timed contacts includes the *time* the timing relay is *energized* or *triggered* plus the set *time delay* period. For example, this timing function is used to sequence the shutdown cycle for motors in machine drive systems. In these applications, off-delay timers with varying delay times turn motors off in an orderly sequence.

The off-delay timer function is also called *delay on de-energize (DODE)*, *delay on break*, and *delay on release*.

The illustration in Figure 7-4(a) describes the operation of a mechanical off-delay timer. Figure 7-4(b) illustrates the operation of an electronic timing relay and indicates the interaction of the external trigger and the off-time delay function. Figure 7-5 indicates the wiring and symbols.

The notation NOTO (*normally open timed open*) is used for the NO contact operation, and NCTC (*normally closed timed closed*) is used for the NC contact operation. Figure 7-5(a) illustrates an off-delay *mechanical* timer with *NEMA* control symbols. Figure 7-5(b) shows an *electronic* off-delay timer with *IEC* control symbols. The IEC symbol shows the B1 external trigger input and separate power inputs A1 and A2. The NOTO and NCTC contacts are identified on each timer relay coil and contact drawing. Figure 7-5(c) provides the NEMA and IEC standard coil and contact symbols for off-delay timing relays and their letter codes.

Components drawn on motor control drawings are in their *de-energized* or "*on the shelf*" state. This state is often called the "*normal*" state. The inclusion of timers in machine control often adds some confusion to the analysis of the operation. As a result, electrical workers must *carefully analyze* machine operations that include on- and off-delay timing devices. Learn these terms now because they are used in this chapter

FIGURE 7-4: Off-delay timing relay contact operation diagrams for pneumatic and electronic timing relays.

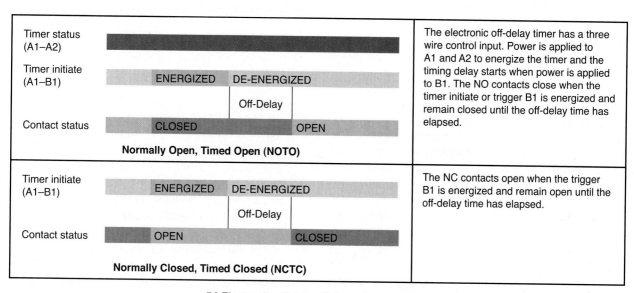

(a) Pneumatic off-delay timing relay operation

(b) Electronic off-delay timing relay operation

and are the foundation for more complex timers covered in Sections 2 and 3.

The term *timing relay* implies that off-delay and on-delay timers have contact configurations such as *SPDT* or *DPDT* that change their state based on input conditions and the timer value. In addition, they have options for *instantaneous* contacts that operate independent of the timer value. *Contact voltage* ratings generally range from 120 to 600V AC and 115 to 250V DC. *Continuous* AC current of 10 amps AC and up to 0.5 amps DC are common. The *coils* are generally rated for 24 and 120V AC. The electronic models have better *accuracy* and *repeatability* than the mechanical devices. Electronic timing relays offer accuracy of ± 10 percent of the range's maximum value and repeatability of ± 0.2 percent of range's maximum value.

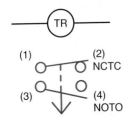

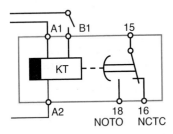

(a) NEMA off-delay timing relay wiring diagram for the pneumatic timer in Figure 7-1(a)

(b) IEC off-delay timing relay wiring diagram for the electronic timer in Figure 7-1(c)

Letter Code	NEMA		IEC
Coil NEMA – TR IEC – KT	TR		KT
Contacts NEMA – TR IEC – KT	NO	NC	NO and NC
	NOTO	NCTC	NCTC NOTO

(c) NEMA and IEC off-delay timing relay coil and contact symbols plus the letter codes

Electrical workers use device *graphic symbols* to recognize *on-delay* and *off-delay* timing relays on control diagrams. After identifying the symbol, an understanding of the operation of NOTC, NCTO, NOTO, and NCTC contacts is necessary. Finally, analysis is performed to determine the source of a problem or the procedure for a system upgrade. Following this process is demanding because mastery of all of the timing relay concepts is required. The follow steps aid in mastering the process:

A. Learn the NEMA and IEC symbols for on- and off-delay type timing relays.

- Imagine the relay symbols in Figures 7-4 and 7-5 placed on a flat surface. The ∧ would stand ON the surface, and so it is the ON-delay. The ∨ would fall OFF the surface, and so it is the OFF-delay.

- Associate ON-delay with the delay starting when timers are turned ON (energized). Associate OFF-delay with the delay starting when mechanical timers are turned OFF (de-energized) or when electronic timers have the external trigger signal removed.

B. Learn the names of the contacts for on- and off-delay type timing relays.

- On-delay has NOTC and NCTO—off-delay has NOTO and NCTC. Notice that both start off NO and NC, and the second two letters are either TC or TO. *No* letters are repeated in the on-delay timer (NOTC and NCTO), but the O and C are *repeated* in the off-delay timer (NOTO and NCTC).

C. Learn the timing function of on- and off-delay timer contacts (NOTC, NCTO, NOTO, and NCTC)

- The first two letters, NO and NC, indicate the state of the timing contact before the timing relay is activated. NO timing contacts are open and NC timing contacts are closed.

- The information communicated by the second two letters depends on the type of timing relay.

- For an on-delay (timing starts when timer is energized), the second letters indicate the state of the timing contacts after the time period and until the timer is de-energized.

- For an off-delay it is the state of the timing contacts after the time period. However, timed contacts change when the timer is energized (mechanical) or externally triggered (electronic). Removal of the trigger or power starts the delay time. The contacts remain changed until after the timing period has elapsed.

7-2 MECHANICAL TIMERS

There are two mechanical timers that are used in industrial applications—the *synchronous timer* and the *dashpot timer*. Both timers use non-electronic means to produce a timing interval.

Synchronous Timer

The *synchronous timer* is a timing device that opens and closes a contact using the position of the analog clock hand. Synchronous timers are available with SPST or SPDT contacts with flush, surface or DIN rail mounting configuration. Figure 7-6 shows a surface mount synchronous timer with a dial face and descriptions of the device's features. Note the manual switch and the ON/OFF operator in the figure. The *off/auto/on* manual switch selects the operation mode. *Trippers* are gold and silver pegs inserted on the periphery of the rotating dial. As the dial rotates, the trippers contact the *on/off operator* at the upper left. The gold tripper closes the contact, the silver opens it. This tripper color code permits a quick glance at the clock face to programmed times. A red power indicator is available on some models.

The on and off duration for the synchronous time control is determined by the speed at which the dial rotates. The motor that drives the clock is AC operated and maintains its speed based on the frequency of the AC power source. If the AC power is interrupted, the time is lengthened by the time of the interruption, and the timer must be manually reset to insure proper operation.

The resolution of the timer is determined by the slot increments of the dial face. This timer has 15 minute intervals; therefore, the best resolution is 15 minute increments. This lower resolution limits the use of these timers in industrial processes. The timer *accuracy* is based on the frequency accuracy of the power source. The synchronous timer is well suited for work-site lighting and sprinkler system control where highly accurate starting and stopping points are not required.

Dashpot Timers

Dashpot timers are one of the oldest style of timers in uses today; however, electronic timers are used in most new designs. Dashpot timers are timing devices that provide a time delay by controlling the rate of fluid flow through a constricted orifice. Think of the narrow neck of an hourglass. The diameter of the neck controls the rate at which sand flows from the top chamber to the lower chamber. The smaller the diameter of the neck, the longer time it takes for the sand to reach the lower chamber. The diameter of the orifice in a dashpot timer is either fixed or adjustable. The adjustment is typically accomplished with a needle valve or a thumbwheel knob. The fluids used in

FIGURE 7-6: Synchronous timer.

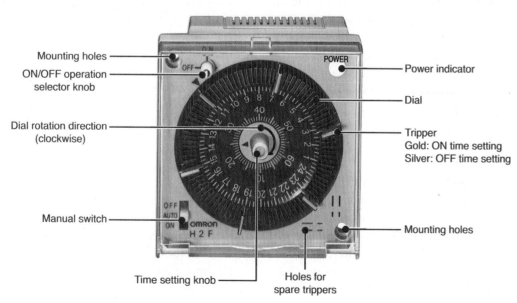

Courtesy of Omron Corporation.

Figure 7-7 illustrates a work-site sprinkling system where the synchronous timer is located in the wall-mounted control panel. The synchronous timer in the exploded view controls the length of time that the sprinklers are on. When the gold tripper on the clock dial contacts the on/off oper-ator, the contact is closed, and the sprinklers turn on. When the silver tripper on the clock dial contacts the on/off oper-ator, the contact opens, and the sprinklers turn off. Note that the sprinklers cycle on and off three times in 24 hours.

FIGURE 7-7: Sprinkler system control with clock timer.

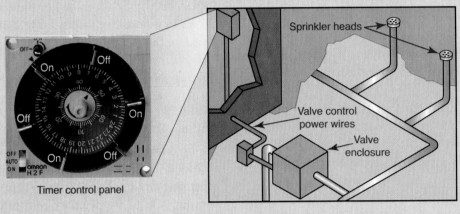

Timer control panel

dashpot timers are air and oil. Figure 7-1(a) illustrates an air type dashpot timer.

Pneumatic Style Dashpot Timers—The time delay of dashpot timers is mechanically produced: however, electromagnetic coils are used to initiate the timing process. The diagram in Figure 7-8 illustrates the operation of a pneumatic dashpot timing relay. Note that the needle valve adjusts the size of the orifice. When the size of the orifice is decreased, inlet air flows more slowly through the orifice and extends the length of the time delay. By increasing the size of the orifice, the time delay is reduced as air flows more quickly through the orifice. Pneumatic timers are usually accurate within a few seconds. They also have narrow timing ranges with settings from 0.1 to 180 seconds and are most accurate near their median range.

When the solenoid in Figure 7-8 is energized, the rod pushes against the bellows, and air is forced out of the bellows through the check valve. When the solenoid is de-energized, the rod is pulled away from the bellows, and the spring attempts to returns the bellows to its original position. However, the bellows expansion is limited by the rate of air flow through the air inlet. The rate at which the air enters is dependent on the position of the needle valve. When the bellows

FIGURE 7-8: Operation of pneumatic dashpot off-delay timing relay.

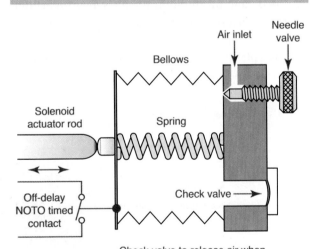

Check valve to release air when timer is energized and the spring compresses and bellows collapses

returns to its original position, the NOTO contacts open. Therefore, the NOTO contacts are closed while the solenoid is energized and for time delay set by the position of the needle valve.

Dashpot timers are manufactured with coil volt-ages ranging from 24 volts to 480 volts with 24 volt

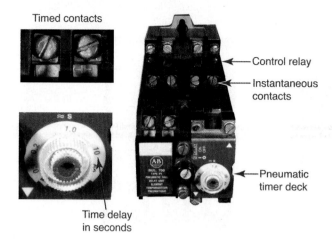

FIGURE 7-9: Pneumatic timing relays.

Timed contacts

Control relay

Instantaneous contacts

Pneumatic timer deck

Time delay in seconds

and 120 volt the most common. The accuracy and repeatability of pneumatic timers is affected by air density, which is changed by heat, humidity and barometric pressure. As a result, air quality changes the flow rate through the needle valve and the time delay value. Figure 7-1(a) shows the older style dashpot pneumatic timing relay. The timer in Figure 7-9 is a newer model pneumatic timer that mounts atop a control relay. The control relay's standard NO and NC contacts act as instantaneous contacts, and the mounted timer has a set of timed contacts shown in the enlarged view. When the timer is attached to control relay the combination is consider a timing relay device.

Fluid Style Dashpot Timers—Fluid type dashpot timers use oil instead of air with an orifice between the holding reservoir for the oil and a diaphragm assembly. Fluid types are more accurate than pneumatic timers because the oil density is only affected by temperature. However, the oil type is more sensitive to contaminants, and so the oil must be free from dirt and foreign substances for proper operation.

7-3 NON-PROGRAMMABLE ELECTRONIC TIMERS

The electronic or solid-state timer is a timing device whose time delay is generated by electronic components enclosed in the device. The solid-state timer provides a very accurate timed delay, some with an

accuracy of 0.01 second. The time delay ranges from fractions of a second to hundreds of minutes. They are well-suited for timing events in industrial processes. Many solid state timers are designed as plug-in modules for quick replacement. Solid state timers are much more accurate than dashpot timers because they have no moving parts such as bellows, which are affected by heat, humidity or pressure. Electronic timers can replace synchronous timers and dashpot timers in most applications. Figure 7-10(a) shows a solid state timer side view with timer data and wiring diagram. Note that the dial on the top, Figure 7-10(c), of the unit is used to set the time delay. Terminals A and B are the input power lines for the timer. The timer has DPDT contacts.

There is a solid state timer to meet almost every condition and requirement in commercial and industrial motor control applications. They are available in a wide variety of input voltages, mounting configurations and timing functions. A common mounting configuration is the *plug-style* base that accepts round or blade-type terminations. The plug-style bases are usually manufactured in *8-* and *11-pin* configurations. Timers without external triggers usually have 8-pin bases and timers with external trigger requirements use the 11-pin configuration. Figure 7-12(a) shows an on-delay solid state timer with a plug-style 8-pin base. The knob on the top of the timer is used to set the time delay on the 1.8 to 180 second *absolute* scale. The wiring diagram for the timer is on the side of the case and also in Figure 7-12(b). The on-delay is triggered from the timer power or input pins 2 and 7. Figure 7-12(c) shows the connections to an 11-pin timer base when an external trigger is present. The term "dry-contact" on the external control switch indicates that the external switch contacts must have low current switching characteristics. The timer is powered at pins 2 and 10, and closing the control switch initiates the timer. When the control switch is opened the off-delay time delay action starts. Most timers work on AC or DC power.

Single function timers, like the timing relay in Figure 7-12(a), rarely have instantaneous contacts. As with most electronic devices, the contacts of solid state timers have limited current carrying capacity, usually less than 10 amperes. Solid state timers are manufactured with single and multiple timing ranges and timing functions.

FIGURE 7-10: Electronic timing relay.

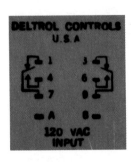

(a) Plug type on-delay electronic timing relay

(b) Plug type wiring diagram

(c) Top view of plug type electronic timing relay mounted in base

TECH NOTES

Timer models have a range of time delay values. The list of ranges in Figure 7-11(a) is an example of the options available. The dial on the face of the timer is often a relative scale dial with a scale from 0 to 1 or 0 to 10. Figure 7-11(b) illustrates a relative scale dial. The following procedure is used to select a time delay with the relative scale dial. The 0 to 1 scale represents 0 to 100% of the time range present in the relay. For example, a 25 second delay on a timer with range of 0.05 to 1 minute is determined as follows.

1. Divide the desired activation time (25 seconds) by the maximum time limit of the relay (60 seconds). Make sure units of both numbers are the same.

2. $25 \div 60 = 0.416$

3. Rotate the setting knob to just past the 0.4 mark in Figure 7-12(b). If the dial is 0 to 10, then set it just past the 4. Set the dial at 41.6 if the scale is 0 to 100. The plug type relay in Figure 7-10 has relative dial on the top used to set the time for the delay time-bases available.

FIGURE 7-11: Sample timing ranges and relative dial for time delay value.

Timing range
0.05...1 sec
0.15...3 sec
0.5...10 sec
1.5...30 sec
0.05...1 min
0.15...3 min
0.5...10 min
1.5...30 min
0.05...1 hour
0.15...3 hour
0.5...10 hour
3.0...60 hour

(a) Sample electronic timer timing ranges

(b) Relative dial for setting time delay value

FIGURE 7-12: Solid-state timer with plug or tube style base.

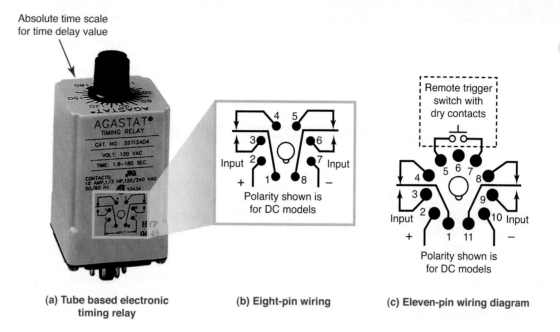

(a) Tube based electronic timing relay

(b) Eight-pin wiring

(c) Eleven-pin wiring diagram

7-4 TROUBLESHOOTING TIMING DEVICES

Troubleshooting timers includes three basic steps— (1) Visually inspect for damage or deterioration, (2) verify that the correct power is applied to the timer, and (3) verify proper timer contact operation. Electronic timers are non-repairable devices, but some dashpot timer failures are repairable. If the timer is determined to be bad, then it is replaced. The timers in this chapter have similar troubleshooting techniques, but the synchronous timer, the dashpot timer and the electronic timers have some unique failure modes that are addressed.

Troubleshooting Synchronous Timers

The synchronous timer opens and closes a contact depending on the position of the hands or dial of a clock. If the timer is suspect, first verify that the clock hands or dial is rotating. If it is not rotating or rotating at the wrong speed, then replace the timer if:

1. Nothing is obstructing its rotation such as dirt or a grime buildup
2. The input AC voltage is the correct level and frequency.

If it rotates, then perform the following steps.

1. Verify that the voltage across open contacts is the switched voltage. If power to the contacts is removed, then a digital multimeter (DMM) indicates if continuity is present or not present.
2. Verify that the voltage across closed contacts is near zero. A higher reading indicates excessive resistance. If power to the contacts is removed, then a digital multimeter (DMM) indicates if continuity is present or not present.

Figure 7-13 provides a list of observed symptoms for failed or faulty synchronous timers and the possible reasons for the symptom that should be investigated.

Troubleshooting Dashpot Timers

Dashpot timers provide a time delay by controlling the rate of fluid flow through a constricted orifice. Proper fluid flow is key for the operation of the dashpot timer. If oil filled timer is suspect, replace the unit. If a pneumatic timer is suspected, cycle the bellows

FIGURE 7-13: Synchronous timer troubleshooting guide.

Observed Symptom	Possible Reason for Failure
Failure in the insulation of control wires	Moisture inside timer enclosure; corrosive fumes; excessive heat from other maintenance work in area; voltage surges or short circuits; foreign material build up on insulation material
Burned contacts or contacts welded close	Incorrect fuse or circuit breaker size; burned or welded contacts from inductive loads produced excessive arcing or excessive contact current; severe vibration; contact ratings insufficient for application
Failure to time out	Mechanical binding in motor or gears driving clock hands; worn parts in clock mechanism; bad or damaged motor; no voltage at motor terminals; excessive dirt or foreign material build up.

Timing devices are used in time-based control systems to manage the operation of energy-consuming loads in a building. The management involves turning loads on and off at specific times and adjusting time schedules for loads in various areas of a building. Time-based-control includes seven-day settings, daily multiple-time-period scheduling, and timed overrides.

Seven-day settings allow the electrical worker to individually set system on-off times for each day of the week.

Daily multiple-time-period scheduling allows the system to accommodate unusual building occupancy. The heating-cooling system, the lighting and other loads are scheduled to operate during multiple independent time periods. Finally, timed overrides allow the occupants of a building to change a zone from an unoccupied mode to an occupied mode for temporary usage. An important advantage timed operation provides is the ability to balance power loads more effectively for energy cost savings.

and replace if necessary. Also, cycle the needle valve from the shortest delay, fully out, to the longest delay, nearly fully in. Cycle the timer several times to clear any obstructions affecting the timing.

If the timer contacts are not changing state, then perform the following steps.

1. Verify that nothing is obstructing the needle valve movement such as dirt or a grime buildup.
2. Verify the input coil voltage is the correct level.
3. Open load contacts or terminals should have the voltage being switched across them. Other readings indicate contacts not opening or supply voltage problems. A continuity check is the preferred method, but power leads need to be removed to perform the checks with a DMM.
4. Closed load contacts or terminals should have a near zero the voltage measurement across them. A higher reading indicates excessive contact resistance. A continuity check is the preferred method, but power leads need to be removed to perform the checks with a DMM.

Figure 7-14 provides a list of observed symptoms for failed or faulty dashpot timers and the possible reasons for the symptom that should be investigated.

Troubleshooting Electronic Timers

The electronic timer generates its time delay by electronic components enclosed in the device. Defective electronic timers are just replaced. These troubleshooting tips are applicable to the on-delay and off-delay timers. If the timer is suspect, first verify the time-delay adjustment knobs turn freely and are free of dirt and grime buildup. The following troubleshooting procedure applies when the timer is suspect.

1. Verify the correct voltage is supplied to the control circuit that drives the timer.
2. Verify the correct input voltage to the timer.
3. Open load contacts or terminals should have the voltage being switched across them. Other readings indicate contacts not opening or supply voltage problems.

FIGURE 7-14: Dashpot timer troubleshooting guide.

Observed Symptom	Possible Reason for Failure
Failure in the insulation of control wires	Moisture inside timer enclosure; corrosive fumes; excessive heat from other maintenance work in area; voltage surges or short circuits; foreign material build up on insulation material
Burned contacts or contacts welded close	Incorrect fuse or circuit breaker size; burned or welded contacts from inductive loads produced excessive arcing or excessive contact current; severe vibration; contact ratings insufficient for application
Failure to time out or reset	Leaking bellows, mechanical binding in mechanism; worn parts; foreign material in needle valve air passage; shorted or open solenoid, no solenoid voltage; excessive dirt or foreign material build up
Sluggish timing operation	Environmental conditions—temperature, humidity, and barometric pressure—are not within specification

FIGURE 7-15: Electronic timer troubleshooting guide.

Observed Symptom	Possible Reason for Failure
Failure in the insulation of control wires	Moisture inside timer enclosure; corrosive fumes; excessive heat from other maintenance work in area; voltage surges or short circuits; foreign material build up on insulation material
Burned contacts or contacts welded close	Incorrect fuse or circuit breaker size; burned or welded contacts from inductive loads produced excessive arcing or excessive contact current; severe vibration; contact ratings insufficient for application
Overheating	Too high ambient temperature; moisture in enclosure; excessive load current; power voltage not within specifications

4. Closed load contacts or terminals should have a near zero the voltage measurement across them. A higher reading indicates output solid state device failure.

Figure 7-15 provides a list of observed symptoms for failed or faulty electronic timers and the possible reasons for the symptom that should be investigated.

CRITICAL CONCEPTS

The need-to-know content from Chapter 7 is summarized in the following statement.

- The normally closed, timed open (NCTO) contact configuration means that when the timer is turned on, the time delay starts. When the timed-delay is complete, the contacts change from closed to open. When the timer is turned off, the contacts return to the closed position.

- The normally open, timed closed (NOTC) contact configuration means that when the timer is turned on, the timed-delay starts. When the timed-delay is complete, the contacts change from open to closed. When the timer is turned off, the contacts return to the open position.

- The off-delay electronic timer has power applied to the electronics and a trigger signal used to initiate the timer and start the time delay. The contacts change state when the trigger signal is active. They remain in the changed state after the trigger signal is deactivated for the duration of the set delay. After the delay period the contacts return to their original position.

- The synchronous timer is a timing device that opens and closes a contact depending on the position of the hands or dial of a clock.

- The dashpot timers are timing devices that provide a time delay by controlling the rate of fluid flow through a constricted orifice.
- The on-delay timer is a timing device on which a set time delay is initiated when the timer is turned on. When the set time delay elapses, the contacts change positions.

QUESTIONS

1. Describe how the timer contacts operate for the NOTC configuration.
2. Describe how the timer contacts operate for the NCTO configuration.
3. Describe how the timer contacts operate for the NOTO configuration.
4. Describe how the timer contacts operate for the NCTC configuration.
5. How does a synchronous timer operate?
6. What is the basis of the accuracy of a synchronous timer?
7. Describe the operation of a dashpot timer.
8. In dashpot timers, what is the advantage of using oil rather than air as the flowing fluid?
9. Why are electronic timers well-suited for timing events in industrial processes?
10. Describe the operation of an on-delay timer.
11. Describe the operation of an off-delay timer.

CHAPTER 8

Control Diagrams and Drawings

GOALS AND OBJECTIVES

The primary goals for this chapter are to identify and differentiate between wiring diagrams, schematic diagrams, ladder diagrams, and logic functions in ladder drawings and to describe the functions of each drawing.

After completing this chapter, you will be able to:

1. Identify and describe the purpose and the function of wiring diagrams.
2. Identify and describe the purpose and the function of schematic diagrams.
3. Identify and describe the purpose and the function of ladder diagrams and the associated numbering systems.
4. Identify and describe the purpose and the function of logic functions in ladder drawings.

8-1 WIRING DIAGRAMS

Wiring diagrams illustrate the physical connection between the electrical components in a machine or production system. When possible, wiring diagrams show the *actual locations* of components in the circuit. For example, in Figure 8-1(c), the dashed rectangle around the temperature and power switch indicates that they are both in the temperature control box. Note that the pictorial for the heater is shown in Figure 8-1(a) and the NEMA symbols as shown in Figure 8-1(b).

Manufacturers usually include wiring diagrams as part of the electrical equipment's documentation. The wiring diagram in Figure 8-1(c) is relatively simple, but a production machine's wiring diagram is complex; as a result wiring diagrams are rarely used to determine circuit operation or for troubleshooting. However, wiring diagrams are widely used by electrical

FIGURE 8-1: Pictorial and wiring diagram.

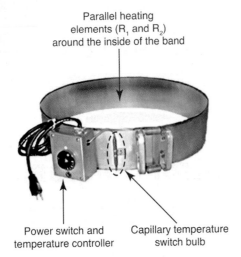

Parallel heating elements (R₁ and R₂) around the inside of the band

Power switch and temperature controller

Capillary temperature switch bulb

(a) Pictorial diagram of a 50 gallon drum heater

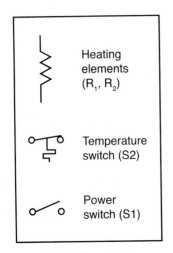

Heating elements (R_1, R_2)

Temperature switch (S2)

Power switch (S1)

(b) NEMA symbols

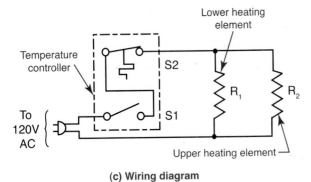

Temperature controller

Lower heating element

S2

S1

To 120V AC

R_1

R_2

Upper heating element

(c) Wiring diagram

workers when *installing* and *maintaining* electrical equipment.

8-2 SCHEMATIC DIAGRAMS

Schematic diagrams use graphic symbols to show connections between components and functions of an electrical circuit. These diagrams do not show the *physical relationship* between electrical components or the *physical size* or *appearance* of the components. Schematic diagrams are essential when troubleshooting because they enable the electrical worker to trace a circuit paths without regard to *size, shape,* or *location* of the components. Figure 8-2 illustrates the schematic drawing for the drum heater in Figure 8-1(a). Note that the components are drawn so that series and parallel current paths are easily identified for electrical analysis. Also, the NEMA symbol drawing is in Figure 8-2(a), and the IEC is in Figure 8-2(b).

FIGURE 8-2: Heater circuit schematics.

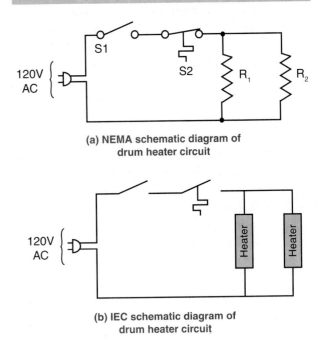

120V AC

S1

S2

R_1

R_2

(a) NEMA schematic diagram of drum heater circuit

120V AC

Heater

Heater

(b) IEC schematic diagram of drum heater circuit

8-3 ONE-LINE DIAGRAMS

One-line diagrams (OLD) or *single-line diagrams* (SLD) cover a board spectrum of electrical drawings. Some of the graphic symbols used in these diagrams are illustrated in Figure 8-3. For example, OLDs are used for: *power grids over large regions, power substations, service entrance to building,* and *machine control power flow.* Most of these OLDs consist of *single lines* and *graphic symbols* that illustrate the relative locations and electrical interconnections of elements used in assembling the power system. These elements include: *generators, transformers, transmission and distribution lines, circuit breakers, power control centers, disconnects, junction boxes, loads,* and *motors. Power riser diagrams* are one example of OLDs.

A one-line diagram is a simplified notation for representing a three-phase power OLD system. Figure 8-4 shows an *OLD* or *power riser* for a service entrance to a building. Showing all three phases would create a complex drawing with great detail that offers little potential advantage in describing the total system power flow. One conductor is used to represent all three phases; as a result, it is a form of block diagram graphically depicting the paths for power flow between the system elements. Use the OLD symbols in Figure 8-3 to identify the items in the power riser in Figure 8-4.

The arrangement of control elements are shown as a one line diagram in Figure 8-5. Each control element is annotated with its function such as chipper and feed conveyor. Note that the drawing shows the type and size of raceways between the control elements such as the conduit size between the chipper and feed conveyor. In addition, wire sizes, color, number of conductors and nomenclature are often shown.

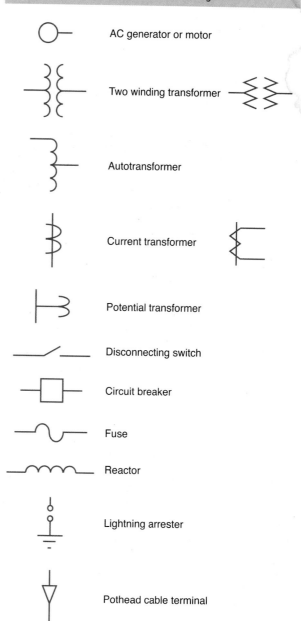

FIGURE 8-3: Symbols used in one-line diagrams.

AC generator or motor

Two winding transformer

Autotransformer

Current transformer

Potential transformer

Disconnecting switch

Circuit breaker

Fuse

Reactor

Lightning arrester

Pothead cable terminal

8-4 LADDER DIAGRAMS

Ladder diagrams illustrate the electrical *relationship* between all components in a control circuit. Electrical workers use ladder diagrams to *analyze* machine and process control circuits and to determine the *interac-* tion between control devices. While *physical placement* and *relationship* between devices is not identified in ladder diagrams, these diagrams are the most widely used motor control drawings for control circuit analysis.

Ladder diagrams, Figure 8-6, are characterized by two vertical lines, called *rails,* and many horizontal

FIGURE 8-4: One-line diagram for service entrance.

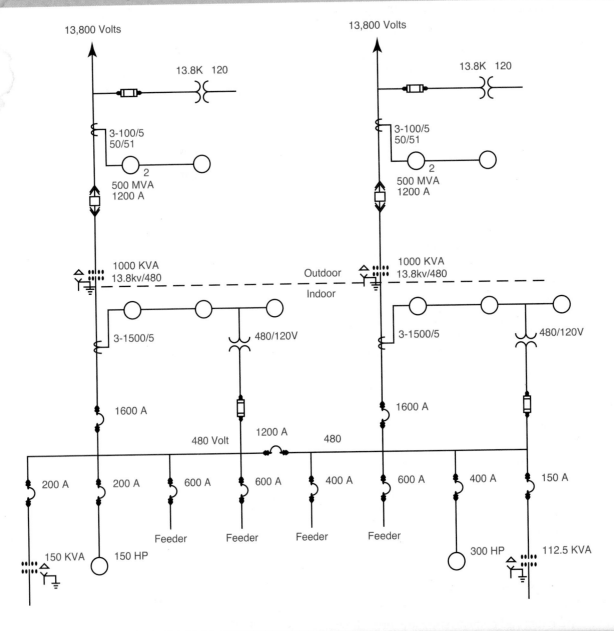

TECH NOTES

Numerous software programs are used to produce one-line diagrams. Component symbol libraries are used to build the diagram and lines indicating power flow interconnect the symbols. In some of the programs, the symbols are active objects that can be turned on or off in a simulated fashion on the computer screen. With this feature, paths of power are symbolized by the interconnections in the diagram logic. When an upstream device's state is turned off in the computer diagram, the down stream devices' logical state responds to upstream action. As a result, power outages for any power flow system are for training and for main and branch circuit trouble analysis.

Another advantage offered by the software to electrical workers is information for the facility manager. The component symbols on the OLD are active and linked to a database. Selecting a symbol on the computer screen displays basic information about the device, which includes: *electrical voltage and current ratings, model number and serial numbers, manufacturer information,* and *emergency point of contact information.* In addition, in some applications the OLD on the computer is linked to components in the power flow system and their status is monitored in real time so problems are displayed when a fault occurs.

FIGURE 8-5: One-line diagram for control elements.

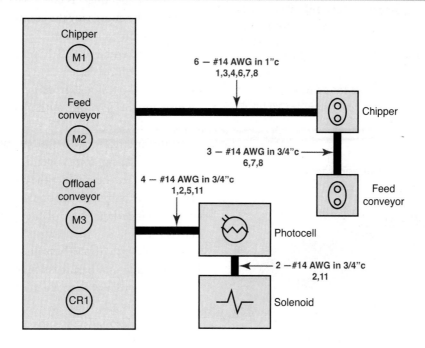

FIGURE 8-6: Ladder structure components—rails and rungs.

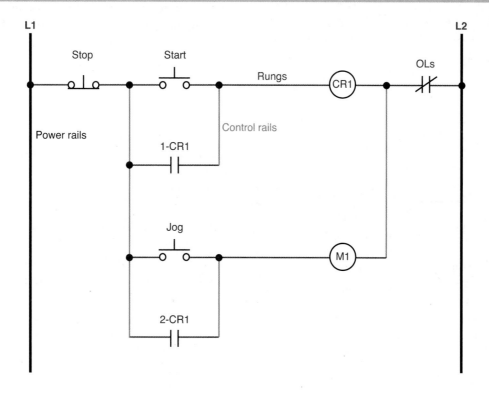

A bulk material transfer conveyor is shown in Figure 8-7(a), and the associated control schematic is shown in Figure 8-7(b). When the operator presses the *STOP* pushbutton, the off-delay timer TR1 is activated. The conveyor continues to run until TR1 time delay has expired. The time delay allows for the bulk material to be completely off-loaded from the conveyor before it stops. The conveyor is then ready to be started for its next operation.

FIGURE 8-7: Bulk material conveyor application.

(a) Bulk material transfer conveyor

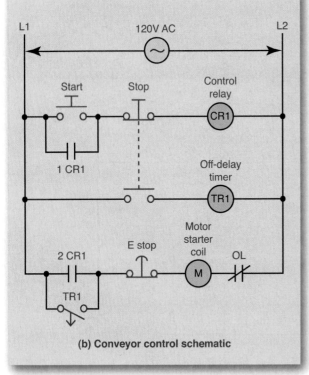

(b) Conveyor control schematic

lines, called *rungs*, hence the name *ladder diagrams.* The rails are identified as *line 1* (L1) and *line 2* (L2) and are the power source for the control circuit. As a result, they are often called the *power rails.* The horizontal lines, connected between L1 and L2, contain the input and output control circuit devices. Ladder diagrams are often read like a book, from *left to right,* with *inputs* devices on the *left* and *output* devices on the *right.* However, ladders with IEC symbols are often drawn vertically and read top to bottom. With power applied to L1 and L2, the *state* (open or closed) of the input device's contacts determines the *condition* (active or not active) of the output device on the rung. Therefore, each rung is an individual control circuit with power applied across the inputs and an output. Rungs are numbered sequentially from top to bottom starting with the number one. Rung numbering is for reference and does not indicate the order of output activation. Figure 8-6 highlights the rails and rungs in a ladder diagram.

Most ladder diagrams show a single-phase control circuit connected to L1 and L2. Generally, control voltage is obtained from the branch circuit power source or through a control transformer connected to the branch circuit power source. The control transformer provides a lower voltage (24V/120V) for the control circuit while the three-phase motor operates with the higher voltage (208/240V/480V). The ladder rails are always noted as L1 and L2 independent of the voltage level and *never* referred to as *hot* and *neutral*.

Ladder Diagram Structure

The *placement* of input and output devices in ladder diagram rungs is governed by *two basic rules*. A load is defined as any device that has a voltage drop across it. The rules are:

- *Only one output device or load is permitted per circuit path.*
- *Any number of input devices in any logical circuit combination is permitted in a rung.*

Figure 8-8(a) illustrates an automatic mixing tank with FS1 sensing liquid at a full tank level and FS2 sensing liquid at an empty tank level. Mixing starts when liquid rises above the empty tank sensors and continues for 30 minutes after the full tank sensor is activated. After the full tank mix cycle the drain valve is opened and the liquid drains with the mixer active until the liquid is below the empty tank sensor. Figure 8-8(b) illustrates the ladder diagram that controls the mixing tank. Note that each of the rungs is an individual circuit powered by L1 and L2. In addition, the rung outputs are not necessarily activated in the order of the ladder rungs from top to bottom. The mixer power circuits are not shown.

FIGURE 8-8: Ladder logic control circuit for automatic mixing tank.

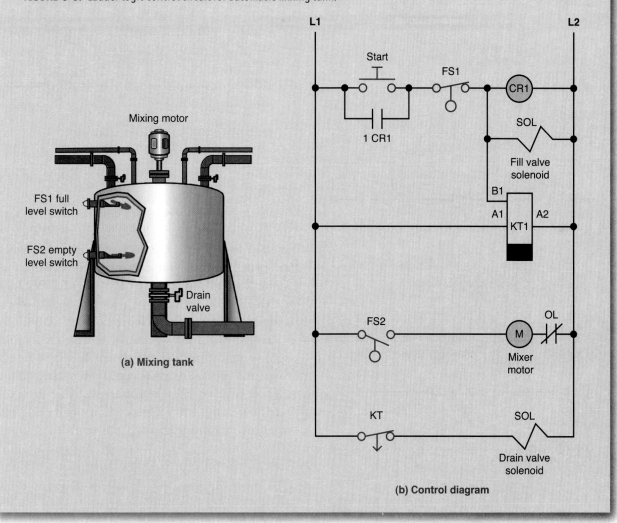

(a) Mixing tank

(b) Control diagram

Figure 8-9 illustrates the *correct* and the *incorrect* placement of output devices in a ladder rung. Connecting two 120V AC loads in series results in a 240V AC voltage drop. The voltage between L1 and L2 is 120V AC, and so each output in Figure 8-9(b) has only 60V AC applied. As a result, neither output operates properly. For a load to operate correctly, the voltage drop must equal the potential difference between L1 and L2.

For proper operation, loads are connected in parallel as shown in Figure 8-10. When the loads are in parallel, they operate properly because the voltage from L1 to L2 is applied across each load.

Control input devices are connected in the rung between L1 and a load. Figure 8-11 illustrates how three rungs with three different input devices activate control relay coils. Each rung is a *complete circuit* and includes at *least one* control device, a pushbutton, limit

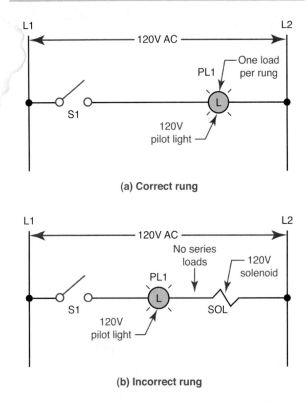

(a) Correct rung

(b) Incorrect rung

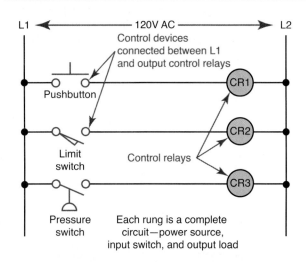

FIGURE 8-10: Illustrates two output devices connected in parallel and activated by a single push button.

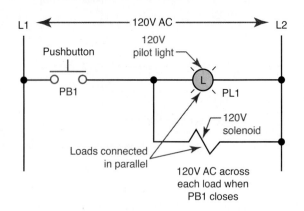

Multiple input devices are connected to the same load as shown in Figure 8-12. In Figure 8-12(a) two control devices, a flow switch and a pressure switch, are connected in series to control the coil of a magnetic motor starter. Current only flows from L1 to L2 and activates the motor starter when both the flow switch and the temperature switch are closed.

In Figure 8-12(b) two control devices, a foot switch and a temperature switch, are connected in parallel to control the coil of a magnetic motor starter. Either the foot switch or the temperature switch controls current flow from L1 to L2 through the input device, the magnetic motor starter, and the overloads.

Common Motor Control Ladder Diagrams

The start/stop push button ladder diagram in Figure 8-13 is used frequently to control motor starters. The function of each control element is presented along with the operational sequence. The ladder diagram in the figure shows only the pushbuttons, motor starter coil, overloads, and pilot light. The power circuit to switch the three phase power is not shown.

This motor starter configuration requires an operator to manually depress the Start pushbutton to start the motor. The motor starter coil is energized by pressing the momentary Start button. An auxiliary contact on the magnetic starter forms a parallel holding circuit around the momentary Start pushbutton contacts. This holding contact passes current around the released

switch or pressure switch, and *only one* output device, a control relay. No *limit* is placed on the number of control *input devices* used in a rung to make the output device function properly. Input devices are connected in *series* or *parallel* to activate the load when the input condition, specified by the production process, is satisfied.

FIGURE 8-12: Series and parallel input devices.

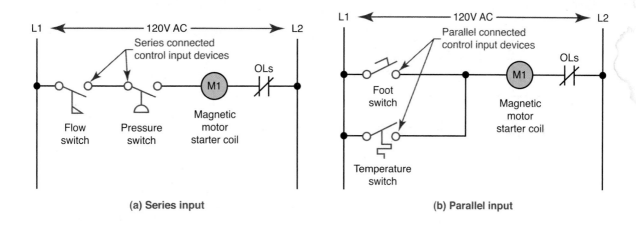

(a) Series input

(b) Parallel input

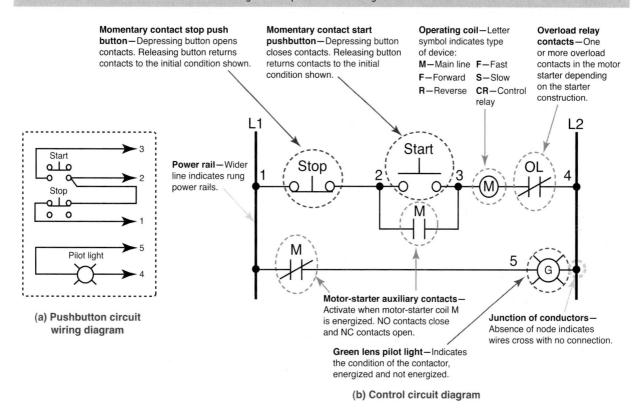

(a) Pushbutton circuit wiring diagram

(b) Control circuit diagram

Start pushbutton and keeps the motor starter coil energized. In the advent of a power failure, the starter drops out, the holding circuit contacts open, and the motor stops. The motor is not energized when power is restored, but is restarted with the Start pushbutton. Pressing the momentary stop button has the same effect as a power failure. The starter drops out and a restart requires depressing the start pushbutton.

The *wiring diagram* and *ladder diagram* in Figure 8-14 illustrates a complete motor control circuit with a three position (Hand, Off, Auto) selector switch for motor control. The *wiring diagram*, Figure 8-14(a),

FIGURE 8-14: Motor control diagrams.

Selector switch position	Contact X	Contact Y
H	Closed	Open
O	Open	Open
A	Open	Closed

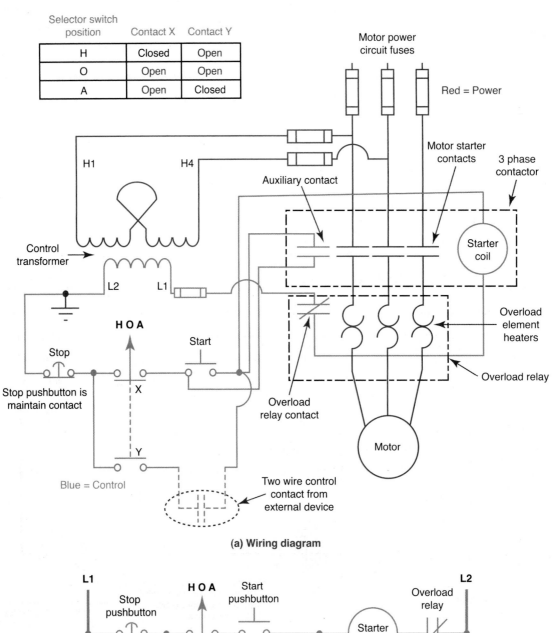

(a) Wiring diagram

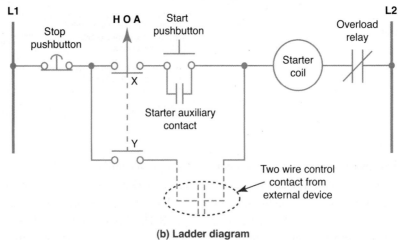

(b) Ladder diagram

shows all the devices and the wire paths required for control. However, installation and troubleshooting with this diagram is difficult. The *ladder diagram*, Figure 8-14(b), is not as useful for wire paths but ideal for installation and troubleshooting. Study both diagrams until you can identify and understand the components and the wiring in each diagram.

Ladder Numbering Systems

Complex ladder diagrams are required to represent complex motor control circuits. These complex lad-

der diagrams often stretch over several pages. To help electrical workers analyze and understand these large ladders, the ladder diagram has a standard numbering system. The numbering system uses rung numbers, numerical cross references and numerical wire identification.

Rung Numbering—*Rung numbering* assigns each rung of a ladder diagram with a unique number. The first rung is usually identified with the number 1, the second rung number 2, and so on. Figure 8-15 illustrates

FIGURE 8-15: Ladder rung numbering convention.

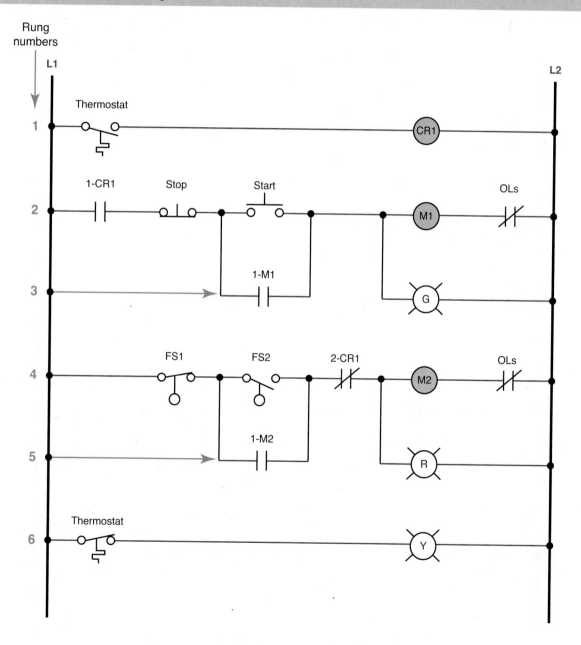

the rung numbering system. Note that the rung numbers are placed to the left of the rungs.

Numerical Cross Referencing—*Numerical cross referencing* is used in conjunction with the rung numbering system. The numerical cross referencing system links coils on a rung with the coil's contacts that are located on other rungs. Frequently, the rung with the coil and the rung with the coil's contacts are separated by ten or more ladder rungs. To quickly locate these contacts, the rung number for each contact is placed inside parentheses to the right of the L2 power rail as shown in Figure 8-16. The number inside the parentheses indicates the rung number(s) where the contacts for the coil are located. A number inside the parentheses that is underlined or over scored indicates a NC contact location. If the number is not underlined it indicates the location of NO contacts.

For example, note the parentheses (2, 4) to the right of rung 1 of Figure 8-16. The 2 in the parentheses indicates that on rung 2, there is a NO contact for the coil CR1. The 4 in the parentheses indicates that on rung 4, there is a NC contact for the coil CR1.

FIGURE 8-16: Coil and contact reference numbering convention.

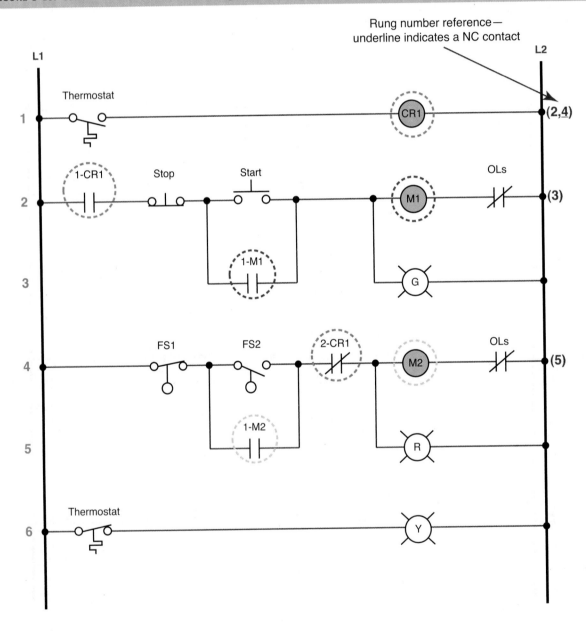

Numerical Wire Identification—The rung numbers and numerical cross references aid electrical workers in understanding and troubleshooting motor control circuits. The numbers used in these systems identify rungs on drawings and never materialize on the actual components in the field. Some type of wire identification method is required to correctly connect the control circuit conductors to their electrical components. Imagine opening a control panel and finding 100 red wires with no wire markers. Unfortunately, there is no standard numerical wire identification method. In fact, in most large industrial plants the electrical engineering staff develops a wire identification method specific to their installation. These identification methods encode *panel location and identification*, *type of control circuit*, and *wire purpose*. Two of the most common generic numerical wire identification methods found in commercial and industrial applications are discussed. Both methods are based on the premise that all wires that do not cross a component in the diagram are considered electrically the same and therefore have the same wire number. Wires crossing a component, for example a contact or coil, are not electrically the same and are assigned different wire numbers. Most wire numbering methods start with the first rung on the diagram and work left to right and then top to bottom.

Method one, which is shown in Figure 8-17, starts with all wires directly connected to L1 that do not cross any component and designates these wires as #1. Starting at the top left of the diagram with rung #1, a new number should be designated for each wire that crosses a component. If the next device is in series, the #2 will designate the wire connecting the first device to the second. If the next components are in parallel, the wires connecting both devices have the same wire number (#2 in this case). Wires that are electrically the same are marked with the same number. The next number is not used until all wires that are electrically the same are marked. The next number is assigned to each new wire until all wires are given a wire designation. Once the first wire directly connected to L2 is designated, all other wires directly connected to L2 are marked with the same number. The number identifying wires directly connected to L2 typically differ from circuit to circuit. The number of components in rung #1 of a drawing determines the wire number for conductors directly connected to L2. The number of components in the first line of a ladder diagram often differs between drawings.

FIGURE 8-17: Wire numbering system—method one.

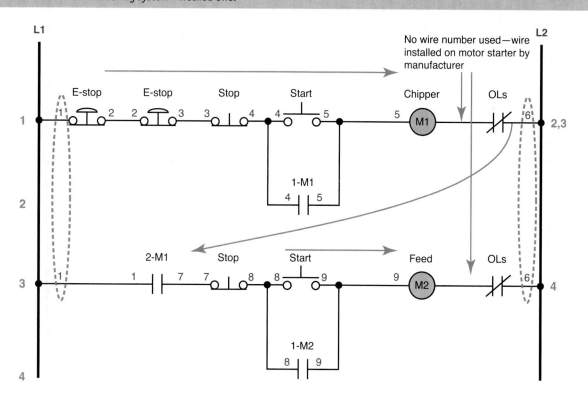

Method two as shown in Figure 8-18 is very similar to method one, with the following changes. After all wires directly connected to L1 are designated #1, the wires directly connected to L2 are marked as #2. After all the wires with #1 and #2 are marked, the remaining numbers are assigned in sequential order starting from the top left of the diagram using the same technique as the previous method. This wire numbering method is preferred by most electrical workers because the wires directly connected to L2 keep the designation of #2, even if devices are later added to the first rung of the drawing. Additional devices are often added to a circuit after the initial drawing and installation to meet customer requirements. When the wire numbering system is established, many field wires are usually marked. In such situations, it is acceptable to identify the new wires by the next number in sequence from the final circuit number rather than renumbering the entire control circuit drawing.

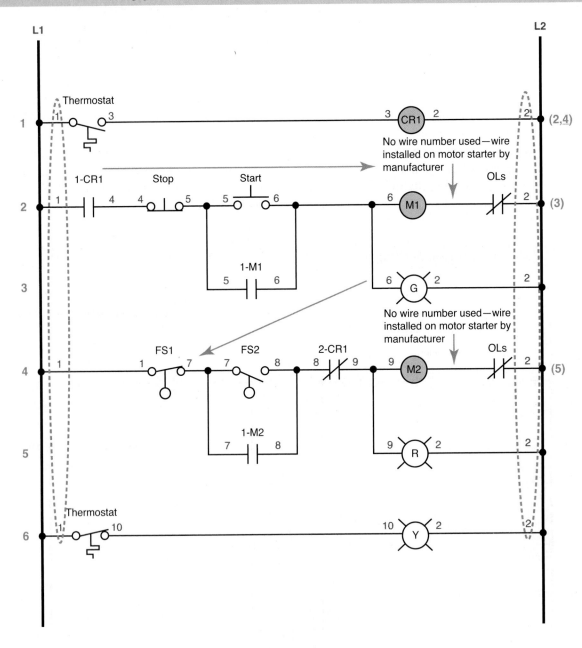

FIGURE 8-18: Wire numbering system—method two.

8-5 LOGIC FUNCTIONS

The three fundamental *logic functions* used in ladder diagrams are *AND, OR,* and *NOT*. Ladder diagram control rungs include inputs, such as switch contacts, near the L1 rail and an output or parallel outputs, such as solenoids, coils, and lights, near the L2 rail. The ladder diagram inputs determine if the output(s) are energized or not energized. Based on the control system requirements, these three logic functions or combinations of these logic functions are used to energize or not energize the rung loads. The logic functions used in ladder diagrams are described in the following sections.

AND Function

The *AND function* is used when two or more inputs are in series in the circuit. The AND function also implies that all inputs must be active or contacts must be closed to energize the load. An example of AND logic is a stamping machine with two normally open pushbuttons as illustrated in Figure 8-19(a). The machine operator places a piece of material in the press. The press only stamps the material when the operator presses both pushbuttons. Pressing one pushbutton AND the other pushbutton completes the current path to the solenoid, which moves the press to stamp the material.

OR Function

The *OR function* is used when two or more inputs are in parallel. The OR function also implies that any of the inputs can be active or any contact can be closed to energize the load. An example of the OR logic is a conveyor that is used to load boxes on a truck with two normally open pushbuttons as illustrated in Figure 8-19(b), A pushbutton is mounted on both sides of the conveyor, and when either pushbutton is pressed, the conveyor line moves until the pushbutton is released. The pushbutton is pressed until a box is near the end of the conveyor. The operator releases the pushbutton, takes the box from the conveyor and loads it on the truck. One pushbutton OR the other pushbutton must be closed to send the signal to start the conveyor motor.

NOT Function

In ladder logic diagrams, the *NOT function* is associated with a rung that has a NC contact on an input device controlling the output device as shown in Figure 8-19(c). When the input device, for example, a limit switch, is NOT active or NOT actuated, the output device is energized.

FIGURE 8-19: Ladder diagram input logic functions.

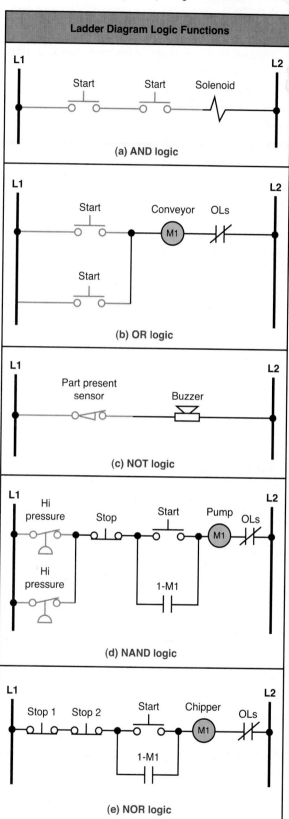

NAND Function

The *NAND function* is a combination of the AND and the NOT functions. An example of NAND logic is a manufacturing process using a hydraulic pump as illustrated in Figure 8-19(d). A pressure switch monitors the system for high pressures and shuts down if the pressure is too high. If the single pressure switch monitoring the system malfunctioned, the system could experience an accidental shut down. As a precaution, two identical pressure switches set at the same pressure are installed. Under normal conditions, any over-pressure would actuate both switches at the same time. If one switch malfunctions, the other switch keeps the system operational. The control circuit for this application uses the normally closed contact on each pressure switch. Remember, NOT logic energizes the load when the control signal is not active. Therefore, the output is de-energized only when both pressure switches are active (open). Thus the NAND function is present because pressure switch 1 AND pressure switch 2 are active for a NOT active output.

NOR Function

The *NOR function* is a combination of the OR and the NOT functions. An example of NOR logic is two normally closed STOP pushbuttons connected in series as illustrated in Figure 8-19(e). If either STOP pushbutton is pressed, the load is de-energized. Therefore, the output is de-energized only when either pushbutton switches are active (open). Thus the NOR function is present because either Stop1 OR Stop2 are active for a NOT active output.

Two and Three Wire Control

The terms *two-* and *three-wire* control describe the number of control wires frequently found in the raceway from the input (initiating pilot devices) to the output (loads). Figure 8-20(a) indicates that only *two control wires* between the inputs and outputs are necessary for load control. Two-wire control is often referred to as *low voltage release* because the lower voltage in the control circuit is switched by the input pilot device. It is also called *automatic control* because no operator action is required for an input signal and activation of the load. Figure 8-20 (b) and (c) illustrate examples of two-wire control. The circuit in Figure 8-20(b) automatically control motors without operator attention. When a power failure occurs while the contacts of the pilot device are closed, the starter drops out. When power is restored, the starter

automatically energizes through the closed contacts of the pilot device. Figure 8-20(c) shows a two-wire control application with a sump pump controlled with a float switch. The float switch (input) starts the pump automatically as needed. Note a switch is added to manually energize the systems. At that point the two-control level switch controls the pump motor.

> **FIGURE 8-20:** Two-wire control for motor starter ladder diagrams.

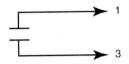

(a) The term "2-wire" control is derived from the fact that in the basic circuit, only two wires are required to connect the pilot device to the starter.

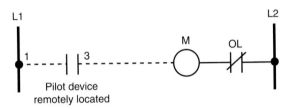

(b) This ladder diagram is a two-wire control technique with a maintained contact pilot device in series with the starter coil. An emergency stop is not shown but is necessary in applications where the NEC requires the device.

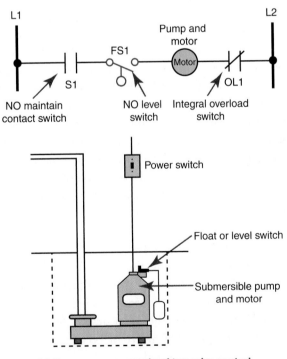

(c) Sump pump example of two-wire control

The pump has an integral overload protection device built into the pump enclosure.

Three-wire control, the most commonly used motor starter control, requires three wires between the inputs and outputs. Numerous three-wire control configurations, dictated by the control application, are used in industry. Several of the most frequently used applications are illustrated in Figure 8-21. Study

FIGURE 8-21: Three-wire control with example ladder diagrams.

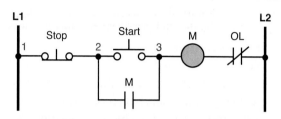

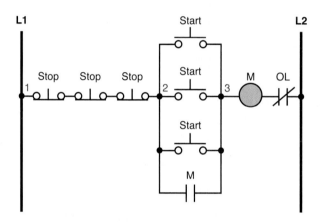

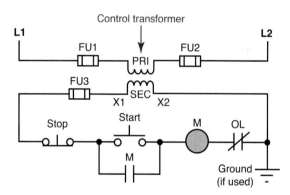

(a) The term "3-wire" control is derived from the fact that in the basic circuit, at least three wires are required to connect the pilot devices to the starter.

(b) Low voltage protection is a 3-wire control technique with momentary contact pushbuttons or similar pilot devices to energize the motor starter coil.

(c) Multiple Stop pushbuttons in series and Start pushbuttons in parallel permit starting and stopping the system from multiple places in the work cell.

(d) Operator safety and the need for a low voltage control circuit require the use of a control transformer. This provides a control circuit voltage lower than line voltage.

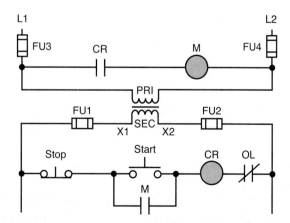

(e) Starter coils with high VA ratings require a large control transformer. The ladder diagram indicates how a control relay permits a transformer with a low VA rating because the motor starter coil is moved out of the low voltage control circuit. Both sides of the secondary are fused in this circuit, but a single fuse at X1 and a ground at X2 are often used.

these configurations until you understand the differences present.

Three-wire control is sometimes called *semi-automatic control* because operator action is required to initiate an input signal. An example of three-wire control is a motor starter controlled by momentary START/STOP pushbuttons. The pushbuttons must be pressed to energize or de-energize the motor starter.

Note that Figure 8-13 shows a three-wire motor control circuit with a light to indicate when the motor starter is not energized. Figure 8-14 shows a selector switch control circuit with a Hand and Auto position. In the *Hand* mode it operates like a three wire control system with a start and stop pushbutton. However, two-wire control is used in the *Auto* position. Note that the stop mushroom pushbutton is a maintain contact type device. Compare Figures 8-20, 8-21, 8-13, and 8-14 to help understand the differences between two- and three-wire control concepts.

The three-wire motor control circuit in Figure 8-22 compares the NEMA and IEC symbol standards. Review both standards until you recognize similar symbols present in each.

8-6 CIRCUIT DEVELOPMENT

A big challenge for the electrical worker is when a customer requires the installation of a machine or process control circuit, and there are no drawings. Essentially, the installation job expands into a design-build project and requires the electrical contractor to develop the entire control circuit. Situations like this truly test the knowledge, skill, and attitude of an electrical worker. Thus, circuit development is an important skill for an electrical worker to master.

Development Steps

The *first step* in developing a control circuit is to determine the desired circuit operation and prepare a preliminary list of components necessary to complete the circuit. For example, an exhaust fan that is used to vent a hot mechanical room requires, at a minimum, a *motor starter* and a *temperature switch* (thermostat). The electrical worker must know the environmental parameters such as the *temperature settings* and *dead-*

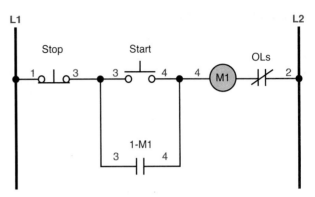

FIGURE 8-22: Comparison of NEMA and IEC motor starter symbols.

(a) NEMA symbol three-wire starter ladder diagram

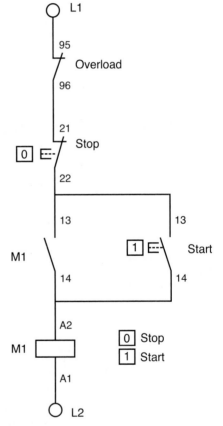

(b) IEC symbol three-wire starter ladder diagram

band range required for the proper operation of the exhaust fan. This information is required for the drawings as well as component purchase.

The *second step* is to create a ladder diagram. Ladder diagrams are often the most useful type of drawing for this type of application. Note—do not spend a large amount of time on the neatness of the initial drawings because normally there are numerous changes to the first draft.

Ladder Diagram Development

Start the ladder diagram by creating the two vertical power rails and labeling them L1 and L2. Note—some complicated circuits require a large space between L1 and L2. Before drawing the horizontal rungs, there are some rules used in control circuit drawings to consider. Each current path of the ladder that connects L1 to L2 must have a load such as a solenoid, an indicator light, a horn or a buzzer. If two or more loads are required to be energized simultaneously, they are drawn in parallel.

Contacts of input control devices such as limit switches, pushbuttons and relays are placed in series with loads. Figure 8-23 illustrates a ladder diagram with pushbuttons (the input control devices) and a motor and a pilot light (the loads). Note that the *stops* are in series (an AND function) and the *starts* are in parallel (an OR function).

Loads are placed on the right side of the drawing next to L2 and contacts are placed on the left side next

to L1. One exception to this rule is the placement of the normally closed contact(s) controlled by the motor overload protection. These contacts are normally drawn on the right side between the motor starter coil and L2. In addition, devices that start a load are usually connected in parallel, while devices that stop a load are usually connected in series.

Ladder Diagram Nomenclature

Input control devices in diagrams are identified with the appropriate nomenclature for the device. Pushbuttons are labeled with their intended use such as start or stop, while other devices are identified by name such as limit switch or flow switch. All loads in ladder diagrams have abbreviations to indicate the type of coil, color of pilot light or other type of load. For example, M for coils and motor starters, and CR for control relays. Many times an additional numerical suffix is used to differentiate multiple devices of the same type. A control circuit with three motor starters might identify the coils as M1, M2 and M3 in the diagram. Additional labeling near devices in a drawing assists in the understanding of the circuit. For example, the M1 contactor for a heater bank is labeled "Tank 1 Heater." Abbreviations are used in place of the entire device name. For example, limit switch 3 is labeled LS3 or pressure switch 2 as PS2. Pilot lights use

FIGURE 8-23: Ladder diagram structure for input and loads.

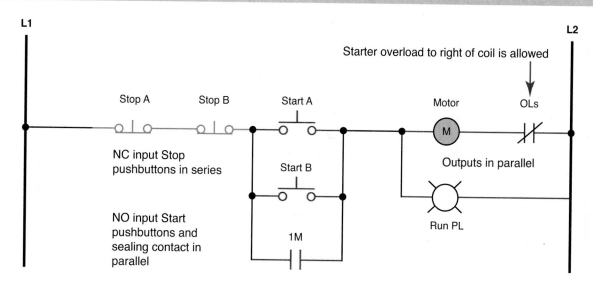

abbreviations of R for red, G for green, A for amber and so forth.

All contacts in a circuit are identified by the device that controls the operation of each contact. An auxiliary contact on motor starter 2 (M2) is designated 1-M2. This designation is assigned to the first contact controlled by M2 starting from the top left of the diagram. Any additional contacts controlled by the starter and located further down on the diagram are designated 2-M2, 3-M2, and so forth. Similarly, contacts on control relays are identified as 1-CR1 and 2-CR1. The rules and standards for drawing and labeling ladder diagrams vary throughout the industry. Large industrial facilities often have a ladder diagram style unique to their organization. In addition, different methods are used in geographical regions of the world. However the ladder diagram is drawn, the fundamental concepts of control circuits are the same. Figure 8-24 illustrates typical rung numbering, coil and contact referencing,

and labeling used on the ladder diagram. Wire numbering is not included in the illustration.

Ladder Diagram Application

A ladder diagram is needed for the *mulching operation system* illustrated in Figure 8-25. The system operates as follows: the mulching operation uses a large chipper to shred whole logs into mulch and stores the chips in a hopper. To prevent jams, the *chipper* motor is started before the *feed* conveyor drops logs into the chipper. An *offload* conveyor dumps the shredded mulch into a storage hopper. The offload conveyor automatically starts and stops when the feed conveyor starts and stops. The *hopper* uses a solenoid to open and close a chute at the bottom of the hopper to release the mulch into a truck. A sensor at the top of the hopper prevents an overflow of mulch from the hopper. The chipper, feed conveyor, and hopper solenoid are controlled with START and STOP pushbuttons.

FIGURE 8-24: Numbering contacts and loads.

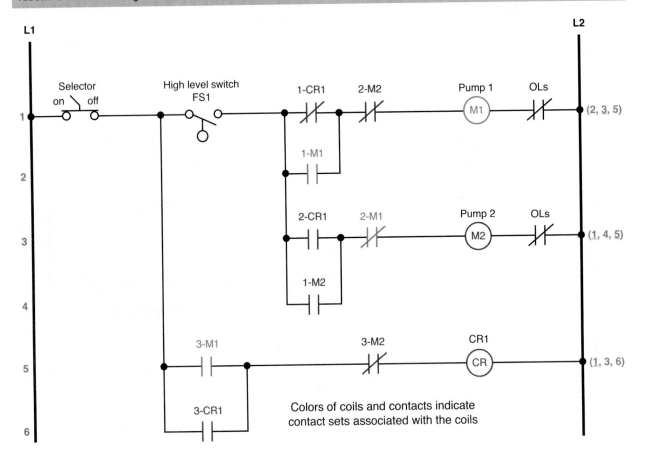

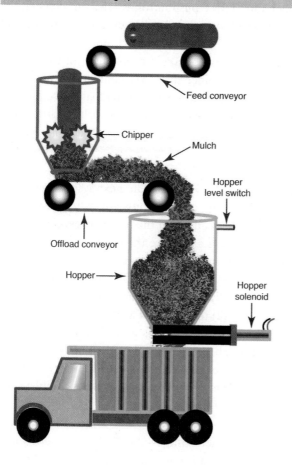

FIGURE 8-25: Mulching operation.

Feed conveyor

Chipper

Mulch

Hopper
level switch

Offload conveyor

Hopper

Hopper
solenoid

Understanding system operation is a critical first step before ladder diagrams are generated. With the operation understood, build relay ladder logic to satisfy each step of the operation: chipper, feeder, offloader, and hopper. The last step is to combine the rungs into a system ladder diagram.

Chipper Ladder Rungs—Draw the L1 and L2 rails for the chipper ladder. The first load to be energized in this system is the chipper motor, so place the motor starter coil, labeled M1 "Chipper Motor Starter," next to the left L2 rail. Add overload contacts between the motor starter coil and the L2 rail. Next determine the input logic required to start the chipper motor. Use a standard start/stop pushbutton combination with an auxiliary contact, 1-M1, from the motor starter to seal in the momentary start pushbutton. Use Figure 8-21(b) as a guide. Connect all components to each other and to L1 and L2. The complete chipper diagram is shown in Figure 8-26(a).

The chipper rungs are now analyzed for proper operation. When control power is applied to L1 and L2, there is no complete circuit through the chipper motor starter coil. At this point, the chipper motor is not running. Pressing the START pushbutton completes the electrical path and current flows through the coil, starting the chipper motor. When the motor starter coil energizes, the normally open auxiliary contact closes and provides an alternate current path (holding circuit) to the coil after the START pushbutton is released. Pressing the STOP pushbutton breaks the current path to the coil and opens the circuit. Also, the overload relay on the motor starter opens the chipper motor rung in the event of a chipper motor overload current.

Feeder Ladder Rungs—Draw the L1 and L2 rails for the feeder ladder and place the symbol for a coil directly to the left of L2. Label the coil M2 "Feed Motor Starter" and place the symbol for the OLs (normally closed contact) between the coil and L2. Identify the input logic required for the feeder conveyor to start. The operation statement stipulates that the feeder motor is energized with a START/STOP pushbutton, but not until the chipper is energized. So the input logic is NOT STOP pushbutton AND START pushbutton AND chipper energized. An AND input logic is needed with three contacts. Place the symbols for the START and STOP pushbuttons using the example three wire control in Figure 8-21(b), like the chipper ladder. A normally open auxiliary contact controlled by the feed conveyor motor starter is connected in parallel with the START pushbutton to act as a holding circuit. Place this contact on a separate rung below the START pushbutton and label it 1-M2. Remember, the feed conveyor cannot start unless the chipper is running. So a second normally open auxiliary contact from the chipper contactor, labeled 2-M1, is placed in the input logic between L1 and the STOP pushbutton contacts. This completes the AND input logic for control of the feeder conveyor motor. The feed ladder diagram is complete and shown in Figure 8-26(b).

The feeder rungs are now analyzed for proper operation. When control power is applied to L1 and L2, there is no complete circuit through the feed conveyor motor starter coil. The normally open auxiliary contact from the chipper motor starter (2-M1) closes only

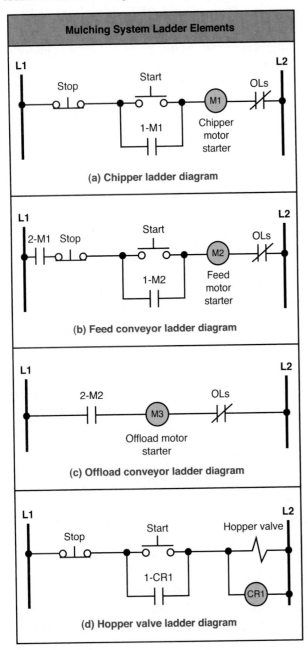

FIGURE 8-26: Ladder diagrams for mulching system.

Mulching System Ladder Elements

(a) Chipper ladder diagram

(b) Feed conveyor ladder diagram

(c) Offload conveyor ladder diagram

(d) Hopper valve ladder diagram

closes and provides an alternate current path to the coil when the START pushbutton is released. Pressing the STOP pushbutton breaks the current path to the coil and opens the circuit. If the chipper stops, contact 2-M1 opens and breaks the current path to the feed conveyor coil. Since the 2-M1 contact and the STOP pushbutton contact form an AND logic circuit, either can stop the feeder motor. The overload protection (OLs) also opens the circuit when a motor overload occurs.

Offload Ladder Rungs—The next system operation to control is the offload conveyor, which starts and stops automatically with the feed conveyor. Draw the L1 and L2 rails and place the symbols for the motor and the OLs on the right side of the drawing near the L2 rail. Label the coil M3 "Offload Motor Starter." Use a normally open auxiliary contact from the feed conveyor (M2) to both start and stop the offload conveyor coil. This contact is placed in series with the motor and labeled 2-M2. Whenever coil M2 (the feed conveyor) is energized, the offload conveyor coil is energized. The offload ladder diagram is complete and shown in Figure 8-26(c).

Hopper Ladder Rungs—As logs are shredded into mulch, the offload conveyor fills the large storage hopper. A START and STOP pushbutton controls a solenoid that opens and closes a chute at the bottom of the hopper, releasing the mulch into a truck. Draw the power rails and then draw the symbol for a solenoid coil directly to the left of L2 and label the symbol as "Hopper Valve." Solenoids are not motor starters, so no OLs are needed in the rung. Duplicate the START/STOP three wire control used for the chipper in the rung next to the L1 rail. Because solenoids are not normally configured with auxiliary contacts, a different method is needed to provide a holding circuit. A normally open auxiliary contact attached to a control relay is connected in parallel with the START pushbutton to act as a holding circuit. The control relay is energized whenever the solenoid is energized. So the control relay coil is placed on a separate rung below the solenoid and in parallel with the solenoid. Label the control relay as CR1 and the auxiliary contact under the START pushbutton as 1-CR1. When the START pushbutton is pressed, a current path is

when the chipper is running and prevents the feed conveyor from starting until the chipper is energized. This type of control is called *electrical interlocking*. Contact 2-M1 is closed while the chipper is running, but the feed conveyor does not start until the START pushbutton is pressed and the electrical path is completed through the coil. When the feed conveyor coils energizes, the normally open auxiliary contact (1-M2)

completed to both the solenoid and the control relay. The holding contact (1-CR1) closes to maintain a current path once the START pushbutton is released. The hopper ladder diagram is complete and shown in Figure 8-26(d).

Mulching Operation Ladder Diagram

A sensor is installed at the top of the hopper to monitor the level and prevent the hopper from overflowing with mulch. The sensor prevents additional mulch from filling the hopper, but does not interfere with loading trucks. Since the offload conveyor starts and stops with the feed conveyor, use a contact from the sensor to control the feed conveyor. Place the normally closed contact of the sensor in series with the feed conveyor coil. Locate the contact between 2-M1 and L1 and label it "Level Switch." The input logic for the feed conveyor motor now is level switch AND chipper energized AND NOT STOP AND START. When the hopper is near capacity, the sensor opens the contact and stops both the feed conveyor and the offload conveyor. The complete mulching operation ladder diagram is built with the chipper rungs, the feeder rungs, the offload rungs, and the hopper rungs and is shown in Figure 8-27.

FIGURE 8-27: Mulching system ladder diagram.

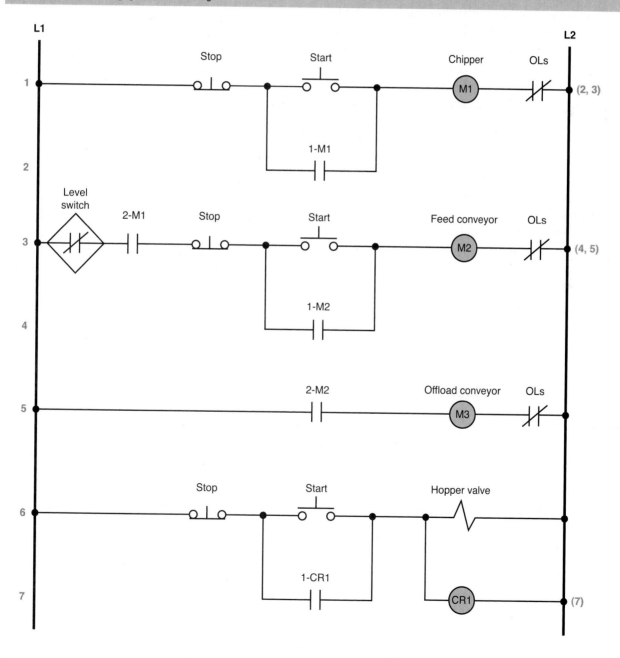

CRITICAL CONCEPTS

The need to know content from Chapter 8 is summarized in the following statements.

- Schematic diagrams show connections and functions of an electrical circuit with graphic symbols where an electrical circuit is an assembly of conductors and electrical devices through which current flows.
- Wiring diagrams illustrate the physical wire terminations of the electrical components in a motor control circuit.
- One-line diagrams consist of single lines and graphic symbols that illustrate the relative locations and connections of devices installed in the field.
- Ladder diagrams illustrate the electrical relationship between all components in a control circuit.
- Ladder diagrams are characterized by two vertical lines, called rails, and labeled L1 and L2, and many horizontal lines, called rungs.
- Connect only one load on a rung, whereas each rung contains one or more input current paths.
- Rung numbering assigns each rung of a ladder diagram with a unique number. The first rung is usually identified with the number 1, the second rung number 2, and so on.
- The numerical cross referencing system locates auxiliary contacts controlled by coils in the control circuit.
- Wire identification methods associate the connections of the control circuit conductors to their electrical components.

- Motor control circuits operate using the three basic electrical logic functions of AND, OR, NOT or combinations of these functions.
- Two- and three-wire control indicates the number of wires in the motor control circuit from the pilot devices to the motor starter.

QUESTIONS

1. Why are schematics good to use when troubleshooting control circuits?
2. Describe the purpose of wiring diagrams.
3. What are one-line drawings?
4. What are the purpose of the rails and rungs of a ladder diagram?
5. Describe how input devices are used on a ladder diagram.
6. Describe how loads are used on a ladder diagram.
7. How are rungs numbered?
8. Describe how numerical cross referring is used in ladder diagrams.
9. What is the purpose of wire identifications in ladder diagrams?
10. Describe how the AND, OR, NOT, NAND, and NOR logic functions are used in ladder diagrams.
11. List examples of devices used in two-wire control and name the most common devices used in three-wire control.
12. Describe the steps to build a ladder diagram from a system description.

Evolution of Motor Controls: Transitioning from Magnetics to Electronics

GOALS AND OBJECTIVES

The primary goals for this chapter are to briefly describe semiconductor theory and describe the solid state devices that are used in subsequent chapters. In addition, some basic troubleshooting techniques are presented.

After completing this chapter, you will be able to:

1. Describe the operation and function of N-type material and P-type material.
2. Describe the function and operation of the standard diode, the zener diode, the light emitting diode, and the photodiode.
3. Describe the function and operation of the standard transistor, the field effect transistor, the phototransistor, and the optocoupler.
4. Describe the function and operation of the silicon controlled rectifier, the triac, and the diac.
5. Describe troubleshooting techniques used for electronic devices.

9-1 INTRODUCTION TO SOLID STATE DEVICES

Electromechanical control devices such as relays and contactors rely on a *magnetic field* to actuate the solenoid and close the device contacts, which permits current flow. This form of motor control has been used for many years and is very reliable. However, electrome-chanical devices consist of many moving parts and each contributes to a possible device failure. With no moving parts, *solid state devices* or *semiconductors* are generally more reliable than electromechanical devices.

Semiconductor Theory

Matter is a collection of *atoms*, which are the *building blocks* for the materials used in electrical and electronic devices. Atoms have three parts: *protons*, *neutrons*, and *electrons*. *Protons* and *neutrons* make up the *nucleus* of the atom, and the *electrons* circle about the nucleus in *orbits* that are called *shells*. In the nucleus, the protons have a *positive* charge, and the neutrons have *no electrical* charge. The orbiting electrons have a *negative* charge. The *number* of protons always equals the number of electrons in an atom. The value of that number depends on the material; for example, copper has 29 and silicon has 14. The number of neutrons in an atom may be equal to the number of protons but is less in light atoms and greater in heavy atoms. Since an atom has equal numbers of electrons (negative charge) and protons (positive charge), their charge is *zero*.

Semiconductors are constructed from either *germanium* or *silicon* atoms. The basic semiconductor material, called *intrinsic* silicon or germanium, is *purified* to remove atoms of all other material. The result is a nearly pure crystal of the semiconductor. For example, purified silicon has no more than one impurity atom in 10 billion silicon atoms. Purification to this degree is the same as a railroad boxcar of sugar with an impurity of a single grain of salt. Figure 9-1 illustrates an intrinsic silicon crystal. Figure 9-1(a) shows the silicon atoms linked by *four* electrons from each atom. Figure 9-1(b) shows a larger portion of the crystal with most electrons not shown. Note that four electrons broke away from their atoms and are *free* to move inside the material. The atom that lost an electron has a *hole*, the absence of an electron, in the place where the free electron formally occupied.

The pure silicon crystals have a *few free electrons* to support some current flow but not a significant current flow. As a result, they are *not conductors* and *not insulators*, so they are called *semiconductors*. A pure silicon crystal is illustrated in Figure 9-2 with a DC source connected across the material. Free electrons are attracted to the positive side of the crystal by the positive side of the DC source. For every free electron that leaves the semiconductor on the positive side (left), a replacement electron enters the semiconductor on the negative side (right). Inside the silicon electron action is dynamic. As electrons break free others recombine with holes. The number of free electrons moving across the silicon remains the same. The overall movement is electrons flowing from right to left and holes flowing from left to right. This movement of electrons is called drift current.

Doping Silicon Atoms

Pure silicon, which is not a good conductor, is modified before it is used to produce semiconductor devices, like diodes and transistors. The silicon crystal's structure is altered by a doping process. *Doping* is the addition of *impurity atoms* into the crystal structure of the semiconductor when the material is in a liquid state. The doping quantity ranges from a few impurity atoms per billion silicon atoms to a few impurity atoms per million silicon atoms. The number of impurity atoms added determines the operating characteristics of the semiconductor device. When doped, some silicon atoms in the crystal structure are replaced by impurity atoms. Depending on the type of impurity atoms used, the new crystal structure becomes either *N-type material* or *P-type material*. N-type and P-type materials are the basic building blocks for semiconductors used in motor control.

FIGURE 9-1: Pure silicon crystal.

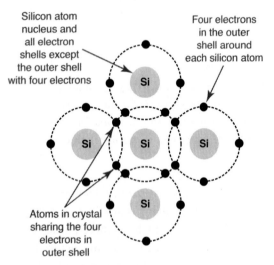

Silicon atom nucleus and all electron shells except the outer shell with four electrons

Four electrons in the outer shell around each silicon atom

Atoms in crystal sharing the four electrons in outer shell

(a) Pure silicon crystal structure

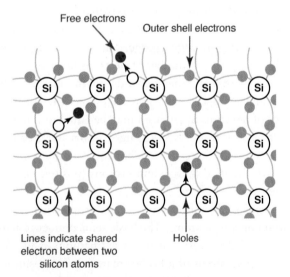

Free electrons

Outer shell electrons

Lines indicate shared electron between two silicon atoms

Holes

(b) Pure silicon crystal with three free electrons and three holes

FIGURE 9-2: Current conduction in a pure silicon semiconductor.

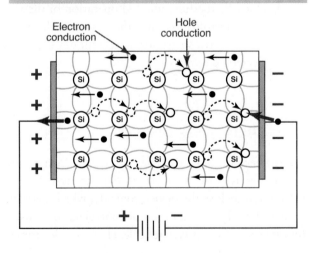

Electron conduction

Hole conduction

N-type Semiconductor Material

N-type material is created by doping the silicon with impurity atoms that have *five electrons* in their outer shell. That is one more than the *four* in the silicon outer shell. Doping impurities that produce N-type material include: *arsenic, bismuth,* and *antimony*. Figure 9-3 illustrates a silicon crystal structure with an *antimony* (Sb) impurity atom surrounded by four silicon atoms.

The antimony atom has *five* electrons, but only four of the five are required when the antimony atom is in the silicon crystal lattice. As a result, the impurity atom's fifth electron is *cut loose* and *free* to move in the N-type silicon to carry current. The *number* of these *free electrons* is primarily determined by the *amount* of impurity atoms (Sb) added to the pure silicon material. Therefore, the *resistance* of the material and its ability to *conduct* a current is linked to the *number* of Sb impurity atoms present.

When the antimony's extra electron leaves, the region of the crystal where the impurity is held takes on a *positive charge*, called a *positive ion*. This happens because the positive charges in the Sb nucleus have one *positively charged proton* not balanced by the missing *negative electron*. N-type material gets that *name* from the *excess* number of negative *free electrons*. The numerous free electrons make it an excellent conductor of current when a voltage is applied across the material. When voltage is applied to the N-type material, the electron current flows from negative to positive as shown in Figure 9-4.

P-type Semiconductor Material

P-type material is created by doping the silicon with impurity atoms that have *three electrons* in their outer shell. That is one less than the four in the silicon outer shell. Doping impurities that produce P-type material include: *gallium, boron,* and *indium*. Figure 9-5 illustrates a silicon crystal structure with a *boron* (B) impurity atom surrounded by four silicon atoms.

The boron atom has *three* electrons, but four are required when the boron atom is in the silicon crystal lattice. This absence of an electron or missing electron in the crystal is called a *hole*. To satisfy the need

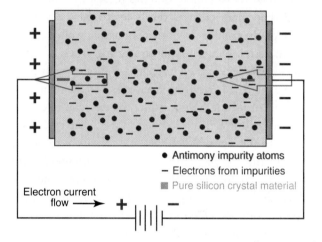

FIGURE 9-4: N-type material with current flow supported by impurity atom electrons.

- ● Antimony impurity atoms
- − Electrons from impurities
- ■ Pure silicon crystal material

Electron current flow ⟶

FIGURE 9-3: Antimony impurity added to pure silicon producing free electron in N-type material.

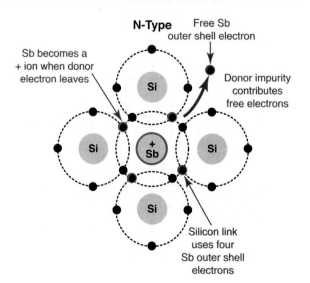

N-Type

Free Sb outer shell electron

Sb becomes a + ion when donor electron leaves

Donor impurity contributes free electrons

Silicon link uses four Sb outer shell electrons

FIGURE 9-5: Boron impurity added to pure silicon producing free hole in P-type material.

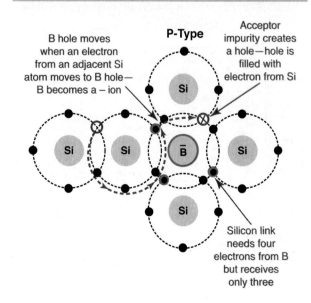

B hole moves when an electron from an adjacent Si atom moves to B hole— B becomes a − ion

P-Type

Acceptor impurity creates a hole—hole is filled with electron from Si

Silicon link needs four electrons from B but receives only three

for four electrons at the impurity site, an electron from a neighboring silicon atom slides around to fill the hole. This movement is illustrated in Figure 9-5. Note as the electron moves in one direction the hole moves in the opposite direction. The *number* of holes is primarily determined by the *amount* of impurity atoms (B) added to the pure silicon material. Therefore, the *resistance* of the material and its ability to *conduct* a current is linked to the *number* of B impurity atoms present.

When the boron's hole is filled with an electron from a neighboring silicon atom, the region of the crystal where the impurity is held takes on a *negative charge,* called a *negative ion.* This happens because the B atom has an additional electron (the one that filled the hole) that is not balanced by the *positive protons* in the nucleus. P-type material gets that *name* from the *excess number* of *holes* present. Conduction in P-type material uses the holes to pass electrons through the conductor when a voltage is applied across the material. Figure 9-6 illustrates the process. When an electron leaves the P-type material on the left side, a hole is created. Electrons from atoms to the right slide around to fill the hole just like the electron filled the hole in Figure 9-5. As electrons move to the left, holes move to the right. When the hole arrives at the right side of the P-type material, an electron enters from the lead to fill the hole. So electrons are moving through the material by moving around the shell of the atoms from one hole to the next from the negative to the positive side the of the crystal. The current flow in P-type material is illustrated in Figure 9-6. Note that

apparent hole movement is from left to right and is equal to the electron movement from right to left.

9-2 PN JUNCTION DIODES

The union of P- and N-type materials produces a single-junction PN diode. The two materials are connected with a chemical process. Figure 9-7 illustrates a PN junction after the material has been joined. When the materials are joined the following actions occur:

- N-type material has many free electrons and positive ions.
- P-type material has many holes and negative ions.
- When the P and N materials unite, electrons from the N side move across the junction and fill the holes on the P side. This electron movement leaves only positive ions at the N side of the junction and negative ions at the P side.
- The region on each side of the junction is an insulator (no free charge carrier present) with only ions present. The region is called the *depletion* region.
- The movement across the junction is stabilized by the depletion region charge, and the newly formed diode looks like the unbiased PN junction shown in Figure 9-7.

FIGURE 9-7: PN diode junction without bias and diode symbol.

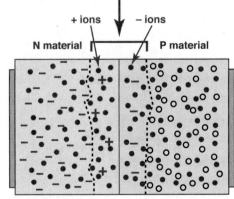

FIGURE 9-6: P-type material with current flow supported by impurity atom holes.

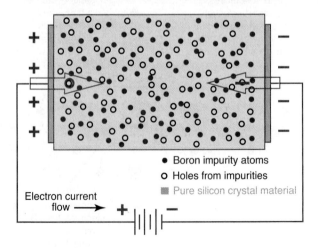

Unbiased PN Junctions

Figure 9-7 shows the P and N diode in an *unbiased* state with a depletion region *devoid* of any *free charge carriers*. After the junction is formed, the negative ions concentrated in the P material at the junction halt the flow of electrons (like charges repel) to the P side.

The negative and positive ions in the depletion region create an *internal barrier voltage* or *electric field* of approximately 0.6 volts for a silicon small signal diode.

Forward Bias Operation

Figure 9-8 shows a forward biased PN junction. A PN junction is forward biased when the polarity of the external voltage source is wired to the diode leads as shown in the figure. In the forward bias mode, the depletion region collapses, and the level of current flow is set by the external current limiting resistance. The following conditions describe forward bias operation:

- The forward bias circuit makes the *P* or *anode* end of the diode more positive than the *N* or *cathode* end. The depletion region barrier voltage (Figure 9-7) is overcome by the external source, when the source is greater than 0.6 volts for a silicon diode (the barrier voltage) and 0.2 volts for a germanium device.
- When the barrier voltage is overcome, the free electrons move through the N material, cross the NP junction, and then use the holes in the P material to flow out of the P side of the diode. Every electron pulled out of the P material is replaced with an electron from the source into the N material.
- The voltage drop across the diode is approximately equal to the barrier voltage of the junction.
- The low forward bias resistance of the diode requires an external series resistor to limit current flow through the diode. The direction of electron current flow is shown.

Reverse Bias Operation

Figure 9-9 shows a PN junction and the external circuit needed for the reverse bias mode. The depletion

FIGURE 9-8: Forward bias operation of PN junction and diode.

FIGURE 9-9: Reverse bias operation of PN junction and diode.

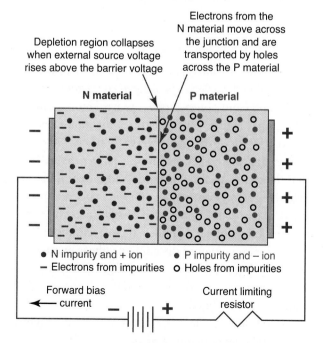

Depletion region collapses when external source voltage rises above the barrier voltage

Electrons from the N material move across the junction and are transported by holes across the P material

N material   P material

- N impurity and + ion   • P impurity and − ion
- Electrons from impurities   ○ Holes from impurities

Forward bias
← current

Current limiting resistor

Depletion region enlarges as the reverse bias voltage increases and current flow across the junction drops to near zero because the P material has insufficient free electrons

N material   P material

- N impurity and + ion   • P impurity and − ion
- Electrons from impurities   ○ Holes from impurities

Leakage reverse
current →

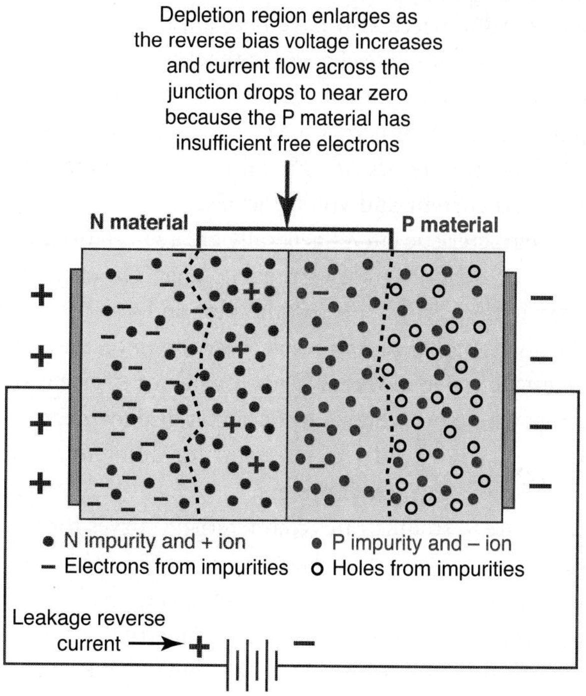

region of a PN junction widens beyond the no-bias width, and current flow drops to near zero. The following conditions describe reverse bias operation:

- The reverse bias circuit makes the N or *cathode* end more positive than the P or *anode* end. This bias causes the depletion region to enlarge in proportion to the external reverse bias as electron and hole charge carriers are pulled back from the junction.
- Few N material free electrons enter the external wire because the P side has few free electrons to cross the junction and replace them. So, the reverse bias current is small. This makes the diode an open circuit in the reverse bias mode. The small current that does flow is called *leakage current*.

The diode is a semiconductor device that allows current flow in only one direction.

9-3 DEVICE CHARACTERISTIC CURVES

The operation of a semiconductor device is defined by the component's *characteristic curves*. Devices have either a *single* characteristic curve or a *group* of curves called a *family* of characteristic curves. Characteristic curves show the *relationship* between the device's *terminal current* and *terminal voltage*. It describes how changes in one parameter (*voltage* or *current*) affects the other parameter (*current* or *voltage*). Most semiconductor devices also have *temperature* characteristics curves that relate changes in the device temperature to changes in device voltage or current. A few special purpose semiconductors have characteristic curves to describe how *levels of light* on the device determine terminal current and voltage levels.

Characteristic curves generally are a *graph* of device terminal *current* versus terminal *voltage*. The current is usually the vertical axis on the plot and voltage is on the horizontal axis. As a result, *every point* on the characteristic curve plot represents a value of *device resistance*. Therefore, characteristic curves display *resistance* between any two device *terminals* for different values of *voltage* and *current* present.

Figure 9-10 illustrates characteristic curves for four different resistor values. Note that an *open circuit* (infinite resistance) is a *horizontal line* (green), and a *short circuit* (zero resistance) is a *vertical line* (red). All resistance values between opens and shorts have a slope like the blue lines of 0.5 ohms and 2 ohms. *Linear*

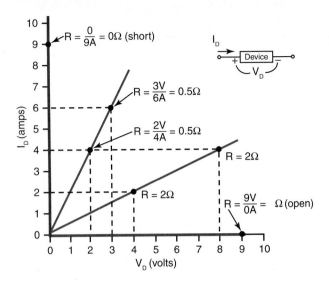

FIGURE 9-10: Characteristic curves for resistors.

(straight) *lines* on a characteristic curve represent the *same* resistance value. A *curved line* indicates a *changing* resistance value.

9-4 SEMICONDUCTORS FOR MOTOR CONTROL

Since the invention of the semiconductor diode by *Russell Ohl* in 1940, hundreds of different types of semiconductor devices have been created. The ones used most often in motor devices are described in this section.

Small Signal and Power Diodes

Diodes come in *numerous sizes, package configurations,* and with various *operational characteristics*. The *small signal* and *power* diodes are used more than any other type. Figure 9-11 illustrates the *diode symbol*, the diode forward and reverse bias *characteristic curves*, and pictures a ten ampere *power diode*. Note that the terminals are the anode and the cathode. The *positive terminal* or *anode* is P-type material, and the *negative terminal* or *cathode* is N-type material. When forward bias voltage is applied, diode resistance is *high* (a horizontal line) until the applied voltage exceeds the *barrier voltage* (0.6 for silicon). After the barrier voltage is exceeded the diode resistance drops to a *low* value (a vertical line).

In *reverse bias* the diode resistance is very high (a horizontal line) with only *leakage current* flowing until

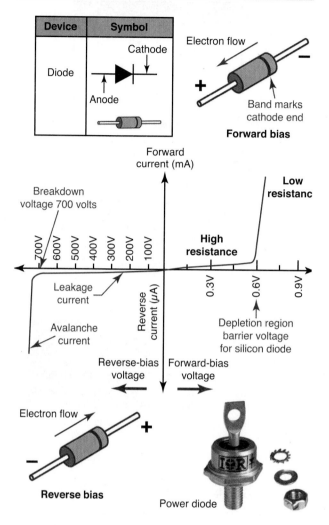

FIGURE 9-11: Small signal and power diode characteristic curve and example power diodes.

Device	Symbol
Diode	Cathode / Anode

Electron flow

Forward bias

Band marks cathode end

Forward current (mA)

Breakdown voltage 700 volts

700V 600V 500V 400V 300V 200V 100V

Low resistanc

High resistance

Leakage current

Reverse current (μA)

Avalanche current

0.3V 0.6V 0.9V

Depletion region barrier voltage for silicon diode

Reverse-bias voltage | Forward-bias voltage

Electron flow

Reverse bias

Power diode

the breakdown point (700V DC) is reached. At *breakdown*, the reverse voltage is high enough to *pull electrons* from the atom's shells in the P material. When the action starts, it is like the first rock in an avalanche rock slide, which knocks other rocks free. The first electron knocks others free and the diode resistance falls to a low value. If the current is limited in the *avalanche region*, the diode is not harmed and returns to normal operation when the reverse voltage falls below the breakdown value. Leakage current before breakdown is in the micro-ampere range, and forward current maximum values depend on the diode type and size. *Peak inverse voltage* (PIV) is the maximum reverse bias voltage that a diode can withstand. The PIV ratings for diodes generally range from a few volts to several thousand volts. The PIV rating is also the breakdown voltage in the reverse bias mode.

Diode applications are numerous in motor control devices and circuits. The diode's ability to limit current flow to a *single direction* makes it an ideal *rectifier* to convert *AC voltage* to pulsating *DC voltage*. *Rectification* is the most common application for silicon power diodes.

Zener Diodes

The *zener diode* is a PN junction that operates like a small signal diode in the *forward direction* but is designed to operate in the *zener mode* in the *reverse breakdown region*. Figure 9-12 illustrates the zener *diode symbol*, the zener diode *characteristic curve*, and shows a picture of *low power zener*. The forward barrier voltage and forward current characteristics are like a standard diode for voltage applied in the forward direction. However, when a voltage is applied to a zener diode in the reverse direction, the current remains near zero until the *zener voltage* (V_Z) is reached. At that point breakdown occurs with a *sharp knee*, and *reverse current* is only limited by the *external* series resistance or the *load*. As in the signal diode, the slope of the zener curves indicates where internal resistance is high (horizontal curve) and low (vertical curve). Like the forward voltage drop of a standard diode, the reverse voltage drop or zener voltage remains essentially *constant* over a wide range of *zener currents*.

The zener voltage is determined by the *level* of doping or number of impurity atoms added to the P and N material during manufacturing. Zener voltages from a few volts to hundreds of volts are available. Zener voltage accuracy varies from +/− 20 percent for standard devices to less than +/− 1 percent for precision devices. Zener applications are numerous; however, the most common application for a zener is *voltage regulation*.

Light Emitting Diodes

A *light-emitting diode* (LED) is a semiconductor diode that produces light when the diode is forward biased. Figure 9-13 illustrates the operation and provides examples of the many colors now available. Electrons in that N material are *freed* from their atoms when they absorb sufficient energy to break free from the nucleus. This additional electron energy is *thermal* energy and energy from the *external electric field*. In the forward bias mode, the free electrons in the N material cross the PN junction and move into a hole in the P material. This process, called *recombination*,

FIGURE 9-12: Zener diode characteristic curve and example low power zener.

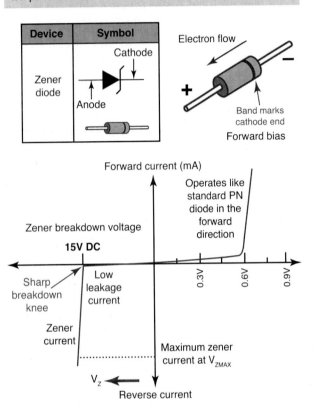

Device	Symbol
Zener diode	Cathode / Anode

Electron flow
−
+
Band marks cathode end
Forward bias

Forward current (mA)

Operates like standard PN diode in the forward direction

Zener breakdown voltage

15V DC

Sharp breakdown knee

Low leakage current

0.3V   0.6V   0.9V

Zener current

Maximum zener current at V_{ZMAX}

V_z

Reverse current

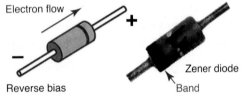

Electron flow
−   +
Zener diode
Reverse bias
Band

reunites the electrons with an atom's nucleus. In this process the electrons release the energy absorbed earlier to get free. Depending on how the semiconductor is doped, the released energy is radiated at wavelengths of visible light. As a result, the higher the LED forward current the greater the illumination from the electron energy loss.

The LED manufacturers normally use a combination of *gallium* and *arsenic* with silicon or germanium to construct LEDs. By adding other impurities to the base semiconductor, different wavelengths of light or colors are produced as Figure 9-13 illustrates. LEDs

FIGURE 9-13: LED operation and color options.

Device	Symbol
Light-emitting diode	Cathode / Anode

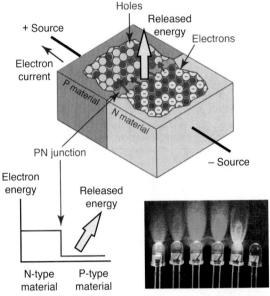

+ Source

Electron current

Holes

Released energy

Electrons

P material

N material

PN junction

− Source

Electron energy

Released energy

N-type material   P-type material

LED diode color options

are also available that produce infrared light, which is not visible to the human eye. As with standard diodes, the anode and cathode leads are identified with a *geometric feature* on the case. The cathode lead of the LED is generally identified by the *flat side* of the device enclosure, a *notch* cut into the package, or with *lead length*. Always verify the diode lead polarity with manufacturers' or suppliers' data sheets before replacing an LED in a device.

Photodiodes

The photodiode is a diode that is *switched* on (low reverse bias resistance) and off (high reverse bias resistance) by light. The photodiode is constructed like a *standard diode* but contains a *lens* to focus the light on the P material near the PN junction as shown in Figure 9-14. The reverse bias PN junction in Figure 9-9 had near *zero* current flow across the PN junction. The absence of current flow resulted from the lack of free electrons in the P material. Electrons could not be pulled from the N material by the reversed bias supply because the P material did not have sufficient free electrons to replace them.

FIGURE 9-14: Photo diode operation and example device.

FIGURE 9-15: Transistor P and N materials and electronic symbols.

Device	Symbol
Photodiode	Cathode / Anode

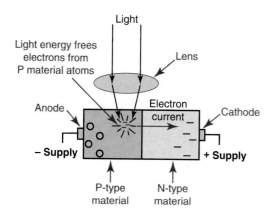

Photodiode

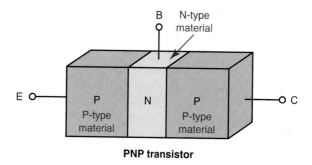

Device	Symbol
PNP transistor	Base (B) — Collector (C) / Emitter (E)
NPN transistor	Base (B) — Collector (C) / Emitter (E)

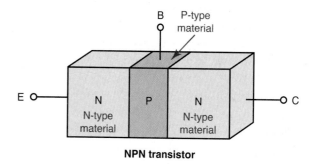

PNP transistor

NPN transistor

The photodiode in Figure 9-14 is reversed biased, like the PN junction in Figure 9-9, and has near zero reverse current when the light source is off. When light is applied, the *light energy* gives electrons in the P material sufficient energy to break loose from their atoms and become *free electrons*. The increased electric field at the junction and the reverse biased supply pulls these electrons across the junction. As a result, a reverse *electron current flow* is established as shown in the figure. In effect, the *resistance* of the photodiode is *high without light*, and *proportionally reduced* when the photodiode is *exposed to light*.

Bi-Polar Junction Transistors

The *transistor* is a solid state device formed with either two *P type materials* and *one N-type material* (PNP transistor) or *two N type materials* and *one P-type material* (NPN transistor). Figure 9-15 shows the two versions of this three layer device with *two junctions* present. The center material is called the *base*. The material at one end is the *collector*, and at the other end is the *emitter*. Transistors are often called *bi-polar junction transistors* (BJT) based on this symmetrical construction. The symbol for each type of BJT is illus-

trated in the figure. While symmetrical in appearance, they are not symmetrical in operation. Since the size and doping of each layer is different, the emitter and collector leads are not interchangeable.

The transistor is a *three-terminal device* with the important feature that the current through two terminals is controlled by small changes in current or voltage at the third terminal. This control feature allows the device to *amplify* small AC signals or act as a discrete switch. These two operations, *amplification* and *switching*, are the basis of a host of electronic functions performed by the transistor.

Transistor Amplification—Transistor *amplification* or *gain* is best described with an NPN configuration as illustrated in Figure 9-16. The first requirement for

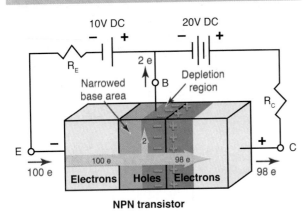

FIGURE 9-16: Transistor current gain illustration.

10V DC — + 20V DC — +

R_E

2 e

B

Narrowed base area

Depletion region

R_C

E —

2

100 e   98 e

C

100 e

Electrons   Holes   Electrons

98 e

NPN transistor

amplification is the *bias* applied to the two junctions. The BJT has the base-emitter junction *forward biased* (P base is more positive than N emitter). Note the *small* blue depletion region because the base-emitter junction is *forward biased* (shown in Figure 9-8). Electron current flow across the base-emitter junction is established due to the forward bias. In this description, 100 electrons of current flow is assumed.

The base-collector junction is *reverse biased* (N collector is more positive than P base). Note the *large* blue depletion region because the base-collector junction is *reverse biased* (shown in Figure 9-9). The depletion region has only *negative ions* (base side of junction) and *positive ions* (collector side of junction) and *no charge carriers.*

A second requirement for amplification is a *thin base region.* The device is intentionally implemented with a narrow base width during BJT fabrication. The large base-collector depletion region reduces the distance across the narrow base before emitter electrons reach the edge of the collector-base depletion region. When the 100 electrons cross from the emitter into the thin base region, these free electrons have two options.

- *Combine* with a hole in the thin base region, called the *recombination process,* and *emerge* from the base as an electron current in the base lead.
- *Move through* the thin base region, across the collector-base depletion region, and end up in the BJT collector. Electrons are moved through the base by the *large* positive electric field established by the *ions* in the collector-base depletion region and the *reverse bias* external voltage. These electrons *emerge* from the collector as an electron current in the collector lead.

Recombination in the base is not instantaneous. With a thin base region and large electric field present, most of the emitter electrons never have a chance to recombine. Instead they move across to the collector. In the example, Figure 9-16, for every 100 electrons leaving the emitter, 98 reach the collector. If 200 leave the emitter, then 196 (2 × 98) reach the collector and 4 exit at the base lead. The *ratio* remains the *same* for all values of base and emitter electron flow. With an understanding of how electrons respond upon entering the base from the emitter, a restatement of the action leads to an understanding of BJT gain. Restated, in order for 2 electrons to flow out of the base, 98 electrons must flow out of the collector. Therefore, the collector current is 49 (98 divided by 2) times the base current. This ratio of *collector current* divided by *base current* is called *beta* (β), which is the *current gain* for the transistor. Therefore:

A transistor with a forward biased base-emitter and a reverse biased base-collector, that is operating in the linear mode, has a collector current equal to β times the base current.

Transistor Circuits—As a *three-element* and *three-terminal* device, the transistor has three possible circuit configurations. These circuits are identified by the *terminal* that is *common* to both the *input* and the *output.* Figure 9-17 illustrates the three circuit configurations for the NPN transistor, where Figure 9-17(a), (b), and (c) depicts the *common emitter, common base,* and *common collector* respectively. The common terminal is often the signal ground as shown in the figure. As a result, the three circuits are often called *grounded emitter, grounded base,* and *grounded collector.* Figure 9-18 shows some of the many transistor case sizes and configurations. In general, the larger the case the higher the transistor power rating. Note power transistors have a mounting hole to bolt the transistor to a heat sink.

Figure 9-19(a) shows an NPN transistor in the common emitter configuration, and Figure 9-19(b) shows its characteristic curves. The curves depict a series of base currents for a range of collector-emitter voltages and show the *saturation region,* the *cutoff region,* and the *active region.* The transistor operates as a *switch* when it's in the saturation or cut-off region. In saturation, the voltage drop from the collector to emitter terminals is a few tenths of a volt (like a closed switch contact), so the transistor is in the *on state.* In this state

FIGURE 9-17: Transistor common circuits.

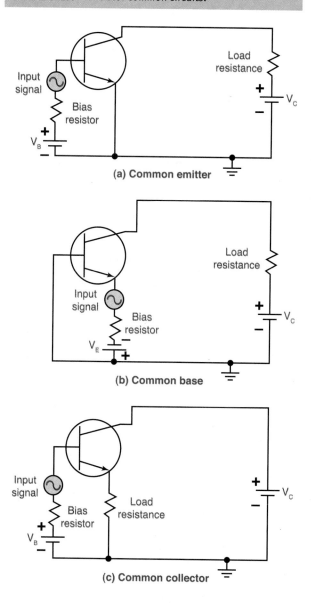

(a) Common emitter

(b) Common base

(c) Common collector

FIGURE 9-18: Transistor case sizes and configurations.

FIGURE 9-19: Transistor common emitter configuration and characteristic curves.

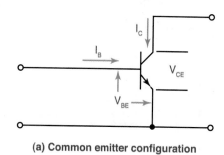

(a) Common emitter configuration

(b) Characteristic curves

the base-emitter junction is *forward biased,* and the base current is greater than the value needed to produce the maximum collector current.

In cutoff, the collector to emitter is an open circuit (like an open switch contact), so the transistor is in the *off state.* The base-emitter junction is *reversed biased,* and zero base current is present. The *active region* produces linear operation. In this mode, a *small change* in base current (microamps) produces a *large* and *proportional change* in collector current (milliamps). The transistor operates as a *linear amplifier* when operation is in the active region.

Field Effect Transistors

The *field effect transistor* (FET) is a three-terminal device where the current flows through two terminals and is controlled at the third. Unlike the standard transistor, the FET is controlled by a voltage at the third terminal rather than by a current. Another difference is the transistor is a bipolar device, and the FET is a unipolar device. The FET devices are well suited for controlled switching between a conducting state and a non-conducting state. Two popular FETs are the

FIGURE 9-20: Junction field effect transistors.

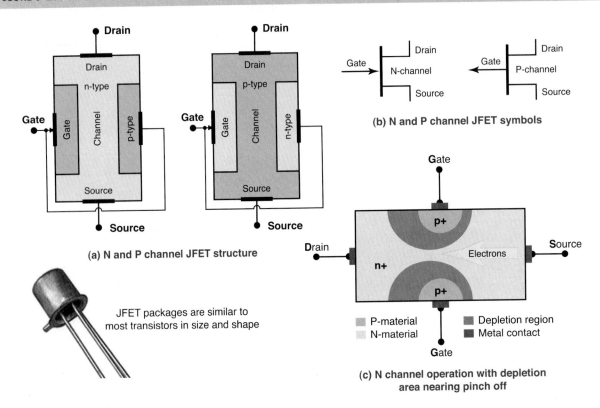

(b) N and P channel JFET symbols

(a) N and P channel JFET structure

JFET packages are similar to
most transistors in size and shape

P-material
N-material
Depletion region
Metal contact

(c) N channel operation with depletion
area nearing pinch off

junction FET (JFET) and the *metal oxide semiconductor FET* (MOSFET). The FETs are characterized by *high input impedance* since the control voltage is applied to a reverse-biased junction or across an insulator. Typical input impedances for these devices are: JFET—thousands of Megaohms and MOSFET—millions of Megaohms.

The *junction FET* (JFET) PN structure and its schematic symbol are shown in Figure 9-20 for the N-channel and P-channel JFET. The three terminals of the JFET, *drain, source, and gate,* are analogous to the *collector, emitter,* and *base* of a standard transistor. The current flow between the source and the drain is controlled by voltage on the gate. Also, the N-channel JFET is analogous to the NPN transistor, and the P-channel to the PNP. In the PN structure for the JFET, note that a solid bar, made of either *N-type* or *P-type* material, forms the *main body* of the device. The gate is formed by diffusing semiconductor material, N for a P type bar and P for an N type bar, into each side of the main bar. Figure 9-20 illustrates the results of this diffusion. The portion of the bar between the deposits of gate material has a *smaller cross section* than the rest of the bar and forms the *channel* connecting the source and the drain.

A *zero* gate voltage allows *maximum* current flow through the channel. When the gate and source are *reverse biased* the depletion area in the channel *increases* and channel current *decreases* proportionally. Figure 9-20(c) shows the channel with the depletion region, which is an insulator, blocking about half of the channel width. When the depletion region extends over the entire channel width, channel current (drain to source) is zero. This zero channel current state is called *pinch off.* The gate voltage that produces zero channel current is call the *pinch off voltage.*

The *metal oxide semiconductor FET* (MOSFET), like the JFET, is either a P-channel type or N-channel type. However, the MOSFET operates in one of two basics modes—the *depletion mode* or the *enhancement mode.* The MOSFET has four terminals—*gate, source, drain,* and *substrate.* The schematic symbols for the four variations are shown in Figure 9-21 along with a typical MOSFET device. The depletion mode MOSFET has a *heavily doped* channel and the enhancement mode MOSFET has a *lightly doped* channel. While the MOSFET is a four terminal device, the substrate contact is often connected to the source inside the device package. The circuit symbols shown in the figure have this internal connection present.

FIGURE 9-21: MOSFET circuit symbols and typical device case.

FIGURE 9-22: MOSFET operation.

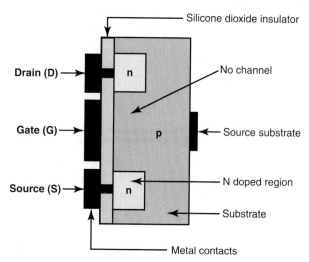

(a) MOSFET circuit symbols depletion mode above and enhancement mode below—P channel on the left and N channel on the right

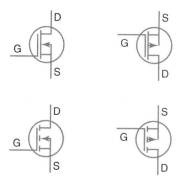

(b) Typical power MOSFET device

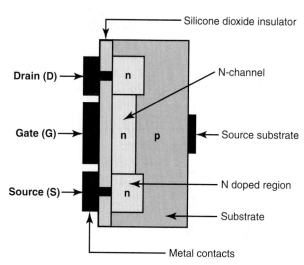

(a) MOSFET in off condition with no channel

(b) MOSFET in on condition with N channel

The construction of an *N-channel* MOSFET is shown as a cross section in Figure 9-22. Heavily doped N-type regions are diffused into a P-substrate or base. A metal oxide, insulating layer is then formed over the channel, and a metal gate layer is deposited over the insulating layer. There is no electrical connection between the gate and the rest of the device.

The operation of the MOSFET is similar to the JFET. The current flow between the source and the drain is controlled by voltage on the gate. A positive gate to source voltage in Figure 9-22 draws electrons into the channel between the two N materials. Electrons from the heavily doped N material build an N channel and conduction between drain and source starts. P channel devices work with a negative gate voltage to control conduction.

Phototransistors

The *phototransistor* is a solid state device that combines a photodiode and transistor. A lens on the top of the transistor case focuses light on the base region of the semiconductor. Figure 9-23 illustrates the *construction, symbols,* and examples of *two* and *three lead*

devices. The *three-lead* device is turned on by *light* through the lens or with *current* at the base terminal. In a *two-lead* phototransistor, the *light* is the only external stimulus used to turn on the collector—emitter current flow. In both type devices, a cover/lens over the junctions allows light to reach the semiconductor. The cover allows *light* to fall on the collector-base region, which stimulates the current flow between the *emitter* and *collector*. The enlarged collector-base junction in Figure 9-23 works as a *reverse biased photodiode* with built in gain. The phototransistor conducts current as a function of the light intensity. The light intensity and collector to emitter resistance are *inversely* proportional. The higher the light intensity the lower the resistance. The relatively small base current produced by the light is amplified by the transistor current gain, *beta* (β). The collector to emitter current depends on the *light intensity* and the *beta* of the phototransistor. In the absence of light, the phototransistor turns off and only *leakage current* flows. This current is called the *collector dark current*.

Optocouplers

A solid state *optocoupler*, shown in Figure 9-24, includes an *infrared emitting diode* (IRED) input stage and a *phototransistor* output stage. *One-way* transfer of electrical signals from the IRED (emitter) to the phototransistor (detector) occurs through a *glass dielec-*tric separating the input stage from output stage. Linking the input to the output with light assures *total electrical isolation* between the input and output. The IRED emitted light wavelength is compatible with the phototransistor's detection capability. Attention to the input drive requirements and the output drive capability of the device is necessary for reliable data transfer. Signal flow is *unidirectional* or *bidirectional* depending on the type of device selected. The device in Figure 9-24 is unidirectional. The bidirectional devices have an input stage and an output stage for each direction of data transmission.

Silicon Controlled Rectifiers

The *silicon-controlled rectifier* (SCR) was introduced in the early 1960s. The SCR is a *three-terminal, four-layer* semiconductor that is built with alternating P-type material and N-type material as shown in Figure 9-25. The *circuit symbol, characteristic curve,* and example *devices* are also illustrated.

The three terminals are the *anode, cathode,* and *gate.* The anode and cathode of the SCR are similar to the anode and cathode of a *diode.* The *gate* is the *control point* or *trigger* for the device. The SCR is often described as two transistors, a PNP above an NPN with two junctions shared. These devices control currents of several hundred amperes and operate in circuits at very high voltages. As its name suggests, the SCR is a *rectifier,* so it passes current only in *one direction.* When turned *on* (conducting or shorted), they provide a *low resistance* current path from *anode to cathode.* When turned *off* (not conducting or open), no current flows from *anode to cathode.* SCRs are used

FIGURE 9-23: Photo transistor configuration and circuit symbols.

Device	Symbol	
Phototransistor	Three leads	Two leads

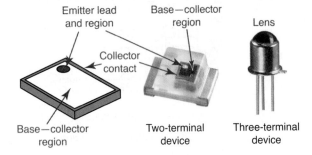

Emitter lead and region
Base—collector region
Lens
Collector contact
Base—collector region
Two-terminal device
Three-terminal device

FIGURE 9-24: Optocoupler circuit and four pin DIP package.

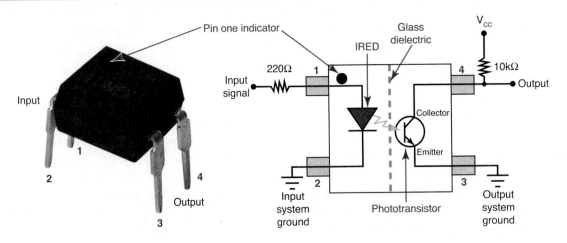

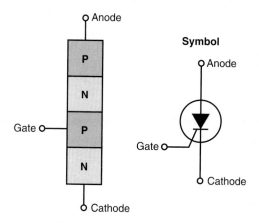

Symbol

Four layers—three junctions

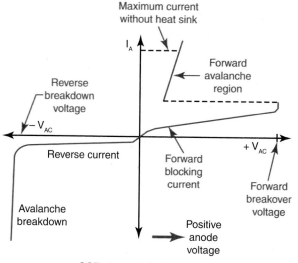

SCR characteristic curve

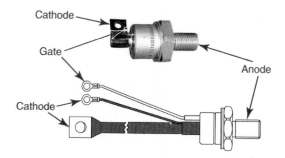

High current SCR models

When controlling AC power, the SCR turns on at some point in the *positive half* of the AC voltage cycle. It turns off at the 180 degree point in the cycle when the voltage passes through zero. When the SCR turns on late in the positive half of the cycle the average power to the load is *low*. However, if the SCR turns on early in the positive half of the AC cycle then the average power is *larger*. As a result, the *average power* delivered to the load is *controlled* by the *turn on point* in the positive half of the AC voltage cycle. This offers a significant advantage over other devices used to control the average power delivered to a load. In other type devices, the power not consumed by the load is *dissipated* in the form of heat in the controlling device. Efficiency is *low* and energy is *wasted*. The SCR does not start conducting until the desired starting voltage point in the AC cycle waveform is reached. As a result, no current flows during the portion of the cycle not required to achieve the desired average power value. When the SCR conducts, the anode to cathode resistance is near zero; therefore, heat loss in the SCR switching device after power is applied to the load is near zero. Efficiency is *enhanced* and energy is *not wasted* in the switching process.

In most applications, an SCR with an anode voltage greater than the cathode voltage is put in the conduction mode with a trigger from the gate. However, anode to cathode voltage greater than the *forward breakover voltage* also causes the SCR to conduct without a *gate trigger* present. *Forward breakover voltage* is the positive anode to cathode voltage required to switch an SCR into a *conductive state*. As gate voltage increases, the breakover voltage necessary for the SCR to conduct decreases. At some value of gate voltage, called the *gate trigger voltage*, the SCR is placed into the conduction state for any positive anode voltage. Low-current SCRs operate with an anode current of less than 1 milliamp, and high-current SCRs handle load currents in the hundreds of amperes.

The SCR characteristic curve is shown in Figure 9-25. Note that the voltage-current characteristic curve of an SCR indicates that it operates much like a standard diode in reverse bias. When an SCR is forward biased but not in full conduction, there is also a small forward leakage current (*forward blocking current*). This current remains relatively constant until the forward breakover voltage is reached or the device is triggered with a gate voltage. At that point, the current increases rapidly and is often referred to as the *forward*

almost exclusively to control AC power delivered to a load. When used with an AC voltage source, the negative half cycle automatically turns the SCR off when the voltage passes through zero. SCRs provide fast switching action like most other solid state devices.

avalanche region. In the forward avalanche region, the current is only limited by external load resistance.

An SCR operates like the contacts of a single directional current switch—an SCR is either *conducting* (closed contact) or *not conducting* (open contact). An SCR *conducts* (fires) when the applied voltage is above the forward breakover voltage (V_{BRF}) or when the *gate trigger voltage* is applied with the anode positive with respect to the cathode. The SCR conducts as long as the current stays above the *holding current* and the *anode remains positive* with respect to the cathode. *Holding current* is the minimum current necessary for an SCR to continue conducting. An SCR returns to its off state when the SCR's anode to cathode voltage drops to a value too low to maintain the holding current. Once an SCR has been turned on by the gate current, the gate current loses control of the SCR forward current. Even if the gate current is completely removed, the SCR remains on until the anode voltage drops to zero or the anode current falls below the minimum current to hold the SCR in conduction.

Triacs

The *triac* was developed to control *AC current flow* to a load for *both halves* of the AC cycle. It operates like a pair of SCRs connected in a *reverse parallel configu-ration*. The triac is a *three-terminal device* that is built with *multi-layers of N-type* and *P-type* materials as shown in Figure 9-26. The terminals of a triac are the *gate, main terminal 1* (MT1), and *main terminal 2* (MT2). Note that there is *no* designation of anode and cathode. Current flows in *either* direction between *MT1* and *MT2*.

In the non-conduction state, the triac blocks current flow between MT1 and MT2. Conduction is initiated by a *momentary trigger pulse* applied to the gate. The triac characteristic curve in Figure 9-26 shows the characteristics of a triac when triggered into conduction. When compared to the SCR characteristic curve in Figure 9-25, the reverse bias curve is just the mirror image of the forward bias operation. Unlike the SCR, the triac controls current flow during both halves of the AC cycle. For the triac, the trigger pulse circuit produces either a negative or positive trigger pulse that occurs at any point in the positive or negative half-cycle of an AC signal. Therefore, the average current supplied to the load varies based on the trigger point. False triggers are produced by high voltage fast rise time spikes across the anode and cathode. This is often called the *dv/dt effect*. Triacs have lower maximum current levels compared to SCRs with maximum currents in the 50 ampere range. Triacs, like

FIGURE 9-26: Triac configuration and characteristic curve.

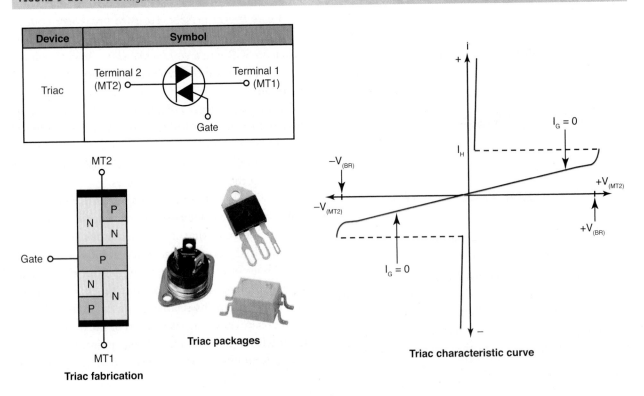

Triac packages

Triac fabrication

Triac characteristic curve

SCRs, are available in a variety of package sizes and mounting configurations.

Diacs

The *diac* is a *two-terminal, three-layer, bidirectional* solid state device as shown in Figure 9-27. Each PN junction is almost identical to the other, but unlike a transistor, the PN junctions of a diac are *heavily* and *equally* doped. It is termed *bidirectional* because current can flow in both directions and the diac is generally used as a triggering device. Therefore, it can be connected in a circuit regardless of polarity. The diac acts like two zener diodes that are connected in series with either the anodes or cathodes joined. This means either diac terminal can be connected to the trigger gate of a device. Note the terminals are marked as A1 and A2.

Diacs allow rapid current increases in both directions after breakdown. The current increase occurs in the negative resistance region as shown in Figure 9-27. A *negative resistance characteristic* occurs when a rise in the device current is accompanied by a drop in the device's terminal voltage. A diac's negative resistance region starts when the voltage across the diac reaches breakover voltage. The diac rapidly switches from a high-resistance state to a low-resistance state when breakdown occurs in either direction. Because a diac is a bidirectional device, it is ideal for controlling triacs, which are also bidirectional devices.

9-5 TROUBLESHOOTING ELECTRONIC DEVICES

The electronic devices discussed in this chapter are generally troubleshot after they are removed from the circuit. However, circuit tests are possible with selected test equipment and a full understanding of how the circuit operates. Common test equipment used in troubleshooting electronic devices include: volt/ohm meters (VOMs), digital multimeters (DMMs), and/or oscilloscopes.

Testing solid state devices generally focuses on determining that the PN junctions present in the devices are operating properly. A second option is to verify that the device characteristic curve has not changed or been degraded. There are three options:

- Remove the device from the circuit and measure the device junctions with a VOM in the ohms mode and check the reading against the values in the table in Figure 9-28. Note the current produced in the diode by the test device is listed under junction current.
- Remove the device from the circuit and measure the device with a DMM in the diode mode and check the reading against the values in the table in Figure 9-28.

FIGURE 9-27: Diac configuration and characteristic curve.

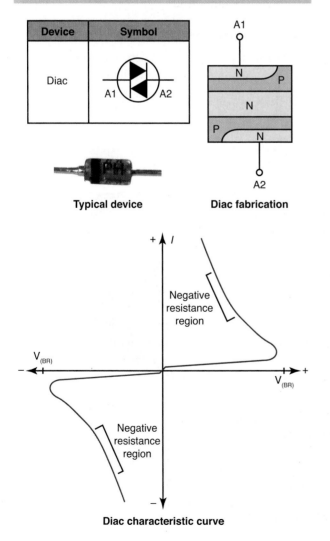

Typical device   **Diac fabrication**

Diac characteristic curve

FIGURE 9-28: VOM and DMM resistance and voltage values for operational PN junctions.

	VOM	VOM	DMM
Range	Rx1	Rx100	Diode test
Junction current	35 mA–50 mA	0.5 mA–1.5 mA	0.5 mA–1 mA
Germanium	8 Ω–19 Ω	200 Ω–300 Ω	0.225 V–0.325 V
Silicon	8 Ω–16 Ω	450 Ω–800 Ω	0.4 V–0.6 V

- With the circuit active, measure junction voltages and verify that forward biased junctions have correct voltage drop and reverse biased junctions have the applied voltage across the open diode circuit.

In general, if the junction works in the forward bias mode, then the junction is not defective.

Troubleshooting Diodes

The method to test a suspected *diode* with one leg removed from the circuit depends on the testing modes available on the DMM or VOM used. In general, the test leads are placed across the diode first in one direction (red lead to P or anode side and black lead to N or cathode side) and then reversed. The former connection is the forward bias measurement and the latter the reverse bias. These two measurement connections for a DMM in the diode test mode are shown in Figure 9-29. Note the enlargement of the DMM mode selector and ohms and diode positions. Analysis of the readings for these connections is provided in the figure as well.

In troubleshooting *zener diodes*, validating that they provide voltage regulation is a good test of a suspect zener. If the zener is not providing regulation, the zener diode is replaced. An oscilloscope is used for testing the operating characteristics of a zener diode as shown in Figure 9-30.

Troubleshooting Transistors

Transistors typically become defective from excessive current or temperature and fail with a junction that is open or at some constant resistance. The junctions of a transistor are tested with a DMM set to the diode

---

FIGURE 9-29: Troubleshooting diodes.

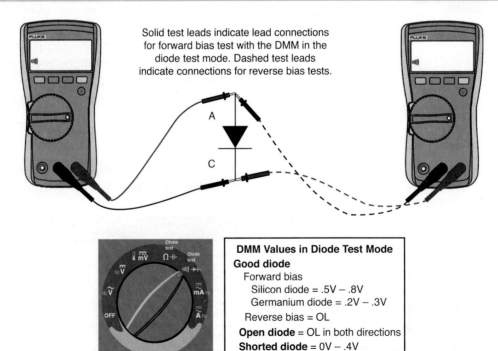

Solid test leads indicate lead connections for forward bias test with the DMM in the diode test mode. Dashed test leads indicate connections for reverse bias tests.

DMM Values in Diode Test Mode
Good diode
Forward bias
Silicon diode = .5V – .8V
Germanium diode = .2V – .3V
Reverse bias = OL
Open diode = OL in both directions
Shorted diode = 0V – .4V

FIGURE 9-30: Troubleshooting zener diodes.

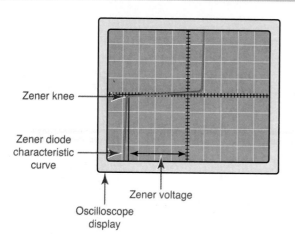

FIGURE 9-31: Troubleshooting transistors.

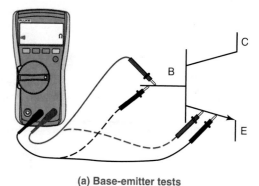

(a) Base-emitter tests

(b) Base-collector tests

test mode using the same procedure used for a single junction diode. The test lead connection for the base-emitter junction are shown in Figure 9-31(a) and the tests for the base-collector junction are shown in Figure 9-31(b). The forward bias connections for the NPN device are illustrated with solid test leads and the reverse bias with dashed test leads. Use the analysis box in Figure 9-29 to evaluate meter measurements.

In most cases, if both junctions are operational, then the transistor is operational. However, characteristics, like transistor gain, often decrease with age and with use in harsh environmental conditions. A specialized transistor tester is required if the junctions test good, and additional tests on the transistor characteristics are necessary.

Troubleshooting Silicon Controlled Rectifiers

An oscilloscope is used to test an SCR under operating conditions, but the DMM is used as a quick test to verify if a suspect SCR is good. To test the SCR with a VOM or DMM, the meter must have a source voltage in the ohms mode higher than the gate trigger voltage of the SCR. Verify the meter source voltage before using it to test the SCR. Figure 9-32 illustrates the testing of an SCR with the DMM set to the Ω (ohm) scale. The steps are as follows:

Step 1: Connect the DMM's negative lead to the cathode.

Step 2: Connect the DMM's positive lead to the anode.

- The DMM should read high resistance or OL to indicate an open circuit.

Step 3: Short the gate to the anode. With the anode more positive than the cathode and a gate trigger present, the SCR should turn on.

- The DMM should read low resistance, near zero ohms. Remove the anode to gate short and verify that the low resistance reading remains.

Step 4: Reverse the DMM leads—the positive lead on the cathode and the negative lead on the anode.

- The DMM should read high resistance or OL to indicate an open circuit.

Step 5: Short the gate to the anode. The SCR should not turn on because the anode is negative with respect to the cathode.

- The high resistance or OL reading should remain.

Troubleshooting Triacs

An oscilloscope is used to test a triac under operating conditions, but the DMM is used as a quick test to verify if a suspect triac is good. Figure 9-33 illustrates the testing of a triac with the DMM. The DMM should have sufficient source voltage to trigger the triac as described in the previous SCR DMM tests. To test a

FIGURE 9-32: Troubleshooting SCRs.

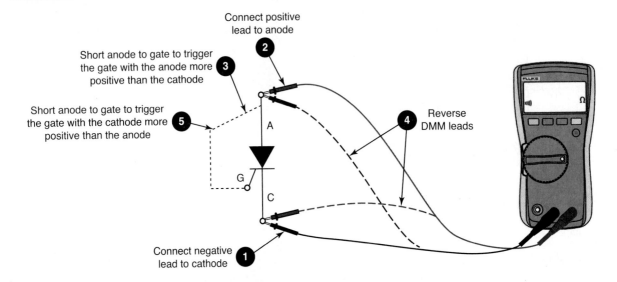

Connect positive
lead to anode
2

Short anode to gate to trigger
the gate with the anode more **3**
positive than the cathode

Short anode to gate to trigger
the gate with the cathode more **5**
positive than the anode

Reverse **4**
DMM leads

A

G

C

Connect negative **1**
lead to cathode

FIGURE 9-33: Troubleshooting triacs.

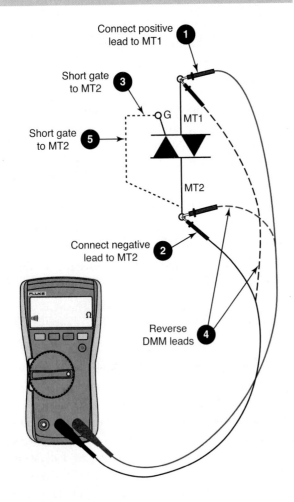

Connect positive **1**
lead to MT1

Short gate **3**
to MT2

Short gate **5**
to MT2

G MT1

MT2

Connect negative **2**
lead to MT2

Reverse **4**
DMM leads

triac, set the DMM on the Ω (ohm) scale, and perform the following steps:

Step 1: Connect the positive lead to MT1.

Step 2: Connect the negative lead to MT2.

- The DMM should read high resistance or OL to indicate an open circuit.

Step 3: Short the gate of the triac to MT2.

- The DMM should read near zero ohms, and the reading should not change after the short is removed.

Step 4: Reverse the DMM leads—the negative lead on MT1 and the positive lead on MT2.

- The DMM should read infinity or OL to indicate an open circuit.

Step 5: Short the gate of the triac to MT2.

- The DMM should read near zero ohms, and the reading should not change after the short is removed.

Troubleshooting Diacs

If a diac is suspect to being *shorted,* a DMM is used to troubleshoot as shown in Figure 9-34. To test a diac for a short circuit, set the DMM on the Ω (ohm) scale, and perform the following steps:

Step 1: Connect the DMM leads to the diac terminals and record the resistance reading.

FIGURE 9-34: Troubleshooting diacs.

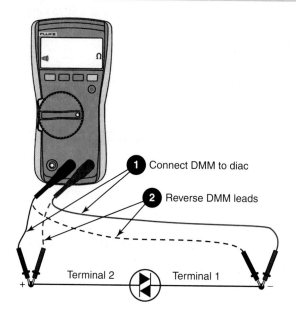

① Connect DMM to diac

② Reverse DMM leads

Terminal 2   Terminal 1

FIGURE 9-35: Troubleshooting diacs with an oscilloscope.

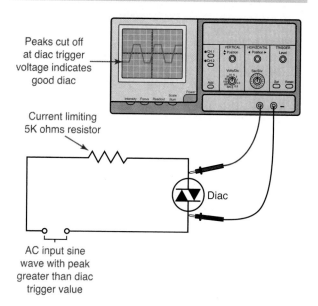

Peaks cut off at diac trigger voltage indicates good diac

Current limiting 5K ohms resistor

Diac

AC input sine wave with peak greater than diac trigger value

Step 2: Reverse the DMM leads and record the resistance reading.

• Both readings should be a high resistance or OL to indicate an open circuit.

If a diac is suspect to being *open*, an oscilloscope is used to troubleshoot as shown in Figure 9-35. To test a diac for an open circuit, set up the test circuit as shown in the figure, connect the oscilloscope, and apply power to the circuit. If the oscilloscope trace is an AC sine wave with the peaks cut off, the diac is good.

CRITICAL CONCEPTS

The need to know content from Chapter 9 is summarized in the following statements.

• Three fundamental particles contained in atoms are protons, neutrons, and electrons. Protons and neutrons make up the nucleus of the atom, and the electrons orbit the nucleus in shells.

• Doping is the addition of impurities to the crystal structure of the semiconductor. By controlling the doping quantity, the operating characteristics of the semiconductor are controlled.

• N-type material is created by doping the region of a crystal with atoms of an element that has more electrons in its outer shell than the crystal.

• P-type material is created by doping the region of a crystal with atoms of an element that has fewer electrons in its outer shell than the crystal.

• Diodes are devices that conduct electricity in one direction only and are made of P-type material (the anode) and N-type material (the cathode).

• A light-emitting diode (LED) is a semiconductor diode that produces light when current flows through it, and the photodiode is *switched* on and off by light.

• The transistor is a three-terminal device with the important feature that the current through two terminals is controlled by small changes in current or voltage at the third terminal.

• The transistor operates as a switch when it's in the saturation or cut-off region and an amplifier when it's in the active region.

• The field effect transistor (FET) is a three-terminal device where the current flows through two terminals and is controlled at the third. Unlike the standard transistor, the FET is controlled by a voltage at the third terminal rather than by a current.

• The phototransistor is a solid state device that combines the effect of a photodiode and the switching capability of the transistor, and the optocoupler is a solid state device that consists of an infrared emitting diode as the input stage and a phototransistor as the output stage.

- The SCR is a three terminal, four-layer semi-conductor that is built with alternating P-type material and N-type material. The three terminals are the anode, cathode, and gate, where anode and cathode are similar to the anode and cathode of a diode, and the gate is controls the SCR operation.
- The triac is a three-terminal device that is built with multi-layers of N-type and P-type materials and operates like a pair of SCRs connected in a reverse parallel arrangement.
- The diac is a two-terminal, three-layer, bidirectional solid state device. It is termed bidirectional because current can flow in both directions and generally used as a triggering device and can be connected in a circuit regardless of polarity.
- The electronic devices are generally troubleshot after they are removed from the circuit. Testing a device that is in the circuit may give a false reading because other devices may be connected in parallel with the device under test. Common test equipment used in troubleshooting is a digital multimeter (DMM) and/or an oscilloscope.

QUESTIONS

1. Describe semiconductor doping and its purpose.
2. Describe how P-type and N-type material is developed.
3. What are semiconductor holes?
4. Describe the function of the depletion region in a diode.
5. What is a zener diode?
6. What is the functional difference between an LED and a photodiode?
7. Describe the differences between a standard transistor and a field effect transistor.
8. What is the difference between a JFET and a MOSFET?
9. Describe the operation of a phototransistor and an optocoupler.
10. Describe the operation of a SCR.
11. What are the differences between a SCR and a triac?
12. How does a diac function and what is its circuit application?

CHAPTER 10

Solid State Devices

GOALS AND OBJECTIVES

The primary goals for this chapter are to identify solid state devices, and to describe the operation of and applications for these discrete control devices in manufacturing systems. In addition, troubleshooting tips and procedures for typical failure modes are presented.

After completing this chapter, you should be able to:

1. Identify and describe photoelectric devices and the scanning methods used.
2. Identify and describe the inductive, capacitive and ultrasonic proximity sensors.
3. Identify and describe the Hall Effect sensor and the actuation methods used.

10-1 SOLID STATE INPUT DEVICES

Solid state input devices or sensors are the *eyes, ears* and *tactile senses* of the machines in industrial and commercial systems. Three distinctive characteristics of discrete solid state sensors are (1) a *single-input condition* or *set-point* triggers a change in the device output state, (2) the output of the device swings between two conditions, *activated* and *de-activated* and (3) the unique models used for control of repetitive and line type automation systems. The sensors that are covered in this chapter are *discrete* devices whereas *analog* devices are covered in a later chapter.

The mechanically- and automatically-operated input devices that are covered in earlier chapters rely on external forces such as *pressure, motion, temperature change* or *fluid flow* to actuate the device. As a result of these external forces, a set of contacts in the device change state when acted upon by these forces. Solid state input devices have no moving parts and do not rely on *direct contact* with any object or process parameter. As a result, these sensors are often called *non-contact* sensors. The solid state input devices include *photoelectric devices, proximity devices* (capacitive, inductive and ultrasonic), and *Hall-effect* devices.

10-2 SENSOR OUTPUT INTERFACES

Sensors are solid state devices with numerous options for switching the attached load. Output circuits include: *transistors* (BJT), *field effect transistors* (FET), *metal oxide semiconductors* (MOS), *triacs, silicon controlled rectifiers* (SCR), and *relay contacts*. Each output interface offers a unique advantage for the interface to the system controller. Figures 10-1 and 10-2 illustrate sensor output interfaces using the IEC and NEMA symbol standards, respectively. In every case, the external load is matched to the *voltage* and *current* specification for the sensor. A description of each of these output configurations follows.

FIGURE 10-1: IEC sensor output switching devices and loads.

IEC Sensor Symbol	Output Switching Device	Load Power Switched
 (a) NPN transistor	Current sinking NO output (white) for DC loads with an NPN transistor as the output switching device.	Any DC voltage load with the load connected between positive supply voltage and the output of the sensor. BJT output has the lowest current rating but fastest switching times.
 (b) PNP transistor	Current sourcing NO output (black) for DC loads with a PNP transistor as the output switching device.	Any DC voltage load with the load connected between ground or neutral and the output of the sensor. BJT output has the lowest current rating but fastest switching times.
 (c) NPN and PNP transistors	Current sinking (white) and sourcing (black) NO outputs for DC loads with NPN and PNP transistor outputs for switching either load types. A NO (white) and NC (black) option is also available.	Any DC voltage load with the load connected as indicated for sinking or sourcing output. BJT output has the lowest current rating but fastest switching times.
 (d) SCR output driver	An SCR switches the output for an AC or DC load. The load and DC source are placed across the brown and blue lines. A bridge circuit in the output permits the DC SCR device to switch either AC or DC powered loads.	Any AC or DC powered load with the load connected between brown and blue outputs of the sensor. Current switching capability is much larger than BJT outputs.
 (e) Relay, FET, MOS, or Triac driver	A relay, FET, MOS, or Triac are used as switching devices for this type of sensor output. AC switching is the most common with the load either in the blue or brown lines.	Primarily AC loads are used, but DC is switched in some devices. Large current switching is possible with the relay and Triac output devices.

Transistor Outputs

The *bipolar junction transistor* (BJT) or *transistor* is used most often to link solid state sensors to their loads. The interface has two configurations; *current sinking* and *current sourcing* as shown in Figures 10-1 and 10-2, sections (a) and (b). Current-sinking sensor outputs control DC power loads and have an NPN transistor in the sensor output circuit. In current sinking, the NPN output transistor acts as a switch to ground for one lead of the load; therefore the other lead of the load is connected to the positive DC source. Therefore, a current-sinking sensor output has current flowing into the output of the sensor and then to ground through NPN transistor switch. In contrast, the PNP sensor output circuit has a current-sourcing characteristic for use with DC loads. When the sensor is active, the output transistor acts as a switch to the positive DC power-supply source for one lead of the load. The other lead of the load is connected to ground.

FIGURE 10-2: NEMA sensor output switching devices and loads.

NEMA Sensor Symbols
NO NPN sinking or NO PNP sourcing—three wire sensor
(a) Normally open (NO) sensor
NC NPN sinking or NC PNP sourcing—three wire sensor
(b) Normally closed (NC) sensor
NC and NO sourcing contacts available—four wire sensor
(c) Complementary normally open and normally closed
NO—two wire sensor
(d) Normally open (NO) sensor
NC—two wire sensor
(e) Normally closed (NC) sensor

NPN and PNP Sensors with NO and NC Outputs

The interface in Figure 10-1(c) illustrates a dual output sensor with NO contacts in both the current sinking and current sourcing output modes. The NPN output supports current sinking and the PNP provides current sourcing.

SCR and Triac Outputs

The SCR output is illustrated in Figure 10-1(d). Most SCR sensor interfaces switch AC and DC loads. In some sensors, the SCR is replaced with a triac to perform the same switching function.

Relay and Other Outputs

The relay output in Figure 10-1(e) has a SPST contact, but SPDT are often present. The external source for the load is either AC or DC with no specific polar-ity requirements. The voltage supply for the load has 100 percent *isolation* from the power source used for the sensor electronics. Typical contact ratings are 3 A at 250V AC or 3 A at 30V DC. The FET and MOS solid state output devices also switch AC and DC loads but do not have the power switching capability of the relay. Study Figures 10-1 and 10-2 until the advantages of each output interface device is clear.

10-3 PHOTOELECTRIC DEVICES

Photoelectric devices are solid state devices that use light to detect the presence of objects without physical contact. They use the level of light present at the photoelectric device to detect the presence or position of a product or the position of a machine during operation. Photoelectric devices are commonly used in operations where the recognition of objects is difficult or impossible with mechanical or automatic switches. For example, the weight of some objects is too light for a limit switch to detect while others are too heavy, causing possible damage to the switch. In other situations, the temperature or corrosive nature of the process material prevents direct contact with a mechanical or automatic switch.

Photocells

Photocells (also called day-light switches) are unique photoelectric devices that only react to ambient light. They are commonly used to control *site* and *exterior lighting* in residential, commercial and industrial applications. Figure 10-3 illustrates a common photocell switch. Photocell switches include a *photocell* to measure the level of light present, an *electronic circuit* to condition the signal from the photocell, and one or more *contacts* for control of external loads. The photocell resistance varies in proportion to the level of light on the surface of the device. When the light on the photocell surface increases, the circuit resistance decreases. The electronic circuit produces a change in the output contacts at a specific light level or photocell resistance. Photocells use *lens* and *positioning* to avoid nuisance switching during momentary lighting changes such as vehicle headlights or clouds. Many photocell switches have a built in time delay ranging from 15 seconds to 1 minute to verify

FIGURE 10-3: Photocell switch.

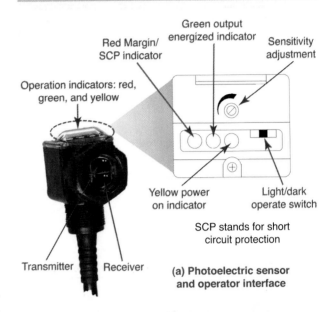

(a) Photoelectric sensor and operator interface

a valid change in the measured light level before triggering a change in the output. Although photocells are available in several voltage configurations, the most common voltages are 120V AC and 277V AC.

Photoelectric Device Operation

To improve the reliability of the photoelectric device operation, a built-in light source is integrated into the photoelectric device. This eliminates the dependence on ambient light to trigger the photocell. As a result, two components are present in photoelectric devices— a *light source,* which transmits light, and a *receiver,* which detects the presence of the light source. Figure 10-4(a) shows a photoelectric device with its transmitter and receiver marked. Figure 10-4(b) shows the IEC and NEMA symbols for the device. Photoelectric devices sense the presence of an object or part when the part either *breaks a light beam* or *reflects a beam of light* to a receiver. The change in light is the result of the *presence* or *absence* of the object, or as the result in a change of the *size, shape, reflectivity* or *color* of an object. Four parameters are commonly used to describe photoelectric devices operation: *response time, sensitivity, operating margin,* and *light/dark operation.*

Response time is measured by the number of light pulses per second that a photoelectric device transmits to detect an object. The greater the number of pulses the faster the response in detecting small moving targets. As a result, fast response times become

Letter Code	NEMA	IEC
	NO	NO
NEMA – PRS IEC – SQ		
	NC	NC

(b) NEMA and IEC photoelectric sensor contact symbols and letter code

important when the operation requires the detection of very small objects, objects moving at a high rate of speed, or both. Response times vary from 0.2 milliseconds to 60 milliseconds, with the vast majority of control applications operating at response times in the lower range.

Sensitivity is the trigger point to change the status of the output. Sensitivity is set by adjusting the threshold value for received light or the intensity of light, which triggers the photoelectric device to produce an output. The majority of photoelectric switching devices have sensitivity adjustments that adjust the threshold for triggering. The adjustment is made after installation to calibrate the sensor. Photoelectric switches are

A conveyer system is used to load a truck with boxes. As a box approaches the end of the conveyor, a dock person takes a box from the conveyor and puts it on a truck. Figure 10-5 illustrates system set-up and the ladder diagram that controls the starting and stopping of the conveyor. Pressing the *start* pushbutton completes the circuit to the control relay *CR1*, thus closing the auxiliary contacts *1-CR1* and *2-CR1*, and starting the conveyor motor. If the photoelectric device detects a box near the end of the conveyor, the NC contact of the photoelectric device opens, stopping the conveyor. When the box is removed, the photoelectric device NC contact closes, restarting the conveyor.

FIGURE 10-5: Conveyor control ladder diagram.

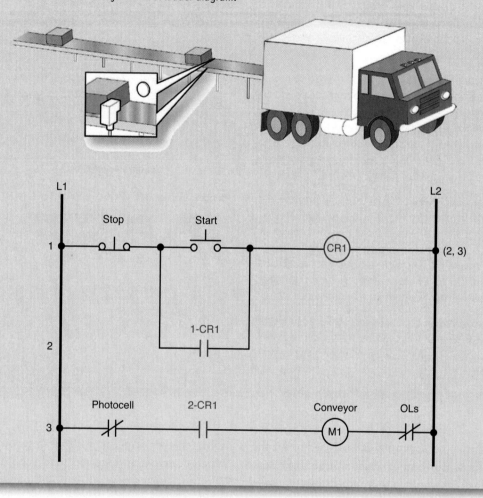

calibrated starting at the lowest trigger threshold setting and working toward the higher settings until the proper device operation is obtained. Using a lower trigger threshold or brighter light transmitters reduces phantom switching caused by excessive ambient light. Also, these settings permit easier detection of clear or translucent objects.

Operating margin is the ratio of the available level of light at the sensor's receiver to the minimum level of light required to trigger the sensor. If the operating margin is one, then the minimum level of light is present for triggering the sensor. With a margin of one any change in the ambient conditions, for example, increased dust in the air, results in unreliable sensor operation. In most applications an operation margin of 2.5 or higher is desired. The sensor manufacturer's data includes graphs of sensing distance versus operation margin values.

The conveyor control described in the previous application sidebar occurs frequently in manufacturing. As a result, a sensor solution is offered by some manufactures that automates the process. The Rockwell solution is called *zone control*. Review the system drawing in Figure 10-6 as you read the description of the operation. The conveyor is broken into zones, four in this example, with each started and stopped with a pneumatic valve. Each zone has a photoelectric sensor and all these components interface to a conveyor zone controller. The controller has two normally open maintain contact pushbutton switch options: *singular release* and *slug release*.

Loading Product—When power is applied to the system and product enters zone four, the system automatically starts and stops zone conveyors to produce an equal length gap between product as shown in Figure 10-6(a). This ensures zero pressure between products throughout the system. When product reaches the discharge zone (1), the conveyor stops and waits for a release signal.

Singular Release of Product—Two release options are available: singular release, Figure 10-6(b), and slug release, Figure 10-6(c). Singular release moves only the product in zone one and all other zones are stationary. As the product clears the zone one sensor, the upstream zones advance one zone. Product continues to discharge until the singular release pushbutton is reset to the original open state.

Slug Release of Product—Slug release moves all products on the conveyor simultaneously. When the slug release push button is released, the remaining products resume normal accumulation.

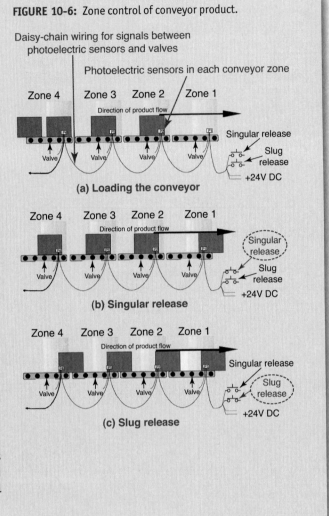

FIGURE 10-6: Zone control of conveyor product.

(a) Loading the conveyor

(b) Singular release

(c) Slug release

Light operate and *dark operate* are used to set the condition of a sensor output when a target is present or absent. The light operate output setting triggers a change in the sensor output when the receiver receives sufficient light from the light source. With the dark operate setting, the sensor outputs change when light levels on the receiver drop. Some photoelectric sensors support both modes selectable by a switch.

Photoelectric Scanning Methods

Photoelectric devices use a process called *scanning* to measure the change in light intensity caused by the presence or absence of objects or targets in the path of the light source. When a target is detected by a change in light level at the sensor's receiver, the input

light receiver triggers a solid state output device, which controls an external load such as a solenoid or motor starter. Several scanning methods are used by photoelectric switches in commercial and industrial applications. Factors that determine the best scanning technique include the following: *distance to the target, size of the target, reflectance level of the target, position of the target, difference in target reflective properties compared to the background,* and *environmental conditions*. The most common scanning methods are *direct, retroreflective, polarized,* and *diffuse* scans.

Direct Scan *Direct scan* (transmitted beam or thru-beam) is a scanning method in which the transmitter and receiver are placed opposite each other. The light beam from the transmitter shines directly on the receiver. The target must pass directly between the transmitter and the receiver. In this method, the receiver is aligned with the transmitter beam to capture the maximum amount of light emitted from the transmitter. Direct scanning is a more reliable method where the environment tends to have impurities in the air that may disperse the beam or when monitoring over a large range. Since the beam travels directly from the transmitter to the receiver, direct scan provides *long-range sensing, has fewer alignment issues,* and *has less interference from impurities in the air* such as dust, dirt or mist. Figure 10-7(a) illustrates the direct scan method. Note that the light beam from the transmitter is broken when the target passes between the transmitter and the receiver.

Retroreflective Scan—*Retroreflective scan* is a scanning method in which the transmitter and receiver are housed in the same enclosure. The transmitted beam is reflected back to the receiver from a reflector. This scanning method is easy to initially calibrate and less likely to require frequent re-calibration as a result of excessive machinery vibration. Retroreflective scans are not commonly used in applications where the surface of the product to be sensed is shiny or reflective. These surfaces reflect the transmitted light back to the receiver, generating a false reading. Also, retroreflective scanning is used in applications where sensing is possible from only one side. Figure 10-7(b) illustrates the retroreflective scan method. Note that the light beam from the transmitter is broken when the target passes between the transmitter and the reflector.

Polarized Scan—*Polarized scan* is a scanning method in which the receiver responds only to the depolarized reflected light from a *special reflector* or *polarized sensitive reflective tape.* Polarized scanning and retro-reflective scanning share many of the same operational characteristics. Both types have a transmitter and receiver that are housed in the same enclosure. Also, both rely on the light beam from the transmitter to be reflected back to the receiver. The primary difference between these two types is that polarized

FIGURE 10-7: Direct scan and retroreflective scan photoelectric sensors.

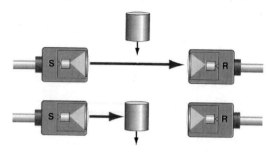

(a) Direct scan (transmitted beam or thru beam)

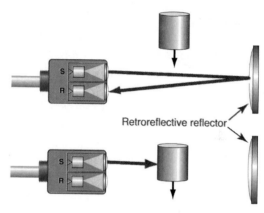

Retroreflective reflector

(b) Retroreflective scan

scanning relies on a special reflector or reflecting tape to return the transmitted light to the receiver. Polarized photoelectric sensors have polarizing filters in front of the transmitter and receiver that are perpendicular to each other. The light is transmitted in one specific plane and the reflector returns the light in both planes, as seen in Figure 10-8(a). As a result, the receiver filter passes the light into the photo sensors. If the light is reflected back to the receiver from the surface of an object, it returns in the same polarized plane as the transmitted beam. Therefore, it never passes through the polarizing filter on the receiver. When the polarized light is reflected from an object's surface, for example, the outside surface of a plastic bottle, no change in the polarized beam is produced. This is called a *first surface reflection.* However, any reflection from a second surface, for example, the inside surface of the plastic bottle,

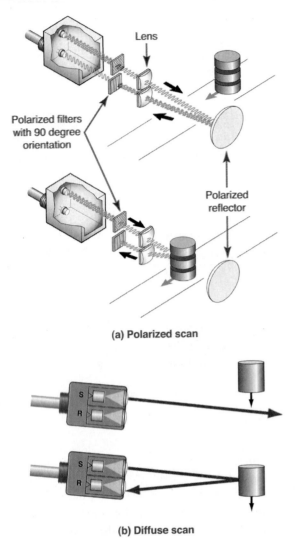

FIGURE 10-8: Polarized scan and diffuse scan photoelectric sensors.

Lens

Polarized filters with 90 degree orientation

Polarized reflector

(a) Polarized scan

S
R

S
R

(b) Diffuse scan

changes the polarization so the reflection looks like the polarized target signal. This is called a *second surface reflection* and produces false sensor outputs. Polarized scan is not affected by ambient light sources and is useful when detecting shinny or reflective materials. Figure 10-8(a) illustrates the polarized scan method. Note that the light beam from the transmitter is broken when the target passes between the transmitter and the reflector.

Diffuse Scan—*Diffuse scan* is a scanning method in which the transmitter and receiver are housed in the same enclosure. In this scan, a small percentage of the transmitted beam is reflected back to the receiver from the target. The diffuse scan does not rely on a reflector to return the light to the receiver. Diffuse scanning is a specialized scanning technique used not only to determine when an object has moved into position, but also to identify the specific location of the object. The sensitivity is set to simply detect an object or to detect a certain point on an object that may be more reflective. Often, this is accomplished using various colors with different reflective properties. In addition, manufacturers offer transmitters with *infrared, visible red, green* or *white* light sources. Diffuse scanning is calibrated to the exact material or object being scanned. If this method is used to detect exact points on an object, the object must be in the same position each time it is scanned for the method to properly function. Figure 10-8(b) illustrates the diffuse scan method. Note that the light beam from the transmitter is reflected back from the target to the receiver.

TECH NOTES

The scanning method used for an application generally depends on the environment. In many applications, several scanning methods work, but one is usually best. Figure 10-9 illustrates applications, advantages, and precautions for the scanning methods of photoelectric devices. Note that diffuse scan sensors are available in five different models to satisfy a variety of applications. Also, note that the final entry is Fiber Optics, which is not a scanning method, but an aid to photoelectric sensors.

(continued)

FIGURE 10-9: Overview of photoelectric sensor applications, advantages, and precautions.

Scanning Method	Applications	Advantages	Precautions
Transmitted beam	General purpose sensing Parts counting	• High operation margin for contaminated environments • Longest sensing distances • Not affected by second surface reflections • Probably most reliable when you have highly reflective objects	• More expensive because of separate light source and receiver required, more costly wiring • Alignment important • Avoid detecting objects of clear material
Retroreflective	General purpose sensing	• Moderate sensing distances • Less expensive than transmitted beam because simpler wiring • Ease of alignment	• Shorter sensing distance than transmitted beam • Less operation margin than transmitted beam • May detect reflections from shiny objects (use polarized instead)
Polarized retroreflective	General purpose sensing of shiny objects	• Ignores first surface reflections • Uses visible red beam for ease of alignment	• Shorter sensing distance than standard retroreflective • May see second surface reflections
Standard diffuse	Applications where both sides of the object cannot be accessed	• Access to both sides of the object not required • No reflector needed • Ease of alignment	• Can be difficult to apply if the background behind the object is sufficiently reflective and close to the object
Sharp cutoff diffuse	Short-range detection of objects with the need to ignore backgrounds that are close to the object	• Access to both sides of the object not required • Provides some protection against sensing of close backgrounds • Detects objects regardless of color within specified distance	• Only useful for very short distance sensing • Not used with backgrounds close to object
Background suppression diffuse	General purpose sensing Areas where you need to ignore backgrounds that are close to the object	• Access to both sides of the target not required • Ignores backgrounds beyond rated sensing distance regardless of reflectivity • Detects objects regardless of color at specified distance	• More expensive than other types of diffuse sensors • Limited maximum sensing distance
Fixed focus diffuse	Detection of small targets Detects objects at a specific distance from sensor Detection of color marks	• Accurate detection of small objects in a specific location	• Very short distance sensing • Not suitable for general purpose sensing • Object must be accurately positioned
Wide angle diffuse	Detection of objects not accurately positioned Detection of very fine threads over a broad area	• Good at ignoring background reflections • Detecting objects that are not accurately positioned • No reflector needed	• Short distance sensing
Fiber optics	Allows photoelectric sensing in areas where a sensor cannot be mounted because of size or environment considerations	• Glass fiber optic cables available for high ambient temperature applications • Shock and vibration resistant • Plastic fiber optic cables can be used in areas where continuous movement is required • Insert in limited space • Noise immunity • Corrosive areas placement	• More expensive than lensed sensors • Short distance sensing

Figures 10-10 and 10-11 illustrate photoelectric sensors in a variety of applications in packaging and material handling. The sensing task is stated below the illustrations, and the solutions are described to the right.

FIGURE 10-10: Application of direct scan, standard diffuse scan, retroreflective scan and diffuse scan with background suppression photoelectric sensors.

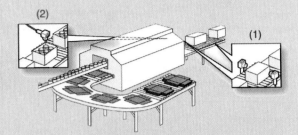

Detect the front edge of the cardboard box with a direct scan sensor pair (1). Detect the jars with six standard diffuse sensors (one sensor per jar) (2). The transmitted beam pair acts as a gating sensor, letting the six diffuse sensors know when to look for caps.

(a) To detect six (6) jars with white metallic lids inside of an open cardboard box

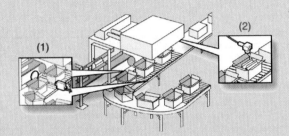

Using retroreflective photoelectric sensor and target (1) to detect the leading edge of the box so that the box is positioned correctly for the insertion of the flour. Then confirm the presence of the flour using a background suppression sensor (2). Once this is done, the box is sealed and plastic wrapped.

(b) Sense presence of corrugated box and baking flour so that the box can be plastic wrapped

Courtesy of Rockwell Automation, Inc.

FIGURE 10-11: Application of diffuse scan background suppression, polarized retroreflective scan and fiber optic photoelectric sensors.

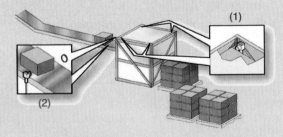

Use a diffuse background suppression photoelectric sensor (1) mounted at the corners of palletizer to sense when it is full and ready for next layer of boxes. Use polarized retroreflective photoelectric sensor and target (2) to count boxes entering palletizer. Initiate table movement and indicate when pallets are full.

(a) Sense correct number of packages on a pallet before its wrapping and removal

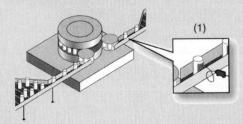

Use fiber optic diffuse photoelectric sensor (1) for a precise determination and measurement of the label placement by mounting small fiber optic head close to the passing bottles. Mount the sensor body away from the bottle conveyor.

(b) Ensure labels are on bottles and that the location is correct

Courtesy of Rockwell Automation, Inc.

Fiber Optic Switches—Fiber optic switches function like photoelectric devices with the added feature of a more compact package. Fiber optics is the technology that uses a thin flexible glass or plastic optical fiber to transmit or receive light. The transmitter and receiver of a fiber optic switch are housed in the same unit with two optical fibers (one for the transmitter and one for the receiver) protruding from the package. The two optical fibers are generally contained in a single cable, which is connected to the switch. The effective scanning distance for most fiber optic switches is a function of the scanning method present. Fiber optic switches are available with most standard scanning methods such as direct, retroreflective, and diffuse. Figure 10-12(a) shows the fiber optic cable, and Figure 10-12(b) shows the fiber optic switch.

FIGURE 10-12: Fiber optic photoelectric sensor control body and fiber cables.

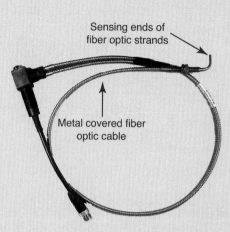

(a) Fiber optic sensor cable and sensing tip

(b) Fiber optic sensor body, transmitter, receiver, and control circuits

10-4 PROXIMITY SENSORS

Proximity sensors are solid state devices that detect the presence of an object by means of an *electronic* sensing field. The two most frequently used are the *inductive* and *capacitive* type sensors with *electromagnetic* and *electrostatic* fields respectively. Proximity sensors detect the presence of solids such as metal, glass, plastic, and most liquids. They detect small objects such as transistors and very large objects such as automobiles. Proximity sensors are encapsulated solid-state circuits suitable in high-vibration conditions, wet locations, and fast-switching applications.

Proximity sensors are available in many shapes and sizes to meet the requirements of industrial and commercial applications. One of the most common shapes is the *cylindrical barrel* configuration that houses the sensor in a threaded metal or polymer barrel. Barrel style inductive proximity sensors are shown in Figure 10-13(a). Barrel styles are produced with and without *shields* as illustrated in Figure 10-13(a). Figure 10-13(b) illustrates the NEMA and IEC proximity sensor symbols.

The threaded housing allows the switch to be easily adjusted when set into a mounting frame. Other less common enclosure styles include rectangular and miniature types. The majority of proximity devices work with control voltages of 12 volts to 24 volts, but some devices have line voltage ratings up to 220 volts. Three proximity sensors are discussed in this section: *inductive*, *capacitive*, and *ultrasonic* sensors.

Inductive Proximity Sensor

Inductive proximity sensors detect the presence of a ferrous or nonferrous metal object when it comes

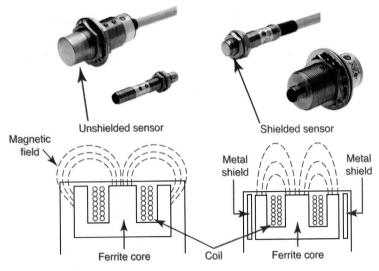

Unshielded sensor

Shielded sensor

(a) Inductive proximity sensors models with shielded and unshielded cores

Courtesy of Rockwell Automation, Inc.

Letter Code	NEMA	IEC
	NO	NO
NEMA – PRS IEC – SQ		
	NC	NC

(b) NEMA and IEC symbols and letter codes

TECH NOTES

Proximity sensors have a scanning head that produces an electronic sensing field used to detect the target. The sensing field must be kept clear of interference for proper operation. Interference is any object other than the desired target. Interference comes from *metal objects* close to the sensor or from *other sensors*. Clearance is required around sensors for proper operation, but the clearance requirements vary for *shielded* versus *unshielded* and among manufacturers of the devices. Figure 10-14 illustrates the minimal sensing distance for flush and non-flush-mounted tubular sensors from Rockwell Automation. Other sensor geometries have different clearance requirements so reference to the data sheet for the device is necessary.

FIGURE 10-14: Flush and non-flush mounted tubular proximity sensors.

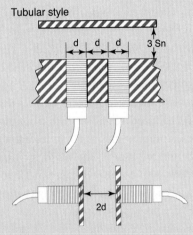

(a) Clearance dimensions for tubular inductive proximity sensors with flush mount and nearby conductive material

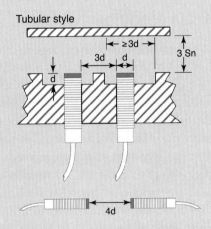

(b) Clearance dimensions for tubular inductive proximity sensors with non-flush mount and nearby conductive material

Note: d is the diameter of the tubular sensing surface and Sn is the minimal sensing distance. Flush mounting in a metal surface produces a shielded sensor.

within a specific distance of a high frequency electromagnetic field radiating from the sensor. Figure 10-15(a) illustrates the inductive proximity sensor operation. Inductive proximity sensors are designed to operate by generating an electromagnetic field and detecting the eddy current losses generated when a ferrous or non-ferrous metal target object enters the field. The sensor consists of a coil on a ferrite core, an oscillator, a trigger-signal level detector, and an output circuit. A standard target, Figure 10-15(b), is used to collect operational data for the sensor data sheet. A standard target is typically a square, one mm thick mild steel plate, with side lengths equal to the diameter of the active face or three times the nominal switching distance, whichever is greater.

As a metallic object approaches the field, eddy currents are induced in the object. The eddy currents in the metallic object absorb some of the radiated energy from the sensor, resulting in a change of amplitude in the sensor's oscillator as shown in Figure 10-15(c). A sensor circuit monitors the change in amplitude and activates a solid state switch at a specific level. This switch changes the sensor's output as shown in Figure 10-15(c). As the metallic object moves away from the sensor, the amplitude of the oscillator returns to its initial value and the output returns to its original state.

Figure 10-13(a) illustrates the effects of shielding on the inductive proximity sensor's field. Shielded construction includes a metal band which surrounds the ferrite core and coil area. Unshielded sensors do not have this metal band. Shielded models have a narrower or focused magnetic field compared to unshielded. However, shielding reduces the range of the sensor.

Inductive proximity sensors detect ferrous metallic objects and non-ferrous metallic objects such as copper, aluminum and brass. The only criterion is the material must conduct an electric current. The *type of metal* and the *size of the object* are factors that determine the effective sensing range of a detector. Ferrous metals are detected up to two inches away while most non-ferrous metals are detected within one inch of the device.

Capacitive Proximity Sensor

Capacitive proximity sensors detect the presence of an object when it comes within a specific distance of an electrostatic field generated by a capacitor at the end

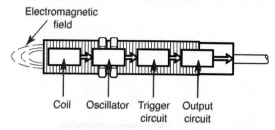

FIGURE 10-15: Operation of inductive proximity sensor.

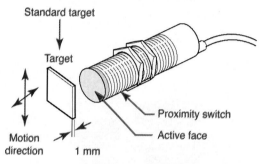

(a) Block diagram of internal circuits
of an inductive proximity sensor

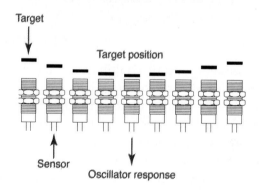

(b) Standard target is used to collect data
for the sensor data sheet

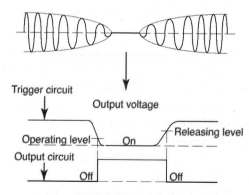

(c) Oscillatory response to target
position and changes in the trigger
and output circuit

Courtesy of Rockwell Automation, Inc.

Figure 10-16 illustrates inductive sensors in a variety of applications in packaging and material handling. The sens-

ing task is stated below the illustrations and the solutions are described to the right.

FIGURE 10-16: Application of inductive proximity sensors.

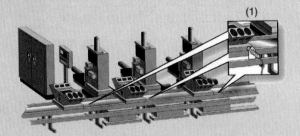

(1)

Use three inductive proximity sensors (1) to detect an engine block at each station. The three stage milling operation on the blocks starts after verification that all three engine block machining pallets are present and in the correct position.

(a) To detect the presence of an engine block at each work station

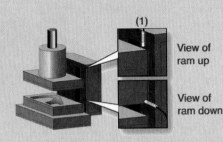

(1)

View of ram up

View of ram down

Sense the up and down positions of the ram using proximity switches (1). To prevent injury, photoelectric sensors (not shown) are often used at the operator entry point for the machine to sense that the operator's hands are out of press area when the press is actuated. Also, two-hand control is frequently used to keep the operator's hands out of the press when the stamping cycle is started.

(b) Sense the position of the ram press. Safety issues might include two-hand and pinch point control.

Courtesy of Rockwell Automation, Inc.

of the sensor. Figure 10-17(a) illustrates the shielded and unshielded capacitive proximity sensors, and Figure 10-17(b) shows the NEMA and IEC sensor symbols. Shielded sensors are constructed with a metal band surrounding the probe. This helps to direct the electrostatic field to the front of the sensor and results in a more concentrated field. Shielded construction allows the sensor to be mounted flush with the surface and not have false triggers. Materials with low dielectric constants are more difficult to detect, so shielded sensors with highly concentrated electrostatic fields are used.

Unshielded sensors do not have a metal band surrounding the probe and hence have a less concentrated electrostatic field. Many unshielded models are equipped with compensation probes for more stable operation with dirty or wet sensing heads. Unshielded capacitive sensors are also more suitable than shielded types for use with *plastic sensor wells,* an accessory designed for liquid level applications. The sensor well is mounted through a hole in a tank and the sensor is placed into the well. The dielectric constant of the plastic is small compared to the dielectric constant for the liquid in the tank. As a result, the sensor detects the presence of a liquid through the plastic well.

Capacitive proximity sensors are designed to operate by generating an electrostatic field and detecting changes in this field caused when a target approaches the sensing face. The sensor's internal components are a *capacitive probe, an oscillator, a signal rectifier, a filter circuit* and *an output circuit* as shown in Figure 10-18. Note in Figure 10-17 that only one plate of the capacitor is in the end of the sensor. The sensed object acts as the second plate for the capacitor. In the absence of a target, the oscillator is inactive. As a target approaches, it raises the capacitance of the probe system. When the capacitance reaches a specified threshold, the oscillator is activated, which triggers the output circuit to change states. The capacitance of the probe system is determined by the *target's size, dielectric constant* and *distance from the probe.* The larger the size and dielectric constant of a target, the more it increases capacitance. The shorter the distance between target and probe (distance between the capacitor's plates), the more the target increases capacitance.

As an object approaches the sensor, there is an increase in the electrostatic field due to the object's dielectric constant. *Dielectric constant* is a measure of the electrostatic lines of flux of a material. Objects

FIGURE 10-17: Capacitive proximity sensor models, ladder diagram contact symbols and letter codes.

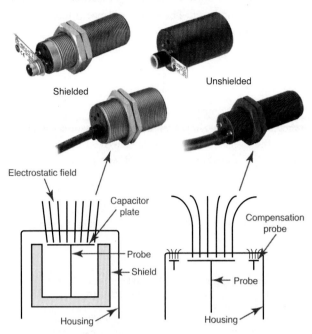

(a) Capacitive proximity sensors models with shielded and unshielded plates

Letter Code	NEMA	IEC
	NO	NO
NEMA – PRS IEC – SQ		
	NC	NC

(b) NEMA and IEC symbols and letter codes

Courtesy of Rockwell Automation, Inc.

FIGURE 10-18: Block diagram of internal circuits of a capacitive proximity sensor.

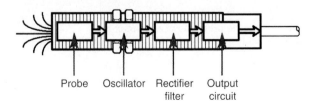

Probe Oscillator Rectifier Output
filter circuit

detected by the sensor have a dielectric constant of greater than 1.2, which is the threshold for most material. For example, the dielectric constant of mica is 7, cement powder is 5 to 10, and dry wood is 2 to 6.

Capacitive proximity sensors are designed to work with a broad spectrum of materials including metals (ferrous and non-ferrous), glass, plastic and liquids. The maximum sensing range for most capacitive proximity sensors is about one inch regardless of the type of material sensed. The operational effective sensing distance depends on the physical and electrical (dielectric constant) characteristics of the object to be detected.

Ultrasonic Proximity Sensor

Ultrasonic proximity sensors are solid state sensors that detect the presence of an object by emitting a high frequency sound signal and detecting the reflected sound from the target object. Since ultrasonic sensors use sound, the *surface* of the target object is more important than its *composition*. Objects with smooth surfaces are more easily detected than objects with irregular or round surfaces. Figure 10-19(a) illustrates

FIGURE 10-19: Ultrasonic sensors.

(a) Barrel type ultrasonic sensor

(b) Ultrasonic sensor response to surface shape and texture

a barrel-style ultrasonic proximity sensor and Figure 10-19(b) shows the operation. Note with an irregularly shaped target, the reflected sound bounces in many directions with less returning to the sensor. Ultrasonic sensors are used to determine the distance between an object and the sensor by measuring the amount of time between the emitted sound pulse and the returning echo. The time measurement is converted into a distance that is represented by a voltage or current level. The electrical parameter is then used to trigger a change in output contacts.

Figure 10-20 illustrates capacitive proximity sensors in a variety of applications in packaging, automotive, and material handling. The sensing task is stated below the illustrations, and the solutions are described to the right. Figure 10-21 illustrates ultrasonic proximity sensors in two applications labeled (a) and (b). In (a), an ultrasonic sensor is used to detect the level of the liquid in a tank. In (b), sensors are use to verify that the box is properly filled with cans.

FIGURE 10-20: Application of inductive and capacitive proximity and diffuse photoelectric scan sensors with background suppression.

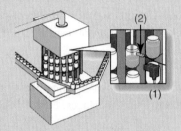

Sensing the presence of the bottle (1) is performed with a photoelectric sensor. A capacitive proximity sensor (2) used at the filling station ensures the glass mustard bottles are filled to the designated "Fill Level" every time. The advantage of using the capacitive proximity sensor is that it will ignore the glass while sensing the presence of the mustard.

(a) Bottle filling station requires a check for presence of bottle and fill level in the bottles

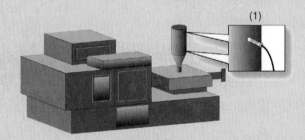

A capacitive sensor (1) is placed into the wall of the hopper to sense the level of the pellets present. In some applications the sensors detect the presence of the material through the hopper walls and in others the sensors are placed thorough holes in the tank so they are in contact with the product. Multiple sensors permit high and low level sensing.

(b) Sense presence of plastic pellets in the hopper of an injection molding machine producing automotive bumpers

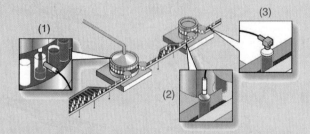

Three types of sensors are used in this application: *photoelectric, inductive proximity,* and *capacitive proximity.* Capacitive sensor (1) mounted about 2 mm from the container checks fill level; inductive proximity sensor (2) mounted over bottle checks for foil seal; and presence of lid/cap is verified (3) with a background suppression photoelectric sensor.

(c) Detect the fill levels in nonmetallic containers, confirm the presence of aluminum foil across the bottle top, and verify that a cap/lid is on the container

Courtesy of Rockwell Automation, Inc.

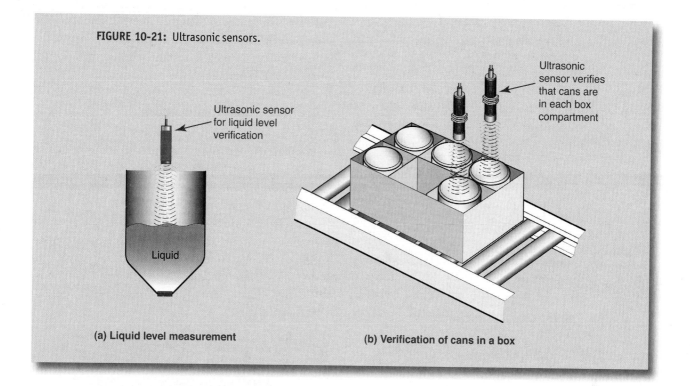

FIGURE 10-21: Ultrasonic sensors.

Ultrasonic sensor for liquid level verification

Liquid

(a) Liquid level measurement

Ultrasonic sensor verifies that cans are in each box compartment

(b) Verification of cans in a box

Inductive, capacitive, and ultrasonic proximity sensors have unique advantages for some applications, which are summarized as follows:

Inductive proximity sensors have:

- Reliable operation in every application with metal parts that pass close (typically less than 2 in.) to the sensor face and when: (1) The environment is moist and dirty or surface detection is not needed, (2) A blind zone (range segment where part is not detected) is not tolerable, and (3) When color detection is not needed

Capacitive proximity sensors have:

- Reliable operation when the material is not metal, photoelectric cannot be used, and the part passes 0–30 mm (1.18in) from the face

- The ability to "see through" certain container material and detect objects inside
- Offer reliable operation in harsh environment conditions like high humidity

Ultrasonic proximity sensors have:

- Large object detection capability up to 15 m (49ft) but with significant blind zones
- Good immunity from background noise, but slow response times
- Poor detection of soft objects like cloth and foam

Ultrasonic sensors are used to monitor the level in a tank, detect metallic and nonmetallic objects, and detect other objects that easily reflect sound waves. Soft materials such as foam, fabric, and rubber are difficult for ultrasonic sensors to detect and are better detected by photoelectric or other proximity sensors. Ultrasonic sensors are ideal for use in the food and beverage industry because they detect clear objects such as glass or plastic, which are difficult to detect with photoelectric sensors.

10-5 HALL EFFECT DEVICES

Hall Effect devices are solid state sensors that detect the presence of a magnetic field. In 1879, Edward Hall discovered an electrical-magnetic phenomena what is now called the Hall Effect. Hall crafted an experiment using a thin rectangular piece of gold connected to two electrodes with a current flowing through the gold film. When a magnet was placed perpendicular to the face of the gold film, he observed a difference of potential across the other two sides of the film perpendicular to the current flow. Hall also noted the difference of potential was directly proportional to the strength of the magnetic field. General features of Hall-effect-based sensing devices are:

- Total solid state operation that leads to a long life (30 billion operations in a keyboard test)
- Over 100 kHz switching speed
- A broad temperature range (–40 to +150°C) with no moving parts
- Interfaces directly to digital logic and is highly repeatable

Figure 10-22 illustrates the operation of the Hall-effect sensor. When a perpendicular magnet field nears the face of the semiconductor material, a voltage (Hall voltage) is produced. When the magnet is removed, the voltage drops to zero. In most Hall-effect sensors, the control current is held constant, and the position of the permanent magnetic is sensed.

Hall Effect Sensor Configuration

Hall-effect sensors are manufactured in a wide array of configurations. Two of the more common types of sensor configurations are the *proximity style* sensor and the *component block style* sensor. The proximity style sensor is cylindrical in design and similar to the barrel style inductive and capacitive proximity switches. Figure 10-23 illustrates Hall-effect sensor styles. The general purpose style allows for easy installation and calibration, and is used most often in indus-

FIGURE 10-23: Hall effect sensors.

(a) Hall effect current sensor

(b) General purpose Hall effect sensor

FIGURE 10-22: Hall effect sensor.

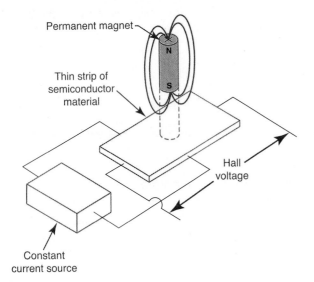

trial applications. For commercial and residential security applications, the sensor is a two piece device with one piece housing the sensor package and the other containing the permanent magnet.

Hall Effect Sensor Actuation Methods

The Hall-effect sensor is activated when the magnetic field interacts with the sensor semiconductor. In most cases, actuation is achieved with a fixed sensor and a moving permanent magnet. The sensor is activated by many methods, but the most popular methods are *linear actuation*, *lateral actuation*, *pendulum actuation*, *vane actuation*, and the *electromagnetic actuation*.

Linear Actuation Method—*Linear or convergent* actuation is where the magnet moves toward and away from the sensor on the same axis as the sensor as shown in Figure 10-24(a). For the device to properly function, the sensor is calibrated with the magnetic field positioned as close as possible to the center of the sensor. Convergent actuation sensors are commonly used in security applications where the sensor is mounted in the doorframe and the magnet is mounted on the door.

Lateral Actuation Method—In *lateral or perpendicular* actuation, the magnet moves perpendicular across the face of the sensor at a constant distance as shown in Figure 10-24(b). Depending on the type of device, the sensor is positioned so that the path of the magnet travels across the narrowest section of the sensor face. In lateral actuation, the permanent magnet travels less distance to activate the device than in other types of actuation.

Pendulum Actuation Method—With *pendulum* actuation, the magnet swings back and forth across the face of the sensor as shown in Figure 10-25. This method is a combination of the convergent and the perpendicular methods. The actuation occurs when the magnet is in line with the sensor. If the magnet has multiple poles, it is possible to have more than one actuation per swing of the magnet.

FIGURE 10-24: Linear and lateral Hall effect switches.

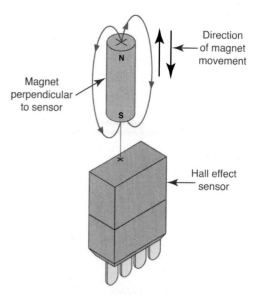

(a) Linear or head-on Hall effect switch

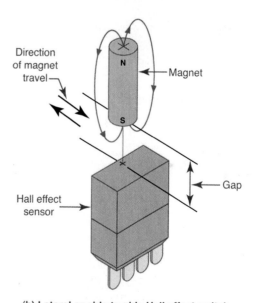

(b) Lateral or side to side Hall effect switch

Vane Actuation Method—*Vane* actuation is an activation method in which iron vane shunts or redirects the magnetic field away from the Hall-effect sensor. Figure 10-26(a) illustrates a linear vane and Figure 10-26(b) a rotary vane. When the iron vane is moved through

FIGURE 10-25: Pendulum motion Hall effect switch.

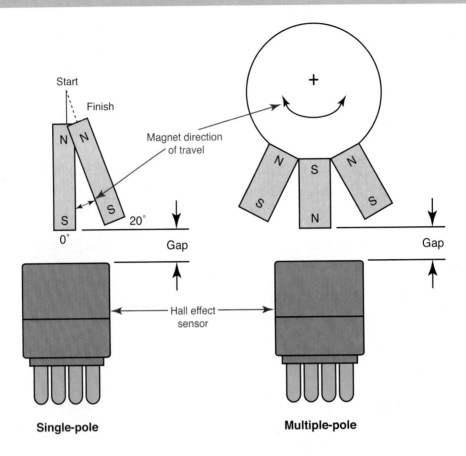

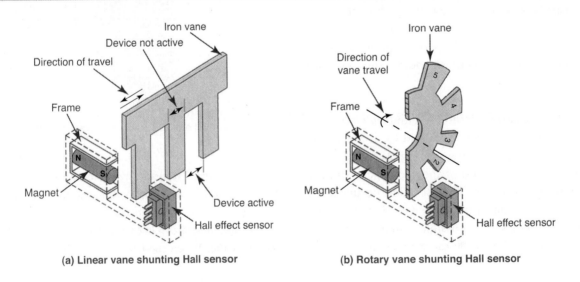

FIGURE 10-26: Linear and Rotary vane applications with Hall effect switch.

(a) Linear vane shunting Hall sensor   (b) Rotary vane shunting Hall sensor

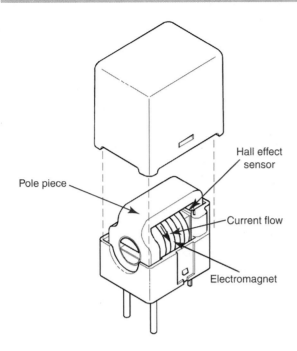

FIGURE 10-27: Electromagnetic actuation of Hall effect device.

Pole piece

Hall effect sensor

Current flow

Electromagnet

Figure 10-28 shows the Hall-effect sensor used for monitoring a conveyor operation. In this application, a barrel-style sensor is mounted to the frame of the conveyor. A magnet that is mounted on the tail pulley rotates past the sensor every revolution. When the tail pulley magnet is not present, the generator produces a voltage from the magnet inside the sensor. However, when the magnet on the tail pulley passes it cancels the magnetic flux and the sensor output drops. The presence of pulses indicates that the conveyor is running. If the conveyor stops, the constant output from the sensor alerts the operator. This Hall-effect sensor application is sometimes referred to as *zero-speed monitor*.

FIGURE 10-28: Hall effect sensor used to sense revolutions of a tail pulley.

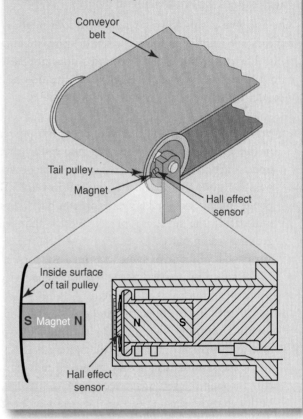

Conveyor belt

Tail pulley

Magnet

Hall effect sensor

Inside surface of tail pulley

S Magnet N

N S

Hall effect sensor

an air gap between the magnet and the sensor, the sensor is activated and de-activated sequentially at the speed that the vane is moving through the gap.

Electromagnetic Actuation Method—The *electromagnetic* actuation has an electromagnet attached to the Hall-effect sensor as shown in Figure 10-27. The method does not rely on a permanent magnet that moves across the sensor. When the specified level of current is applied to the electromagnet, a magnetic field to activate the sensor is produced. As more current flows through the coil of wire, the stronger the magnetic field.

The zero-speed application of a Hall-effect sensor is also accomplished by specialized switching devices. These specialized devices use centrifugal force to close switch contacts when the motor reaches a specific speed. The concept of zero-speed monitoring is important in many processes, particularly those involving large conveyor systems. Typically, belts, gears, or chain drives are installed between the motor and the conveyor. If the conveyor stops as a result of a jammed product, the entire system must be shut down before damage occurs.

10-6 TROUBLESHOOTING SOLID STATE DEVICES

The different types of solid-state sensors introduced in this chapter require unique troubleshooting methods. There are, however, some common tips that apply to all the sensor types. Before starting device-specific troubleshooting, verify that the sensing field of these devices is not obstructed. Also, visually inspect the device and the device lens (if applicable), verifying it is clean and free of debris. Finally, make sure that you know how the device is expected to perform in the system. Verify that you have the operating characteristics for each sensor for each manufacturer.

Troubleshooting Photoelectric Devices

The following tips may be helpful if the problem appears to be in the photoelectric sensor or sensor controls. The following order of the tips does not indicate a preferred sequence. Review all the tips and consider those that apply to the sensor problem.

- Verify by measurement that the sensor has power in the specified range. Verifying power to other operating equipment connected to the same power buss is a good method for testing for power. LED power indicators signal power is present but do not indicate if the level is correct. Verify that all grounds are in place.
- Verify that all control switch settings are correct. Make sure the protective seal on any sensitivity adjustment control is still intact.
- If available, use the operation indicator on the sensor to determine if the sensor electronics recognize that a part is present. If the system permits, check the sensing distance by manually moving a part through the sensor's detection field.
- Verify that the sensing distance was not reduced due to a change in the ambient temperature or light.
- Verify that alignment for transmitters and receivers of direct scan devices has not changed and that placement of reflective targets is proper.

Troubleshooting Proximity Devices

The following tips may be helpful if the problem appears to be in a proximity sensor or sensor amplifier. The following order of the tips does not indicate

a preferred sequence. Review all the tips and consider those that apply to the sensor problem.

- Verify by measurement that the sensor has power in the specified range. Checking other operating equipment connected to the same power bus is a good method for testing for power. LED power indicators signal power is present but do not indicate if the level is correct. Verify that all grounds are in place.
- Verify that all control switch settings are correct. If applicable, make sure the protective seal on any sensitivity adjustment control is still intact.
- Verify that all switch settings are correct.
- If available, use the operation indicator on the sensor to determine if the sensor electronics recognize that a part is present. If the system permits, check the sensing distance by manually moving a part through the sensor's detection field.
- Verify that a foreign object is not creating a problem on one of the sensing heads.
- Verify that the velocity of the parts past the sensor has not changed to a value that exceeds the frequency response of the unit.
- Verify that the effective sensing distance was not reduced due to a change in the ambient temperature or a change in supply voltage.

Troubleshooting Hall Effect Devices

The following tips may be helpful if the problem appears to be in the Hall-effect sensor or sensor controls. The following order of the tips does not indicate a preferred sequence. Review all the tips and consider those that apply to the sensor problem.

- Verify that the sensor has power in the specified range. Verifying power to other operating equipment connected to the same power buss is a good method for testing for power. Verify that all grounds are in place.
- Verify that the magnet is positioned properly for the actuation method used in the application. If the system permits, check the sensor operation by manually moving a magnet through the sensor's detection field.
- Verify that the effective sensing distance was not reduced due to a change in the ambient temperature or a change in the supply voltage.

CRITICAL CONCEPTS

The need-to-know content from Chapter 10 is summarized in the following statements.

- Photoelectric devices are solid state devices that provide accurate detection of objects without physical contact.
- There are two components present in photoelectric devices—a light source, which transmits light, and a receiver, which detects the presence of the light source.
- Response time is determined from the number of light pulses per second that a photoelectric device transmits to detect an object. Sensitivity is the operating point or the intensity of light which triggers the photoelectric device and produces a change in the output.
- Direct scan is a scanning method in which the transmitter and receiver are placed opposite each other. The light beam from the transmitter shines directly on the receiver.
- Retroreflective scan is a scanning method in which the transmitter and receiver are housed in the same enclosure, and the transmitted beam is reflected back to the receiver by a reflector.
- Polarized scan is a scanning method in which the receiver responds only to the depolarized reflected light from a special reflector or polarized sensitive reflective tape.
- Diffuse scan is a scanning method in which the transmitter and receiver are housed in the same enclosure, and a small percentage of the transmitted beam is reflected back to the receiver from the detected object's surface.
- Inductive proximity *sensors* detect the presence of a metallic object when it penetrates a high frequency electromagnetic field that radiates from one end of the sensor.
- Capacitive proximity *sensors* detect the presence of an object when it penetrates the electrostatic field generated by one plate of a capacitor located at the end of the sensor.
- Ultrasonic proximity sensors are solid state sensors that detect the presence of an object by emitting a high frequency sound signal and detecting the reflected sound from the target object.
- Hall Effect devices are solid state sensors that detect the presence of a magnetic field.
- The Hall-effect sensor is activated by convergent actuation, perpendicular actuation, pendulum actuation, vane actuation, and the electromagnetic actuation methods.

QUESTIONS

1. Describe how photocells operate.
2. Describe the response time and sensitivity of a photoelectric device.
3. What is the direct scan method?
4. What is the retroreflective scan method?
5. What is the polarized scan method?
6. What is the diffuse scan method?
7. Describe the operation of the inductive proximity sensor.
8. Describe the operation of the capacitive proximity sensor.
9. Describe the operation of the ultrasonic proximity sensor.
10. How does a Hall-effect sensor work?
11. Describe three methods of Hall-effect sensor actuation.

CHAPTER 11

Solid State Relays

GOALS AND OBJECTIVES

The primary goals for this chapter are to *identify solid state relays*, and to *describe the operation of and applications of non-programmable styles and programmable styles*. In addition, troubleshooting tips and procedures for typical failure modes are presented.

After completing this chapter, you should be able to:

1. Identify and describe non-programmable solid state relays including switching methods and illustrate NEMA and IEC symbols.
2. Describe the advantages and disadvantages between the solid state relays and electromechanical relays.
3. Identify and describe programmable logic relays.

11-1 NON-PROGRAMMABLE RELAYS

The *non-programmable solid state relay* (SSR) is an electronic device that performs the same function as an electromechanical relay. Because the SSR is a device with no moving parts or contacts, switching is performed electronically. The SSR is an encapsulated module with a variety of methods for installation into the control circuit. Mounting options include *tube base* and *square base plug, DIN rail, panel mount*, and *heat sink mounting* types. Plug in type SSRs

have less current switching capability than heat sink mounted models. Switched AC load currents from 3 amps to 40 amps are common depending on the style and mounting options.

SSR Configurations

Solid state devices are packaged in many different type enclosures. Figure 11-1 depicts six commonly used SSR packages from Rockwell Automation. The common name of each is provided in the figure. Popular plug-in

FIGURE 11-1: Six solid state relay styles from Rockwell Automation.

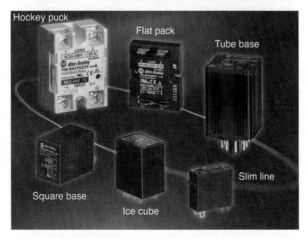

Courtesy of Rockwell Automation, Inc.

types have 8-, 11-, and 14-pin base styles. An option that is offered for some enclosures is an *LED indicator* for on/off status monitoring. Because SSRs are available as plug-in devices, they are easily removed and quickly replaced. In addition, various sockets are available that can be soldered on a printed circuit board (PCB) or mounted on a panel or DIN rail assembly. Another popular PCB-mounted enclosure is the dual-in-line package (DIP).

Figure 11-2(a) shows a NEMA style SSR and the control wiring diagram. The relay has a DC control voltage and a DC single pole solid state switch. Note the input voltage range and output voltage and current limit values circled on the case. The ladder diagram symbols are displayed in Figure 11-2(b). Figure 11-3(a) shows the IEC style SSR and the IEC style control wiring diagram. Inputs and outputs have standard numbering with A1 and A2 for inputs and 1L and 2T for the output. The AC control voltage is identified on the case and the single pole solid state output switches 48 to 480V AC. The IEC ladder diagram symbols are displayed in Figure 11-3(b).

The SSR is configured to operate as two independent circuits—input and output. The input side receives a signal from the source, and the output side actuates

FIGURE 11-2: NEMA style of solid state relay.

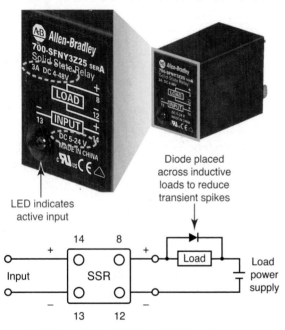

(a) DC control and DC load NEMA style square base SSR with LED indicator and wiring diagram

Letter Code	NEMA	
	NO	NC
NEMA – SSR		

(b) NEMA ladder diagram symbols and letter code

Courtesy of Rockwell Automation, Inc.

FIGURE 11-3: IEC style of solid state relay.

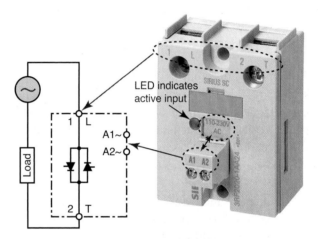

(a) AC control and AC load IEC solid state relay with LED indicator and wiring diagram

Letter Code	IEC	
	NO	NC
IEC – SCCR		

(b) IEC ladder diagram symbols and letter code

Courtesy of Siemens.

the load. The input and output sides are not electrically interconnected, to permit different input and output voltage sources. For example, while the source voltage for the input side is 12V DC, the output controls a 120V AC load.

The *input section* of an SSR performs the same function as the coil of an electromechanical relay. Some SSRs have a fixed input voltage of 12V DC, but most SSRs have an input voltage range such as 3V DC to 32V DC. However, some SSRs accept AC voltage inputs up to 277V AC. The input voltage range allows the SSR to operate with most electronic devices. The input signal is used to actuate the output section of the SSR. Optical coupling or opto-isolation is the most common technique used to link SSR inputs to outputs. Input signals activate a photo diode. The photo diode turns on a photo transistor in the output circuit, which activates the load. The only link between the input and output circuits is the light from the photo diode.

The *output section* of an SSR performs the same function as the contacts of an electromechanical relay. SSRs switch low-level DC voltages or AC voltages up to 480V AC. Some SSRs have two- and three-pole configurations, but a single pole output is most common. The output section uses different electronic devices depending on the type of load being switched. Figure 11-4 lists the common input and output switching devices used in an SSR and the type of load that the switching device drives.

SSR Switching Methods

Solid state relays operate with several different switching methods. Circuit parameters such as the type of load are important factors in the selection of the switching method. The most common switching methods used in SSRs are *zero switching, instant-on,* and *peak.*

Zero Switching—When the *zero switching method* is used in an SSR, the load is switched on when the

---

FIGURE 11-4: SSR input devices, control circuits, and output switching devices.

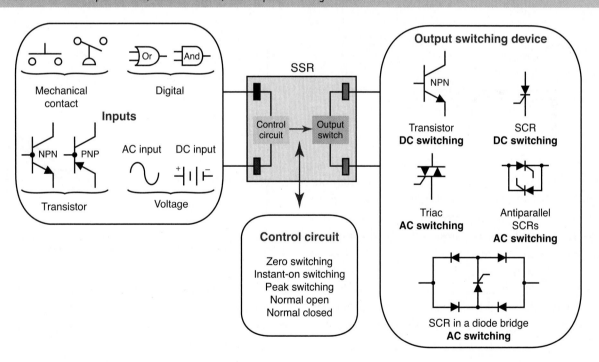

Solid state relays can be connected in parallel to obtain multi-contacts that are controlled by one input device. Figure 11-5 illustrates three SSRs connected in parallel to control a three-phase circuit that drives resistive heating elements.

FIGURE 11-5: Parallel SSRs switch three phase power to a three phase heater.

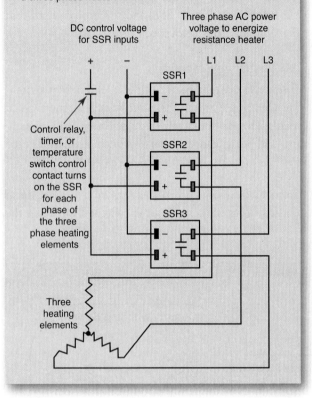

FIGURE 11-6: Zero switching of single phase immersion heater in a tank.

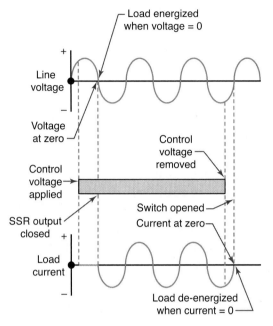

(a) Zero switching SSR operation

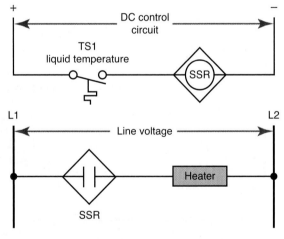

(b) Zero switching ladder application

sine wave of the control voltage crosses the zero axis. Figure 11-6(a) illustrates the zero switching method. Figure 11-6(b) displays a typical ladder diagram with an SSR contact and separate wiring diagram of the control circuit. This method is the most widely used with resistive loads. Since the current and voltage are in phase in a resistive load, the SSR turns the load on and off when the current and voltage are at or near zero. An SSR with zero switching is used to control loads such as heating elements, soldering irons and extruders for forming plastic products.

Instant On—When the *instant-on method* is used in an SSR, the load is switched on immediately when the control voltage is present. It functions exactly as an electromechanical relay. Both types of relays energize the output at the exact time the input signal is received. Figure 11-7 illustrates the instant-on switching method.

Instant-on relays are used when the controlled load is a combination of resistance and reactance, with the reactive portion of the load usually inductive. Because the voltage and current are not in phase in the inductive portion of the circuit, there is no advantage to connect to or disconnect from the load at any specific time. An SSR with instant-on switching controls loads such as *contactors, magnetic motor starters, magnetic valves, small motors, lighting systems,* and *magnetic brakes.* The power and control ladder diagram in Figure 11-6(b) is the same for all SSR output control methods.

FIGURE 11-7: Instant on SSR output control and operation.

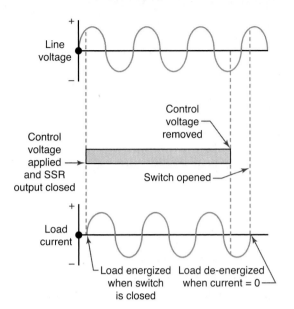

FIGURE 11-8: Peak switching method of SSR control and operation.

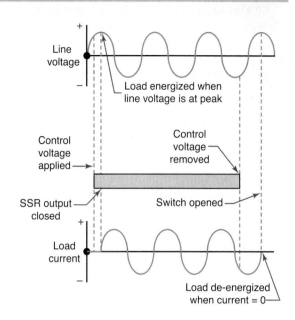

Peak Switching Method

Peak Switching Method—When the *peak switching method* is used in an SSR, the load is switched on when the load voltage is at its peak and not when the input control voltage is applied. Figure 11-8 illustrates the peak switching method. In this method, the load is mostly reactive and the current and voltage are approximately 90 degrees out of phase. The SSR breaks the output circuit when the control voltage is at the peak of the sine wave. When a reactive voltage is at or near peak value, the current is at or near zero. Peak switching SSRs are used to control loads that are mostly inductive or capacitive. An SSR with peak switching controls loads such as *transformers, larger motors, small DC motors,* and *heavy inductive* devices. The power and control ladder diagram in Figure 11-6(b) also applies to the peak switching output control method.

SSR Control Schemes

The SSR provides the same control as an electromechanical relay; however, the SSR's operation is quite different from the electromechanical relay. As a result, the use of the SSR in two-wire and three-wire control schemes require external components in some applications.

The single pole single throw SSR integrates into *two-wire control schemes* with few modifications. Figure 11-9(a) illustrates an SSR used to control an AC load

FIGURE 11-9: Two-wire control with SSR.

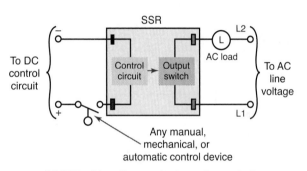

(a) SSR wiring diagram for two-wire control

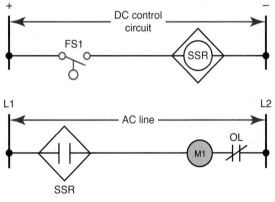

(b) Ladder diagram with control ladder and power ladder illustrated

FIGURE 11-10: Ladder diagram changes for Figure 11-9 when SSR control and load use AC power.

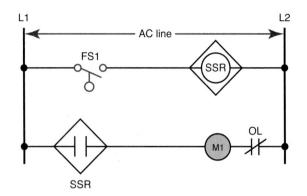

with a float switch or any manual, mechanical, or automatic control device. Figure 11-9(b) illustrated the ladder diagrams (control and power) for this two-wire control scheme. Note the AC load is a motor starter coil and the overloads in the ladder diagram.

Some SSRs use AC control inputs. The ladder in Figure 11-10 illustrates how the ladder diagram in Figure 11-9(b) changes when the SSR's AC input voltage is the same as the output switched AC voltage.

In *three-wire control schemes,* a single-pole SSR requires a holding circuit. In AC systems, the simplest method is to add an additional SSR with the output terminal across the start switch. The inputs are placed

in parallel with the input of the SSR controlling the process load. In SSR systems with DC input control voltage, an SCR is used for the holding circuit. Figure 11-11 illustrates an SSR and a silicon controller rectifier (SCR) controlling an AC load (motor starter and overloads). A start pushbutton in parallel with the SCR triggers the gate and allows current to flow

FIGURE 11-11: SSR in a three wire control ladder with SCR used to seal start pushbutton.

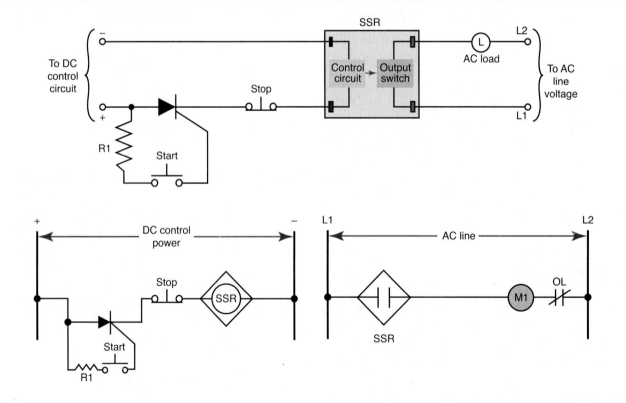

through the SCR providing the holding circuit after the start momentary switch is released. A stop push-button in series with the SSR and the SCR interrupts the current flow and turns off the SCR.

SSR Circuit Considerations

The solid state relay is more susceptible to *temperature rise* and *voltage spikes* than the electromechanical relay. External devices, such as heat sinks, varistors, and semiconductor fuses, are used to eliminate these conditions and extend the useful life of the SSR.

Temperature rise affects all electronic components, including the SSR. If the SSR is not properly cooled, over time the heat dramatically reduces the life of the relay. Heat sinks are the most common devices used to help dissipate excess heat developed in electronic circuits. SSRs are mounted directly to the metal, usually aluminum, heat sink. Fins on the heat sink increase the surface area use to radiate the heat from the SSR. Thermal grease is often used to increase the heat flow from the SSR to the heat sink.

Voltage spikes are produced by switching inductive loads and are superimposed on the AC voltage. If overvoltage protection is not provided, transient voltage spikes may damage the solid state circuit or cause false triggering of the output devices. A *metal-oxide varistor* (MOV), which looks like a disc capacitor, is added across the output terminals of the SSR. A MOV is a voltage variable resistor with a high resistance at low voltages (normal operating voltage) and a low resistance at high voltages (voltage levels produced by transient spikes). Therefore, when voltage spikes occur, the MOV resistance drops and shunts the current from the spike through the MOV, thus protecting the SSR switching devices.

Semiconductor fuses are another reliable way to protect solid state relays. They are also referred to as current-limiting fuses and provide extremely fast opening (about 2 msec) while restricting pass-through current far below the current level that could destroy the SSR. While they are expensive, they provide a means of fully protecting SSRs against rapid rise, high overload currents. Every SSR has an I^2T rating, which is used to identify a matching fuse rating for protection. Devices such as electromechanical circuit breakers and fast/slow blow fuses cannot react quickly enough to protect the SSR in a shorted condition and are not recommended for SSR protection.

Figure 11-12 illustrates a solid state relay installed on a heatsink with an inline fast semiconductor fuse and a varistor across the output terminals.

Solid State Relays Versus Electromechanical Relays

The solid state relays offer several advantages over electromechanical relays. Because the SSR is an electronic device, they typically have a longer operational life and faster switching capabilities. The SSR also features multiple switching modes and can easily be interfaced with electronic components. The SSRs have some disadvantages as well. They usually have a single pole and must be protected from excessive

---

TECH NOTES

Solid state relays cannot always be applied in exactly the same way as electromechanical relays. Knowing the type of load that connects to the SSR is important when an SSR is being installed or replaced. Three common heavy-duty loads that an SSR drives are transformers, motors and lamps.

When a transformer is the load, extremely high current surges commonly occur. The zero crossing turn on and off characteristic of SSRs minimize the surge, but does not prevent it. From the practical and economic standpoint, the best choice is an SSR, which is overrated to withstand the large surges.

When a motor is the load, special problems are created for solid state relays. High initial surge current is drawn because their stationary impedance is usually very low. As a motor rotates, it develops a counter electromagnetic force (CEMF) that opposes the flow of current. The back EMF generally adds to the applied line voltage and creates overvoltage conditions during turn off. It should be noted that overvoltage or CEMF from the motor cannot be effectively dealt with by adding an MOV. The MOV is typically designed for brief high voltage spikes and may be destroyed by sustained high energy conduction. It is therefore important that SSRs are chosen to withstand the highest expected sustained voltage.

Lamps often have turn on currents that are ten times their steady state ratings. The surge characteristic of SSRs with thyristor output switches have a similar surge carrying capability. As a result, SSRs are often used to switch incandescent lamps. However, SSRs are not recommended for switching mercury or fluorescent lamp loads.

FIGURE 11-12: SSR protected with fuse for over-current conditions.

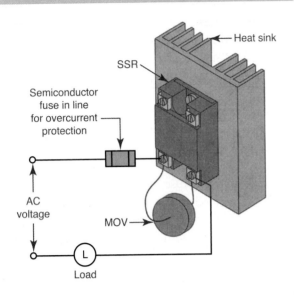

heat and voltage spikes. Figure 11-13 lists the advantages and limitations of the electromechanical relay and the solid state relay.

11-2 PROGRAMMABLE LOGIC RELAYS

A *programmable logic relay* (PLR) is a solid state device, which contains discrete DC and AC input interfaces and discrete DC and AC output interfaces. The inputs are logically linked to the outputs with a software program to meet the control requirements of industrial applications. The control functions include *relays* (electromechanical contacts or solid state switch outputs), *timers* and *counters*. For example, some PLR devices have up to 15 separate timers, which provide the on-delay, off-delay and one-shot functions. The PLR input interfaces to devices such as pushbuttons and limit switches to control output loads such as lamps, solenoids and motor starters. Figure 11-14 illustrates a programmable logic relay. PLRs are powered by DC (12–24 volt) or AC (100–240 volt) power sources.

The PLR is ideal for small machine applications such as car washes and packaging machines. Features of the PLR include the following:

- Custom high speed processor, rivaling small programmable logic controllers

FIGURE 11-13: Electromechanical relays compared to solid state relays.

Electromechanical Relays	
Advantages	**Limitations**
Normally multi-pole, multi-throw contact arrangements	Contact wear reduces the useful device life
Low initial cost	Rapid switching applications or high current loads, shortens contact life
Resistant to temperature rise and voltages spikes	Generates electromagnetic noise and interference on the power lines
No leakage current through open contacts in the non-energized state	Poor performance when switching high inrush currents
No voltage drop across closed contacts in the energized state	

Solid State Relays	
Advantages	**Limitations**
No contact wear produces a longer life	Normally only one contact available per relay
No contact arcing to generate electromagnetic interference	Leakage current is present when the device is not energized and output should be an open circuit
Very fast switching capability	Heat sinks are generally required to improve relay life
Different switching methods available	Voltage drop across the output terminals of up to 2 volts is present when the device is energized and output should be a short circuit

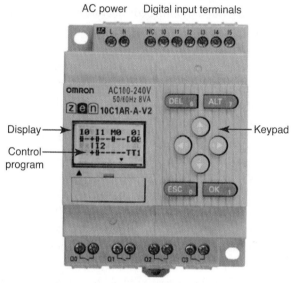

The PLR programming software allows the PLR to be adapted to a variety of applications. The software provides the ability to monitor operating conditions of inputs and outputs on the PLR screen. The active and not active state of inputs and energized and not energized state of outputs is easily determined. This information is useful for analysis of system operation and for troubleshooting system faults. Manufacturers provide PLR program development software for a personal computer (PC); so that the programming can be accomplished off-line on the PC, and then download to the PLR.

The programming software has a simulator mode to test the selected functions before downloading the data to the PLR. With the ability to simulate discrete or analog input changes and monitor outputs, program logic problems are identified before the control program is downloaded to the PLR.

TECH NOTES

FIGURE 11-14: Programmable logic relay.

AC power   Digital input terminals

Display
Control program

Keypad

Output terminals

Courtesy of Omron Corporation.

- Readable screen, typically a 12 × 4 character LCD display for I/O bit status and timer and counter preset and accumulated values
- Front panel interface for programming and operator program editing
- High speed inputs for rapidly changing signals
- Relay outputs, which allows direct control up to 1/3 horsepower motors
- Real time clock built-in
- DIN rail or panel mount capability
- Memory module for storing program or transferring to other PLRs
- Built-in serial communication data channel for linking to a PC for off-line programming

In applications that need multiple relays or anticipate circuit changes, the programmable logic relay is a good choice. Control devices are programmed into the PLR using standard ladder diagrams. Only the inputs such as pressure or temperature switches and output loads such as lamps and solenoids are wired to the PLR. The PLR has several advantages over discrete components such as: the PLR logical control is programmed into software so physical wiring of relay contacts is not necessary; a range of control devices and control functions are available such as control relays and numerous timer functions; changes to the control logic requires only a change in the program and no rewiring of physical devices; and the PLR is a relatively low cost option.

11-3 TROUBLESHOOTING SOLID STATE RELAYS AND PROGRAMMABLE LOGIC RELAYS

Three basic fault modes for a *solid state relay* are: (1) the SSR fails to de-energize the load, (2) the SSR fails to energize the load, and (3) the SSR operation is intermittent or erratic. There are a variety of conditions that cause improper relay operation. First verify that power levels are within specifications. Excessive heat and surge currents are the most common causes of solid state relay failure. Therefore, before a replacement of a load device or in a new installation, make sure that the surge characteristics of the load are within the operating parameters of the SSR. This includes both the inrush current as well as the steady state condition.

Load Fails to De-energize

Failure to de-energize the load is a condition that occurs when: the load power is not present or too low; the SSR output device is shorted due to excessive or prolonged high load current; the sensor input voltage never drops below SSR input drop out value; the leakage current for the solid state output driver is larger than the turn on current for the output device; or voltage spikes cause a false trigger of a solid state output element. Make the following measurements to verify that the input and output conditions are within specification.

1. Measure the sensor and load circuit voltage.
2. Measure the current drawn by load.
3. Measure the input sensor's activated and not-activated voltage at the SSR input.
4. Measure the output leakage current when the SSR output is in the non-energized state.
5. If voltage spikes on an output are suspected, check the noise on the output with an oscilloscope.

Load Fails to Energize

Failure to energize the load is a condition that occurs when the input control device is faulty; the control device signal is not reaching the SSR input; the SSR input is bad; the SSR output drive circuit is bad; or the output device failed. Make the following measurements to verify the input and output conditions are within specifications.

1. Measure the SSR input control voltage with input sensor active and not active.
2. Measure the voltage at the output of the SSR when input conditions indicate that the output should be energized.
3. Measure and verify that the input current to the SSR is within specified limits and that the input is not open.
4. Measure the voltage drop across the SSR when the relay is energized. Verify that the voltage drop across the SSR is not reducing the voltage available to energize the load.

Intermittent and Erratic Operation

Erratic SSR operation occurs because of loose terminal connections, power source not operating within specifications, or ambient temperature out of range. Make the following measurements to verify that the input and output conditions are within specification.

1. Verify that wires are in good condition and that all terminal terminations are tight. For PCB-mounted relays, verify that solder connections are not cracked or damaged.

2. Verify that the input wires are not near the output wires because noise can be coupled from output to input.
3. Verify that the load voltage and current are within specifications.

Troubleshooting PLRs

The PLRs are combinations of SSRs with the inputs and outputs linked by logic in a computer program. As a result, most of the troubleshooting tips for SSRs also apply to faults in PLRs. However, the addition of a program for control adds another dimension to the troubleshooting challenge.

General troubleshooting considerations for PLR systems include the following:

- It is rare that two different and independent parts of a system fail simultaneously. However, one device failure can cause a second different but related device to fail. If you suspect that two devices failed, verify that a common fault could cause both failures.
- In general, external devices attached to the PLR are the cause for improper operation more often than a failed PLR.
- If a new installation operates improperly, the cause could be either hardware, the software program, or both. If the installation fails after operating correctly for a number of complete cycles of the process, the problem is most likely hardware. It is rare for a software program to change without human intervention. If the system fails after an update to the program, the most likely cause is a programming logic error in the new program or improper editing of the old program.
- If one output is operating improperly and all others are functioning correctly, the problem is most likely related to the inputs that logically control that output or the output circuit. Verify that all input voltages to the PLR from the devices are correct. Verify that the output(s) from the PLR have the correct drive voltage. If input and output devices are good, systematically moving the inputs and outputs to different input and output terminals on the PLR helps to isolate the specific fault. After each move the program must be modified to include the new location for the input or output.

- If none of the outputs or a majority of outputs fail to operate on a PLR controlled system that has been performing properly, then the PLR is most likely the problem.

CRITICAL CONCEPTS

The need-to-know content from Chapter 11 is summarized in the following statements.

- The non-programmable solid state relay (SSR) is an electronic device that performs the same function as an electromechanical relay, but its switching is performed electronically.
- The input section of an SSR performs the same function as the coil of an electromechanical relay.
- The output section of an SSR performs the same function as the contacts of an electromechanical relay.
- When the zero switching method is used in an SSR, the load is switched on and off when the AC voltage powering the load crosses the zero axis.
- When the instant-on method is used in an SSR, the load is switched on immediately when the control voltage is present.
- When the peak method is used in an SSR, the load is switched on and off when the control voltage is present and the load voltage is at its peak.
- The solid state relay is more susceptible to temperature rise and voltage spikes than the electromechanical relay. However, external devices are used to minimize the effect of each of these conditions.
- Semiconductor fuses are the only reliable way to protect solid state relays. They provide extremely fast opening (about 2 msec) while restricting pass-through current far below the fault current that could destroy the SSR.
- The SSR typically has a longer operational life and faster switching capabilities than an electromechanical relay.
- A programmable logic relay (PLR) is a solid state device, which contains control functions that can be selected and adapted to meet the requirements of industrial and commercial applications.
- The PLR control functions include relays (electromechanical contacts or solid state switch outputs), timers and counters.
- Three basic improper operations of a solid state relay are: (1) the relay fails to turn off the load, (2) the relay fails to turn on the load, and (3) the relay operates erratically.

QUESTIONS

1. Describe the two sections of an SSR.
2. Describe the zero switching method that is used in an SSR.
3. Describe the instant-on method that is used in an SSR.
4. Describe the peak method that is used in an SSR.
5. How is an SSR protected from temperature rise and voltage spikes?
6. What are semiconductor fuses?
7. List the differences between an SSR and an electromechanical relay.
8. What the three basic improper operations of a solid state relay?

CHAPTER **12**

Motor Control Centers and Special Purpose Starters

GOALS AND OBJECTIVES

The primary goals for this chapter are to describe the layout, function, installation and maintenance of motor control centers, and to identify and differentiate between the following special purpose starters—*autotransformer, primary resistor, part winding, wye-delta, solid state, soft-start,* and *reversing starters.*

After completing this chapter, you will be able to:

1. Describe the layout, function, installation and maintenance of *motor control centers.*
2. Identify and describe the purpose and the function of reduced voltage starters, including *auto-transformer, primary resistor, part winding, wye-delta, solid state,* and *soft start starters.*
3. Identify and describe the purpose and the function of *reversing* starters.

12-1 MOTOR CONTROL CENTERS

Power and data distribution systems in large commercial and industrial operations are complex and widely divergent in application and operation. *Motor control centers* (MCCs) assist in managing the power control and distribution for process control hardware in company systems. The MCC is an efficient method to mount, power, and organize electrical motor control, automation, and power distribution systems. Motor control centers consist of totally enclosed free-standing structures or sections that are bolted together. These sections house control units, power distribution bus bars, and wireways for incoming and outgoing power, load, and control wires. The control units consist of components such as *combination motor starters, branch feeder devices, AC drives, soft starters,* and *meters.* Each unit is mounted in an individual, isolated compartment having its own door. Typically, MCC dimensions are 20 inches wide (including a 4 inch vertical wireway trough) by 90 inches high (plus a base channel and a removable top lifting channel) by 15 to 20 inches deep.

All the major manufacturers of motors, motor control systems, and automation control components also provide motor control centers. In this chapter, general information on motor control centers from various manufacturers is presented, providing the electrical worker with a comprehensive overview of motor control centers. However, when the electrical worker is *tasked* with *installing, operating,* or *maintaining* an MCC, the manufacturer's manuals are used.

Figure 12-1 illustrates a typical motor control center. The call outs and their numbers highlight areas of the MCC in the figure and are included in the following description. Motor control centers have compartments to house individual control units (2), which are mounted from the front side. Steel covers (7) enclose the structure at the top, sides and at the rear. A vertical copper ground bus (20) and a horizontal copper ground bus (8) is located in each MCC structure and provides grounding for each unit. A 24V DC bus provides distribution of control voltage to each unit in an MCC and is generated by a power supply unit (5). A vertical bus system (13) installed in each vertical section is connected to the horizontal bus to feed the individual control units. The vertical bus is isolated by a full height vertical barrier (6). This labyrinth barrier provides isolation and insulation, plus an automatic shutter to cover the openings for each control unit.

At the bottom of each section, a door (18) provides ready access to the bottom horizontal wireway (19) and neutral bus. The bottom of each section is completely open to provide unrestricted bottom entry for cable and conduit. Channel sills are installed across the bottom of the control center. A vertical wireway (16) extending the full height of the control center is located to the right of each unit compartment. This wireway is covered by two hinged doors (15) and contains cable supports to secure wire bundles and cables. The verti-

FIGURE 12-1: Motor control center.

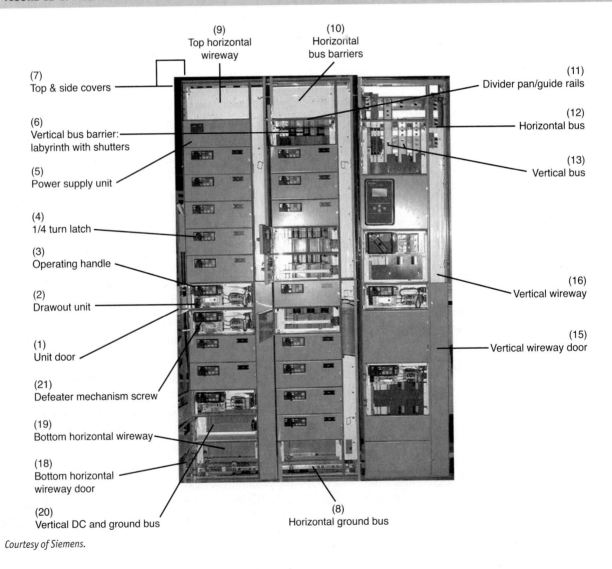

(9) Top horizontal wireway

(10) Horizontal bus barriers

(7) Top & side covers

(11) Divider pan/guide rails

(6) Vertical bus barrier: labyrinth with shutters

(12) Horizontal bus

(5) Power supply unit

(13) Vertical bus

(4) 1/4 turn latch

(3) Operating handle

(2) Drawout unit

(16) Vertical wireway

(1) Unit door

(21) Defeater mechanism screw

(19) Bottom horizontal wireway

(15) Vertical wireway door

(18) Bottom horizontal wireway door

(20) Vertical DC and ground bus

(8) Horizontal ground bus

Courtesy of Siemens.

cal wireway joins the horizontal wireway at the top and bottom to provide unobstructed space for internal wiring. The horizontal and vertical wireways are shown in Figure 12-2.

The term *unit* (sometimes called a bucket) refers to a control or plug-in assembly such as a combination starter or meter. It also refers to equipment that is actually mounted into the section such as a large feeder or the main fusible disconnect. The control units (2) in Figure 12-1 are a completely self-contained packages consisting of a steel enclosure, operating handle and electrical components. The unit slides into the compartment on guide rails (11) to provide easy withdrawal and reinsertion and to ensure precise alignment of the units with the vertical bus. Each control unit is held in place by a single quarter-turn latch (4), which is engaged when the unit is fully mated with the vertical bus. Each structure has a separate door (1), which is held closed by quarter-turn fasteners. In the ON

position, the operating handle (2) interlocks with the unit door to prevent its opening. In this position, authorized personnel open the door by turning the defeater mechanism screw (21). With the unit door open and the operating handle in the ON position, another interlock to the divider pan prevents removal of the unit. This same interlock prevents insertion of the unit unless the handle mechanism is in the OFF position. To ensure that units are not energized accidentally or by unauthorized personnel, the handle mechanism can be padlocked in the OFF position. Figure 12-3(a) illustrates a MCC unit that contains motor starter components including contactor, overload protection, and disconnect. Figure 12-3(b) illustrates a multiple unit with fused protected motor drive.

Feeder and Internal Power Busses

The *feeder power bus* enters the MCC either from overhead or underneath and supplies three-phase AC, generally 208 to 600V AC. The electrical worker needs to know how the feeder bus is fed to the MCC to eliminate difficult wire bends and/or costly field changes required to properly terminate an awkward cable feed. The feeder power bus is used to develop different power levels such as *secondary power, lower voltage AC, single phase AC* and *DC power*.

The amount of *feeder bus current* available varies from installation to installation, depending on the impedance of the electric source. For example, if the available fault current is 12,000A, the MCC must be rated to withstand 12,000A of fault current while the overcurrent protective device clears the fault. Fault-current ratings of electrical devices are available in semi-standard rating such as 10,000A, 14,000A, 18,000A, and 22,000A. The fault current withstand rating of an MCC is determined by the lowest rated device within the MCC. If an MCC bus structure is rated to withstand 42,000A, and a circuit breaker is installed with a fault-withstand rating of 18,000A, then the entire MCC assembly is rated 18,000A.

The *internal power bus* distributes power to the control units via a *horizontal* and a *vertical* bus. The MCC internal busses are shown in Figure 12-4. Bus material is usually copper; however, in some installations aluminum is used to reduce costs. When aluminum is used, special washers are required because

FIGURE 12-2: Vertical and horizontal wireways at right side and top and bottom of back panel of MCC.

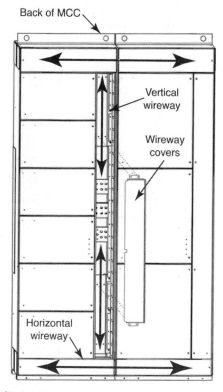

Back of MCC

Vertical wireway

Wireway covers

Horizontal wireway

Courtesy of Rockwell Automation, Inc.

FIGURE 12-4: MCC power bus.

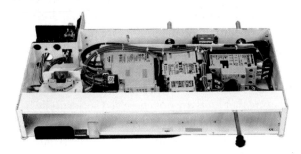

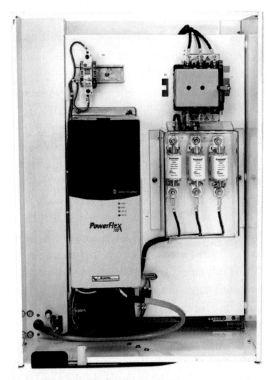

(a) Single unit module with branch feed disconnect, motor starter, motor overload protection, and other control elements

(b) Eight unit module with fuse protected motor drive

Courtesy of Rockwell Automation, Inc.

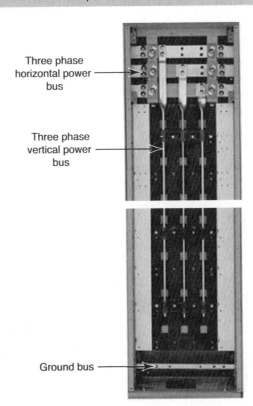

(a) Upper and lower half of MCC showing power bus layout

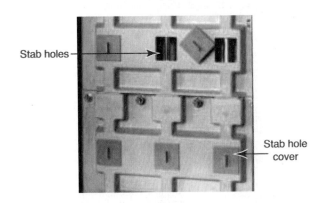

(b) Power bus covered by insulator with stab holes and stab hole covers visible

Courtesy of Siemens.

aluminum's thermal expansion is greater than copper. These spring loaded washers keep bolts from loosening with temperature change. Also, due to its lower conductivity than copper, a larger aluminum bus is needed to handle the same level of current.

Some environments present a corrosive atmosphere to the copper bussing, which possibly leads to bus fail-

ure. Coating the copper bus with tin protects it from corrosion. Coating copper bus with silver is effective in some environments, but it can form relatively thick, insulating layers of silver sulfide and tarnish. The electrical worker should be aware if the MCC is in a corrosive industrial environment such as in *pulp plants, wastewater treatment facilities, fossil fuel-based power generating plants,* and *marine facilities.*

Classifications and Wiring Types

Motor control centers are classified based on the interconnection method and the unit wiring is typed based on the connection styles. The MCC *classes* are 1 and 2 and *wiring types* are A, B, and C. Their descriptions are as follows:

Class 1—Independent Units—Class 1 motor control centers consist of mechanical groups of combination motor control units, branch feeders, other units, and electrical devices arranged in a convenient assembly. The manufacturer completes wiring between components within each unit. Wiring between units is not required.

Class 2—Interconnected Units—Class 2 MCCs are the same as Class 1 MCCs with the addition of manufacturer-furnished electrical interlocking and wiring between units as specifically described in the overall control system diagrams.

Type A—User (field) wiring connects directly to device terminals internal to the unit. This wiring type is provided only on Class 1 MCCs.

Type B—User (field) control wiring connects to unit terminal blocks in or adjacent to each motor control unit. User load (power) wiring for Size 3 or smaller combination motor control units connects as follows:

> *Type B–D*—User load (power) wiring connects directly to the device terminals, which are located immediately adjacent to and are readily accessible from the vertical wireway.

> *Type B–T*—User load (power) wiring connects to factory-wired power terminal blocks located in or adjacent to each unit.

User load (power) wiring for Size 4 or larger combination motor control units and branch feeder units connects directly to the unit device terminals.

Type C—User (field) control wiring and load wiring on Size 3 or smaller motor control units connects to master terminal blocks mounted at the top or bottom of those vertical sections containing control units. Size 3 or smaller units are factory-wired from unit-located terminal blocks to the master terminal blocks. Size 4 or larger units connects directly to the device terminals. As an option, user load (power) wiring for all sizes of motor control units may connect directly to the device terminals within the MCC units.

Units and Compartments

Motor control centers are available with many combinations of units and compartments both *removable* (called *draw-out* or *withdrawable*) and *fixed*. Figure 12-5 shows a fixed unit with many of the features identified.

Removable units have *line, load, control, network,* and *protective earth* (PE) connections. The units use a sliding track and mechanical lever for ease of insertion and removal. Figure 12-6(a) illustrates a two module removable unit. Figure 12-6(b) illustrates the mounting plate that connects the unit to the MCC. Note that the PE connection mates with the mounting plate first, then the guide pins, and finally the connectors.

Terminations compartments or blocks are either fixed or removable. Figure 12-7 illustrates a fixed terminal block. In the removable termination compartment, the

FIGURE 12-5: Fixed compartment unit.

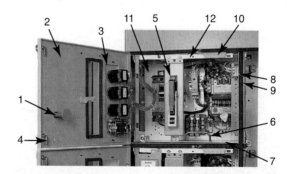

1) Starter reset mechanism
2) Door
3) Pilot device panel
4) Locking latch
5) Disconnect operating handle
6) Supplementary installation handle
7) Bottom unit barrier plate
8) Control terminal blocks
9) Swing plate with terminal blocks
10) Racking lever
11) Back plate
12) Top barrier plate

Courtesy of Siemens.

FIGURE 12-6: Withdrawable MCC modules.

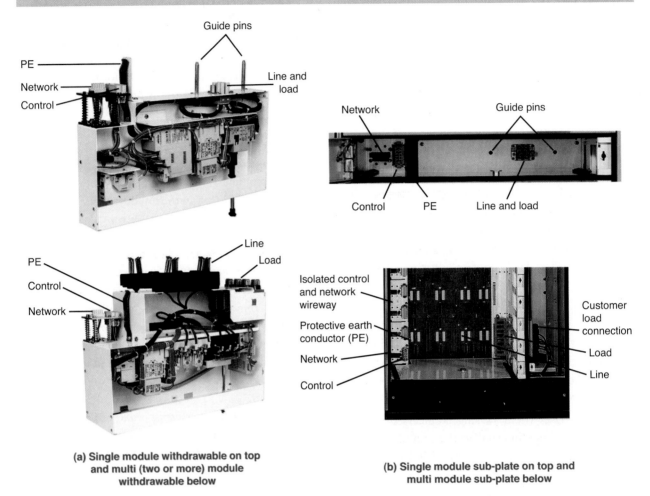

(a) Single module withdrawable on top
and multi (two or more) module
withdrawable below

(b) Single module sub-plate on top and
multi module sub-plate below

Courtesy of Rockwell Automation, Inc.

FIGURE 12-7: MCC terminal blocks.

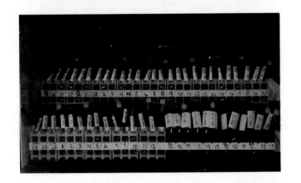

terminal blocks are rack mounted to permit withdrawal of the entire assembly for ease of wiring during installation and maintenance. Typically, wiring is brought from the horizontal wireway to the terminal block for Size 3 and smaller combination motor control units. The larger sizes are generally carried into the vertical wireway and under the bottom side of the unit to terminations within the unit.

Meter compartments are used for power management of three-phase systems and include *analog ammeters* and *voltmeters*, *digital meters* and *power monitors*. Figure 12-8 illustrates the digital meter unit and the ammeter/voltmeter unit. The *digital meter* measures *line-neutral voltages*, *line-line voltages*, and the instantaneous averaged peak values of measured *phase currents*. The *power monitors* display current and voltage parameters in real time and typically includes event logs and trend analysis. *Current* and *potential transformers* are often necessary to condition the voltage and current levels to values used by the metering devices.

Installation and Maintenance

The *installation procedure* of a motor control center is dependent on the manufacturer and the application. Before any installation work is begun, consult all manufacturer drawings and applicable contract drawings for the installation. Give particular attention to the physical location of units in the control center and their relation to existing or planned raceway. Provide for future raceway entrance prior to control center installation. The following steps provide the electrical worker with general guidelines for MCC installation.

1. Locate the motor control center in the area shown on the building floor plans. If the MCC is installed where it is exposed to water/moisture, use the appropriate NEMA/IEC enclosure. This enclosure would be the primary protection from the elements.

2. Since control centers are assembled at the manufacturer on smooth and level surfaces to assure correct alignment of all parts, control centers should be securely mounted on a level surface. Leveled channel sills under both the front and rear of the MCC are used to provide this level base. If sills are grouted in concrete, the mounting bolts should be screwed in place and remain until the concrete has hardened.

3. For bottom entry, position the motor control center so that the conduit stubs or floor openings are located in accordance with floor plan drawings. If optional bottom plates are supplied, the plates may be removed and drilled for conduit entry.

4. Install the MCC in its final position, progressively leveling each section and bolting the frames together if they are separated. If necessary, secure the MCC to walls or other supporting surfaces.

5. Ground and bond the MCC in accordance with NEC guidelines and the manufacturer directives.

6. Complete all internal wiring and adjustments in accordance with the equipment installation manual, and then close all unit and wireway doors.

7. Unless the MCC has been designed for unusual service conditions, do not locate where it will be exposed to ambient temperatures above 40°C (104°F), corrosive or explosive fumes, dust, vapors, dripping or standing water, abnormal vibration, shock or tilting.

The *maintenance procedure* of a motor control center is dependent on the equipment and the application. Periodic preventative maintenance programs are established for motor control centers to avoid unnecessary downtime. At a minimum, checks are made semi-annually. If the equipment within the MCC is subjected to heavy duty or highly repetitive operation, more frequent maintenance may be necessary. The following checks are typical for semi-annual and annual maintenance programs.

Semi-Annual Maintenance

1. Perform an overall visual inspection.
2. Check all indicators, meters, and instruments for proper operation.
3. Make sure all bolted connections are secure.
4. Verify operation of heaters and thermostats.
5. Check for undue noise and vibration that might loosen bolted connections.
6. Look for evidence of moisture in the switchgear.
7. Note unusual amount of ozone odor, which is a by-product of arcing.

Annual Maintenance

1. Bolted connections should be tight. Discoloration, excessive corrosion, brittle or discolored insulation may indicate an overheated connection.
2. Inspect all cables for tight connections and ample support.
3. Inspect control wiring for signs of wear and damage. Replace suspected wire.

4. Examine resistors and other devices prone to over-heating.
5. Open all hinged doors and remove bolted panels.
6. Clean insulation thoroughly.
7. Withdraw and clean all draw-out components.
8. Clean the stationary portion of the switchgear by wiping with a clean cloth. Use dry, compressed air in inaccessible areas.
9. Remove the covers of all panel devices where possible. Check wiring for secure connections. Clean contacts on relays and switches wherever necessary and permitted by code and manufacturer's procedures. Replace covers.
10. Remove air filters when used. Flush with clean water if necessary.

12-2 REDUCED VOLTAGE STARTERS

Reduced voltage starters apply a low voltage to the motor at startup, and then when the motor is at its running speed, a higher voltage is applied. The majority of industrial applications use three-phase AC motors because of their simplicity, ruggedness, and reliability. Reduced voltage starting is typically not used for single phase motors because they are smaller, typically less than five horsepower, and are started directly from the line voltage. So reduced voltage starters are applied to three-phase motors and DC motors. Three phase motors are used in every conceivable industrial application and DC motor industrial applications include portable power equipment such as forklift trucks, dollies, and small locomotives.

DC Motors

During turn-on, when the motor is connected directly to the power source, the DC motor current is limited only by the resistance of the windings. Large DC motors have less resistance and higher starting currents; therefore a higher likelihood of damage to the motor when started at full line voltage. A starting *rheostat* (Figure 12-9) or *solid-state starter* provides a safer reduced voltage start. DC motor drives, dis-

FIGURE 12-9: Rheostat motor starters.

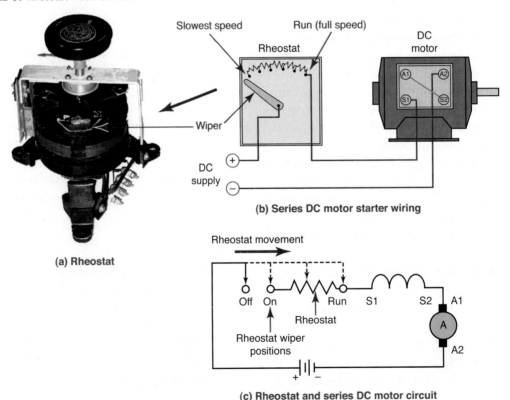

(a) Rheostat

(b) Series DC motor starter wiring

(c) Rheostat and series DC motor circuit

DC Motors Using Rheostats—The starting rheostat is connected in series with the power line and the DC motor as shown in Figure 12-9. The resistance of the rheostat reduces the motor starting voltage, and the resistance is lowered when the motor is at running speed. The rheostat is manually controlled, which means the operator determines the starting voltage and the running voltage. Note in the figure that in the full speed position, the rheostat resistance is zero. Rheostats control DC motor speed; however, they are not energy efficient because the energy withheld from the motor to slow the speed is dissipated in the rheostat. As a result, the rheostat is not the current choice for low voltage DC motor starting or speed control.

cussed in a later chapter, have replaced reduced voltage staring techniques in many DC motor applications.

AC Motors

Small horsepower AC motors are normally started using the full line voltage. These motor starters are the most efficient and an inexpensive method for starting small horsepower motors. However, many applications require large horsepower motors where full-voltage starters cannot be used. With a full voltage starter, the motor windings are directly connected to the power line. As a result, the high inrush current for a large horsepower motor causes interference on the power distribution system. This problem is not an issue for small motors, which produce a negligible disturbance. Most power distribution systems are not designed for huge current fluctuations on their power grid. Large current fluctuations result in *voltage drops, poor voltage regulation,* and *harmonic issues* on the industry's power system and on the utility power grid. In some cases, utility companies put limitations on the amount of inrush current or current spikes permitted on their systems.

An alternative is reduced voltage starters, which lessen the impact on the power distribution system by reducing inrush current. Hence, reduced voltage starting techniques are commonly used to limit the inrush currents of large motors. Techniques that are used in reduced voltage starting for AC motors include *autotransformer, primary resistor, part winding, wye-delta, solid state* and *soft-start starters.*

12-3 AUTOTRANSFORMER STARTERS

Autotransformer starting is one of the *most efficient* and *effective* reduced voltage starting techniques. Autotransformer starting is best suited for applications requiring *long startup times* with *high torque* and *low starting current* limitations. This starting technique delivers the *most torque per line ampere* of any reduced voltage starting method. In general, *autotransformer starters* have a low primary current and a higher secondary current due to the turns ratio present in the autotransformer. Also, with the autotransformer present, the motor terminal voltage is not dependent on the load current. While, the current to the motor *changes* because of the motor's dynamic characteristics, the voltage to the motor is *relatively constant.*

Autotransformer starters are constructed with a *single inline winding* with *multiple* voltage taps *switched* by timer controlled contactors. The timer controls the contactors, which engage and disengage the autotransformer windings taps. The motor is typically switched off the low voltage starter to line voltage when the motor has accelerated to 75 percent of running speed. The windings of the autotransformers are typically tapped at 50%, 65% and 80% of the line voltage value that results in inrush currents of the same percentage.

This starter offers more reduction of line current than any other reduced voltage starting method. The multiple taps on the autotransformer provide adjustments to the voltage and current to meet different motor starting requirements. Autotransformer starters are the *best option* when *maximum starting torque* and *minimum starting current* are required for applications with *frequent starts* or *long acceleration* periods. Autotransformer starters are generally used with *squirrel cage* type motors and not with *wound rotor* and *synchronous* types.

An autotransformer starter with an autotransformer in each leg of the three phase supply has two disadvantages: *cost* and *open transition conditions.* The cost is relatively high, and *open transition conditions* occur where the motor is disconnected from the supply when changing from reduced voltage to full voltage.

Open Transition Autotransformer Starter Circuit

Figure 12-10 illustrates an autotransformer starter circuit with open transition. The control circuit consists of contactors *1S*, *2S*, and *R* and an on-delay timer *TR1*. Note that the motor is connected to three power lines *L1*, *L2*, and *L3* directly when contactor *R* is closed or through the autotransformer 65% taps when contactor *2S* is closed. Contactor *1S* connects the three autotransformers together.

When the *start* pushbutton is pressed, the timer *TR1* is energized. Instantaneous contact *1-TRl* closes to form the holding circuit for the *start* pushbutton. Instantaneous contact *2-TR1* closes and completes the current path to the starting contactor *1S*. When contactor *1S* energizes, the three *1S* contacts in the power circuit close and connect the autotransformers together. Auxiliary contact *2-1S* closes to energize the second starting contactor *2S*, which closes three *S2* contacts in the power circuit and connects the autotransformers to the three power lines *L1*, *L2*, and *L3*. At this point, the motor is connected to the line through the autotransformer taps and begins to accelerate the motor at a reduced voltage.

After the preset time delay, timed contacts *3-TR1* (NOTC) and *4-TR1* (NCTO) change state. Contact *4-TR1* opens and de-energizes contactor *1S*. Contactor *2S* continues to be energized through a holding contact *1-2S*. Contact *3-TR1* closes and energizes the run contactor *R*. The three *R* contacts in the power circuit close and connect the motor directly to the line

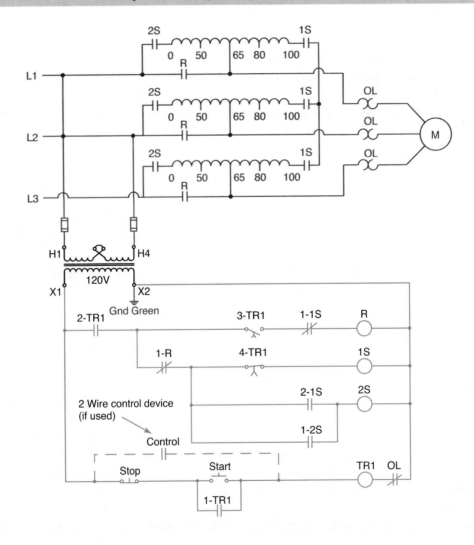

FIGURE 12-10: Autotransformer low voltage motor starting with open transition.

at full voltage. In addition, the *R* contactor opens a normally closed auxiliary contact *1-R* that de-energizes contactor *2S* and disconnects the autotransformer from the circuit.

The dashed two-wire control is shown if the motor is started under automatic control from a process sensing device, such as a level switch. Any of the discrete process switches discussed earlier could be used singly or in some logical combination to start the motor.

Closed Transition Autotransformer Starter Circuit

Figure 12-11 illustrates an autotransformer low voltage starter with closed transition. When two autotransformers are used for the autotransformer starter in an *open delta configuration*, a *closed transition start* is

possible with motor input T2 always connected to the three phase supply. The control circuit is not changed but the middle autotransformer is replaced with a parallel set of contacts from the *R* and *2S* contactors. The T2 leg of the motor is never broken from the L2 line because the *R* contact closes before the *2S* contact opens. Note in the figure that the *2S* coil is energized through the 2-TR1 instantaneous contact, the NC *R* contact and then sealed in with a NO contact from *2S*. Thus, *2S* is de-energized when *R* is energized. Therefore, the T2 leg of the motor never has an open transition. The two-wire control is not shown but can be added as shown in Figure 12-10.

In both circuits the shut down process is the same. As long as the motor is running at full voltage, timer

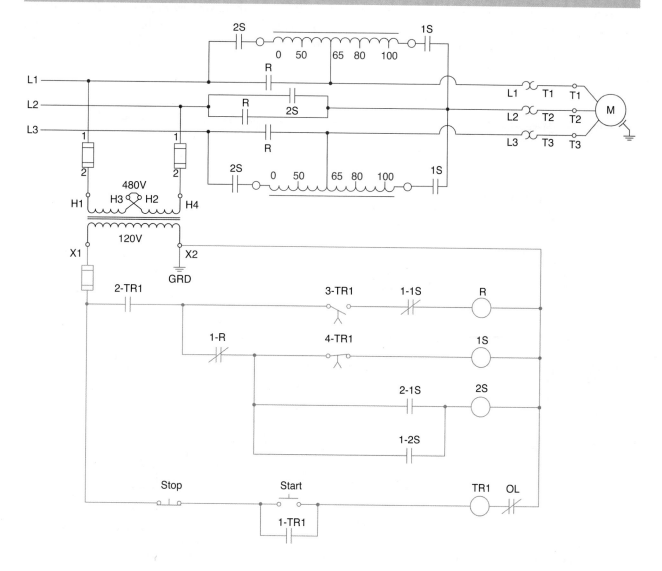

FIGURE 12-11: Autotransformer low voltage motor starting with closed transition.

TR1 and contactor *R* are energized. Only an overload condition or pressing the *stop* pushbutton stops the motor and resets the circuit.

Wiring Diagram for Autotransformer Starting

The diagrams illustrated in Figures 12-10 and 12-11 are useful for understanding the *operation* of the power and control circuits in motor controls. However, *wiring* the control cabinet requires a *wiring diagram*. A sample wiring diagram for an autotransformer starting circuit is illustrated in Figure 12-12(a). The start contactor has five NO power contacts, which is two more than the standard three-phase motor starter contactor. Trace out the wiring for the control and power circuits so the relationship between the diagrams is clear.

The power circuits in Figures 12-10 and 12-11 have overload heaters that carry FLC for the motors. Often FLC is large and a current transformer is required to provide a scaled down motor current for overload detection. Figure 12-12(b) shows two frequently used configurations: *current transformers* and *individual overload*

heaters for each phase and a *solid state overload circuit* with input from a *current transformer* from each phase.

12-4 PRIMARY RESISTOR STARTERS

Primary resistor starting is a reduced voltage starting technique that connects a resistor in series with each power phase that supplies the motor. When the motor starts, a *voltage drop* occurs across the added primary resistors that results in a reduced voltage and current to the motor. Once the motor accelerates to about 75 percent of the full run speed, a timer controlled contactor closes contacts that are in parallel with the primary resistors. The contacts connect the motor directly to full line voltage. Primary resistor starting is used in operations requiring a *slow* and *consistent* start.

Typically, these starters drop the *voltage* and *current values* to about 80% of the normal line voltage. In contrast, autotransformer starters use about 65%. Primary resistor starters offer *closed transition* starting

FIGURE 12-12: Wiring diagram for autotransformer starting motor controller and alternative motor overload wiring options.

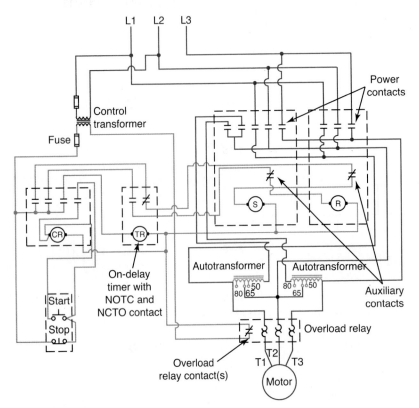

(a) Wiring diagram for closed transition starting motor control

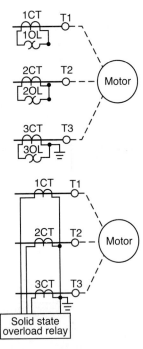

(b) Overload configurations using current transformers in place of the standard overload relay used wiring diagram and operate with almost any *type of motor*. As the motor accelerates, the voltage drop across the resistors decreases because the motors surge current drops, which produces a smoother acceleration and transition between reduced and full voltage operation. Frequent or prolonged starting creates considerable *heat*; as a result, the design includes resistor heat dissipation.

Primary Resistor Starter Circuit

Figure 12-13 illustrates the primary resistor starter circuit. When the *start* pushbutton is pressed, contactor *M1* and on-delay timer *TR1* are energized. Auxiliary contact *1-M1* closes to form the holding circuit. Contactor *M1* closes the three *power circuit contacts* and connects the motor to the line voltage through a resistor. The voltage drop across each resistor reduces the voltage supplied to the motor. After a preset time delay, the NOTC timed contact *1-TR1* closes and energizes contactor *C*. The contactor's three contacts in the power circuit *bypasses* the resistors and connects the motor directly to the full line voltage. The two-wire control is not shown but can be added as shown in Figure 12-10.

The circuit in Figure 12-13 shows a primary resistor starter with a single resistor in each phase leg. When smoother acceleration is required, two or more parallel resistors are added with additional timers and contactors to control the change in resistance. The initial parallel resistor is large, which creates the greatest voltage drop. As subsequent resistors are progressively added in parallel the total resistance drops, which allows increasingly higher voltages and currents to the motor. With this configuration, motor speed is increased in steps.

12-5 PART WINDING STARTERS

Part-winding starters use a motor starting technique that applies power to part of the motor windings at turn-on and then connects the remaining windings for full speed. The *voltage* and *current* reductions are achieved by temporarily modifying the wiring configurations to the motor. A part winding starter is only used with a *dual voltage motor* capable of part winding starting.

The windings of dual voltage motors have two sets of coils in each winding. These coils are connected in series for the higher voltage and in parallel for the lower voltage. Part winding starters are connected to one set of coils at turn-on and both sets of coils in parallel when the motor is at its running speed. One

FIGURE 12-13: Primary resistance low voltage motor starting.

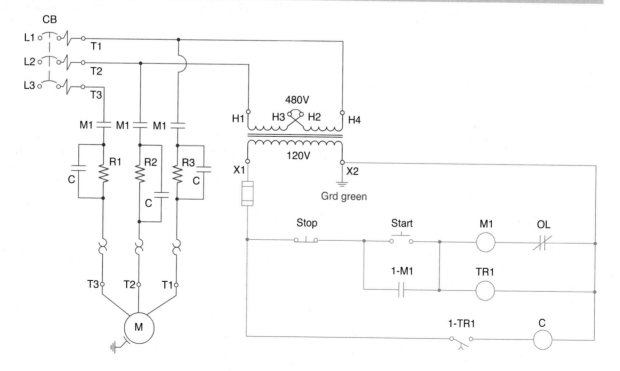

set of coils has a higher resistance than two coils in parallel; thus a reduced inrush current flows through the one set of coils at turn-on. Although dual voltage motors are used in part winding starting, the motor must be operated at the lower voltage. To operate at the higher voltage, the coils are connected in series for the correct voltage drop across the windings. If only one set of coils are connected to the higher voltage for part winding starting, the resulting current flow would quickly damage the motor.

Two motor starters and an on-delay timer are used in part winding starters. Both starters switch half of the full load current (FLC) of the motor because once the motor is at running speed, the two starters effectively divide the FLC between them. When selecting the overload protection, it is a good practice to measure the phase currents and size overload protection based on the readings. The current measurements are for selecting overload protection, which is intended to protect the motor windings and not the conductors. The conductors that supply the motor are normally protected by an overcurrent protective device such as a circuit breaker or fuse on the line side of the starters. This overcurrent protective device is sized to protect the motor conductors and accommodate inrush currents. The motor circuit conductors on the line side of the starters are sized to the FLC of the motor.

Part winding starters are popular because no specialized equipment is required. They are among the *least expensive* types of starters to *purchase, install,* and *maintain.* Although they offer closed transition starting, this type of starting is not suited for *long startup times* or *high inertia loads.* Both sets of winding coils are connected to the line after only a few seconds or the motor may be damaged. In most cases, part winding starters are used with a 230/460 volt dual voltage wye-connected motor operating at 230 volts.

Part Winding Starter Circuit

Figure 12-14 illustrates a part winding starter circuit. When the *start* pushbutton is pressed, the motor starter *M1* and the on-delay timer *TR1* are energized. Auxiliary contact *1-M1* closes to form the holding circuit. Starter *M1* closes three contacts, thus connecting one set of winding coils to the line. At this point, the motor begins to accelerate at a reduced current: After a preset time delay, timed contact *1-TR1* closes and energizes starter *M2.* Starter *M2* closes three contacts, thus connecting the second set of winding coils

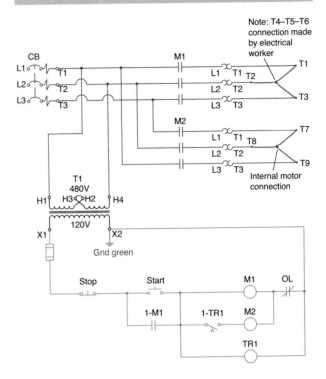

FIGURE 12-14: Part winding low voltage motor starting.

to the line. The two-wire control is not shown but can be added as shown in Figure 12-10.

12-6 WYE-DELTA STARTERS

Wye-delta motors are available with *internal connections* that produce a *wye* or *delta* configuration. They are also available with *no internal connections* so electrical workers can configure them as either wye or delta. The *field configured* type motors are used for wye-delta low voltage starting configurations. The field configured motors are either *six* terminals or *twelve* terminals depending on the number of winding present in the motor stator. Figure 12-15(a) shows a *six terminal* wye motor winding with a single winding in the stator for each phase. Figure 12-15(b) shows a *six terminal* delta motor winding with a single winding in the stator for each phase. The standard terminal numbering used for the six terminal motor configurations is shown in the figure.

Wye-Delta Low Voltage Starter Operation

Understanding the operation of wye-delta low voltage starters begins with a review of how the line voltage distributes across the stator windings for wye and delta

FIGURE 12-15: Standard lead numbers for six terminal winding motors.

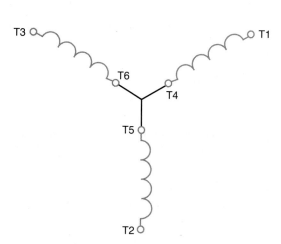

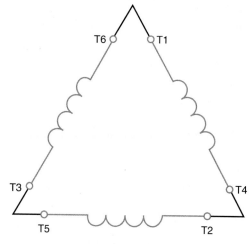

(a) Six terminal stator winding
motor wired for wye operation

(b) Six terminal stator winding
motor wired for delta operation

In some older systems a twelve terminal wye-delta motor is used in the reduced voltage starting mode. Figure 12-16 shows a *twelve terminal* type motor with two windings in the stator for each phase. The standard terminal numbering used for the twelve terminal motor configurations is shown in the figure.

FIGURE 12-16: Standard lead numbers for twelve terminal wye-delta motors.

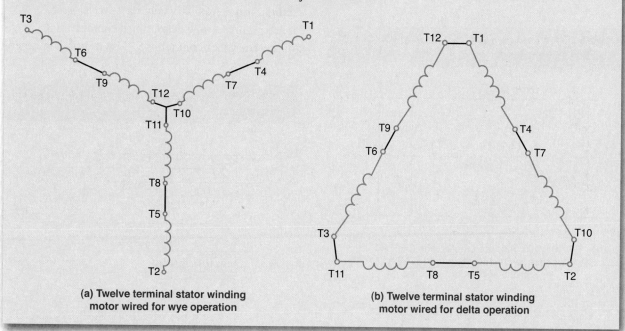

(a) Twelve terminal stator winding
motor wired for wye operation

(b) Twelve terminal stator winding
motor wired for delta operation

configured motors. Figure 12-17 illustrates the *voltages across* the winding for the *wye* and *delta* motor operation. When connected in the wye configuration, Figure 12-17(a), motor windings are connected together at one point (terminals 4, 5, and 6). Each phase of the line voltage is applied to the opposite ends of the wind-ings (terminals 1, 2, and 3). Note that each stator wind-ing has about 58 percent (it is not half because the line voltages are not in phase with each other) of the line voltage applied. Starting current is reduced because the windings are in series. The motor remains connected in a wye configuration throughout the timer controlled acceleration. After the acceleration in the wye configuration is reached, the motor is connected in a delta configuration, Figure 12-17(b), for full run speed operation. Note terminal connections are T1 to T6, T3 to T5, and T2 to T4 with the line voltages L1, L2, and L3 applied to jumpers at T1, T2, and T3 respectively. In the delta configuration each motor winding has the full phase to phase voltage applied across a stator winding for maximum horsepower. So the *wye winding* configuration is used to *start* the motor, and the *delta winding* configuration is used to *run* the motor.

Two configurations, *open transition* and *closed transition,* are available with wye-delta starters. *Open transition* starters require *two contactors, a motor starter,* and an *on-delay timer* with a *NCTO contact. Closed transition* starters add an additional *contactor* to switch in added *resistors* for each phase. With open transition starting, current fluctuations are present when the starter switches from wye to delta. These fluctuations are reduced when the wye configuration is held until the motor approaches its *full run* speed or by using the additional contactor and resistors.

Wye-delta starters are one of the least expensive options, especially for larger horsepower motors. They are easy to install and maintain because they require no special components. However, wye-delta starters require a special motor that adds to the cost of the installation. Wye-delta starters are best suited for applications where low staring torque and minimal line current are required.

Wye-Delta Starter Circuit

Figure 12-18 illustrates a wye-delta starter circuit, and Figure 12-19 condenses the power circuit into a single diagram. Refer to both during the analysis of the circuit operation that follows.

When the *start* pushbutton is pressed, the on-delay timer *TR1* is energized. Instantaneous contact *3-TR1* closes to form the holding circuit. Instantaneous contact *1-TR1* closes and energizes contactor *S* and contactor *M1*. Contactor *S* closes three contacts that connect one end of each motor winding together through terminals T4, T5 and T6. This forms the center point for the temporary wye connection the motor uses during acceleration. Contactor *M1* closes three contacts and connects motor terminals Tl, T2 and T3 to the line. At this point, the motor accelerates and operates as a wye-connected motor. Auxiliary contact *2-S* opens, locking out contactor *M2* while the motor operates in the wye configuration. Auxiliary contact *1-M1* closes.

After a preset time delay, timed contact *2-TR1* opens and de-energizes contactor *S.* The motor is momen-

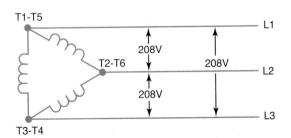

FIGURE 12-17: Analysis of stator winding applied voltage in wye-delta low voltage starters.

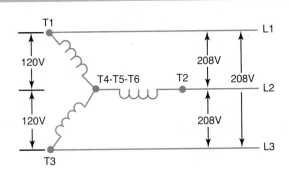

(a) Wye configured motor with 208V AC phase to phase voltage and 120V AC across each stator winding

(b) Delta configured motor with 208V AC phase to phase voltage and 208V AC across each stator winding

FIGURE 12-18: Wye-delta low voltage motor starting with open transition.

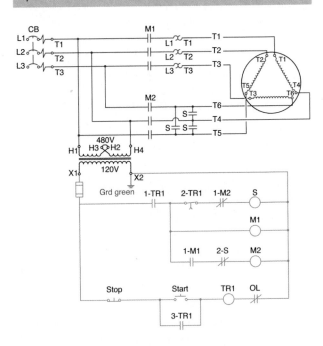

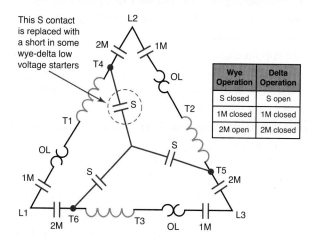

This S contact is replaced with a short in some wye-delta low voltage starters

	Wye Operation	Delta Operation
	S closed	S open
	1M closed	1M closed
	2M open	2M closed

tarily disconnected from the line (open transition). Auxiliary contact 2-S closes and contactor M2 is energized. Contactor M2 closes three contacts, thus connecting the motor to the line in a delta configuration. In most wye-delta starters, contactor S and contactor M2 are electrically and mechanically interlocked. The two-wire control is not shown but can be added as shown in Figure 12-2.

12-7 SOLID STATE AND SOFT STARTERS

Solid state starters use electronic components to control the voltage and current to the motor. In these starters, a *silicon controlled rectifier* (SCR) controls the voltage and current to the motor during acceleration. An SCR has three terminals—a *cathode, anode* and *gate*. When a signal is applied to the gate, it acts as a "trigger" that turns the SCR *on* (cathode to anode near zero resistance. The SCR turns off when the AC input voltage drops to zero in the cycle. Since solid state devices have no moving parts, there is virtually no time delay during the switching. *Triggering* the SCR *on* at specific intervals during each positive cycle of the sine wave controls the *value* of the *voltage* and *current* delivered to the motor from near *zero* to *50 percent*. When two SCRs are used, Figure 12-20, power control is extended to 100 percent. The gate signals start conduction in the SCRs at any point along the positive or negative half of the sine wave. For example, the trigger signal in Figure 12-20 occurs at the positive and negative peak sine wave values. As a result, the power delivered to the load is at the 50 percent level. A gate control circuit is used to set the trigger point in the AC

voltage cycle. The earlier in a half-cycle that the gate is triggered, the longer the SCR remains on and the greater the voltage and current supplied to the load.

Solid State Starter Circuit

Figure 12-21 illustrates a solid state reduced voltage starter. It consists of a *start* contactor, *S*, a *run* contactor, *R*, and a *current transformer CT* to sense motor current flow. Note that the *start contactor* contacts, *S*, are in series with the SCRs, and the *run contactor* contacts, *R*, are in parallel with the SCRs. The motor is started with the *S* contactor *activated* and the *R* contactor *not activated*. With the *S* contacts *closed*, the acceleration of the motor is controlled by the SCRs.

FIGURE 12-20: AC operation of SCR pair in a solid state motor starter.

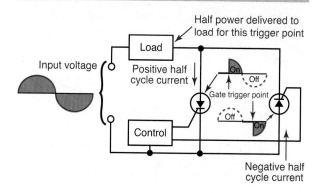

FIGURE 12-21: SCR solid state starter operation.

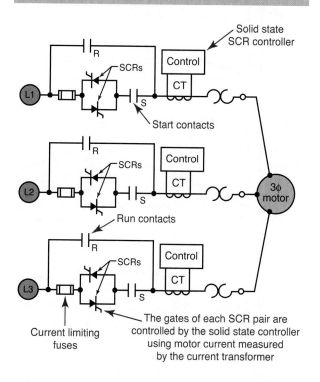

The solid state electronics uses the motor current level to determine when the solid state control triggers the SCR gates. The SCRs control the motor until it reaches running speed at which time the *run* contactor, *R*, energizes and the start contactor, *S*, de-energizes. This connects the motor directly to L1, L2, and L3, and the SCRs are turned off.

Solid state starters provide the smoothest acceleration and greatest control of current for motors than any other starting technique. Figure 12-22 compares across-line starts to a solid state motor control starting for *applied voltage*, *current*, *torque*, and *speed*. Note the vast improvement in motor control parameters with the solid state starter. When a solid state reduced voltage starter is sized correctly for the load and mounted to properly dissipate heat, years of reliable service results.

Soft Starters

Soft starters are electronic devices that offer greater control during the *starting* and *stopping* of a motor. These starters offer adjustable *ramp-up* (soft start) times by gradually increasing the voltage and current supplied to the motor. The ramp-up time is based on an adjustable preset time on the motor controller. Most soft start controllers offer *ramp-down* (soft stopping) control that reduces motor voltage and current during deceleration. Like solid state starters, soft start controllers are used in applications that require *smooth* starting and stopping. Figure 12-23 illustrates the soft starting and soft stopping motor starter with front panel controls to set motor operation parameters. Figure 12-24 displays the motor *voltage profile* used in soft starting and stopping applications. Also,

FIGURE 12-22: Comparison of voltage, current, torque, and speed for across line voltage starts and solid state reduced voltage starts.

FIGURE 12-23: Soft start motor starter with settings for overload class, starting voltage, starting time, and stopping time.

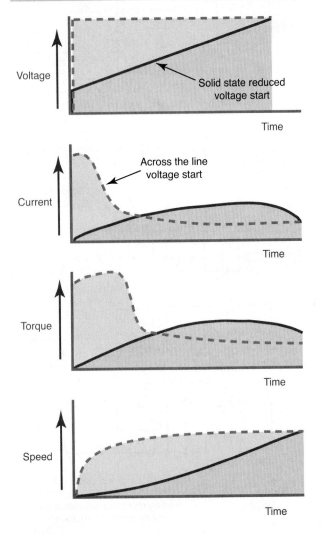

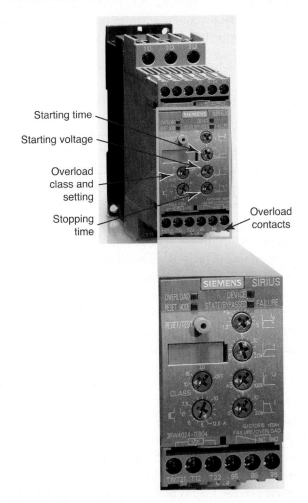

Courtesy of Siemens.

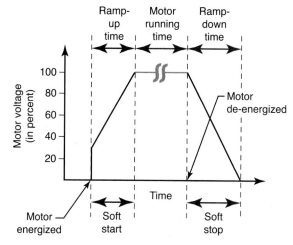

(a) Soft start motor starter ramp-up or starting time, run time motor voltage, and ramp-down or stopping time for motor

Courtesy of Siemens.

Suggested Setting	Startup Parameters	
Application	**Start voltage %**	**Starting time s**
Conveyor belt	70	10
Roller conveyor	60	10
Compressor	50	20
Small fan	40	20
Pumps	40	10
Hydraulic pump	40	10
Stirrers	40	20

(b) Typical table supplied by manufacturer for setting ramp-up or starting times based on common applications

Figure 12-25 lists the advantages, disadvantages and applications of the reduced voltage starters for AC motors. Although reducing the starting voltage in comparison to load requirements is the primary consideration for selecting a starting method, cost is also a factor. The cost varies for each reduced starting technique and is listed in the figure.

FIGURE 12-25: Comparison of reduced voltage starters.

Starter	Advantages	Disadvantages	Applications
Autotransformer	Provides the highest torque per ampere of line current; suitable for long starting periods; motor current is greater than the transformer primary current during starting	Most expensive, low power factor; large physical size	Blowers, pumps, compressors, conveyors
Primary resistor	High power factor and smooth acceleration on startup; less expensive than autotransformer	Requires expensive resistors that dissipate high heat in long starts; poor efficiency at low torque	Conveyors, belt and gear drives
Part winding	Least expensive; small physical size; most dual motors can be started with this starter	Unsuitable for high inertia loads; motors over 230V AC require special design; motor overheats if startup is greater than five seconds	Pumps, blowers, fans, reciprocating compressors
Wye delta	Suitable for high inertia loads; good efficiency for high torque and best for frequent starts; good where inrush current is restricted	Requires a special motor; provides lower starting torque; momentary inrush current when delta contactor is closed	Centrifuges, centrifugal compressors
Solid state	Voltage gradually applied during startup; adjustable braking and acceleration time; built-in self-calibration features	Higher cost; requires protection against electrical transients and requires ventilation	Hoists, packing and conveyor equipment, machine tools

TECH NOTES

a typical table of motor *voltage* and *starting* times for common production applications is illustrated.

12-8 REVERSING STARTERS

In addition to the reduced voltage starters, *reversing starters* are used in industrial processes that require the motor to run *forward* and *backward*. Reversing the direction of a motor is accomplished manually with *switches* or electromagnetically with *solenoids*. Although motors can be reversed with mechanical means such as *gearboxes*, the most economical and feasible solution is a switching device that controls the direction of the motor. The direction is controlled by a variety of mechanisms such as *drum switches* (see Chapter 2), *manual and magnetic starters* and *solid state* devices. This chapter focuses on three-phase motors with electromagnetic starters due to their common use in commercial and industrial applications. Motor control circuits use reversing starters (sometimes called *forward/reversing starters*), which are commonly found in hoists, cranes, turntables, conveyor systems, and in a variety of industrial machine processes. A three phase motor reverses its direction when any two of the input power lines are interchanged. Although interchanging any two of the input lines reverses the motor, the industry standard is to interchange *L1* (phase A) and *L3* (phase C) with no change in L2 (phase B) as shown in Figure 12-26.

Electromagnetic reversing starters consist of two, interconnected three-pole contactors on a common back plate with a single overload relay assembly. Usually, one contactor is designated as *forward* and the other contactor is designated *reverse*, hence the name *forward/reverse* starter. The two contactors are interconnected with bus bars or heavy gauge wires. Only one overload relay assembly is needed because three phase motors gener-

ally draw the same current regardless of the direction of rotation. Figure 12-27 illustrates the forward and reverse contactors and the single overload assembly. The interconnected wiring of NC auxiliary contacts from each contactor creates an electrical interlock.

Mechanical and Electrical Interlocks

Motor control circuits with reversing starters use *interlocks* to inhibit both contactors energizing at the same time. Also, the rapid reversal of a motor's direction could damage the driven machinery, endanger personnel and destroy the motor if the starter did not have interlocks. Starters are generally equipped with both *electrical* and *mechanical* style interlocks. Electrical interlock wiring, visible in Figure 12-27, is connected to auxiliary contacts as shown in Figure 12-28. An NC auxiliary contact from the forward and reversing contactors is used to *electrically interlock* each contactor. The NO contacts act as *memory* or a *sealing* contacts on the forward and reversing pushbuttons. The NC contact *electrically isolates* the contactor that is not energized.

Figure 12-28 illustrates the ladder diagram for the *mechanical* and *electrical interlocking* of a reversing starter. Note the auxiliary contacts *2-R1* and *2-F1* provide the electrical interlocking. The NC contact *2-F1* is controlled by the forward coil and connected in series

FIGURE 12-27: Typical forward/reversing contactor.

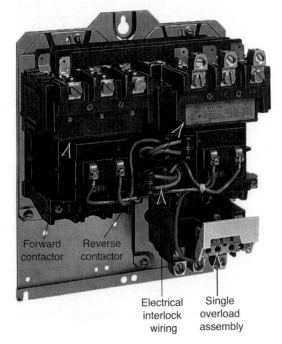

Forward contactor   Reverse contactor

Electrical interlock wiring   Single overload assembly

Courtesy of Rockwell Automation, Inc.

FIGURE 12-26: Reversing three phase motors.

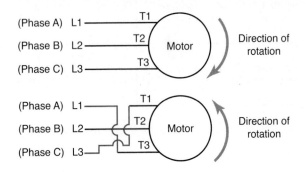

with the reverse coil. The NC contact *2-R1* is controlled by the reverse coil and connected in series with the forward coil. When the forward coil is energized, the *2-F1* contact is opened and prevents power flow in rung 3, which isolates the reverse coil. If the reverse coil is energized, the *2-R1* contact is opened and blocks power flow in rung 1, which isolates the forward coil. Reversing starters are normally factory wired for electrical interlocking, but electric workers should be knowledgeable in mounting and connecting these contacts in the field. The combination of mechanical and electrical interlocking is usually sufficient for most motor control circuits with reversing starters.

Mechanical interlocking is one of the most *common* and *reliable* methods used in reversing starters. A mechanical interlock is a mechanism installed between the two contactors of a reversing starter as shown in Figure 12-29. Figure 12-29(a) shows the interlock in the neutral position when both contactors are de-energized. When the coil of the *forward* contactor is *energized*, the mechanical interlock moves to *physically block* the movement of the *reverse* contactor as shown in Figure 12-29(b). Even if the coil of the reverse contactor is energized, the reverse contactor does not close because the mechanical interlock is physically blocking the movement of the reverse contactor. The forward contactor must de-energize before the reverse contactor can operate. Likewise, if the reverse contactor is energized, the mechanical interlock prevents the operation of the forward contactor as shown in Figure 12-29(c).

Pushbutton Interlocking

Some reversing motor control circuits use *pushbutton interlocking*, which provides another level of protection. Pushbutton interlocking uses both the NO and the NC momentary contacts of the forward and reverse pushbuttons. Figure 12-30 illustrates the ladder diagram for the mechanical, electrical and pushbutton interlocking of a reversing starter. The NC contact of the reverse pushbutton *REV* is in series with the NO contact of the forward pushbutton *FOR*. The NO contact of *REV* pushbutton functions as another stop pushbutton in the forward circuit. The NO contact on *REV* pushbutton

FIGURE 12-28: Electrical and mechanical interlocking of forward/reversing contactors.

Electrical interlock—2-R1 contact electrically isolates rung 1 when the R1 coil is energized. The 2-F1 contact electrically isolates rung 3 when the F1 coil is energized.

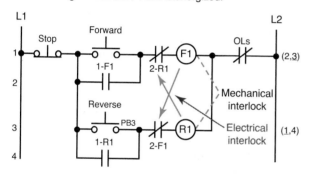

FIGURE 12-29: Mechanical interlock between forward and reverse contactors.

(b) Forward contactor energized—cam rotates to block any movement of the armature in the reverse contactor

(a) Both contactors de-energized— cam is in a neutral position

(c) Reverse contactor energized—cam rotates to block any movement of the armature in the forward contactor

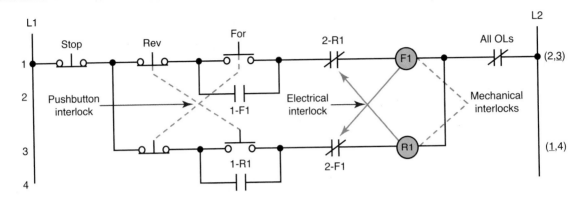

FIGURE 12-30: Mechanical interlock, electrical and pushbutton interlocks on forward/reversing starter.

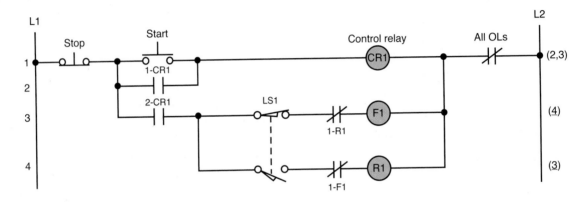

FIGURE 12-31: Automatic reversal ladder diagram for grinder application.

is used as the start pushbutton for the reverse circuit. When the REV pushbutton is pressed, the NC contact opens the current path to the forward circuit and at the same time closes the NO contact to complete the current path to the reverse circuit. Likewise, the same interlocking scheme is used to interlock the reverse circuit. When the FOR pushbutton is pressed, the NC contact opens the current path to the reverse circuit and at the same rime closes the NO contact to complete the current path to the forward circuit.

Automatic Reversing Starters

Limit switches provide an automatic motor control circuit that reverses the direction of the motor at fixed points. A typical application is a grinding machine where its table is reversed end of travel in each direction. Figure 12-31 illustrates a ladder diagram for a motor control circuit with limit switches. When the *start* pushbutton is pressed, the control relay *CR1* is energized. Auxiliary contact *1-CR1* forms the holding circuit for the *start* pushbutton, and *2-CR1* pro-

vides a current path for the limit switch. The grinder motor runs in the forward direction until the maintain-operator limit switch is actuated (opening the NC contact and closing the NO contact), and then the grinder motor runs in the reverse direction.

12-9 TROUBLESHOOTING SPECIAL PURPOSE STARTERS

The troubleshooting techniques in Chapter 6 are applied with the modifications for reduced voltage and reversing starters that follow. For reduced voltage starters, verify the voltage delivered to the motor from the power circuits during starting and running.

Troubleshooting Reduced Voltage Starters

Measure the voltage at the motor from the reduced voltage power circuit during starting and running. The voltage during running should be equal to the line voltage for all reduced voltage starting techniques. The starting voltage values depend on the reduced voltage starting technique.

- For autotransformer starting, the measured voltage should be a percentage of the line voltage depending on the tap used.
- For primary resistor starting, the measured voltage should be between ten and fifty percent of the line voltage.
- For part winding and wye-delta starting, the measured voltage should be the value of the line voltage.
- For solid state starting, the measured voltage should be between fifteen and fifty percent of the line voltage based on the starter settings.

Troubleshooting Reversing Starters

Reversing starter failure is often due to problems in the power circuit or the control circuit. The power circuit connects the loads to the main power line. Troubleshooting the power circuits involves determining the point in which system power is lost. Troubleshooting the control circuits involves using a ladder diagram to analyze the control logic and determine if a control element failure could cause the observed symptoms. Test points are selected and measurements made to locate the faulty component.

When troubleshooting the power circuit, first verify that the line to line voltage is correct. Next, follow the voltage path, measuring the voltage at the fuse or circuit breaker, the voltage out of the starter, and the voltage at the motor.

The first step in control circuit troubleshooting is verification that control power is present. Next, use voltage measurements to verify that overloads and all NC contacts are closed. Cycle NO contacts, where possible, to verify that they are closed when activated. From the test data determine if the problem is in the control circuit.

CRITICAL CONCEPTS

The need to know content from Chapter 12 is summarized in the following statements.

- Motor control centers consist of totally enclosed, dead front, free-standing structures or sections that are bolted together, which support and house control units, common bus bars for distributing power to the control units, and a network of wireway and conductor entrance areas for accommodating incoming and outgoing load and control wires.
- The feeder power bus enters the MCC either from overhead or underneath and supplies three-phase AC, generally 208 to 600V AC.
- Motor control centers are classified based on their interconnection method and the unit wiring is typed based on the connection styles. The MCC classes are 1 and 2 and wiring types are A, B, and C.
- Reduced voltage starters apply a low voltage to the motor at startup, and then when the motor is at its running speed, a higher voltage is applied.
- Autotransformer starters are constructed with inline single, multiple-tapped windings connected to timer controlled contactors, where the windings are typically tapped at 50%, 65% and 80% of the line voltage value, thus reducing the startup current.
- Primary resistor starting is a reduced voltage starting technique that connects a resistor in series with each phase that supplies the motor.
- Part-winding starters use a motor starting technique that applies power to part of the motor windings at turn-on and then connects the remaining windings for normal speed.
- Wye-delta starters only use a six-lead motor that can be connected in either a wye or delta configuration, where the wye winding configuration is used to start the motor, and the delta winding configuration is used to run the motor.
- Solid state starters use electronic components to reduce the voltage and current to the motor. In these starters, a silicon controlled rectifier (SCR) controls the voltage and current to the motor during acceleration.
- A motor reverses its direction when any two of the input power lines are interchanged.
- Electromagnetic reversing starters consist of two, interconnected three-pole contactors on a common back plate with a single overload relay assembly, where one contactor is designated as forward and the other contactor is designated reverse.
- Starters are generally equipped with both electrical and mechanical style interlocks. Electrical interlock wiring is connected to auxiliary contacts, and mechanical interlock is a mechanism installed between the two contactors of a reversing starter.
- Limit switches provide an automatic motor control circuit that reverses the direction of the motor at predetermined points.

QUESTIONS

1. What is a motor control center?
2. Explain the function of horizontal and vertical wireways.
3. What is the function of the feeder power bus?
4. What the advantages and disadvantages of using copper and aluminum bus material?
5. Describe the autotransformer method of reduced voltage starting.
6. Describe the primary resistor method of reduced voltage starting.
7. Describe the part winding method of reduced voltage starting.
8. Describe the wye-delta method of reduced voltage starting.
9. Describe the solid state method of reduced voltage starting.
10. How is a motor's direction reversed?
11. How are electrical and mechanical interlocking implemented in reversing starters?
12. How do limit switches provide automatic motor reversing?

CHAPTER **13**

Programmable Timers

GOALS AND OBJECTIVES

The primary goals for this chapter are to describe multifunction timers, timing function applications, and programmable timer functions such as retentive timers, non-retentive timers and real time clock timers. In addition, programming techniques and applications of programmable logic relays are addressed.

After completing this chapter, you will be able to:

1. Describe the purpose and operation of multifunction timers for on-delay and off-delay timer functions.
2. Describe the operation of one-shot and repeat-cycle timer functions.
3. Describe the operation of retentive and non-retentive timers.
4. Describe basic techniques for programming timers of the programmable logic relay.

13-1 PROGRAMMABLE TIMER FUNCTIONS

Timer manufacturers offer a range of programmable timing functions such as: *on-delay, off-delay, on- and off-delay, one-shot, fleeting off delay,* and *repeat cycle (flasher)*. A *multifunction timer* as shown in Figure 13-1

provides four of these outputs in the one timer package. The different timer functions are often selected with a *dip switch* settings. Note the table from the side of the relay as shown in Figure 13-1(a) illustrates the dip switch settings for the timing functions and the range of the time delay. Study the front panel interface and timing functions in Figure 13-1.

A common characteristic of multifunction timers is a *trigger signal* to initiate (start) the timing function as well as return (reset) the contacts to their original state. The most commonly used timing functions are *on-delay, off-delay, one-shot,* and *repeat cycle*. On- and off-delay timing functions date back to the original pneumatic timing relays. The other timing functions became available with the introduction of solid state timers. The NEMA and IEC standard timer symbols listed in Chapter 7 apply to on- and off-delay timers, and no symbol standards exist for the other timing functions. The NEMA and IEC standards for NO and NC contacts are used for the other timer functions along with the coil and letter code for the on-delay timer.

On-Delay Timer Function

Figure 13-2(a) illustrates how an on-delay timer in a multifunction timer performs. The timer has power

FIGURE 13-1: Dip switch selectable multifunction IEC timer.

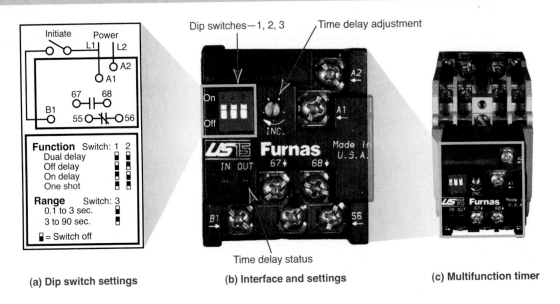

(a) Dip switch settings **(b) Interface and settings** **(c) Multifunction timer**

FIGURE 13-2: On-delay timer function in a multifunction timer.

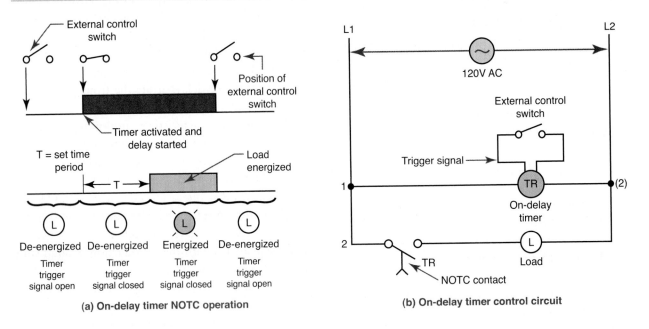

(a) On-delay timer NOTC operation **(b) On-delay timer control circuit**

applied continuously, and the timer is activated with a trigger signal when the NO external control switch contacts close. The load is energized after the set time period by a change in the state of the NOTC contact in the timer. Note that the load receives power only after the set time period has elapsed and until the exter-

nal control signal is removed from the timer. The load remains energized as long as the external control switch remains closed. The load de-energizes when the external control switch is opened.

The external contacts shown represent the NO contacts from any *manually, mechanically,* or *process*

The control circuit in Figure 13-2(b) is used frequently with motors in industrial applications. Often the start of a motor is delayed until other process events occur. For example, pump motors are delayed until the pumps are primed or until the automatic bearing oiling system has lubricated the bearings. Also, air handler motors are delayed until the heater or cooler is powered for some time period.

Some automated work cells have light curtain security systems to sense when someone enters the work area. The control system in Figure 13-2(b) could be used to delay an alarm and the shutdown of the automated system until an authorized operator enters the proper security code to override the security breach signal. For the security system application, the load is an intrusion alarm that sounds after a set delay. The delay allows an operator time to key in an access code. The code checking system has a NC contact placed in rung 2 of the ladder to inhibit the alarm for a valid code entry.

operated switch. In industrial processes, timers are frequently triggered by *pushbuttons, limit switches, and discrete temperature, pressure, flow,* and *level* sensors.

Off-Delay Timer Function

Figure 13-3 illustrates how an off-delay timer in a multifunction timer would perform. As in the on-delay type, the power is applied continuously. Also, the timer is activated with a *trigger signal* produced by a change in the NO external control contacts. The load is energized when the trigger signal is applied to the timer and the timer's NOTO contact closes. The time delay starts when the trigger signal is removed, but the load remains energized until after the set time delay elapses.

As in the on-delay timer, the external contacts represent the NO contacts from any *manually, mechanically,* or *process operated* switch; such as, *pushbuttons, limit switches, and discrete temperature, pressure, flow,* and *level* sensors. Also, the on-delay and off-delay programmable timers often have NCTO and NCTC contacts respectively.

One-Shot Timer Function

The *one-shot* timer or *interval* timer is a timing device where the timed contacts change state immediately when the timer's trigger contacts are closed or power is applied to the timer. When the one-shot function is part of multifunction timer, trigger contacts are present. If the timing relay has a dedicated one-shot

FIGURE 13-3: Off-delay timer function in a multifunction timer.

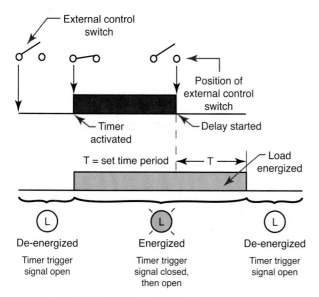

(a) Off-delay timer NOTO operation

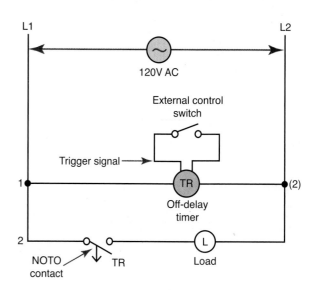

(b) Off-delay timer control circuit

Figure 13-4 shows a projector for a PC with an off-delay timer controlling the cooling of the projector bulb. The projector power switch controls the projector lamp power and the trigger signal for the off-delay timer. When the NO DPST projector power switch is activated, power is applied to the projector lamp and the trigger signal is applied to the off-delay timer. The NOTO timer contacts close and start the projector lamp fan motor. When the projector power switch is moved the original open position, the lamp power is removed and the set delay in the timer is started. The NOTO contacts remain closed as the time delay elapses, which keeps the lamp cooling fan powered. This protects the projector bulb from overheating when power is removed and the cooling fan stopped by providing a proper cool down with the one to two minute extended cooling time.

FIGURE 13-4: Projector cooling fan control with off-delay timer.

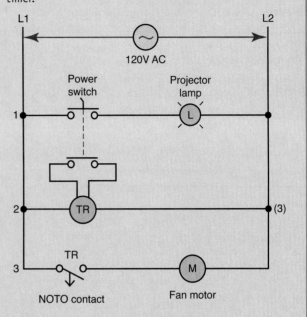

function, then power on trigger is often present. This type is called *supply voltage controlled* timers.

Figure 13-5 illustrates the timing diagram for a supply voltage controlled one-shot. Triggered when power is applied, the timed contacts change state and remain in that state for a set time delay. After the time delay has elapsed, the timed contacts return to their original state. The timer input power or the trigger contact remain active after the timed contacts return to their original state. If input power is interrupted during the timing operation, the time delay is cancelled. However, when power is restored to the timer, the time delay restarts immediately with a full time delay period. One-shot timers are used in applications where the trigger time is *longer* than the preset timing period and for controlling loads for a set period of time.

Repeat-Cycle Timer Function

The *repeat-cycle* timer or *recycle* timer is a timing device in which the timed contacts cycle open and close repeatedly once the timer is active or triggered. The cycling of the contacts continues until the power is removed from the timer or the trigger signal is removed. Timers are either *symmetrical, equal on/off time periods,* or *asymmetrical, unequal on/off time periods.* Options for *start on* or *start off* are also available. Figure 13-6 shows a repeat-cycle timer and the wiring diagram. Note the two knobs on top—one sets the on-time period and the other the off-time period. Like most plug-in timers, the terminal layout and connections are printed on the side of the timer.

Figure 13-7 illustrates the timing diagram for the repeat-cycle timer. The control switch supplies power to

FIGURE 13-5: One shot timing diagrams.

Timer Diagram				Description
Timer status	ENERGIZED		DE-ENERGIZED	When the timer is energized, the timed-delay (T1) starts, the timed contacts change state from open to closed, and the load is energized. When T1 is complete, the timed contacts open and the load is de-energized.
		T1		
Contact status	OPEN	CLOSED	OPEN	
Load status		ENERGIZED	DE-ENERGIZED	

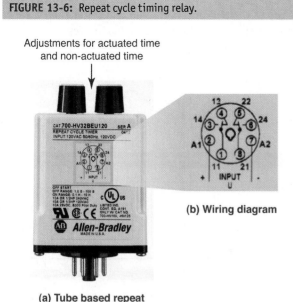

FIGURE 13-6: Repeat cycle timing relay.

Adjustments for actuated time
and non-actuated time

(b) Wiring diagram

**(a) Tube based repeat
(flashing) timing relay**

the timer. The time periods T1 and T2 are adjustable. If they are equal, the timer function is *symmetrical*. If they are unequal, the timing function is *asymmetrical*. Note that the load receives power during the T1 time period. The load de-energizes during the T2 time period. Note that the top line in the figure shows the position of the control switch, and the bottom shows the condition of the load.

Timing Function Options

Additional options available for programmable timers include:

- *On- and off-delay* timers that are *combined* into a single function are also available. The output is either symmetrical (equal on and off delays) or asymmetrical (length of on and off is selectable) for the on and off delays.
- *Repeat cycle* timers are available with *first pulse on* or *first pulse off.*

FIGURE 13-7: Repeat cycle timing diagrams.

Timer Diagram								Description
Timer status	ENERGIZED					DE-ENERGIZED		When the timer is energized, the timed-delay (T1) starts. During T1 timing contacts close, and the load is energized. When T1 is complete, timed-delay (T2) starts. During T2, timing contacts are open, and load is de-energized. The cycle is repeated until the timer is de-energized or the trigger signal is removed.
		T1	T2	T1	T2	T1		
Contact status	OPEN	CLOSED	OPEN	CLOSED	OPEN	CLOSED	OPEN	
Load status		ENER	DE-EN	ENER	DE-EN	ENER	DE-ENERGIZED	

Figure 13-8(a) illustrates a product mixing tank where timers are used to control the mixing process for material in the tank. The drain and fill solenoid valves open when energized. The process is initiated with the start pushbutton. Full level switch, FS1, and the empty level switch, FS2, sense the level of the liquid in the tank. The mixer motor agitates the tank contents after the tank is filled and for the duration of the 30 minute fill and mix cycle. The process is started with a momentary pushbutton by the operator and is stopped at any point in the process by the stop pushbutton. As the tank fills, the empty level switch, FS2, starts the 30 minute fill and mix process. When the liquid reaches the FS1 full level switch, the fill valves are de-energized and mixing of the liquid starts. The mixer motor is energized for 2 minutes and de-energized for 1 minute by a recycle timer. After the 30 minute fill and mix cycle is complete, the tank is drained.

The control circuit for the process is illustrated in Figure 13-8(b). Two timers are used for control.

A repeat cycle timer is used for the 2 minute on and 1 minute off mixing motor control. An on-delay timer is used to control the 30 minute fill and mix cycle. Study the control circuit in Figure 13-8(b) and the timing diagram in Figure 13-8(c). The start pushbutton energizes CR1 through the closed NCTO contacts of the on-delay timer TR1. CR1 contacts energize the two fill solenoids through the NC FS1 level switch contact. A second CR1 contact seals in the Start PB. The TR1 30 minute timer trigger is activated by the FS2 low level switch. When the tank is full, FS1 changes state, which de-energizes the fill solenoids and starts the recycle timer and the mix process. When the 30 minute on-delay timer, TR1, times out, 1-TR1 (NC times open) opens to de-energize CR1 and 2-TR1 (NO times closed) closes to energize the drain solenoid and start the drain cycle. When the liquid drops below the FS1 full tank level switch the trigger to recycle timer TR2 is open and mixing ceases.

(continued)

APPLICATION

When the liquid falls below the FS2 low level switch the trigger to TR1 is open and the on-delay timer contacts return to their original state. This closes the drain valve and prepares the start rung for another process cycle.

FIGURE 13-8: Mixing tank control system.

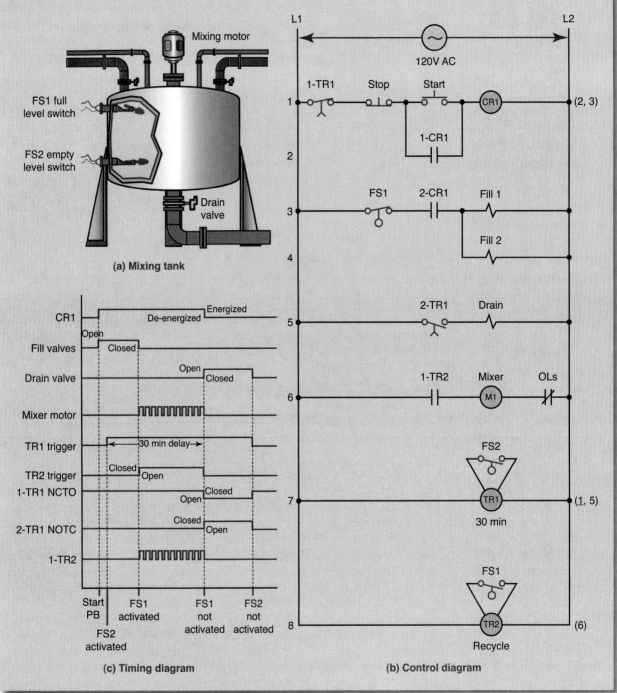

(a) Mixing tank

(c) Timing diagram

(b) Control diagram

- *Wye-delta starters,* covered in Chapter 12, often use a timer in the starting control circuit. When the timer is energized, it closes the wye contactor instantaneously and starts the timing period. When the set time delay has elapsed, the wye contactor returns to its original condition. Then after a sufficient delay for breaking the power lines, the delta contactor closes.

13-2 PROGRAMMABLE LOGIC RELAY

The *multifunction timers* provide a variety of timing functions that are manually selected with *dip switch* settings. Selecting the timer function by switch settings is a rudimentary method of programming. The *programmable logic relay* (PLR), which was introduced in Chapter 11, offers a more versatile method of programming timer functions. In addition, the PLR has a variety of programmable functions such as: *counters, timers, real time clocks (RTC), comparators*, and *Human Machine Interface (HMI) information displays*. This section addresses only the timer function in the PLR. An Omron PLR was illustrated in Chapter 11, Figure 11-14, and the Teco PLR is shown in this chapter as Figure 13-9 with a description of the front face controls. Review the functions of the front panel controls in the Teco PLR figure.

When a timer is needed to control a process, the timer *type* and *function* are selectable in the PLR and are *programmed* to produce the required operations. Programmable timer functions include *retentive* timers, *non-retentive* timers, and *real time clock* timers.

A *retentive timer* is a timer that maintains its current accumulated time value when its control input signal is interrupted or power to the timer is removed before the preset time is reached. A *non-retentive timer* is a timer that does not maintain its current accumu-

lated time value when its control input signal is interrupted or power to the timer is removed before the preset time is reached. The non-retentive timer resets the accumulator to zero and the full time delay is applied at the next application of the control input signal. In both timers, the output contacts of the timer are activated when the accumulated time reaches the preset value. Figure 13-10 illustrates the retentive and the non-retentive timer functions. Note the preset time is set to six seconds in the figure.

The PLR has internal timer functions that are programmed into the control circuit rather than hard-wired. The internal timer functions are generally programmed with ladder diagrams. Retentive timers are programmed with a *preset time* and a *time base*. Non-retentive timers are programmed in a *specific mode* such as the *on-delay, off-delay, one-shot*, or *recycle* with a preset value and a time base. The *preset value* is used to set the amount of time that a timer counts before completing an operation. *Time base* is used to set the precision of a timer. For example, a preset value of 300 with a time base setting of 0.01 seconds is equal to 3 sec (the product of the preset value and time base). A preset value of 300 with a time base of 1 second equals 300 sec. Time base is typically set to 0.01, 0.1, or 1 seconds.

Real time clock timers energize and de-energize output contacts at preset times of the day and days

FIGURE 13-9: PLR and front panel control functions.

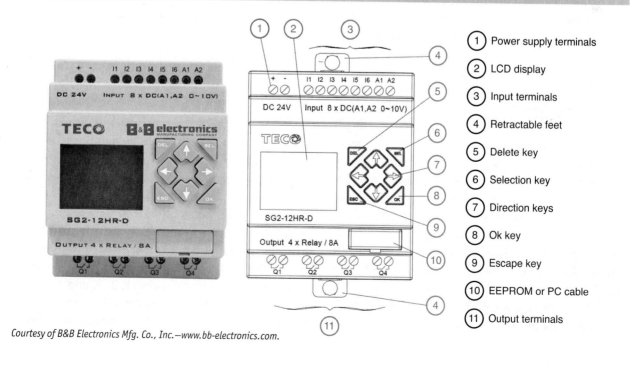

Courtesy of B&B Electronics Mfg. Co., Inc.—www.bb-electronics.com.

FIGURE 13-10: Timer functions.

Timer Diagram		Description
(a) Retentive timer		When the timer is energized, the timing function is on. When the timer is de-energized, the timing function is off. Accumulated time is maintained when the timer is de-energized. When the accumulated time reaches 6 sec. (the preset time), the timer contacts are energized.
Timer status: ENERGIZED — ENERGIZED — DE-ENERGIZED Timing function: ON — OFF — ON — OFF Accumulated time: 0 to 3 sec — 4 to 6 sec Contact status: DE-ENERGIZED — ENERGIZED — DE-ENERGIZED		
(b) Nonretentive timer		When the timer is energized, the timing function is on. When the timer is de-energized, the timing function is off. Accumulated time is set to zero when the timer is de-energized. The timer must remain energized for 6 sec (the preset time) before the timer contacts are energized.
Timer status: ENERGIZED — ENERGIZED — DE-ENERGIZED Timing function: ON — OFF — ON — OFF Accumulated time: 0 to 3 sec — 0 to 6 sec Contact status: DE-ENERGIZED — ENERGIZED — DE-ENERGIZED		

of the week. The real time clock timer of the PLR is typically based on *military time*, which is a 24hr based clock. The 24hr based clock uses the hour numbers 0 to 23; whereas the 12hr based clock uses the hour numbers from 1 to 12 for both AM and PM. For example, 1:00 PM is the same as 13:00 in military time.

PLR Programmable Timers

This chapter addresses *operation, programming* and *electrical interface* for the *programmable* timers and the *real time clock* (RTC) timers. The PLR includes a built-in LCD display and keypad as shown in Figure 13-9. The keypad and display are most often used for changing timer *set points, modes* and *updating the RTC*. Although logic programming can be accomplished using keypad and display, it is rather slow and tedious. Programming through the computer interface is the *recommended* procedure. The computer programming is accomplished with software supplied by the PLR manufacturer. The PLR is *connected* to the communication port on the computer via a cable supplied by the PLR manufacturer as shown in Figure 13-11. Note the EEPROM port (see number 10 Figure 13-9) is used as the input to the PLR. After the program is *developed* and *tested* on the computer, it is *downloaded* to the PLR through this interface for use in the control system. This chapter discusses only the basics of programmable timers using the programming guidelines in the PLR user manual supplied by the manufacturer.

FIGURE 13-11: Interface between PLR and PC.

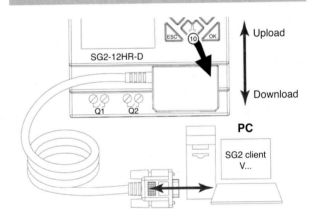

Courtesy of B&B Electronics.

Programmable On-Delay and Off-Delay Timers

The PLR has *fifteen* separate timers (indicated by the hex numbers 1 to F) that can be used throughout a program. Each timer can be set in any one of *eight modes* of operations, which are various configurations of the *on-delay* and the *off-delay* timers. Figure 13-12(a) illustrates the ladder diagram timer symbol with number code for parameter description, and Figure 13-12(b) lists the configuration parameter descriptions for the timers. Note that the timer *unit parameter* (number in location 2) has four choices (1, 2, 3, and 4), allowing delay times with maximum values of 99.9 sec, 999.9 sec, 9999 sec to 9999 min respectively. When

FIGURE 13-12: Timer ladder diagram symbol and parameter descriptions.

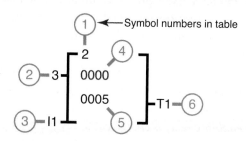

(a) Ladder diagram timer symbol with the number code for the description of each configuration parameter

Symbol	Description	
①	Timer mode (0–7)	
②	Timer unit:	1 : 0.00–99.99 sec
		2 : 0.0–999.9 sec
		3 : 0–9999 sec
		4 : 0–9999 min
③	ON: the timer reset to zero	
	OFF: the timer continues to time	
④	Current timer value	
⑤	Timer preset value	
⑥	Timer coil number (T1 to TF total: 15 timers)	

(b) Description of six configuration parameters—the parameter in location 3 is the reset input contacts (I1), which performs the On and Off function described in 3 row of the chart

FIGURE 13-13: On-delay PLR ladder command block, timing diagram, and programming interface.

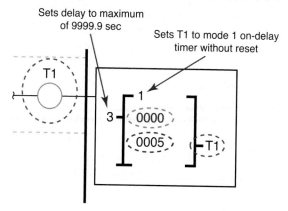

(a) Ladder display of on-delay timer instruction block

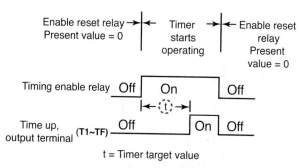

t = Timer target value

(b) Timing diagram for T1 ladder

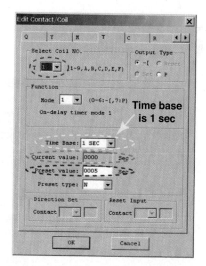

(c) Program dialog box for entering timer data—color coded dashed circles indicate common data among the figures

programming a timer, the PLR client software requests that a number be entered for each of the timer parameters in the timer ladder area, Figure 13-12(a), from the values that are listed in Figure 13-12(b).

An on-delay timer starts when the timer *enabling relay* (inputs at the top of the PLR in Figure 13-9) is energized. The on-delay timer times up to a fixed preset value and stops timing when the *current time* is *equal* to the *preset value*. The current time is *non-retentive* and resets to *zero* when the timer *enabling relay* is *de-energized* before the preset value is reached. Figure 13-13(a) illustrates a typical programmed ladder rung with the timer symbol associated with the ladder rung containing the timer coil symbol. The *preset value* is set at five seconds. The timer *status bit* T1 is on when the timer accumulator reaches the current preset value of five. Observe in Figure 13-13(a) the notations in the timer symbol—the *timer mode* is 1 (on-delay timer with no reset), the *timer unit* is 3 (0–9999 seconds), and the *timer number* is T1. Figure 13-13(b) displays the timing diagram for the on-delay PLR. Figure 13-13(c) illustrates the dialog box that is used to program the parameters of the on-delay timer in the PLR software. Color coded dashed markers show the relationship between the programming dialog box and the timer ladder rung values.

Off-delay timer programming is similar to the on-delay. The off-delay *timer status* bit T1 is energized immediately when the enabling relay is activated. The off-delay timer, illustrated in Figure 13-14, starts when the enabling relay is de-energized and holds the T1 status bit true for this time delay duration. The time delay *equals* a fixed preset value and stops timing when the *current time* is equal to the *preset value* of 10. Figure 13-14(a) and (b) illustrates the *timer symbol* and the *timing diagram* for the off-delay timer. The preset value is set at ten seconds. The current time (accumulator value) is non-retentive and *resets to zero* when the timer *reset relay is energized* or when the *timer enabling relay is energized*. Study the timing diagram and notice the two points in the diagram where the timer is interrupted. First by a reset before the preset time is reached and later by energizing the enabling

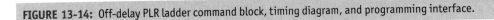

FIGURE 13-14: Off-delay PLR ladder command block, timing diagram, and programming interface.

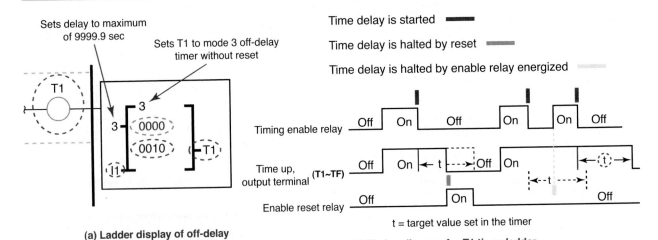

(a) Ladder display of off-delay timer instruction block

(b) Timing diagram for T1 timer ladder

(c) Program dialog box for entering timer data— color coded dashed circles indicate common data among the figures

relay before the preset time is reached. Observe the notation in the software dialog box, Figure 13-14(c) and in the timer symbol—the *timer mode* is 3 (off-delay timer with a reset), the *timer unit* is 3 (0–9999 seconds), and the *timer number* is T1. The reset is activated with input contacts *I1*. Color coded dashed markers show the relationship between the programming dialog box and the timer ladder rung values.

Programmable Real Time Clock Timers

The PLR has fifteen separate *real time clock* (RTC) timers that can be used throughout a program. Each RTC timer can be set in any one of five *modes of operations*, Figure 13-15(a) illustrates the ladder diagram RTC timer symbol, and Figure 13-15(b) lists the configuration parameters for the RTC timer in a table. The function of the ten numbers on the RTC symbol is described in the table. Note that the RTC mode parameter has three choices—*internal coil*,

which is the auxiliary contacts, *daily*, and *consecutive days*. When programming a RTC timer, the PLR programming software requires that a number be entered for each of the timer parameters as listed in Figure 13-15(b).

The daily mode allows the RTC timer to activate based on a fixed time across a selectable number of days per week. Figure 13-16(a) illustrates the RTC timer symbol connected to a ladder rung, and Figure 13-16(b) shows the timing diagram. Figure 13-16(c) shows the software input dialog box for the RTC parameters. When the RTC timer is enabled, the timer output R1 is activated from 8:00 to 17:00 on Tuesday through Friday. The current time in the symbol is 11:41. Note the notations on the timer symbol—the timer mode is 1 (daily) and the timer number is R1.

PLR Input and Output Circuits

Two input circuit options, discrete switch contacts and solid state sensors, for PLRs are illustrated in Figure 13-17. In Figure 13-17(a) six IEC discrete input contacts switch symbols are shown as single pole enabling relay inputs. The switches use a positive voltage source, which is used to power the PLR. Note the input power common is also the ground reference for the enabling relay inputs. The switches use the Figure 13-17(b) shows the wiring configuration for three wire solid state sensors. The black (BK), brown (BN), and blue (BL) leads of the current sourcing sensors are connected as illustrated. One of the solid state sensors is a discrete type and is the enabling signal for a discrete input. The second is an analog type and is an enabling signal for an analog input. Discrete inputs have a solid line and analog have a dashed line.

Two output circuit options are shown in Figure 13-18. Figure 13-18(a) is a NO relay contact for switching AC or DC powered loads. Figure 13-18(b) is an open collector transistor output used to switch low power DC loads that draw less than half of an ampere. Inputs and outputs have fuse protection for over-current protection and peak voltage limiting devices (zeners) to protect against over-voltage conditions. The loads have noise suppression in the form of an RC circuit in Figure 13-18(a) and a diode for inductive transient reduction in Figure 13-18(b).

FIGURE 13-15: Real time clock ladder symbol and parameter descriptions.

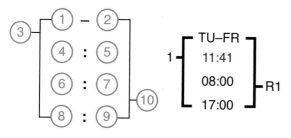

(a) RTC ladder symbol and number code for description of the ten parameters

Symbol	Description
①	Input the first week to RTC
②	Input the second week to RTC
③	RTC mode 0~2, 0: internal coil, 1: daily, 2: consecutive days
④	RTC displays the hour of present time
⑤	RTC displays the minute of present time
⑥	Set RTC hour ON
⑦	Set RTC minute ON
⑧	Set RTC hour OFF
⑨	Set RTC minute OFF
⑩	RTC coil number (R1~RF total: 15 RTCs)

(b) RTC parameter descriptions

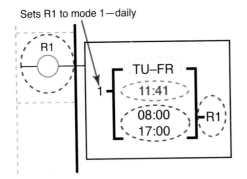

Sets R1 to mode 1—daily

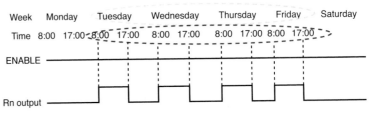

(a) Ladder display of real time clock instruction block

(b) Timing diagram for R1 timer ladder

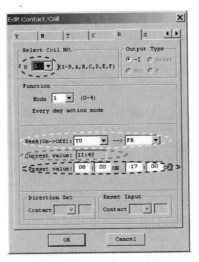

(c) Program dialog box for entering RTC timer data— color coded dashed circles indicate common data among the figures

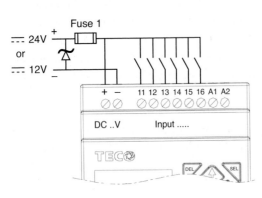

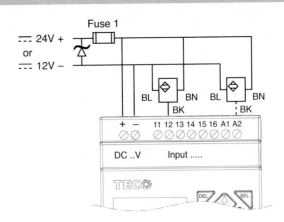

(a) Discrete switch contact—six inputs

(b) Discrete solid state sensor inputs

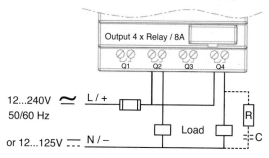

(a) NO relay contact outputs

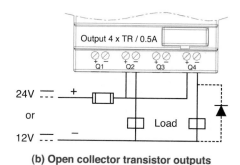

(b) Open collector transistor outputs

13-3 PROGRAMMABLE TIMER APPLICATIONS

Programmable timers are used in a variety of industrial applications in which specific timer functions are used in the process. An example follows that uses a PLR to control the opening and closing of a large industrial door. Many industrial companies have large doors that are operated by sensors. In this application, the door automatically opens if a person or vehicle approaches from either inside or outside as detected by photoelectric sensors. The door remains open for 30 seconds after there is no person or vehicle in the area.

The implementation of an automatic door control application is shown as a PLR wiring diagram in Figure 13-19(b) and as the ladder diagram in Figure 13-19(c) with a description of the interface sensing devices in Figure 13-19(a). The NO outdoor and indoor photoelectric sensors are designated as B1 and B2, respectively. Limit switch S1, NC, detects when the door is fully open, and limit switch S2, NC, detects when the door is fully closed. The limit switches prevent the motor from running when the door is fully closed or

fully open. The door is opened by motor contactor MC1 and closed by motor contactor MC2. Note that the timer T1 configuration data is located in a block to the right of the ladder.

In the wiring diagram, Figure 13-19(b), the sensors, the limit switches, and the motor contactors are connected to the input/output terminals of the PLR. Note that sensor B1 is addressed as I1, sensor B2 as I2, limit switch S1 as I3, and limit switch S2 as I4. Also, MC1 is connected to PLR at Q1 and addressed in the program as Q1 and MC2 is connected and addressed as Q2.

Refer to the ladder diagram in Figure 13-19(c) as you read the following description. Rung 001 of the ladder diagram turns on M1 if sensor S1 is activated (a person or vehicle is approaching the door from the outdoors. Rung 002 turns on M1 if sensor S2 is activated (a person or vehicle is approaching the door from the indoors). Note that in rung 003 a M1 contact seals the sensor contacts when the timer is de-activated. When M1 is turned on, the motor contactor MC1 in rung 006 opens the door. Rung 004 turns on M2 if both sensors are de-activated and the door is not fully closed. Rung 005 initiates the on-delay timer T1 if both sensors are de-activated (no one in the area). Note that the on-delay timer is preset to 30 seconds. After the T1 times out, the sensor inputs I1 and I2 are not energized, and MC2 closes the door as shown in Rung 007.

13-4 TROUBLESHOOTING PROGRAMMABLE TIMERS

Review the suggested troubleshooting tips for PLRs in Chapter 11. Additional tips suggest that external observations and measurements be made before any functional tests are performed on the PLR. First, make the following observations and measurements to verify that the input and output conditions are within specification.

- Verify that the wiring is not damaged and the proper size if recent maintenance has been performed, and verify that the connections to the PLR terminals are tight. For DIN rail mounting, verify the PLR is securely attached. For direct mounting, verify that the attachment hardware is secure.

FIGURE 13-19: Door control application with PLR controller.

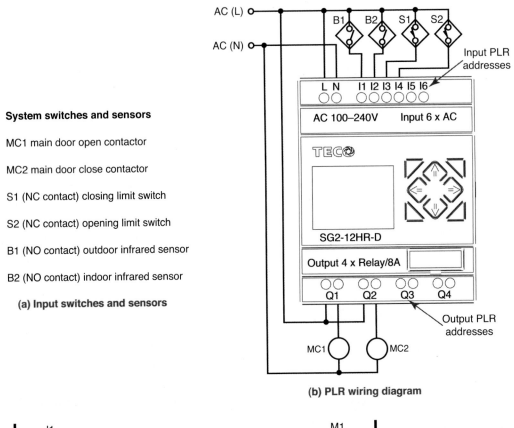

System switches and sensors

MC1 main door open contactor

MC2 main door close contactor

S1 (NC contact) closing limit switch

S2 (NC contact) opening limit switch

B1 (NO contact) outdoor infrared sensor

B2 (NO contact) indoor infrared sensor

(a) Input switches and sensors

(b) PLR wiring diagram

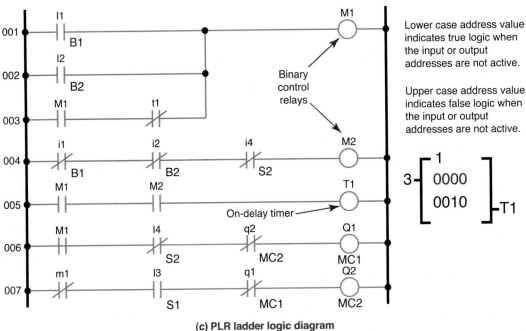

Lower case address value indicates true logic when the input or output addresses are not active.

Upper case address value indicates false logic when the input or output addresses are not active.

(c) PLR ladder logic diagram

- Verify that the input wires are not near the output wires because noise can be coupled from output to input.
- Verify that the input voltage and current are within specification.

If all external measurements suggest that the problem is within the PLR, then use the built-in simulator program to verify correct timer operation. To use the simulator, the PLR is connected to a PC that has the PLR client software installed. The simulator icons lead the electrical worker through the test and evaluation steps of the timer program to verify its correct operation in the application.

CRITICAL CONCEPTS

The need to know content from Chapter 13 is summarized in the following statements.

- The one-shot timer or *interval* timer is a timing device in which the contacts change position immediately when the timer is powered on or an external trigger is applied and stay in that position for a set time delay.
- The repeat-cycle timer or recycle timer is a timing device in which the contacts cycle open and close repeatedly once the timer is activated.
- A retentive timer is a timer that maintains its current accumulated time value when its control input signal is interrupted or power to the timer is removed.
- A non-retentive timer is a timer that does not maintain its current accumulated time value when its control input signal is interrupted or power to the timer is removed.
- Real time clock timers energize and de-energize output contacts at preset times of the day and days of the week.
- The programming of a PLR is accomplished on a PC using client software supplied by the PLR manufacturer.
- After the PLR program is developed and tested on the PC, it is downloaded to the PLR for use in the system.

QUESTIONS

1. Describe the operation of a one-shot timer.
2. What type of applications use one-shot timers?
3. Describe the operation of a repeat-cycle timer.
4. Describe the operation of a retentive timer.
5. Describe the operation of a non-retentive timer.
6. What is a real time clock?
7. What are the parameters that are selectable in programming a PLR on-delay and off-delay timers?
8. What are the parameters that are selectable in programming a PLR real time clock?

CHAPTER 14

Function Specific Control Devices

GOALS AND OBJECTIVES

The primary goals for this chapter are to identify and describe function specific control devices such as *latching relays*, *phase sequence relays*, *frequency relays*, *voltage sensors*, *sequencing devices* and *counters*.

After completing this chapter, you will be able to:

1. Identify and describe the purpose and function of specific devices such as latching relays, phase sequence relays, frequency relays, and voltage sensors.
2. Describe the purpose and operation of sequencing devices.
3. Describe the purpose and operation of up counters and down counters.

14-1 LATCHING RELAYS

A *latching relay* is defined as follows:

A latching relay is a relay that maintains its contacts in the last position without a continuously energized coil but with a mechanical mechanism or through remnant magnetism until reset electrically.

Three types of latching relays are available: *mechanical, bistable or impulse,* and *magnetic* relay. Latching relays have *one* or *two* coils, are available in *AC* and *DC* voltage models, and have *one* or *two* inputs. When two inputs are present, one puts the contacts in the *active state* and the other resets the contacts to their *original state*. If one input is present, every application of energy *toggles* the relay to the opposite state. Relays are typically available for DC (12 to 110V DC) or AC (24 to 240V AC) control voltage and switching contacts are available for 10 amps at 120V AC. Contact configurations range from a SPDT to 6PDT. Some relays use internal diodes that permit either AC or DC control voltage.

Mechanically Latching Relays

Electromechanical relays are manufactured with two electromagnet coils—one a *latch coil* and the other an *unlatch coil*. Latching relays are manufactured in multiple configurations including *general purpose* and *machine tool* type relays and are available in a variety of enclosures such as tube and flat tab plug-in (generally 8- and 11-pin) and printed circuit board modules. Figures 14-1 and 14-2 illustrate a typical latching relay.

When the latch coil of the relay is energized, the coil changes the contact position as in a standard electromechanical relay. At the same time, a mechanical mechanism engages and holds the relay contacts in the latched position even after the latch coil is de-energized. To return the relay contacts to their original position,

FIGURE 14-1: Tube base style mechanical latching relay.

FIGURE 14-2: NEMA style mechanically latching relay with higher current switching capability.

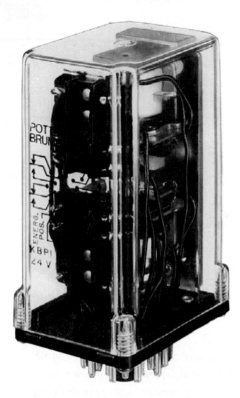

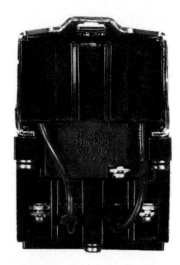

the unlatch coil is energized. When the unlatch coil is energized, it trips the mechanical mechanism, which returns the relay contacts to their original position. Figure 14-3 illustrates the mechanically latched and unlatched conditions. Some latching relays have a manual lever that if pressed, unlatches the coil. The latching relay is normally not rated for continuous duty so continuous power to the coils often damages the relay.

Many latching relays contain contacts that prevent continuous power being applied to the coil after it has been energized. These contacts are usually called coil *clearing contacts*. Figure 14-4 illustrates the use of clearing contacts where L is the latching coil and U is the unlatch coil. When the *ON* pushbutton is pressed, coil L is energized and the relay changes to the latch position. The normally closed L contact, which is connected in series with the L coil, opens and disconnects power to the L coil. At the same time, the normally open U contact, which is connected in series with the U coil closes, to allow the U coil to be energized when

the *OFF* pushbutton is pressed. When coil L energized, it also closed the normally open L contact, turning on a yellow lamp. The lamp is turned off by pressing the *OFF* pushbutton and energizing coil U. This process causes the latching relay to return to the normal position. Note that the coil clearing contacts prevent power from being applied continuously to the latching relay

FIGURE 14-4: Example of clearing contacts for energized coil.

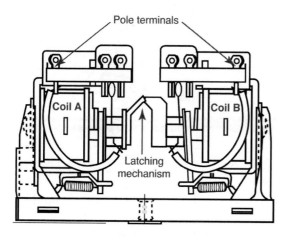

(a) Latched state—coil A energized and then released

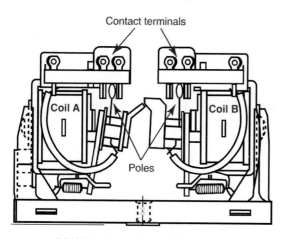

(b) Unlatched state—coil B energized and then released

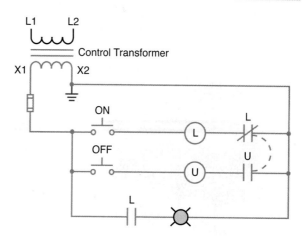

coils in case either momentary pushbutton is depressed for an extended period of time.

Impulse and Bi-stable Latching Relays

Impulse or *bi-stable* latching relays have a single coil and a mechanical mechanism that transfers the contacts to the opposite state. When the relay coil is pulsed for a minimum of 50 ms with the control voltage, a transfer to the opposite contact occurs. An impulse latching relay and the transfer mechanism are shown in Figure 14-5. When the relay is energized, the solenoid plunger retracts and the guide pin moves

from its starting position to position 1, then 2, and then 3 as noted in Figure 14-5(b). This movement rotates the cam, and the switch contact changes position. When the plunger is released, the guide pin returns to its original position, noted as position 4 on Figure 14-5(b).

Magnetic Latching Relays

Magnetic latching relays require one pulse of coil power to move their contacts to the opposite state. A second pulse, opposite in current direction, reverses the magnetic force to return the contacts to the original state. After the armature is moved in *contact* with the electromagnet core by an applied voltage, the core has sufficient *residual magnetic force* to hold the relay pulled in. Repeated pulses at the same input or with the same polarity have no effect. Contacts are returned to their original state by the application of a voltage that *cancels* the *residual magnetic force* permitting the armature to drop out. Figure 14-6(a) shows a typical magnetic latch relay for general purpose control applications.

Magnetic latching relays are useful in applications where dropping out of the contacts in the event of a power failure causes process problems. Magnetic latching relays have either *single* or *dual* coils. On a single coil device as shown in Figure 14-6(b), the relay pulls in when power is applied with one polarity, and drops out when the polarity is reversed. On a dual coil device as

FIGURE 14-5: Impulse latching relay.

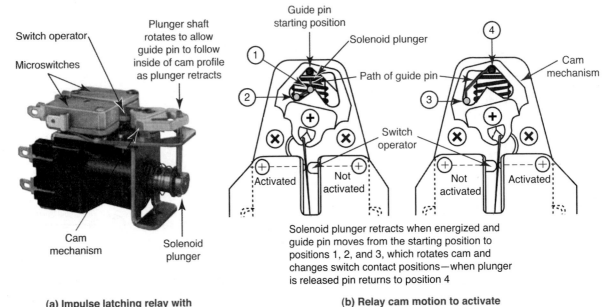

Guide pin
starting position

Solenoid plunger

Plunger shaft
rotates to allow
guide pin to follow
inside of cam profile
as plunger retracts

Path of guide pin

Cam
mechanism

Switch operator

Microswitches

Switch
operator

Activated   Not
activated

Not
activated   Activated

Solenoid plunger retracts when energized and
guide pin moves from the starting position to
positions 1, 2, and 3, which rotates cam and
changes switch contact positions—when plunger
is released pin returns to position 4

Cam
mechanism

Solenoid
plunger

(a) Impulse latching relay with
microswitch contacts mounted on top

(b) Relay cam motion to activate
microswitch operators when solenoid is energized

Courtesy of Tyco Electronics Corporation.

FIGURE 14-6: Magnetic latching relays.

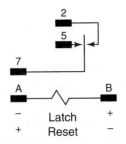

(a) Magnetic latching
general purpose relay

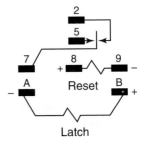

(c) Two coil DC or AC magnetic
latching SPST relay

(b) Single coil DC magnetic
latching SPST relay

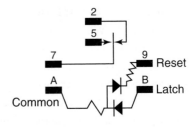

(d) Single coil AC magnetic
latching SPST relay

Courtesy of Tyco Electronics Corporation.

shown in Figure 14-6(c), a *pull-in coil* and a *drop-out coil* are used to transition between the two states. AC controlled magnetic latch relays as shown in Figure 14-6(d) have single coils that employ *steering diodes* to differentiate between pull-in and drop-out commands. Note that a series resistor is used for the drop-out current since a smaller magnetic force is sufficient to overcome the residual magnetism.

14-2 PHASE SEQUENCE RELAYS

Phase sequence relays are electronic devices that monitor a three-phase input for phase failures such as *out of sequence* phases, a *lost* phase, or a *too high* or *too low* input voltage level. If there is a phase failure, the relay output of the device changes state—usually closed contacts are opened. Typically, phase sequence relays have one or two SPDT outputs and two or three light emitting diode (LED) indicators. Figure 14-7(a) illustrates a phase sequence relay. Figure 14-7(b) illustrates the front panel. Note the four LED lamps provide power-on, relay status, and alarm indications. Three adjustment knobs are shown—*OVER*, which sets acceptable over-voltage limits, *UNDER*, which sets acceptable under-voltage limits and *T*, which sets operating time. The operating time is a time delay before an alarm is triggered when one of the measurements moves outside of set limits. This eliminates nuisance alarms due to short disturbances on the power grid. Figure 14-7(c) illustrates the wiring diagram. Note that the two SPDT relay outputs have the NC contact, the NO contact, and the wiper available at the terminal block.

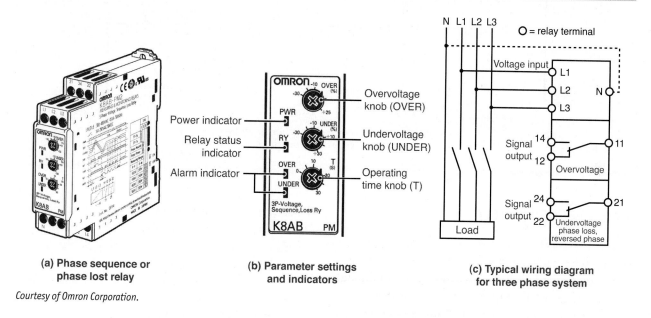

FIGURE 14-7: Phase sequence or phase lost relay.

(a) Phase sequence or phase lost relay

(b) Parameter settings and indicators

(c) Typical wiring diagram for three phase system

Courtesy of Omron Corporation.

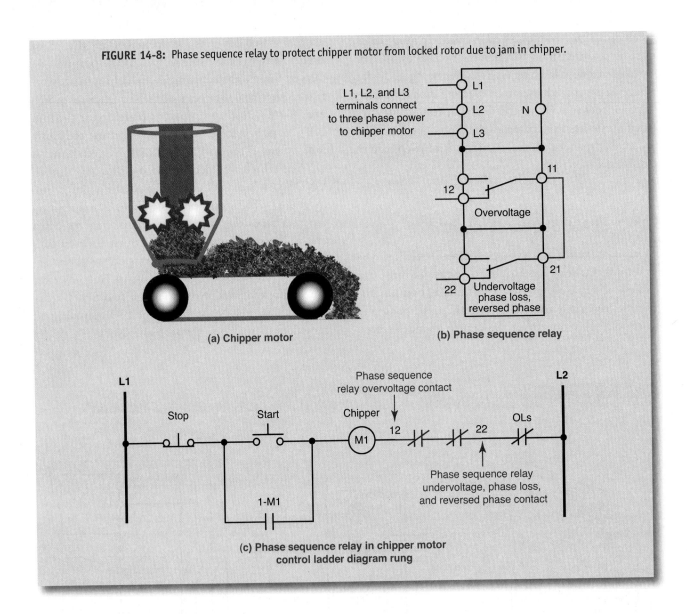

FIGURE 14-8: Phase sequence relay to protect chipper motor from locked rotor due to jam in chipper.

L1, L2, and L3 terminals connect to three phase power to chipper motor

(a) Chipper motor

Overvoltage

Undervoltage phase loss, reversed phase

(b) Phase sequence relay

Phase sequence relay overvoltage contact

Stop   Start   Chipper

Phase sequence relay undervoltage, phase loss, and reversed phase contact

(c) Phase sequence relay in chipper motor control ladder diagram rung

14-3 FREQUENCY RELAYS

Frequency relays are electronic devices that monitor a single-phase voltage input for a change in frequency. If the frequency falls below or rises above a nominal frequency, generally 60Hz, the relay output of the device changes state—normally closed contacts are opened. Typically, frequency relays have one or two SPDT outputs and one or two LED indicators. Figure 14-9(a) illustrates a frequency relay, and how it interfaces with the system wiring. Note that the LED lamps provide power-on and alarm indications, and the adjustment knob allows selectable frequency deviation increments. Frequency deviations from 0.5Hz to 3Hz in 0.5Hz increments are available. The alarm LED is on when the change in frequency is greater than

the setting on the frequency deviation selector. Two SPDT relay contacts are available as shown. This type of frequency relay has many applications but is used most often with wound rotor motors.

14-4 VOLTAGE SENSORS

Voltage sensors are electronic devices that monitor AC and/or DC voltage levels and provide an output when the voltage is out of specification. The two most commonly used are *overvoltage/undervoltage* relay and *voltage band* relay. When used as an undervoltage relay, they protect equipment that is required to operate above a minimum voltage. When used as an overvoltage relay, they protect equipment against excessive voltage conditions.

FIGURE 14-9: Frequency relay.

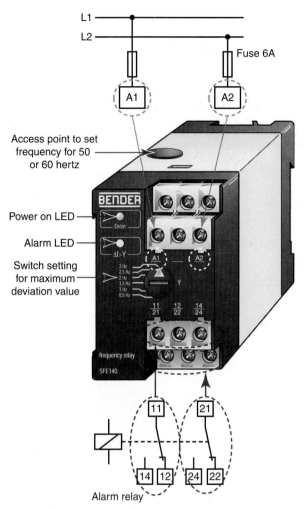

Access point to set
frequency for 50
or 60 hertz

Power on LED

Alarm LED

Switch setting
for maximum
deviation value

Alarm relay

Courtesy of Bender.

FIGURE 14-10: Voltage sensors.

Courtesy of Pace Scientific.

or DPDT set of switch contacts that change state when a voltage fault is detected. Other performance specifications include maximum *AC voltage* (typically, 600V AC), *frequency* (50Hz to 60Hz), *response time* in the milliseconds, and *accuracy* of 0.5 percent or less. Voltage sensors commonly include LED indicators of voltage conditions. Other options include auxiliary contacts for remote indicator lights plus analog and digital visual indicators. Voltage sensors are designed to survive industrial shock and vibration and standard manufacturing environments.

14-5 SEQUENCING DEVICES

Sequencing refers to a predetermined step-by-step process that accomplishes a specific task. Sequencing devices include *pump sequencers* or *alternators* and *motor driven sequence* switches. Pump sequencers control industrial equipment such as *pumps, compressors,* and *air conditioners* so that the equipment has uniform wear. Motor driven sequence switches provide sequential switch control.

Pump Sequencers

Pump sequencers are sequencing devices that automatically alternate between two pumps based on *running time* or every *on-off cycle.* The alternation between loads evens the wear on the pumps. Loads are alternated based on selectable running time such as 7, 14, or 30 days. The load that is energized *first* is referred

The voltage band relay protects equipment that is required to operate within an *upper* and *lower voltage limit.* As long as the operating voltage remains within the upper and lower voltage set points, the internal relay stays energized. If the operating voltage moves outside this range, the relay drops out. In addition, some voltage sensing devices provide application specific outputs for monitoring *sine waves, pulse trains, frequency* and *modulated frequency* outputs. Self-powered devices are commonly available as portable and handheld products. Voltage sensors generally mount on or in tube sockets, square pin bases, DIN rails, or printed circuit boards. Wires are also attached through terminal lugs. Figure 14-10 illustrates a DIN rail mounted voltage sensor.

Electrical voltage sensors vary in terms of *performance specifications, optional features,* and *environmental operating conditions.* However, all devices provide a SPDT

FIGURE 14-11: Pump sequencer.

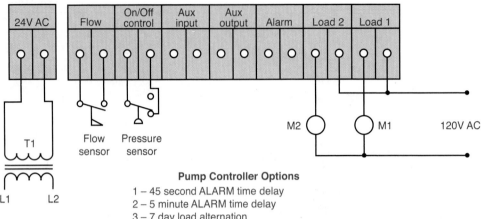

Pump sequencer

Pump Controller Options

1 – 45 second ALARM time delay
2 – 5 minute ALARM time delay
3 – 7 day load alternation
4 – 14 day load alternation
5 – 30 day load alternation
6 – Alternate load on every on-off control cycle

to as the *lead load,* and the *second* load is referred to as the *lag load.* Figure 14-11 illustrates a pump sequencer wired for a dual pump system using 24V AC for sequencer power.

The pump sequencer in Figure 14-11 alternates operation between pump 1 (M1) and pump 2 (M2) to maintain 45 psi in a tank. Pump 1 is the lead pump, and pump 2 is the lag pump. A pressure switch is wired to the *on/off control* input, and a flow switch is wired to the *flow* input. The *flow* input verifies the operation of the pumps. The pump sequencer is programmed to alternate the pumps on every on-off cycle. The pump sequencer starts the *lead pump* when system pressure drops below 45 psi, and the contacts of the pressure switch are closed as shown in Figure 14-11. The lead pump remains on until system pressure is above the deadband setting on the pressure switch and the NC contact opens. When system pressure once again falls below 45 psi, the *lag pump* is turned on and remains on until system pressure is above the switch deadband. Each pump is run on alternate cycles.

Pump sequencers have a programmable alarm circuitry to indicate a pump failure. For example, when the system pressure falls below 45 psi, the lead pump is turned on. If the flow switch is not closed after two minutes (this number is selectable) of operation, it indicates that the pump is not operating. Therefore the sequencer turns off the lead pump and turns on the lag pump. In addition, the alarm relay is energized, indi-

FIGURE 14-12: Alternating relays.

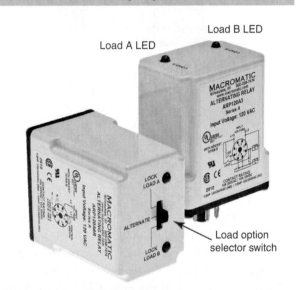

Load B LED

Load A LED

Load option
selector switch

Courtesy of Macromatic Industrial Controls, Inc.

cating that a pump has failed. The failed pump is not used until the system is reset, generally after corrective action has been taken.

Alternating Relays

Alternating relays are used in special applications where the load usage requires equal run time between two loads. An alternating relay is illustrated in Figure 14-12. The alternating action is initiated by an

The initial state for the alternate pump controller in Figure 14-13 shows the control input float switch is open, the relay contacts are in the load A position (load A LED is on), and both pump contacts, M1 and M2, are off. When the control float switch closes, it energizes load M1. As long as the control float switch remains closed, load M1 remains energized. When the control float switch opens, load M1 is turned off, and the alternating relay *toggles* to the load B position. A red LED marked load B glows. When the control float switch closes again, it energizes load M2. When the control float switch opens, load M2 is turned off, the alternating relay toggles back to the load A position, and the process is repeated again. On relays with DPDT contacts, the extra contact is used to control remote pilot lights indicating the load that is energized.

FIGURE 14-13: Alternating relay control for two pump systems.

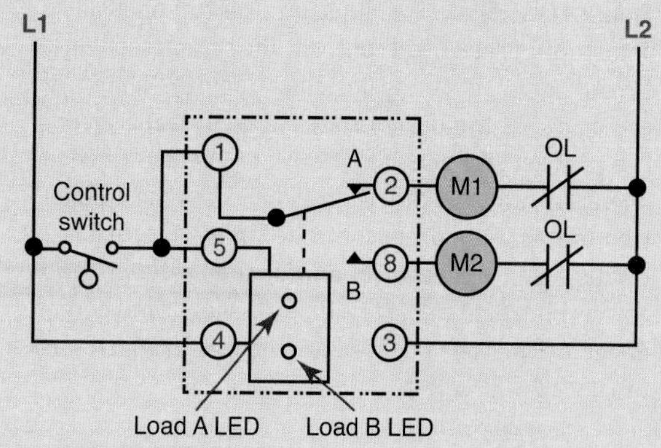

external control switch such as a *float switch, manual switch, timing relay, pressure switch,* or *other isolated contact.* Each time the initiating switch is opened, the alternating relay contacts change state, thus alternating the two loads. The LED indicators show the status of energized load. Alternating relays are available in either SPDT or DPDT output configurations and are used with one or two control switches. Models have optional three position selector switches to allow the unit to alternate the two loads as normal, or lock the relay to one load or the other. Locking the alternating relay to one load permits maintenance operations on the other load.

Motor Driven Switches

Motor driven switches have a motor-driven timing cam that controls switches, for example, the switch control for movie theater illumination. The four-step lighting sequence for theater illumination is as follows:

1. High brightness for the cleaning crew
2. Medium brightness during the pre-show time, allowing for patrons to find seats
3. Low brightness for the showing of the previews
4. Totally off for the showing of the movie

Another example of motor driven sequencing is the cleaning of an industrial tank to prepare it for the next mixing cycle. The steps in the cleaning sequence are the *pre-rinse cycle, the soap release, the wash cycle, the post-rinse cycle,* and the *drying cycle.* Figure 14-14

shows the sequential steps for the tank cleaning process. Note that the sequence numbers are in the first column, the step numbers are in the second column, and the sequencing patterns are in columns three through seven. The sequencing patterns (columns three to seven) are labeled with the cleaning actions, which are soap, fill, wash, drain, and dry. The number 1 in these

FIGURE 14-14: Sequence table.

1	2	3	4	5	6	7
Machine Sequence	Sequencer Step	Soap	Fill	Wash	Drain	Dry
	0	0	0	0	0	0
1	1	0	1	0	0	0
1	2	0	0	1	0	0
1	3	0	0	0	1	0
2	4	1	0	0	0	0
3	5	0	1	0	0	0
3	6	0	0	1	0	0
3	7	0	0	0	1	0
4	8	0	1	0	0	0
4	9	0	0	1	0	0
4	10	0	0	0	1	0
5	11	0	0	0	0	1

Early motor driven switches or sequencers used a motor and gear box to rotate a drum with horizontal slots. Figure 14-15 shows a unit used to control pneumatic actuators and electrical controls. The slots accept plastic tabs or posts at any position along the length of the drum. As the drum rotates at a constant speed, the tabs actuate pneumatic valve or electrical switch operators, which in turn control devices in the production process. The drum controller in the figure has a combination of electrical and pneumatic switching devices. The accuracy of this type of sequencer is determined by the speed control for the motor, which was usually a DC voltage.

FIGURE 14-15: Motor driven drum sequencer.

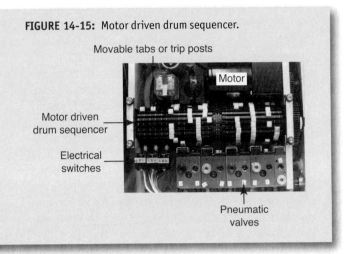

Movable tabs or trip posts

Motor

Motor driven drum sequencer

Electrical switches

Pneumatic valves

---

pattern columns indicates that the cleaning action is activated. Conversely, the number 0 in these pattern columns indicates that the cleaning action is de-activated. For example, in step 6, which is the second step in sequence 3, the wash cycle is activated, and all other actions are de-activated.

14-6 COUNTERS

Many industrial applications use counters to record the number of events within a system. Application examples include the *number of products produced*, *number of items that fill a carton*, and *number of rejected parts*. *Counters* are mechanical and/or electronic devices that count the total number of inputs and provide an output (mechanical or solid state contacts) at a pre-determined or preset number. In addition, most counters display the current count value. Counters are available as *mechanical devices* and *electronic devices* that count up, count down or count up and down. Long before electronic counters became common, mechanical devices were used to count events. They typically consist of a series of disks mounted on an axle, with the digits 0 through 9 marked on the edge of the disk. Such counters were originally used to control manufacturing processes. However, the low cost of electronic display forced the mechanical devices into the legacy category.

Mechanical Counters

Mechanical counters, as shown in Figure 14-16, use shaft rotations to increment or decrement numerical wheels, thus displaying an accumulated count. Counters are available with a pushbutton reset, a lever reset, or no reset. Actuating the reset causes the counter dis-

play to indicate all zeros. The no-reset style of counter is typically used as a time totalizer or elapsed time meter, which totals the time a piece of equipment has been powered on.

Electronic Counters

Electronic counters, as shown in Figure 14-17, have a numerical readout and are programmed to count up, count down, or count up and down depending on the

FIGURE 14-16: Mechanical industrial counters.

FIGURE 14-17: Electronic counters.

application. A simple programming procedure selects operating mode and function. Input pulses drive the counter's electronics, which in turn drive the readout. Front panel reset, remote reset or no-reset styles are available. Electronic counters have replaced mechanical counters in most industrial and commercial applications.

Up Counters

The *up counter* accumulates input pulses and provides an output after the preset count value is reached. Up counters have a count input or a count input and a reset input. The single input up counter is reset when power is removed. In the dual input counter, the reset input is used to set the accumulated count to zero. The count input adds one to the accumulated number for each cycle of the input. When the preset count value is reached, the counter's output contacts are activated—NO contacts are closed, and NC contacts are open. Figure 14-18 illustrates the single input and dual input counters. Note that the counter is preset to twelve

(number of bottles in a case). When the counter reaches twelve, the control relay CR1 is energized and resets the counter, indicating that a case is filled.

A typical application of an up counter is shown in Figure 14-19, where soft drink bottles are move along on a conveyor. A photoelectric sensor in the direct mode provides an output each time a soft drink bottle passes the sensor. The output of the photoelectric sensor is the input to an up counter, which keeps track of the bottles that have been produced. Figure 14-19(b) is a pictorial of the bottles on the conveyor, and Figure 14-9(c) is the timing diagram for the counting operation. Note that time *a* is when the bottles break the light beam, and time *b* is when the light beam passes between the bottles.

APPLICATION

FIGURE 14-19: Bottle counting application using photoelectric sensor trigger signal.

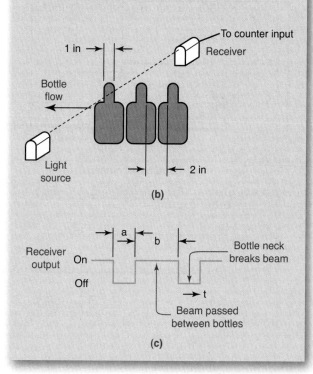

(a)

(b)

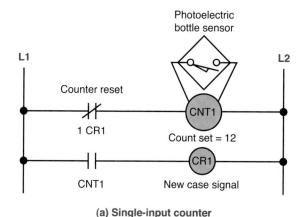

FIGURE 14-18: Case bottle filler using up counter.

(a) **Single-input counter**

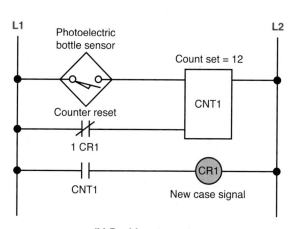

(b) **Dual-input counter**

Up/Down Counters

The *up/down counter* accumulates input pulses from two inputs and provides an output after the preset count value is reached. Figure 14-20 illustrates an up/down counter that is used to count parts in a conveyor queue. Figure 14-20(a) shows a pictorial of the conveyor and Figure 14-20(b) the ladder and timing diagrams. Note that sensor S1 adds counts to the accumulated total, and sensor S4 subtracts counts from the accumulated total. A third input resets the accumulated count to zero. In the timing diagram, note that the counter value is incremented and decremented, but the output only changes state when the counter value reaches the preset value (a count of four). When the queue is full (counter value is 4 and counter output is active) the NC counter contact opens. This prevents the pneumatic actuator from energizing when sensor S1 is active. The part continues down the conveyor to the next assembly machine. Sensors S2 and S3 are for queue feed control.

FIGURE 14-20: Up/down counter control of parts queue.

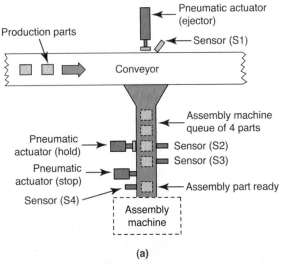

(a)

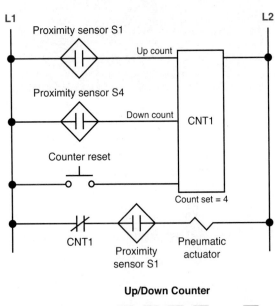

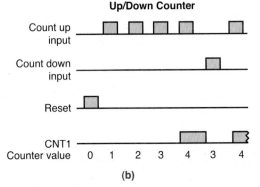

(b)

An up/down counter is used in a parking garage to operate a *LOT FULL* sign as illustrated in the Figure 14-21 ladder diagram. Sensors are at the entrance and exit of the garage and provide the count up and the count down signals, respectively. As each car enters the garage, the counter *CNT1* is incremented by one. As each car exits the garage, the counter is decremented by one. When the accumulated count reaches the preset value (the total number of cars that the garage holds), the counter outputs illuminates the *LOT FULL* sign. If one car leaves, the accumulated count is decremented, and the *LOT FULL* sign is extinguished. Note the alternate symbols used for electronic sensors here and in Figures 14-18 and 14-20.

FIGURE 14-21: Parking garage counter ladder diagram.

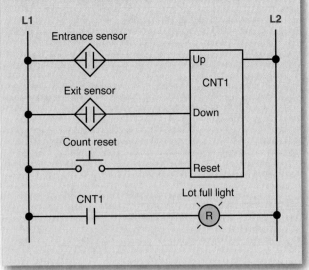

CRITICAL CONCEPTS

The need to know content from Chapter 14 is summarized in the following statements.

- Latching relays are electromechanical relays with two electromagnet coils—one a latch coil and the other an unlatch coil.
- Phase sequence relays are electronic devices that monitor a three-phase input for phase failures such as out of sequence phases, a lost phase, or an unacceptable input voltage level.
- Frequency relays are electronic devices that monitor a single-phase voltage input for a change in frequency.
- Voltage sensors are electronic devices that monitor AC and/or DC voltage levels and provide an output when the voltage is out of specification.
- Impulse or bi-stable latching relays have a single coil and a mechanical mechanism that transfers the contacts to the opposite state.
- Pump sequencers evens the wear on the loads by automatically alternating between the two loads based on running time or every on-off cycle.
- Alternating relays are used in special applications where the load usage requires equal run time between two loads.
- Mechanical counters use shaft rotations to increment or decrement numerical wheels, thus displaying an accumulated count.

- Electronic counters have a numerical readout and are programmed to count up, count down, or count up and down depending on the application.
- Up/down counters accumulate input pulses from two inputs and provides an output after the preset count value is reached, where one input adds counts and one input subtracts counts from the accumulated total.

QUESTIONS

1. Describe the operation of a latching relay.
2. How are clearing contacts used with latching relays?
3. Describe the operation of a phase sequence relay.
4. Describe the operation of a frequency relay.
5. Describe the operation of a voltage sensor.
6. Describe the operation of a impulse relay.
7. What is the purpose of a pump sequencer?
8. What is the function of an alternating relay?
9. How does a mechanical counter differ from an electronic counter?
10. Describe the operation of an up/down counter.
11. What is the purpose of the reset input on an up/down counter?

CHAPTER **15**

AC Motor Speed Control

GOALS AND OBJECTIVES

The primary goals for this chapter are to identify and describe *non-electronic* and *electronic AC motor speed control circuits* and *drives*. In addition, an introduction to *variable frequency* and *vector* drives for AC motors is presented.

After completing this chapter, you will be able to:

1. Describe manual, time-operated, and frequency control of the speed of a wound rotor motor.

2. Describe the function of motor speed control circuits that use silicon control rectifiers and triacs.

3. Describe the basic components of a variable frequency drive and how it controls the speed of an AC motor.

4. Describe the operation of closed-loop and open-loop vector drives.

5. Describe the operation of dynamic and regenerative braking.

Motors convert *electrical* energy to *mechanical* energy. Depending upon the motor size and design, motors typically convert electrical energy to mechanical energy at a 75 percent or higher rate. Some type of motor is used in nearly all industrial equipment and processes. The *alternating current* (AC) motor uses alternating current to produce rotation torque and operates with a *single-phase* or a *three-phase* voltage input. The *AC induction motor* is the most common, but other types of AC motors used in industry include: *wound rotor, synchronous,* and *consequent pole*. The AC motor consists of a *rotor,* which is the rotating part of the motor and the *stator,* which is the stationary part of the motor. AC motors operate on the principle of a *rotating magnetic field.* In three-phase motors, the phases are 120 degrees out of phase, which causes the motor to rotate when connected to the voltage source. The *direction of rotation* is determined by the *connection* sequence of the input voltage lines at the motor input terminals. The speed of a three-phase AC motor is determined by many different factors such as the *number of poles, percentage of slip,* and *frequency.* Figure 15-1 illustrates an AC motor, a cutaway view of an AC motor, and single- and three-phase connections.

(continued)

TECH NOTES

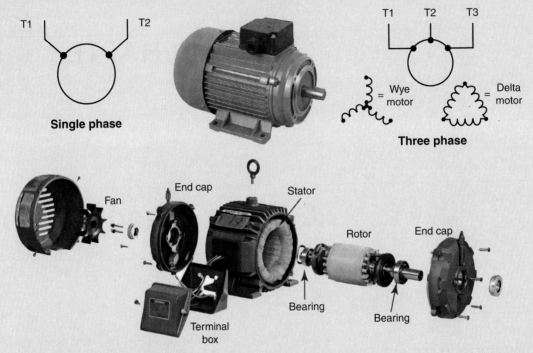

FIGURE 15-1: AC motor, single and three phase, with identification of major components.

Single phase

T1 T2

Three phase

T1 T2 T3

= Wye motor

= Delta motor

Fan

End cap

Stator

Rotor

End cap

Bearing

Bearing

Terminal box

Courtesy of Baldor Electric Company.

Motors are specified by the following factors: *enclosure style, voltage, insulation and temperature rise, torque, speed/slip,* and *service factor.*

Enclosure style—NEMA and IEC standards specify enclosure styles for all operational environments. Examples include: *open drip-proof, totally enclosed (non-ventilated, fan cooled, or air over), explosion proof,* and *dust ignition proof.* Tables in each standard specify enclosure characteristics.

Voltage—Single phase motors have 115/230 standard voltages, and three phase motors use the following standard voltages 190/380, 200, 200/400, 230/460, 208-230/460, 460 and 575. Definite purpose motors have non-standard voltage values.

Insulation and temperature rise—Motor insulation systems are classified by the maximum total operational temperature without adverse affects on design life. The maximum total temperature has three components: *ambient temperature* (temperature of the atmosphere, 40° C is the standard), *temperature rise* (the change in temperature of the motor windings during operation), *hot spot allowance* (temperature variation within the motor at spots in the

stator slots or coil head, 10° C is considered a standard value).

Torque—NEMA has defined four standard design classes A, B, C, and D of squirrel cage polyphase induction motor, and Figure 15-2(a) lists the torques associated with each class. Also, different loads present different torque requirements at four operational points as described in Figure 15-2(b).

Speed/slip—Speed on a synchronous motor is affected by the *power frequency* and *number of poles.* Standard 60 Hz motors are available with synchronous speeds of 3600, 1800, 1200 or 900 rpm. The actual operating speed of an AC induction motor is determined by the synchronous speed and the slip. Slip is the difference between the speed of the rotating magnetic field (which is always synchronous) and the actual rpm. Slip generally increases with an increase in motor torque; therefore, actual operating speed generally decreases with an increase in the driven load torque.

Service factor—The service factor of a motor is a multiplier which, when applied to the rated horsepower, indicates a permissible horsepower loading that may be carried under the conditions specified for the service factor.

FIGURE 15-2: AC motor torque characteristics.

NEMA Design	Starting Torque	Starting Current	Breakdown Torque	Full Load Slip	Typical Applications
A	Normal	High to medium	Normal	5% maximum	Broad variety (i.e. fans and pumps)
B	High	Low	Normal	5% maximum	Broad variety (i.e. common in HVAC application with fans, blowers, and pumps)
C	High	Low	Normal	5% maximum	High inertia starts (i.e. positive displacement pumps, loaded conveyors and compressors)
D	Very high	Low	—	5 to 13% maximum	Very high inertia starts (i.e. cranes, hoists, punch presses)

(a) NEMA design classes for squirrel-cage polyphase induction motors

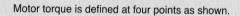

Motor torque is defined at four points as shown.

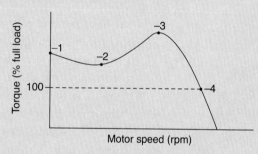

1. Breakaway or starting 2. Minimum or "pull-up" 3. Breakdown or "pull-out" 4. Full load

(b) Motor torque points

15-1 NON-ELECTRONIC WOUND ROTOR SPEED CONTROL

Non-electronic speed control is used on three-phase wound rotor motors. The wound rotor has three separate rotor windings. Each winding of the rotating rotor is connected to a slip ring as shown in Figure 15-3.

Manual Speed Control of Wound Rotor Motors

Manual control is achieved by connecting each rotor winding to an external resistance. The amount of resistance determines the starting current and motor speed. Three pole, make-before-break rotary switches, like Figure 15-4(a), permit manual speed control of small wound rotor motors. The number of rotary switch contacts matches the number of taps on the external resistors. The rotor leads are labeled M1, M2, and M3. Note that the resistor has five taps, and the switch is

shown with the maximum amount of resistance between the rotor windings. In this maximum rotor resistance position, the limit switch's NO contacts are closed. The motor control circuit requires this switch position with maximum resistance present for starting the motor as Figure 15-4(b) illustrates. As the switch is rotated, there is less resistance in the rotor circuit, and the motor speeds up. When the resistance is removed, the rotor windings are shorted together by the three switch poles, and the motor is at full speed. The limit switch NO contacts open when the switch poles move away from the held closed starting position. Figure 15-4(b) shows a standard motor start/stop starting ladder diagram with the wound rotor resistance speed control limit switch integrated into the control. The NO held closed limit switch assures that the maximum rotor resistance is present when the wound rotor motor is started.

FIGURE 15-3: Wound rotor wiring configurations and slip rings.

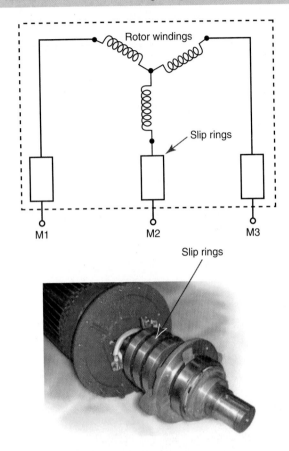

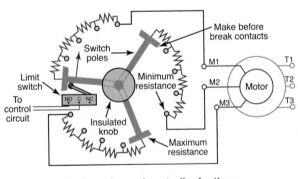

Slip rings

FIGURE 15-4: Rotor resistance speed controller for three phase wound rotor motor.

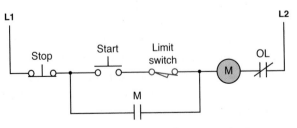

(a) **Manual speed controller for three phase wound rotor motor**

(b) **Control circuit for three phase wound rotor motor manual speed controller**

Time-Operated Wound Rotor Motor Speed

Another method of speed control for the wound rotor motor uses a *time-operated circuit* as shown in Figure 15-5. Four pushbuttons select a motor speed from slowest to highest. Note that switches S1, S2, and S3 control the amount of resistance in the rotor circuit. In addition, three time delay relays, TR1, TR2, and TR3, control when the motor accelerates to a higher speed. For example, if the motor has been running at the second speed for more than 5 seconds, and the highest speed is selected, the motor speed immediately increases to the third speed, and 5 seconds later increases to the fourth or highest speed. If the motor is running at a higher speed, and a lower speed is selected, the motor rpm decrease to the lower speed without delay.

Frequency Controlled Wound Rotor Motor Speed

A third method of speed control for the wound rotor motor uses changes in frequency of the input voltage to adjust the motor speed. In *frequency control*, the frequency of the rotor's induced voltage drops as the rotor's speed increases. The diagram in Figure 15-6 illustrates frequency control of wound rotor motor. Note that frequency relays, S1 and S2, are connected across rotor windings M2 and M3. Also, note the capacitor C1 is connected in series with one of the frequency relays.

Pressing the *START* button energizes the *M* contactor and connects the stator winding to the line. Thus a voltage with a 60Hz frequency is induced in the rotor. The 60Hz frequency energizes the frequency relays *S1* and *S2* and opens their NC contacts. The rotor is now turning at the lowest speed due to maximum resistance in series with each phase winding. The increase in speed causes the frequency to decrease. This causes the *C1* capacitive reactance to increase, so *S1* is de-energized and *S1* contacts return to their NC position. With less resistance, motor speed increases causing additional reductions in induced voltage and frequency. As a result, *S2* is de-energized, and *S2* contacts return to their NC position. With two of the three resistance banks removed from the rotor winding, the motor is running at maximum speed.

The remaining resistance in the motor winding is the main disadvantage. However, frequency control has an advantage over other types of control in that it is very responsive to changes in motor load. For example, with the application of light load the motor accelerates and increases speed rapidly. With a heavy load

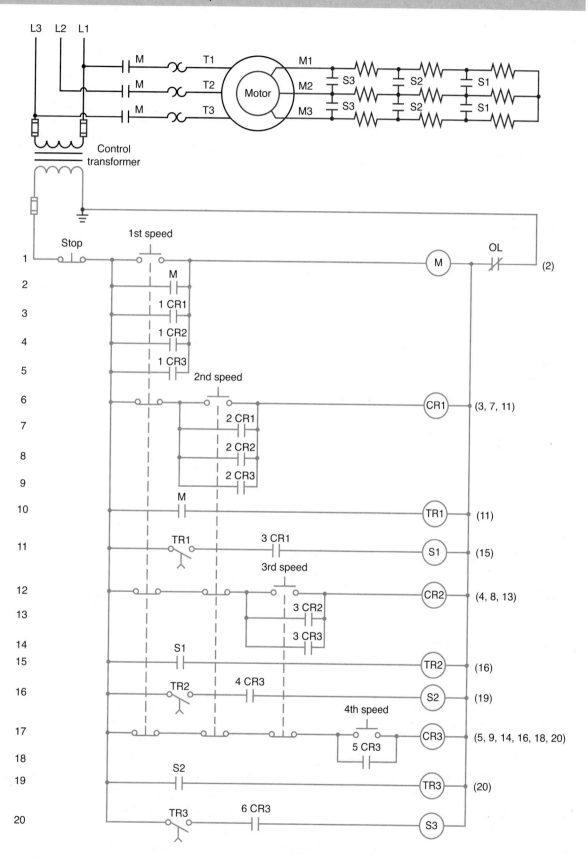

FIGURE 15-5: Time-operated wound rotor motor speed.

FIGURE 15-6: Frequency controlled wound rotor motor speed control.

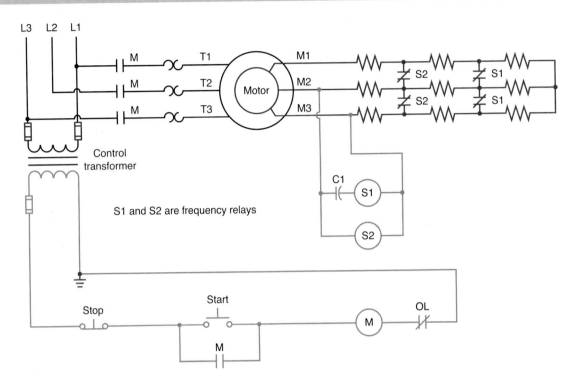

applied, the larger inertia is overcome with a slower increase in speed.

15-2 SINGLE-PHASE SPEED CONTROL

Although most AC motors used in industry are *three-phase*, there are many applications for the *single phase* motor. They operate from a 120V AC or a 240V AC source and are generally small or *fractional horsepower* motors. Single phase speed control is accomplished with *electronic circuitry*, typically with *thyristor* components such as the *silicon controlled rectifier* (SCR) used in the *antiparallel mode* or the *triac*. The thyristor controls the power to the motor by changing the firing angle of the AC sine-wave that drives the motor. The firing angle is the point in each sine-wave where the thyristor in series with the motor turns on. Since the thyristor is not conducting ahead of the firing angle, no current is flowing, so it is an energy efficient method for AC motor speed control.

Triac Speed Control for Single Phase Motors

The diac/triac circuit in Figure 15-7 controls the speed of a single phase AC motor. The setting of R2 determines the phase difference between the input volt-

FIGURE 15-7: Single phase AC induction motor electronic speed control.

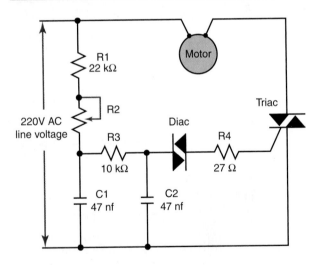

age sine wave and the voltage across C2. This sets the triac *triggering angle* and the power delivered to the motor that sets the *motor speed*. Each half cycle the input voltage charges C2 through R1, R2, and R3 until the voltage applied across the diac reaches its AC breakover level or trigger voltage. When the diac conducts, the voltage on C2 discharges into the gate of the triac, switching it on. The voltage across C1 par-

The synchronous speed of an AC motor is directly proportional to the frequency of the AC power applied to the motor. As the frequency increases, the motor speed increases. As the frequency decreases, the motor speed decreases. The speed of a motor is equal to 120 times the motor frequency divide by the number of poles per phase. For example, a 4-pole (per phase) motor connected to a 60 Hz source has a synchronous speed of 1800 RPM. Increasing the frequency by 2 Hz raises the synchronous speed to 1860 RPM. Note that the motor speed calculations are shown is Figure 15-8.

FIGURE 15-8: Revolutions per minute formulas.

$$RPM = \frac{120 \times f}{\text{number of poles per phase}}$$

$$= \frac{120 \times 60}{4} = 1800$$

$$RPM = \frac{120 \times f}{\text{number of poles per phase}}$$

$$= \frac{120 \times 62}{4} = 1860$$

tially restores the voltage across C2 after triggering the triac. The width and amplitude of the trigger signal is kept constant by R4. The triac is bidirectional so it triggers at the same firing angle for the positive and negative AC cycle. The triac on-time during each half cycle of the AC input dictates the speed of the motor.

15-3 VARIABLE FREQUENCY DRIVES

A *variable-frequency drive* (VFD) is an electronic device for controlling the rotational speed of an AC motor by changing the frequency of the electrical power supplied to the motor. Variable-frequency drives are also called *adjustable-frequency* drives (AFDs), *variable-speed* drives (VSDs), or *scalar* drives. The early VFDs were very large and rather expensive, but technological advancements in the 1990s reduced the physical size and the overall cost. This led to a rapid expansion in the VFD market. The size and affordability of today's VFD, coupled with its operational flexibility, have positioned the VFD as the AC motor drive of choice. Figure 15-9 illustrates the VFD connected to an AC motor. Note that a lower frequency voltage output yields a lower motor speed, and a higher frequency, higher motor speed. The VFD is

FIGURE 15-9: AC motor speed control.

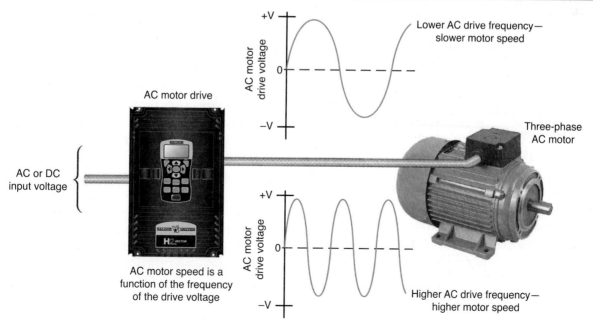

Lower AC drive frequency—slower motor speed

Three-phase AC motor

AC motor drive

AC or DC input voltage

AC motor speed is a function of the frequency of the drive voltage

Higher AC drive frequency—higher motor speed

Courtesy of Baldor Electric Company.

widely used in applications such as ventilations systems for large buildings and used on pumps, conveyors, and machine tool. They are also used on fans to save energy by allowing the volume of air moved to match the system demand.

Drive Operation

The operation of the VFD involves three electronic components—a *converter*, a *DC bus*, and an *inverter*. These components and their associated input and output signals are shown in Figure 15-10. Note that the output of the converter is the input to the DC bus whose output is the input to the inverter. The first component is the *AC to DC converter*, which converts AC input voltage into pulsating DC voltage, Figure 15-10. Converters are basically rectifier circuits that are used to convert the AC sine waveform into either half- or full-wave rectified DC waveform. The second component is the DC bus, which performs the *DC voltage conditioning*, Figure 15-10. The DC bus filters and smoothes the pulsating DC output to ensure that the waveform resembles a pure DC waveform. The DC output is the input to the inverter, which is a *DC to AC converter*.

The inverter converts the filtered DC waveform to a pulsating DC waveform. This waveform simulates an AC sine wave at a fixed effective peak voltage adjustable over a wide frequency range, Figure 15-10. So the VFD converts an AC input voltage at a fixed peak amplitude and at line frequency (50 or 60 hz) to a variable frequency AC output voltage used to change the speed of AC motors.

The VFD AC output is a *pulse width modulation* (PWM) waveform as noted in Figure 15-10. The inverter controls the width (duration) and polarity (direction) of the pulsating DC waveform to produce an effective AC sine wave from an *energy* standpoint. The narrowest pulse simulates the AC waveform when the waveform amplitude is close to a value of zero at 0 degrees. As the pulse width grows, the PWM waveform simulates the AC waveform moving away from zero amplitude with the widest pulse simulating the peak value of the AC waveform at 90 degrees. As time continues, decreasing the pulse width simulates the waveform returning to the zero at 180 degrees. At the point the waveform passes through the zero axis, the inverter changes the polarity of the DC output to simulate the AC waveform in the opposite direction. The inverted output is repeated to complete the AC sine wave. The average value of the PWM is, in effect, a sine wave. By controlling the width or modulation of the PWM waveform, the VFD produces a variable frequency output waveform, which controls the speed of an AC motor. In other words, the VFD controls the PWM waveform to maintain a constant voltage/frequency (V/Hz) pattern to the motor.

Figure 15-11 illustrates the electronic schematic of an AC drive. Note that the converter consists of a step-up transformer and a full bridge rectifier; the DC bus section is an inductor-capacitor (LC) filter; and the inverter section consists of transistor switches driven by control logic. Note the three outputs (A, B, and C) of the inverter drive a three-phase motor. The waveforms of each of the three phases A, B, and C are shown in Figure 15-11.

Many drives have serial inputs that can be used for monitoring control system parameters, and output contacts that control external devices. The control section generally has communication ports that allow the VFD to interface with other smart devices such as computers and controllers. These drive concepts and input/output control are expanded upon in Chapter 20.

FIGURE 15-10: Variable frequency drive voltage conditioning overview.

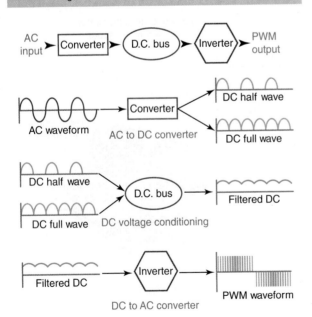

FIGURE 15-11: VFD electronic circuit overview.

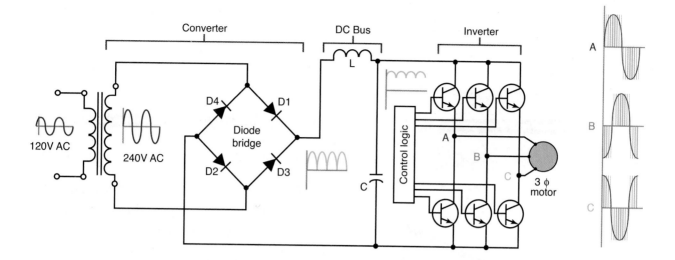

TECH NOTES

Pulse width modulation (PWM) is currently the most popular method used in the VFD applications. The *advantage* of VFDs is that they are designed to easily control the speed of most AC motors found in the field. Their *reliability, relatively low cost,* and *functionality* make them one of the best choices for AC motor control applications. The PWM drives offer efficiency ratings of 92% to 96%. They also inject minimal harmonic feedback on the power source.

Their *disadvantage* is that they are generally limited to normal torque loads. In some installations, they cause motor overheating and insulation breakdown due to high frequency switching of electronic components. Normally, this is only a problem with older motors not rated for VFD use. Even though these drives produce few harmonics, they generate line-side power harmonics. These line-side harmonics pose significant power quality issues for power distribution systems.

Braking

Braking of motors is used to reduce the time for a motor to stop rotating after power is removed from the terminals. The techniques applied are *mechanical braking,* like the drum brakes used on older automobiles, and *electrical braking,* which uses the electromagnetic characteristics of the motor. Figure 15-12 illustrates a mechanical braking system.

Electrical braking uses four techniques: *injection, flux, dynamic,* and *regenerative* braking. *Injection braking* injects DC current into two of the three windings of the motor. *Flux braking* is similar to injection braking but all three of the phases are involved, and motor flux is used for braking. *Dynamic* and

regenerative braking are the most commonly used in AC motors.

AC motors have excess energy created when the load drives the motor during deceleration, rather than the motor driving the load. The VFD can redirect the energy through resistors (dynamic braking) or back to the AC power supply (regenerative braking). In *dynamic braking,* the drive connects a resistance across the DC bus to absorb the energy. For smaller horsepower motors, the resistance is built into the drive. External resistance modules are used for higher horsepower motors. *Regenerative braking* is similar to dynamic braking, except the excess energy is redirected to the AC supply.

FIGURE 15-12: Mechanical friction brake.

Open

Closed

TECH NOTES

The VFD is successfully competing with the conventional electromagnetic motor starter. The functionality of the VFD to operate as forward/reverse starters, with soft start ramp-up and -down capabilities and the flexibility for speed control, are making the VFD the device of choice for many conventional motor starting applications. In fact, the VFD is replacing the reduced voltage starter in many applications. Technology advancements and more efficient manufacturing processes have reduced drive size to the point where many VFDs are now comparable in size to a similarly-rated NEMA motor starter. Depending on the manufacturer and the drive functions, the cost is higher than a similarly rated NEMA device, but the added functionality of the VFD establishes it as a viable alternative to the traditional motor starter. However, price may prohibit the use of the VFD in applications where the functionality of the VFD is never used. Additionally, the harmonics generated by the VFD can pose significant power quality issues for distribution systems. So, power distribution systems not designed for harmonic disturbances are not a good application for the VFD.

15-4 VECTOR DRIVES

The standard *variable frequency drive* or *scalar drive* outputs a PWM pattern that maintains a constant V/Hz pattern to the motor under ideal conditions. The motor's reaction to the PWM pattern is dependent upon the load conditions. The scalar drive has no information about load conditions. If for example, it outputs a 40Hz waveform to the motor, and the motor rotates at a speed equivalent to 38Hz, the scalar drive doesn't know.

The *vector drive* uses feedback to further modify the PWM pattern to maintain more precise control of the operating parameter—*speed* or *torque*. The drive uses the feedback information to calculate the exact vector sum of voltage and frequency to attain precise control. The drive constantly updates the vector sum to maintain control. In other words, the device tells the motor what to do, then checks to see if it did it, then changes its command to correct for any error. Vector drives are marketed under a variety of names such as *flux vector drives* and *sensorless vector drives*. Two types of vector drives are available—*closed loop* and *open loop*—based on how they receive feedback information. Figure 15-13 shows a vector drive with a display and keypad. The drive controls motor speed and torque with the precision and the responsiveness for the most demanding applications. It is available for 3/4 to 250 horsepower motors and for voltage ranges between 120 to 600V AC.

The *closed-loop* vector drive uses a shaft encoder on the motor to give shaft rotation data back to the drive. The drive alters the PWM pattern to adjust for any change as indicated by the shaft encoder. For torque control, the feedback allows the drive to adjust the pattern so that a constant level of torque is maintained regardless of speed. If the feedback data indicate that the torque requirement is wrong, the drive corrects it. The closed-loop vector drive controls an AC motor to develop continuous full torque at zero speed, which makes them suitable for crane and hoist applications. In those applications, the motor produces full torque before the brake is released. This prevents the load from dropping when the brake is released.

The *open-loop* vector drive is actually a misnomer because it is actually a closed loop system, but the feed-

FIGURE 15-13: Variable frequency vector drive.

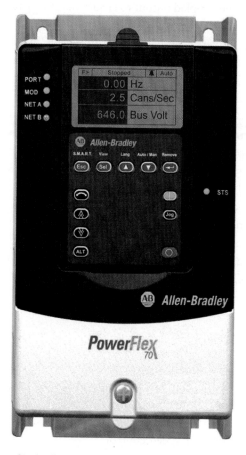

Courtesy of Rockwell Automation, Inc.

TECH NOTES

The vector drive offers unmatched control of speed, torque, and power of an AC motor. The torque capabilities are comparable to other drives and provide lower maintenance and installation costs. However, the vector drive generally requires an AC motor and the vector drive to be matched with the motor and drive parameters known. In addition, the vector drive is more complex than the VFD. Vector drives also have a higher purchase price than other drives. Applications that do not require the high performance of the vector drive are satisfied with a lower cost variable frequency drive.

15-5 TROUBLESHOOTING AC MOTOR DRIVES

When a motor circuit is not operating properly, voltage and current measurements are taken to determine or isolate the problem. This section provides general troubleshooting steps, whereas Chapter 20 provides drive troubleshooting to identify internal problems and configurations setup problems. The general troubleshooting steps in this section include narrowing problems down to a specific system and eliminating external problems such as power source or motor load.

Voltage measurements establish that the voltage is present and at the specified level. Voltage measurements determine circuit problems such as blown fuses or improper grounding. Perform the following troubleshooting steps using voltage measurements to establish the location of the fault:

1. Measure the disconnect voltage. With the power ON, measure the voltage across each phase. The phase to phase voltage measurements should be within two percent of the specified level. If those voltages are not within two percent, check for problems in the power source.
2. Check fuses and/or circuit breakers. With all power removed, replace blown fuses and reset tripped circuit breakers. Try to determine why circuit protection devices tripped before restoring power to the system.
3. With the drive energized, measure the voltage into the drive. The voltage into the drive should be within two percent of the specified level. If the voltage into the drive is not within two percent,

back loop comes from within the drive instead of an external encoder. For this reason, they are referred to as *sensorless vector drives*. The drive creates a mathematical model of the motor operating parameters and keeps it in memory. As the motor operates, the drive monitors the output current, compares it to the model and determines from previously captured data what the different current effects mean in terms of the motor performance. Then the drive executes the necessary corrections just as in the closed-loop vector drive. The only drawback is that as the motor gets slower, the ability of the drive to detect the subtle changes becomes more difficult. At zero speed, it is generally accepted that an open-loop vector drive is not reliable enough to use on cranes and hoists. For most other applications, it performs well.

check for power problems between the disconnect and the drive.

4. With drive energized and activated, measure the voltage out of the motor drive. The voltage out of the drive should be within two percent of specified value with the motor at full speed. If the motor drive voltage is not within two percent, check for motor drive problems with drive diagnostic software or built-in procedures.

Make current measurements to record motor load conditions—*under loaded, fully loaded,* or *overloaded.* With the drive energized and activated, measure the current in each motor phase. The difference in each phase current should be less than ten percent, and not greater than the FLC value on the name plate. A difference greater than ten percent or currents over the FLC value indicates a motor overload due to process problems or a problem in the motor.

CRITICAL CONCEPTS

The need to know content from Chapter 15 is summarized in the following statements.

- Small wound rotor motors are often controlled manually by a three-pole, make-before-break rotary switch.
- Time-operated circuit controls the speed of the motor with pushbuttons and time delay relays.
- Frequency control operates on the principle that the frequency of the induced voltage in the rotor decreases as the speed of the rotor increases.
- Thyristor control the power to the motor so that as the load on the motor changes, the speed is held relatively constant.

- A converter is a device that converts AC voltage into DC voltage, and the DC filter smoothes the uneven, rippled output to ensure that the waveform resembles a pure DC waveform.
- The inverter converts the filtered DC waveform to a pulsating DC waveform, which simulates an AC waveform. The pulsating waveform is a pulse width modulation (PWM) waveform.
- Closed-loop vector drives use a shaft encoder to constantly monitor the motor speed and rotor position.
- Open-loop vector drives use a feedback loop that comes from within the drive instead of an external encoder.
- In dynamic braking, the drive connects a resistance across the DC bus to absorb the energy. Regenerative braking is similar to dynamic braking, except the excess energy is redirected to the AC supply.

QUESTIONS

1. Describe the operation of motor speed control by the manual, time-operated and frequency control methods.
2. Describe how the SCR and the triac are used in motor speed control.
3. Describe the function of the converter, the DC filter and the inverter in a variable frequency drive.
4. Describe how pulse width modulation controls the speed of a motor.
5. Describe the difference between an open-loop and a closed-loop vector drive.
6. Explain why variable frequency drives are not a good choice for power distribution systems.
7. Describe dynamic and regenerative braking.

CHAPTER 16

DC Motor Starting and Speed Control

GOALS AND OBJECTIVES

The primary goals for this chapter are to identify and describe *manual* and *automatic* DC motor starting and solid state DC motor speed control drives. In addition, *dynamic* and *regenerative* braking techniques for DC motors are presented.

After completing this chapter, you will be able to:

1. Describe manual and automatic DC motor starting techniques.
2. Describe the operation of solid state DC motor speed control.
3. Describe dynamic and regenerative braking.

TECH NOTES

Before variable frequency drive technology was developed, direct current (DC) systems were one of a few options for variable speed motors. Although DC systems are not used as often today, many commercial and industrial locations retain DC equipment that has been in use for decades and continues to perform adequately. A cut away of a DC motor is illustrated in Figure 16-1 showing the rotor and field windings plus the brushes and commutators.

There are several reasons why DC motors are popular and still in use today. The rotational speed of most DC motors is started and controlled by simply using a variable resistor device known as a rheostat. The DC motor normally has high operational torque characteristics that enhance performance. For short periods of time, a DC motor can increase torque by as much as five times their normal rated motor torque. In addition, DC motors maintain their rated torque over a wide range of motor speeds. DC motor characteristics are illustrated in Figure 16-2. Note that the amount of applied voltage is proportional to motor speed, and the amount of applied current is proportional to motor torque.

FIGURE 16-1: DC motor with rotor windings, field windings and commutator indicated.

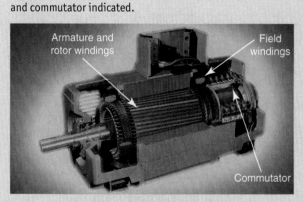

Armature and rotor windings

Field windings

Commutator

Courtesy of Siemens.

The stability of DC voltage as a power source is an advantage over AC power sources, which typically has switching voltage spikes and harmonics. However, DC voltage has some

(continued)

major drawbacks. Because DC must be derived from AC, it is not readily available and the conversion process is inefficient. Also, system voltage drop limits the distance DC volt-age can be transmitted, whereas AC voltage is transmitted over long distances through the use of transformers.

FIGURE 16-2: Speed/voltage and torque/current DC motor characteristics.

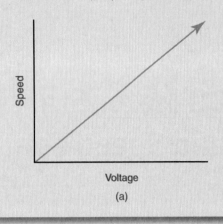

(a)

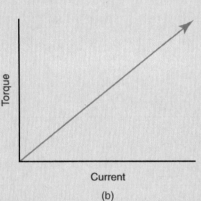

(b)

16-1 DC MOTOR STARTING

The DC motor is started *manually* with a *rheostat*, like an AC motor, in an automatic mode using *contactors* or *drives*. While manual rheostat starters are rarely used in new applications, they are still in use on older systems so the electrical worker needs to know the principles of operation. New and upgraded DC systems use electronic drives like the DC drive and motor illustrated in Figure 16-3.

Rheostat Starter

The rheostat starter is a multiple-tapped resistor that starts and accelerates a motor to the rated speed manually. In addition, the starter rheostat limits armature current in the motor during starting and accelerating. Figure 16-4 shows a typical starting rheostat with a contact that is moved over an exposed winding so resistance from the contact to one coil end is varied from near zero to the maximum value of the coil. This contentiously

FIGURE 16-3: DC motor and electronic speed control with access door open.

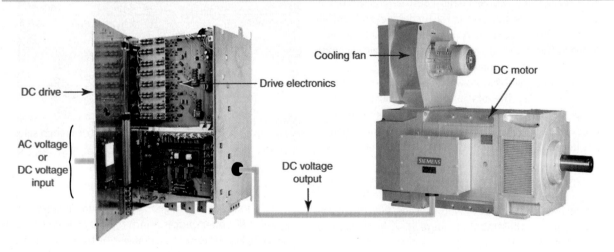

Courtesy of Siemens.

FIGURE 16-4: DC motor speed control rheostat.

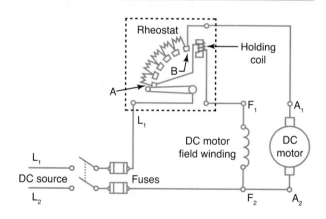

FIGURE 16-5: Rheostat motor starter.

ture and the maximum rheostat resistance is connected across the source. Also at point A, the field winding in series with the holding coil is connected across the source. The initial armature current is limited by the starting resistance value. The shunt field, connected across the line at point A, current is a maximum, which produces high starting torque. Moving the arm toward point B reduces armature circuit resistance and accelerates the motor to full rpm. At point B the field current is reduced due to rheostat resistance, but the armature is directly across the source. The rheostat arm moves quickly from point A to point B because of the heat generated in the start sequence. Because of the heat, rheostats are often placed in ventilated enclosures.

Finally, the holding coil and the shunt field series circuit creates an *open-field* release. DC shunt field motors have a run away rpm condition if the shunt field opens. The holding coil prevents this dangerous situation by releasing the rheostat arm if shunt current falls to zero. A spring return pulls the arm back to point A. In addition, a below normal source voltage also releases the holding coil, which causes the rheostat arm to reset to position *A*.

Contactor Starter

Contactors used in DC motor starters are constructed and operated in the same manner as AC contactors. DC contactors use a solenoid to make and break the contacts. When the solenoid is energized, movable contacts mounted on the plunger assembly are forced against the stationary contact, closing the circuit, and connecting the motor to line power. When the power is removed from the coil, a spring assembly opens the circuit and returns the contacts to the normal state.

The DC contactors are available in multiple pole configurations, but most are one set of single pole contacts. DC contactors have standard coil voltage ratings of 12, 24, 48, 120 and 240V DC. Contactors are selected based on the applications such as *DC controls, motor loads* or *resistive heating*. Once the use and maximum continuous load is determined, the contactor is then selected by the ampere rating. DC contactors are available in ampere ratings from 10 to 1,200A DC. However, contactors designed for special applications such as melting ore in the steel industry have ampere ratings of several thousand amperes.

Arc suppression is more of an issue with DC contactors than with AC contactors. DC voltage does not pass through zero as the AC voltage, so the DC current stays above the zero axis and maintains a constant

variable DC output is produced by the circuit in Figure 16-5. The rheostat in the figure is different from the one in Figure 16-4 because it is not continuously variable. In the circuit the movable arm or contact jumps over six winding contact. This produces six different voltage levels to start the DC motor. Field current through an electromagnet holds the rheostat arm in the full voltage position when maximum rpm is attained.

The full connection diagram for a typical three-terminal rheostat is shown in Figure 16-5. The rheostat connects a DC shunt motor and the input voltage source. With the rheostat arm at contact A, the arma-

FIGURE 16-6: Arc chute operation.

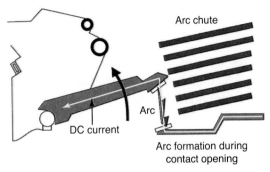

(a) Arc chute at start of contact opening sequence

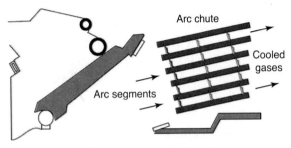

(b) As contacts open arcs are pulled into chute by heated air

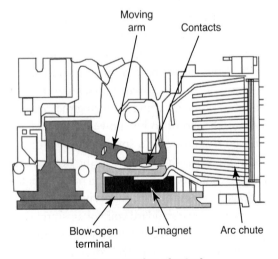

(c) Cross section of actual contactor with arc chute

Courtesy of Schneider Electric.

current flow to the motor. Therefore, the current flowing through the contacts of a contactor remains high when the power is disconnected. This creates an arc that is more difficult to contain and quench. It is especially true in systems powered by an unfluctuating waveform from sources like batteries or DC generators. *Making* and *breaking* the contacts as quickly as possible helps

FIGURE 16-7: DC magnetic arc blowout coil.

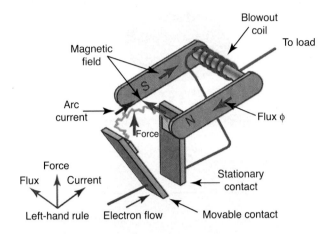

extinguish the arc promptly and extends the life of the contacts and contactor.

Arc chutes are devices that are added to contactors to quickly quench the arcs produced when the contacts open and close. The arc chute operation is illustrated in Figure 16-6. As the contactor contacts open, the arc chute segments cool and move the arc away from the contacts. Moving the arc away preserves the integrity of the contacts, thus yielding a longer service life. Arc chutes typically absorb greater than *eighty percent* of the energy released during the interruption of current flow.

In addition to arc chutes, most DC contactors have a DC magnetic *arc blowout coil* to assist with arc suppression. Blowout coils produce a magnetic field that "blows" out the arc. The magnetic blowout coil produces a magnetic field between the breaking contacts that forces the arc up. Rather than arcing in a straight line from contact to contact, the arc is forced up increasing the length of the arc causing it to dissipate faster. Figure 16-7 illustrates the electro-magnetic blowout coil and its effect on the arc. Blowout coils work on the left-hand rule principle. Current flowing normal to a magnetic field produces a force on the current conductor or current arc. See vectors in Figure 16-7.

16-2 SOLID STATE SPEED CONTROL

Solid state DC drives are more efficient in controlling the speed and torque of DC motors than rheostats, and the overall cost is less. Because solid state drives do not use resistors, energy is not wasted in the form of heat. Solid state drives are divided into two separate operational sections—the *power section* and the *control section*.

FIGURE 16-8: Waveforms for different stages of an AC-to-DC converter.

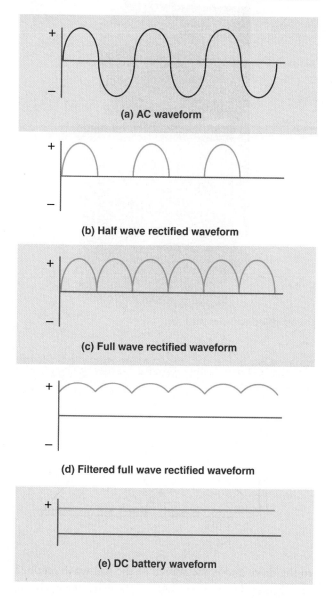

(a) AC waveform

(b) Half wave rectified waveform

(c) Full wave rectified waveform

(d) Filtered full wave rectified waveform

(e) DC battery waveform

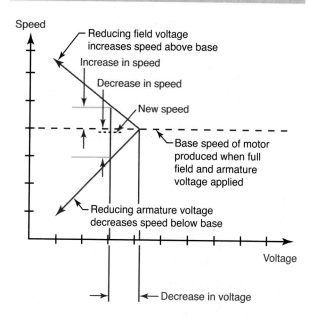

The power section supplies the DC voltage to the motor with an AC-to-DC converter. Figure 16-8(a) through (d) illustrates the waveforms in the conversion process. Figure 16-8(e) illustrates a DC battery waveform for comparison.

The output level of the power section is determined by the control section. The control section of a solid state drive is capable of varying the motor speed above and below the *base speed*. The base speed is the speed in RPM at which the motor runs with full line voltage applied to the armature and the field. DC motors have three wiring configurations, series, shunt, and compound. The speed control technique depends to some degree on the wiring configuration, but in each case, control of the armature and field voltage is used to control the speed. Figure 16-9 illustrates the relationship between *motor speed* and *armature and field* voltage for a *shunt wired* motor. Note that reducing the field voltage, increases the speed, and reducing the armature voltage, decreases the speed. As a result, the decrease in the voltage across the shunted motor armature and field has little effect on the motor speed. The change in voltage across the armature and field cancel out, and the speed remains near constant at the base value. This characteristic allows a shunt DC motor to maintain a constant speed for all reasonable loads. However, independent variations in the armature voltage or the field current changes the motor speed.

Speed Control with an SCR

Figure 16-10(a) illustrates an SCR circuit that controls the speed of a DC motor. The speed is controlled from zero RPM to the base speed of the motor. The gate trigger circuit varies the amount the time that the SCR is on during each cycle of the input AC voltage. The SCR on-time varies the amount of armature current, thus the speed of the motor. The longer the SCR is on, the faster the speed as shown in Figure 16-10(b). Note that input AC voltage is connected to the SCR and the motor field winding through the bridge rectifier.

FIGURE 16-11: DC motor electronic drive.

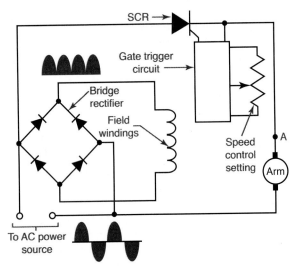

(a) DC motor speed control circuit

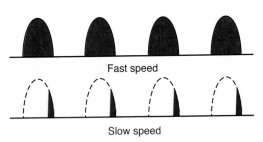

Fast speed

Slow speed

(b) SCR motor drive waveforms at point A in circuit above

Courtesy of Rockwell Automation, Inc.

FIGURE 16-12: DC motor drive ramp up and ramp down speed profile.

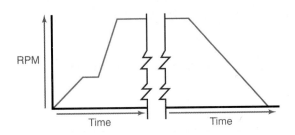

Digital DC Drives

Digital DC drives provide control points to set the desired speed of the motor. Motor speed information is fed back to the drive to compensate for any variations. Data regarding the motor speed is normally delivered from a tachometer or encoder that monitors the shaft speed of the motor. The drive compares the feedback signal to the set point and makes the necessary speed corrections. Drives with a shaft monitoring feedback device are normally accurate to 0.05%. The control section of the drive is also capable of controlling the rotational direction of the motor by reversing the polarity of the voltage. DC drives often have braking capability built into the control section. Braking allows for additional control of the motor in applications such as hoisting and lowering loads, where speed control and braking are critical for proper operation.

Figure 16-11 illustrates a solid state digital DC drive. The solid state digital DC drive integrates easily into automation systems. Three-phase AC power is connected to the drive and is the source of the full-wave rectified and filtered DC power used by the drive. Front panel control allows for programmed setting, such as speed set points and diagnostic testing. The drive uses the latest technology in high density power devices and manufacturing techniques to provide a compact, reliable package. Features of the drive include *multiple digital and analog inputs and outputs, semiconductor fuse protection, modular construction* and *strategically located components*, which allow for fast, easy maintenance.

DC drives use a *ramping* method to *accelerate* and *decelerate* the motor. Ramping smoothly and steadily brings the motor up to speed or decreases the speed to bring the motor to a smooth and quick stop. The ramp up and ramp down parameters are shown in Figure 16-12. The parameters are programmed into

FIGURE 16-13: DC motor braking options.

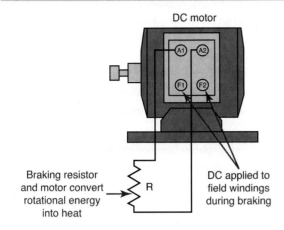

(a) DC motor with braking resistor

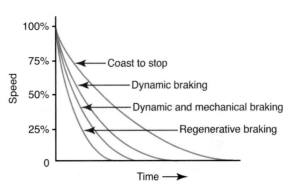

(b) DC motor braking options and effectiveness

the DC drive and are easily reset at any time by re-programming the drive. Ramping works well for small to intermediate loads. Motors connected to heavy loads are not normally stopped with ramping alone because the large inertia of the load continues to rotate the motor after the ramp down voltage has stopped. Ramping is effective in stopping large inertia loads when used with an electric braking system. The ramp down slope slows the load, and the brake brings the load to a complete stop. Slowing the load before the brake is applied helps reduce the wear on the braking components.

Dynamic and Regenerative Braking

Dynamic braking is a motor braking technique where the motor is operated as a DC generator after main power is removed. With the field winding connected to DC power, the motor functions as a generator because the rotating armature is cutting lines of flux and producing a current flow. The leads of the armature are reconnected to braking resistors that create a load and dissipate the generated energy. This brings the motor to a rapid stop. The smaller the braking resistor the faster the stopping time and the hotter the resistor temperature. Figure 16-13(a) shows the resistors connected to the DC motor, and Figure 16-13(b) illustrates the relationship between motor speed and time for four braking methods. In some instances, a friction brake is used in conjunction with dynamic braking. The dynamic braking slows the motor, and the friction brake stops the motor.

Regenerative braking returns the regenerated power of a DC motor back to the power source. As

APPLICATION

Figure 16-14 is a ladder diagram that illustrates dynamic braking. Pressing the *START* pushbutton energizes the starter. Auxiliary contact 3-M1 is used for the holding circuit. Contact 1-M1 connects the main power to the armature of the motor. Contact 2-Ml opens the circuit to the load resistor while the motor is energized. Pressing the *STOP* pushbutton de-energizes the starter and opens contact 1-M1. Contact 2-Ml closes and completes an internal loop connection between the load resistor and the armature. This internal connection creates torque in the opposite direction of the motor rotation and assists in bringing the motor to a stop.

FIGURE 16-14: DC motor ladder diagram for speed control.

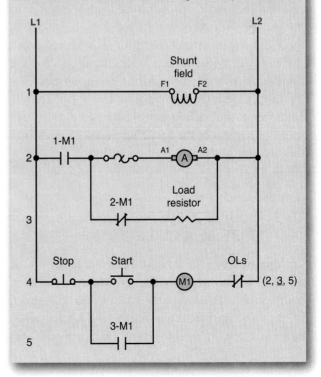

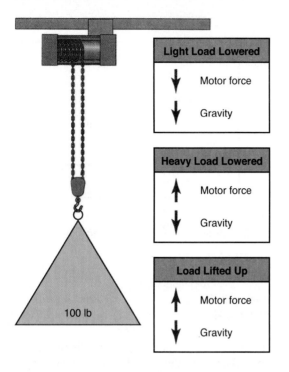

FIGURE 16-15: DC motor braking application.

Light Load Lowered
↓ Motor force
↓ Gravity

Heavy Load Lowered
↑ Motor force
↓ Gravity

Load Lifted Up
↑ Motor force
↓ Gravity

100 lb

shown is Figure 16-13(b), regenerative braking decelerates the motor faster than dynamic braking. When a motor lifts a load, the motor force turns the lifting shaft to overcome the downward force of the load. However, when a motor lowers a load, the motor force provides a torque to the shaft that controls the rate that the load drops. For some loads, gravity pulls the load down faster than the speed of the motor. In those cases a smooth deceleration is produced when the motor provides an opposing torque to slow the shaft rotation caused by gravity. *DC regenerative control drives* detect this condition and automatically adjust the torque of a motor to maintain a controlled speed regardless of the load. Figure 16-15 illustrates this concept with three load conditions.

16-3 TROUBLESHOOTING DC MOTOR STARTERS AND DRIVES

Troubleshooting rheostat and contactor starters is simpler than troubleshooting DC drives. However, many motor drives monitor and automatically turn off the motor if there is a problem, which helps maintain a safe system for equipment and electrical work-

ers. First, make a quick visual check of the DC motor. With the motor off, *remove foreign material* from the grooves between the commutator bars and from the brush holders and posts and then verify that the *brushes move freely in the holder,* the *spring tension* on each brush *is about equal* and every brush and commutator has a *properly polished surface.* Perform maintenance on the motor if required.

Troubleshooting DC Motor Starters

A visual inspection of the rheostat starter and the contactor starter is the first step in troubleshooting DC starters. The visual inspection includes a check for *excess dirt accumulation, burns* or *damaged starter components.* The rheostat is a variable multiple-tapped resistor and is tested at each of its taps. Each tap is a different resistor value; therefore, it is tested with a DMM like any resistor. For the contactor starter, follow the troubleshooting steps in Chapter 6 for contactors.

Troubleshooting DC Drives

Use the internal diagnostics for the DC motor drive to locate the fault. The drive *detects* and *displays* common *circuit faults* and/or *fault numbers* to help identify the problem area. Common drive faults are *power loss, motor overload condition, overvoltage* or *undervoltage condition, high drive operating temperature condition,* and *ground fault condition.* Refer to the drive user manual to determine the possible causes described by the fault or the fault number. Figure 16-16 illustrates some examples of fault numbers and fault descriptions for a DC drive.

CRITICAL CONCEPTS

The need to know content from Chapter 16 is summarized in the following statements.

- The rheostat starter is a multiple-tapped resistor that starts and accelerates a motor to its nominal rated speed in one rotational direction.
- The holding coil in series with the shunt field provides an open-field release.
- Arc chutes are devices that are added to contactors to quickly quench the arcs produced when the contacts open and close.

FIGURE 16-16: Troubleshooting DC drives.

Fault Codes		
No.	**Fault**	**Description**
F2	Auxiliary input	Check remote contacts, source, and wiring.
F3	Power loss	Put voltage monitor on AC line to record low voltage or line power interruption.
F4	Undervoltage	Put voltage monitor on AC line to record low voltage or line power interruption.
F5	Overvoltage	Put voltage monitor on AC line to record high line voltage or transient conditions. If bus overvoltage is due to motor regeneration, extend the decel time or install dynamic brake.
F6	Motor stalled	Increase acceleration time or reduce load so drive output current remains below the maximum current parameter.
F7	Motor overload	Locate the cause of the excessive load on the motor and correct the problem.
F8	Heatsink over temperature	Check for bad fan motor, faulty fan motor controller, and blocked or dirty heat sink fins. Verify that the NEMA enclosure is properly sized and consistent with the current ambient temperature.
F12	Overcurrent	Check for programming errors. Check for excess load, improper DC boost setting, or other causes of excess current.
F13	Ground fault	Check the motor, drive, and external wiring for a ground fault condition.

- Blowout coils provide a magnetic field that blows out the arc, allowing the arc to be extinguished rapidly and with less space between the contacts.
- The DC drive compares a feedback signal to the speed set point and makes the necessary speed corrections.
- Ramping is a type of accelerating and decelerating method used on DC drives.
- Dynamic braking is a motor braking technique where the motor is reconnected as a DC generator after it is disconnected from the main power.
- Regenerative braking is a method of motor braking in which the regenerated power of a DC motor that is coming to a stop is returned to the input power supply.

QUESTIONS

1. Describe how a rheostat starts and accelerates a DC motor.
2. What is the purpose of a holding coil in series with the field winding?
3. What is the purpose of arc chutes?
4. What is the purpose of blowout coils?
5. Explain the relationship between motor speed and the armature voltage and field voltage.
6. Describe how an SCR controls the speed of a DC motor.
7. What two devices feedback motor speed to the DC drive?
8. Describe dynamic braking operation.
9. Describe regenerative braking operation.

SECTION 3

CHAPTER 17

Analog Signals Used in Motor Control

GOALS AND OBJECTIVES

The primary goals for this chapter are to identify and describe *analog signal types, analog inputs* and *outputs*. In addition, *analog switches* and *signal converters* that are used in motor control are described.

After completing this chapter, you will be able to:

1. Describe the analog signal types used in motor control.
2. Discuss analog input and output parameters.
3. Describe the operation and function of analog switches and signal converters.

17-1 ANALOG SIGNAL TYPES

An analog signal is a continuous value (i.e. 0 to 5 volts) as opposed to a discrete signal, which has an on and off state (i.e. 0 volts or 5 volts). A third type is a digital signal, which has a limited number of discrete steps within a range. An analog signal is like a volume control with a range of values between zero and full-scale. The magnitude of an analog process signal is proportional to the value of the measured process parameter and takes the form of a current or voltage. Generally, *current signals*, with a very low source resistance, are less sensitive to electrical noise from *welders* and *electric motor starters* than voltage signals. There is a wide range of analog input signal types generated by analog transducers and sensing devices. Figure 17-1(a) shows the many different analog *transducer output* signal types used in process control. Analog controllers have a more limited selection of input signal types for the interface with the sensor outputs. Figure 17-1(b) lists frequently used process analog input signals. As a result of the smaller number of input signal types, an interface device called a signal conditioner is required.

Analog signals are converted between volts, amperes, or pressure by signal conditioning devices to match the input requirements of the process controller or data collector. For example, an analog ±300mv DC sensor output is converted to a 0 to 5V DC signal required at the input of a process controller. A span of −300mv to +300mv is made proportional to a span of 0 to 5V. Signal conditioners convert the output values in Figure 17-1(a) to the required value in Figure 17-1(b). Figure 17-2 shows a DIN rail mounted universal signal conditioner that converts analog signal data from a broad input range [Figure 17-1(a)] to a standard output range [Figure 17-1(b)].

FIGURE 17-1: Analog DC signal ranges used with industrial analog sensors and processors.

Transducer Outputs	
Voltage	**Current**
0–60 mV	0–5 mA
0–100 mV	0–10 mA
0–200 mV	0–20 mA
0–300 mV	±5 mA
0–500 mV	±10 mA
0–1 V	±20 mA
0–2 V	4–20 mA
0–2.5 V	**Pressure**
0–5 V	3–15 psi
0–10 V	
0–20 V	
±60 mV	
±100 mV	
±200 mV	
±300 mV	
±500 mV	
±1 V	
±2 V	
±2,5 V	
±5 V	
±10 V	
±20 V	

(a) Sensor analog output signals

Process Inputs	
Voltage	**Current**
0–10 V	0–5 mA
±10 V	0–10 mA
0–5 V	0–20 mA
±5 V	4–20 mA
1–5 V	**Pressure**
	3–15 psi

(b) Process analog input signals

Note: Blue highlight indicates the most frequently used values.

FIGURE 17-2: Universal signal conditioner showing front panel and DIP switch settings.

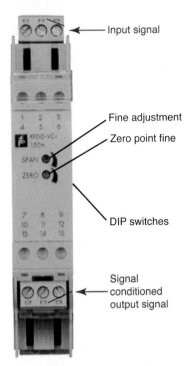

(a) Universal signal conditioner front panel

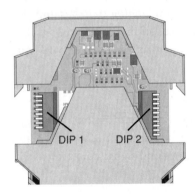

(b) DIP switches to select input and output signal levels

17-2 ANALOG INPUTS

Many analog devices that monitor system parameters provide only a low-level analog signal. Often, these low-level signals are analog inputs to solid-state operational amplifiers or op amps, which output a high-level signal needed by other system devices. Figure 17-3 depicts the symbol for the op amp. The basic op amp is a five-terminal device—two input terminals, an output terminal and two power-supply terminals. The input terminals are identified as + and −, which does not indicate polarity, but rather what happens to the

FIGURE 17-3: Operational amplifier input and output interface.

FIGURE 17-4: Operational or instrumentation amplifiers.

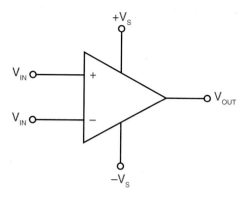

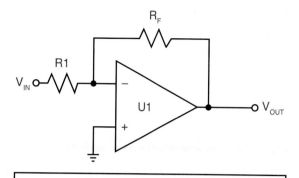

The negative input terminal of the op amp is at a virtual ground. The gain of the op amp is equal to the ratio of the feedback resistor divided by the input resistor. The input impedance at V_{IN} for the analog input signal is equal to the input resistor.

(a) Inverting amplifier

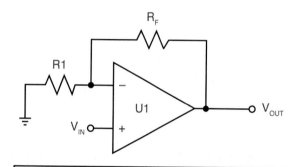

The negative input terminal of the op amp is approximately equal to the analog input voltage. The gain of the op amp is equal to one plus the ratio of the feedback resistor divided by the input resistor. The input impedance at the + input point for the analog input signal is equal to input resistance of the op amp times the ratio of the open-loop gain of the op amp divided by its closed-loop gain.

(b) Non-inverting amplifier

output signal when different magnitudes and polarity of input signals are applied to the amplifier's inputs. The + input terminal is called the *non-inverting input,* which means if a positive analog signal is on this input, then the output signal is positive. Conversely, a negative input yields a negative output. The – input is called the *inverting input,* which means if a positive analog signal is on this input, and then the output signal is negative. Conversely, a negative input yields a positive output.

There are many configurations of op amps, but the inverting and non-inverting are most common configurations. Figure 17-4 illustrates the inverting and non-inverting op amps. Note that the output voltage that is fed back to the input cancels a part of the input voltage thus reducing the extremely high open loop gain of the op amp to a gain necessary for the application. This function is called *negative feedback.* The level of the feedback is determined by the resistors, so the resistor values determine the close-loop amplifier gain. The DIP switch settings for the signal conditioner example shown in Figure 17-2 determine the number and value of op-amp feedback resistors. The switches configure the internal amplifiers for the input and output voltage or current conditioning required for the process application.

Note that the *analog input impedance* for the non-inverting op amp is much higher than the inverting op amp because it is a function of the open loop gain of op amp. Also, note that the power supply terminals are not shown. In the industry, schematics are typically drawn without these terminals shown in order to avoid clutter. Op amp power supplies are typically plus and minus 15 volts, but other voltages are often used as well.

17-3 ANALOG OUTPUTS

The output impedance of the op amp is near zero so it is an ideal driver of output loads. Two phenomena affecting analog outputs are *output saturation* and *output offset.* Op amp output signal peaks swing between the positive and negative power supply values. When the product of the op amp gain and input signal produce an output voltage less than the output maximum, op amp operation is in the linear region. However, if the product is larger than the output maximum, then the output is clipped and operation is in the saturated region. The typical op amp drops about two volts of the total supply voltages on internal circuitry. So the maximum output voltage swing of an op amp powered from ±15 volt supplies is approximately ±14 volts or 28 volts peak-to-peak. Figure 17-5 illustrates this phenomenon.

A small voltage, produced by DC bias currents, is present at the op amp inputs. This voltage, called the input offset, is multiplied by the open loop gain of the op amp, creating a DC-offset voltage at the output. This means that when an AC signal is applied at the input, the output voltage swings around a small DC voltage as opposed to zero volts. This is called the *output offset*. This phenomenon is as shown in Figure 17-6.

FIGURE 17-6: Op-amp DC offset voltage.

FIGURE 17-5: Op-amp clipped output waveform.

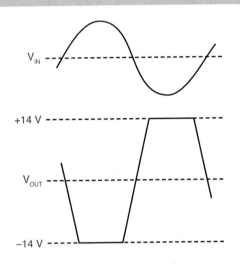

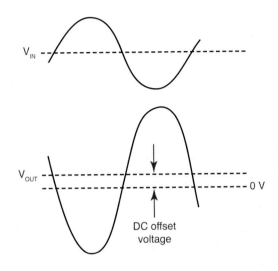

The DC offset voltage is partially eliminated by the addition of a resistor between the + input terminal of the op amp and ground as shown in Figure 17-7(a). This resistor labeled R_B is calculated as follows: $R_B = R1 \times R_F / (R1 + R_F)$. Because the resistor R_B does not totally eliminate the output offset voltage, some op amps have null offset terminals for critical applications where output offset must be eliminated. Referring to Figure 17-7(b), the 10kΩ potentiometer is adjusted to obtain 0 volts at the V_{OUT} when the inputs are connected to 0 volts.

FIGURE 17-7: Input offset current adjustment.

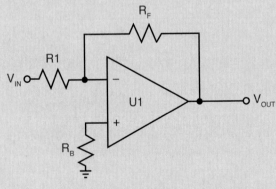

(a) Inverting amplifier without offset voltage adjustment

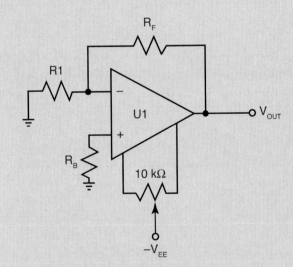

(b) Inverting amplifier with offset voltage adjustment

17-4 ANALOG SWITCHES AND SIGNAL CONVERTERS

Analog switches and converters are used in a variety of motor control applications. Analog switches pass analog signals, both voltage and current, in applications where fast switching time is needed. Voltage-to-current, current-to-voltage and current-to-pressure are common converters that are used in industrial applications where analog signals drive process and measurement devices.

Analog Switches

The *analog switch* is a solid state device that operates in a similar manner to a solid-state relay. Like solid-state relays, analog switches use *field effect transistors* (FETs) to transition between states. However, in the case of solid-state relays, optical isolation allows the transfer of higher voltage signals than analog switches, but it also makes them slower. Switching time for solid-state relays is typically 500 to 1000ns, whereas for analog switches, the time is 20 to 100ns.

Figure 17-8 illustrates the analog switch symbol in two package configurations. Note that one package has an enable input (EN) in addition to the control input (IN). The switching element is an FET, and the control input to the switch is a standard logic voltage, usually +5 volts. The logic voltage input is converted by internal circuitry to a suitable voltage for switching the FET. Generally, a logic zero on the control input causes the FET switch to have a high resis-

FIGURE 17-8: Analog switches.

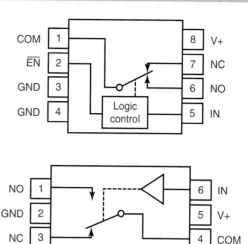

tance, so that the switch is open, and a logic one on the input causes the FET switch to have a low resistance, so that the switch is closed. Analog switches are usually manufactured as integrated circuits in packages that contain multiple switches of *two*, *four* or *eight*.

Unlike a relay, the analog switch does not provide electrical isolation between the analog signal and the control signal. Therefore, the analog switch is not used in high-voltage circuits where such isolation is needed. Also, because there is only a low current path between the input and output, the maximum current allowed through the switch is smaller than that in a typical relay. There are also some constraints on the polarity

Figure 17-9 illustrates a gain adjustment circuit. Note that the op amp is in the inverting configuration. The single pole, triple throw (SP3T) analog switch has a very low on-resistance and is a break-before-make style, which provides minimal signal distortion as the different gains are selected by the process. The analog switch has three control inputs (not shown) for each process selectable gain setting.

FIGURE 17-9: Multigain amplifier with analog gain switch.

APPLICATION

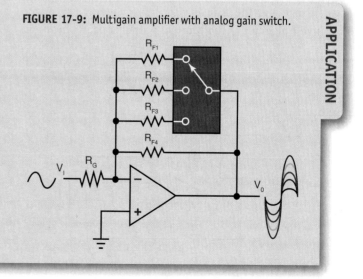

and range of voltages of the signal being switched. Important parameters of an analog switch are:

- Closed-resistance is the resistance of the FET when switched on, which commonly ranges from five ohms to a few hundred ohms.
- Open-resistance is the resistance of the FET when switched off, which is typically a number of Mega-ohms or Giga-ohms.
- Signal range is the minimum and maximum voltages allowed for the signal to be passed through. If these are exceeded, the switch may be destroyed.

Voltage-to-Current Converters

Some industrial applications require a current source rather than a voltage source to link the sensors to the process system. If the sensor output is a current value, for example 4 to 20 milliamps, then wire resistance, which produces a voltage drop from the current flow, does not introduce any error in the measurement since the data are stored in the current value. Also, the low source impedance of the current output reduces the negative effect of noise in the signal. The *voltage-to-current converter* shown in Figure 17-10 converts the input voltage to an output current that is linear and proportional to the input voltage. Circuits like this are often used in signal conditioners (Figure 17-2) for voltage to current conversions.

In this converter, the load is connected in the feedback loop, and the input signal is applied to the inverting input of the op amp. The load is the feedback resistance. In this circuit, the load current flows through R1. This causes the voltage at the non-inverting input to change with the change in the input voltage. This effectively maintains a load current proportional to the input voltage. The current through the load is $I_L = V_{IN} / R1$. In the equation, the stability of R1 is the only factor that affects the relationship between the load current and the input voltage. This is not a concern because highly stable resistors are readily available.

Current-to-Voltage Converters

A reverse function of the voltage-to-current converter is the *current-to-voltage converter*. Its input is a current source, and its output is a voltage proportional to the input current. Figure 17-11 shows the op amp used as a current-to-voltage converter. This configuration accommodates those analog devices that have current output. Note that the input current source is connected directly to the inverting input of the op amp. All the current from the input source flows through the feedback resistor because the inverting input has high input impedance.

With the inverting input terminal of the op amp at a virtual ground, the voltage drop across the feedback resistor is also the output voltage, which is $V_{OUT} = I_{IN} \times R_F$. The output voltage is directly proportional to the input current. And as in the voltage-to-current converter, the stability of R_F is only factor that affects the output linearity.

Current-to-Pressure Converters

A current-to-pressure converter (I/P) converts a 4 to 20 ma analog signal to a proportional and linear 3 to 15 psi pressure output. Figure 17-12 shows a current-to-pressure converter, which is ideal for a pneumatic control system. It translates the analog output from a control system into a precise, repeatable pressure value to control *pneumatic actuators/operators, pneumatic*

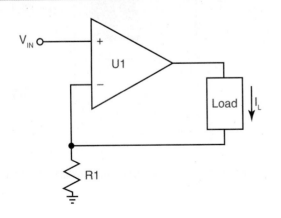

FIGURE 17-10: Voltage-to-current converter.

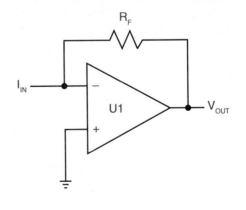

FIGURE 17-11: Current-to-voltage op-amp converter.

FIGURE 17-12: Current-to-pressure converter.

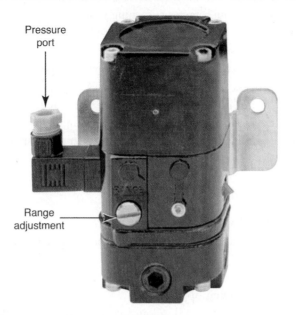

Pressure port

Range adjustment

Reproduced with the permission of Omega Engineering, Inc., Stamford, CT, 06907 USA www.omega.com

valves, *dampers* and *vanes*. In addition, I/P converters are available in a variety of housings for cabinet, field and rail installations.

17-5 MEASURING ANALOG SIGNALS

Oscilloscopes are commonly used to measure the amplitude of an analog signal. In addition to the amplitude of the signal, an oscilloscope shows wave shape, frequency, distortion, and relative timing of two related analog signals. Some modern digital oscilloscopes analyze and display the spectrum of a repetitive event. Special-purpose oscilloscopes, called spectrum analyzers, have sensitive inputs and display spectra in the GHz range.

In addition to oscilloscopes, data acquisition devices measure analog signals by digitizing them for computation in a controller or computer. Measuring analog signals with a data acquisition device is not always as simple as wiring the signal source leads to the device. Knowledge of the nature of the signal source, a suitable configuration of the data acquisition device, and an appropriate cabling scheme is required to produce accurate and noise-free measurements. Figure 17-13 shows a block diagram of a typical data acquisition system. Note that a pre-amp connects the analog signal to be measured to the acquisition interface module (AIM). The AIM filters and digitizes the analog signal and passes the signal to the digital acquisition system. The integrity of the acquired data depends upon the entire analog signal path. An understanding of the types of signal sources and measurement systems is a prerequisite to the application of good measurement techniques.

The most common analog signal measured by data acquisition devices is a voltage. Current and frequency are used to indicate the parameter value in applications where the signal is carried over long cabling in harsh environments. In virtually all applications, the signal form is ultimately converted back into a voltage signal before measurement. Refer to Chapter 5 for the measuring technique for grounded and floating signal sources.

FIGURE 17-13: Data logging of analog signals.

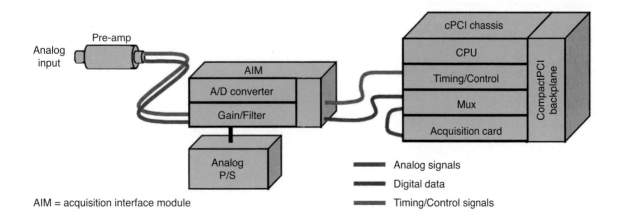

AIM = acquisition interface module

CRITICAL CONCEPTS

The need to know content from Chapter 17 is summarized in the following statements.

- An analog signal is a continuous waveform, as opposed to a discrete signal, which has two states (on and off), or a digital signal, which has a limited number of steps within a range.
- The positive input terminal of an op amp is called the non-inverting input, which means if a positive analog signal is on this input, then the output signal is positive. Conversely, a negative input yields a negative output.
- The negative input of an op amp is called the inverting input, which means if a positive analog signal is on this input, and then the output signal is negative. Conversely, a negative input yields a positive output.
- Output saturation occurs when the output signal is limited to the power supply voltages because the input signal level is a magnitude such that the closed loop gain drives the output beyond the power supply inputs.
- When an AC signal is applied at the input, the output voltage swings around a small DC voltage as opposed to zero volts. This is called the output offset.

- The analog switch is a solid state device that operates in a similar manner to a solid-state relay but with a much faster switching time.
- Voltage-to-current, current-to-voltage and current-to-pressure are common converters that are used in industrial applications where analog signals drive process and measurement devices.
- In addition to oscilloscopes, data acquisition devices measure analog signals by digitizing them for computation in a digital controller or computer.

QUESTIONS

1. What is an analog signal?
2. What are some common analog signal ranges used in motor control?
3. Describe the operation of a non-inverting and inverting op amp.
4. Describe analog output saturation and DC offset.
5. Explain the operation of an analog switch.
6. What is the range of the on-resistance and off-resistance of an analog switch?
7. Describe the various converters used in motor control.
8. Describe the operation of a data acquisition system.

CHAPTER 18

Analog Devices

GOALS AND OBJECTIVES

The primary goals for this chapter are to identify and describe the function of *analog input devices* such as transducers and *analog output devices* such valves and recorders.

After completing this chapter, you will be able to:

1. Describe the function and operation of analog input devices such as temperature, pressure, flow and position sensing devices.
2. Describe the function and operation of analog output devices such as valves and recorders.

18-1 ANALOG INPUT DEVICES

The control of industrial processes depends on accurate measurements of process variables by *analog input devices*, which are called *transducers* or *sensing devices*. *Transducers* convert a variable such as *temperature, position, flow,* or *pressure* into an analog signal that is used by the control system. Transducers have two parts: a *sensor* and a *transmitter*. The *sensor* is a device that is sensitive to changes in the process variable being measured. The *transmitter* is a device that converts small analog signals from a sensor into larger, more usable analog signals. This chapter covers the most frequently used devices in manufacturing applications. Sensors are grouped by

the process parameter measured. The four major sensor groups are *temperature, position, pressure,* and *flow*. Also, the chapter discusses bridge circuits, which are used to condition the analog input signal for the system or process controller.

18-2 TEMPERATURE SENSING DEVICES

Temperature is a physical property of a system that describes degrees of hot and cold. Stated differently, temperature is the *degree* or *intensity* of heat present in a substance or material and is expressed on any one of several comparative scales. The three scales used most often are: *Celsius, Fahrenheit,* or *Kelvin*. Temperature is the most important parameter in many industrial processes. Process temperature controllers maintain a set temperature value by executing a control action when the temperature exceeds or falls below the set point. The temperature sensing devices are classified by the electrical parameter that changes with a change in the temperature. They include:

* **Resistance as a function of temperature**—The two devices commonly used are *Resistance Temperature Detectors* (RTD) and *Thermistors*.
* **Voltage as a function of temperature**—The two devices commonly used are *Thermocouples* and *Solid State Temperature Sensors*.

Resistance Temperature Detection Sensors

The *resistance temperature detector (RTD)* is a temperature-sensing device that exhibits a change in resistance in a metal as a function of the change in the metal's temperature. Most often RTDs use *platinum, copper, nickel,* and *tungsten* to sense temperature change. The RTD has a proportional and approximately linear change in resistance for a change in the metal's temperature. The RTD is used to measure temperatures from −184 to +815 degrees Celsius. They are available in many styles to satisfy a variety of industrial control applications. Figure 18-1 illustrates three RTD styles that are mounted on the stator of a motor to monitor motor temperature.

The *change* in resistance of the RTD is *converted* to a change in *voltage* or *current* to match the input requirements of the control system. Figure 18-2 depicts an RTD in a bridge circuit with a solid-state operational amplifier (op-amp) connected to points X and Y of the bridge. Note that the RTD is represented as a *variable resistor* and labeled R_T. When the resistance of the RTD is at room temperature, the resistor R_2 is adjusted to balance the bridge, which sets the bridge output to zero volts and zero volts at the amplifier output. The bridge is balanced when R_3 and R_T are equal, and R_1 and R_2 are equal. When the temperature of the RTD changes, the RTD resistance changes, and the bridge is no longer balanced. This causes a voltage difference across the bridge at X and Y that is amplified by the op-amp. In addition to the two-terminal RTD, *three-* and *four-terminal devices* are available for more accurate measurements. The three-terminal RTD eliminates errors caused by *lead wire resistance*, and the four-terminal RTD eliminates errors caused by *lead wire resistance* and reduces errors caused by *noise*.

Thermistors Sensors

Thermistors are electronic components that exhibit a large change in resistance with a change in thermistor body temperature. The word thermistor is a contraction of the words *therm*al re*sistor*. Thermistors have either a *negative temperature coefficient* (NTC) of resistance or a *positive temperature coefficient* (PTC) of resistance. The NTC thermistors exhibit *decreasing resistance* with *increases in temperature* and *increas-*

FIGURE 18-1: Stator RTD temperature sensors.

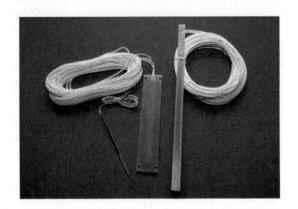

Courtesy of RTD Company.

FIGURE 18-2: Two wire RTD temperature sensor in a bridge circuit.

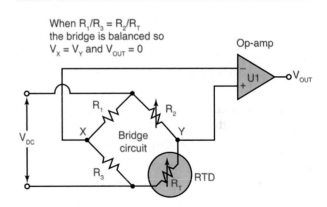

ing resistance with *decreasing temperature*. The PTC thermistors exhibit *increasing resistance* with *increases in temperature* and *decreasing resistance* with *decreasing temperature*. Figure 18-3 illustrates the *resistance-temperature* relationship of the NTC and the PTC thermistors.

The NTC thermistors use metals such as *manganese, cobalt, copper,* and *nickel*. PTC thermistors use *barium titanate*. They operate over a temperature range of −200°C to +1000°C. Thermistors are generally available in two enclosure styles: 1) Glass covered and formed into shapes such as *beads, probes* and *rods* and 2) Metal covered and formed into shapes such as *chips, disks,* and *washers*. Thermistors are used in a wide variety of applications from cooling systems to heaters. *Ease* of installation and *low cost* are the primary advantages of thermistors.

Thermocouple Sensors

Thermocouples are temperature-sensing devices that produce a millivolt level voltage when the temperature increases. In the early 1800s, *Thomas Seebeck* discovered that heating the junction where two wires of dissimilar metals are joined produces a small potential difference and generates a current flow. This discovery, which he named the *Seebeck effect,* is what are now called *thermocouples*. Figure 18-5 illustrates the operation of a single junction (iron and constantan) thermocouple. A voltmeter indicates the thermocouple output.

Note that in Figure 18-5, as the voltmeter completes the circuit, two more junctions are formed between the dissimilar metal thermocouple wire and the voltmeter leads. As a result, a small voltage is produced. This voltage is opposite to the voltage produced by the thermocouple junction, causing an error in the voltage reading. However, if these new junctions are at zero volts, then the voltmeter reads the correct voltage. These junctions are placed into a *reference block,* which holds the junctions at zero volts.

FIGURE 18-3: PTC and NTC thermistor characteristic curves.

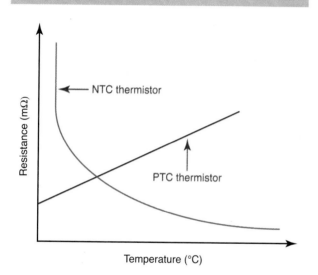

The control of a fan motor is a typical application of a NTC thermistor as shown in Figure 18-4. A rise in temperature causes the thermistor resistance to decrease and more current flows in the circuit. With sufficient current flow, the solid-state relay is energized, which turns on the fan motor. A decrease in temperature causes an increase in the resistance of the thermistor, and the relay is de-energized, shutting off the fan motor.

FIGURE 18-4: Thermistor controlled cooling fan.

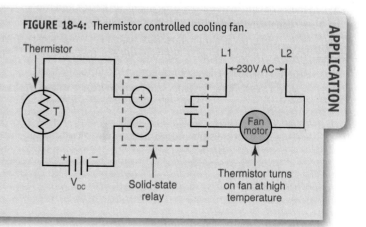

APPLICATION

FIGURE 18-5: Thermocouple operation.

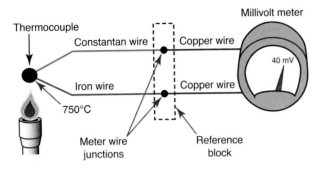

Due to the millivolt output level of the thermocouple, a transmitter is required. Thermocouple transmitters are high-gain amplifiers with analog outputs generally 0 to 10 volts or 4 to 20 mA. Thermocouple transmitters include potentiometers to adjust the lower and upper limits of the output. Connections between the transmitter and the thermocouple wires are twisted, shielded pair to ensure the integrity of the low level voltage. Thermocouple wires, listed in Figure 18-6(a), are made from various metallic materials. Note that the list includes the temperature range and letter designating

FIGURE 18-6: Thermocouple materials.

Type	Thermocouple Materials	Temperature Range (°C)
B	Platinum and 6% or 30% rhodium	0 to +1800
E	Chromel and constantan	−190 to +1000
J	Iron and constantan	−190 to +800
K	Chromel and alumel	−190 to +1370
R	Platinum or platinum and 13% rhodium	0 to +1700
S	Platinum or platinum and 10% rhodium	0 to +1765
T	Copper and constantan	−190 to +400

(a) Thermocouple materials and temperature ranges

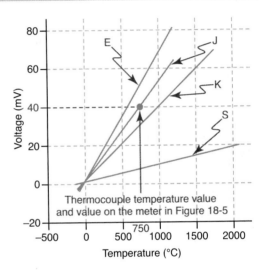

(b) Materials voltage versus temperature curves

Industrial processes use a large quantity of RTDs and thermocouples because temperature is one of the most frequently measured process parameters. Distributed Control Systems (DCS) and Programmable Logic Controllers (PLC) are the electronic control systems used most often to control the industrial process. These systems sense the process parameter with sensors, like the RTD and thermocouple, and compare the measured value with a programmed set point. The process system controls the process parameter with a program based on measured process temperatures and the set point

value. As a result of the large number of applications, DCS and PLC systems have input modules designed specifically for RTD and thermocouple sensors. The RTD modules have built in bridges, and the thermocouple modules have amplifiers designed to handle the low thermocouple voltages. In addition, the thermocouple modules supply the reference junction for the interface to the thermocouple wires. Figure 18-7(a) has a comparison for the RTD and thermocouple sensors. An image of both devices used to measure air flow and motor stator temperatures is shown in Figure 18-7(b).

(continued)

FIGURE 18-7: Comparison of RTD and thermocouple sensors and stator temperature sensor.

Feature	RTD	Thermocouple
Accuracy	More accurate	Less accurate
Temperature range	−200 to 600°C	−200 to 2000°C
Initial cost	More expensive	Less expensive
Sensitivity	Across a variety of lengths	Point sensing only
Response time	1 to 7 seconds	Less than 0.1 second
Robustness	Good	Good, subject to drift
Reference junction	Not required	Required
Long-term stability	Excellent	Good, subject to drift
Output	Resistance (0.4 ohm/ohm/°C), highly linear	Voltage (10–40 microvolts/°C), approximately linear
Electrical noise resistance	Less susceptible	More susceptible

(a) Comparison of RTD and thermocouple operational characteristics

← RTD temperature sensor
← Thermocouple temperature sensor

(b) RTD and thermocouple sensors for motor air flow and stator temperature measurements

Courtesy of RTD Company.

the type. Figure 18-6(b) shows the graph of *temperature* versus *output voltage* for four of the more common thermocouple types. Note that at zero degrees Celsius the thermocouple output voltage is equal to zero volts.

Solid State Temperature Sensors

Solid state temperature sensors are electronic devices whose voltage output is linear and proportional to a temperature scale, typically Celsius. A typical device is illustrated in Figure 18-8(a). Cellular phones usually include one or more solid state sensors to measure battery pack temperatures, and laptop computers might have four or more solid state sensors for checking temperatures in heat generating assemblies. Solid state temperature sensors cannot always replace the traditional industrial temperature sensors, such as RTDs, thermistors, and thermocouples, because their operational temperature range is typically −55 to 150°C. However, within this limited range solid state temperature sensors offer some advantages. Sensor and circuits on a single integrated circuit chip are very small and sensors can be used to determine *minimum* (minimum temperature from T_1, T_2, and T_3), *average* (average of T_1, T_2, and T_3), and *differential* ($T_1 − T_2$) temperatures. Figure 18-8(b) illustrates circuits for these three types of measurements. In addition they are used for thermocouple cold junction compensation and temperature control applications with linearity requirements of ±0.8°C, repeatability of ±0.1°C, and long term drift of ±0.1°C/month.

FIGURE 18-8: Solid state temperature sensor and typical circuits.

AD590 is a
two-lead device

(a) AD590 solid state temperature sensor

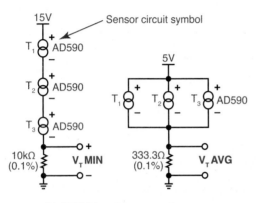

(b) AD590 in minimum and average temperature sensing circuit

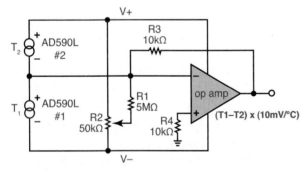

(c) AD590 in differential temperature sensing circuit

18-3 POSITION SENSING DEVICES

Position sensing devices measure *motion* and *distance* in both the *linear* and *rotary* directions. The three most frequently used position sensors include the *linear* and *rotary potentiometers* and the *linear variable differential transformer* (LVDT).

Potentiometer Position Sensors

Linear potentiometers are position sensing devices that produce a resistance output proportional to the linear *displacement* or *position*. Linear potentiometers are

FIGURE 18-9: Linear potentiometer.

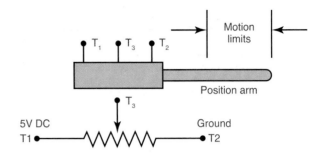

rectangular or *cylindrically* shaped *variable resistors* with *wire-wound* or *conductive plastic* resistance elements. When a voltage, for example 0 to 5V DC is applied across the resistance element, the output voltage on the wiper is a linear function of the wiper displacement. As a result, wiper position measurements are converted to a 0 to 5V DC set of values. Figure 18-9 depicts the linear potentiometer position sensor with its three leads labeled T_1, T_2 and T_3. A voltage (5V DC) is applied across T_1 and T_2 and the output voltage is from T_3 to T_2. Note the *wiper* moves with the *position arm*, so the sensor output voltage (0 to 5V DC) is a function of the position arm on the resistor. The potentiometer acts as *variable voltage divider*. For example, with a 1500-ohm linear potentiometer, the resistance between the position arm and wiper lead and either of the other two leads can vary from zero to 1500 ohms depending on the position of the position arm and wiper.

An important specification for linear potentiometers is the *motion limits* or *travel distance. Accuracy* and *linearity* are stated as a percentage of the *full scale* output. Also important are the *total resistance, resistance tolerance* and *life expectancy.* Typically linear potentiometers have a life span in the millions of strokes. Typical applications include position tracking piston strokes and the x and y locations for an indexing table.

Rotary potentiometers are position sensing devices that produce a change in the output proportional to a rotational position of the wiper shaft. Electrically they operate the same as a linear potentiometer. Figure 18-10 depicts the rotary potentiometer with leads T_1, T_2, and T_3. Two leads connect to the ends of the resistor and the third lead connects to a wiper of the pot's rotational shaft. A voltage is applied to the ends of the resistance, for example 5V DC and ground. When the wiper rotates through its range the voltage from T_3 to T_2 varies from 5V to 0V DC. For example, in the middle of the range when the wiper is at

FIGURE 18-10: Rotary potentiometer.

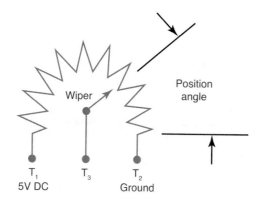

FIGURE 18-11: Linear variable differential transformer (LVDT).

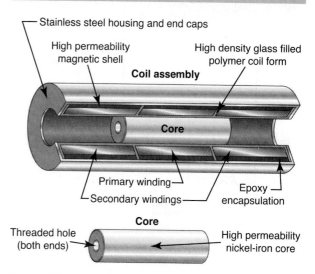

Courtesy of Macro Sensors Div. of Howard A. Schaevitz Technologies.

the halfway point in the rotation, the voltage at the wiper is 2.5V DC.

Legacy potentiometers have a reputation for poor reliability and short lifetime. However, current potentiometer technology combined with improved mechanical design has substantially improved both of those characteristics. In many cases the life of new linear and rotary potentiometers in a process are longer than the life of the unit they are monitoring.

Linear Variable Differential Transformer Position Sensors

The *linear variable differential transformer* (LVDT) is a linear position sensing device, consisting of a *transformer* with a *movable core* as shown in Figure 18-11. The transformer's internal structure consists of a stationary primary winding centered between a pair of identically wound secondary windings. The coils are wound on a one-piece hollow form of thermally stable polymer. The windings are protected against moisture and external magnetic fields, and then placed into a cylindrical stainless steel housing.

The moving element of an LVDT, called the *core,* is a tubular armature of magnetically permeable material that is free to move axially within the coil's hollow bore. The core is attached to a displacement arm, similar to the linear potentiometer. The position of this displacement arm determines the position of the core and the output of the LVDT. The LVDT output then indicates the location of the production element driving it. The core is threaded on both ends to permit attachment to the process system.

In operation, the LVDT's primary winding is energized by an AC voltage known as the *primary excitation.* The LVDT's electrical output signal is the

differential AC voltage between the two secondary windings. The value of this voltage is set by the axial position of the core within the LVDT coil. This AC output voltage is signal conditioned to a DC voltage or current compatible with the control system.

The three graphics in Figure 18-12 illustrate how the magnetic field coupled through the core changes the output of the two secondary coils as the core moves left and right. The two secondary coils are wound so the output from S_2 is 180 degrees out-of-phase with the output from S_1. Therefore, a core position in the *middle* induces equal but opposite phase AC voltages in each secondary. As a result, the outputs for the secondary coils cancel, and the sensor output is zero. This is called the *null* output point, as shown in Figure 18-12(b).

In operation, the magnetic flux is coupled by the core to the adjacent secondary windings, S_1 and S_2. At the null point between S_1 and S_2, equal flux is coupled to each secondary so the voltages, E_1 and E_2, induced in windings S_1 and S_2 respectively, are equal. As a result, the differential voltage output, $(E_1 - E_2)$, is essentially zero. As shown in Figure 18-12(a), if the core is moved closer to S_1 than to S_2, more flux is coupled to S_1 and less to S_2. Therefore, the induced voltage E_1 is increased while E_2 is decreased, resulting in the differential voltage $(E_1 - E_2)$. Conversely in Figure 18-12(c), if the core is moved closer to S_2, more flux is coupled to S_2 and less to S_1. Therefore, E_2 is increased as E_1 is decreased, resulting in the differential voltage $(E_2 - E_1)$.

FIGURE 18-12: LVDT primary and secondary coupling voltage output.

FIGURE 18-13: LVDT AC and DC output for full core movement.

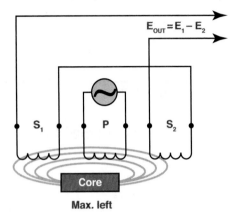

Max. left

(a) Core full left maximum coupling to secondary one

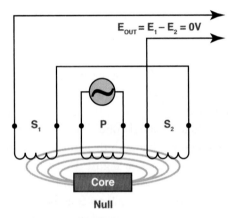

Null

(b) Core center—null position with equal secondary coupling and zero output

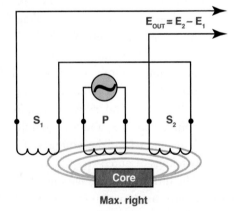

Max. right

(c) Core full right maximum coupling to secondary two

Courtesy of Macro Sensors Div. of Howard A. Schaevitz Technologies.

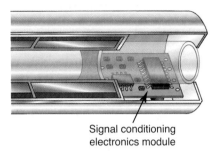

Signal conditioning
electronics module

(a) Signal conditioning inside the LVDT

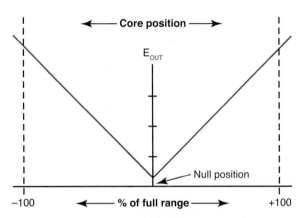

(b) AC outputs from core full left to core full right passing through the null position

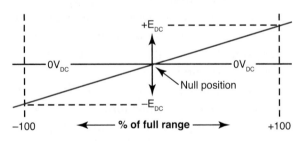

(c) DC output for full left to full right core movement after signal conditioning

Courtesy of Macro Sensors Div. of Howard A. Schaevitz Technologies.

Electronics inside the LVDT, see Figure 18-13(a), converts the AC output to DC. Figure 18-13(b) displays the AC output voltages as the core moves from *full left* to *full right* passing through the *null* point. The AC output is converted to a linear DC output, Figure 18-13(c), which is −10V DC to +10V DC for the equivalent left to right movement of the core.

LVDT linear position sensors measure movements as small as a few millionths of an inch up to several inches. Larger LVDT sensors are capable of measuring positions up to ±20 inches (±0.5 m). Because an LVDT operates on electromagnetic coupling principles in a friction-free structure, it can measure infinitesimally small changes in core position. This infinite resolution capability is limited only by the LVDT signal conditioner *noise* and the output display's *resolution*. These same factors also give an LVDT outstanding repeatability. LVDTs have a long mechanical life because the moving core slides inside the magnetic winding polymer tube. Long life is important in high reliability applications such as aircraft, nuclear installations and industrial process control and factory automation systems.

18-4   PRESSURE SENSORS

Pressure sensing devices detect the *force* exerted by one object on another. They output an analog signal *proportional* to the amount of applied pressure or to the amount of deformation caused by the applied pressure. Pressure sensing devices are classified as follows: *deflection and differential pressure sensors, piezoelectric and solid state sensors,* and *direct pressure sensors.*

Deflection Pressure Sensors

Deflection pressure sensing devices measure the movement of a mechanical element and convert it into an analog signal. Figure 18-14 illustrates a deflection pressure device that uses a diaphragm to detect changes in pressure. The diaphragm is mounted in a cylinder, with space on both sides. One space is open to the atmosphere, and the other is connected to the measured pressure source. When the pressure port is open to the atmosphere, the diaphragm has no deflection. Applied pressures above and below the atmospheric level produce a deflection proportional to the pressure. The deflection is sensed and converted to a proportional analog voltage or current output.

Bourdon Tube Sensors

Bourdon tubes, another deflection pressure sensing device, are shown in Figure 18-15. In this application an LVDT is used to convert the mechanical movement of the bourdon tube into an analog pressure value. The *bourdon tube* is a hollow metal tube fixed in place at the open end and free to move at the closed end. The

FIGURE 18-14: Pressure sensors.

(a) Pressure sensor

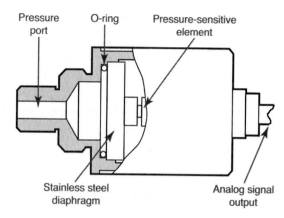

(b) Pressure sensor construction

Courtesy of Omron Corporation.

cross section of the tube is shown in Figure 18-15(a) with *no pressure* present and with *pressure* applied. The pressure forces the *oval* shaped tube geometry to become more *round* as shown in the figure. This change in tube shape causes a curved tube to *straighten* and produce a *deflection* proportional to the pressure at the free end of the tube. Note this change in the figure. The bourdon tube is mechanically connected to the core of the LVDT with a mechanical linkage system. The actual linkage is more complex than the simplified version used for illustration purposes. The deflection of the tube moves the core, thus yielding a voltage change that is proportional to the pressure. The tube is bent into various zero pressure shapes including: the *letter C,* as illustrated in Figure 18-15(b), a *spiral* or a *helix.* The greater the number of spirals the greater the deflection under pressure. *Bronze, steel,* or *stainless steel* is typically the metal used for the tube.

Differential Pressure Sensors

The *differential pressure sensing device* is a variation of the deflection pressure device in Figure 18-14. The differential pressure sensing device replaces the atmospheric pressure on one side of the diaphragm with a second system pressure. When two system pressures are applied, one to each side of the diaphragm, the diaphragm moves in the direction of the lowest pressure. Therefore, the movement of the diaphragm represents the difference in the two pressures. The diaphragm movement changes a potentiometer or LVDT element to produce a proportional electrical output.

Piezoelectric Pressure Sensors

Piezoelectric pressure sensing devices operate on the *piezoelectric effect* discovered in the late 1800s by *Jacques* and *Pierre Curie*. The piezoelectric effect occurs when applied pressure on a crystal causes crystal deformation and a voltage change proportional to the deformation. Because the internal impedance of the crystal is large and the voltage is small, an amplifier is used to generate a usable voltage. Figure 18-16 illustrates a piezoelectric pressure sensor. The diaphragm deflects when pressure is applied, and a rod transfers the movement directly to a piezoelectric crystal. The pressure on the crystal causes a small voltage to be produced, which is proportional to the applied pressure.

Solid State Pressure Sensors

The *solid-state pressure sensing device*, like the piezoelectric pressure sensor, produces an output proportional to the pressure exerted on one side of a diaphragm. A small deflection of the diaphragm causes implanted resistors to exhibit a change in resistance value. The sensor converts this change into a voltage that represents a proportional and linear pressure reading. In addition, this solid state device has temperature compensation and calibration capability to make it immune from environmental changes. The solid state pressure sensor shown in Figure 18-17 is packaged to be mounted on a printed wiring board. Note that a *stovepipe port* is present for a pressure tube connection.

FIGURE 18-15: Bourdon tube pressure sensor.

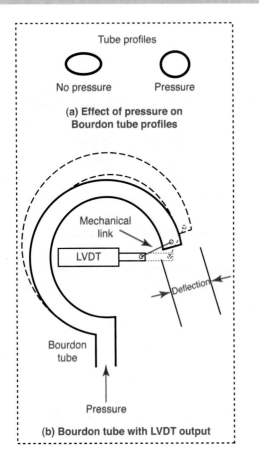

Tube profiles

No pressure   Pressure

(a) Effect of pressure on Bourdon tube profiles

Mechanical link

LVDT

Deflection

Bourdon tube

Pressure

(b) Bourdon tube with LVDT output

FIGURE 18-16: Piezoelectric pressure sensor.

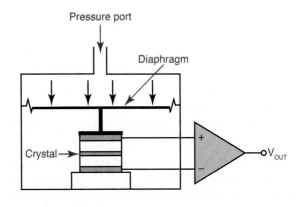

Pressure port

Diaphragm

Crystal

V_{OUT}

FIGURE 18-17: Solid state pressure sensor with port for pressure tube.

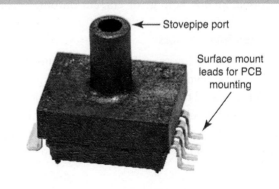

Stovepipe port

Surface mount leads for PCB mounting

System pressure measurement data are enhanced by replacing an electromechanical pressure switch with a solid-state pressure sensor. For example, in a liquid tank, the switch provides a discrete change at one liquid level. In contrast, the pressure sensor provides a continuous reading of liquid level. However, the continuous reading is an analog value and requires a different type of interface module.

Strain Gage and Load Cell Pressure Sensors

Direct pressure devices measure the amount of deformation of a body due to an applied pressure or force. Deformation is a fractional change in length of material that is either positive (*tensile or elongated change*) or negative (*compression or foreshortened change*). If this change in length is occurring in a copper wire, then the change results in a change in the *resistance* of the wire. Devices designed to detect tensile and compression change are called *strain gages*. Direct pressure sensing *strain gages* have fine wire or metallic foil arranged in a grid pattern. The grid pattern maximizes the amount of metallic wire or foil that is elongated or foreshortened when the pressure is applied. A strain gage is illustrated in Figure 18-18.

FIGURE 18-18: Strain gage wire pattern.

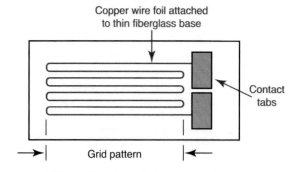

(a) Simplified view of strain gage wire layout

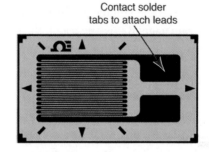

(b) Strain gage from Omega—dark area is copper and light area is thin carrier material

Reproduced with the permission of Omega Engineering, Inc., Stamford, CT, 06907 USA www.omega.com

The grid pattern of a strain gage is bonded to a thin backing, called the *carrier,* which is attached directly to the test specimen. Therefore, the pressure experienced by the test specimen is transferred directly to the strain gage, which responds with a linear change in the wire length and electrical resistance. Because the wire grid is thin copper foil, it compresses or elongates the same distance as the test specimen as shown in Figure 18-19(a). Proper strain gage operation and accurate measurements require careful attention to the manufacturer's instructions for strain gage bonding onto the test specimen. A typical mount for a strain gage is illustrated in Figure 18-19(b).

FIGURE 18-19: Strain gage mounting and operation.

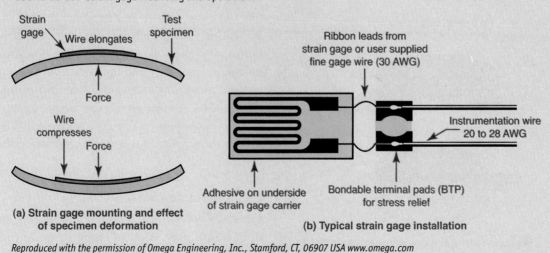

(a) Strain gage mounting and effect of specimen deformation

(b) Typical strain gage installation

Reproduced with the permission of Omega Engineering, Inc., Stamford, CT, 06907 USA www.omega.com

Strain gage resistance changes due to deformation of the test element are not large. While the change in strain gage resistance due changes in temperature are also small, they often add significant error into the strain gage measurement. The temperature change error is eliminated with a compensation strain gage placed in the bridge circuit. This second strain gage, called the *dummy gage*, is added into the bridge, Figure 18-20(a), in place of resistor R₂. The strain gage that is sensing the force is called the *active* gage. The second strain gage is oriented perpendicular to the active gage and the line of force. As a result, the dummy gage resistance is not changed by test element deformation. The dummy gage does not affect the force measurement, but changes with changes in temperature. Since both gages are changing the same amount due to temperature, the changes cancel in the bridge output. This canceling effect occurs because the two gages are in opposite legs of the bridge.

Figure 18-20 illustrates a *strain gage* in a *bridge circuit* and a *load cell*. The output voltage of the bridge is V_O, and the voltage applied to the bridge is V_{EX}. The strain gage, R_G, is one leg on the bridge, and R_T, the balance resistor, is in the opposite leg on the bridge. When there is no force applied to the strain gage, the bridge is balanced, and V_O is zero volts. The bridge is balanced with R_T so the output is zero. Balancing is necessary to compensates for resistance variations and for preloading. Preloading is the small amount of pressure normally applied to the strain gage by the process before an actual pressure measurement is made. When a force is applied to the test specimen, the strain gage resistance changes. The bridge output voltage changes proportional with the deformation of the wire in the strain gage from the pressure applied to the test element.

A common application for strain gages is a *weight measuring device* called a *load cell*. Two pancake type load cells are shown in Figure 18-20(b). Pancake load cells are available in 14 ranges from 100 lbs. through 50,000 lbs. Hold down bolt holes are provided through the outer diameter, and a threaded hole is provided through the center for pushing or pulling from either side. The sensing element incorporates bonded foil strain gages sealed for protection against industrial environments.

FIGURE 18-20: Strain gage bridge circuit and load cell application device.

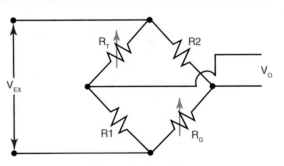

(a) Strain bridge circuit

(b) Load cells with strain gage sensors

Courtesy of RDP Electrosense.

18-5 FLOW SENSORS

Sensing the flow of *solids*, *liquids*, and *gases* is an important measurement in industrial processes. The measurement of *flow rate* indicates the volume of fluid passing a specific point in a process per some unit of time. The data is used to determine if process pumps are working and the efficiency of the pumping system. Flow rate is also used to indicate if process valves are functioning properly and tank drain cycles are working. In this section, the *paddlewheel*, the *turbine*, the *vortex*, the *electromagnetic*, the *ultrasonic* flow, and the *mass* flow sensing devices are covered. The type of flow device used is determined in part by the flow material measured.

Paddlewheel Flow Sensors

Paddlewheel sensing devices, illustrated in Figure 18-21(a), are installed inside a pipe so the flowing fluid causes its paddlewheel to rotate. The flow

Flow rate is defined as the volume of material passing a fixed point per unit of time. The material is a solid, liquid, or gas. For example, in river dredging operations, the flow rate of sand and river soil mixed with water is measured with a flow sensor. The data is used to determine the amount of solid material removed. All natural gas pipelines distributing gas to multiple regions have flow sensors to determine the amount of gas delivered to a local distributor. These two very different applications require different types of flow meters and control systems. However, in each case the flow rate of material in a pipe is equal to the velocity of the material (meters per second) times the cross-sectional area of the pipe.

causes the paddlewheel to rotate, and its revolutions are converted into an analog signal. Generally, a magnet is mounted to the paddles so that as they spin, a magnetic sensor converts rotation of spin to electronic pulses. The output is typically available as a square wave whose frequency is a function of the flow rate. A calibration table converts pulse rate to an analog voltage. Figure 18-21(b) illustrates a paddlewheel sensing device. Note the flow input port is on the left and flow exits on the opposite side. The presence of flow and the movement of the paddlewheel are visible in the front of the sensor. In addition, a data display shows the flow rate, flow total, and *liquid temperature*. The paddlewheel is a low-cost device and is used in applications where a high degree of accuracy is not required.

Turbine Flow Sensors

Turbine sensing devices are installed in a pipe and operate on the principle that fluid moving through a pipe past the vanes of a turbine causes the turbine blades to rotate. Figure 18-22(a) shows a turbine device installed in a pipe. The operation is similar to the paddlewheel,

FIGURE 18-21: Paddle wheel flow sensors.

(a) Paddle wheel sensor operation

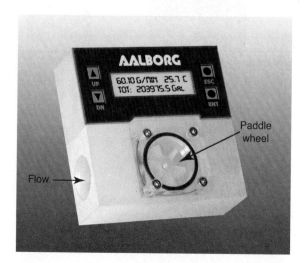

(b) Paddle wheel sensor with paddle and flow indicated

Courtesy of AALBORG Instruments & Controls, Inc.

FIGURE 18-22: Turbine flow sensors.

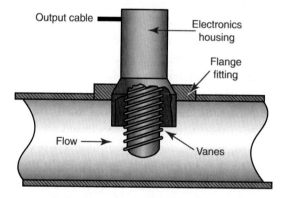

(a) Turbine sensor operation

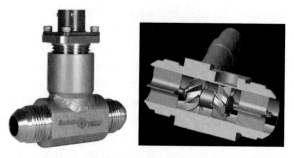

(b) Turbine flow sensors

Courtesy of Flow Dynamics, Inc.

where the *rate of spin* determines the *rate of flow*. High-quality jewel bearings and nickel-tungsten carbine turbine shaft are used for long life and low friction. The flange fitting ensures correct depth placement of the turbine. The rotation of the rotor is typically detected by a *Hall-effect sensor* and converted to square wave voltage pulses. The pulses are proportional to the velocity of the flow and accurate to +/− 0.1 percent of the full scale reading. Turbines have greater accuracy than the paddlewheel flow sensors. Figure 18-22(b) shows a dual turbine flow device as a cut-away solid model and as an operational unit. The flow is straightened by the fixed vanes, and then spins the first turbine in a clockwise direction. The fluid spins the second turbine in a counter-clockwise direction with the fluid hitting the turbine vane at ninety degrees because of the first turbine. As a result, fluid flow energy is transferred to the second turbine more efficiently. This allows measurement of lower flows and better repeatability. An operational sensor is also pictured in the figure. Turbine flow meters are used to determine diesel engine flow consumption and the flow of fluid in hydraulic actuators in earth-moving equipment. They are also used to measure gasoline consumption, and coolant and transmission fluid flows in those machines.

Vortex Flow Sensors

The *vortex flow sensing device* includes a non-streamlined object (a *bluff body*) that is placed in the fluid flow. When fluid flow strikes the bluff body, a series of vortices (whirlpools or eddies) are produced. Figure 18-23(a) illustrates the vortices around the bluff body in the fluid flow. Note that the bluff body is shown as a *trapezoid*, but other shapes where the width is a large fraction of the pipe diameter work as well. These vortices occur at the instance where *alternating low-pressure zones* are generated in the downstream flow. The alternating vortices are spaced at equal distances. In the devices, the sensor is either a *piezoelectric-* or *capacitance*-type. The sensor detects the pressure oscillation around the bluff body and produces a low voltage output signal that has the same frequency as the vortex oscillations. The oscillation frequency is *proportional* to the flow rate. Signal conditioning converts the oscillation output into an analog output voltage that indicates the flow rate. Figure 18-23(b) shows two vortex flow sensors of different size. One has a flange mount the other is designed to be inserted into a pipe at a pipe joint. The bluff body is visible in the right image.

Electromagnetic Flow Sensors

The *electromagnetic flow sensor*, Figure 18-24, uses Faraday's principle of magnetic conduction. Faraday's law states that *a moving conductor (the liquid) has a current induced in it that is directly proportional to the strength of the magnetic field and the velocity of the moving conductor.* If the strength of the magnetic field is *constant*, then the magnitude of the induced *current* and resulting *voltage drop* is *proportional* to the *velocity* of the moving conductor. These sensors provide reliable flow measurements in most *conductive fluids*—some examples include: *water, sewage, wastewater, clarified water, replenishment at sea (RAS) systems, chemicals, heavy sludge, paper and pulp stock slurries, mining slurries, acids,* and *cooling tower water.* This sensor is especially well suited for industrial appli-

FIGURE 18-23: Vortex flow sensors.

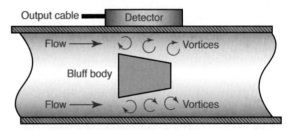

(a) Vortex sensor operation

(b) Vortex flow sensors

Courtesy of AALBORG Instruments & Controls, Inc.

cations that require *non-intrusive* flow measurements. In addition to a conductive liquid, another requirement for adoption is an adequate length of straight pipe where the sensor is installed. Typically, a minimum of 15 pipe diameters of straight pipe is required up stream from the sensor to develop a symmetrical flow profile.

Figure 18-24(a) illustrates the electromagnetic flow sensor installation. The flow sensor has a small insertion depth so minimal pressure drop occurs. Sensor electrodes are at twelve percent of the pipe diameter, which is the nominal velocity point when symmetrical flow profiles are present. The sensor in the figure has been enlarged to show construction details, so it extends deeper than normal into the pipe.

The sensor applies *alternating polarity* square wave pulses, Figure 18-24(b), to the electromagnet coil in Figure 18-24(a). *Voltage* measurements are made at the *electrodes* with the *electromagnet off,* to measure ambient background noise, and then with the *electromagnet on* in both polarities. The difference in the electromagnet on and electromagnet off voltage measurements is proportional to flow. Once fluid velocity is measured, then various volumetric flow measurements are obtained from pipe diameter data.

Figure 18-25 shows an installation of the electromagnetic flow sensor in a main water pipe. Numerous options are available for collecting data both at the site of the measurement or at remote monitoring locations. The system typically provides measurement accuracy of ± one percent of full scale in pipe diameters of 4 to 120 inches (102 to 3048 mm).

Ultrasonic Flow Sensors

The operation of *ultrasonic flow sensing devices* is based on measuring the change that a liquid medium causes

FIGURE 18-24: Electromagnetic flow sensors.

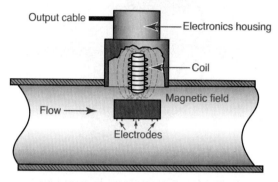

(a) Sensor operation with coil and electrodes shown

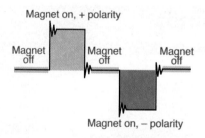

(b) Sensor pulsed electromagnetic field

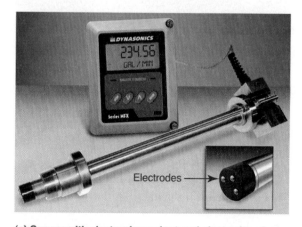

(c) Sensor with electronic readout and electrodes shown

Courtesy of Dynasonics, Division of Racine Federated, Inc.

FIGURE 18-25: Electromagnetic flow sensor in municipal clean water system.

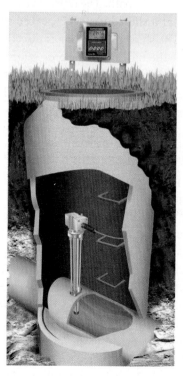

Courtesy of Dynasonics, Division of Racine Federated, Inc.

on ultra high frequency sound. Three types of ultrasonic flow sensors draw upon this technology: *doppler* sound type, *transit time* sound type, and *hybrid,* a combination of doppler and transit-time. The doppler type uses a measured *change in the frequency* of the sound, and the transit time uses a measurement of the *change in the speed* of the sound waves. Both of these techniques are based on work by *Christian Johann Doppler* in the mid 1800s. He observed that a sound wave transmitted into a liquid medium had its reflected signal modified by the velocity and direction of the fluid flow. If a fluid is moving towards a sensor, the frequency of the returning signal *increases,* and as fluid moves away from a sensor, the frequency of the returning signal *decreases.* The frequency *difference,* the reflected frequency minus the originating frequency, is used to calculate the fluid flow rate. Sensors used today apply two different ultrasonic techniques, called *doppler* and *transit time.* The sensors used in these applications have both an ultrasonic *generator* and *receiver* built into the same device. The operation of the doppler type operation is illustrated in Figure 18-26(a).

Doppler mode operation starts with the flow meter *transmitting* an ultrasonic sound from its transmitting transducer into the flowing liquid. The sound is reflected by sonic reflectors, gas bubbles or particulate, suspended within the liquid back to a *receiving* transducer. The sonic reflectors move in the liquid through the sound transmission path. The reflected sound comes to the receiver at a shifted frequency, called the *Doppler frequency.* The shift in frequency is directly related to the speed of the moving particle or bubble. This frequency data is *signal conditioned* into electrical signal levels for use in industrial process control. A typical doppler type sensor is shown in Figure 18-26(b).

Several precautions for doppler ultrasonic flow sensors include:

- The liquid flowing within the pipe must contain 100 ppm of useful sonic suspended reflectors. Useful reflectors are particles greater than 35 microns in size or a volume of particles greater than 100 microns that is 25% of the overall particle volume. The suspended *micron reflectors* in the liquid under the sensors are illustrated in Figure 18-26(a).
- The reflecting material must travel at the same velocity as the fluid for good accuracy.
- A significant portion of the ultrasound energy generated by the transducer must reach the sonic reflectors. As a result, externally mounted sensors,

FIGURE 18-26: Ultrasonic doppler and transit time flow sensors.

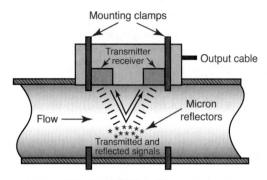

(a) Doppler ultrasonic flow sensor operation

(b) Doppler ultrasonic flow sensor on pipe

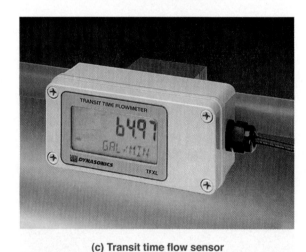

(c) Transit time flow sensor

Courtesy of Dynasonics, Division of Racine Federated, Inc.

like in Figure 18-26(b), must be capable of passing through the pipe material.
- The pipe must be completely filled with liquid when measurements are made.

Transit time mode operation starts by transmitting and receiving a frequency modulated burst of sound energy between two transducers. The burst is first transmitted in the direction of fluid flow and then against fluid flow. Sound energy in a moving liquid is carried faster when it travels in the direction of fluid flow (downstream) as compared to the sound speed against the direction of fluid flow (upstream). The difference between the two travel times is used in the sensor electronics to calculate the fluid flow rate. A typical transit time sensor is shown in Figure 18-26(c).

The *hybrid ultrasonic flow meters* utilize both *Doppler* and *transit time* sound techniques and have the ability to automatically select the correct technology to calculate the flow rate. These hybrid flow meters measure liquid flow by using both Doppler and transit time ultrasonic hardware. This automatic selection process for the measurement type, provides the most accurate measurement for the conditions present in the application. Typically measurement accuracy is one percent of flow rate with a response time of less than one second. Flow speeds from 0.15 to 30 feet per second (0.05 to 9 meters per second) are measured and converted into an analog output signal.

Mass Flow Sensors

Mass flow sensors directly measure the flow rate of fluids and are especially useful to measure gas flow rates. With a margin of error of less than 0.1 percent, they are one of the most accurate flow measuring sensors. The two most frequently used types of mass flow sensors are the *thermal* mass flow sensor and the *Coriolis* mass flow sensor.

The *thermal mass flow* sensor operates independently of *density, pressure,* and *viscosity.* There are three implementations of the thermal mass flow sensor: *constant temperature thermal mass flowmeters, constant power thermal mass flowmeters,* and *calorimetric or energy balance thermal mass flowmeters.*

Constant temperature—This type has three elements: two *RTD temperature sensors* and a *heater.* One RTD sensor is in the liquid or gas to measure the operational temperature of the fluid and establish the base temperature. The heater and the second RTD sensor are combined into a single unit and placed slightly down stream from the first RTD sensor. The temperature of the second RTD is heated to a constant temperature by the heater. As the passing fluid cools the second RTD, the flow controller increases the heater current to keep the RTD at a constant temperature. The current required by the

heater is proportional to the flow rate of the liquid through the sensor.

Constant power—This type has the same number of elements and element configuration as the constant temperature. However, the heater has a constant current applied. Therefore the second RTD's temperature reading drops as the flow rate increases and removes heat from that unit. The first RTD again acts as base line reference temperature for the system. The flow rate is proportional to the change in temperature of the second RTD.

Calorimetric—The thermal mass flow sensor, Figure 18-27(a) uses a heated element located between two RTD sensors. The upstream RTD establishes the base line fluid temperature. The fluid passing the heater absorbs heat based on the mass density and flow rate of the fluid. The downstream RTD measures the increase in the fluid temperature, and from that temperature change and the type of fluid, the flow rate is determined by the controller. The tem-

FIGURE 18-27: Mass flow sensors.

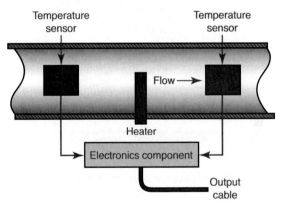

(a) Calorimetric type mass flow sensor operation

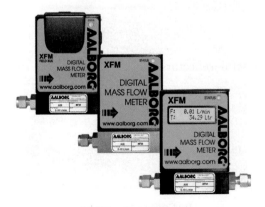

(b) Mass flow sensors

Courtesy of AALBORG Instruments & Controls, Inc.

perature difference between the sensors is directly proportional to the mass flow rate. Figure 18-27(b) illustrates three styles of thermal mass flow sensors.

The *Coriolis flow sensor* uses a vibrating U-shaped tube to measure fluid flow rate based on an inertial force phenomenon. This phenomenon, called the *Coriolis effect,* was identified by *Gustave-Gaspard Coriolis* in the mid-1800s. The fluid to be measured runs through a U-shaped tube that is vibrated with an angular harmonic oscillation, as shown in Figure 18-28(a). The fluid flowing through the tube causes the tube to deform in a twist, and the amount of twist is directly proportional to the fluid flow. Sensors detect the amount of twist and a signal conditioner produces a proportional analog output for the fluid flow rate. The Coriolis mass flow sensor does not require temperature compensation, which is an advantage over the thermal mass flow sensor. Figure 18-28(b) shows a Coriolis sensor.

FIGURE 18-28: Coriolis flow sensors.

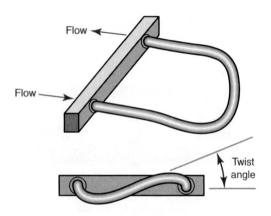

(a) Coriolis mass flow sensor vibrating tube

(b) Coriolis flow sensors

Courtesy of Krohne, Inc.

18-6 ANALOG OUTPUT DEVICES

The control of industrial processes depends on accurate and responsive *analog output devices* such as *valves* and *recorders*. Valves are solenoid controlled (two positions—open or closed) or analog controlled (open positions from zero percent to 100 percent). Both analog controlled and solenoid controlled valves need to be understood by electrical workers. Solenoid valves are generally limited to small-diameter pipes and are not applicable for direct control of fluid through large-diameter pipes. However, the solenoid valve is used as a *pilot* or *lead* valve to actuate a larger valve, which controls large diameter pipe flow.

Discrete Control Valves

Discrete control valves generally fall into two categories: *solenoid valves* and *spool valves*. An example of each type is illustrated in Figure 18-29. A *solenoid control valve* is an electromechanical device that is used to control the flow of air or fluids such as water, inert gas, light oil and refrigerants. Solenoid valves are the simplest output device and are used extensively in industrial control systems.

Solenoid valves are generally two position, energized and de-energized. The control is either two-way or three-way depending on the application requirements. A study of Figure 18-29(a) indicates that a de-energized valve has a spring to force the solenoid core down to close the valve. When the coil is energized a magnetic field draws the core up by overcoming the spring force, which allows flow through the valve body. The magnetic field overcomes the opposing spring force. The most common fluid controlled by this valve type is water or air in a pneumatic cylinder. Three-way valves, with input, output, and exhaust ports, are often used for pneumatic cylinder control. One condition allows compressed air to flow to the cylinder. The other state allows air in the cylinder to flow out through the exhaust port when the cylinder piston retracts. Figure 18-30(a) illustrates the flow symbols for two- and three-way solenoid valves. Two options for two-way are shown and one option for three-way. The locations of input (In), output (Out), and exhaust (Exh) ports change depending on the model solenoid selected.

Valve Symbols

Valve symbols and port designations for two-way and three-way solenoid valves are shown in Figure 18-30(a). Figure 18-30(b) illustrates valve symbols for spool

FIGURE 18-29: Solenoid control valves.

(a) Cut-away view of a solenoid valve

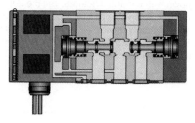

(b) Operational two-way solenoid valve

(c) Cut-away spool valve

(d) Operational spool valve

valves with two- and three-way valves with two and three ports. The individual components of the spool valve symbol are as follows:

Large blocks—represent the number of valve positions.

Small block with the slash through it—represents the solenoid and is attached to the large block that indicates the flow direction when the solenoid is energized.

The symbol $\wedge$—represents the spring and is attached to the large block that indicates the flow direction when the solenoid is de-energized.

Letters A, B, P, and T—indicate the ports of the valve.

The Tee inside the large blocks—indicates that the port is closed.

Arrows—illustrate the direction of the flow in and out of the ports.

Proportional Control Valves

Proportional valves are analog controlled devices, which adjust the flow over a range of zero to 100 percent. Valves are configured with a variety of closing mechanisms that include: *gate valves, butterfly valves, ball valves,* and *globe valves.* The globe valve is used for discussion on process valves in this section.

The rate of flow through the valve is proportional to an input analog signal. The analog input is typically a ramp signal that transitions the valve opening between two values. The three valve types are widely used for fluid flow control in every conceivable industrial application. In addition, valves are used by municipal utilities for water and waste water movement and in the distribution of fluids such as gasoline, oil, and natural gas between regions of the country.

Figure 18-31(a) illustrates a cutaway view of a proportional control valve with a detailed view of the proportional control spring-loaded diaphragm in Figure 18-31(b). Control pressure enters the port and

Current-to-pressure converter—A current-to-pressure converter allows the pneumatic assisted control valves to operate over the range of full open to full closed. The converter is either part of the valve assembly or mounted near the valve assembly and is known as an *I/P converter*. The converter changes a current signal (I) to a pressure signal (P). Input current signal generally varies over a range of 4 to 20 mA, and the output pressure from 3 to 15 pounds per square inch (psi). Therefore, when the current is at 4mA, the pressure is at 3psi and with a 20ma input, the output is at 15psi. With those defined limits, the proportional relationship between current and pressure is expressed as follows: (I − 4) / 16 = (P − 3) / 12, where I is in mA and P is in psi.

TECH NOTES

FIGURE 18-30: Valve symbols.

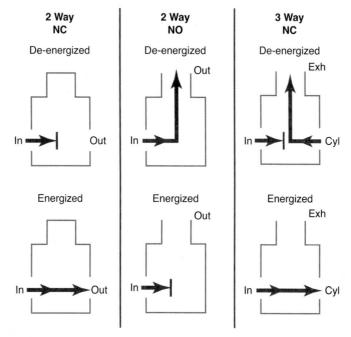

(a) Solenoid valve symbols

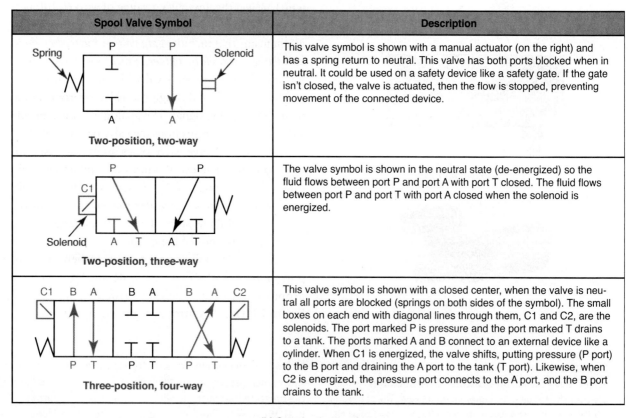

Spool Valve Symbol	Description
Two-position, two-way	This valve symbol is shown with a manual actuator (on the right) and has a spring return to neutral. This valve has both ports blocked when in neutral. It could be used on a safety device like a safety gate. If the gate isn't closed, the valve is actuated, then the flow is stopped, preventing movement of the connected device.
Two-position, three-way	The valve symbol is shown in the neutral state (de-energized) so the fluid flows between port P and port A with port T closed. The fluid flows between port P and port T with port A closed when the solenoid is energized.
Three-position, four-way	This valve symbol is shown with a closed center, when the valve is neutral all ports are blocked (springs on both sides of the symbol). The small boxes on each end with diagonal lines through them, C1 and C2, are the solenoids. The port marked P is pressure and the port marked T drains to a tank. The ports marked A and B connect to an external device like a cylinder. When C1 is energized, the valve shifts, putting pressure (P port) to the B port and draining the A port to the tank (T port). Likewise, when C2 is energized, the pressure port connects to the A port, and the B port drains to the tank.

(b) Spool valve symbols

applies a force on the diaphragm inside the valve head. As the pressure overcomes the compression springs, the valve stem moves down. The downward movement closes the valve by moving the *globe valve plug* toward the *valve seat*. For all applications except steam or very hot liquid, the flow is as indicated in Figure 18-31(a). The pressure on the bottom of the plug makes opening the valve easier and protects the packing from long period of pressure. The direction is reversed for heated flows so that plug and stem remain heated after closing and do not contract due to cooling.

The valve in Figure 18-31 uses air pressure to control the opening on the valve from 0 to 100 percent. The control signal is commonly a 4 to 20 mA analog output from a process control system. The variable current signal is passed through an I/P converter (current to pressure converter) so the signal applied to the control valve is a 3 to 15 psi pressure. The valve is calibrate for full open at 3 psi and full closed at 15 psi. These valves are mainly used to control the flow of liquid through large-diameter pipes and in explosive atmosphere applications such as chemical processing.

Motor Driven Process Valves

The second *prime mover* for a proportional valve is an *electric motor*. Motors are used to control the opening and closing of valves and are geared for very fine control of the flow value. In general, control valve *response time* is *slower* with motors than with pneumatic actuators. However, all types of valves have options to add motor driven actuators in place of the pneumatically controlled valve. For slow transition systems where response time is not an issue, the use of a motor driven value eliminates the need for pneumatics in the control loop. Typical applications include a mixing valve to control water temperature and damper positioning in a heating or air conditioning system. Figure 18-32

FIGURE 18-31: Pneumatic proportional control valve.

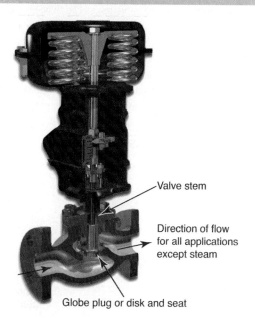

Valve stem

Direction of flow for all applications except steam

Globe plug or disk and seat

(a) Cut away of pneumatic actuated proportional control valve

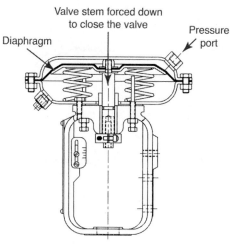

Valve stem forced down to close the valve

Diaphragm

Pressure port

(b) Pneumatic actuated spring loaded diaphragm

Courtesy of Dresser, Inc.

FIGURE 18-32: Motor driven mixing valve.

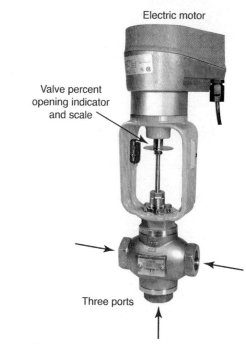

Electric motor

Valve percent opening indicator and scale

Three ports

Courtesy of Baumann, Inc.

A *mixing* and *diverting* valve application with motor-driven three-way valves is shown in Figure 18-33. Figure 18-33(a) shows a cut away of the mixing valve with the valve plug and three ports identified. When the plug is at the full up position, 100 percent flow moves between port C and L. When the plug is at the full down position, 100 percent flow moves between port C and U. If the plug is at the midpoint then flow moves in or out of all three ports. For example, if C is the input then L and U each pass 50 percent of the input.

Figure 18-33(b) shows a *heat exchanger* application. Process systems in thousands of industries use heat exchangers to control the temperature of a process liquid. The heat exchanger illustrated in this figure has concentric pipes. The inside pipe carries the process liquid, and the pipe surrounding the inside pipe carries the heating medium. Therefore, the heated medium surrounds the pipe passing the process fluid. A study of Figure 18-33(b) indicates that the *diverting* valve (a name often given mixing valves in this application) controls the flow of the purified process water. The heat exchanger is used to heat the process water with heated water from a boiler.

In many applications *steam* is used as the heating medium.

A study of the diverting valve indicates that *100 percent* of the process water goes through the heat exchanger if the valve plug is in the *full up* position. Conversely, a plug position at *full down* diverts all the process water through the valve and *0 percent* passes through the heat exchanger. With one input and two outputs the valve diverts the flow in either one direction or the other.

A study of the mixing valve indicates that *100 percent* of the heating water goes through the heat exchanger if the valve plug is in the *full up* position. Conversely, as the valve plug moves up, some of the heating water passes through the heat exchanger and the balance bypasses the heat exchanger and flows directly to the return. With two inputs and one output the valve mixes the flow. This is an ideal application for motor driven valves because a heat exchanger does not require the fast response time of a pneumatic control valve. The control system sets the two valve positions through their respective electric drive motors to produce purified process water that is at the correct temperature for the next stage in the production process.

FIGURE 18-33: Mixing and diverting valve application.

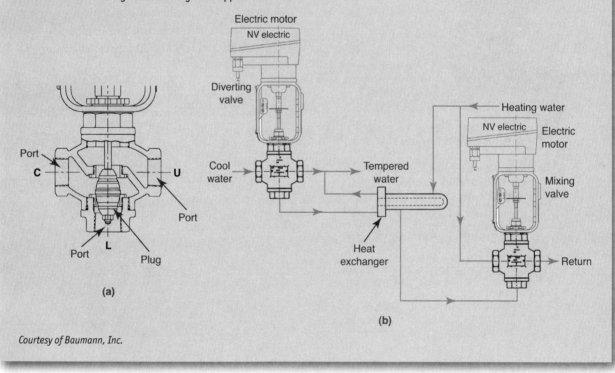

(a)

(b)

Courtesy of Baumann, Inc.

illustrates a mixing valve with an electric motor actuator and three ports. The use of the ports is application specific, any one can be an input or an output. For mixing applications, two ports are inputs, and the blend of the inputs exits at the third port. In heat exchanger applications, one port is the input and two are outputs.

Recorders

Recorders are analog output devices that *document* industrial and commercial process *data* for a variety of applications. There are two general classifications of recorders—*classic* (strip chart and circular chart) and *paperless*. The *classic* provides a *paper copy* of the data, whereas the *paperless* provides an *electronic copy* of the data.

Figure 18-34(a) illustrates a circular chart recorder, and Figure 18-34(c) shows a linear strip chart recorder. The paper speed of the strip chart recorder is adjustable, typically from 0.02 to 200 inches per hour. The circular chart recorder is typically a ten inch paper disc and available with one or multiple recording pens. Each pen has the capability to monitor different process outputs. Popular models of paper process data recorders have numerous electronic features included. Figure 18-34(b) shows a digital display on the front cover of a paper circular recorder. These recorders are well suited to record any process parameter presented as a voltage/current signal.

Figure 18-35 illustrates a paperless recorder with a multicolored display. The paperless recorders have replaced classic chart recorders in many applications. Typical input options and capability of the paperless systems are listed in the figure. Note the ability to establish *mathematical* and *logical relationships* with multiple inputs, the *alarm options, relay outputs,* and *network capability.* Also, data are stored on small *Secure Digital (SD) memory cards* for easy transfer and analysis.

The display modes, illustrated in Figure 18-36, are selectable from a variety of formats such as *vertical* and *horizontal line charts* and *digital* readouts. In addition, they have the capability to communicate the recorded data to other systems via hardwire or on a network. Future process systems are more likely to include paperless recorders because of the increased functionality.

FIGURE 18-34: Process data paper recorders.

(a) Circular paper data recorders

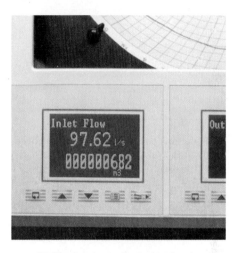

(b) Electronic readouts on circular paper data recorders

(c) Strip chart paper recorders with electronic data displays

Courtesy of ABB, Inc.

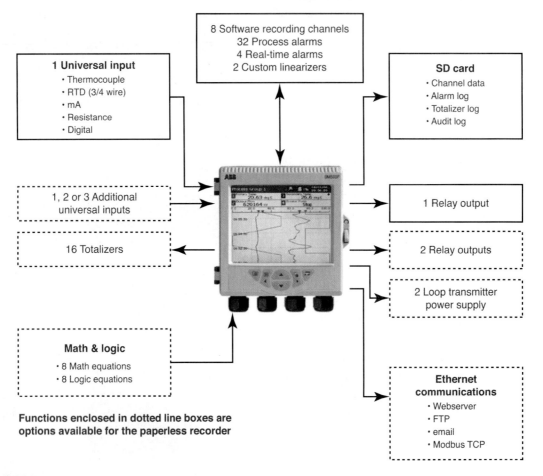

Courtesy of ABB, Inc.

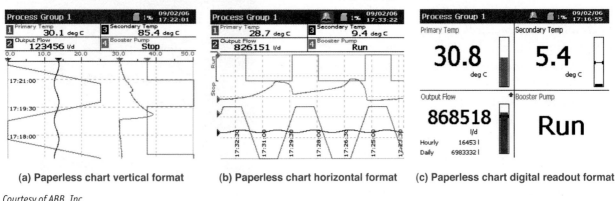

(a) Paperless chart vertical format　　(b) Paperless chart horizontal format　　(c) Paperless chart digital readout format

Courtesy of ABB, Inc.

18-7 TROUBLESHOOTING ANALOG DEVICES

Before you start troubleshooting, remember that analog devices from different manufacturers have different operating characteristics, so the first requirement is to know how the devices in the system operate. The following are some general points, which an electrical worker should investigate first.

- Verify that the device is properly installed.
- Verify that no foreign objects are impeding the operation of the device.
- Verify that the device has power in the specified range. Checking other operating equipment connected to the same power lines is a good method for testing for power.
- Consult the device manufacturer's manual for troubleshooting tips.

Troubleshooting Temperature Sensing Devices

With the resistive temperature detectors (RTDs) and thermistors, an *ohmmeter check* is a simple way to validate that the device is operational, but the device must be removed or isolated from the circuitry. However, before isolating the device, make sure the leads are intact and not broken. With the ohmmeter connected to the device, heat the device and verify that the resistance changes. With an RTD, the resistance increases only a few ohms. The increase in resistance is much greater for the thermistor than the RTD. Whereas with a negative temperature coefficient thermistor, the resistance decreases. The manufacturer's data sheet, which specifies the device's temperature characteristics, is an important reference. When a temperature sensor is subjected to a temperature change, and its resistance doesn't change, it is defective and should be replaced.

With thermocouples, an accurate millivoltmeter is needed to measure the thermocouple output as a function of temperature. Most thermocouple manufacturers provide thermocouple testers, including a millivoltmeter, power supply and reference junction compensation. Simply connect the thermocouple to the tester and select the temperature range, and the tester provides the measurement.

Troubleshooting Strain Gages

Strain gages act like resistive sensing devices in a bridge circuit. If the input voltage to the bridge is correct, then a physical load should be applied to validate the operation of the device. The manufacturer's data sheet specifies the range of loads for the device. Choose a value in the midrange and measure the output voltage, which is expressed as: *Output Voltage = Output maximum voltage × test load / maximum load*

TECH NOTES

Troubleshooting Example—A strain gage operates up to a maximum pressure of 600 pounds, and its output is 3mv per volt of input voltage, which is set at 8V. To validate the operation, choose the test load at 300 pounds, and measure the output voltage.

Recalling: Output Voltage = Max output voltage × test load / maximum load

Substituting: Output voltage = (3mv/V × 8V) × 300lb / 600lb

Output Voltage = 12mv

Troubleshooting Control Valves

When validating the operation of a control valve, disconnect the control signal from the controller, and turn off the fluid flow to prevent unwanted flow during troubleshooting. Cycle the valve between 0 and 100 percent with the appropriate input source to verify the full limits of the valve operation. For proportional control valves, review Figure 18-37. Study the list of observed symptoms for failed or faulty valves and possible reasons for the symptom to be investigated.

FIGURE 18-37: Positional control valve troubleshooting guide.

Observed Symptom	Possible Reason for Failure
Valve has no response	Valve stem will not move due to corrosion; valve gate will not move due to corrosion; improper pressure for the input signal; pressure connector may be corroded; pilot pressure is out of specification; diaphragm is ruptured or has a hole; filter is contaminated
Valve operates erratically	Input signal is unstable; filter is contaminated; orifice is contaminated; valve stem sticks due to corrosion; valve sticks due to corrosion; process pressures are too high

CRITICAL CONCEPTS

The need to know content from Chapter 18 is summarized in the following statements.

- *Transducer* is a device that receives one type of energy and converts it to another type of energy and generally includes a sensor and a transmitter. *Sensor* is a device that is sensitive to energy such as heat, pressure, motion and light. *Transmitter* is a device that converts small signals into larger, more usable signals.
- A resistance temperature detector (RTD) is temperature-sensing device that detects a change in resistance in a metal as a function of temperature.
- Thermistors are electronic components that exhibit a large change in resistance with a change in its body temperature.
- Thermocouples are temperature-sensing devices that produce a small voltage in the millivolt range as a function of temperature.
- Linear potentiometers produce a resistance output proportional to the displacement or position, and rotary potentiometers produce a resistance output proportional to a rotational position.
- The linear variable differential transformer (LVDT) is a position sensing device, consisting of a transformer with a movable core attached to the item whose position is to be measured.
- The bourdon tube is a deformed hollow metal tube opened at one end and sealed at the other, generally in the shape of the letter C, which straighten under pressure, thus providing a displacement, which is proportional to the pressure.
- In piezoelectric pressure sensing devices, pressure is applied to a crystal; the crystal deforms and produces a small voltage, which is proportional to the deformation or pressure.
- When pressure is applied to the strain gage, it responds with a linear change in electrical resistance, which is proportional to the applied pressure.
- In paddlewheel flow sensing devices, the flow causes the paddlewheel to rotate and its revolutions are proportional to the flow rate. The turbine flow sensing device, whose operation is similar to the paddlewheel, where the rate of spin is measured to calculate the flow rate.

- The vortex flow sensing devices includes a non-streamlined object placed in the fluid flow, which creates vortices in a downstream flow and the difference in vortices pressures is used in the calculation of flow rate.
- Electromagnetic flow sensing devices measure the electrical charges in flowing fluid, which are proportional to the fluid velocity.
- Ultrasonic flow sensing devices calculate the fluid flow rate based on the fact that the frequency difference between reflected frequency and the originating frequency produced by the sensor.
- A solenoid control valve is an electromechanical device that is used to control the flow of air or fluids such as water, inert gas, light oil and refrigerants.
- Proportional valves are analog controlled devices, which adjust the flow over the range of zero percent to 100 percent.

QUESTIONS

1. Explain the relationships between sensors, transmitters and transducers.
2. Explain the operation and construction of a thermocouple.
3. Under what conditions would you choose a positive temperature coefficient thermistor over a negative temperature coefficient thermistor?
4. Explain the operation of a resistive temperature detector.
5. Explain the operation of the bourdon tube pressure sensing device.
6. Describe the construction of a strain gage.
7. What do paddlewheel flow and turbine flow sensing devices have in common?
8. Explain the operation of a vortex flow sensing device.
9. On what principle to electromagnetic flow sensing devices operate?
10. Describe the operation of a solenoid valve.
11. What function does the solenoid valve symbol serve?
12. Explain the operation of a proportional control valve.

CHAPTER 19

Solid State

GOALS AND OBJECTIVES

The primary goals for this chapter are to detail *techniques for working with solid state devices* and to address advanced *techniques for troubleshooting solid state devices and controls*.

After completing this chapter, you will be able to:

1. Describe methods of connecting solid state devices to input and output modules.
2. Describe the best practices for handling solid state devices.
3. Describe troubleshooting of smart solid state devices and controls.

19-1 WORKING WITH SOLID STATE DEVICES AND CONTROLS

Solid state components are the basic *building blocks* of commercial and industrial electronic equipment. The electrical worker generally comes in contact with solid state devices or controls on a daily basis. This chapter addresses the *signal* and *grounding* requirements for connecting solid state devices to a variety of input and output modules. In addition, best practices for handling solid state devices are presented.

Connecting Solid State Devices

The electrical worker is expected to connect solid state devices to a variety of input and output module configurations with numerous input and output field devices that have a variety of voltages and currents present. The *DC modules* often have a *current sinking* or *sourcing* feature while *AC modules* are both *current sourcing* and *sinking*. The current sinking and sourcing concept discussed in Chapter 10 is expanded here with descriptions of the interfaces circuits used. Figure 19-1 illustrates and describes current sinking and current sourcing for a sensor module. The *sourcing sensor* normally uses a *PNP* output transistor for the output circuit, and an NPN is used for a *sinking sensor*. In addition, note how the field device power supply is connected to provide the correct current flow for the sinking and sourcing input modules in the figure.

There are many different types of *input circuits* used in the input modules of controllers and motor drives. Four of the most common input circuits, *AC/DC*, *DC current sinking*, *DC current sourcing*, and *transistor transistor logic* (TTL), are illustrated and described in Figures 19-1 and 19-2. Figure 19-1(a) and (b) show the configuration of DC input current sinking and sourcing, respectively. Figure 19-2(a) addresses the AC/DC input module and Figure 19-2(b)

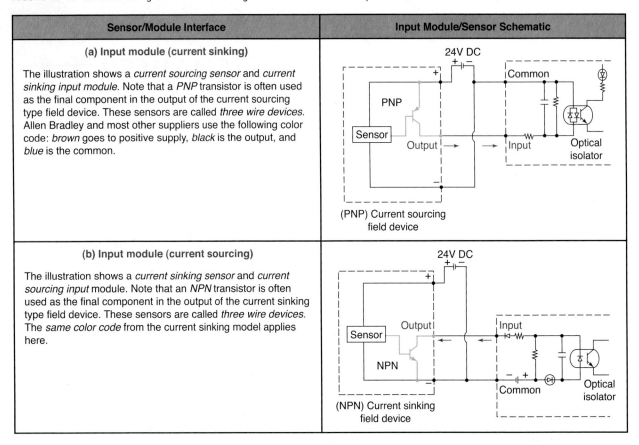

Sensor/Module Interface	Input Module/Sensor Schematic
(a) Input module (current sinking) The illustration shows a *current sourcing sensor* and *current sinking input module*. Note that a *PNP* transistor is often used as the final component in the output of the current sourcing type field device. These sensors are called *three wire devices*. Allen Bradley and most other suppliers use the following color code: *brown* goes to positive supply, *black* is the output, and *blue* is the common.	
(b) Input module (current sourcing) The illustration shows a *current sinking sensor* and *current sourcing input* module. Note that an *NPN* transistor is often used as the final component in the output of the current sinking type field device. These sensors are called *three wire devices*. The *same color code* from the current sinking model applies here.	

addresses the TTL input module. Note that the schematics in the figure indicate the *power* and ground connections.

The input circuits in Figure 19-2 have *opto-isolation* between the *field device power* and the *controller* or *motor drive system power*. *Noise* and *operational* problems are eliminated when the power and grounds of the input system are *isolated* from and *independent* of the field device. The isolation is produced with a *light emitting diode* (LED) and photoelectric transistor. The input resistor *limits* input current, and the capacitor *filters* input noise. Note that the current sinking and sourcing types have *one* diode in the opto-isolator, and the AC types have *two* LEDs in opposite directions to handle the bi-directional AC current. In some cases, an LED provides an *indication* on the front of the module when an *input signal* is present.

The *inverting trigger circuit*, called a Schmidt trigger, in the TTL interface in Figure 19-2(b) produces a deadband so the output does not switch on and off as

the input moves above and below the trigger point. In addition, it *inverts* the input signal, so that a true input produces a zero or false condition for use in controller programming.

There are many different types of *output circuits* used for controllers and motor drive output modules. Three of the most common output circuits are illustrated and described in Figure 19-3. Figure 19-3(a) addresses the *current sinking DC output* module; Figure 19-3(b) addresses the *AC output* module; and Figure 19-3(c) addresses the *current sinking TTL output* module. Note that the schematics in the figure indicate the power and ground connections.

Like the input circuits, the output circuits have *opto-isolation* between the field device power and the controller or motor drive system power. The isolation is a diode and transistor as shown at the far left of the schematic and is produced with a LED and photo-triggered transistor. The circuits operate the same as the input opto-isolators. Many modules also have an

FIGURE 19-2: AC/DC and TTL input modules.

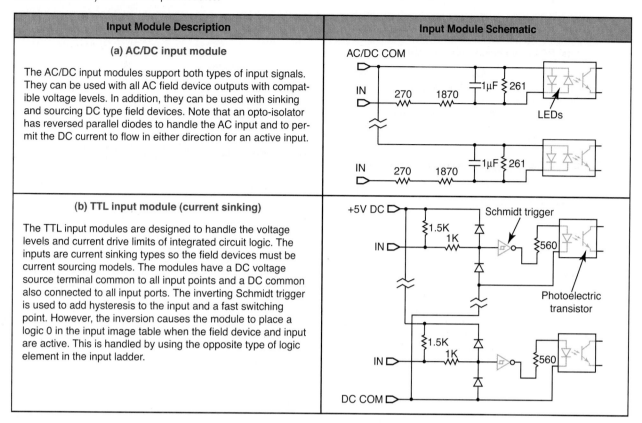

Input Module Description	Input Module Schematic
(a) AC/DC input module The AC/DC input modules support both types of input signals. They can be used with all AC field device outputs with compatible voltage levels. In addition, they can be used with sinking and sourcing DC type field devices. Note that an opto-isolator has reversed parallel diodes to handle the AC input and to permit the DC current to flow in either direction for an active input.	
(b) TTL input module (current sinking) The TTL input modules are designed to handle the voltage levels and current drive limits of integrated circuit logic. The inputs are current sinking types so the field devices must be current sourcing models. The modules have a DC voltage source terminal common to all input points and a DC common also connected to all input ports. The inverting Schmidt trigger is used to add hysteresis to the input and a fast switching point. However, the inversion causes the module to place a logic 0 in the input image table when the field device and input are active. This is handled by using the opposite type of logic element in the input ladder.	

LED on the front of the module to *indicate* when an *output signal* is present.

The TTL inverter in Figure 19-3(c) produces the output voltage and drive necessary for the TTL field devices. In addition, the inverter inverts the output signal, so a true output from the opto-isolator produces a false output condition and an off field device. When this module is used, an inversion of the ladder logic output state is produced at the output field devices. For example, if the input to the module is true, then the input to the field device connected to this module is false. As a result, the field devices are energized when the module has a zero input level applied.

Handling Solid State Devices

Virtually *all* solid state devices are subject to damage by an *electrostatic discharge* (ESD) event. An ESD event is the *rapid flow* of electrons between two bodies of unequal charge. It also *occurs* between one charged body and ground with an electronic circuit being the path of least resistance between the two. While some devices can withstand tens of thousands of ESD volts before damage, some are damaged by less than 200 volts. The sensitivity of solid state devices to ESD is *classified* according to the voltage levels that may cause potential damage. There are three classes, which are listed in Figure 19-4. To avoid ESD damage to devices, it is important that *proper precautions* and *handling procedures* be understood and followed.

Electrical workers cannot rely on their senses with hardware susceptible to ESD. While the worker did not have any sensation of an ESD event, the circuit did and damage was done. All solid state device manufacturers and electrical workers should be aware of the adverse results ESD voltage has on product reliability, along with the impact on product quality and cost. Figure 19-5 illustrates two common ESD caution and warning symbols on the protective packaging containing its products and on printed wiring boards and control modules.

FIGURE 19-3: DC, AC, and TTL output modules.

Output Module Description	Output Module Schematic
(a) DC output module (current sinking) The *sinking output* modules have a current flow into the output terminal when the output is active. For *compatibility*, the field device must have a sourcing type of input. All of the grounds for all output points, called DC COM, on the module are connected to the DC ground. A positive DC voltage is applied for power to the V DC terminal. Note that an *opto-isolator* is used to separate the power for the output field device from the PLC power. The sinking output circuit is shown with NPN type transistors for the opto-isolators and the output drive. A sourcing version of this circuit is also available where the NPN is replaced with a PNP transistor and the power and common lines are interchanged.	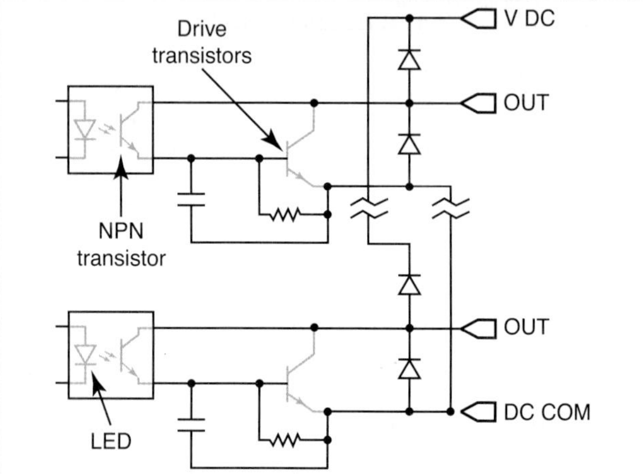 *(schematic: Drive transistors, NPN transistor, LED, V DC, OUT, OUT, DC COM)*
(b) AC output module The AC/DC output modules use a *Triac* to turn on the output field device. AC power is applied to the L1 terminal. All output field devices are placed between the OUT terminal and AC neutral. As a result, all AC field devices used with this module have similar voltage and current specifications.	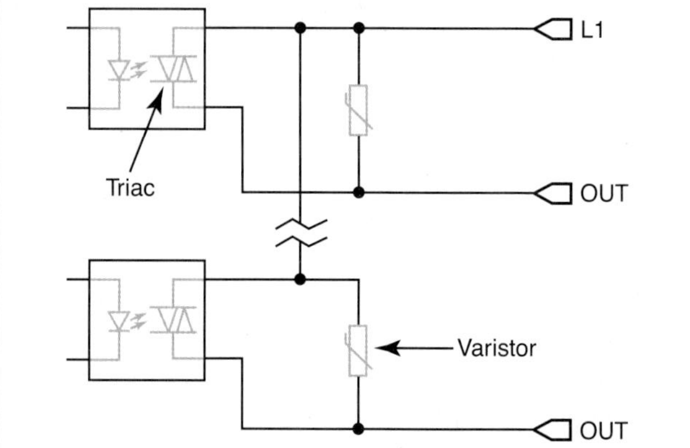 *(schematic: Triac, Varistor, L1, OUT, OUT)*
(c) TTL output module (current sinking) The *TTL output modules* are designed to handle the voltage levels and current drive requirements of *integrated circuit* logic. The outputs are current sinking types so the field devices must be current sourcing models. The modules have a DC voltage source terminal (+5V DC) connected to all output ports and a common ground (DC COM) also connected to all output ports. The transistor in the opto-isolator would make the output a sourcing type but the TTL inverter adds inversion to the output signal, making it a sinking output. As a result, the inverter forces a not active (false) output on the module when the module input is active (true). This is handled by changing the rung logic so the rung coil is not energized for an energized condition of the field device.	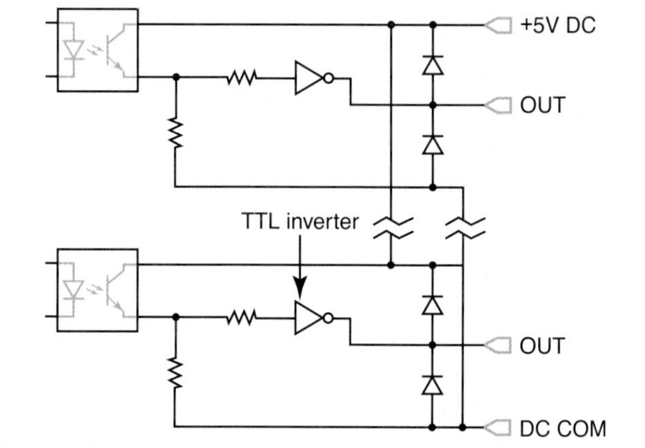 *(schematic: TTL inverter, +5V DC, OUT, OUT, DC COM)*

FIGURE 19-4: ESD classification codes.

Class	Sensitivity Level
Class 1	Less than 1,000 volts
Class 2	1,000 to 4,000 volts
Class 3	4,000 to 15,000 volts

Wherever ESD sensitive devices, assemblies and equipment are handled, *best practices* that are implemented in industry dictate the use of a *protected work area*. The protected area is constructed, equipped and maintained with the necessary ESD protective materials and equipment to insure that voltages are below the sensitivity level of the most ESD sensitive item handled in the work place. The Electronics Industry Alliance (EIA) document of requirements for handling electrostatic discharge sensitive devices (EIA-625) is a good specification to use as a reference. It identifies the key elements in handling ESD devices. It also provides a check list for performing an ESD handling audit. All items included in the protected work area are tested at a prescribed frequency to insure their continued effectiveness. Test records are maintained for at least two years. An ESD protected work area includes the following items:

- Grounded ESD protective work surfaces
- ESD safe flooring (mats or permanent installed ESD flooring)
- Personnel grounding (wrist straps or ESD shoes in conjunction with grounded ESD flooring)
- Removal or control of static generating sources so that no voltages are present greater than the threshold established for safe ESD handling of the most sensitive device used.
- Usage of ESD smocks when personnel's clothing generates charges greater than the established threshold
- Installation of air ionizers where essential equipment and material exceed the established threshold
- Identification of ESD safe workstations

To maintain a high level of quality, audits are performed on each operation where *processing, handling,* and *storage* of ESD sensitive devices occur. Each operation is audited at least annually with audit records kept for a minimum of two years. The ESD training programs help ensure all personnel have a basic understanding of safe handling procedures and are capable of applying their knowledge in the workplace. Training records should also be maintained for a minimum of two years. There are various types and brands of *inspection, test, measuring,* and *monitoring* equipment involved in proper ESD operations. Test equipment is selected based on the need to measure voltages of the established threshold and greater. It must be capable of measuring all the elements of the ESD work area.

The equipment also needs to be properly maintained and controlled by a calibration system.

19-2 ADVANCED TROUBLESHOOTING OF SOLID STATE DEVICES AND CONTROLS

Troubleshooting techniques for basic solid state devices are discussed in three chapters. Solid state device troubleshooting basics are covered in Chapter 10, troubleshooting techniques for analog devices are discussed in Chapter 18, and network devices are covered in Chapter 23. This chapter discusses troubleshooting techniques for *smart or intelligent solid state devices* and controls, and complements the topics in the three other chapters. A *smart* or *intelligent device* contains a solid state circuit or chip that provides communication and diagnostic capabilities for the device. These devices often have a *microprocessor* included in their electronics. The microprocessor permits the device to use messaging conventions that allow individual devices, such as photoelectronic sensors or motor starters, to *communicate* with each other over a single cable. The added intelligence permits a wealth of information and data to be accessed from the device over the communication line, called a *network*. The network information includes not only the *value* of the measured parameter, but *additional data* useful for troubleshooting and *configuration*. These intelligent devices *reduce* system wiring and *increase* system control and monitoring. Figure 19-6(a) provides a visual image of a system with smart input devices connected to a device level network called *DeviceNet*. Note that the primary controller is a *programmable logic controller* (PLC) with a network module called a *DeviceNet Scanner*. The network cable is a single small cable with connections, called *drops,* to the attached smart devices, like the variable frequency drive (VFD) for an AC or DC motor control.

The E3 overload is a standard overload relay used with a contactor for a motor starter application. The overload and contactor are not smart devices. However, with the addition of the DeviceNet interface, Figure 19-6(b), the overload is placed on the data network. The DeviceNet communication side-mount module integrates the motor starter overload relay into the system control network. The DeviceNet module provides: *I/O (2 inputs and 1 output) for local connection*

FIGURE 19-6: Smart devices on a DeviceNet network.

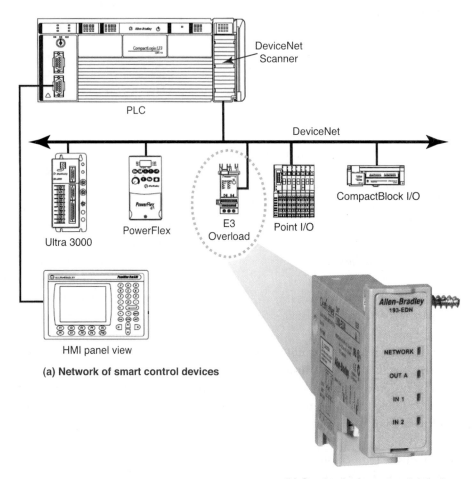

(a) Network of smart control devices

(b) Overload relay network interface

of motor starter-related I/O, overload warning, jam protection, underload warning, access to average motor current (percentage of FLC setting), percentage of thermal capacity usage, device status, trip and warning identification, and *trip history.* All of this data plus data from other smart devices on the network are available for analysis by electrical workers on the networked HMI panel. As a result, the motor performance data helps electrical workers *identify* problems when systems fail and *spot* problems in advance of a failure to prevent system down time.

Troubleshooting smart systems is aided by the *self-diagnostic capabilities* of the smart devices. Each smart device monitors itself and other system devices. To locate a system fault, the electrical worker needs to understand the system operation. Armed with system knowledge, they use software programs operated from a central unit such as a programmable logic controller (PLC) or a human machine interface (HMI). Training in the system software program is needed for efficient troubleshooting.

The network cable system is designed so that new branches or drops can be added when required. Quick replacement of faulty devices is easy because the smart devices are connected at the drop points with terminal blocks or electrical connectors. In addition, troubleshooting these smart systems is aided by the system's ability to record a history of good and faulty performance. For example, the exact time any input is energized (turned on) or de-energized (turned off) is recorded and documented. This information not only aids troubleshooting but also is used for determining production time and scheduling preventive maintenance.

CRITICAL CONCEPTS

The need to know content from Chapter 19 is summarized in the following statements.

- The four most common input modules that are interfaced by solid state devices are AC/DC, DC sinking, DC sourcing, and TTL modules.
- The three most common input modules that are interfaced by solid state devices are AC, DC, and TTL modules.
- Virtually all solid state devices are subject to damage by an electrostatic discharge (ESD) event.
- An ESD event is the rapid flow of electrons between two bodies of unequal charge.
- Wherever ESD sensitive devices, assemblies and equipment are handled, best practices implemented in industry dictate the use of a protected work area.
- A smart device contains a solid state circuit or chip that provides communication and diagnostic capabilities for the device.
- Troubleshooting smart systems is aided by the self-diagnostic capabilities of the smart devices. To locate a system fault, the electrical worker needs to understand the system operation and use a software program operated from a central unit.

QUESTIONS

1. Describe the input circuit for the AC/DC, DC sinking, DC sourcing, and TTL input modules.
2. Describe the output circuit for the AC, DC, and TTL output modules.
3. What is an ESD event?
4. Name five items that an ESD protected work area includes.
5. What does a troubleshooter use when attempting to locate a fault in system with smart devices?

CHAPTER 20

Variable Frequency Drives

GOALS AND OBJECTIVES

The primary goals for this chapter are to describe the *concepts, setup guidelines* and *set points* of variable frequency drives. In addition, applications, maintenance, and troubleshooting techniques are discussed.

After completing this chapter, you will be able to:

1. Describe open-loop and closed-loop variable frequency drive systems.
2. Discuss the guidelines for installing and starting variable frequency drives.
3. Describe variable frequency drive set points.
4. Discuss various variable frequency drive applications and maintenance and troubleshooting techniques.

20-1   DRIVE CONCEPTS

The basic *function* of a drive is to *control* the flow of *energy* from the *power source* to the *motors* used in industrial processes. The energy is supplied to the process through the motor shaft. Two physical quantities, *torque* and *speed,* describe the state of the shaft, and both must be controlled. Initially, drives provided either *torque control* or *speed control.* When the drive provides torque control, the speed is determined by the load. Likewise, when operated in speed control mode, the torque is set by the load. DC motors were first used as drives because they could easily achieve the required speed and torque without the need for sophisticated electronics. However, AC drive technology available today matches the excellent performance of DC motor control, such as fast torque response and speed accuracy. At the same time, the AC motor provides a rugged, inexpensive and maintenance free device. Figure 20-1

FIGURE 20-1: Family of variable speed drives for a range of motor sizes.

Courtesy of ABB, Inc.

There are AC drives and DC drives. A variable frequency drive (VFD) refers to AC drives only and a variable speed drive (VSD) refers to either AC Drives or DC Drives. The VFD controls the speed of an AC motor by varying the frequency to the motor. The VSD, referring to DC motors, controls the speed by varying the voltage to the motor. However, numerous other terms are used in industry to identify the solid state drive systems that control AC and DC motors. Some other terms electrical workers may encounter to indicate a solid state motor control is present include: SCR (Silicon Controlled Rectifier) Drives, Variable Speed Drives, Adjustable Speed Drives, Electric Motor Drives, Electronic Motor Drives, AC Motor Controllers, AC Inverters, and Pulse Width Modulation (PWM) Drives. In this chapter, the term VFD is used because the primary focus is on AC motor drive systems.

shows a family of seven AC drives from ABB, Inc. ABB offers more than forty different drive models and even more options for the models to handle applications in *material handling, mining and cement, rubber and plastics, food and beverage, consumer goods, textile, water/waste water, automotive, oil and gas,* and *pulp/paper*. With this broad range of applications, electrical workers are very likely to work on systems with motor drives.

Based on recent estimates, *sixty-five percent* of the total electrical energy generated in the North America is consumed by rotating equipment. Of this total, approximately *sixty* percent is consumed by centrifugal or flow related applications such as *fans, blowers, compressors,* and *pumps*. Drive technology offers a cost-effective method to match *driver speed* to *load demands* and represents an opportunity to *reduce* operating costs and *improve* overall productivity. Solid state drives control the *speed, torque, direction* and resulting *horsepower* of a motor by monitoring motor operational parameters such as speed and current. When motor parameters are fed back to the drive, the control is called *closed-loop control*. Unmonitored control systems or *open-loop systems* provide no feedback data of actual motor parameters, such as speed. *Monitored control* systems or *closed-loop* systems provide direct feedback of motor operation data through electrical signals. Some of the newer drive technologies provide the speed and torque control of a closed-loop system without physical measurements of motor speed. The motor operation is determined from the motor voltage and current, and corrections are made based on the power delivered to the motor. The electrical worker needs to understand both the traditional closed-loop type motor controller and the newer drives that extract the feedback data from an analysis of the power delivered.

Open-Loop Systems

In the *open-loop system* as shown in Figure 20-2, the variable frequency drive (VFD) has no feeback data for motor speed or torque. These systems often have a *speed reference tachometer* used to display the present RPM of the motor. However, this does not automatically compensate for an incorrect motor speed. To achieve the desired speed on an open-loop system, the operator adjusts the speed manually. These systems work well in installations that have constant load characteristics and do not require continuous regulation once the motor is brought up to the desired speed. The primary advantages of open-loop systems are lower initial cost and easier installation and calibration. In most applications, open-loop systems are installed and brought online faster than closed-loop systems.

FIGURE 20-2: Open loop VFD operation.

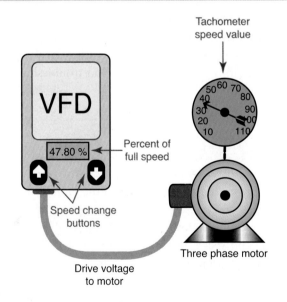

Tachometer speed value

VFD

47.80 %

Percent of full speed

Speed change buttons

Drive voltage to motor

Three phase motor

Closed-Loop Systems

In the *closed-loop system* shown in Figure 20-3, motor speed and torque data are automatically fed back to the VFD. Closed-loop systems consist of the *drive, comparator, sensor* and an *amplifier*. The speed sensor reports the motor RPM to the comparator. The comparator compares the sensor signal to the motor RPM *set point*. The drive electronics use the comparator output to bring the motor RPM to the set point value. Once the system speed parameters or set-points are programmed into the VFD, the drive operates without the need for manual adjustment.

The two standard RPM feedback sensors are *tachometer/generators* and *optical encoders*. Tachometer/generators are connected directly to the motor shaft or to a rotating section of the load such as a gear shaft or pulley. The tachometer/generator sensor produces a *feedback voltage* that is *directly proportional* to the *speed* of the motor. When the speed of the motor increases, the tachometer/generator output voltage increases. Conversely, as the motor speed decreases, the voltage also decreases. Optical encoder sensors generate pulses that represent shaft RPM. The pulse data is converted to shaft RPM in the drive and compared to the RPM set point value.

Speed Control Concepts

Speed control is used in the acceleration and deceleration of a motor. The *speed ramp up* capabilities of VFDs allow the motor and connected machinery to start slowly and gradually accelerate to the desired speed as shown in Figure 20-4. The *ramp-up* is *smoother* than a *stepped acceleration* that is used in the soft start method. The length of time preset for the speed ramp-up is varied from a few seconds to 120 seconds or more depending on the drive capabilities. The ramp-up is used in applications that are sensitive to quick, jerky starts or excessive torque.

Speed ramp down is a function of VFDs and provides very smooth deceleration and stopping of the motor. Ramping down brings the motor to a full stop in a predetermined time. Depending on drive parameters, ramp down times vary from fractions of a second (when used with dynamic braking) to more than 120 seconds. Ramping down smoothly stops the load more quickly than simply allowing the motor to coast to a stop.

Most VFDs have multiple speed control inputs. Each input generally has a preset function assigned to that control input. Some applications require the motor to run at different speeds at different specific points in the process. Each of these specific operational speeds is assigned to a different input point on the drive. For example, if a mixing application needs to be operated at three different speeds and for varying lengths of time, timing signals are sent to separate VFD speed control inputs at the pre-established time, and the VFD changes the speed of the mixer to match process requirements.

FIGURE 20-3: Closed loop VFD operation.

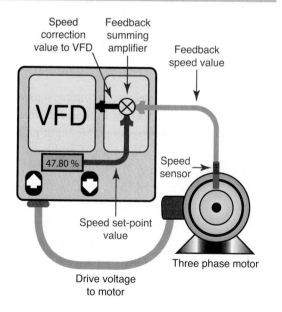

FIGURE 20-4: Stepped versus ramped acceleration.

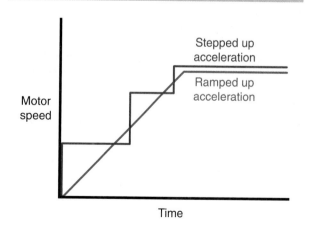

Harmonic interference is a growing concern in many motor control installations. Years ago, all loads were linear in nature, but today, electrical loads are becoming more non-linear due to the extensive use of switched mode power supplies found in electronic equipment. *Harmonics* are high-frequency voltage and current distortions within the power system normally caused by electronic equipment such as VFDs, computers and uninterruptible power supplies. Harmonics are the result of electronic loads that do not have a constant current draw; but rather draw current in pulses during the peak of a voltage waveform. These harmonics have different effects on electrical systems. Harmonics cause *overheating* of electrical components such as transformers, motor conductors and motor windings. They are responsible for *nuisance tripping* in circuit breakers, while under normal load conditions due to component overheating. Another problem is *higher than normal currents* in a grounded neutral conductor of a three phase, four-wire, wye system. This has become very prevalent in areas with large PC loads. Often a larger neutral is installed to help compensate for the higher current. It is possible for harmonics to produce currents on the neutral that exceed those of the current carrying phase conductors.

To lessen the impact of harmonics generated by VFDs, inductors, called *line reactors,* are installed in the power lines to the drive. Figure 20-5(a) shows a unit with three line reactors enclosed in one package. Line reactors are basically inductors that consist of tightly wound coils of wire. The greater the number of windings in the coils of wire, the higher the inductance rating of the reactor. The magnetic field of inductors opposes any current changes. This counteracts the rapid fluctuations of the current caused by harmonics. Reactors are often required in installations that consist of multiple drives on the same circuit. Although reactors are not the solution for harmonic issues, installing the correct reactors in a circuit is a good first step to correct many power quality problems caused by VFDs. Figure 20-5(b) illustrates line reactors in the input power lines to the VFD.

FIGURE 20-5: VFD drive and line reactors.

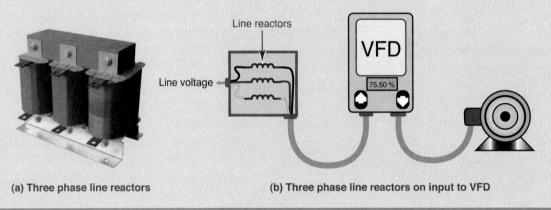

(a) Three phase line reactors

(b) Three phase line reactors on input to VFD

Operational Concepts

Figure 20-6(a) illustrates a typical VFD wiring diagram and connections with NEMA symbols. Note that the VFD is operating a small horsepower, three phase motor in an open-loop system. The three phase power source is connected to the VFD through line reactors at the input line terminals L1, L2, and L3, and the motor feed conductors are connected to the output terminals T1, T2, and T3. There is no direct connection between the input and output line terminals that is common with electromechanical motor starters. The VFD features input and output sections that perform the same basic functions as in traditional motor control circuits and permit the drive to interface with external components. Based on programmed parameters, the input section receives the incoming signals to the drive and the output section executes desired motor control actions. The programmable input points provide connections for devices such as pushbuttons, limit switches, process switches or pilot devices.

In Figure 20-6(a), the drive's digital inputs are interfaced to external devices, and the digital output contacts control other external devices. Programmable Logic Controllers (PLCs) often provide input signals for VFDs, while the output of a VFD serves as source for input to the PLC. Additional input and output drive components include an analog output speed indicator and a manual speed potentiometer. The analog speed indicator is an output device that displays the actual operating speed of the motor in real time. The

FIGURE 20-6: VFD wiring diagram and connections.

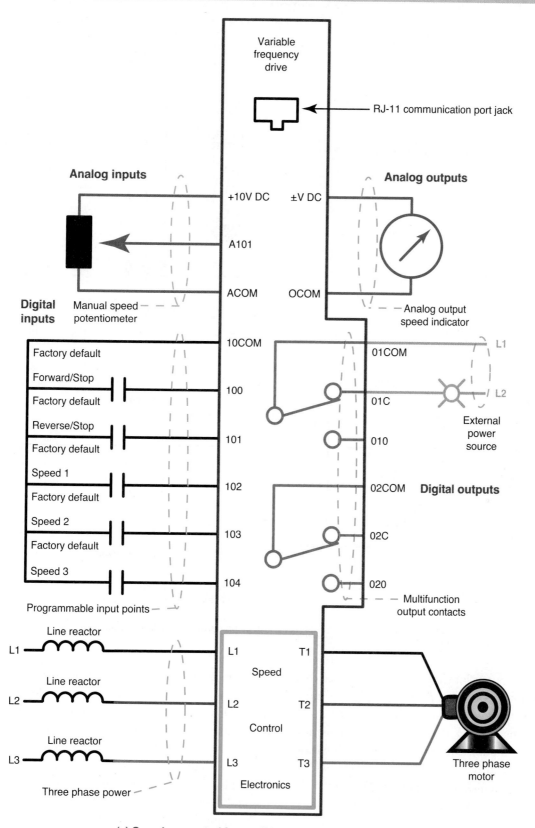

(a) Open-loop control for small hp motor with NEMA symbols

FIGURE 20-6: (Continued)

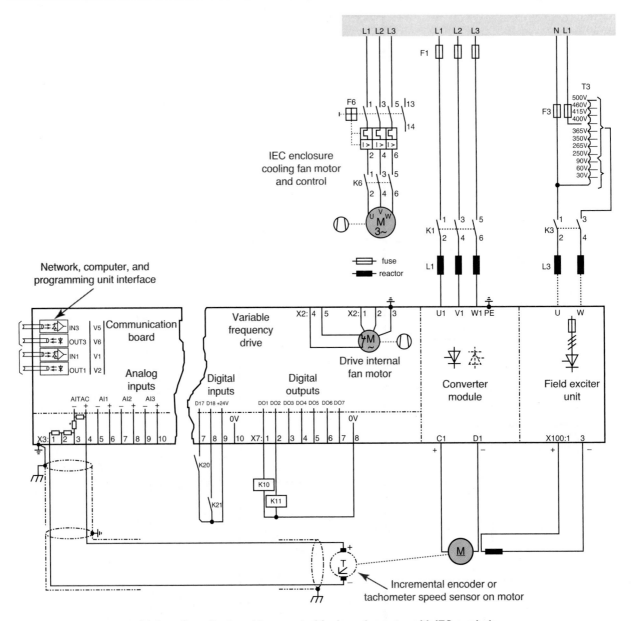

(b) A portion of a closed-loop control for large hp motor with IEC symbols

manual speed potentiometer is an input device that provides manual control of the motor speed. A modular RJ-11 jack provides a *serial communication port* for interfacing with a computer. The connection enables the computer software to remotely program and monitor the drive. The VFD is configured with a variety of communication ports that allow the drive to directly interface with PLCs, thus bypassing some of the programmable input points and multifunction output contacts.

Figure 20-6(b) illustrates a portion of a VFD wiring diagram and connections with IEC symbols. Note that the VFD is operating a large horsepower, three phase motor in a closed-loop system. An *incremental encoder* or *tachometer* speed sensor on the motor shaft provides the feedback to this closed-loop VFD system. The VFD has both analog and digital inputs and analog and digital outputs. The VFD is configured with a communication board that allows the drive to directly interface with the network, computers, or

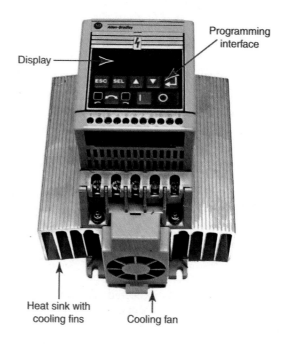
In a cooling tower application, the VFD in Figure 20-6(a) controls the main fan motor in the tower. The fan is started by replacing the normally open contact between inputs 10COM and 100 with the normally open contact of a START pushbutton. The three factory default speed settings operate the motor at different speeds. A thermostat monitors the water temperature of the cooling tower and closes the appropriate input contact to increase or decrease the fan speed. When cooling loads are high, the thermostat signals the drive to operate the fan motor at the highest speed. The multifunction output contacts provide connections to devices such as indicator and alarm lights, bells and buzzers. For example, an indicator light is inserted in the circuit between O1COM and O1C and illuminates as long as the contacts remain closed.

PLCs, which bypasses the programmable input and output terminals.

20-2 SETTING UP THE VFD

Many drive failures are the result of improper VFD setup, which includes *installation* and *configuration*. A carefully organized setup procedure assures better equipment operation and system reliability plus simplifies future troubleshooting. In fact, successful installation of nearly any electrical equipment or system benefits from an orderly, well-planned start-up process.

Installation

Important installation considerations include *temperature* and *line power quality requirements*, along with *electrical connections*, *grounding*, *fault protection*, *mounting*, *motor protection*, and *environmental parameters*.

Temperature—Environmental considerations are a primary concern when installing VFDs as these factors have a significant impact on drive *performance* and *reliability*. The VFD produces substantial heat during drive operation. If the enclosure surrounding the drive is not well ventilated or not in a climate controlled environment, the buildup of excess heat may damage the VFD components over time. Ensuring the drive remains cool is a primary concern when installing a VFD. Wet and corrosive environments also damage sensitive electronic equipment. Large fluctuations in ambient temperatures result in condensation forming inside drive enclosures and possibly damaging components. Factory enclosures of large VFDs should have a NEMA rating appropriate to the level of protection for the installation's environment. The same precautions are used when installing a smaller VFD in a control cabinet.

Mounting—The VFD is manufactured in a wide variety of mounting configurations. Figure 20-7 illustrates an older model VFD installed on a heat sink with a built-in cooling fan. Some VFDs are DIN-rail mountable and easily installed in control cabinets.

Electrical Connections—Many startup difficulties result from incorrect wiring. A variety of cable types are acceptable for VFD installations. For many installations, unshielded cable is adequate as long as signal and power cables are segregated. In all cases, long parallel runs are to be avoided and wire gauge are not to be reduced when using higher temperature wire. *Unshielded*, *shielded*, and *armored* cabling is used in VFD installations.

- *Unshielded Cabling*—Thermoplastic High Heat-resistant Nylon-coated (THHN) wire or similar

FIGURE 20-7: Older model VFD on heat sink with cooling fan.

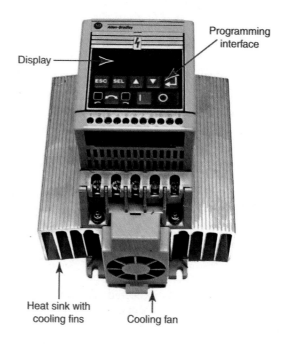

Display

Programming interface

ESC SEL ▲ ▼

Heat sink with cooling fins

Cooling fan

is acceptable for VFD installation in *dry* environments provided adequate free air space and/or conduit fill rate limits are observed. Use THWN wire for installation in wet areas. Any wire chosen must have a minimum insulation thickness of 15 Mils and not have large variations in insulation concentricity.

- *Shielded Cabling*—Shielded cable is generally used in installations with sensitive equipment such as *weigh scales, capacitive proximity switches* and other devices that are *affected* by electrical noise in the distribution system. Applications with *large numbers* of drives in a single location, imposed *EMC* (electromagnetic compatibility) regulations or many *communication networks* are also good candidates for shielded cable. In addition, the increased impedance of shielded cable extends the distance between motors and drives in network applications.

- *Armored Cabling*—Cable with *continuous aluminum cover* or *armor* is often recommended in VFD applications and in specific industries. It offers most of the advantages of shielded cable and also provides added *mechanical strength* and *resistance* to moisture. It permits concealed and exposed installations and removes the requirement for conduit.

Grounding—In addition to running a grounding conductor back to the electrical service entrance, a grounding conductor is brought back from the motor to the VFD's internal grounding terminal. This *direct motor ground* to the VFD is required to *minimize interference* and for *proper operation* of the ground-fault protection function.

Fault Protection—Many VFD's for larger horsepower motors have short-circuit protection (usually in the form of fuses) already installed by the manufacturer. External fuses are normally used on 1/3 to 5 hp motors. Follow the manufacturer's recommendations when installing or replacing fuses in the VFDs, especially the torque-bolt guidelines.

Motors—The squirrel cage motor is the most common AC motor used with VFDs. Most squirrel cage motors operate well with the PWM (pulse-width-modulated) waveform delivered by VFDs and damage-free operation under standard load and drive conditions is expected. However, exercise care when installing VFDs on older motors not designed to operate with PWM drive power waveforms. Load side line reactors, which give PWM waveforms a more traditional sine wave characteristic, help older motors tolerate the PWM drive power. Figure 20-8 illustrates the smoothing effect on the PWM output waveform of the VFD.

Startup

An organized start-up procedure assures better equipment operation and system reliability while simplifying troubleshooting. In addition to a fast and smooth startup, other major benefits of an organized start-up procedure are as follows.

- A better understanding of all component and system functions.
- Documentation of data for warranty purposes.
- Accumulation of baseline information and values to speed future troubleshooting and proper maintenance.

Prior to startup, read and follow all cautionary notes and warnings provided by the VFD manufacturer. The notes are found in the equipment manual and on VFD equipment labels. Next, read the VFD manual and highlight the features and adjustments that you expect to use. Pay particular attention to connection terminals for power and control and locate these within the VFD control enclosure. Finally, make a physical inspection of the VFD installation and look for the following:

- Any moisture or debris such as metal shavings inside the equipment.
- Damage or dents to the enclosure, damaged or loose components and wires, and disconnected terminal connectors.
- Possible restrictions to air flow at the cooling fans or heat sink.
- Un-removed shipping blocks or tapes at power contactors, relays, and other components.

In addition to the VFD, make a *visual inspection* of the entire system including *motors, disconnect switches, circuit breakers, controls, load components,* and *control devices*. Finally, make a thorough check of the following items:

- Connections (line, load, and ground).
- Motor (horsepower, full-load amps, voltage, and rotation).

FIGURE 20-8: Smoothing effect of line reactor on PWM from VFD.

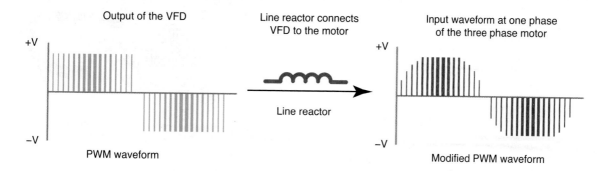

- VFD (input/output voltages, maximum output current).
- Protective devices (circuit breaker, fuses, overloads, thermal devices).
- Disconnects (in place and sized correctly).
- Incoming line power voltage measurements to the VFD (A-B phase, B-C phase, C-A phase).

The following *test equipment* is recommended to be available for an effective and efficient startup.

- True RMS multimeter capable of reading AC/DC voltages up to 750 volts.
- True RMS clamp-on ammeter capable of reading the VFD's maximum current output.
- Photo tachometer to verify shaft output speed at load.
- Current/voltage signal generator to generate a reference analog signal to VFD such as 4 to 20mA or 0 to 5V. This is extremely useful on HVAC applications where the building automation system designed to control the VFD is not ready at time of start-up.
- Oscilloscope to check wave shapes of VFD output to motor. These wave shapes are compared to those provided in the startup manual, or recorded for future comparison during troubleshooting or maintenance. The scope also can be used to check volts/hertz ratio.

Finally, make up a complete check of all electrical and mechanical components, ensuring that they are set correctly. Components include: *valves, dampers, limit switches, steady-state voltage* and *current values.* A proper startup is considered complete only when the VFD is operated at full load. This is important because meaningful drive adjustments can be made. Verify this by actually checking the FLC and comparing the value

to that on the motor nameplate. When a startup command is given, watch, listen, and smell for anything unusual. Recommendation—once startup has been accomplished, allow the system to run a few hours before taking test readings for future comparison.

20-3 VFD CONTROL SET POINTS

Setup procedures for a VFD are vendor specific, so procedures described in this section provide general guidelines and with specific examples for drives supplied by ABB, Inc. Experience in the field indicates that when electrical workers become proficient with VFD setup for one vendor, learning another manufacturer's drive is not difficult. A typical VFD from ABB with a description of interface options is shown in Figure 20-9. Note that the drive has programming and display panel options that are interfaced to the drive as shown.

The control set points of a VFD establish the *speed, directional rotation,* and *stopping* parameters for the motor. The motor name plate data and the set points, which are determined by the industrial process parameters, are loaded into the VFD. The process to transfer the data uses a variety of interfaces, software programs, and computer type devices. Most often, loading control set point is accomplished through the interface located on the VFD. The interface uses a handheld controller that communicates to the VFD via a communications port, or through a communication jack and cable connected directly to PC. Each type of interface has advantages and disadvantages. When using the VFD interface located on the drive, no additional hardware is required. Generally, this interface offers easy access for an electrical worker to *check parameters* or make minor *programming changes.* The interface for the ABB drive is the FlashDrop handheld programmer, which is

FIGURE 20-9: VFD drive interface description.

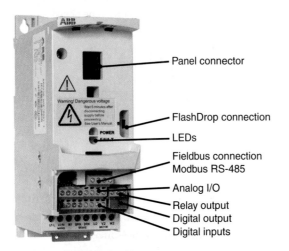

Panel connector

FlashDrop connection

LEDs

Fieldbus connection
Modbus RS-485

Analog I/O

Relay output

Digital output

Digital inputs

(a) Drive interface descriptions

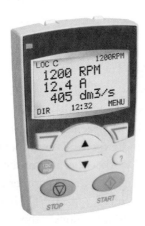

**(b) Drive programming and
display interface—plugs into
panel connector identified
in figure above**

**(c) Drive terminal cover—snaps
into drive below display interface**

Courtesy of ABB, Inc.

shown in Figure 20-10. The handheld programmer plugs into the drive at the FlashDrop connection slot noted in Figure 20-9(a). The handheld unit duplicates the display panel shown in Figure 20-9(b).

Companies with numerous ABB drives often use a blank panel instead of the display and use a handheld

FIGURE 20-10: FlashDrop handheld programmer for ABB drive.

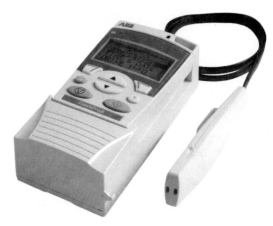

Courtesy of ABB, Inc.

unit at each drive to make parameter and setup changes. The primary *disadvantage* of the drive display and the handheld display is *functionality*. The displays are normally small and hard to read, and because of the smaller screen, most programming parameters are abbreviated. This can cause difficulties in navigating the program if the electrical worker is unsure of the abbreviations. Another option for changing drive parameters is a remote panel box with a potentiometer to change drive speed settings. Figure 20-11 shows an electrical worker making a speed adjustment on an ABB drive from a remote panel box.

Drive Programming

Most major drive manufacturers provide additional programming functionality through drive software on a personal computer (PC). For example, ABB offers DriveWindow software for their larger drives and DriveWindow Light 2 for the smaller drive sizes. The software is used with a *laptop PC* at the site of the drive installation or through a *data network*. Handheld programmers usually offer increased functionality when compared to drive mounted programming interfaces but cannot approach the benefits offered by PC-based software. The PC offers greater flexibility because more detailed information on the drive parameters is viewed simultaneously on screen. Additionally, because of the increased functionality offered by a software-based interface, more special drive features can be accessed on a PC-based interface. Figure 20-12 shows a closed-loop drive system with drive parameter programming performed by an electrical worker from a remote desktop computer.

Courtesy of ABB, Inc.

FIGURE 20-12: Closed-loop drive application with electrical worker working remotely to monitor or change drive status.

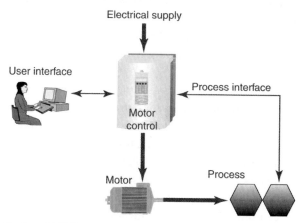

Courtesy of ABB, Inc.

In general, drive software has computer screens or dialog boxes to perform the following drive setup and control functions:

- **Display drive status**—monitors and displays the value of all drive and motor parameters in real time and in a trend display for a preset time period. The software often provides a quick look at important parameters in AC drive status such as those in Figure 20-13.
- **Parameter update**—provides access to view drive parameter data and to change motor drive parameter values. Figure 20-14 illustrates a detailed look at all parameters in a parameter browser dialog box and a trend display on a monitor screen.
- **Error Messages and Alarms**—displays error and alarm messages generated by the drive.

FIGURE 20-13: Quick look at parameter status on programming screen.

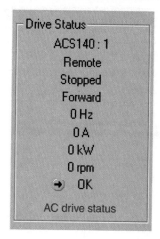

FIGURE 20-14: Parameter browser and monitor.

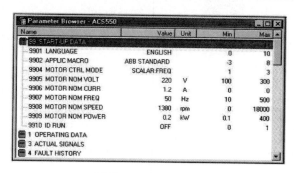

(a) Parameter browser

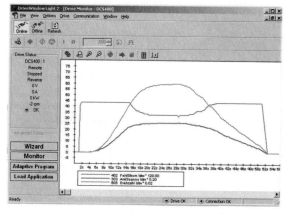

(b) Monitor screen

Most drives are programmed through the use of PC menus and sub-menus. These sub-menus are shown in their entirety on the PC versus one line at a time on VFD direct interfaces or a few lines at a time on hand-held devices. In the programming mode, drive parameter are also set with a drive control bar. Figure 20-15(a)

FIGURE 20-15: Drive control command bar.

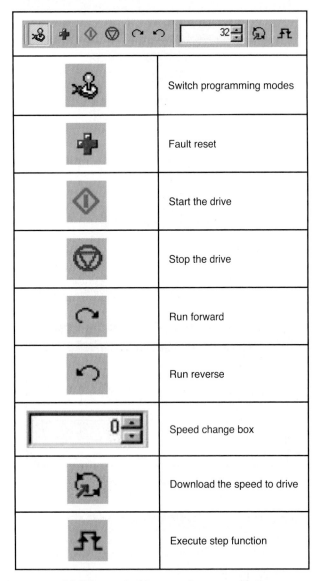

(a) Drive control icons and command bar

	Switch programming modes
	Fault reset
	Start the drive
	Stop the drive
	Run forward
	Run reverse
	Speed change box
	Download the speed to drive
	Execute step function

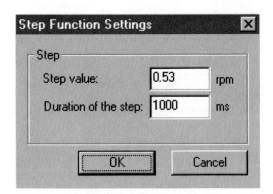

(b) Speed step function dialog box

illustrates the control bar and associated icons. Each of the drive's parameters is easily changed with an icon selection. In the case of the speed step function, step speeds and step time durations are selected and downloaded to the drive from the programming software. Figure 20-15(b) illustrates the speed set dialog box.

20-4 VFD APPLICATIONS

In the past, many motor control applications requiring speed control used DC drives and motors or AC motors attached to gear boxes or pulley assemblies connected to the driven machinery. Although somewhat inefficient, DC drives offered the capability to easily change the motor speed. Today, the VFD combines the controllability of DC drives with the efficiency of AC motors. Even the tendency of AC drives to deliver less torque at lower rotor speeds is being overcome in newer generations of drives. The VFD is used in many industrial and commercial applications, generally classified by load type as follows:

- **Constant torque loads**—These loads represent 90% of all general industrial machines (other than pumps and fans). Examples of these load types include general machinery, hoists, conveyors, printing presses, positive displacement pumps, some mixers and extruders, reciprocating compressors, as well as rotary compressors.
- **Constant horsepower loads**—These loads are most often found in the machine-tool industry and center driven winder applications. Examples of constant horsepower loads include winders, core-driven reels, wheel grinders, large driller machines, lathes, planers, boring machines, and core extruders.
- **Variable torque loads**—Variable torque loads are most often found in variable flow applications such as fans and pumps. Examples of applications include fans, centrifugal blowers, centrifugal pumps, propeller pumps, turbine pumps, agitators, and axial compressors.

Heating, Ventilation, and Air Conditioning System

Heating, ventilation, and air conditioning (HVAC) applications are one of the most common commercial installations for VFDs. In the past, HVAC systems employed AC motors that operated at a predetermined RPM. These motors drove fans in HVAC units and provided a steady and unchanging air pressure. To ensure sufficient air pressure delivery, the motors were often oversized and dampers were installed in air handlers to control air flow. This configuration performed adequately for many years. In fact, they continue to be used today on smaller, as well as legacy HVAC systems. The main drawback of this design is inefficiency. Adjustable dampers in air handlers function similarly to variable resistors in an electrical circuit. When too much air is delivered, dampers close or narrow to reduce air flow. Restricting the air flow results in wasted energy, just like variable resistors in an electrical circuit. Furthermore, the back-pressure developed by the restricting dampers in an HVAC system makes the fan motor work harder to deliver more air in what is essentially an over-pressurized system. In many new HVAC installations, VFDs control the fan motor speed

and, therefore, the amount of air supplied to the HVAC system. These VFD driven systems supply only enough airflow for proper system efficiency in real time, without the need for restricting dampers. Figure 20-16 illustrates and describes a VFD-controlled HVAC system. Note that the circled numbers in the illustration match the numbers in the description.

Turf Irrigation System

The turf irrigation system as shown in Figure 20-17 uses VFDs to control the water pressure that is delivered to the golf course. It also has a liquid fertilizer tank with a VFD and pump to add fertilizer to the watering system. Figure 20-17(a) illustrates a VFD and pump that moves liquid fertilizer from the holding tank to the irrigation system for the golf course. Note the VFD prohibits pump operation when liquid is below the tank level sensor. Figure 20-17(b) illustrates the VFDs that maintain the proper water pressure at the irrigation

---

FIGURE 20-16: VFD used in an industrial HVAC system.

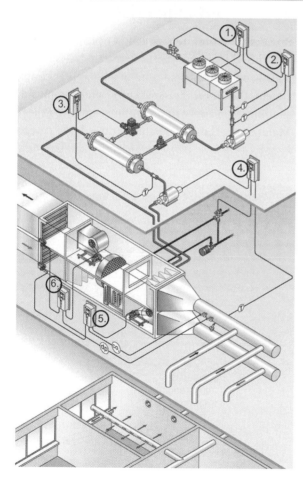

1. Liquid cooler fans are controlled according to the temperature of the condenser water outlet. Condenser water temperature is kept constant with closed-loop VFD drive. To prevent unnecessary cooling, liquid cooler fans are not started until the condenser water pump exceeds maximum speed. If water temperature falls too low, circulation can be stopped with a solenoid valve. Fans can also be programmed to run fixed speed for a certain time, e.g. once a week, to avoid condensation in the motors.
2. Condenser water pump is controlled with a closed-loop VFD drive according to the temperature of the condenser water. Operation is enabled when the chilled water pump and the chiller compressor are running.
3. An AC drive optimizes compressor motor speed to actual cooling demand. The compressor is controlled according to the temperature of the chilled water. The compressor's minimum speed is 60 percent of its normal speed. Operation is enabled when chilled water pump and condenser water pump are running.
4. Chilled water pump circulates chilled water in a cooling coil according to the temperature of the supply air. Operation is enabled when the duct temperature rises above a preset level and chiller compressor is running.
5. Room air quality is controlled by changing the speed of the supply fan according to the CO_2 content of the exhaust air. The outdoor air damper will be opened when the fan is started. Operation is enabled when the damper is fully open (damper end switch).
6. Room pressure is controlled by changing the speed of the return fan according to the exhaust duct pressure. Return fan keeps up constant under pressure in the exhaust duct by using closed-loop VFD drive control. Exhaust air dampers will be opened when the fan is started. Operation is enabled when damper is fully open (damper end switch).

Courtesy of ABB, Inc.

FIGURE 20-17: Golf course irrigation system.

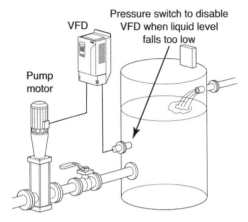

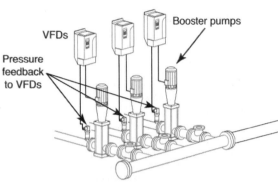

(a) Holding tank for irrigation fertilizer liquid with VFD pump control and level sensor

(b) Booster pumps located halfway across golf course with VFDs to maintain proper pressure at irrigation heads

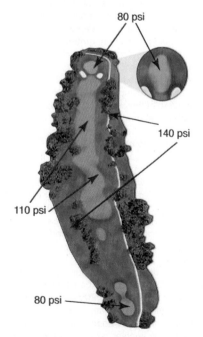

(c) Golf course irrigation requirements

heads in a closed-loop system. Note that water pressure is fed back to the VFDs, which drive the booster pumps. Customizable programs permit the selection of a variety of pressure set points for different areas of the golf course such as the greens, tees, and fairways.

Constant Level Control System

The constant level control system is shown in Figure 20-18. The VFD controller receives a 4 to 20 mA signal, which is proportional to the tank water level, from the level sensor. The VFD, operating from the sensor signals, determines the level in the tank. When the level is at the desired set point, the discharge of the pump is equal to the recharge of the well. If the recharge rate goes up, the transducer detects that the water level is rising and the pump needs to pump faster, so the VFD drives the pump at a higher RPM. Likewise, if the recharge rate goes down, the transducer detects a drop in the water level, and the VFD slows the pump down.

20-5 MAINTAINING THE VFD

Preventative maintenance (PM) programs ensure a VFD provides many years of trouble-free service. The VFD has the elements found in a computer controlled system, therefore, the same safety and equipment precautions that apply to a computer apply to the VFD. Maintaining the VFD includes three basic categories: *keep it clean; keep it dry;* and *keep the connections tight.*

FIGURE 20-18: VFD well pump motor to control level of water in well.

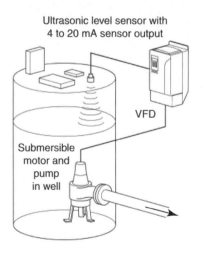

Although "re-torquing" as a way of checking tightness is common in many PM procedures, it violates basic mechanical principles and does more harm than good. A screw has maximum clamping power at a torque value specific to its size, shape, and composition. Exceeding that torque value permanently reduces the clamping power of that screw by reducing its elasticity and deforming it. Loosening and then re-torquing still reduces elasticity, which still means a loss of clamping power, such as doing this to a lock washer results in a permanent 50% loss. What should you do? Use an infrared thermometer to note hot connections. Check their torque. If they have merely worked loose, retighten them. Note which screws were loose, and be sure to give them a check at the next PM cycle. If they are loose again, replace them.

Keeping the VFD Clean

Generally, VFDs fall into the NEMA 1 category (side vents for cooling airflow) or NEMA 12 category (sealed, dust-tight enclosure). Drives that fall in the NEMA 1 category are susceptible to dust contamination. Dust on VFD hardware diminishes the airflow, resulting in lower performance from heat sinks and heat sink fan. Dust from factory fans usually accumulates on equipment near the fans. Dust on an electronic device can cause malfunction or even failure. Dust absorbs moisture, which also contributes to failure. Periodically spraying air through the heat sink fan is a good PM measure. Discharging compressed air into a VFD is a viable option in some environments, but typical plant air contains oil and water. To use compressed air for cooling, ensure that the air is *oil-free and dry*, which requires a specialized, dedicated, and expensive air supply. However, the risk of generating electrostatic charges (ESD) remains. A non-static generating spray or a reverse-operated ESD vacuum reduces static build-up. These vacuums, and cans of non-static generating compressed air, are available through companies that specialize in static control equipment.

Keeping the VFD Dry

Moisture is generally not a problem when the VFD is installed in a clean, dry area of a mechanical room. However, dehumidifiers installed close to the mechanical room could present a problem—water dripping from the dehumidifier into the VFD. Over time, the VFD accumulates enough water to produce circuit board corrosion or component failure. Periodic checking of other equipment installed near the VFD is a good maintenance action. Relative to condensation, some VFD manufacturers include a type of condensation protection in older models. If the VFD is operated all day every day, the normal radiant heat from the heat sink should prevent condensation.

Keeping Connections Tight

This maintenance action may sound basic, but checking connections is a step many miss or do incorrectly. Heat cycles and mechanical vibrations lead to substandard connections. Re-torquing bolts and screws is not a good procedure because further tightening an already tight connection ruins the connection. Poor connections eventually lead to arcing. Arcing at the VFD *input* could result in *nuisance overvoltage faults, clearing of input fuses,* or *damage to protective components*. Arcing at the VFD *output* could result in *overcurrent faults* or *damage* to the power components. For example, a loose start/stop signal wire can cause uncontrollable VFD stops. A loose speed reference wire can cause the drive speed to fluctuate, resulting in scrap, machine damage, or personnel injury.

20-6 TROUBLESHOOTING THE VFD

When troubleshooting a VFD, one of the first steps is to *identify* the malfunctioning section of the drive circuit. The problem may be located in any of the following: *input devices, output devices, programming* or VFD *internal* components.

To check an input device, the electrical worker should verify on the control diagrams, which input devices are used with the VFD and which devices may be directly related to the problem. For example, if a VFD is used for reversing a motor and the forward operation is working but the reverse is not, this may indicate a problem with a switch or other device acting as the reverse input. If the input devices are working normally, the problem is in another part of the device. Often the status of the motor circuit is determined by observing the drive data. Drives indicate operational parameters for the motor. If the motor is not operating, the problem could be anywhere in the motor and motor control circuit. Sometimes VFD inputs are the outputs of a PLC that interface with the entire control process. Troubleshooting input devices differs, depending on the type of device. To troubleshoot a PLC, the electrical worker must have a working knowledge of PLCs to competently diagnose problems.

Drive outputs are often control indicators that provide useful information when the system malfunctions. The output of a drive may also interface with a PLC through an output port or a communication port.

Most programming problems are identified and corrected during startup. Once the drive is functioning properly, programming is generally eliminated as the source of the problem. Software related failures rarely occur after startup unless program updates are made. During startup, the parameters of the drive may not have been properly programmed for the desired operation. When such a problem occurs, the best course of action is to access the program and verify the parameters agree with field conditions and process requirements. Whenever a program change is planned, backup the original program before any changes are made. If the parameters of the drive are not listed on drawings, the electrical worker should record all of the current parameters before making any changes. Modifications of program parameters are made one parameter at a time to observe the system response. If the change in a parameter does not correct the problem, reset the parameter to the original value and change the next parameter related to the problem. Program parameters should not be changed randomly trying to find a solution to the problem.

The final problem area is the drive itself. Internal drive problems often require a factory technician who has received training specifically for that manufacturer's drive. This type of training is usually reserved for factory technicians and most electrical workers generally consider internal drive problems outside their scope of work. In some cases, simply replacing the drive is a cost effective solution that does not require a factory trained technician. Generally, electrical workers should not attempt to repair drives, as it may void the warranty.

CRITICAL CONCEPTS

The need to know content from Chapter 20 is summarized in the following statements.

- In an open-loop system, the motor provides no speed information feedback to the VFD, and in a

closed-loop system, motor speed and torque data are automatically fed back to the VFD.

- The speed ramp up allows the motor and connected machinery to start slowly and gradually accelerate to the desired speed, and the speed ramp down provides very smooth deceleration and stopping the motor.

- Important installation considerations include temperature and line power quality requirements, along with electrical connections, grounding, fault protection, mounting, motor protection, and environmental parameters.

- Prior to VFD startup, read and follow all caution notes and warnings provided by the VFD manufacturer, and then, make a physical inspection of the VFD installation.

- Test equipment such a multimeter, ammeter and oscilloscope is recommended to be available for an effective and efficient startup.

- The control set points of a VFD establish the various speeds and directional rotation of a motor. The set points are determined by the industrial process parameters and inputted to the VFD by a variety of interfaces.

- Maintaining the VFD includes three basic categories: keep it clean; keep it dry; and keep the connections tight.

- When troubleshooting a VFD, one of the first steps is to identify the malfunctioning section of the drive circuit. The problem may be located in any of the following: input devices, output devices, programming or internal components.

QUESTIONS

1. Describe the open- and closed-loop operation of a VFD.
2. Relative to a VFD, what is ramp up and ramp down?
3. When installing a VFD, when would armored cabling be chosen over shielded cabling?
4. In addition to a fast and smooth startup, what are other major benefits of an organized startup procedure?
5. List some test equipment that should be available for an effective and efficient VFD startup.
6. What are three basic categories in maintaining a VFD?
7. When troubleshooting a VFD, what are the general areas that the problem may be located?

CHAPTER 21

Programmable Logic Controllers

GOALS AND OBJECTIVES

The primary goals for this chapter are to describe *programmable logic controller (PLC) concepts* and to identify and describe *stand-alone controllers and modular PLCs*. In addition, the integration of the PLC into motor control systems is described.

After completing this chapter, you will be able to:

1. Describe the basic concepts and components of a PLC.
2. Explain the operation and function of stand-alone and modular PLCs.
3. Describe how the PLC is integrated into motor control.

21-1 PLC CONCEPTS

The *Programmable Logic Controller* (PLC) is a special purpose industrial computer designed for use in the control of a wide variety of manufacturing machines and systems. The term *industrial computer* means that the PLC is a computer designed to operate in the harsh *physical* and *electrical noise* environments of production plants. They are also specialized electronic devices, so they are not just a personal computer (PC) that was ruggedized and moved to the factory floor. Because PLCs are computers, they must be programmed using

a programming language. While *Ladder Logic* (LD) is a common programming language for PLCs, there are four other *programming languages* in the IEC 61131-3 international standard that are used—*Function Block Diagrams* (FBD), *Structured Text* (ST), *Instruction List* (IL), and *Sequential Function Charts* (SFC). Most PLC manufactures use a proprietary ladder logic programming language, such as Allen Bradley's RSLogix 5, RSLogix 500 or RSLogix 5000 and Siemen's STEP 7. While these languages are similar they are *not identical* and *not interchangeable*. A ladder logic diagram is very similar to the relay ladder diagrams used for electromechanical applications, which is discussed in Chapter 8. However, detailed discussion of PLC programming language is beyond the scope of the text.

PC Versus PLC

The PC and PLC have some things in common and many things that make them different. The architecture of the PC and PLC systems are similar with both featuring a *motherboard, processor, memory,* and *expansion slots.* The processor in the PLC includes a *central processing unit* (CPU), which is composed of a *microprocessor* and *computer-type architecture.* This structure is identical to the technology used in the PC. Generally, PLCs do not have *removable* storage media like compact disks (CDs) or *fixed* storage media like hard disk drives. However, they have solid state memory to store programs and process data. The PLC does not have *a* monitor, but a human machine interface (HMI) in the form of a flat screen display to show process or production machine status is often present. PCs are generally designed to do *many* jobs, but the programmable logic controller performs only *one* chore, sequential and process control of production processes.

Will PC and PLC technologies converge? According to vendors like Allen-Bradley and Siemens the answer is someday, but the PC will never replace the PLC. In some current applications, the PC is performing PLC type control that allows the PC to simulate the actions of a PLC. Technical differences notwithstanding, the PC and PLC industries are starting to look more alike every day.

PLC System and Components

Figure 21-1 illustrates a block diagram of a PLC system and its components. Note that the PLC system includes a number of different components and modules. The heart of the PLC is the *PLC processor.* The processor is surrounded by *input modules, output modules,* and a *power supply.* Programming is performed by either a *hand-held programmer* or by a *personal computer* connected directly to the processor or through a network connection. The processor communicates with input and output devices directly using the input and output modules. Note that a variety of input devices and output devices are listed in the figure. *Special communication modules* interface with a variety of common networks such as *Ethernet/IP* and *DeviceNet,* which are described in Chapter 23.

For *stand-alone* PLCs like the Allen-Bradley MicroLogix 1000, the component modules in Figure 21-1 are integrated into a *single unit,* whereas for *modular* PLCs like the Allen-Bradley ControlLogix systems and older SLC 500 models, the modules are mounted in a *rack* as shown in Figure 21-2. The rack

FIGURE 21-1: Programmable logic controller system.

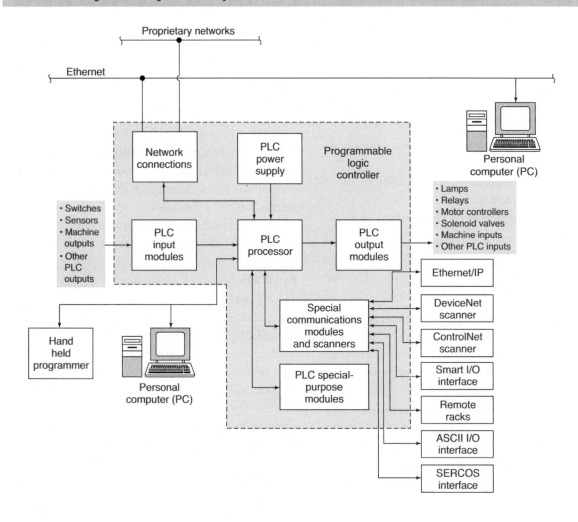

FIGURE 21-2: ControlLogix and SLC 500 programmable logic controllers.

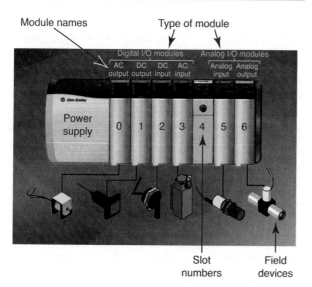

(a) **Front panel and rack with seven modules for ControlLogix PLC**

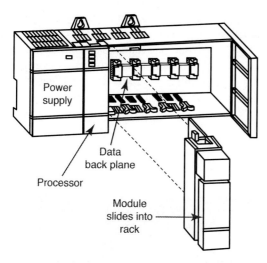

(b) **Module and rack interface for SLC 500 PLC**

Courtesy of Rockwell Automation, Inc.

provides *mechanical support* and all the *electrical interconnections* plus the data interface between all of the PLC modules using the backplane bus structure. The *backplane* is a printed circuit board that delivers power to the modules and provides a data bus to exchange data between the modules and the CPU. Modules slide into the rack and engage connectors on the backplane to access the backplane's power and data buses. The number of slots in the rack is determined by the number and type of modules required for the control application.

The *input and output (I/O) interface* used in PLCs take two forms: *fixed or modular*. The fixed type is associated with the stand-alone PLC systems where all of the features are integrated into a single unit. The number of I/O ports is fixed with each model and cannot be changed. The modular PLC system uses the rack to hold the I/O modules, so the number and type of I/O are variable by selecting from the broad array of interface modules. The *input* interface provides the link between the PLC processor and the *external devices* that *measure* the process conditions. The devices used most often include: *switches, sensors, machine outputs*, or *PLC outputs*. Input devices are often called *field devices* indicating that they are not a part of the PLC hardware. The PLC input modules are both a *physical interface* for the connection of wires and an *electrical/data interface* to determine the on/off state or voltage level from the attached field device. The fixed and modular *output* interface provides the connection between the PLC processor and the external devices such as *lamps, relays, motor* and *heater* contactors, *solenoid valves*, and *machine* inputs. The term *field device* is also used to address the wide range of output devices attached to a PLC system. Again, the output module is both a location for *termination of wiring* and a *supplier* of drive power to activate the output field device.

PLCs in Industry

Every aspect of industrial systems from *power generation* to *automobile production* to *food* and *liquid* packaging uses PLCs to expand and enhance the manufacturing system. Industrial electrical systems are generally divided into *discrete parts* manufacturing and *process* manufacturing.

Discrete parts manufacturing represents the production of durable goods such as automobiles, refrigerators and components used in larger and small products. Discrete parts manufacturing uses PLCs that perform numerous control functions. Sample applications include: *drilling, shearing, press feeding, progressive die control, material handling, robotic control,* and *part positioning.* The PLC handles *motion control* with servos and stepper motor drivers and with AC and DC motor controllers, *product movement tracking* and *control* with discrete switches and electronic sensors, data concentration with data collection and logging, and with system status displays at human machine interface (HMI) panels.

In addition to shaping parts, the PLC is used to interface and control the operation of the parts of a machine along the production line. The PLC is used to control the speed of the production line, divert production to other lines when there is a problem, track product movement, check product quality, package products, and maintain production documentation such as inventory and scrap. Figure 21-2(a) illustrates the numerous different types of modules available for PLCs to control all parts of the manufacturing process. Note the variety of different devices from *solenoid* and *display* outputs to different discrete input *switches* and *sensors* for the ControlLogix PLC in the figure.

APPLICATION

Figure 21-3(a) illustrates a material handling application for peanut butter filled crackers. Crackers from the baking area move into the robot cell in stacks on the rear moving conveyor. Crackers are positioned on a second moving conveyor for the peanut butter filling. A three axis servo driven Delta robot, controlled by an Allen Bradley ControlLogix PLC with motion control modules, moves the crackers between conveyors. The robot and conveyor motion systems are all controlled by the PLC; as a result, synchronizing the locations and movement is possible from a single program. In addition, all switches and sensors plus safety control devices are integrated into the PLC control. Figure 21-3(b) shows a typical PLC control panel with ControlLogix PLCs, input/output control devices, and wiring terminals mounted on DIN rails.

FIGURE 21-3: PLC controlled sandwich cracker production system.

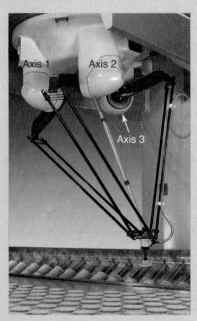

(a) Three axes servo robot

Courtesy of Rockwell Automation, Inc.

(b) ControlLogix PLCs for motion and production control

Process manufacturing produces consumables such as *food, gas, paint, paper* and *chemicals*. Most of the processes require industrial systems to perform a variety of operations that mix, separate, or cook the process material. This system opens and closes valves and controls motors in a programmed sequence and at the selected time. The PLC runs these processes and allows for easy process modifications if the time, temperature

APPLICATION

The production of paper in a paper mill requires an unparalleled use of production technology. A simplified view of paper production is illustrated in Figure 21-4. The front end of the production process requires logs of either hard or soft wood depending on the type of paper produced. The logs are stripped of bark and chipped into small wood chips. In some processes the chips are cooked, then ground into pulp, and then the pulp is cooked again. A bleaching process is used before color dye is applied. In some paper mills this front end process produces pulp for as many as four paper finishing machines. Paper finishing machines start with a *head box* that applies the processed pulp on a flannel or mesh belt. The finishing machines are often 50 to 60 feet wide and over a 300 feet long. Paper moves through the machines at speeds of 80 feet per second.

These machines have hundreds of motor drives, pumps, valves, motors, and related process elements. In addition, the control system has thousands of switches and sensors to measure and display hundreds of process parameters. Control of the paper mill is provided by distributed control systems (DCS) for many of the processes and by programmable logic controllers (PLCs) for most of the discrete control functions. It is not uncommon to have PLC programs with thousands of rungs of ladder logic code, hundreds of pages of function block diagrams, or hundreds of lines of instruction list or structure text code. For example, The finishing machine in the figure has thirty-four motor driven rollers over which the paper passes when it leaves the head box and moves to the finished paper roll. With the paper moving at 80 feet per second, each roller must turn at a coordinated rpm that keeps the proper tension on paper through all of the finishing processes. Complex systems like these under PLC control are operated and maintained by electrical workers. These workers have a thorough understanding of paper production process operation and the many control technologies used to keep the process running.

FIGURE 21-4: Paper production process.

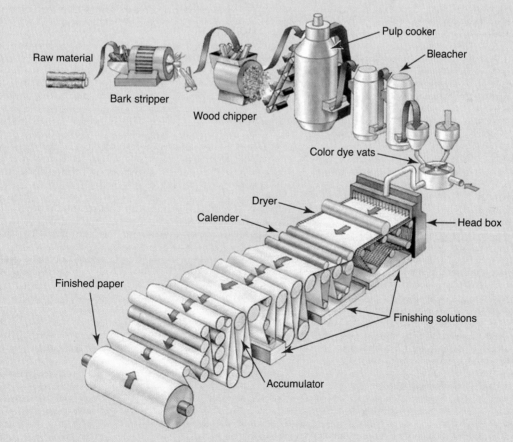

or flow requirements of the system or products changes. The PLC not only controls industrial processes, but also supports preventative maintenance functions and process reports, which are used to determine the efficiency of the manufacturing system. Manufacturers provide a variety of PLCs that are adaptable to perform nearly all industrial operations and are generally categorized in two styles—*stand-alone* and *modular*.

21-2 STAND-ALONE CONTROLLERS

For *stand-alone controllers* like the Allen-Bradley MicroLogix 1000, the PLC component modules are *integrated* into a single unit, and each unit is configured with a *fixed number* of I/O ports. Figure 21-5(a) illustrates the MicroLogix 1000 controller. The controller is a compact design with units available having up to 32 I/O ports in multiple configurations of analog and digital. The I/O options and electrical configurations make it ideal for many applications. Figure 21-5(b) illustrates the hand-held programmer that lets the operator *create* and *modify* programs for

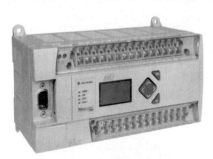

(a) MicroLogix 1000 PLC

(b) MicroLogix 1000 handheld programmer

Courtesy of Rockwell Automation, Inc.

the MicroLogix Controller. In addition, the hand-held programmer allows the operator to monitor programs through features such as *fault text messages* and *fault trace monitoring*.

Installation

The following discussion provides an overview of the installation of the MicroLogix 1000 controller. Complete installation instructions are found in the manufacturer's user or installation manual. The controller is installed horizontally or vertically with mounting screws or on a DIN rail. Figure 21-6 illustrates the controller mounted horizontally on a DIN rail. The power, ground and I/O wiring connections to the controller are made with lugs as shown in the figure or wired directly without lugs.

The controller accepts both discrete inputs and analog inputs. The discrete inputs are either *sinking* or *sourcing*. In the sinking mode, the input is energized when a positive voltage is applied (current flowing into the PLC input terminal), and in the sourcing mode, the input is energized when a ground or negative voltage is applied (current flowing out of the PLC input terminal). Figure 21-7(a) illustrates discrete switch and sensor inputs connected to the controller for both sinking and sourcing connections. For analog inputs, the controller does not supply analog loop power, so a power supply is used that matches the transmitter specifications. Figure 21-7(b) shows analog voltage and current connections at both the input and output terminals. Unused inputs are normally jumpered together to reduce electrical noise. Figure 21-7(c) illustrates the 2-wire, 3-wire, and 4-wire connections for analog inputs. The analog controller inputs have digital filters to reduce the effects of electrical noise on the input signals. However,

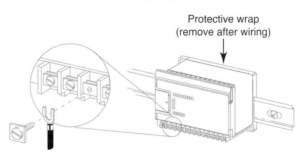

Protective wrap (remove after wiring)

Courtesy of Rockwell Automation, Inc.

because of the variety of applications and environments where the controllers are installed, it is impossible that all electrical noise is eliminated. Several steps can be taken to further reduce the effect of the noise—use shielded cabling, route cabling away from AC wiring, and route the cables in a grounded metallic conduit. Cable termiation points are marked on the PLCs in Figure 21-7.

Controller output channels that are connected to inductive loads such as *motor starters* and *solenoids*

FIGURE 21-7: MicroLogix signal interfaces for discrete and analog devices.

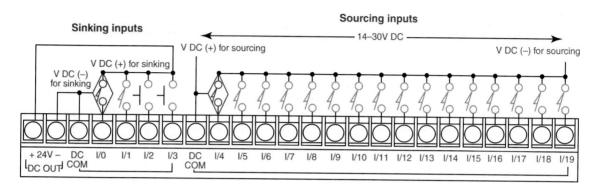

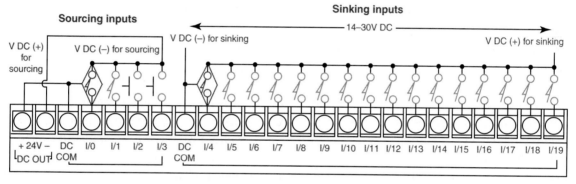

(a) Current sinking and sourcing MicroLogix 1000 inputs

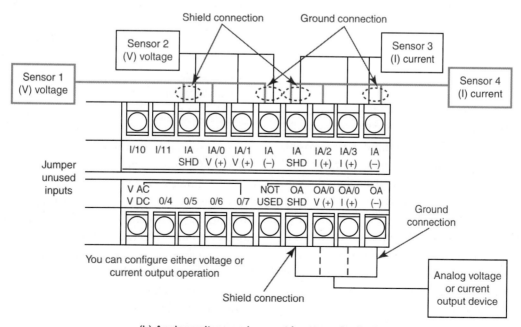

(b) Analog voltage and current inputs and outputs

Courtesy of Rockwell Automation, Inc.

FIGURE 21-7: (Continued)

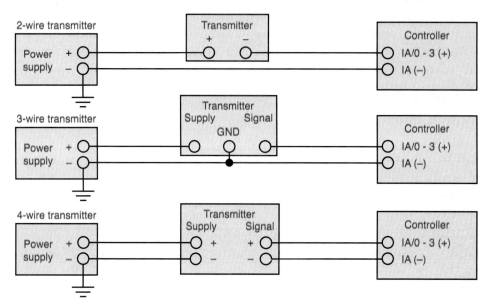

(c) **Sensor inputs with 2-wire, 3-wire, and 4-wire sensor inputs**

require the use of *surge suppressor* to protect the controller outputs. Suitable surge suppression methods include a *varistor,* an *RC circuit* or a *diode.* These components must be appropriately rated to suppress the spike producing characteristics of the inductive load. If the load is connected to a controller transistor output, then a diode is connected across the load. If the load is connected to a controller triac output, then a varistor is connected across the load. The controller manufacturer usually has a list of recommended surge suppressors for various inductive loads.

21-3   MODULAR PLCs

For modular PLCs like the Allen-Bradley *SLC 500* and *CLX 5000,* the component modules are mounted in slots in a rack or chassis. Modular processors, power supplies, I/O modules, memory options, and communication interfaces allow for a configurable and expandable system. Figure 21-8 illustrates the modularity concept of the SLC 500 PLC. The modular PLCs are designed to withstand the vibrations, thermal extremes, and electrical noise associated with harsh industrial environments. The system is configurable for the number of I/O, the amount of memory, and the communication networks that are required by the control application. If requirements change, I/O modules or communication interfaces are removed or added.

Allen-Bradley CLX 5000

The Allen-Bradley *ControlLogix (CLX) modular system* allows the user to design, build, and modify the system efficiently with cost savings in training and engineering. It provides *discrete, motor drive, motion, process,* and *safety control* together with *communication* and *state-of-the-art I/O* in a small package. Figure 21-9 illustrates a CLX 5000 package. The controller is placed into any slot of the chassis and multiple controllers are permitted in the same chassis. Multiple controllers in the same chassis communicate with each other over the backplane like controllers communicate over networks but each operates independently. The ControlLogix architecture provides a wide range of input and output modules to span many applications from *high-speed digital* to *process control.* The ControlLogix architecture allows input information and output status to be shared among multiple ControlLogix controllers.

Each I/O module mounts in a ControlLogix chassis and requires a *removable terminal block* (RTB) to connect the I/O module to system wiring. Figure 21-10 illustrates the RTB interface. The RTB is not part of the module. It plugs into the front of the I/O module and is available in a screw clamp and a spring clamp style. The *interface module* (IFM), which provides an output terminal block for digital I/O modules, is an alternative to the RTB. The factory-wired cable is used to match the I/O module to the IFM. This wiring system is shown in Figure 21-10.

FIGURE 21-8: PLC modular systems.

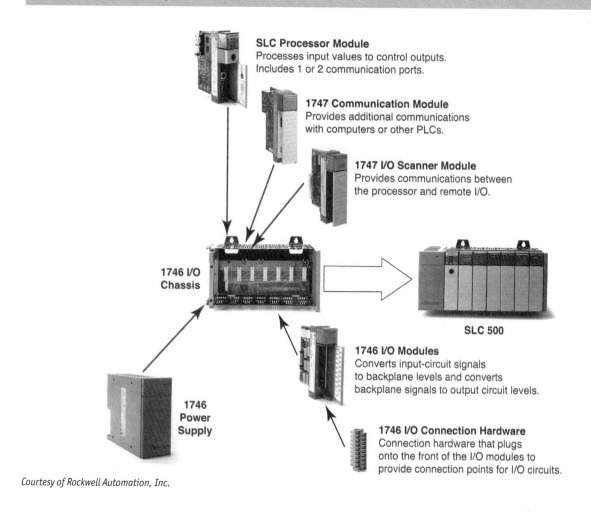

SLC Processor Module
Processes input values to control outputs.
Includes 1 or 2 communication ports.

1747 Communication Module
Provides additional communications
with computers or other PLCs.

1747 I/O Scanner Module
Provides communications between
the processor and remote I/O.

**1746 I/O
Chassis**

SLC 500

**1746
Power
Supply**

1746 I/O Modules
Converts input-circuit signals
to backplane levels and converts
backplane signals to output circuit levels.

1746 I/O Connection Hardware
Connection hardware that plugs
onto the front of the I/O modules to
provide connection points for I/O circuits.

Courtesy of Rockwell Automation, Inc.

FIGURE 21-9: ControlLogix PLC.

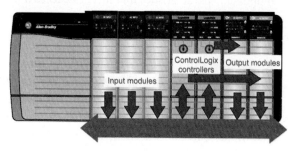

ControlLogix
controllers

Output modules

Input modules

Courtesy of Rockwell Automation, Inc.

FIGURE 21-10: ControlLogix module terminal blocks for I/O terminations.

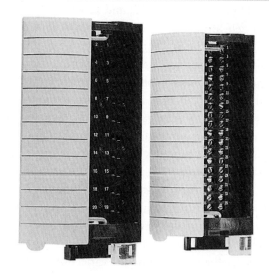

Courtesy of Rockwell Automation, Inc.

Allen-Bradley SLC 500

The Allen-Bradley *SLC 500* is a small chassis-based family of programmable controllers with *discrete, analog,* and *specialty I/O,* and *peripheral* devices. The SLC 500 family delivers power and flexibility with a wide range of communication configurations, features, and

FIGURE 21-11: SLC 500 family of PLC processors and modules.

Courtesy of Rockwell Automation, Inc.

FIGURE 21-12: Remote chassis for SLC 500.

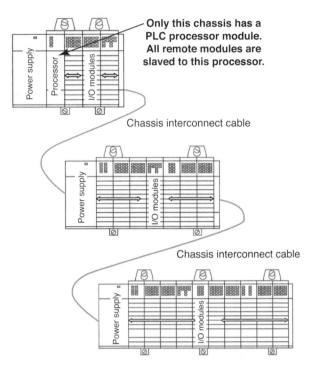

Only this chassis has a PLC processor module. All remote modules are slaved to this processor.

Chassis interconnect cable

Chassis interconnect cable

Courtesy of Rockwell Automation, Inc.

memory options. The RSLogix 500 ladder logic programming package provides flexible editors, point-and-click I/O configuration, and diagnostic and troubleshooting tools that help maximize productivity. Figure 21-11 illustrates the SLC 500 family of controllers and modules.

At a minimum, the SLC 500 modular hardware consists of a *processor module,* I/O modules, and a power supply in one chassis. Systems can be configured with two or more local chasses, which permit up to thirty I/O or communication modules. The multiple local chasses are connected together with interconnect cables, thus extending the backplane as shown in Figure 21-12.

The SLC 500 *I/O modules* are available with 4, 8, 12, and 16-channels or I/O terminations, and LED indicators on the front of each module display the status of each I/O point. The 4, 8, 12, and 16-channel modules have self-lifting pressure plates that accept two #14 AWG wires. The 32-channel modules are equipped with a 40-pin header and a removable wiring connector. The connector is assembled with the wire type and length that meets the application requirements. Input modules are available for *digital* and *analog* signals and discrete modules supporting DC *sinking* and DC *sourcing* inputs. Output modules are available with *solid-state AC, solid-state DC,* and *relay contact* type outputs. High current solid-state output modules have fused common lines with a blown-fuse LED indicator. The analog I/O modules have user-selectable voltage or current inputs, removable terminal blocks and diagnostic feedback. In addition, a variety of specialty modules are available such as *thermocouple modules, resistance temperature detector (RTD) modules, step-*

per motor control modules, and *servo motor control* modules.

Selecting PLC Components

Modular PLCs are built by *selecting components* that fulfill the requirements for the control application and installing them into the rack or chassis. Selection is based on component characteristics that meet or exceed application requirements. The following typical steps are used in the selection process to build a PLC system.

Step 1—Select *I/O modules* based on the combination and quantity of digital and analog inputs and outputs required by the application. If field-side diagnostics, electronic fusing, or individually isolated inputs/outputs is needed, select the appropriate module.

Step 2—Select *integrated motion control modules* based on the need for a digital or analog interface module for controlling motor drives or actuators. If associated cabling and terminal blocks are needed, select appropriate ones for specified drives and motors.

Step 3—Select *communication modules* and associated network cabling for the system network plus additional modules and cabling if a redundant system is required.

Step 4—Select processor/*controller modules* with sufficient memory to meet the requirements plus memory cards and replacement batteries.

Step 5—Select the *chassis* with sufficient slots plus slot fillers for empty slots and the appropriate cabling if more than one chassis is required.

Step 6—Select one *power supply module* for each chassis or a *power supply bundle* if a redundant power supply system is required.

21-4 INTEGRATING PLCs INTO MOTOR CONTROL SYSTEMS

Controlling motors with PLCs is the most efficient way to accomplish the task. The stand-alone PLC or modular PLC with motor control modules is used to interface with the motor. The programming capability of the PLC permits changes in motors and application requirements and provides a diagnostic ability. This section describes a motor control system for a stepper motor and servo motor using a stand-alone PLC and a modular type PLC.

Motor Control System

Figure 21-13 illustrates the range of options available when PLCs are integrated into a motor control system. Any PLC from a legacy PLC, like the Allen Bradley PLC-5, to newer models like the MicroLogix and ControlLogix PLCs are used to control DC and AC motors. Information is accepted from a variety of input devices like *operator manual switches, automatic switches, process switches and sensors, PC programming station*, and *human machine interface (HMI) panel*, like the PanelView touch sensitive screen process display. Outputs drive a variety of output devices like *motor starters, indicators, panel lights, motor drives, a PC programming station*, and *HMI display*. The electrical worker controls the motors through pushbuttons or the HMI. Motor control is also automated with automatically controlled switches and sensor inputs integrated into a ladder logic program in the PLC. The system permits electrical workers to view system status and apply diagnostic tools for troubleshooting. Not shown are the power distribution and circuit protection components that are included in the motor control system.

Stepper Motor Control

Stepper motors are covered in detail in the next chapter. In this section the integration of the stepper motor with the PLC is introduced. As the name implies, the stepper motor rotates in steps as opposed to the continuous rotation present in AC and DC motors. The PLC *stepper motor control module* is placed into a slot in the SLC 500 backplane and is a programmable interface to the motor. Ladder logic program instructions permit changes in the motor shaft position as a part of the total process control ladder logic program. Stepper rotation is programmable in either direction up to plus and minus eight million steps of absolute position. Figure 21-14 illustrates the interface between the SLC 500 and a stepper motor and the motor translator. The PLC generates the move pulse train and the motor translator converts the pulse train to power signals that move the motor. Most permanent magnet type stepper-motor applications are open loop, which implies that position feedback incremental optical encoder is not used. However, most stepper controllers have a closed loop option if a position feedback incremental encoder is necessary. Feedback would be present if the force from the process controlled element was sufficient to overcome the residual magnetic force in the stepper holding it in the desired position. Since stepper motors are lower torque devices, a gear train or other mechanical link is normally used between the stepper motor and the process controlled element to improve resolution or amplify the torque. Often, the mechanical advantage in the system isolates the stepper from process forces and eliminates the need for closed-loop control. Variable reluctance steppers have lower residual holding power and a closed-loop system would likely be used when they are the prime mover in the application.

The module operates in three modes—*configuration, command* and *diagnostic*.

- In the *configuration mode*, the module is setup through the SLC processor to perform operations required by the application. Operations include— set the inputs to be used, set the active level of the inputs that are used, and select the type of encoder that is used.
- In the *command mode*, all stepper motor operations are performed. The move operations include: absolute, relative, hold, and resume moves. Also immediate stops and preset stops are programmable options.

FIGURE 21-13: PLC links to motor control.

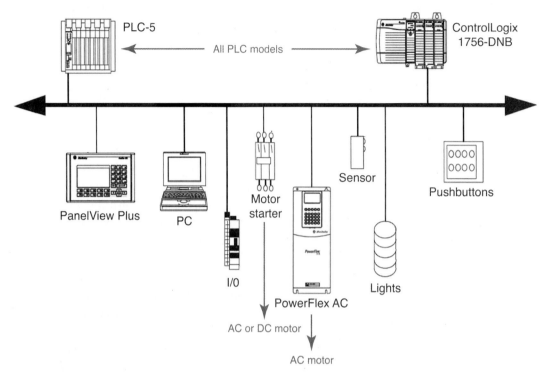

Courtesy of Rockwell Automation, Inc.

FIGURE 21-14: PLC stepper motor controller.

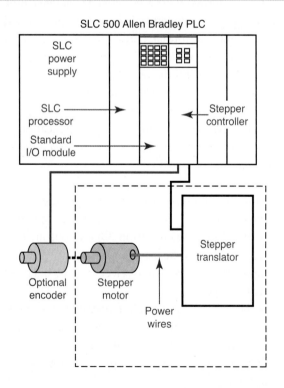

- In the *diagnostic mode,* the program and the wiring are tested by installing loop-back wires at the stepper motor translator. The number of step pulses transmitted should equal the number received at the end of the move. If they are not equal, the system is experiencing problems due to electrical noise. The SLC stepper module has five diagnostic LED indicators located on the module front panel. The *LED layout, module location,* and *operational description* are shown in Figure 21-15.

Figure 21-16 illustrates the terminals on the stepper control module with I/O signal names listed. After the module is installed into the designated slot in the SLC 500 chassis, the input and output device wires are attached to the terminal block based on interface requirement of the application. Output and input signals are isolated from the stepper-motor translator with several types of interface circuits including: *differential, optocoupler with common supply* and *individually isolated optocouplers.* Each terminal accommodates two #14 AWG wires, which are connected to captive screws on the module. The release screws on the terminal block

FIGURE 21-15: PLC stepper motor controller LED indicators.

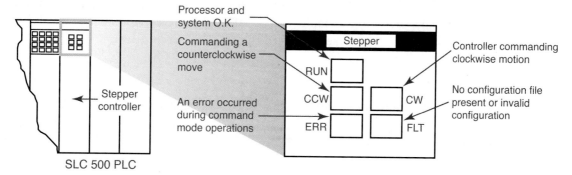

Courtesy of Rockwell Automation, Inc.

FIGURE 21-16: PLC stepper motor control module terminals.

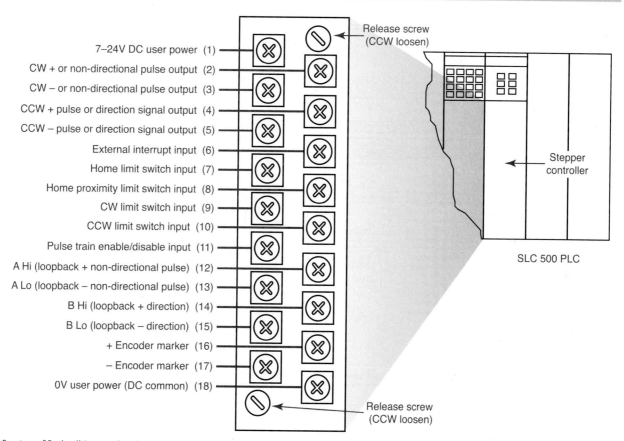

Courtesy of Rockwell Automation, Inc.

allow the replacement of the module without removing any interface wires from the terminal block.

Servo Motor Control

Servo motors are covered in detail in the next chapter. In this section, the integration of the servo motor with the PLC is introduced. The servo motor is a special purpose DC or AC motor that always operates in the close-loop control mode. As a result, the servo motor has integrated feedback sensor(s) that permit highly accurate and repeatable control of motor speed and degree of rotation. The PLC *servo motor control module* is placed into a slot in the SLC 500 backplane and is a programmable interface to the motor's servo drive electronics. Ladder logic program instructions permit changes in the motor shaft position or rotation speed as a part of the total process control ladder logic program. Typically, each servo module controls one servo motor or axis of rotation in the pro-

cess. Motion control includes both linear or rotary movement through rotational and linear motors or with mechanical linkages. Figure 21-17 illustrates the SLC 500 and the termination panel, which interfaces to the encoder, servo driver, and servo motor. The

FIGURE 21-17: PLC servo module, termination panel, drive, and servo.

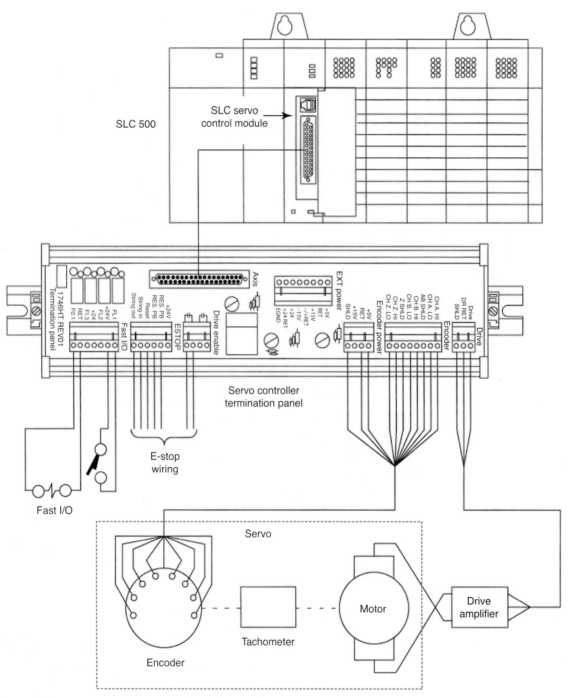

Courtesy of Rockwell Automation, Inc.

FIGURE 21-18: PLC servo module.

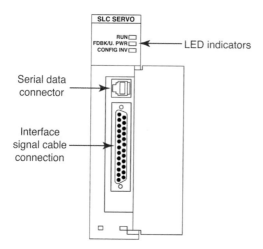

input and output devices are wired to the termination panel in accordance with the type of interface required by the application. Types of interface include differential, optocoupler with common supply and individually isolated optocouplers. The user controlled Emergency Stop (E-stop) circuit is defined in the servo motor module user manual.

The servo motor module operates in a similar set of *configuration, command,* and *diagnostic* modes as described in the stepper motor module. Figure 21-18 shows the servo module with its door open. The connector is the interface to the termination panel, and the LEDs indicate power and operational status. The module requires external +5V DC and +/− 15V DC power and monitors encoder feedback, position and error after initial power up and homing, and inputs and outputs.

CRITICAL CONCEPTS

The need to know content from Chapter 21 is summarized in the following statements.

- The Programmable Logic Controller (PLC) is a special purpose industrial computer designed for use in the control of a wide variety of manufacturing machines and systems.
- The PC is generally designed to do many jobs, but the PLC performs only one chore, sequential and process control of production processes.

- The PLC expands and enhances industrial electrical systems that are generally divided into discrete parts manufacturing and process manufacturing.
- The component modules of the stand-alone PLC are integrated into a single unit, and each unit is configured with a fixed number of I/O ports.
- The stand-alone PLC is installed horizontally or vertically with mounting screws or on a DIN rail, and wiring connections are made with lugs or without lugs.
- The modular PLC consists of a processor module, I/O modules in one chassis with a power supply. Systems can be configured in two or more local chasses, up to thirty I/O or communication modules. The multiple local chasses are connected together with interconnect cables.
- For modular PLCs, input modules are available for digital and analog signals and discrete DC sinking and DC sourcing inputs. Output modules are available with solid-state AC, solid-state DC, and relay contact type outputs.
- Modular PLCs are built by selecting components that fulfill the requirements for the control application and installing them into the rack or chassis. Selection is based on component characteristics that provide the closest match to application requirements.

QUESTIONS

1. Describe the differences and the similarities between the PC and the PLC.
2. Describe the installation process for the Allen-Bradley MicroLogix 1000.
3. Describe the installation process for the Allen-Bradley ControlLogix 5000.
4. Describe the installation process for the Allen-Bradley SLC 500.
5. Describe the purpose of the configuration, the command, and the diagnostic modes of a PLC stepper motor control module.
6. What is the purpose of the release screws on a PLC stepper motor control module?
7. What types of motor movement are controlled by a PLC servo motor control module?
8. Name three common interfaces to a PLC servo motor control module.

22

Special Motor Control Applications

GOALS AND OBJECTIVES

The primary goals for this chapter are to identify and describe the function of *synchronous, stepper,* and *servo motors,* plus the control methods for these motors are discussed.

After completing this chapter, you will be able to:

1. Describe the operation and control of synchronous motors.
2. Describe the operation and control of stepper motors.
3. Describe the operation and control of servo motors.

22-1 SYNCHRONOUS MOTORS

The *synchronous motor* is a three-phase motor in which the rotor turns at the same speed as the magnetic field of the stator. With an induction motor, the rotor rotation is slightly less than the rotation rate of the magnetic field of the stator. The difference between these two speeds is the *slip,* which is zero in the synchronous motor.. The initial cost of a synchronous motor is more than an induction motor due to the expense of the wound rotor and synchronizing circuitry. These initial costs are often offset by the following *advantages.*

- Precise speed regulation makes the synchronous motor an ideal choice for certain industrial processes and as a prime mover for generators.
- Response to digital input pulses provides open-loop control, making the motor simpler and less costly to control.
- Synchronous motors have speed/torque characteristics that are suited for direct drive of large horsepower, low-rpm loads such as reciprocating compressors.
- Synchronous motors operate at an improved power factor, thereby improving overall system power factor and eliminating or reducing utility power factor penalties. An improved power factor also reduces the system voltage drop and the voltage drop at the motor terminals.

The main difference between the synchronous motor and the induction motor is the rotor construction. The rotor construction uses permanent magnets, Figure 22-1, and wound coil technology with two winding elements: the *salient pole winding,* and the *damper or amortisseur winding,* Figure 22-2. The *salient pole* windings are coils of wire that are wound on laminated cores to form the rotor of the motor. Salient means *projecting out,* hence the salient poles project outward from the shaft of the motor. The *amortisseur* (squirrel cage) windings are sets of bars

FIGURE 22-1: Synchronous motor elements.

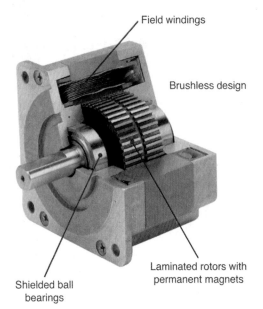

Field windings

Brushless design

Shielded ball bearings

Laminated rotors with permanent magnets

Courtesy of Kollmorgen.

FIGURE 22-2: Synchronous motor salient pole and amortisseur winding.

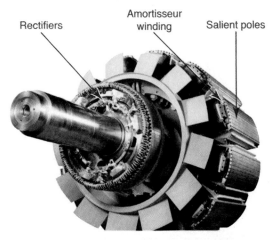

Rectifiers

Amortisseur winding

Salient poles

(a) Salient pole rotor winding with pole wires on laminated cores and amortisseur winding

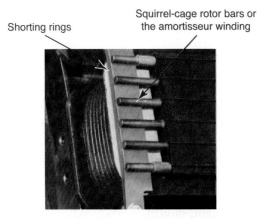

Shorting rings

Squirrel-cage rotor bars or the amortisseur winding

(b) Squirrel-cage rotor bars and a shorting ring on each side of the rotor

Courtesy of ABB, Inc.

with shorting rings similar to those in the induction motor.

Operation and Control

Two phases in synchronous motor control are *start up* and *attaining synchronous speed*. At start up, the three-phase input voltage is applied to the stator, generating a rotating magnetic field in the stator, which cuts through the rotor coils. The *amortisseur* windings are located near the surface of the pole faces of the synchronous motor. These windings *dampen* any speed fluctuations that may occur as a result of sudden load changes and permit the motor to operate as an induction motor until synchronous speed is reached. When the rotor speed nears the speed of the stator field, DC power (the *exciter*) is applied to the rotor. Since adjacent rotor poles have different polarities, each pole is attracted and locked in step to the

rotating stator magnetic field. The amount of force required to lock the rotor into synchronization is called *pull-in torque*. The rotor is operating at synchronous speed—turning at the same speed of the stator field. Since the rotor turns at the same speed as

The synchronous frequency is equal to the input AC voltage frequency times 120 divided by the number of poles or

$$\text{Synchronous frequency} = 120 \times \text{frequency} / \text{number of poles}$$

For example, a 12-pole synchronous motor operating at 60Hz has a synchronous frequency of $120 \times 60 / 12 = 7200 / 12 = 600$ RPM

The synchronous speed increases as the number of poles decrease. The following table lists synchronous speeds at 60Hz for the corresponding number of poles.

Number of Poles	Synchronous Speed (RPM)
2	3600
4	1800
6	1200
8	900

the rotating stator field, no cutting action occurs between the stator field and the amortisseur windings. This action eliminates current flow in the amortisseur windings, and motor no longer operates as an induction motor.

Figure 22-3 illustrates a typical *DC exciter circuit*, which sets the speed of the synchronous motor. The solid state controller energizes the relays K1, K2, and K3, which controls the timing of the application of the DC power and the removal the rotor shunting resistor. The resistor provides a current path to dissipate the current generated in the rotor field prior to synchronous speed. If the load increases after synchronous speed is attained, rotor torque is increased with an increase in the DC excitation. However, if the motor becomes overloaded, the rotor and stator lose synchronous operation. The torque at which synchronization is lost is called the *pull-out torque*.

System Power Factor Improvement

Most of the AC motors used in industry are induction motors, and their loads are inductive; hence a lagging power factor. *Lagging power* factor is *undesirable* because the power costs more since the input must supply more current to satisfy the required load consumption. The disadvantages of lagging power factors are three. The first is that transmission lines and other power circuit elements are usually more reactive than resistive. In some circuits, additional voltage-regulating equipment is required for satisfactory operation of the equipment using power. The second disadvantage is the inefficient utilization of the transmission equipment since more current flow per unit of real power transmitted is necessary due to the reactive power also carried in the power lines. If the current necessary to satisfy

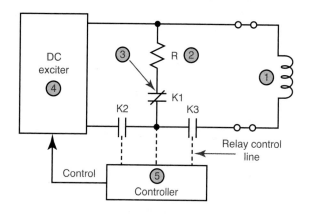

FIGURE 22-3: Typical DC exciter circuit for synchronous motor rotor.

① Synchronous motor commutator and rotor

② Field resistor discharges current prior to synchronous operation

③ Relay K1 is de-energized after synchronous operation

④ DC exciter (usually a regulated DC power supply) provides controllable power

⑤ Controller sequences the K1, K2, and K3 relays leading to synchronous operation

reactive power could be reduced, more useful power could be transmitted through the system. The third disadvantage is the cost of the increased power loss in transmission lines. The increased power loss is due to the unnecessary reactive power which is in the system. The reactive power losses vary as the square of the reactive current or as the inverse of the power factor. In many cases, power companies impose a penalty charge if industrial sites run a power factor below an agreed upon value. So, it is important for industrial plants to keep their power factor as close to *100% (unity)* as

---

FIGURE 22-4: Power factor correction from parallel AC motor operation.

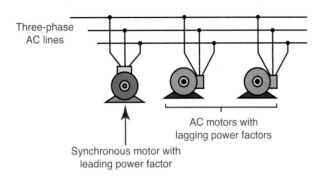

Three-phase AC lines

AC motors with lagging power factors

Synchronous motor with leading power factor

FIGURE 22-5: Stepper motor and stepper motor control electronics.

Courtesy of Applied Motion Products.

economically feasible. Synchronous motors operate at an excellent power factor, thereby improving overall system power factor and eliminating or reducing utility power factor penalties. The power factor of the synchronous motor is a function of the DC field excitation. The DC exciter sets the field excitation, thus creating a leading power factor. Figure 22-4 illustrates a synchronous motor connected to the input power lines with other motors, thus the power factor is improved, moving it closer to unity.

22-2   STEPPER MOTORS

The *stepper motor* converts electronic digital pulses into mechanical rotational steps. Every revolution of the stepper motor is divided into a discrete number of steps, and the motor is sent a separate pulse for each step. The stepper motor only takes one step at a time, and each step is the same size. Since each pulse causes the motor to rotate a precise angle, the motor's position is controlled without any feedback mechanism. As the digital pulses increase in frequency, the step movement changes into continuous rotation, with the speed of rotation directly proportional to the frequency of the pulses. Figure 22-5 shows stepper motors with the electronic controller integrated onto the motor. NEMA standards specify motor sizes from a NEMA 11 to a NEMA 34.

Stepper Motor Types

Stepping motors come in two varieties, *permanent magnet* and *variable reluctance*. There are a number of variations of the basic permanent magnet stepper, which are called *hybrid* stepper motors. The hybrid group includes:

Unipolar Motors—The unipolar type has six coil wires because each of the two windings has a center-tapped connection. With the center tap connected to positive power, the motor direction is determined by the end of the coil that is switched to ground. The motor in Figure 22-6 illustrates this type of winding configuration.

Bipolar Motors—The bipolar type has the same construction as the unipolar but the center tap on the winding is not present. Wiring is simplified but controlling the direction of rotation requires a more complex controller.

Bifilar Motors—The bifilar motor is a six lead device that is configured as unipolar or bipolar depending on the connection of the six leads. It is essentially a unipolar motor with the center tapped point created external to the motor by joining two of the winding connections.

Multiphase Motors—The multiphase motor has the three winding connected in either a delta or wye configuration. A five phase is also used with five winding and ten leads. This hybrid type has more torque and higher resolution.

Lacking a label on the motor, the *permanent magnet* and *variable reluctance* types are identified by manually *rotating* the rotor with no power applied. Permanent magnet motors tend to *cog* as you twist the rotor with your fingers. The rotor *locks* on each field pole as you rotate. Variable reluctance motors almost *spin freely* (a slight cog is sometimes felt because of residual magnetization in the rotor). *Resistance reading*

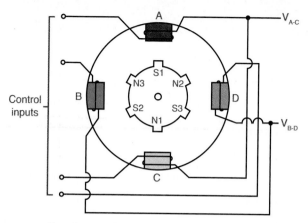

FIGURE 22-6: Unipolar stepper motor rotor pole and stator winding operation.

Note: Stator windings are labeled A, B, C, and D.
Rotor poles are labeled N1, S1, N2, S2, N3, and S3.

on the field winding distinguishes between the two varieties as well. *Variable reluctance* motors usually have *three* or *four windings,* with a common return, while *permanent magnet* motors usually have *two independent windings,* with or without center taps.

Stepping motors come in a wide range of angular resolution. The coarsest motors typically turn 90 degrees per step, while high resolution permanent magnet motors provide 1.8 or even 0.72 degrees per step. Controllers drive most permanent magnet and hybrid motors in half-steps, and some controllers can handle smaller fractional steps or microsteps.

Stepper Motor Operation

When the motor receives a digital pulse energizing the stator winding, the shaft of the stepper motor turns (steps) a specific angular distance then remains at that position until the next incoming digital pulse. The shaft is driven clockwise or counterclockwise, at various pulse rates. Thus, the stepper motor is capable of incrementally controlling the velocity, distance and direction of its mechanical load. In this chapter, three common stepper motors—*the permanent magnet (PM), the variable reluctance (VR),* and *the hybrid*—are discussed. Finally, some stepper motor terms that the electrical worker may encounter are as follows:

- **Stepping Rate**—the maximum number of steps the motor makes in one second
- **Step Angle**—the number of degrees the motor moves per step

- **Holding Torque**—the maximum load-originating torque that the motor stands without moving from its position with the stator energized
- **Detent Torque**—the maximum load-originating torque that the motor stands without moving from its position with the stator de-energized. Its value is typically ten percent of the holding torque.

Permanent Magnet Stepper Motors

The *permanent magnet stepper motor* consists of stator windings and rotor magnets and operates under the principle that unlike magnetic poles attract and like magnetic poles repel. Figure 22-6 is a cross-sectional view of a permanent magnet stepper motor with a four-pole stator and a six-pole rotor. Only one stator winding is energized at a time as the north pole. The stator winding that is the north pole attracts the closest rotor tooth that is a south pole.

For the rotor position shown in the Figure 22-6, winding A is energized as a north pole and rotor pole S1 is aligned to it. This rotor-position is zero degrees. The motor controller increments the rotor through the following steps.

1. The motor controller de-energizes winding A and energizes winding B as a north pole. This causes rotor pole S2, which is closest to B, to align itself with B, causing the rotor to turn 30 degrees clockwise.
2. Next the controller de-energizes winding B and energizes winding C as a north pole. This causes rotor pole S3, which is closest to C, to align itself with C. The rotor has turned another 30 degrees.
3. This stepping action continues in this manner with the sequence for one complete rotation listed in Figure 22-7.

Note in Figure 22-7 that in the *Stator Windings* block, the energized stator winding has an N in its column. The *Rotor Poles* columns indicate the stator winding that is aligned with that rotor pole. The figure lists the steps for a complete rotation of the rotor, from zero degrees back to zero degrees (360 degrees) in 30 degree steps (the step angle).

Variable Reluctance Stepper Motors

The *variable reluctance stepper motor* consists of electromagnetic stator windings as in the permanent

FIGURE 22-7: Stepper motor rotor pole and stator winding alignment for rotation.

Angular Position	Stator Windings				Rotor Poles					
	A	B	C	D	S1	N2	S3	N1	S2	N3
0°	N	–	–	–	A					
30	–	N	–	–					B	
60	–	–	N	–			C			
90	–	–	–	N	D					
120	N	–	–	–					A	
150	–	N	–	–			B			
180	–	–	N	–	C					
210	–	–	–	N					D	
240	N	–	–	–			A			
270	–	N	–	–	B					
300	–	–	N	–					C	
330	–	–	–	N			D			
360	N	–	–	–	A					

Note: Rotor positions from 0° to 360° indicate a clockwise rotation.

magnet stepper motor, and a non-magnetized toothed rotor. The motor shaft rotates to a position that minimizes the magnetic reluctance of the flux path. The variable reluctance motors have much less *holding torque* and effectively zero *detent torque* as compared to the permanent magnet motors because the rotor is non-magnetic. In addition, the variable reluctance motor generally operates at a higher stepping rate (up to 15,000 steps per second) than the permanent magnet motor.

Figure 22-8(a) is a cross-sectional view of a three-winding variable reluctance stepper motor with twelve stator windings and eight rotor teeth. Note that the stator windings are set thirty degrees apart, and the rotor teeth are forty-five degrees apart.

Note that the rotor teeth are labeled T1 through T8, and the stator winding labeled A has four poles alternating between N and S magnetic poles around the motor. However, to avoid clutter in the figure, the B and C windings and connections are omitted, but all winding connections, drawn in Figure 22-8(b) are as follows:

• *Stator winding A* is at the twelve, three, six and nine o'clock positions.

• *Stator winding B* is at the one, four, seven and ten o'clock positions

• *Stator winding C* is at the two, five, eight and eleven o'clock positions

The variable reluctance stator windings are sequentially energized and de-energized as in permanent magnet stepper motor control. The rotational direction is clockwise, and the step angle as shown in Figure 22-8 is fifteen degrees, which is the difference between the positions of the stator poles and rotor teeth—thirty degrees and forty-five degrees, respectively.

The inability of stepper motors to exactly follow the step command results in overshoot followed by oscillations as shown in Figure 22-9. With the *permanent magnet stepper motor* the oscillations dissipate rather quickly because the magnetic rotor clings to the energized magnetic field of the stator windings. However, the *variable reluctance stepper motor* has no permanent magnets, and the oscillations do not dissipate quickly and are rather severe when the load exhibits a high inertia. If the oscillations have not dissipated prior to the next step, the variable reluctance motor could take a backward step.

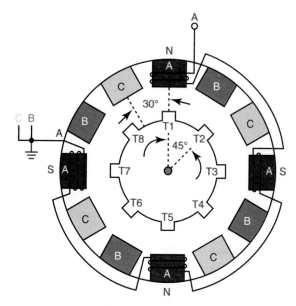

(a) Cross-section of the three-winding variable reluctance stepper with winding A shown. Windings on B and C would be connected in a similar fashion.

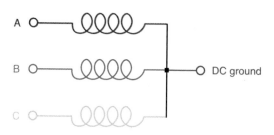

(b) Connection of three-winding for the reluctance motor cross-section in (a)

FIGURE 22-9: Stepper motor overshot response to position change.

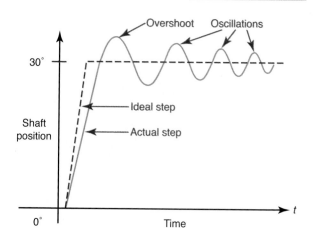

Damping Variable Reluctance Steppers

Damping is implemented in the variable reluctance motor to suppress the step oscillations. A rather inexpensive electrical damping method is resistive or capacitive damping as shown in Figure 22-10(a) and (b), respectively. In the *resistive damping* method, a small amount of current is allowed to flow through the resistors to the two de-energized windings, resulting in a slight reverse torque applied by these two windings. The effect is that the rotor's acceleration is slightly reduced, therefore limiting the overshoot.

The *capacitive damping* method, Figure 22-10(b), allows a charged capacitor in parallel with the winding to discharge into the winding when the winding is de-energized. This results in a reverse torque applied to the rotor to damp oscillations.

FIGURE 22-10: Resistor and capacitor damping of step response for stepper motor.

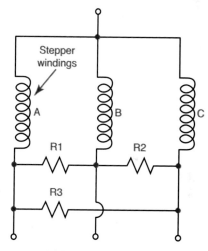

(a) Resistor damping

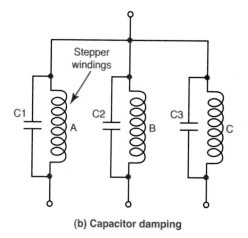

(b) Capacitor damping

Hybrid Stepper Motors

The *hybrid stepper motors* combine the best characteristics of the *permanent magnet* and the *variable reluctance* motors. They are constructed with multi-toothed stator poles and a permanent magnet rotor. Typically, hybrid motors have 200 rotor teeth and rotate at a 1.8 degree step angle. Because they exhibit high static and dynamic torque and run at very high step rates, hybrid stepper motors are used in a wide variety of commercial applications including *computer disk drives, printers/plotters*, and *CD players*. Industrial applications of stepper motors include *robotics, machine tools, pick and place machines, automated wire cutting and wire bonding machines*, and *precise fluid control devices*. Hybrid stepper motors have three basic step modes, which are *full, half* and *microstep*. Motor drives are available with either *switch-selectable* or *software-selectable* step modes.

- The *full step mode* has 200 full steps per revolution of the motor shaft. Dividing the 200 steps into the 360 degrees of rotation equals a 1.8 degree full step angle. Essentially one digital pulse from the driver is equivalent to one step.
- *Half step* means that the step motor is rotating at 400 steps per revolution. In this mode, two adjacent windings are energized, causing the rotor to rotate half the distance, or 0.9 degree step angle. Although it provides approximately thirty percent less torque, half-step mode produces a smoother motion than full-step mode.
- The *microstep* is a relatively new stepper motor technology that controls the current in the motor winding to a degree that further subdivides the number of positions between poles. Drivers are capable of dividing a full step (1.8 degrees) into 256 microsteps, resulting in 51,200 steps per revolution, or 0.007 degree/step. Microstepping is typically used in applications that require accurate positioning and smoother motion over a wide range of speeds. Like the half-step mode, microstepping provides approximately thirty percent less torque than full-step mode.

Stepper Motor Drives

The stepper motor drives are *solid state devices* that control the step and direction of the motor. Figure 22-11(a) illustrates the *block diagram* of a typical microstep driver. The *microstep controller board* for the stepper motor is illustrated in Figure 22-11(b). The step, direction, and enable inputs are optically-isolated, logic level signals. Note the switch selectable step resolution and the self-test are inputs to the microstep sequencer. When selected, the self-test feature rotates the motor at 1/4 revolution in each direction at 100 steps/second. The motor current is also switch selectable from 0.4A to 3.5A per phase. Note that an additional switch selectable feature allows the motor current to be reduced by fifty percent if the motor is at rest for more than one second. Drives are also available with integral DC power supplies and fault protection for situations such as *over-voltage, under-voltage*, and *over-temperature*.

Stepper motor drive selection depends on the application's torque and speed requirements. Figure 22-12 illustrates a *typical torque-speed* curve. Drive manu-

---

FIGURE 22-11: Stepper motor controller block diagram and controller board.

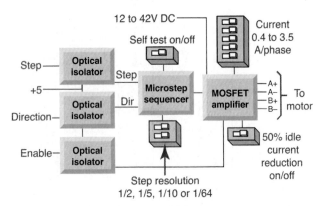

(a) Block diagram of microstep controller for stepper motor

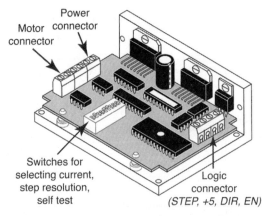

(b) Microstep controller board for stepper motor

Reproduced courtesy of Omega Engineering, Inc., Stamford, CT, 06907 USA www.omega.com with permission of Applied Motion Products, Inc.

FIGURE 22-12: Torque versus speed curves for stepper motor.

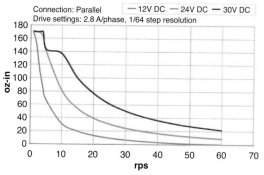

Connection: Parallel
Drive settings: 2.8 A/phase, 1/64 step resolution
— 12V DC — 24V DC — 30V DC

Reproduced courtesy of Omega Engineering, Inc., Stamford, CT, 06907 USA www.omega.com with permission of Applied Motion Products, Inc.

facturers supply the torque-speed curves for their stepper motors. If the torque and speed requirements are met by multiple step motors, the drive is selected based upon the needs of the motion system such as *step/direction*, *stand-alone*, *programmable*, *analog inputs*, and *micro-stepping*. The manufacturer's motor list is based on extensive testing by the manufacturer to ensure optimal performance of the stepper motor and drive combination.

In some applications, stepper motors are driven by a programmable logic controller with an I/O stepper module. Figure 22-13(a) shows Siemens PLCs, stepper motors, and PLC stepper control modules.

FIGURE 22-13: PLC stepper motor control module and interface.

(a) PLC, stepper motors, and PLC control module

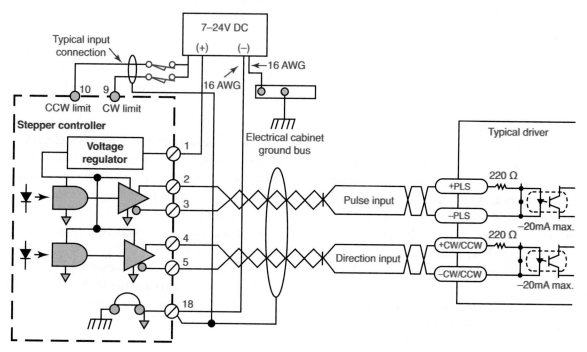

(b) PLC stepper module and stepper driver interface

Courtesy of Siemens (part a) and Rockwell Automation, Inc. (part b).

Stepper PLC modules are capable of providing up to 250 kHz pulse train output for micro-stepping applications. The stepper modules are usually used for open loop stepper applications because stepper motors are most often used without position feedback. The module offers unique features with built-in loop diagnostics that permit monitoring of the commands to the module.

A typical PLC stepper motor module interface that drives the stepper electronics is shown in Figure 22-13(b). This Allen Bradley SLC 500 PLC interface includes inputs from normally closed limit switch contacts to indicate that stepper motor shaft rotation reached the clockwise and counter clockwise limits. The limit switch contacts are often used to indicate linear movement limits when the stepper rotation is converted to linear motion with a rack and pinion type of drive system. Other interface parameters include the pulse and directional inputs on terminals two through five. Control options not used and not shown in the figure include the *external interrupt* to stop a move with an external contact and the *home limit* or *proximity switch* to indicate the home move position.

22-3 SERVO MOTORS

The *servo motor* is a *position* or *motion* correcting motor that responds to a *control signal*. The servo motor shaft is driven to a specific angular position as commanded by the control signal. As long as the control signal is present, the servo motor maintains the angular position of the shaft. When the control signal is changed, the angular position of the shaft follows the change. The *servo motor* is generally part of a *servo system* that operates in a closed-loop system called a *servo loop*. The block diagram of a servo loop is shown in Figure 22-14. The three basics blocks are the *servo amplifier, the servo motor* and *the feedback sensors*. The servo amplifier consists of an *input stage* that develops a drive signal for the *output stage*. The drive signal is basically the difference between the *input control signal*, V_{CS}, and the *velocity* and *position feedback signal*, V_{FS}, from the sensors.

In general, servo motors are just a *DC* or *AC motor*; however, specific capabilities must be incorporated to

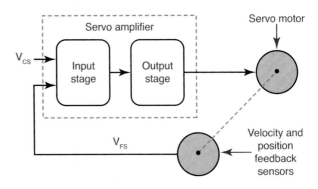

FIGURE 22-14: Servo motor control system.

qualify the DC or AC motor as a servo type device. The capabilities include:

- Sufficient torque to hold a load in a fixed position
- Operation at standstill and over a range of speeds without overheating
- Smooth acceleration in the forward and reverse directions

DC Servo Motors

The *DC servo motor* is normally used in computer related devices like printers and scanners, numerically controlled (NC) machinery, or other applications where starts and stops are made quickly and accurately. In the DC servo motor, the voltages applied to the *field winding* and to the *armature winding* are supplied from *different sources*. Most DC servo systems have a fixed field voltage and an amplifier controlled armature voltage. This voltage application on the DC servo motor differs from the general purpose DC motor where a *single voltage source* drives both the *field winding* and the *armature winding*. The industrial DC servo motor is a rugged design that meets the demanding requirements of motion control such as *X-Y indexing tables, electrical coil winding machines* and *industrial robots*. While some applications are better satisfied by DC servo motor characteristics, the advances in servo motor design makes the AC servo motor an equally good choice. This is especially true in industrial servo robot applications.

Figure 22-15 illustrates an exploded view of a DC servo motor. The characteristics of the DC servo motor are described in torque-speed curves as shown in Figure 22-16. Note that the torque-producing capability

FIGURE 22-15: Exploded view of DC servo motor.

Courtesy of Baldor Electric Company.

FIGURE 22-16: DC servo speed versus torque curves.

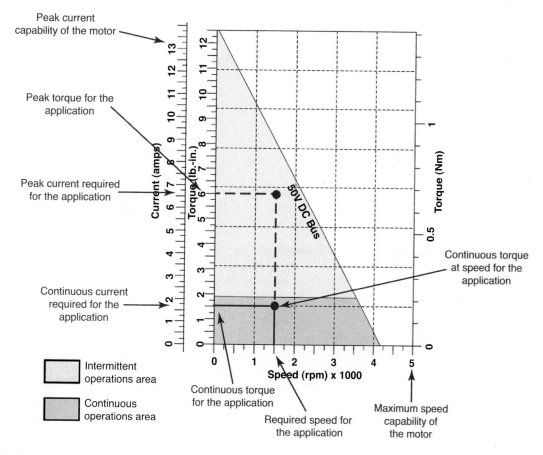

Courtesy of Baldor Electric Company.

of the DC servo motor is greater at lower speeds than at higher speeds. This capability enables the motor to rapidly accelerate from a standstill to the commanded position. As the motor approaches its commanded position, the armature voltage is reduced, enabling the motor to reduce the heating in the armature winding and to deliver a reverse torque to reduce the speed if required.

In constant speed applications, motors are defined in terms of horsepower, which is torque at a base speed. DC servo motors normally operate over a wide speed range. The curves show continuous torque, which is the torque that does not overheat the motor, and peak torque, which is the intermittent acceleration torque. It is also necessary to know the current and voltage required for the motor to operate. The curves have a scale that shows current required for any torque, and voltage required for any speed. As noted in Figure 22-16, an application requires a continuous torque of 1.5 lb-in at a speed of 1,500 RPM. The intermittent or peak torque required for acceleration is 6 lb-in. Therefore, a DC servo motor is selected that meets these requirements from the motor manufacturers' torque-speed curves that are available for every DC servo motor.

AC Servo Motor

The AC servo motor provides high acceleration for rapid positioning in industrial applications where low inertia is present. The voltages applied to the fixed winding and to the control winding are supplied from the same source. These voltages are either in phase or 180 degrees out of phase with each other. If the voltage that drives the control winding is in phase with the fixed winding voltage, then the control winding current lags the fixed winding current by approximately ninety degrees. In this case, the motor turns in the clockwise direction. Conversely, if the voltage that drives the control winding is 180 degrees out of phase with the fixed winding voltage, then the control winding current leads the fixed winding current by approximately ninety degrees. As a result, the motor turns in the counterclockwise direction. Figure 22-17 illustrates an exploded view of an AC servo motor.

The characteristics of the AC servo motor are described in torque-speed curves as shown in Figure 22-18. Interpretation of the curves is similar to the description for the DC servo motor. The curves indicate that the greatest torque is generated at low speed and decreases as the speed increases. At small

FIGURE 22-17: Exploded view of AC servo motor.

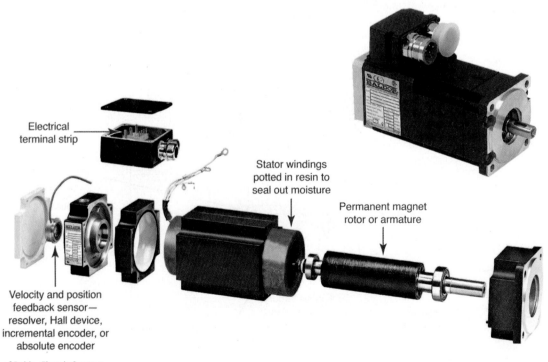

Electrical terminal strip

Stator windings potted in resin to seal out moisture

Permanent magnet rotor or armature

Velocity and position feedback sensor— resolver, Hall device, incremental encoder, or absolute encoder

Courtesy of Baldor Electric Company.

control voltages, the AC servo motor actually provides a reverse torque, which aids in preventing overshoot. If the inertia of the load attempts to make the rotor spin faster than its controlled speed, the fixed-winding magnetic field interacts with the fast-turning rotor, causing current to flow in the reverse direction in the control winding. In general, AC servo motors are preferred over DC servo motors because they are more rugged, have lower maintenance, and are capable of operating at higher temperatures. These reasons are basically the same in non-servo motor selection; however, in servo systems that require high power output, the DC servo motor is typically selected.

In constant speed applications, motors are defined in terms of horsepower, which is torque at a base speed. The AC servo motors normally operate over a wide speed range. The curves show continuous torque, which is the torque that does not overheat the motor, and peak torque, which is the intermittent acceleration torque. It is also necessary to know the current and voltage required for the motor to operate. The curves have a scale that shows current required for any torque, and voltage required for any speed. As noted in Figure 22-18, an application requires a continuous torque of 25 lb-in at a speed of 1,000 RPM. The intermittent or peak torque required for acceleration is 80 lb-in. Therefore, an AC servo motor is selected that meets these requirements from motor manufacturers' torque-speed curves that are available for every AC servo motor.

Servo Motor Controllers

Initially, a simple servo amplifier controlled the motor whose input was the difference between the control signal and the sensor signal, and whose output drove the motor. For the DC servo motor these amplifiers were typically push-pull type amplifiers, built with discrete components and solid state transistors. Amplifiers that drove AC servo motors were typically discrete component choppers, which converted DC pulses to AC sine waves. These simple amplifiers were superseded by microprocessor-based servo drive amplifiers, but today the servo motor controller has replaced the

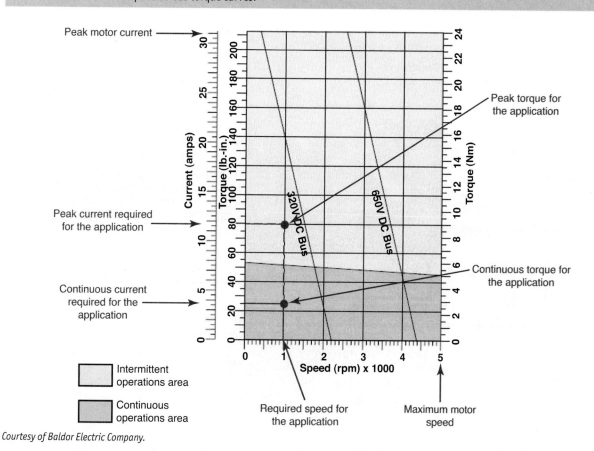

FIGURE 22-18: AC servo speed versus torque curves.

Courtesy of Baldor Electric Company.

servo amplifier for most applications. The servo motor controllers consist not only of an amplifier, which drives the servo motor to the correct position, but also contains circuitry that receives signals from sensors, controls the system, and sends signals to a programmable logic controller that typically controls many servo systems. Figure 22-19 shows a DC servo motor controller. The unit plugs directly into the 115V AC power line and contains its own DC power supply. It controls one or two servo motors, accepts analog input feedback signals in the +/− 10 volts range, and has multi-axes operation capability. This is one example of the many servo motor controllers that are available in the marketplace. These units vary from stand-alone to network-connected units with assemblies suited for a printed wiring board style to a rack mounted style.

FIGURE 22-19: DC servo controller.

Courtesy of Baldor Electric Company.

APPLICATION

Cartoner systems provide the packaging for a wide variety of consumer products ranging from pet foods to breakfast cereal. Because cartoners provide the packaging for products that are directly received by the consumer, they are usually equipped with additional features such as a code-date printer, leaflet, or coupon inserter. These machines are grouped into two main categories: vertical cartoners and horizontal cartoners.

Figure 22-20 illustrates a horizontal cartoner. Note that a PLC controls the servo motor drives over a SERCOS

FIGURE 22-20: Servo driven cartoner system.

Servo drive module   High speed output card

ControlLogix system

SERCOS

Sensor

Glue dispenser

MP-series brushless servo motors

AC induction motor

Kinetix 6000 multi-axis servo drives

Courtesy of Rockwell Automation, Inc.

(SERial COmmunication System) fiber-optic link. SERCOS is a serial real time communication system, generally used for closed-loop data transfer. As incoming product enters the cartoner machine, it is collated into the appropriate pack pattern. A flat case is then selected from the case magazine, opened and positioned for insertion. Individual cartons are pulled into the machine based on their posi- tion. Carton position is determined by sensors that detect the movement of product passing by on the conveyor. With precise timing and positioning provided by the servo motors, three products are placed into their respective cartons with horizontal actuators. Carton flaps are then folded as the case moves into a sealing station where a glue dispenser seals the outside flaps on the carton.

CRITICAL CONCEPTS

The need to know content from Chapter 22 is summarized in the following statements.

- The synchronous motor is a three-phase motor in which the rotor turns at the same speed as the magnetic field of the stator.
- Two phases in synchronous motor control are start up and attaining synchronous speed. At start up, the three-phase input voltage is applied to the stator, generating a rotating magnetic field, which cuts through the rotor coils. When the rotor speed nears the speed of the stator field, DC power (the *exciter*) is applied to the rotor.
- Synchronous motors operate at an improved power factor, thereby improving overall system power factor and eliminating or reducing utility power factor penalties.
- The stepper motor converts electronic digital pulses into mechanical rotational steps.
- The permanent magnet stepper motor consists of stator windings and rotor magnets and operates under the principle that unlike poles attract and like poles repel.
- The variable reluctance stepper motor consists of electromagnetic stator windings as in the permanent magnet stepper motor, and a non-magnetized toothed rotor. The motor shaft rotates to a position that minimizes the magnetic reluctance of the flux path.
- The hybrid stepper motors are constructed with multi-toothed stator poles and a permanent magnet rotor, typically, 200 rotor teeth and a 1.8 degree step angle.
- The microstep stepper motors are capable of dividing a full step (1.8 degrees) into 256 microsteps, resulting in 51,200 steps per revolution, or 0.007 degree/step.

- The servo motor is a position or motion correcting motor that is driven to specific angular position as commanded by a control signal.
- In DC servo motors, an amplifier controls the armature voltage, whereas the field voltage is fixed. In contrast to the general purpose DC motor, one voltage drives both the field winding and the armature winding.
- In the AC servo motor, the voltages applied to the fixed winding and to the control winding are supplied from the same source, but they are either in phase or 180 degrees out of phase with each other.
- The servo motor controller consists not only of an amplifier, which drives the servo motor to the correct position, but also contains circuitry that receives signals from sensors, controls the system, and sends signals to a programmable logic controller that typically controls many servo systems.

QUESTIONS

1. Describe the operation and control of a synchronous motor.
2. How do utility power companies use synchronous motors?
3. What are step angle, stepping rate, holding torque and detent torque as used to describe a stepper motor?
4. Describe the operation and control of a permanent magnet stepper motor.
5. Describe the operation and control of a variable reluctance stepper motor.
6. Explain how the winding voltages are applied to control a DC servo motor.
7. Explain how the winding voltages are applied to control an AC servo motor.
8. Describe the evolution of servo motor controllers.

CHAPTER 23

Network Motor Control

GOALS AND OBJECTIVES

The primary goals for this chapter are to describe the features and functions of industrial networks including *network devices, topologies, and media* and *networked motor control.*

After completing this chapter, you will be able to

1. Describe local area network devices and components.
2. Discuss network topologies and media.
3. Describe the operation and features of Ethernet, ControlNet and DeviceNet.
4. Describe the operation and function of networked motor control.

23-1 INTRODUCTION TO NETWORKS

A *network* is a communication system where two or more intelligent machines or devices are physically and/or wirelessly connected together to share information. Networks require unique features, which permit network management without constant manual intervention, and a set of rules for communication called a *protocol.* Some common network protocols are *file transfer protocol* (FTP), *simple mail transfer protocol* (SMTP) and *industrial* or *Internet protocol* (IP). Networks typically consist of the following distinct components:

- *Enterprise Networks*, which consist of locally connected machines in a company building or group of company buildings
- *Local-area Networks*, which act as data highways within an enterprise network
- *Wide-area Networks*, which connect enterprise networks together
- *Remote Networks*, which link branch offices and single mobile users to a local enterprise network or the Internet.

Figure 23-1 illustrates a typical *enterprise network*, which interconnects company-wide operation into local area networks (LANs) such as financial, engineering and production. Note that *switches* are daisy-chained together and subdivide the enterprise network into LANs. A network switch is critical in the management of an enterprise network. The *network switch* functions as the traffic management system within the network, directing data to the correct destinations. They also connect peripheral devices to the network and ensure maximum cost effectiveness and the ability to

FIGURE 23-1: Enterprise data network.

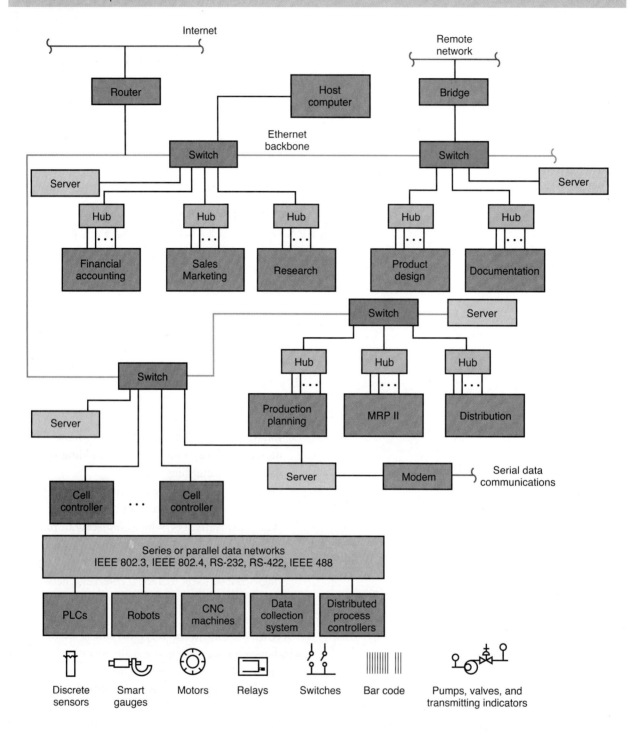

share resources. Each LAN is comprised of the following hardware components:

- **Hubs**—Central connecting devices in a network that are sometimes called a *multiport repeaters.* Hubs regenerate the data bits in order to maintain

a strong signal. Since all devices connected to a hub compete for the network resources, the data transmission rate is reduced. As a result, hubs are not as good for control systems and should not be used for control type data. Note that hubs are not used in the control portion of the network in Figure 23-1.

- **Cables**—Network cables, called the *network media*, are various types of data transmission elements used to physically connect intelligent machines to the network and interconnect network hardware. Network media includes: *single* and *multi-pair twisted pair cables, coaxial cables, fiber optic cables*, and a variety of *wireless technologies*.
- **Servers**—High-powered workstations with a specific function such as *file service, web service*, or *email service*.
- **Interface Cards**—Electronic assemblies that connect individual devices to the network, matching the device type to the cable type.
- **Peripherals**—Network devices such as *printers, plotters, fax machines*, and *backup devices*.

LANs are often expanded because of *increased* data traffic, *addition* of other nodes, or the *distance* between devices on the LAN becomes excessive. The expansion uses one or more of the following components:

- **Bridges**—Bridges are devices that connect two network segments together. These segments may have similar or dissimilar networks. A bridge is inserted into a network to "segment it" so that traffic can be contained within each segment to improve performance.
- **Routers**—Routers are used to segment LANs in order to balance traffic within workgroups and are used as "firewalls" to filter traffic for security purposes and policy management. Routers are also used at the edge of the network to connect remote locations.
- **Repeaters**—Devices used for signal retransmission when the cable length exceeds the specification of the cable type for reliable signal transmission. They transmit received messages from one cable segment to another.
- **Gateways**—The term *gateway* has several different meanings. In some cases, gateways connect different types of networks where they perform the conversion from one network protocol to the other. In other cases, a gateway acts as a go-between, connecting two or more networks that use the same protocols. In this case, the gateway functions as an entry/exit point to the network. Gateways are often used to connect local- and wide-area networks that use a different network protocol and therefore require protocol switching.

TECH NOTES

The transfer of information is dependent on the access speed of the devices or machines and the network media. The rate of transfer is measured in *bits per second* (bps), where bps is also referred to as baud rate. A reciprocal relationship exists between bps and the bit time of the transferred data. (bit time = 1 / bps). For example, if the data bit time is 500 microseconds, then the rate of transfer is 2,000 bps.

Network Media

Network media is the *physical path* over which an electrical or optical signal travels as it moves from one user to another. It is the type of *conductor* used to interconnect the intelligent machines. Four basic factors that determine which media is used in a data network are:

- **Range**—the maximum recommended transmission length between machines.
- **Bandwidth**—specification of the network's maximum frequency range, thus impacting the rate at which a network transfers data. There are two classifications for bandwidth—*broadband* and *baseband*.
- **Noise Immunity**—indication that susceptibility to electromagnetic interference is media dependent.
- **Cost**—a factor because the media with higher performance characteristics generally is more expensive.

The media is possibly the single most important long-term investment made in a network. The choice of media type affects the *type* of network interface cards installed, the *speed* of the network, and the *capability* of the network to meet future needs. Common types of physical network media include: *unshielded twisted-pair (UTP), shielded twisted-pair (STP), coaxial*, and *fiber-optic cables*. The 100-ohm UTP (Unshielded Twisted Pair) type of cable, used for most Ethernet wiring, is divided into six categories designated Cat3, Cat4, Cat5, Cat5e, Cat6, and Cat7. Figure 23-2 compares the media choices.

Human-Machine Interface

The *human-machine interface* (HMI) is where people and technology meet. This people-technology intercept is as simple as the grip on an electromechanical hand tool or as complex as the flight deck controls on a commercial jet. For industrial networks, the *graphic terminal* is the HMI. Graphic terminals offer rugged electronic interface solutions in a variety of

FIGURE 23-2: Network cable comparison.

Media Type	Maximum Length	Speed	Cost	Advantages	Disadvantages
UTP	100 m	10 Mbps to 1,000 Mbps	Least expensive	Easy to install, widely used and widely available	Susceptible to interference, can cover limited distance
STP	100 m	10 Mbps to 100 Mbps	More expensive than UTP	Reduced crosstalk, more resistant to interference	Difficult to work with, can cover limited distance
Coaxial	185 m to 500 m	10 Mbps to 100 Mbps	Relatively inexpensive, but more expensive than UTP	Less susceptible to interference than STP	Difficult to work with, limited bandwidth, damage can bring down network
Fiber optic	2 km to 10 km	100 Mbps to 100 Gbps	Expensive	Security better, used over great distances, not susceptible to interference, very high speed	Difficult to work with and to interface

Note: The UTP speeds are typical, but in newer applications speeds of 10 Gbps and 100 Gbps are used but accommodate shorter cable length.

FIGURE 23-3: HMI devices.

sizes and configurations. These robust devices include hardware, software, and a communications interface that supports the HMI operation. These networked terminals replace traditional wired panels as the input and output mechanism for operator interaction with machines. They are capable of providing process information over a variety of industrial networks.

A popular graphic terminal is the Allen-Bradley PanelView, and Figure 23-3 illustrates a variety of PanelView styles. Most of the HMI panels have a high contrast ratio, making this graphic terminal an excellent choice for bright ambient light applications such as environments using halogen or fluorescent lights. They are available in touch screen or keypad and satisfy the most demanding process control applications. Some HMI panels include training documents and

videos on the operator terminal, so the electrical worker can view short training modules on the terminal.

23-2   NETWORK TOPOLOGIES

Topology is the physical structure of the network. The topology specifies how nodes in a network are connected to each other for communication of data over the network cables. The machines and devices communicating between each other on a LAN and enterprise network are connected together via *three basic topologies*, shown in Figure 23-4. The three basic topologies are:

- **Bus Topology**—All machines are connected to a central network media (cable), which is called the *bus* or *backbone*. Bus topologies like that shown in Figure 23-4(a) typically have network nodes located on the backbone.
- **Ring Topology**—All machines are interconnected in the shape of a *closed loop*. Ring topologies like that shown in Figure 23-4(b) typically have network nodes at points around the ring topology.
- **Star Topology**—All machine clusters are typically connected to a hub or switch. The cluster hub or switch is are connected to a *central router* or a *switch*. All communication passes through the central hubs and switches so bandwidth may be less than the other topologies. Figure 23-4(c) illustrates this type topology.

Additional topologies, such as the tree topology, are constructed using combinations of two of the basic

FIGURE 23-4: Network topology.

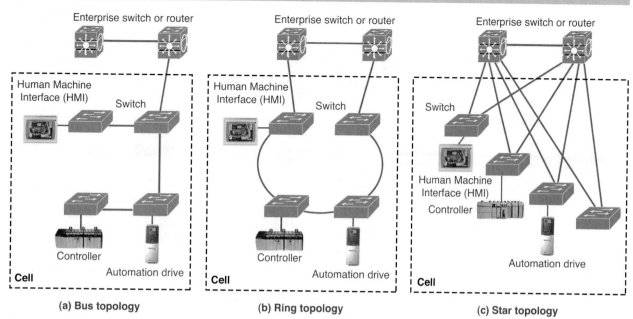

(a) Bus topology   **(b) Ring topology**   **(c) Star topology**

Note: Usually multiple devices are connected to the switches.

three topologies. The tree topology is a combination of the bus and star topologies where groups of star-configured machines are connected to a central bus. The topologies illustrated in Figure 23-4 use network switches, but they are built with *hubs* in place of the switches in some applications. When hubs are used, additional data throughput is lost due to the hub technology.

23-3 FACTORY FLOOR NETWORK

The factory floor network, a part of the enterprise network, is shown pictorially in Figure 23-5. Note that the *factory floor architecture* is flattened into three layers—*Ethernet, ControlNet,* and *DeviceNet/ FOUNDATION Fieldbus.*

- **Ethernet**—The highest level of the network architecture and provides an information layer for enterprise-wide data collection and program maintenance.
- **ControlNet**—The middle level of the architecture and supplies an automation and control layer for real-time input/output control, coordinating update times between applications and messaging.
- **DeviceNet/FOUNDATION** Fieldbus—The lowest level of the architecture and provides a network based integration of individual control devices.

Use the color coded elements in Figure 23-5 to observe the device groupings in each of the networks. Note the

integration of smart motor and servo controllers with smart pilot devices and the use of HMI interfaces to control and view motor and process parameters.

Ethernet and Ethernet/IP

The *Ethernet* system consists of three basic elements: (1) the physical medium used to carry Ethernet signals between devices; (2) a set of network control rules in each Ethernet interface that allow devices to equally share the Ethernet channel; and (3) a standard Ethernet data packet or grouping of bits to carry data over the system.

Each Ethernet-equipped device operates independently of all other devices on the network. All devices attached to the Ethernet have a shared signaling system using the same protocol. Ethernet signals are transmitted serially, one bit at a time, over the shared signal channel to every attached device. Each device listens to the channel, and when the channel is idle, the device transmits its data in the form of an Ethernet frame or packet. After each frame transmission, all devices on the network must contend equally for the next frame transmission opportunity—when the channel is idle.

Ethernet/IP is an open industrial networking standard that uses commercial off-the-shelf Ethernet communication devices and physical media. Ethernet/IP permits devices from different vendors to communicate on the same Ethernet/IP network. This open standard enables

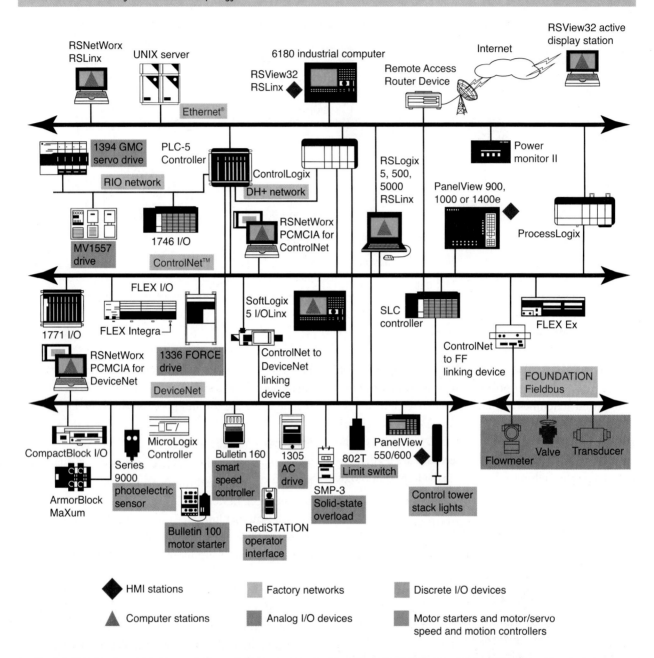

FIGURE 23-5: Factory floor network topology.

TECH NOTES

The nomenclature *xBasey* describes Ethernet media and is interpreted as follows:

- x is the signaling rate in Mbps, unless the letter G is present, then the rate is in Gbps.
- Base is the term that means the signal uses the Ethernet cabling in a baseband scheme as opposed to a broadband. Broadband is a multi-frequency, multi-channel modulating scheme.
- y is the indication of the media type. New media types are continually being developed to support modern applications.

Commonly used Ethernet media types are:

- 10Base5—standard thick coaxial cable
- 10Base2—thin coaxial cable
- 10BaseT—UTP (Unshielded twisted pair)
- 100BaseT—UTP
- 10GBase-LR—long range fiber optics
- 10GBase-T—UTP or STP (shielded twisted pair)
- 10GBase-CR10—copper cable

real-time communications between a wide variety of industrial automation products including *PLC processors, robot controllers, input/output adapters, operator interfaces, motor control center hardware,* and *supervisory control stations.* An application of Ethernet/IP is illustrated in Figure 23-6. Three motor control centers (MCC) are linked by Ethernet/IP. The Allen Bradley ControlLogix system links the factory Ethernet to Ethernet/IP with an Ethernet/IP scanner module. The MCCs have a built-in network system to link intelligent control elements inside the centers. It is possible to control up to 620 motor control devices through the single Ethernet/IP scanner.

ControlNet

ControlNet is an open network standard, which means that any company can develop a ControlNet product without a license fee. ControlNet is a subnetwork of the Ethernet or Ethernet/IP and positioned one level above DeviceNet in the control hierarchy. Its high-speed control and data capabilities significantly enhance input/output performance and user-to-user communications. ControlNet permits all nodes on the network to *simultaneously* access the *same data* from a *single source.* This provides significant advantage over other networks, which allow only *one master controller* on the network. ControlNet also allows

simultaneous broadcast to multiple devices of both inputs and data, thus reducing traffic on the wire and increasing system performance.

ControlNet is highly *deterministic* and *repeatable.* Determinism is the ability to reliably predict when data is delivered, and repeatability ensures that transmit-times are constant and unaffected by devices connecting to, or leaving the network. These two critical characteristics ensure dependable, synchronized and coordinated real-time performance. As a result, ControlNet permits data transfers such as program uploads/downloads and monitoring of real-time data, in flexible but predictable time segments. Electrical workers see ControlNet in applications like Figure 23-5 where the drive provides real time data feedback to the PLC on motor speed or other parameters. Management and configuration of the entire system is performed from a single location on ControlNet or from one location on the Ethernet. ControlNet can link a variety of devices including *motor drives, motion controllers, remote input/output modules, PLCs,* and *operator interfaces.* ControlNet functions as the integrator of complex control systems such as c*oordinated drive systems, weld control, motion control, vision systems, complex batch control systems, process control systems,* and systems with *multiple controllers* and *human-machine interfaces.* Review the devices on the ControlNet network in Figure 23-5.

FIGURE 23-6: MCCs under Ethernet/IP control.

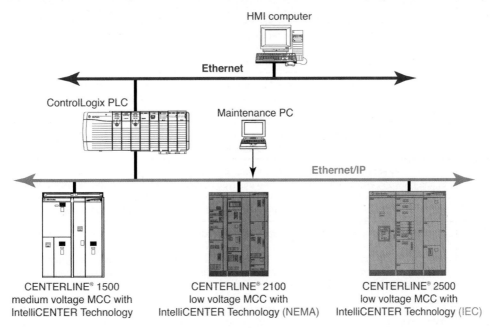

Courtesy of Rockwell Automation, Inc.

Note that the PLC 5 controller has a remote I/O (RIO) network attached for control of drives and servo motors. The PLC 5 is linked to the Ethernet backbone through the Ethernet interface, and connected to the ControlNet and DeviceNet networks with scanner modules. As a result, data from devices on all three networks are available to use in the program in the PLC 5 for the control of the servos and drives.

DeviceNet

DeviceNet is an open network standard, which means that any company can develop a DeviceNet product without a license fee. With many suppliers offering DeviceNet devices, the best combination of devices from multiple suppliers is used to solve the control problem. As a result, DeviceNet is the fastest growing device network in the world with millions of installed devices. DeviceNet operates on multiple messaging formats, which are mixed and matched within a network to achieve the most information-rich and time-efficient information from the network at all times. Some common messaging types are listed in Figure 23-7.

DeviceNet interconnects industrial devices such as *limit switches, photoelectric sensors, valves, motor starters, process sensors,* and *operator interface* devices via a single network. Expensive wiring and failure due to the increase of the number of connections are eliminated. It also reduces the cost and time to install

industrial automation devices while providing reliable interchangeability of components from multiple vendors. The direct connectivity provides improved communication between devices as well as important device-level diagnostics not easily accessible or available through hardwired input/output interfaces.

Figure 23-8 illustrates an example of a DeviceNet network. This illustration emphasizes the many different types of devices that are networked/networkable with this technology. The *ControlLogix, CompactLogix, MicroLogix,* and *SLC* model PLCs interface well to the networks. In addition to these Allen Bradley devices, all major PLC vendors offer a full line of DeviceNet hardware and software. Note that MicroLogix uses a DeviceNet interface device to connect to the network.

Numerous motor starters and VFDs are networked to the DeviceNet. Any that do not have a DeviceNet port as an option, use an interface like the one connecting the smart motor controller. The diagram also emphasizes the ability of all the PLCs to use the DeviceNet network and the other network choices. DeviceNet permits the location of remote I/O like *Point, ArmorPoint, FLEX,* and *CompactBlock* anywhere on the DeviceNet media.

Figure 23-9 illustrates devices that permit control elements not designed for DeviceNet use to be interfaced to the network. For example, the *DeviceNet Starter Auxiliary* (DSA) provides DeviceNet integration options for contactors and discrete sensors without DeviceNet

FIGURE 23-7: DeviceNet message types.

Message Type	Description
Polling	Each device is requested to send or receive an update of its status. This requires an outgoing message and incoming message for each node on the network. This is the most precise but least time efficient way to request information from devices.
Strobing	Requests are broadcast to all devices for a status update. Each device responds in turn, with node 1 answering first, then 2, 3, 4, etc. Node numbers are assigned to prioritize messages. Polling and strobing are the most common messaging formats used.
Cyclic	Devices are configured to automatically send messages on scheduled intervals. This is sometimes called a heartbeat and is often used to indicate that the device is still functional.
Change of State	Devices only send messages when their status changes. This occupies an absolute minimum of time on the network, and a large network using this type often outperforms a polling network operating at several times the speed. This is the most time efficient but sometimes least precise way to obtain information from devices because throughput and response time become statistical instead of deterministic.
Explicit Messaging	The explicit-messaging protocol indicates how a device should interpret a message. Commonly used on complex devices like drives and controllers to download parameters that change from time to time but do not change as often as the process data itself. An explicit message supplies a generic, multipurpose communication path between two devices and provides a means for performing request/response functions such as device configuration.
Fragmented Messaging	For messages that require more than DeviceNet's maximum 8 bytes of data per node per scan, the data can be broken up into any number of 8 byte segments and re-assembled at the other end. This requires multiple messages to send or receive one complete message.

interfaces. The DSA is useful because it integrates a motor starter into the network with four input and two output ports. In addition, the DSA's high-capacity outputs eliminate the need for interposing relays between the DSA and the starter. The DSA is ideal for use with *motor starters, circuit breakers, contactors, motor protectors, soft starters, sensors, reed switches, tracer switches,* and *control protectors.* The interface devices for motor controllers and the MicroLogix Controller mentioned earlier are also shown in Figure 23-9.

FIGURE 23-8: Factory floor network topology.

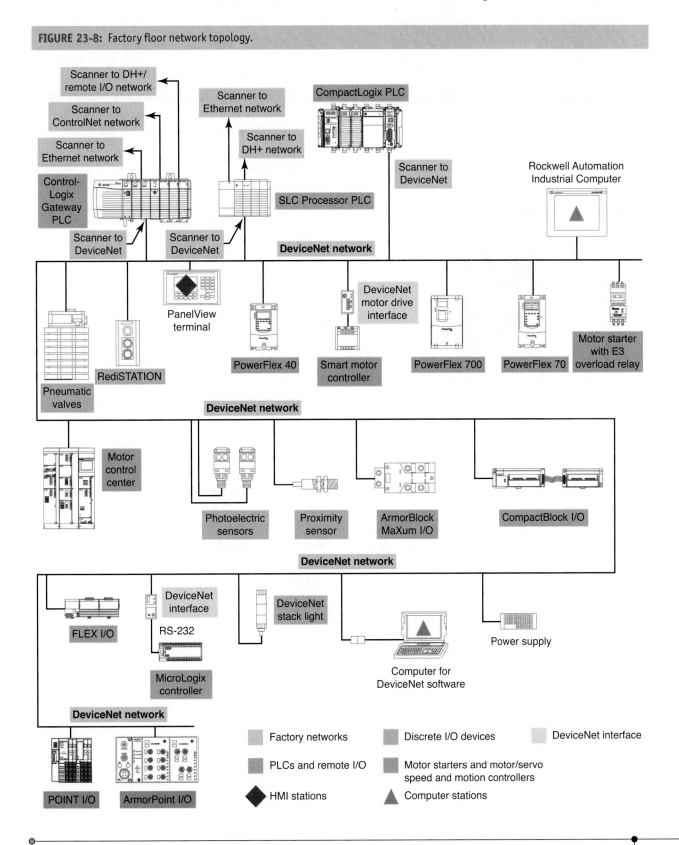

(a) DeviceNet Starter Auxiliary (DSA) module

(b) DeviceNet MicroLogix PLC interface

(c) DeviceNet motor controller interface

Courtesy of Rockwell Automation, Inc.

FOUNDATION Fieldbus

FOUNDATION Fieldbus handles all of the complexities of process management, including *process variables, real-time process control,* and *diagnostics.* It features intrinsic *safety, long wiring run length,* and *delivery* of blocks of data and *device power* over a two-wire system. Although it is tailor-made for analog instruments such as control valves and transmitters, it is often appropriate for on/off valves as well. For example, in continuous processes, it is often logical to tie the on/off valves into the FOUNDATION Fieldbus rather than use conventional point-to-point wiring or a completely different bus network for a small number of discrete valves. And in batch processes that must be *intrinsically safe,* the FOUNDATION Fieldbus is often the only logical choice for networking on/off valves. FOUNDATION Fieldbus is emerging as a leader at this level with strong market share in North America and increasing share throughout the world. Figure 23-5 shows the integration of FOUNDATION Fieldbus into the typical shop floor control architecture.

23-4 NETWORKED MOTOR DRIVES

Although non-networked, stand-alone motor control continues to be used, more information is learned about the processes by taking advantage of data obtained from motor drives connected through communication networks. Smart device networking provides the ability to share operating data across the enterprise and make more informed decisions. This helps ensure quick response, which *reduces downtime* and *boosts productivity.* With the ability of drives to provide detailed operational information over long periods of time, *networked motor control* allows users to better predict *potential problems* and prevent *catastrophic failures.* Moreover, the improved quality and availability of data helps improve troubleshooting speed and accuracy. Rather than relying on obscure fault codes, electrical workers receive simple descriptions to pinpoint specific problems.

For maximum network efficiency, motor control devices are configured to communicate data as often and in whatever format as needed. For example, a drive controlling a rapidly fluctuating process might update every 5 milliseconds, while a motor on a slower changing process updates at a slower update interval. For less critical processes, devices can be configured to communicate only when there is a change-of-state. Information reported by devices in the system could be recorded for later analysis, if needed, or used to generate alarm messages as important events occur in the process. Networked AC drives allow users to set drive configuration options to send *email, page,* or *text-messages* to electrical workers when a *fault* or *alarm* occurs. Electrical workers can click on a hyperlink in the message to launch a Web browser and connect directly to the drive. Additional software tools are then launched that provide complete access to the drive's information, thus enabling a faster response, and preventing further disruption of the process or damage to the motor.

SERCOS

SERCOS (Serial Real-time Communication System) is an open *controller-to-motor drive* interface used for high-speed *serial, real-time* communication of *closed-loop data* over *fiber-optic cables.* The *ring topology* SERCOS interface (called a daisy chain) is installed in a PLC controller. Analog interfaces were designed before intelligent drives, or even before digital controls existed. Using this analog interface with today's intelligent digital drives not only degrades system performance, but also prevents any data such as status, parameters and diagnostics, other than the basic command value from being exchanged. The SERCOS interface allows *reliable, noise-free transmission* of 32-bit data between *drives* and *controls* including: *commands, status, parameters* and *diagnostics*. Figure 23-10 illustrates the SERCOS topology. The SERCOS-interface controls the ring topology data and assigns time slots that ensures collision-free access for the motor drives and

imposes no limit to the number of rings that can be synchronized together. Since SERCOS supports distributed processing, it provides control of time intensive tasks. Note that the encoder feedback from the AC induction motors permits synchronization between the two motor systems. The HMI displays system data and motor performance and permits electrical worker changes to program set points.

FIGURE 23-10: SERCOS ring servo motor drives and serial interface for AC motors.

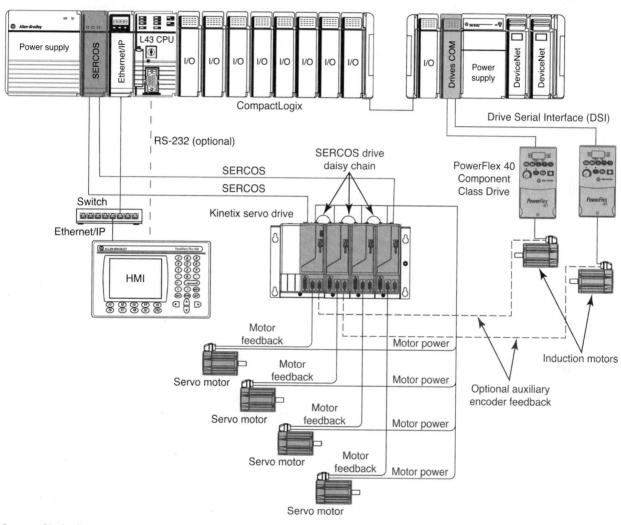

Courtesy of Rockwell Automation, Inc.

23-5 DEVICENET AND CONTROLNET MEDIA WIRING

The physical wiring of DeviceNet networks draws from a number of hardware options. Figure 23-11 shows a machine application with *three motors* connected to three *ArmorStart motor controls*. The three different ArmorStart devices offer different motor starting and braking options. The control of the motors is performed over a DeviceNet network that uses cables to deliver *motor power*, *device power*, and *DeviceNet data*. Cabling components are available for most motor control application requirements.

The *round cable system* DeviceNet wiring in Figure 23-11 is just one of several options depending on the cable selected and the types of connection interfaces used. All DeviceNet cable systems includes device power and data integrated into a single cable system. A second option is the *flat cable system* illustrated in Figure 23-12.

Note that drop points for a number of cabling options are placed along the flat cable. These termination points are placed *anywhere* along the flat cable using the *KwikLink* system. This system uses a cable termination device with an upper and lower half. The termination device is placed anywhere along a flat cable run. When the flat cable is placed between the termination halves, four sharp conductors in the top half of the terminator pierce the flat cable insulation and embed into the four conductors inside the cable. The *caps* at each end of the flat cable in Figure 23-12 are required *cable terminators*. These terminators prevent the data moving through the cable from reflecting back at the end points.

The *ControlNet* requires a cabling system designed to interconnect ControlNet ready devices and PLCs with ControlNet scanner modules. A number of the earlier figures showed a graphical description of a ControlNet configuration. Figure 23-13 illustrates the *wiring* or *cabling system* used with ControlNet.

FIGURE 23-11: DeviceNet motor control network with round cable wiring.

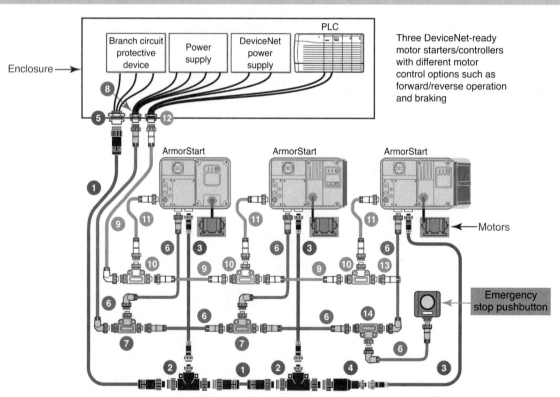

1. 3-Phase power patchcord (trunk)
2. 3-Phase power T-port
3. 3-Phase power patchcord (drop)
4. 3-Phase power reducer
5. 3-Phase power receptacle
6. Control power patchcord
7. Control power T-port (E-Stop IN)
8. Control power receptacle
9. DeviceNet patchcord (trunk)
10. DeviceNet T-port
11. DeviceNet patchcord (drop)
12. DeviceNet receptacle
13. DeviceNet terminator
14. Control power T-port (E-Stop OUT)

Courtesy of Rockwell Automation, Inc.

FIGURE 23-12: Flat cable DeviceNet network with example terminated devices.

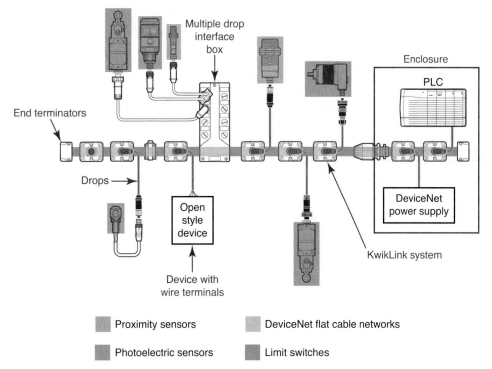

Multiple drop interface box

Enclosure

PLC

End terminators

Drops

DeviceNet power supply

KwikLink system

Open style device

Device with wire terminals

	Proximity sensors		DeviceNet flat cable networks
	Photoelectric sensors		Limit switches

Courtesy of Rockwell Automation, Inc.

FIGURE 23-13: Round cable ControlNet network linking PLC systems.

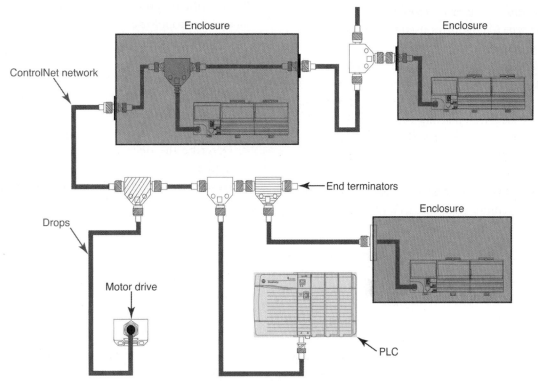

Enclosure

Enclosure

ControlNet network

End terminators

Enclosure

Drops

Motor drive

PLC

Courtesy of Rockwell Automation, Inc.

CRITICAL CONCEPTS

The need to know content from Chapter 23 is summarized in the following statements.

- A network is a communication system where two or more intelligent machines or devices are physically and/or wirelessly connected together to share information by set of rules for communication called a protocol.
- Network devices include hubs are devices that provide nodes on network to which intelligent machines are connected, and servers are high-powered workstations with a specific function such as file service, web service or email service.
- Network components include bridges that connect network segments that may differ at the physical level but are compatible at the communication level; routers connect separate local- and wide-area networks that share the same network protocol; repeaters are used for signal retransmission when the cable length exceeds the specification of the cable type for reliable signal transmission; and gateways connect local- and wide-area networks that use a different network protocol and therefore require protocol switching.
- Network media is the actual physical path over which an electrical or optical signal travels as it moves from one user to another, in other words, it is the type of conductor used to interconnect the intelligent machines.
- Three common topologies are bus topology, where all machines are connected to a central network media, which is called the bus or backbone; ring topology, where all machines are connected to one another in the shape of a closed loop; and star topology, where all machines are connected to a central hub.
- Ethernet consists of three basic elements: (1) the physical medium used to carry Ethernet signals between computers; (2) a set of medium access control rules embedded in each Ethernet interface that allow multiple intelligent machines to fairly arbitrate access to the shared Ethernet channel; and (3) an Ethernet frame that consists of a standardized set of bits used to carry data over the system.
- ControlNet is a sub-network of the Ethernet and positioned one level above DeviceNet in the control hierarchy and permits all nodes on the network to simultaneously access the same data from a single source.
- DeviceNet interconnects industrial devices such as limit switches, photoelectric sensors, valves, motor starters, process sensors, and operator interface devices via a single network.
- SERCOS (Serial Real-time Communication System) is an open controller-to-motor drive interface used for high-speed serial, real-time communication of closed-loop data over fiber-optic cables.

QUESTIONS

1. Describe the function of network switches, hubs and servers.
2. Describe the function of network bridges, routers, repeaters and gateways.
3. Describe nodal connections in the bus, ring, and star topologies.
4. Describe the operation and function of the Ethernet.
5. Describe the operation and function of the ControlNet.
6. Describe the operation and function of the DeviceNet.
7. Describe the operation and function of the fieldbus.
8. Describe the operation and function of SERCOS.

CHAPTER 24

System-Wide Troubleshooting of Motor Control Systems

GOALS AND OBJECTIVES

The primary goals for this chapter are to detail the *basic and advanced techniques* for system-wide troubleshooting through discussion and illustrations.

After completing this chapter, you will be able to:

1. Describe the basic techniques for troubleshooting system-wide faults.
2. Describe the advanced techniques for troubleshooting system-wide faults.

24-1 BASIC TROUBLESHOOTING

Troubleshooting techniques are proven *procedures* that provide a *structure* for the troubleshooting process. It is not always apparent that the experienced troubleshooter and the beginner use the same techniques to find a faulty component. Often experienced electrical workers do many of the *troubleshooting processes* and *logical operations* in their head. The beginner, on the other hand, is encouraged to write down or verbally express the procedures with troubleshooting partner until the techniques are mastered. The basic techniques or logical tools most often used are *block diagrams, bracketing, signal flow, signal flow analysis* and *information funneling*. Troubleshooters may use other words to describe these procedures, but in this chapter these

terms are used. To facilitate the understanding of system-wide troubleshooting techniques, a simple public address (PA) system, an alarm system and a process tank system are used to demonstrate the techniques before they are applied to a motor control system.

Block Diagrams

The block diagram is a set of rectangles used to identify parts of a system. The block diagram of a public address (PA) system is illustrated in Figure 24-1. Note that two *microphones* are used as inputs into the mixer in the figure. The *mixer* allows for the volume and tone levels for microphones to be individually adjusted. The small signal amplifier, called the *pre-amplifier,* amplifies the combined output of both microphones. The *power amplifier* provides additional amplification to drive the two output *speakers*. A *selector switch* is present between the pre-amplifier and power amplifier to connect either the microphones or a compact disc (CD) player into the power amplifier. The CD player has an individual pre-amplifier and volume control included in the unit.

The characteristics of block diagrams are as follows:

- **Complex systems are represented by series of simple rectangles.** The complex parts of the public address system, like the pre-amplifier and power amplifier, are reduced to single rectangle. As a result, very complex system can be represented on a single page.

FIGURE 24-1: Block diagram of public address system.

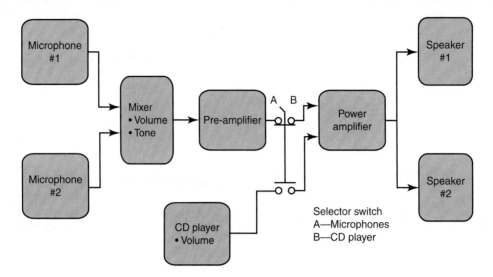

- **Information flows from left to right through the rectangles.** Also notice that the flow of information starts on the left side (sound into microphones) and moves from left to right where the speaker rectangles are located. Restated, inputs are on the left and outputs on the right.
- **Systems and subsystems are represented.** The decision on what to include in a rectangle is usually based on how repairs are performed. If a failed unit is replaced with a spare to return the system to operation, then that entire unit is in a single block in the diagram. However, if components of the unit are replaced when a system fault is traced to the failure of a unit, then a sub-system block diagram of the unit is necessary. For example, the power amplifier has three internal modules that can be replaced. If the fault is traced to the power amplifier, then troubleshooting continues at the subsystem level to locate the block inside the power amplifier that caused the system failure.

The system block diagram is available from two sources. Ideally, the vendor for the equipment provides a system block diagram in the user manual. However, if one is not provided, then the electrical worker creates one for troubleshooting. While the block diagram is necessary for troubleshooting, it is also one of the best learning tools for understanding how the system functions. Without a complete understanding of system operation, identifying system faults and solving system operational problems is little more than a guessing game. A block diagram is easily generated as follows:

1. *Make a list of all of the system components that would be replaced in a system failure.* For example, the selector switch and microphone are single components in the PA system in Figure 24-1 that would be replaced if they failed. The power amplifier has three circuit boards with I/O connectors (Figure 24-2) that are individually replaced if that amplifier was the problem. This is similar to an SLC model Allen Bradley PLC. If the PLC is the problem, then most likely one of the modules, *I/O, power,* or *processor,* would be replaced and not the entire SLC PLC.

   In contrast, the pre-amplifier has many individual components integrated into a single amplifier unit, so the complete amplifier is replaced if it fails. The PLC analogy for the pre-amplifier is a MicroLogix PLC. These PLCs are an integral unit with I/O, power supply, and processor all integrated into one circuit. Entire units, like the pre-amplifier or the MicroLogix PLC, are replaced with a spare because that is the fastest way to get the entire system back into operation. The decision to fix the bad unit after replacement is generally based on cost. In some cases, the cost of repair is too high, and the unit it is discarded.

FIGURE 24-2: Power amplifier block diagram.

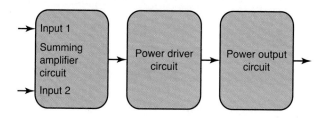

In other situations, a repair facility fixes the unit, and it is returned for use as a spare.

2. *Arrange the list of system components with inputs devices at the top, outputs devices at the bottom, and all remaining system devices in the order that signal or information flows through them.* The list for the PA system in Figure 24-1 has microphones at the top and speakers at the bottom. The mixer is listed under the microphones, and the pre-amplifier and CD player are on the same line since they both feed into the selector switch. The selector switch and power amplifier are just above the speakers.

3. *Put all of the block diagram components into rectangles and apply signal flow techniques to link the rectangles in the diagram.* A major part of the block diagram is the signal flow representation and analysis that starts in the next section.

Bracketing

Bracketing is a technique that uses *external markers* to identify the portion of the system block diagram in which the fault exists. The brackets are initially placed on the system block diagram, but could be moved to a schematic diagram when the fault is narrowed down to a single circuit. A three-step process is used to establish the initial location for the brackets.

1. *Record and study all system symptoms listing all conditions that vary from normal operation.*

2. *Locate points on the system block diagram where abnormal operation is occurring and place a right bracket ( ]) after each abnormal block.* Remember, the signal flow on the block diagrams is from left (inputs) to right (outputs). So in general, the right brackets are placed on the right side of output blocks that are not operating.

3. *Move to the left along the signal flow path from each bad bracket until normal operation is observed. Place a left bracket ([ ) to the right of the block where a normal output was detected.* In general, the brackets are initially placed with simple tests and observations that verify what is working and what is not working.

The application of the brackets to the system block diagram is an entirely mental process for some experience electrical workers; however, the beginner should physically mark them on the block until all the troubleshooting techniques are fully internalized.

Signal Flow Analysis

Signal flow is generally divided into two groups called *power* and *information*. The *power flow* illustrates how power is delivered to all of the components in

---

The PA system in Figure 24-1 is needed in a conference room for a presentation. The system is set up by an electrical worker and tested to verify correct operation. When the electrical worker taps on both microphones there is no sound coming from either speaker. Locate the PA system fault with the following steps. Because this is an application of bracketing, assume the system power and the mixer's volume setting are not the problem.

1. **Record and analyze symptoms.** There is no output from either speaker when a valid input to the system is applied.

2. **Place the right bracket after each faulty output.** The right brackets are placed on the right side of each speaker block as shown in Figure 24-3.

3. **Place the left bracket to the right of the last good or normal output.** The symptoms indicate that the input to the microphones is valid, but the condition of the microphones is not known. Therefore, the left bracket is placed to the left of the microphone block as shown in the figure.

This application shows how the initial bracket positions are placed based on verified system symptoms. However, no new information is generated at this point. The brackets indicate that the fault is somewhere in the total system. Before proceeding with additional checks on the faulty PA system, it is important to learn the concepts associated with signal flow in the block diagrams.

APPLICATION

(continued)

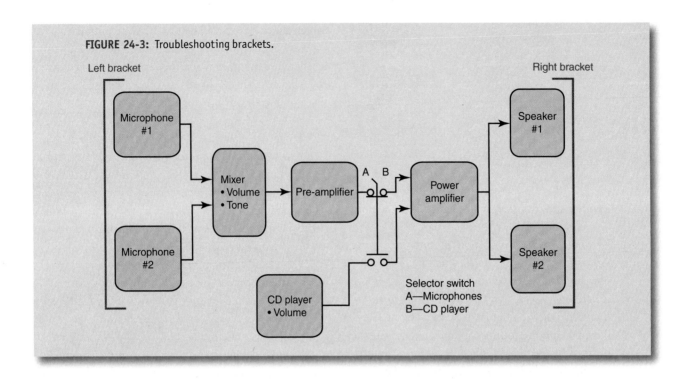

FIGURE 24-3: Troubleshooting brackets.

the system, and *information flow* indicates how information or data flows from sources to destinations.

There are five distinct types of signal flow topologies: *linear, divergent, convergent, feedback,* and *switched paths.* The electrical worker must recognize each type of path because a unique troubleshooting approach is associated with each of the topologies. A description of each type is provided below.

- **Linear**—The linear signal path is a simple series connection of blocks.
- **Divergent**—A divergent signal path is present when a single block feeds two or more blocks. Figure 24-4 is a power flow block diagram for a security system. The divergent path in the figure is the power flowing from the power supply to the three system blocks.
- **Convergent**—A convergent signal path is present when signals from two or more blocks feed into a single block. The two microphones connected to the mixer in Figure 24-1 represent a convergent signal path. A second example is present in the security system in Figure 24-4 where the two power sources connect to the power supply.
- **Feedback**—A feedback signal flow is created when part of the output signal is diverted back to the input of the system and added to the input signal. The block diagram for a process tank control system is

FIGURE 24-4: Power flow block diagram for a security system.

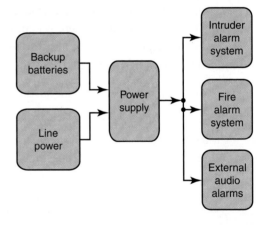

illustrated in Figure 24-5. The *temperature* of the process is measured and fed back to the input where it is compared with the desired temperature called the *set point.* When the set point is higher than the actual temperature, a positive error signal is generated. The amplified *positive error signal* causes the mixer valve to *increase* the temperature of the liquid in the process tank. If the liquid is too hot, a *negative error signal* is generated, and the *opposite action* occurs.

- **Switched paths**—Switched signal flow paths include *linear, divergent,* or *convergent* paths with switches present to change the flow of the signal.

FIGURE 24-5: Feedback block diagram for a process tank system.

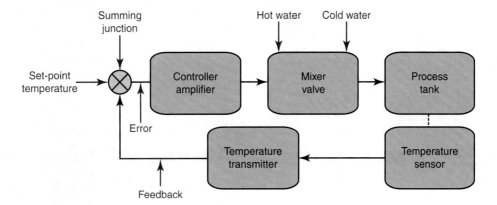

A switched convergent path is present in the PA system (Figure 24-1) where the CD player and pre-amplifier converge at the power amplifier through the selector switch.

Analysis of the signal flow topologies provides a technique to move the brackets to speed the troubleshooting process. The five topologies have rules that are used to search for the faulty system component. The topology rules that direct bracket movement are described below.

- **Linear rule**—When brackets enclose a linear set of system blocks to be tested, the first test point should be located at or just before the *midpoint* of the bracketed area. If the signal is *faulty,* then the right bracket ( ]) moves to that point because the fault is to the left of this point. However, if the signal is valid, then the left bracket ([ ) movers to that point because the fault is in the blocks to the right of this point. Application of this "*divide and conquer*" rule eliminates half of the components with a single check.
- **Divergent rule**—When brackets enclose system blocks with a *divergent path,* the stage before the divergence is fault free if any of the divergent paths are normal. For example, assume that brackets ([ ]) enclose the power supply and all three outputs in the power flow block diagram in Figure 24-4. If a test indicates that power is present at the Fire Alarm system, then it is a valid assumption that the power supply is not the problem. As a result, the left bracket ([ ) is moved to the output side of the power supply.
- **Convergent rule**—When brackets enclose system blocks with a *convergent path,* two rules are applied.

Rule One: If all convergent inputs are required to produce a valid output, then a valid output indicates all inputs paths are fault free. *Rule Two:* If only one convergent input is required to produce a valid output, then each input must be checked to verify that the input paths are fault free. For example, the convergent paths into the power supply in Figure 24-4 would use Rule Two because either source could supply energy to the power supply.

- **Feedback rule**—When brackets enclose system blocks with a feedback path, a change or modification to the feedback path is used to indicate normal operation of the closed-loop system. Figure 24-5 illustrates a block diagram with this topology.
- **Switched path rule**—If brackets contain *linear, divergent,* or *convergent* topologies that are changed by a switch setting, then observe the system when the switch is moved to another position. If the trouble disappears, then the fault is in the path now switched out. If the trouble persists then the fault is in the path common to both switch positions.

Information Funneling

The last basic troubleshooting technique is called *information funneling.* This process is shown graphically in Figure 24-6 with four levels of testing. As the figure indicates, when the brackets on the system block diagram are widely separated the tests selected for identifying the fault tend to be of a more general nature. For example, tests at *level one* might include:

- Verifying that power is present at every unit.
- Verifying that switches required for normal operation are in the on position and level controls are at their nominal settings.

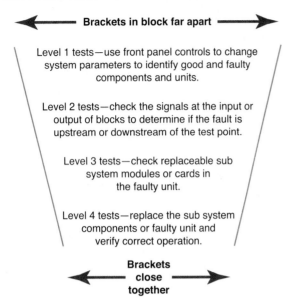

FIGURE 24-6: Funneling analysis.

← Brackets in block far apart →

Level 1 tests—use front panel controls to change system parameters to identify good and faulty components and units.

Level 2 tests—check the signals at the input or output of blocks to determine if the fault is upstream or downstream of the test point.

Level 3 tests—check replaceable sub system modules or cards in the faulty unit.

Level 4 tests—replace the sub system components or faulty unit and verify correct operation.

← Brackets close together →

- Verifying that all cabling has been properly connected.
- Verifying that front panel controls are in the position for normal operation.
- Changing front panel controls or switch settings to see how the symptoms are affected.

Checks at this level are performed quickly, usually don't require the use of any test equipment, don't require that equipment covers be removed, and eliminates some suspected blocks, so the separation between the brackets can be reduced. As a general guideline, the electrical worker should exhaust all possible checks at each level, moving the brackets as close together as possible, before dropping to the lower levels where test are more specific.

At *level two*, fewer suspect blocks are present between the brackets, and test equipment is used to move the brackets closer together. For example, cables are removed from units and measurements are made to verify that a valid input or output signal is present. Work at this level usually involves a number of tests with each test result changing the location of either a left or right bracket. The test equipment most often used includes meters, oscilloscopes, and data analyzers.

At *level three*, tests in the funnel are usually performed when a single unit has been identified as the fault. In some cases, the troubleshooting continues inside the unit on subsystem modules or electronic cards using more precision measurements, but just as often the unit is replaced with a spare.

Level four focuses on replacing faulty units or subsystem components with good spares and verifying that the exchange corrected the problem. Bracketing and funneling work together to help eliminate:

- **Pointless and irrelevant system tests**—troubleshooters are required to focus only on the bracketed trouble area.
- **Redundant system tests**—if the separation between the brackets does not change, a measurement has not provided new information. When this occurs, it is an indication that additional test at the current level may be redundant.
- **Premature system tests**—making detailed test on a single block when the brackets are widely separated yields too precise information for the present situation. Funneling helps focus on the most appropriate test for the current situation.

The system block diagram with the new location for the brackets is shown in Figure 24-7. Using the level one procedure, the location of the fault was narrowed from eight units to just two.

However, no additional new information can be obtained from work on this level, so the test moves to *level two*.

4. A study of the updated system block diagram, Figure 24-7, indicates that the fault must in the linear blocks labeled mixer and pre-amplifier. The "divide and conquer" strategy (see *linear rule* in signal flow analysis) is applied, and a check is made with an oscilloscope at the midpoint in the linear signal between the mixer and pre-amplifier. The output of the mixer is correct,

so the brackets move around the faulty unit, which is the pre-amplifier.

Level three in the information funnel is not used since the pre-amplifier does not have any subsystem components that are replaceable. If the power amplifier were the faulty unit, the tests would continue on the inside of the unit. The test moves to *level four*.

5. The pre-amplifier is replaced with a spare, and the PA system is tested to verify correct operation. The test is successful; the system is ready for operation.

The application illustrates how bracketing, signal flow analysis, and information funneling is used with a system block diagram to locate a bad component with the minimum number of test and in the shortest time.

FIGURE 24-7: System analysis—bracket placement.

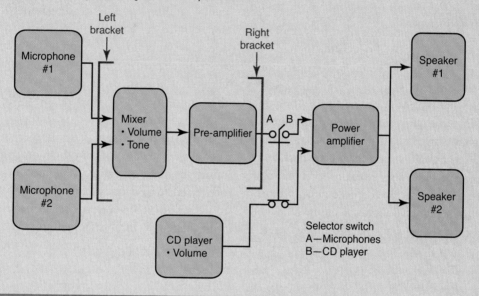

24-2 ADVANCED TROUBLESHOOTING

The advanced troubleshooter uses a combination of tools and techniques that are related to problem solving. The troubleshooter is like a detective, the fault is the crime, and the symptoms are the clues. The following general guidelines should be applied to the solution process as necessary.

- Check that symptoms are a clear and detailed description of what the problem *is* and *is not*. Sometimes stating what is working helps to more clearly see what is not working. Use these guidelines:
  - If possible, personally verify all symptoms. When this cannot be done, rely on written problem descriptions in maintenance logs and from reliable sources.

- Verify that operating controls are in their nominal position before recording and analyzing symptoms.
- Keep an accurate and detailed troubleshooting log for each system that includes: conditions present when troubleshooting starts and changes in the system as troubleshooting progresses.
- Recognize abnormal operation by fully understanding normal operation. Electrical workers have to study normal system operation until every possible operational mode is understood. Abnormal operation has three sources:
  - **Adjustment**—improper adjustment of controls either on the front panel or inside the unit.
  - **Calibration**—the lack of calibration against some universal standard.

- **Component or unit failure**—a component failure in some part of the system. Always look for evidence of a component failure such as noticeable wear, burn, excessive heat marks, or damage from impact.

Troubleshooting Sequence

With the tools in place to approach troubleshooting in a systematic and organized fashion, a general set of steps are developed for use on system faults. The sequence includes:

1. **Define the problem.** Gather all the symptom data for the failure and information on the state of the system when the fault occurred.
2. **Decide what needs to be tested.** Put the brackets on the system block diagram (physically or mentally) to narrow the search for the fault to that part of the system where faulty operations has been verified.
3. **Decide what type of test to perform.** Apply the funneling criteria, which start with changes in the signal flow path to perform broad system test that eliminates some of the suspect units between the brackets. As the brackets narrow the type of test performed becomes more precise with increased use of test equipment. When test fail to provide any new information on the location of the fault, move to the next level of more precise tests.
4. **Correct the problem.** After the faulty unit or component is identified, the problem is corrected by adjustment or replacement of the unit or component.
5. **Verify correct operation.** After a problem is corrected, it is important to thoroughly test the system to verify that the applied fix corrected all of the system problems.
6. **Determine the cause of the failure.** Getting the system back into operation is only half of the solution. If possible determine what caused the unit or component to fail and recommend system changes that would prevent a similar failure in the future.

The first three steps in the sequence are repeated as often as necessary until the fault is located. Symptoms are studied, possible faulty units are bracketed, and the easiest possible changes in the signal flow are applied to eliminate some suspected units. As the brackets move closer together, the test on suspected units gets more precise with test equipment introduced. Throughout the process, symptoms continue to be analyzed. The analysis includes time to *think* about the problem reflecting on results of previous test and possible future test.

Multiple Failures

Systems with multiple failures provide the toughest troubleshooting problems. The first problem is to determine if multiple failures are present. If a single unit or component failure could not cause the symptoms present, then multiple failures are assumed. Multiple failures present two types of symptoms: *related* and *unrelated*. In the related symptom situation, failure of either unit or component would produce the symptom. For example, consider the case of a variable speed pump, which is driven by a motor with a variable speed drive (VFD). Pumping stops if the pump, motor, or VFD fails. So the symptom is related to three components. However, if a pump bearing causes the pump to stall, then the motor fails because a locked rotor and the motor failure cause a failure in the motor drive. The motor and drive failures may be overloads tripping or maybe something more serious. However, the result is multiple failures with related symptoms. When units and components have related symptoms multiple failures could be present, so it is important to check each component before implementing a fix to the trouble.

Actuation of circuit protection devices like fuses, circuit breakers, and overload relays often falls into the two related failure situation. A fuse failure or circuit breaker opening could result from an external event, such as a voltage spike on the power lines. Replacement of the fuse and resetting of the circuit breaker is all that is required. However, circuit protection devices also open when a protected device fails. In those cases both actions have a related cause. As a result, special care in isolating the cause of circuit protection device actuation is important for electrical workers maintaining systems with motors and motor controllers.

The presence of unrelated symptoms indicates that multiple failures could be present in unrelated units or components. While this type of failure is rare, the solution process is the same. Apply the troubleshooting principles to one of the symptom(s) until the fault is corrected, and then repeat the process for the unrelated symptom(s) until the second fault is fixed.

The tools and processes outlined in this chapter provide a basic and advanced approach to troubleshooting system-wide problems. Specific trouble-shooting techniques are available for individual components and machines in the system. Electrical workers must be able to efficiently use both the basic and advanced techniques to solve system-wide problems as quickly as possible.

APPLICATION

The ladder diagram in Figure 24-8 is used to demonstrate how the troubleshooting techniques presented in this chapter are applied. The ladder provides control for the following problem:

A pump fills a mixing tank with process liquid from a supply tank. The fluid is heated in the process tank before delivery to the next process stage. The heater is energized when the liquid is above the low-level float switch FS 2. The tank fill cycle stops when the liquid is above the high-level float switch FS 1. Heating continues until the liquid temperature reaches the set point of the temperature switch TS 1. When the temperature set point is reached the drain valve is energized and the liquid drains. A start push button is used to initiate the

processes, and energize the fill pump. A stop push button is used to stop the pump. When low level float switch, FS 2, is activated (liquid above low level float switch) and the temperature switch is not activated (temperature is below the set point value), a contactor for a heater is energized, and the tank fluid is heated. When the high level float switch, FS 1, is activated (liquid above high level float switch), the fill cycle stops. The heater remains energized until the temperature switch is activated (temperature is above the set point value), indicating that the proper temperature is achieved. At this point, the heater is de-energized and the drain valve is energized to drain the heated liquid to the production process.

FIGURE 24-8: Process tank fill-heat-drain ladder logic (pump and heater power circuits are not shown).

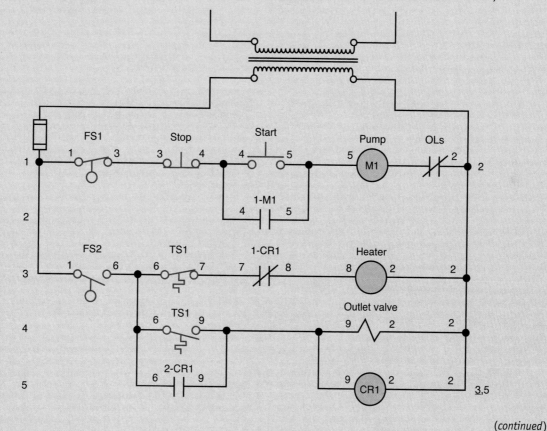

(continued)

The first step is to draw a signal flow diagram for the system. The experienced electrical workers do this in their minds eye. The signal and power flow diagram for the ladder is shown in Figure 24-9. Each component could be a possible problem so the diagram breaks the system into component parts. *Operators* and *contacts* are combined since you are trying to isolate a faulty device; however, all coils and contacts are shown separately. Compare the

signal flow diagram in Figure 24-9 with the ladder logic diagram in Figure 24-8 and identify how each element in the ladder is placed into the signal flow. With experience, the electrical worker can mentally create the signal flow when studying a ladder logic diagram viewed for the first time. The ability to convert the ladder diagram to a signal and power flow sequence is what identifies the good troubleshooter.

Using Figure 24-9, determine where the left and right brackets would be placed to isolate the problem component(s) for each of the following symptoms. Assume no multiple component failures.

Problem: *The three phase power is present and process tank is not filled with fluid, but the pump does not start when the start PB is pressed.*

Solution: *Set left bracket on the left side of transformer because power at the transformer is present, and place the right bracket on the right side of the pump since it does not start. See Figure 24-10. Any one of the components between the brackets could cause the failure of the pump to move process fluid. Note the contactor coil and contactor contacts are*

FIGURE 24-9: Process tank fill-heat-drain control and power block diagrams.

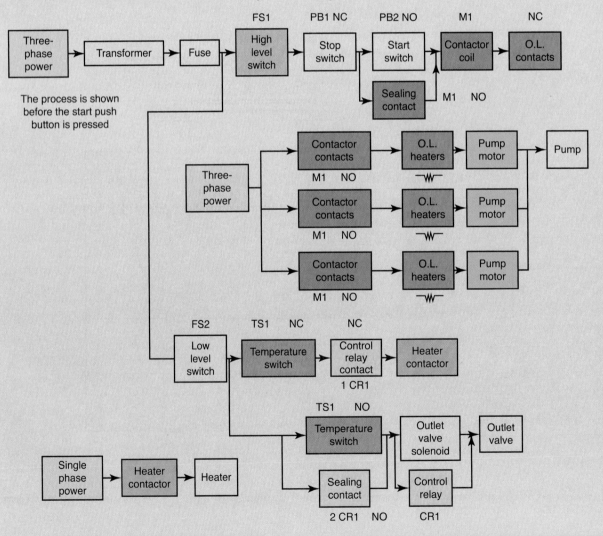

linked electromagnetically. So now all possible faulty elements are identified. Note that the color of the blocks indicates common components.

There are no additional front panel switches that would support additional analysis of the problem (Level 1 tests in funneling). Therefore a voltage test is necessary (Level 2 test in funneling). A test of the voltage between the Start contacts and the contactor coil with the Start PB depressed is recorded (*divide and conquer rule*). The voltage reading is zero. This indicates that the problem is upstream, so the right bracket is moved to the right side of the Start PB. See Figure 24-11. Note: Easy access to the measurement points was considered when selecting points for the measurements.

The next measurement is between the fuse and high level switch (*divide and conquer rule*). A correct voltage level is found. This indicates that the problem is downstream, so the left brackets move to the left side of the high level switch. See Figure 24-12.

With the tank empty the NC contacts of the high level switch should be closed. So the final measurement is made between the high level switch and the Stop switch. No voltage is measured. This indicates that the problem is upstream, so the right bracket is moved to the right side of the high level switch. The right bracket moves to the right side of the high level switch and faulty device is isolated. See Figure 24-13.

Making measurements is often difficult in a large process. Many of the components are at operator panels, some are in control cabinets, and others are on the process system. When additional measurements are required, the ones that would *narrow brackets the fastest* and are *easiest to make* are made first.

A signal flow diagram for a very large system is often not practical to draw. However, the exercise just performed teaches a process for using the troubleshooting tools and procedures that is useful regardless of the system size.

FIGURE 24-10: Initial bracket placement based on symptoms.

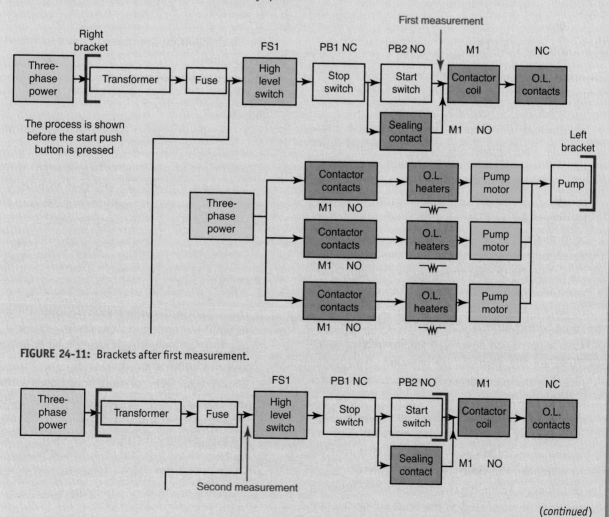

FIGURE 24-11: Brackets after first measurement.

(continued)

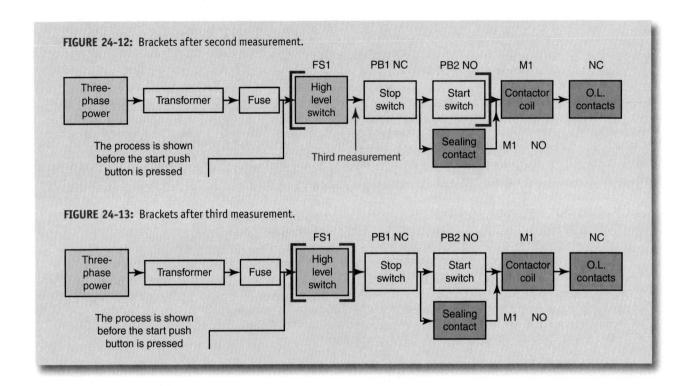

FIGURE 24-12: Brackets after second measurement.

FIGURE 24-13: Brackets after third measurement.

CRITICAL CONCEPTS

The need to know content from Chapter 24 is summarized in the following statements.

- The basic troubleshooting techniques most often used are block diagrams, bracketing, signal flow, signal flow analysis and information funneling.
- The characteristics of block diagrams are—complex systems are represented by series of simple rectangles and information flows from left to right through the rectangles.
- Bracketing is a technique that uses external markers to identify the portion of the system block diagram in which the fault exists. The brackets are initially placed on the system block diagram, but could be moved to a schematic diagram when the fault is narrowed down to a single circuit.
- There are five distinct types of signal flow topologies: linear, divergent, convergent, feedback, and switched paths.
- Analysis of the signal flow topologies provides a technique to move the brackets to speed the troubleshooting process using fixed rules that are used to search for the faulty system component.
- Information funneling is a process where different tests are implemented as the brackets on the system block diagram are moved closer to the suspected fault.
- Advanced troubleshooting techniques provide guidelines and test sequences to isolate the system fault.
- Multiple failures present two types of symptoms: related and unrelated. In the related symptom situation, failure of either unit or component would produce the symptom. The presence of unrelated symptoms indicates that multiple failures could be present in unrelated units or components.

QUESTIONS

1. Describe how the following techniques are used in troubleshooting system faults—block diagrams, bracketing, signal flow, signal flow analysis and information funneling.
2. Describe the general guidelines that are used in advanced troubleshooting of system faults.
3. Describe the testing sequence steps that are used in advanced troubleshooting of system faults.
4. Explain the differences between related and unrelated multiple system failures.

Index